the california indians

a source book

the california indians

A SOURCE BOOK

COMPILED AND EDITED BY

R. F. HEIZER AND M. A. WHIPPLE

SECOND EDITION REVISED AND ENLARGED

UNIVERSITY OF CALIFORNIA PRESS

BERKELEY, LOS ANGELES, LONDON

University of California Press
Berkeley and Los Angeles, California
University of California Press, Ltd.
London, England
Copyright 1951 and 1971 by the Regents of the University of California
Second Edition, 1971

ISBN: 0–520–01770–6 cloth
ISBN: 0–520–02031–6 paper
Library of Congress Catalog Card Number: 72–122951
Printed in the United States of America

3 4 5 6 7 8 9 0

pReface to the second edition

Alfred L. Kroeber's *Handbook of the Indians of California* was written in 1918, submitted for publication in 1923 and published by the Bureau of American Ethnology as its Bulletin No. 78 in 1925. As a compendium of basic information written by the preeminent student of the subject, it has never been supplanted as an authoritative source. The *Handbook* was reprinted in facsimile in 1953, two years after the first printing of the present source book. The present work is in no sense a substitute for Kroeber's book which runs to 1000 pages, describes each tribe separately and in detail, and is a technical monograph in which can be found comprehensive discussions of social and religious systems as well as material culture.

The present collection of essays is intended more for a lay public than a professional audience and is a survey rather than an encyclopedia for reference work. It attempts to offer to the reader interested in the Indians of California a selection of articles and extracts that will provide an introduction to the civilization of the original inhabitants of the state. Because it is aimed at the nontechnical reader, extensive footnotes, detailed citations to the literature, and some illustrations have been omitted. To determine these the reader will have to consult the original published accounts. The few deletions from the original text are indicated by ellipses. Except for these omissions and some minor punctuation and spelling changes, the articles are printed as originally published.

Eleven selections which appeared in the first edition have been omitted, and in their place eighteen others have been introduced. We believe that the present coverage is thereby made rather broader and somewhat more up to date. We are fully conscious of the shortcomings of the collection in terms of its treating with any adequacy the bewildering variety of California Indian social and material culture, and can only say that we have done the best we could in terms of the abundance of published accounts, variety of topics, and limitations of space. In the hopes of compensating for omissions of whole subjects such as medicine, music, mythology, social organization, aesthetics, and ritual, we have added at the end a minimal topical bibliography where the reader may find references to these subjects as well as additional citations to matters discussed in the printed selections. But even here we may be charged with not having done enough, and the present editors can only say that the literature is so extensive, the variety of topics so great, and the restrictions of space so stringent that the reference bibliography cannot be considered as anything more than a sampling.

contents

GENERAL SURVEYS

Elements of Culture in Native California by A. L. Kroeber / 3

The Aboriginal Population of Upper California by S. F. Cook / 66

A New Ecological Typology of the California Indians
by R. L. Beals and J. A. Hester, Jr. / 73

Some Regional Aspects of Native California by S. J. Jones / 84

Californian Indian Physical Types by E. W. Gifford / 97

Linguistic Families of California by R. B. Dixon and
A. L. Kroeber / 105

The History of Native Culture in California by A. L. Kroeber / 112

ARCHAEOLOGY

The Western Coast of North America by R. F. Heizer / 131

San Francisco Bay Shellmounds by N. C. Nelson / 144

Culture Sequences in Central California Archaeology
by R. K. Beardsley / 158

*A Suggested Chronology for Southern California Coastal
Archaeology* by W. J. Wallace / 186

Antiquity of San Francisco Bay Shellmounds by S. F. Cook / 202

Prehistory of the Santa Barbara Area by R. L. Olson / 206

Speculations on the Prehistory of Northwestern California
by A. B. Elsasser and R. F. Heizer / 225

Rock Art in California by Campbell Grant / 231

HISTORICAL ACCOUNTS OF NATIVE CALIFORNIANS

The Colorado River Yumans in 1775 by Pedro Font / 247

The Chumash Indians of Santa Barbara by Pedro Fages / 255

The Yurok of Trinidad Bay, 1851, by Carl Meyer / 262

The Lone Woman of San Nicolas Island by Emma Hardacre / 272

Ishi, the Last Yahi by T. T. Waterman / 285

ETHNOLOGY: MATERIAL CULTURE AND ECONOMY

The Food Problem in California by A. L. Kroeber / 297

Californian Balanophagy by E. W. Gifford / 301

Desert Plant Foods of the Coahuilla by David Prescott Barrows / 306

The Value of Insects to the California Indians by E. O. Essig / 315

California Basketry and the Pomo by A. L. Kroeber / 319

Miwok Houses by S. A. Barrett and E. W. Gifford / 332

Fire-Making of the Wintu Indians by George H. H. Redding / 341

Mines and Quarries of the Indians of California by R. F. Heizer
and A. E. Treganza / 346

Stone-Flaking of the Klamath River Yurok by Paul Schumacher / 360

ETHNOLOGY:
SOCIAL CULTURE

The Tribe in California by A. L. Kroeber / 367

Miwok Lineages and the Political Unit in Aboriginal California
by E. W. Gifford / 375

Yurok National Character by A. L. Kroeber / 385

Yurok Law and Custom by A. L. Kroeber / 391

Modoc Childhood by Verne F. Ray / 424

Mohave Warfare by Kenneth M. Stewart / 431

War Stories from Two Enemy Tribes by Walter Goldschmidt, George Foster,
and Frank Essene / 445

Aboriginal California and Great Basin Cartography
by R. F. Heizer / 459

The World Renewal Cult of Northwest California
by A. L. Kroeber / 464

Yurok Geographical Concepts by T. T. Waterman / 472

Village Shifts and Tribal Spreads in California Prehistory
by R. F. Heizer / 480

Principal Local Types of the Kuksu Cult by A. L. Kroeber / 485

The 1870 Ghost Dance by Cora Du Bois / 496

Death and Burial Among the Northern Maidu by Roland B. Dixon / 500

The Yokuts Dance for the Dead by Stephen Powers / 513

The Mourning Ceremony of the Miwok, 1906,
by C. Hart Merriam / 520

Yurok Shamanism by Robert Spott and A. L. Kroeber / 533

Hupa Sorcery by William J. Wallace and Edith S. Taylor   /   544

Migration and Urbanization of the Indians of California
by S. F. Cook   /   551

Conflict Between the California Indian and White Civilization
by S. F. Cook   /   562

Number and Condition of California Indians Today by R. F. Heizer
and M. A. Whipple   /   572

REFERENCE BIBLIOGRAPHY   /   583

INDEX   /   611

ıllustrations

Boat Types of Native California / 10

Range of Head Form of California Indians / 98

Two Types of Face Form of California Indians / 99

Culture Development in Central California / 163

Oval Metate, Santa Barbara / 211

Shell and Bone Fishhooks, Santa Barbara / 212

Reconstruction of Prehistoric Cultural Changes, Chumash (Santa Barbara) Area / 223

The Painted Cave near Santa Barbara / 233

Elaborate Figures Pecked on Basalt / 234

Mountain Sheep / 235

Chumash Polychrome Painting / 236

A. L. Kroeber and Ishi (1916) / 289

Ishi, the Last Yahi Indian / 290

Roof Plans of Miwok Assembly Houses / 335

Prehistoric Steatite Artifacts / 349

Prehistoric Stone Grinding Implements / 354

Yurok Method of Making Stone Weapons / 361

The Yurok Conception of the World   /   475

Plan of Burning-grounds   /   505

Pie Diagram of the Principal Minorities in California   /   573

maps

1 Native Tribes, Groups, Dialects, and Families of California in 1770 / *see endpapers*

2 Distribution of Types of Native California Boats / 11

3 Distribution of Methods of Disposal of the Dead / 36

4 Distribution of Ritual Cults / 45

5 Diffusion of Ghost Dances / 57

6 Geomorphic Provinces of California / 85

7 Climates of California / 86

8 Indians of California / 88

9 Yokuts Territory / 89

10 The Climax Area of Central California / 93

11 Probable Distribution of California Physical Types / 102

12 Areas and Subareas of Culture in and about California / 116

13 Archaeological Sites in Central California / 160

14 The Rock Art Style Areas of California / 240

15 Distribution of North American Cult Societies / 486

GENERAL SURVEYS

ELEMENTS OF CULTURE
IN NATIVE CALIFORNIA

by
A. L. Kroeber

INTRODUCTION

These pages are intended for readers whose ethnographic interests are at once sufficiently broad and sufficiently intense to absorb local data presented in summarized fashion. The sketch does not endeavor a systematic presentation of the native Californian cultures. Information that is abundant or suggestive in certain aspects, such as its distributional significance, is outlined and discussed. On the other hand, subjects like magic and ritual dress on which knowledge is irregular, miscellaneous, or complicated by intricate considerations have been omitted. Extra-Californian comparisons have been instituted rather sparingly. The purpose has been not so much to relate California as a unit to other American cultures, as to outline the internal relations of the primitive civilization of the area.

Map 1 shows the territory of all the ethnic groups in California (see endpapers).

ARTS OF LIFE

Dress

The standard clothing of California, irrespective of cultural provinces, was a short skirt or petticoat for women, and either nothing at all for men or a skin folded about the hips. The breechclout is frequently mentioned, but does not seem to have been aboriginal. Sense of modesty among men was slightly developed. In many parts all men went wholly naked except when the weather enforced protection, and among all groups old men appear to have gone bare of clothing without feeling of impropriety. The woman's skirt was everywhere in two pieces. A rather narrow apron was worn in front. A larger back piece extended around at least to the hips and fre-

University of California Publications in American Archaeology and Ethnology (1922), 13:260–328.

A more recent attempt to reconstruct aboriginal California history may be found in S. Klimek, *Culture Element Distributions: I, The Structure of California Indian Culture, ibid.* (1935), 36:1–70.

quently reached to meet the front apron. Its variable materials were of two kinds: buckskin and plant fibers. Local supply was the chief factor in determining choice. If the garment was of skin, its lower half was slit into fringes. This allowed much greater freedom of movement, but the decorative effect was also felt and used. Of vegetable fibers the most frequently used was the inner bark of trees shredded and gathered on a cord. Grass, tule, ordinary cordage, and wrapped thongs are also reported.

As protection against rain and wind, both sexes donned a skin blanket. This was either thrown over the shoulders like a cape, or wrapped around the body, or passed over one arm and under the other and tied or secured in front. Sea-otter furs made the most prized cloak of this type where they could be obtained. Land otter, wildcat, deer, and almost every other kind of fur was not disdained. The woven blanket of strips of rabbit fur or bird skin sometimes rendered service in this connection, although also an article of bedding.

The moccasin which prevailed over central and northwestern California was an unsoled, single-piece, soft shoe, with one seam up the front and another up the heel. This is the Yurok, Hupa, and Miwok type. The front seam is puckered, but sometimes with neat effect. The heel seam is sometimes made by a thong drawn through. The Lassik knew a variant form, in which a single seam from the little toe to the outer ankle sufficed. The drawstring varied: the Miwok did without, the Lassik placed it in front of the ankle, the Yurok followed the curious device of having the thong, self-knotted inside, come out through the sole near its edge, and then lashing it over instep and heel back on itself. This is an arrangement that would have been distinctly unpractical on the side of wear had the moccasins been put on daily or for long journeys. Separate soles of rawhide are sometimes added, but old specimens are usually without, and the idea does not seem native. The Californian moccasin is rather higher than that of the Plains tribes, and appears not to have been worn with its ankle portion turned down. Journeys, war, wood gathering are the occasions mentioned for the donning of moccasins; as well as cold weather, when they were sometimes lined with grass. They were not worn about the village or on ordinary excursions.

The Modoc and Klamath moccasin stands apart through Eastern modification. It appears to have been without stiff sole, but contains three pieces: the sole and moccasin proper, reaching barely to the ankle; a U-shaped inset above the toes, prolonged into a loose tongue above; and a strip around the ankles, sewed to the edge of the main piece, and coming forward as far as the tongue. The main piece has the two seams customary in California, except that the toe seam of course extends only to the bottom of the inset. The ankle piece can be worn turned down or up; the drawstring passes across the front of the tongue.

Southern California is a region of sandals; but the desert Cahuilla wore a high moccasin for travel into the mountains. The hard sole curls over the thick but soft upper, and is sewed to it from the inside by an invisible stitch. The upper has its single seam at the back. The front is slit down to the top of the instep, and held together by a thong passed through the edges once or twice. The appearance of this moccasin is Southwestern, and its structure nearly on the plan of a civilized shoe. It reaches well up on the calf.

Moccasins and leggings in an openwork twining of tule fibers were used in northeastern California and among the Clear Lake Pomo as a device for holding a layer of soft grass against the foot.

The skin legging is rarer than the moccasin. It was made for special use, such as travel through the snow.

In southern California, the sandal of the Southwest begins to appear. In its most characteristic form it consists of yucca fiber, apparently folded around a looped frame or string. The Colorado River tribes have abandoned the use of this form of sandal if ever they possessed it. In recent years they have worn simple rawhide sandals; but their very slender opportunities to hunt render it doubtful whether this is a type that antedates the introduction of horses and cattle among them. The Chemehuevi are said to have worn true moccasins. There is no clear report of any sandal north of Tehachapi.

The woman's basketry cap, a brimless cone or frustum, is generally considered a device intended to protect against the chafe of the pack strap. That this interpretation is correct is shown by the fact that in the south the cap is worn chiefly when a load is to be carried; whereas in the north, where custom demands the wearing of the cap at all ordinary times, it is occasionally donned also by men when it becomes of service to them in the handling of a dip-net which is steadied with the head. The woman's cap, however, is not a generic Californian institution. In the greater part of the central area it is unknown. Its northern and southern forms are quite distinct. Their distribution shows them to be direct adjuncts of certain basketry techniques. The northern cap coincides with the *Xerophyllum tenax* technique and is therefore always made in overlaid twining. The range of the southern cap appears to be identical with that of baskets made on a foundation of *Epicampes rigens* grass and is thus a coiled product. There can be no question that tribes following other basketry techniques possessed the ability to make caps; but they did not do so. It is curious that an object of evident utilitarian origin, more or less influenced by fashion, should have its distribution limited according to the prevalence of basketry techniques and materials.

Two minor varieties of the cap occur. Among the Chemehuevi the somewhat peaked, diagonally twined cap of the Great Basin Shoshoneans was in use. From them it had spread in some measure to the typical southern California tribes as far as the Diegueño. This is likely to have been a comparatively recent invasion, since the two types are found side by side among the same people—a condition contrary to prevailing precedent.

The Modoc employ but little overlay twining, and most of their caps are wholly in their regular technique of simple twining with tule materials. The Modoc cap averages considerably larger and is more distinctly flat topped than that of the other northern Californians.

Inasmuch as woven caps and hats are worn all along the Pacific coast to Alaska and through a great part of the Plateau and Great Basin area, the two Californian types are but occurrences in a larger continuous area, and can therefore scarcely be interpreted as having originated quite independently. Rather is central California to be looked upon as a tract that once had and then lost the cap, or possibly always resisted its invasion.

The hair net worn by men clearly centers in the region of the Kuksu religion, but its distribution seems most accurately described as exclusive of that of the woman's cap. Thus the Kato probably used the net and not the cap, the adjacent Wailaki reversed the habit. There are a few overlappings, as among the Yokuts, who employed both objects. The head net is also reported for the Shasta of Shasta Valley, but may have penetrated to them with the Kuksu elements carried into this region in recent years by the Ghost Dance.

Houses

The houses of native California are difficult to classify except in summary fashion. The extreme forms are well differentiated, but are all connected by transitions. The frame house of the Yurok and Hupa is a definite type whose affinity with the larger plank house of the North Pacific coast is sufficiently evident. Southward and eastward from the Yurok this house becomes smaller and more rudely made. Bark begins to replace the split or hewn planks, and before long a conical form made wholly of bark slabs is attained. This in turn, if provided with a center post, need only be covered with earth to serve as the simple prototype of the large semisubterranean house of the Sacramento Valley. Again, the bark is often partly replaced by poles and sticks. If these are covered with thatch, we have a simple form of the conical brush house. This in turn also attains the rectangular form characteristic of the perfect form of plank house, but in other cases is made oval or round and domed, as among the Chumash. In this event it differs from the semisubterranean house only in the lack of earth covering and its consequent lighter construction. A further transition is afforded by the fact that the earth house almost invariably has foliage of some kind as its topmost covering immediately below the earth surfacing. The brush house is often dug out a short distance. The Chumash threw the earth from the excavation up against the walls for a few feet. The earth-covered house proper is only a little deeper and has the covering extending all the way over.

Neither shape, skeleton structure, nor materials, therefore, offer a satisfactory basis for the distinction of sharp types. A classification that would be of value would have to rest on minute analysis, preceded in many cases by more accurate information than is now available. Among numerous tribes the old types of houses have long since gone out of use. Among most of the remainder they have been at least partly modified, and the majority of early descriptions are too summary to be of great service.

Nor does a consideration of the distribution of house forms hold much present promise of fuller understanding. The earth-covered house was made from the Modoc, Achomawi, and Yuki south to the Miwok; then again in the extreme part of southern California. The bark house is found chiefly among mountain tribes, but no very close correlation with topography appears. The well-fashioned plank house is definitely to be associated with the northwestern culture. The earth lodge of the Sacramento Valley region is evidently connected with the Kuksu religion on one side, since the southward limits of distribution of the two appear to coincide. Northward, however, this form of house extends considerably beyond the cult. The southern earth lodge probably has the center of its distribution among the Colorado River tribes. It appears to have penetrated somewhat farther west than the religious influences emanating from this district.

From the Chumash to the southern valley Yokuts, communal houses were in use. Yet the larger specimens of the earth lodges of the Sacramento Valley district must also have sheltered more people than we reckon to a family; and the same is true of the thatched houses of the Pomo.

As regards affiliations outside of California, there is the same uncertainty. Are we to reckon the semisubterranean house of interior British Columbia as one in type with the Navaho hogan simply because the two are roofed with earth; or is the hogan essentially of the type of the plains tepee by reason of its conical shape and tripod foundation? Until such broader problems are answered, it would scarcely be sound to attempt a definitive classification of the dwellings of aboriginal California.

The separate hut for the woman in her periodical illness seems to be a northern Californian institution. Information is irregular, but the groups who affirm that they formerly erected such structures are the Yurok, Karok, Hupa; probably the other northwestern tribes; the Shasta and Modoc;

the northern Maidu; and apparently the Pomo. The Yuki and Sinkyone deny the practice, but their geographical situation renders unconfirmed negative statements somewhat doubtful. South of the Golden Gate, there is no clear reference to separate huts for women except among the Luiseño, and the Yokuts specifically state that they did not build them.

The Sweathouse

The sweathouse is a typical Californian institution if there is any; yet it was not in universal use. The Colorado River tribes lacked it or any substitute; and a want of reference to the structure among a series of Shoshonean desert tribes, such as the Chemehuevi and the eastern Mono, indicates that these must perhaps be joined to the agricultural Yumans in this respect; although an earth sweathouse is reported from the Panamint. The nonuse of the sweathouse among the Yuma and Mohave appears to be of rather weighty historical significance, since on their eastern side the edifice was made by the nomadic tribes of the Southwest, and a related type—the kiva or estufa —is important among the Pueblos.

The Californian sweathouse is an institution of daily, not occasional, service. It serves a habit, not a medicinal treatment; it enters into ceremony indirectly rather than specifically as a means of purification. It is the assembly of the men, and often their sleeping quarters. It thus comes to fulfill many of the functions of a club; but is not to be construed as such, since ownership or kinship or friendship, not membership, determines admission; and there is no act of initiation.

In line with these characteristics, the California sweathouse was a structure, not a few boughs over which a blanket was thrown before entry. It was earth covered; except in the northwest, where an abundance of planks roofed a deep pit. In either case a substantial construction was requisite. A center post was often set up: logs and poles at any rate had to be employed.

Warmth was produced directly by fire, never by steam generated by heated stones. While the smoke was densest, the inmates lay close to the floor. Women were never admitted, except here and there on special ceremonial occasions, when sweating became a subsidiary feature or was wholly omitted.

In general, the sweathouse was somewhat smaller than the living house. This holds of the northwestern tribes, the Yokuts, and the groups of southern California. In the region of the Kuksu religion, the dance house or ceremonial assembly chamber—built much like the sweathouse elsewhere but on a far ampler scale—has come to be known as "sweathouse" among both Indians and whites. It is not likely that this large structure ever really replaced the true sweathouse in and about the Sacramento Valley. The two may generally have existed side by side, as is known to have been the case among the Pomo and Patwin, but the smaller edifice has lost its proper identity in description under the unfortunate looseness of nomenclature; much as among tribes like the Yana, the Indians now speak of "sweathouses" inhabited by families. Some careful because belated inquiries remain to be made to dispel the uncertainty in this matter. It would seem that in the Sacramento Valley region there were three sizes of earth-covered structures: the large dance house, the moderately spaced living house, and the small sweathouse proper.

In extreme northeastern California the Plains form of sweathouse has obtained a foothold: a small dome of willows covered with mats, large enough for a few men to sit up in, heated by steam. This is established for the Modoc, while less complete descriptions suggest the same for the Shasta, Achomawi, and Washo; but among at least some of these groups the steam sweathouse is of modern introduction.

It is notable that there is no indication of any fusion or hybridization of the Californian and the Eastern types of sweathouse even in the region where they border. This condition is typical of cultural phenomena in native America, and probably throughout the world, as soon as they are viewed distributionally rather than in their developmental sequence. Civilizations shade by endless transitions. Their elements wander randomly, as it seems, with little reference to the circumstances of their origin. But analogous or logically equivalent elements exclude each other far more often than they intergrade.

Boats

Native California used two types of boat—the wooden canoe and the tule balsa, a shaped raft of rushes. Their use tends to be exclusive without becoming fully so. Their distribution is determined by cultural more than by physiographic factors.

The northwestern canoe was employed on Humboldt Bay and along the open, rocky coast to the north, but its shape as well as range indicate it to have been devised for river use. It was dug out of half a redwood log, was square ended, round bottomed, of heavy proportions, but nicely finished with recurved gunwales and carved-out seat. A similar if not identical boat was used on the southern Oregon coast beyond the range of the redwood tree. The southern limit is marked by Cape Mendocino and the navigable waters of Eel River. Inland, the Karok and Hupa regularly used canoes of Yurok manufacture, and occasional examples were sold as far upstream as the Shasta.

The southern California canoe was a seagoing vessel, indispensable to the Shoshonean and Chumash islanders of the Santa Barbara group, and considerably employed also by the mainlanders of the shore from Point Conception and probably San Luis Obispo as far south as San Diego. It was usu-

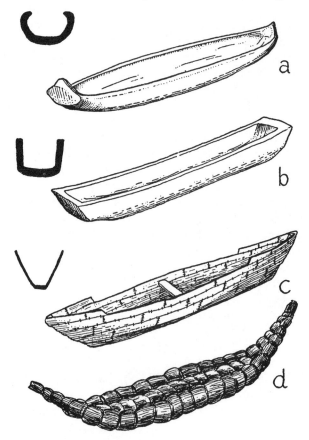

Boat Types of Native California (not to scale). *a*, Yurok (northwestern California) river canoe; *b*, Klamath (northeastern California) canoe; *c*, Chumash plank-canoe; *d*, tule balsa.

ally of lashed planks, either because solid timber for dugouts was scant, or because dexterity in woodworking rendered a carpentered construction less laborious. A dugout form seems also to have been known, and perhaps prevailed among the manually clumsier tribes toward San Diego. A double-bladed paddle was used. The southern California canoe was purely maritime. There were no navigable rivers, and on the few sheltered bays and lagoons the balsa was sufficient and generally employed. The size of this canoe was not great, the beam probably narrow, and the construction light; but the sea is normally calm in southern California and one side of the islands almost always sheltered.

A third type of canoe had a limited distribution in favorable localities in

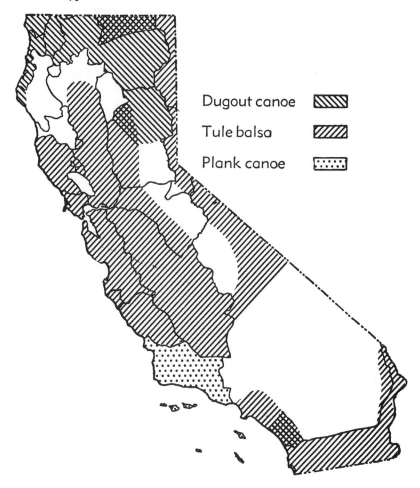

Map 2. Distribution of Types of Native California Boats.

northern California, ranging about as far as overlay twining, and evidently formed part of the technological culture characteristic of this region. A historical community of origin with the northwestern redwood canoe is indubitable, but it is less clear whether the northeastern canoe represents the original type from which the northwestern developed as a specialization, or whether the latter is the result of coastal influences from the north and the northeastern form a deteriorated marginal extension. This northeastern canoe was of pine or cedar or fir, burned and chopped out, narrow of beam, without definite shape. It was made by the Shasta, Modoc, Atsugewi, Achomawi, and northernmost Maidu.

The balsa or rush raft had a nearly universal distribution, so far as drainage conditions permitted; the only groups that wholly rejected it in favor of the canoe being the Chumash and the northwestern tribes. It is reported from the Modoc, Achomawi, Northern Paiute, Wintun, Maidu, Pomo, Costanoans, Yokuts, Tübatulabal, Luiseño, Diegueño, and Colorado River tribes. For river crossing, a bundle or group of bundles of tules sufficed. On large lakes and bays well-shaped vessels, with pointed and elevated prow and raised sides, were often navigated with paddles. The balsa does not appear to have been in use north of California, but it was known in Mexico, and probably has a continuous distribution, except for gaps due to negative environment, into South America.

The balsa was most often poled; but in the deep waters of San Francisco Bay the Costanoans propelled it with the same double-bladed paddle that was used with the canoe of the coast and archipelago of southern California, whence the less skillful northerners may be assumed to have derived the implement. The double paddle is extremely rare in America; like the "Mediterranean" type of arrow release, it appears to have been recorded only from the eastern Eskimo. The Pomo of Clear Lake used a single paddle with short broad blade. The canoe paddle of the northwestern tribes is long, narrow, and heavy, having to serve both as pole and as oar; that of the Klamath and Modoc, whose lake waters were currentless, is of more normal shape. Whether or not the southerners employed the one-bladed paddle in addition to the double-ended one, does not seem to be known.

The occurrence of the double-bladed paddle militates against the supposition that the Chumash plank canoe might be of Oceanic origin. It would be strange if the boat—minus the outrigger—could be derived from the central Pacific, its paddle from the Arctic. Both boat and paddle look like local inventions.

Except for Drake's reference to canoes among the Coast Miwok—perhaps to be understood as balsas—there is no evidence that any form of boat was in use on the ocean from the Golden Gate to Cape Mendocino. A few logs were occasionally lashed into a rude raft when seal or mussel rocks were to be visited.

A number of interior groups ferried goods, children, and perhaps even women across swollen streams in large baskets or—in the south—pots. Swimming men propelled and guarded the little vessels. This custom is established for the Yuki, Yokuts, and Mohave, and was no doubt participated in by other tribes.

Fishing

In fresh water and still bays, fish are more successfully taken by rude people with nets or weirs or poison than by line. Fishhooks are therefore employed only occasionally. This is the case in California. There was probably no group that was ignorant of the fishhook, but one hears little of its use. The one exception was on the southern coast, where deep water appears to have restricted the use of nets. The prevalent hook in this region was a single curved piece cut out of haliotis shell. Elsewhere the hook was in use chiefly for fishing in the larger lakes, and in the higher mountains where trout were taken. It consisted most commonly of a wooden shank with a pointed bone lashed backward on it at an angle of 45 degrees or less. Sometimes two such bones projected on opposite sides. The gorget, a straight bone sharpened on both ends and suspended from a string in its middle, is reported from the Modoc, but is likely to have had a wider distribution.

The harpoon was probably known to every group in California whose territory contained sufficient bodies of water. The Colorado River tribes provide the only exception: the stream is too murky for the harpoon. The type of implement is everywhere substantially identical. The shaft, being intended for thrusting and not throwing, is long and slender. The foreshaft is usually double, one prong being slightly longer than the other, presumably because the stroke is most commonly delivered at an angle to the bottom. The toggle heads are small, of bone and wood tightly wrapped with string and pitched. The socket is most frequently in or near the end. The string leaving the head at or near the middle, the socket end serves as a barb. This rather rude device is sufficient because the harpoon is rarely employed for game larger than a salmon. The lines are short and fastened to the spear.

A heavier harpoon which was perhaps hurled was used by the northwestern coast tribes for taking sea lions. Only the heads have been preserved. These are of bone or antler and possess a true barb as well as socket.

A single example of a Chumash sealing harpoon has been preserved. This has a detachable foreshaft of wood, set in a socket of the main shaft, and tipped with a nondetachable flint blade and a bone barb that is lashed and asphalted on immediately behind the blade.

There is one record of the spear-thrower: also a specimen from the Chumash. This is of wood and is remarkable for its excessively short, broad, and unwieldy shape. It is probably authentic, but its entire uniqueness renders caution necessary in drawing inferences from this solitary example.

The seine for surrounding fish, the stretched gill net, and the dip-net were known to all the Californians, although many groups had occasion to use only certain varieties. The form and size of the dip-net of course differed according as it was used in large or small streams, in the surf or in standing waters. The two commonest forms of frame were a semicircular hoop bisected by the handle, and two long diverging poles crossed and braced in the angle. A kite-shaped frame was sometimes employed for scooping. Nets without poles had floats of wood or tule stems. The sinkers were grooved or nicked stones, the commonest type of all being a flat beach pebble notched on opposite edges to prevent the string from slipping. Perforated stones are known to have been used as net sinkers only in northwestern California and even there they occur by the side of the grooved variety. They are usually distinguishable without difficulty from the perforated stone of southern and central California which served as a digging-stick weight, by the fact that their perforation is normally not in the middle. The north-westerners also availed themselves of naturally perforated stones.

Fish poison was fed into small streams and pools by a number of tribes: the Pomo, Yokuts, and Luiseño are specified, which indicates that the practice was widely spread. Buckeyes and soaproot (*Chlorogalum*) as well as other plants were employed.

Bows

The bow was self, long, and narrow in the south, sinew-backed, somewhat shorter, thin, and broad in northern and central California. Of course light unbacked bows were used for small game and by boys everywhere. The material varied locally. In the northwest, the bow was of yew and shorter and flatter than anywhere else; the wood was pared down to little greater thickness than the sinew, the edge was sharp, and the grip much pinched. Good bows of course quickly went out of use before firearms, so that few examples have been preserved anywhere except low-grade modern pieces intended for birds and rabbits. But sinew backing is reported southward to the Yokuts and Panamint, so that the Tehachapi range may be set as the limit. The Yokuts name of the Kitanemuk meant "large bows." This group therefore is likely to have used the southern self bow. On the other hand, a specimen attributed to the Chumash is sinew backed, thong wound in the middle, and has a three-ply sinew cord. As the piece is narrower than the northern bows and the wood does not seem to be yew, the attribution is probably correct.

The arrow was normally two-pieced, its head most frequently of obsidian, which works finer and smaller as well as sharper than flint. The butt end of the point was frequently notched for a sinew lashing. The foreshaft was generally set into the main shaft. For small game shot at close range one-piece arrows frequently sufficed: the stone head was also omitted, or replaced by a blunted wooden point. Cane was used as main shaft wherever it was available, but nowhere exclusively. From the Yokuts south to the Yuma the typical fighting arrow was a simple wooden shaft without head, quantity rather than effectiveness of ammunition appearing the desideratum. The same tribes, however, often tipped their cane deer arrows with stone.

The arrow release has been described for but three groups. None of these holds agrees, and two are virtually new for America. The Maidu release is the primary one, the Yahi a modification of the Mongolian, the Luiseño the pure Mediterranean, hitherto attributed in the new world only to the Eskimo. This remarkable variety in detail is characteristic of California.

The arrow was bent straight in a hole cut through a slab of wood, and polished with *Equisetum* or in two grooved pieces of sandstone in the north. The southern straightener and polisher is determined by the cane arrow: a transversely grooved rectangle of steatite set by the fire. This Southwestern form extends north at least to the Yokuts; the Maidu possessed it in somewhat aberrant form.

Textiles

Basketry is unquestionably the most developed art in California, so that it is of interest that the principle which chiefly emerges in connection with the art is that its growth has been in the form of what ethnologists are wont to name "complexes." That is to say, materials, processes, forms, and uses which abstractly considered bear no intrinsic relation to one another; or only a slight relation, are in fact bound up in a unit. A series of tribes employs the same forms, substances, and techniques; when a group is reached which abandons one of these factors, it abandons most or all of them, and follows a characteristically different art.

This is particularly clear of the basketry of northernmost California. At first sight this art seems to be distinguished chiefly by the outstanding fact that it knows no coiling processes. Its southern line of demarcation runs between the Sinkyone and Kato, the Wailaki and Yuki, through Wintun and Yana territory at points that have not been determined with certainty, and between the Achomawi (or more strictly the Atsugewi) and the Maidu. Northward it extends far into Oregon west of the Cascades. The Klamath and Modoc do not adhere to it, although their industry is a related one.

Further examination reveals a considerable number of other traits that are universally followed by the tribes in the region in question. Wickerwork and checkerwork, which have no connection with coiling, are also not made. Of the numerous varieties of twining, the plain weave is substantially the only one employed, with some use of subsidiary strengthening in narrow belts of three-strand twining. The diagonal twine is known, but practiced only sporadically. Decoration is wholly in overlay twining, each weft strand being faced with a colored one. The materials of this basketry are hazel shoots for warp, conifer roots for weft, and *Xerophyllum, Adiantum,* and alder-dyed *Woodwardia* for white, black, and red patterns respectively. All these plants appear to grow some distance south of the range of this basketry. At least in some places to the south they are undoubtedly sufficiently abundant to serve as materials. The limit of distribution of the art can therefore not be ascribed to botanical causes. Similarly, there is no easily seen reason why people should stop wearing basketry caps and pounding acorns in a basketry hopper because their materials or technique have become different. That they do, evidences the strength of this particular complex.

In southern California a definite type of basket ware is adhered to with nearly equal rigidity. The typical technique here is coiling, normally on a foundation of straws of *Epicampes* grass. The sewing material is sumac or *Juncus.* Twined ware is subsidiary, is roughly done, and is made wholly in *Juncus*—a material that, used alone, forbids any considerable degree of finish. Here again the basketry cap and the mortar hopper appear but are limited toward the north by the range of the technique.

From southern California proper this basketry has penetrated to the southerly Yokuts and the adjacent Shoshonean tribes. Chumash ware also belongs to the same type, although it often substitutes *Juncus* for the *Epicampes* grass and sometimes uses willow. Both the Chumash and the Yokuts and Shoshoneans in and north of the Tehachapi mountains have developed one characteristic form not found in southern California proper: the shouldered basket with constricted neck. This is represented in the south by a simpler form, a small globular basket. The extreme development of the "bottleneck" type is found among the Yokuts, Kawaiisu, and Tübatulabal. The Chumash on the one side, and the willow-using Chemehuevi on the other, round the shoulders of these vessels so as to show a partial transition to the southern California prototype.

The Colorado River tribes slight basketry to a very unusual degree. They make a few rude trays and fish traps. The majority of their baskets they seem always to have acquired in trade from their neighbors. Their neglect of the art recalls its similar low condition among the Pueblos, but is even more pronounced. Pottery making and agriculture seem to be the influences most largely responsible.

Central California from the Yuki and Maidu to the Yokuts is an area in which coiling and twining occur side by side. There are probably more twined baskets made, but they are manufactured for rougher usage and more often undecorated. Show pieces are usually coiled. The characteristic technique is therefore perhaps coiling, but the two processes nearly balance. The materials are not so uniform as in the north or south. The most characteristic plant is perhaps the redbud, *Cercis occidentalis,* which furnishes the red and often the white surface of coiled vessels and is used in twining also. The most common techniques are coiling with triple foundation and plain twining. Diagonal twining is however more or less followed, and lattice twining, single-rod coiling, and wickerwork all have at least a local distribution. Twining with overlay is never practiced. Forms are variable, but not to any notable extent. Oval baskets are made in the Pomo region, and occasionally elsewhere, but there is no shape of so pronounced a character as the southern Yokuts bottleneck.

A number of local basketry arts have grown in central California on this generic foundation. The most complicated of these is that of the Pomo and their immediate neighbors, who have developed feather-covering, lattice twining, checkerwork, single-rod coiling, the mortar hopper, and several other specializations. It may be added that the Pomo appear to be the only central Californian group that habitually make twined baskets with patterns.

Another definite center of development includes the Washo and in some measure the Miwok. Both of these groups practice single-rod coiling and have evolved a distinctive style of ornamentation characterized by a certain lightness of decorative touch. This ware, however, shades off to the south into Yokuts basketry with its southern California affiliations, and to the north into Maidu ware.

The latter in its pure form is readily distinguished from Miwok as well as Pomo basketry, but presents few positive peculiarities.

Costanoan and Salinan baskets perished so completely that no very definite idea of them can be formed. It is unlikely that any very marked local type prevailed in this region, and yet there are almost certain to have been some peculiarities.

The Yuki, wedged in between the Pomo and tribes that followed the northern California twining, make a coiled ware which with all its simplicity cannot be confounded with that of any other group in California; this in spite of the general lack of advancement which pervades their culture.

It thus appears that we may infer that a single style and type underlies the basketry of the whole of central California; that this has undergone numerous local diversifications due only in part to the materials available, and extending on the other hand into its purely decorative aspects; and that the most active and proficient of these local superstructures was that for which the Pomo were responsible, their creation, however, differing only in degree from those which resulted from analogous but less active impulses elsewhere. In central California, therefore, a basic basketry complex is less rigidly developed, or preserved, than in either the north or the south. The flora being substantially uniform through central California, differences in the use of materials are in themselves significant of the incipient or superficial diversifications of the art.

The Modoc constitute a subtype within the area of twining. They overlay chiefly when they use *Xerophyllum* or quills, it would seem, and the majority of their baskets, which are composed of tule fibers of several shades, are in plain twining. But the shapes and patterns of their ware have clearly been developed under the influences that guide the art of the overlaying tribes; and the cap and hopper occur among them.

It is difficult to decide whether the Modoc art is to be interpreted as a form of the primitive style on which the modern overlaying complex is based, or as a readaptation of the latter to a new and widely useful material. The question can scarcely be answered without full consideration of the basketry of all Oregon.

Cloth is unknown in aboriginal California. Rush mats are twined like baskets or sewn. The nearest approach to a loom is a pair of upright sticks on which a long cord of rabbit fur is wound back and forth to be made into a blanket by the intertwining of a weft of the same material, or of two cords. The Maidu and southern Californians, and therefore probably other tribes also, made similar blankets of feather cords or strips of duck skin. The rabbitskin blanket has of course a wide distribution outside of California; that of bird skins may have been devised locally.

Pottery

The distribution of pottery in California reveals this art as surely due to Southwestern influences. It is practiced by the Yuma, Mohave, and other Colorado River tribes; sporadically by the Chemehuevi; by the Diegueño, Luiseño, Cupeño, Serrano, and Cahuilla; probably not by the Gabrielino; with the Juaneño doubtful. A second area, in which cruder pottery is made, lies to the north, apparently disconnected from the southern California one. In this district live the southern and perhaps central Yokuts, the Tübatulabal, and the Western Mono [Monachi]. This ware seems to be pieced with the fingers; it is irregular, undecorated, and the skill to construct vessels of any size was wanting. The southern Californians tempered with crushed rock, employed a clay that baked dull reddish, laid it on in thin spiral coils, and smoothed it between a wooden paddle and a pebble. They never corrugated, and no slipped ware has been found in the region; but there was some variety of forms—bowls, jars, pots, oval plates, short-handled spoons, asymmetrical and multiple-mouthed jars, pipes—executed in a considerable range of sizes. Designs were solely in yellow ochre, and frequently omitted. They consisted chiefly of patterns of angular lines, with or without the corners filled in. Curves, solidly painted areas, and semi-realistic figures were rarely attempted. The ware was light, brittle, and porous.

The art during the last generation has been best preserved among the Mohave, and seems at all times to have attained greatest development on the Colorado River. But the coast tribes may have been substantial equals before they came under Caucasian influence, except that they decorated less. An affinity with ancient Pima and Seri ware is unmistakable; but it is far from attaining identity. There is no direct or specific resemblance to any present or ancient Pueblo pottery. This argues a local origination under outside influence, not an importation of the art as such; at any rate not from the true Pueblo area. Sonora is rather indicated as the source of stimulation. Potsherds indistinguishable from the modern ware occur in ancient sites on the Diegueño coast. Whether or not they extend to the earlier deposits remains to be ascertained; but they testify that the art is not an entirely recent one. Pottery was not established in California as a mere adjunct of agriculture, its distribution being considerably greater.

Pottery, then, must be reckoned as historically in a class with the religious institutions of southern California: a local growth, due to an ultimate stimulus from the Southwest.

Musical Instruments

The rattle is of three kinds in the greater part of California: the split clap stick for dancing, the gravel-filled cocoon bunch for shamanistic practices, the bundle of deer hoofs for the adolescent girl. South of Tehachapi these are generally replaced by a single form, whose material varies between turtle shell and gourd according to region. The northwest does not use rattles except in the adolescence ceremony; in which some tribes, such as the Hupa and Sinkyone, employ a modification of the clap stick, the Karok, Tolowa, and others the more general deer hoofs. The latter implement is known as far south as the Luiseño but seems to be associated with hunting or mourning ceremonies at this end of the state. The clap stick penetrated to the Gabrielino.

The notched scraper or musical rasp has been reported only from the Salinans.

California is a drumless region, except in the area of the Kuksu cult. There a foot drum, a segment of a large cylinder of wood, is set at the back of the dance house, and held very sacred. Various substitutes exist:

the Yurok beat a board with a paddle, the Maidu strike or rub baskets, the Mohave do the same before a resounding jar. But these devices accompany gambling or shamans' or narrative songs: none of the substitutes replace dance drums.

Whistles of bone or cane are employed far more frequently in dances than the drum—by practically all tribes, in fact, although of course in quite different connections.

The bull-roarer has been reported from several scattered tribes. As might be expected, its use is religious, but its specific service is not well known and may have varied. To the Luiseño it was a summons. It was not used by the northwestern nations.

The only true musical instrument in our sense is the flute, an open, reed-less tube, blown across the edge of one end. Almost always it has four holes, often more or less grouped in two pairs, and is innocent of any definite scale. It is played for self-recreation and courtship. The Mohave alone know a flageolet.

The musical or resonant bow, a sort of jew's-harp, the only stringed instrument of California, has been recorded among the Pomo, Maidu, Yokuts, and Diegueño, and no doubt had a wider distribution. It was tapped as a restful amusement, and sometimes in converse with the spirits.

It is remarkable, although abundantly paralleled among other Indians, that only two instruments capable of producing a melody were not used ceremonially. The cause may be their imperfection. The dance was based on song, which an instrument of rhythm could enrich, but with which a mechanically but crudely produced melody would have clashed.

It is also a curious fact that the comparatively superior civilization of the northwestern tribes was the one that wholly lacked drum, bull-roarer, and musical bow and made minimal employ of rattles.

Money

Two forms of money prevailed in California, the dentalium shell, imported from the far north; and the clamshell-disk bead. Among the strictly northwestern tribes dentalia were alone standard. In a belt stretching across the remainder of the northern end of the state, and limited very nearly, to the south, by the line that marks the end of the range of overlay twined basketry, dentalia, and disks were used side by side.

Beyond, to the southern end of the state, dentalia were so sporadic as to be no longer reckoned as money, and the clam money was the medium of valuation. It had two sources of supply. On Bodega Bay, perhaps also at a few other points, the resident Coast Miwok and neighboring Pomo gathered the shell *Saxidomus aratus* or *gracilis*. From Morro Bay near San

Luis Obispo to San Diego there occurs another large clam, *Tivela* or *Pachydesma crassatelloides*. Both of these were broken, the pieces roughly shaped, bored, strung, and then rounded and polished on a sandstone slab. The disks were from a third of an inch to an inch in diameter, and from a quarter to a third of an inch thick, and varied in value according to size, thickness, polish, and age. The Pomo supplied the north; southern and central California used *Pachydesma* beads. The Southern Maidu are said to have had the latter, which fact, on account of their remoteness from the supply, may account for the higher value of the currency among them than with the Yokuts. But the Pomo *Saxidomus* bead is likely also to have reached the Maidu.

From the Yokuts and Salinans south, money was measured on the circumference of the hand. The exact distance traversed by the string varied somewhat according to tribe; the value in our terms appears to have fluctuated locally to a greater degree. The Pomo, Wintun, and Maidu seem not to have known the hand scale. They measured their strings in the rough by stretching them out, and appear to have counted the beads when they wished accuracy.

Associated with the two clam moneys were two kinds of valuables, both in cylindrical form. The northern was of magnesite, obtained in or near southeastern Pomo territory. This was polished and on baking took on a tawny or reddish hue, often variegated. These stone cylinders traveled as far as the Yuki and the Miwok. From the south came similar but longer and slenderer pieces of shell, white to violet in color, made sometimes of the columella of univalves, sometimes out of the hinge of a large rock oyster or rock clam, probably *Hinnites giganteus*. The bivalve cylinders took the finer grain and seem to have been preferred. Among the Chumash, such pieces must have been fairly common, to judge from finds in graves. To the inland Yokuts and Miwok they were excessively valuable. Both the magnesite and the shell cylinders were perforated longitudinally, and often constituted the center piece of a fine string of beads; but, however displayed, they were too precious to be properly classifiable as ornaments. At the same time their individual variability in size and quality, and consequently in value, was too great to allow them to be reckoned as ordinary money. They may be ranked on the whole with the obsidian blades of northwestern California, as an equivalent of precious stones among ourselves.

The small univalve *Olivella biplicata* and probably other species of the same genus were used nearly everywhere in the state. In the north, they were strung whole; in central and southern California, frequently broken up and rolled into thin, slightly concave disks, as by the Southwestern Indians of today. Neither form had much value. The olivella disks are far more common in graves than clam disks, as if a change of custom had taken place from the prehistoric to the historic period. But a more likely explanation is that the olivellas accompanied the corpse precisely because they were less valuable, the clam currency either being saved for inheritance, or, if offered, destroyed by fire in the great mourning anniversary.

Haliotis was much used in necklaces, ear ornaments, and the like, and among tribes remote from the sea commanded a considerable price; but it was nowhere standardized into currency.

Tobacco

Tobacco, of two or more species of *Nicotiana,* was smoked everywhere, but by the Yokuts, Tübatulabal, Kitanemuk, and Costanoans it was also mixed with shell lime and eaten.

The plant was grown by the northwestern groups such as the Yurok and Hupa, and apparently by the Wintun and Maidu. This limited agriculture, restricted to the people of a rather small area remote from tribes with farming customs, is curious. The Hupa and Yurok are afraid of wild tobacco as liable to have sprung from a grave; but it is as likely that the cultivation produced this unreasonable fear by rendering the use of the natural product unnecessary, as that the superstition was the impetus to the cultivation.

Tobacco was offered religiously by the Yurok, the Hupa, the Yahi, the Yokuts, and presumably by most or all other tribes; but exact data are lacking.

The pipe is found everywhere, and with insignificant exceptions is tubular. In the northwest, it averages about six inches long, and is of hard wood scraped somewhat concave in profile, the bowl lined with inset soapstone. In the region about the Pomo, the pipe is longer, the bowl end abruptly thickened to two or three inches, the stem slender. This bulb-ended pipe and the bulb-ended pestle have nearly the same distribution and may have influenced one another. In the Sierra Nevada, the pipe runs to only three or four inches, and tapers somewhat to the mouth end. The Chumash pipe has been preserved in its stone exemplars. These normally resemble the Sierra type, but are often longer, normally thicker, and more frequently contain a brief mouthpiece of bone. Ceremonial specimens are sometimes of obtuse angular shape. The pottery-making tribes of the south use clay pipes most commonly. These are short, with shouldered bowl end. In all the region from the Yokuts south, in other words wherever the plant is available, a simple length of cane frequently replaces the worked pipe; and among all tribes shamans have all-stone pieces at times. The Modoc pipe is essentially Eastern: a stone head set on a wooden stem. The head is variable, as if it were a new and not yet established form: a tube, an L, intermediate forms, or a disk.

The Californians were light smokers, rarely passionate. They consumed smaller quantities of tobacco than most Eastern tribes and did not dilute it with bark. Smoking was of little formal social consequence, and indulged in chiefly at bedtime in the sweathouse. The available species of *Nicotiana* were pungent and powerful in physiological effect, and quickly produced dizziness and sleep.

Various

The ax and the stone celt are foreign to aboriginal California. The substitute is the wedge or chisel of antler—among the Chumash of whale's bone —driven by a stone. This maul is shaped only in extreme northern California.

The commonest string materials are the bark or outer fibers of dogbane or Indian hemp, *Apocynum cannabinum,* and milkweed, *Asclepias.* From these, fine cords and heavy ropes are spun by hand. Nettle string is reported from two groups as distant as the Modoc and the Luiseño. Other tribes are likely to have used it also as a subsidiary material. In the northwest, from the Tolowa to the Coast Yuki, and inland at least to the Shasta, Indian hemp and milkweed are superseded by a small species of iris— *I. macrosiphon*—from each leaf of which two thin, tough, silky fibers are scraped out. The manufacture is tedious, but results in an unusually fine, hard, and even string. In the southern desert, yucca fibers yield a coarse stiff cordage, and the reed—*Phragmites*—is also said to be used. Barks of various kinds, mostly from unidentified species, are employed for wrappings and lashings by many tribes, and grapevine is a convenient tying material for large objects when special pliability is not required. Practically all Californian cordage, of whatever weight, was two-ply before Caucasian contact became influential.

The carrying net is essentially southern so far as California is concerned, but connects geographically as well as in type with a net used by the Shoshonean women of the Great Basin. It was in use among all the southern Californians except those of the Colorado River and possibly the Chemehuevi, and extended north among the Yokuts. The shape of the utensil is that of a small hammock of large mesh. One end terminates in a heavy cord, the other in a loop. A varying type occurs in an isolated region to the north among the Pomo and Yuki. Here the ends of the net are carried into a continuous headband. This arrangement does not permit of contraction or expansion to accommodate the load as in the south. The net has also been mentioned for the Costanoans, but its type there remains unknown. It is possible that these people served as transmitters of the idea from the south to the Pomo. A curious device is reported from the Maidu. The pack strap, when not of skin, is braided or more probably woven. Through its larger central portion the warp threads run free without weft. This arrangement allows them to be spread out and to enfold a small or light load somewhat in the fashion of a net.

The carrying frame of the Southwest has no analogy in California except on the Colorado River. Here two looped sticks are crossed and their four lengths connected with light cordage. Except for the disparity between the frame and the shell of the covering, this type would pass as a basketry form, and at bottom it appears to be such. The ordinary openwork conical carrying basket of central and northern California is occasionally strengthened by the lashing in of four heavier rods. In the northeastern corner of the state, where exterior influences from eastern cultures are recognizable, the carrier is sometimes of hide fastened to a frame of four sticks.

The storage of acorns or corresponding food supplies is provided for in three ways in California. All the southern tribes construct a large receptacle of twigs irregularly interlaced like a bird's nest. This is sometimes made with a bottom, sometimes set on a bed of twigs and covered in the same way. The more arid the climate, the less does construction matter. Mountain tribes make the receptacle with bottom and lid and small mouth. In the open desert the chief function of the granary is to hold the food together and it becomes little else than a short section of hollow cylinder. Nowhere is there any recognizable technique. The diameter is from two to six feet. The setting is always outdoors, sometimes on a platform, often on bare rocks, and occasionally on the ground. The Chumash did not use this type of receptacle.

In central California a cache or granary is used which can also not be described as a true basket. It differs from the southern form in usually being smaller in diameter but higher, in being constructed of finer and softer materials, and in depending more or less directly in its structure on a series of posts which at the same time elevate it from the ground. This is the granary of the tribes in the Sierra Nevada, used by the Wintun, Maidu, Miwok, and Yokuts, and in somewhat modified form—a mat of sticks covered with thatch—by the Western or mountain Mono. It has penetrated also to those of the Pomo of Lake County who are in direct communication with the Wintun.

In the remainder of California, both north and south, large baskets—their type of course determined by the prevailing style of basketry—are set indoors or perhaps occasionally in caves or rock recesses.

The flat spoon or paddle for stirring gruel is widely spread, but far from universal. It has been found among all the northwestern tribes, the Achomawi, Shasta, Pomo, Wappo, Northern Miwok, Washo, and Diegueño. The Yokuts and Southern Miwok, at times the Washo, use instead a looped stick, which is also convenient for handling hot cooking stones. The Colorado River tribes, who stew more civilized messes of corn, beans, or fish in pots, tie three rods together for a stirrer. The Maidu alone are said to have done without an implement.

SOCIETY

Political Organization

Tribes did not exist in California in the sense in which the word is properly applicable to the greater part of the North American continent. When the term is used it must therefore be understood as synonymous with "ethnic group" rather than as denoting political unity.

The marginal Mohave and the Yuma are the only Californian groups comparable to what are generally understood as "tribes" in the central and eastern United States: namely, a fairly coherent body of from five hundred to five thousand souls—usually averaging not far from two thousand; speaking in almost all cases a distinctive dialect or at least subdialect; with a political organization of the loosest, perhaps; but nevertheless possessed of a considerable sentiment of solidarity as against all other bodies, sufficient ordinarily to lead them to act as a unit. The uniquely enterprising military spirit displayed by the Yuma and Mohave is undoubtedly connected with this sense of cohesion.

The extreme of political anarchy is found in the northwest, where there was scarcely a tendency to group villages into higher units, and where even a village was not conceived as an essential unit. In practice a northwestern village was likely to act as a body, but it did so either because its inhabitants were kinsmen, or because it contained a man of sufficient wealth to have established personal relations of obligation between himself and individual fellow-townsmen not related to him in blood. The Yurok, Karok, and Hupa, and probably several of the adjacent groups simply did not recognize any organization which transcended individuals and kin groups.

In north central California the rudiments of a tribal organization are discernible among the Pomo, Yuki, and Maidu and may be assumed to have prevailed among most other groups. A tribe in this region was a small body, evidently including on the average not much more than a hundred souls. It did not possess distinctive speech, a number of such tribes being normally included in the range of a single dialect. Each was obviously in substance a village community, although the term village in this connection must be understood as implying a tract of land rather than a settlement as such. In most cases the population of the little tribe was divided between several settlements, each presumably consisting of a few households more or less intimately connected by blood; but there was also a site which was regarded as the principal one inhabited. Subsidiary settlements were frequently abandoned, reoccupied, or newly founded. The principal village was maintained more permanently. The limits of the territory of the group were well defined, comprising in most cases a natural drainage area. A chief was recognized for the tribe. There is some indication that his elevation may often have been subject to popular consent, although hereditary tendencies are likely to have been rather more influential in most cases. The minor settlements or groups of kinsmen had each their lesser chief or headman. There was no proper name for the tribe. It was designated either by the name of its principal settlement or by that of its chief. Among foreigners these little groups sometimes bore names which were used much like true tribal names; but on an analysis these almost invariably prove to mean only "people of such and such a place or district." This type of organization is likely to have prevailed as far south as the Miwok in the interior and the Costanoans or Salinans on the coast, and northward to the Achomawi and possibly the Modoc.

The Yokuts, and apparently they alone, attained a nearer approach to a full tribal system. Their tribes were larger, ranging from a hundred and fifty to four hundred or five hundred members; possessed names which usually did not refer to localities; and spoke distinctive dialects, although these were often only slightly divergent from the neighboring tongues. The territory of each tribe was larger than in the Maidu-Pomo region, and a principal permanent village looms with prominence only in some cases.

The Shoshoneans of Nevada, and with them those of the eastern desert fringe of California, possessed an organization which appears to be somewhat akin to that of the Yokuts. They were divided into groups of about the same size as the Yokuts, each without a definite metropolis, rather shifting within its range, and headed by a chief possessing considerable influence. The groups were almost throughout named after a characteristic diet, thus "fish eaters" or "mountainsheep eaters." It is not known how far each of these tribes possessed a unique dialect: if they did, their speech distinctness was in most cases minimal. Owing to the open and poorly productive nature of the country, the territory of each of these groups of the Shoshonean Great Basin was considerably more extensive than in the Yokuts habitat.

Political conditions in southern California are very obscure, but are likely to have been generally similar to those of north central California. Among the Chumash, towns of some size were inhabited century after century, and these undoubtedly were the centers if not the bases of political groups.

The Mohave and other Yuman tribes of the Colorado Valley waged war as tribal units. Their settlements were small, shifting, apparently determined in the main by the location of their fields, and enter little into their own descriptions of their life. It is clear that the Mohave's sense of attachment was primarily to his people as a body, and secondarily to his country as a whole. The Californian Indian, with the partial exception of the Yokuts, always gives the impression of being attached first of all to a spot, or at most a few miles of stream or valley, and to his blood kindred or a small group of lifelong associates and intimates.

It should be added that the subject of political organization is perhaps the topic in most urgent need of investigation in the whole field of California ethnology.

The Chief

Chieftainship is still wrapped in much the same obscurity and vagueness as political bodies. There were no doubt hereditary chiefs in many parts of California. But it is difficult to determine how far inheritance was the formally instituted avenue to office, or was only actually operative in the majority of instances. In general it seems that chieftainship was more definitely hereditary in the southern half or two-thirds of the state than in the north central area. Wealth was a factor of some consequence in relation to chieftainship everywhere, but its influence seems also to have varied according to locality. The northwestern tribes had hereditarily rich men of great influence, but no chiefs. Being without political organization, they could not well have had the latter.

The degree of authority of the chief is very difficult to estimate. This is a matter which cannot be judged accurately from the accounts of relations between native groups and intruders belonging to a more highly civilized alien race. To understand the situation between the chief and his followers in the routine of daily life, it is necessary to have at command a more intimate knowledge of this life before its disturbance by Caucasian culture than is available for most Californian groups. It does seem that the authority of the chief was considerable everywhere as far north as the Miwok, and by no means negligible beyond; while in the northwest the social effect of wealth was so great as to obtain for the rich a distinctly commanding position. Among certain of the Shoshoneans of southern California the chief, the assistant or religious chief, and their wives or children, were all known by titles; which fact argues that a fairly great deference was accorded them. Their authority probably did not lag much behind. Both the Juaneño and the Chumash are said to have gone to war to avenge slights put upon their chiefs. The director of rituals as an assistant to the head chief is a southern California institution. Somewhat similar is the central Yokuts practice of having two chiefs for each tribe, one to represent each exogamous moiety. The chief had speakers, messengers, or similar henchmen with named offices, among the Coast Miwok, the interior Miwok, the Yokuts, the Juaneño, and no doubt among other groups.

The chief was everywhere distinctly a civil official. If he commanded also in battle, it seems to have been only through the accident of being a distinguished warrior as well. The usual war leader was merely that individual in the group who was able to inspire confidence through having displayed courage, skill, and enterprise in combat. It is only natural that his voice should have carried weight even in time of peace; but he seems not to have been regarded as holding an office. This distinction between the chief and the military leader appears to apply even to the Yuma and Mohave, among whom bravery was the supreme virtue.

There were no hereditary priests in California. A religious function often passed from father to son or brother's son, but the successor took his place because his kinship had caused him to acquire the necessary knowledge, not in virtue of his descent as such. At that there was hardly a recognized class of priests. The old man who knew most held the direction of ceremonies; and in the Kuksu region a man became clown, or moki, or kuksu, or some other specific impersonator, rather than a priest as such.

The shaman of course was never an official in the true sense of the word, inasmuch as his power was necessarily of individual acquisition and varied directly according to his supernatural potency, or, as we should call it, his gifts of personality.

Social Stratification

Social classes of different level are hardly likely to develop markedly in so primitive a society as that of California. It is therefore highly distinctive of the northwestern area that the social stratification which forms so important an element in the culture of the North Pacific coast, appears among these people with undiminished vigor. The heraldic and symbolic devices of the more advanced tribes a thousand miles to the north are lacking among the Yurok: the consciousness of the different value of a rich and a poor man is as keen among them as with the Kwakiutl or the Haida.

The northwest is also the only part of California that knew slavery. This institution rested upon the economic basis of debt.

Wealth was by no means a negligible factor in the remainder of California, but it clearly did not possess the same influence as in the northwest. There seems to have been an effort to regulate matters so that the chief, through the possession of several wives, or through contributions, was in a position to conduct himself with liberality, especially toward strangers and in time of need. On the whole he was wealthy because he was chief rather than the reverse. Among the Colorado River tribes a thoroughly democratic spirit prevailed as regards property, and there was a good deal of the Plains sentiment that it behooved a true man to be contemptuous of material possessions.

Exogamy and Totemism

California was long regarded as a region lacking clans, group totems, or other exogamous social units. The Colorado River tribes were indeed known to be divided into clans, and the Miwok into moieties, both carrying certain rather indirect totemic associations. But these seemed to be isolated exceptions. More recent information, however, due mainly to the investigations of E. W. Gifford, shows that some form of gentile organization was prevalent among nearly all groups from the Miwok south to the Yuma; and the principal types which this organization assumes have become clear at least in outline.

In brief the situation is this. Almost everywhere within the area in question, the units are exogamous. Nearly always they are totemic. Descent is invariably patrilinear. In the extreme south or southeast the division of society is on the basis of multiple clans; in the San Joaquin Valley of moieties; between, that is, roughly in the region of the northern part of southern California, there are clans and moieties. Toward the head of the San Joaquin Valley there is a tract over which clans, moieties, and totems are all lacking. This tongue of clanless area may represent intrusive or conservative influence from the desert Shoshoneans on the east. It very likely did not wholly sever the totemic social organizations of central and southern California, for there is no definite information available on the most southwesterly body of Yokuts, the Chumash, the Kitanemuk, or the Gabrielino, and if these groups possessed moieties, clans, or totems, they would connect the two areas into a continuous unit.

It is hardly possible to doubt that the totemic clan or moiety system of California stands in a positive historic relation to that of the Southwest. The fact of its being a patrilinear system, whereas the southwestern Indians reckon descent in the female line, indicates only that the connection is ancient and indirect. Both the chief other North American regions in which totemic clans or moieties prevail, the North Pacific coast and the eastern side of the continent, are divided into patrilinear and matrilinear subareas. The continental distribution is such that it would be more than hazardous to assume the patrilinear institutions of the North Pacific, the East, and the Southwest-California area to have been derived from a common source, and the matrilinear institutions of the same three regions from a second origin. It is as clear as such matters can be that a system of gentile organization developed around three centers—whether these were thoroughly independent of one another or were originally related is a question that need not be considered here—and that within each area, with the growth and diversification of the institution, paternal and maternal reckoning grew up side by side or one after the other. In other words, the impulse toward the division of society on the basis of exogamous hereditary groups is the older. The predominance accorded to one sex or the other in the reckoning of descent is a direction subsequently assumed. Such being the indicated course of continental development, we need be under no hesitation in linking the totemic exogamy of California with that of the Southwest, in spite of its decisive patrilinear character.

As to the age of the institution in the two regions, there can be little doubt that as in most matters probable precedence should be given to the Southwest on the ground of the generally greater complexity and development of its culture. It is only necessary to guard against the hasty inference that, because the connection is almost certain and the radiation from New Mexico and Arizona into California probable, this movement has been a recent one whose course can still be traced by the present location of this or that particular tribe.

The clans of the Colorado River tribes are fairly numerous, a dozen or more for each group. They have no names as such, but are each characterized by the use of a single name borne by all the women of a clan. These women's names can usually not be analyzed, but are understood by the Indians as denotive of an animal or object which is clearly the totem of the clan. This system is common without material modification to all the Yumans of the river, but the totemic references vary considerably, and the women's names even more. The latter must have fluctuated with considerable readiness, since only a small proportion of the total number known are common even to two tribes.

With the Diegueño and Luiseño the system loses many of its characteristics. Totemism, direct or indirect, is wholly lacking. The groups are numerous and small. Their names when translatable are mostly those of localities, or have reference to a locality. The native theory is clearly that each clan is a local kin group. How far this was actually the case, is very difficult to determine positively, since mission residence, and among even the remoter sections of these groups a century or more of Caucasian contact, have rather disintegrated the native life.

With the Cupeño, Cahuilla, and Serrano, the institution is reinvigorated. The local groups persist as among the Luiseño and Diegueño and bear similar names. They are, however, united into two great moieties—named after the coyote and wildcat—which are thus totemic, and which are also the essential units determining exogamy. The clans are numerous, small, and probably consist in the main of actual or even traceable blood kinsmen related in the male line.

From here on northward follows the gap in our knowledge. It is however certain that the Shoshonean Kawaiisu and Tübatulabal, and the southern Yokuts such as the Yaudanchi and Yauelmani, were at least substantially free from the influence of any exogamous system.

When this negative or doubtful zone has been passed through, we find ourselves well in the San Joaquin Valley. Here, among the central Yokuts, according to some slender indications among the Salinans, probably among the northern Yokuts, and among all the Sierra Miwok, clans have wholly disappeared. The exogamous moiety however remains, and its totemic aspects are rather more developed than in the south. The Miwok carry the totemic scheme farthest, dividing the universe as it were into totemic halves, so that all its natural contents are potential totems of one or the other moiety. Among the other groups of this region the totemism is generally restricted to a limited number of birds or animals. Moieties are variously designated as land and water, downstream and upstream, bluejay and coyote, bullfrog and coyote, or bear and deer. The totem is spoken of as the "dog," that is domestic animal or pet, of each individual. Among the Miwok the personal name refers to an animal or object of the individual's moiety, but the totem itself is hardly ever expressed in the name, the reference being by some implication which can hardly be intelligible to those who do not know the individual and his moiety.

The Western Mono, at least in the northern part of their range, have come under the influence of the Miwok-Yokuts system, but this has assumed a somewhat aberrant shape among them. They subdivide each moiety into two groups which might be called clans except for the fact that they are not exogamous. The names of these groups have not yielded to certain translation. The Mono seem to identify them with localities.

Matrilinear descent has once been reported for a single Yokuts tribe, the Gashowu, but is so directly at variance with all that is known of the institutions of the region, as to be almost certainly an error of observation. On the other hand, there are more positive indications, mainly in kinship designations and the inheritance of chieftainship, of a reckoning in the female line among some of the Pomo and Wappo; and these are the more credible because the Pomo lie outside of the exogamic and totemic area of California. The evidence pointing to Pomo matrilineate is however slight, and it is clear that the institution was at most a sort of suggestion, an undeveloped beginning or last vestige, and not a practice of much consequence. This inference is strengthened by the fact that the several Pomo and Wappo divisions conflict in their usages on the points involved.

Totemic taboos are not shown to have been strongly developed in California. Among most groups the totem seems to have been killed and eaten without further thought. Belief in descent from the totem is also weak or absent, except for some introduction of the moiety totems into the cosmogony of the Shoshoneans of the south.

The exogamic groups of California have rather few religious functions. The Colorado River clans seem to have no connection with ritual. The clans of some of the Shoshoneans—Luiseño, Cupeño, possibly Cahuilla—tended to be the bodies that conducted ceremonies, the instruments for ritual execution; although the rites were nearly identical, not peculiar to each clan. It appears also that these ritually functioning groups or parties often included several clans, and always admitted individuals who had become disgruntled with their hereditary groups. It is thus likely that these religious associations really crystallized around chiefs rather than on a clan basis. Indeed, the word for such a group is merely the word for chief. Among other groups of the south, such as the Serrano, the moieties, or their clan representatives in a given locality, appear to have been charged with religious privileges and duties. But the situation remains in need of more intimate elucidation. In the San Joaquin Valley, the moieties assumed ceremonial obligations, usually reciprocal, and evidently in the main in connection with the mourning anniversary; but these arrangements faded out toward the north, among the Miwok.

Marriage

Marriage is by purchase almost everywhere in California, the groups east of the Sierra and those on the Colorado River providing the only exceptions. Among the latter there is scarcely a formality observed. A man and a woman go to live together and the marriage is recognized as long as the union endures. While some form of bride-purchase is in vogue over the remainder of the state, its import is very different according to locality. The northwestern tribes make of it a definite, commercial, negotiated transaction, the absence of which prior to living together constitutes a serious injury to the family of the girl, whereas a liberal payment enhances the status of both bride and groom and their children. In the southern half of the state, and among the mountaineers of the north, payment has little more significance than a customary observance. It might be described as an affair of manners rather than morals. Formal negotiations are not always carried on, and in some instances the young man shows his intentions and is accepted merely on the strength of some presents of game or the rendering of an ill-defined period of service before or after the union. Even within comparatively restricted regions there is considerable difference in this respect between wealthy valley dwellers and poor highlanders: the northern Maidu furnish an interesting case in point.

So far as known the levirate or marriage of the widow by her dead husband's brother was the custom of all Californians except those on the Colorado. The same may be said of the "sororate" or "glorate," the widower's marriage to his dead wife's sister, or in cases of polygamy to two sisters or to mother and daughter. On account of this almost universal occurrence, these customs may be looked upon as basic and ancient institutions. The uniformity of their prevalence in contrast to the many intergrading forms assumed by the marriage act, and in contrast also to the differences as regards exogamy, renders it highly probable that if an attempt be made to bring the levirate and sororate into relation with these other institutions, the levirate and sororate must be regarded as antecedent—as established practices to which marriage, exogamy, and descent conformed.

Various Social Habits

A rigid custom prescribes that the widow crop or singe off her hair and cover the stubble as well as her face with pitch, throughout a great part of central California. This defacement is left on until the next mourning anniversary or for a year or sometimes longer. The groups that are known to follow this practice are the Achomawi, Shasta, Maidu, Wintun, Kato, Pomo, and Miwok; also the Chukchansi, that is the northern hill Yokuts. Among the Southern Yokuts the widow merely does not wash her face during the period in which she abstains from eating meat. Beyond the Yokuts, there is no reference to the custom; nor is it known from any northwestern people.

A mourning necklace is northern. The northwestern tribes braid a necklace which is worn for a year or longer after the death of a near relative or spouse. The Achomawi and Northeastern Maidu, perhaps other groups also, have their widows put on a necklace of lumps of pitch.

A belt made of the hair cut from her head was worn by the widow among the Shastan tribes, that is the Shasta, Achomawi, and Atsugewi. In southern California, belts and hair ties and other ornaments of human hair reappear, but do not have so definite a reference to mourning.

The couvade was practiced by nearly all Californians, but not in its "classic" form of the father alone observing restrictions and pretending to lie in. The usual custom was for both parents to be affected equally and for the same period. They observed food restraints and worked and traveled as little as possible in order to benefit their child; they did not ward illness from the infant by shamming it themselves. The custom might well be described as a semicouvade. It has been reported among the Achomawi,

Maidu, Yuki, Pomo, Yokuts, Juaneño, and Diegueño. Only the Yurok, Hupa, Shasta, and with them presumably the Karok and a few other north-western tribes, are known not to have followed the practice. Here too there are certain restrictions on both parents; but those of the father are much the lighter and briefer.

Fear toward twins is known to have been felt by the Yurok, Achomawi, and Northwestern Maidu of the hills. It is likely to have prevailed more widely, but these instances suggest that the most acute development of the sentiment may have been localized in northern California.

The child's umbilical cord was saved, carefully disposed of, or specially treated. The Diegueño, Luiseño, Juaneño, and Chukchansi Yokuts buried it. The Tachi Yokuts tied it on the child's abdomen. The Hupa and Yurok kept it for a year or two, then deposited it in a split tree.

Kinship Taboos

The taboo which forbids parents-in-law and children-in-law to look each other in the face or speak or communicate, was a central Californian custom. It is recorded for the Kato, Pomo, Maidu, Miwok, Yokuts, and Western Mono; with whom at least the southerly Wintun must probably be included. The Yuki, perhaps the Yana, the Eastern Mono, the Tübatulabal, and the Kawaiisu seem not to have adhered to the practice, whose distribution is therefore recognizable as holding over a continuous and rather regular area whose core is the Sacramento–San Joaquin Valley. There is no mention of the habit in regard to any northwestern or southern tribe. Actually, the mother-in-law is alone specified in some instances, but these may be cases of loose or incomplete record. Accuracy also necessitates the statement that among the Kato and Pomo the custom has not been reported directly, but it is known that they address a parent-in-law in the plural—a device which the Miwok and Western Mono make use of as an allowable circumvention of the taboo when there is the requisite occasion. The Kato and Pomo were shy toward their parents-in-law, but much less scrupulous about rigidly avoiding all communication with them than the Northwestern Maidu.

It may be added that among the Yana and the Western Mono, two far separated and unrelated peoples, brother and sister used plural address. For the Yana it is stated that a certain degree of avoidance was also observed. This custom can be looked for with some likelihood among the intervening nations; but to predict it would be rash. There are many purely local developments in Californian culture: witness the sex diversity of speech among the Yana.

As in other parts of America, no reason for the custom can be obtained from the natives. It is a way they have, they answer; or they would be ashamed to do otherwise. That they feel positive disgrace at speaking brusquely to a parent-in-law is certain; but this sentiment can no more be accounted the direct cause of the origin of the custom than a sense of shame can by itself have produced the manifold varieties of dress current among mankind. It need not be doubted that a sense of delicacy with reference to sexual relations lies at the root of the habit. But to imagine that a native might really be able to explain the ultimate source of any of his institutions or manners, is of course unreasonable.

Disposal of the Dead

The manner of disposing of the dead varied greatly according to region in California. The areas in which cremation was practiced seem to aggregate somewhat larger than those in which burial was the custom, but the balance is nearly even, and the distribution quite irregular (map 3). Roughly, five areas can be distinguished.

The southern Californian area burned its dead.

Interment was the rule over a tract which seems to extend from the Great Basin across the southern Sierras to the Chumash and Santa Barbara Islands. This includes the Chemehuevi, the Eastern Mono, the Tübatulabal, the Southern Yokuts, the Chumash, and perhaps a few of the adjacent minor Shoshonean groups.

A second region of cremation follows. This consists of the entire central Sierra Nevada, the San Joaquin Valley except at its head, the lower Sacramento Valley, and the coast region for about the same distance. Roughly, the range is from the Salinans and Central Yokuts to the Pomo and Southern Maidu.

A second area of burial takes in all of the tribes under the influence of the northwestern culture, and in addition to them the Yuki, at least the majority of the Wintun, and most of the northern Maidu.

The Modoc in the northeastern corner of the state again cremated. For the adjoining Achomawi the evidence conflicts. It is possible that this northern region was connected with the central area of cremation through the Yahi and Northwestern Maidu of the foothills.

It seems impossible to establish any correlation between custom and environment in this matter. Treeless and timbered regions both cremated and in other cases interred.

It does appear that the southern and central culture areas can be described as regions of prevailing cremation, the northwestern culture and the desert as areas of burial. The practice of each of the two interring regions has to some extent penetrated the adjacent parts of the central area. Interment

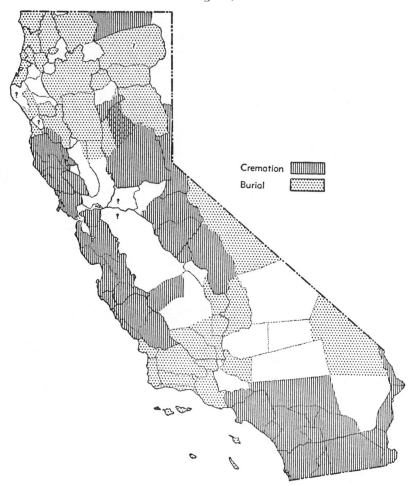

Map 3. Distribution of Methods of Disposal of the Dead.

however extends farther beyond the outer limits of the northwestern culture than almost all other institutions or elements which are definitely characteristic of the northwest, basketry and dentalia, for instance. Furthermore,
there is the curious assemblage of burying peoples from the Eastern Mono
to the Santa Barbara Islands, which can scarcely correspond to any primary
cultural stratum.

War

Warfare throughout California was carried on only for revenge, never
for plunder or from a desire of distinction. The Mohave and Yuma must

indeed be excepted from this statement, but their attitude is entirely unique. Probably the cause that most commonly originated feuds was the belief that a death had been caused by witchcraft. No doubt theft and disputes of various sorts also contributed. Once ill feeling was established, it was likely to continue for long periods. Even a reconciliation and formal peace must generally have left lurking suspicions which the natives' theory of disease was likely at any moment to fan into fresh accusation and a renewal of hostilities.

Torture has been reported as having been practiced by several tribes, such as the Maidu and the Gabrielino. It appears to have been considered merely a preliminary to the execution of captives, which was the victors' main purpose. As a rule, men who could be seized in warfare were killed and decapitated on the spot. Women and children were also slaughtered more frequently than enslaved. There is no record of any attempt to hold men as prisoners.

Scalps were taken in the greater part of California, brought home in triumph, and celebrated over, usually by a dance around a pole. Women as well as men generally participated. Some tribes made the dance indoors, others outside. There was no great formality about this scalp dance of victory. It may often have been celebrated with great abandon, but its ritual was loose and simple. The Mohave and Yuma alone show some organization of the ceremony, coupled with a considerable manifestation of dread of the scalps themselves—a Southwestern trait.

It is rather difficult to decide how far the scalp taken was literally such and how far it was the entire head. A fallen foe that could be operated upon in safety and leisure was almost always decapitated, and his head brought home. Sometimes it is said that this head was danced with. In other localities it was skinned at the first opportunity and the scalp alone used in the dance. The scalp, however, was always a larger object than we are accustomed to think with the habits of eastern tribes in mind. The skin taken extended to the eyes and nose and included the ears. There is no evidence of an endeavor to preserve scalps as permanent trophies to the credit of individuals; nor of a feeling that anything was lost by a failure to secure scalps, other than that an occasion for a pleasant celebration might be missed thereby.

It is significant that it remains doubtful whether the Yokuts, the valley Maidu, and the Pomo took scalps or performed a scalp dance. If they did so, it was clearly with less zest than most of their neighbors. All of the tribes in question are peoples of lowland habitat, considerable wealth, and comparative specialization of culture.

In the northwestern area no scalps were taken, and the victory dance was replaced by one of incitement before battle. In this dance the fully armed warriors stood abreast, with one or more of their number moving before them. With the Yurok and Hupa, and perhaps some of their immediate neighbors also, this dance was particularly made when two hostile parties gathered for a settlement of a feud; and, as might be expected, as often as not resulted in a new fight instead of the desired peace. The northwestern habit of not scalping extended at least as far south as the Sinkyone and as far east as the Shasta. The Wintun on the Trinity River are also said to have taken no scalps and may therefore be supposed to have practiced the associated form of war dance. Finally, there is an echo of the Yurok custom from as far away as the Maidu of the northern Sacramento Valley, who it is said had a war dance performed by armed negotiators.

The battle weapon of California was the bow. Spears have been mentioned as in use by a number of tribes, but all indications are that they were employed only sporadically in hand-to-hand fighting, and not for hurling from the ranks. It is probable that they were serviceable in an ambush or early morning rush upon the unsuspecting sleepers in a village. In a set fight the spear could not be used against a row of bowmen.

Southern California used the Pueblo type of war club, a rather short, stout stick expanded into a longitudinal mallet head. This seems to have been meant for thrusting into an opponent's face rather than for downright clubbing. The Mohave at any rate knew a second form of club, a somewhat longer, straight, and heavy stick, which served the specific purpose of breaking skulls. In central California mentions of clubs are exceedingly scarce. If they were used they were probably nothing but suitable sticks. When it came to hand-to-hand fighting the central Californian was likely to have recourse to the nearest stone. Stones were also favored by the northwestern tribes, but in addition there are some examples of a shaped war club of stone in this region. This club was a little over a foot long and rudely edged, somewhat in the shape of a narrow and thick paddle blade. This type has affiliations with the more elaborate stone and bone clubs used farther north on the Pacific coast.

Slings seem to have been known to practically all the Californians as toys, and in some parts were used effectively for hunting water fowl. The only definite reports of the use of slings in warfare are from the Wintun of Trinity River and the Western Mono; both mountaineers.

The shield, which is so important to the Plains Indian and to the Southwestern warrior, was known in California only to the Mohave, the Yuma, and the Diegueño, that is to say, the local representatives of the Yuman family. It was a round piece of unornamented hide. There is no reference to symbolism, and it appears to have been carried only occasionally. Not a single original specimen has been preserved. Much as tribes like the Mohave speak of war, they very rarely mention the shield, and its occurrence among them and their kinsmen is of interest chiefly as an evidence that the distribution of this object reached the Pacific coast.

Armor enters the state at the other end, also as an extension from a great extra-Californian culture. It is either of elk hide, or of rods twined with string in waistcoat shape. The rod type is reported from the northwestern tribes, the Achomawi, and the northern mountain Maidu. Elkskin armor has been found among the same groups, as well as the Modoc, Shasta, northern valley Maidu, and Wailaki. These closely coincident distributions indicate that the two armor types are associated, not alternative; and that, confined to the northernmost portion of the state, they are to be understood as the marginal outpost of the extension of an idea that probably originated in the eastern hemisphere and for America centers in the culture of the North Pacific coast.

The greater part of central California appears to have been armorless and shieldless.

RELIGION AND KNOWLEDGE

Shamanism

The shamanistic practices of California are fairly uniform, and similar to those obtaining among the North American Indians generally. The primary function of the California shaman is the curing of disease. The illness is almost always considered due to the presence in the body of some foreign or hostile object. Only among the Colorado River tribes is there definite record of belief in an abstraction or injury of the soul. The shaman's usual business, therefore, is the removal of the disease object, and this in the great majority of cases is carried out by sucking. Singing, dancing, and smoking tobacco, with or without the accompaniment of trance conditions, are the usual diagnostic means. Manipulation of the body, brushing it, and blowing of tobacco smoke, breath, or saliva—the last especially among the Colorado River tribes—are sometimes resorted to in the extraction of the disease object.

As contrasted with the general similarity of the practices of the established shaman, there is a considerable diversity of methods employed by the prospective shaman in the acquisition of his supernatural powers. This diversity is connected with a variety of beliefs concerning guardian spirits.

In central California, from the Wailaki and Maidu to the Yokuts, the guardian spirit is of much the same character as with the Indians of the central and eastern United States, and is obtained in a similar way. A supernatural being or animal or other form is seen and conversed with during a trance or dream. Sometimes the spirits come to a man unsought, occasionally there is an avowed attempt to acquire them.

For southern California, information on these matters is still tantalizingly scant, which may indicate that beliefs are meager. The sources of shamanistic power seem to have been deities, monsters, or heavenly phenomena more often than animals or unnamed spirits. Repeated dreams, especially in childhood, seem to produce shamans among the Cahuilla more often than unique experiences of trance or vision type. This is probably an approximation to the point of view of the tribes on the Colorado. It must not be overlooked that the concept of a definite guardian spirit and the institution of shamanism in its common American form are weakly developed among the tribes of the Southwest, especially the Pueblos.

Among the Colorado River peoples it is certain that there was no belief in a guardian spirit of the usual kind. Shamans derived their power by dreaming of the creator or some ancient divinity, or as they themselves sometimes describe it, from having associated before their birth—in other words during a previous spiritual existence—with the gods or divine animals that were on earth at the beginning. The culture of the Colorado River tribes is so specialized that to apply a positive inference from them to the remaining southern Californians would be unsound; but it must be admitted that their status increases the possibility that the latter tribes did not very fully share the central Californian and usual northern and eastern ideas as to the source of shamanistic power.

In northern California, and centering as usual among the northwestern tribes, beliefs as to the source of shamanistic power take a peculiar turn. Among peoples like the Yurok the guardian spirit in the ordinary sense scarcely occurs. The power of the shaman rests not upon the aid or control of a guardian, but upon his maintenance in his own body of disease objects which to nonshamans would be fatal. These "pains" are animate and self-moving, but are always conceived as minute, physically concrete, and totally lacking human shape or resemblance. Their acquisition by the shaman is due to a dream in which a spirit gives them to him or puts them in his body. This spirit seems most frequently to be an ancestor who has had shamanistic power. The dream, however, does not constitute the shaman as such, since the introduced pain causes illness in him as in other persons. His condition is diagnosed by accepted shamans, and a long and rigorous course of training follows, whose object is the inuring of the novice to the presence of the "pains" in his body and to the acquisition of control over them. Fasting and analogous means are employed for this purpose, but the instruction of older shamans seems to be regarded as an essential feature, culminating in what is usually known as the "doctors' dance." This dance is therefore substantially a professional initiation ceremony. There is no doubt that it provided the opportunity for the establishment of shamans' societies as organized bodies; but this step seems never to have been taken in California.

From the Yurok and Hupa this peculiar type of shamanism spreads out gradually, losing more and more of its elements, to at least as far as the Maidu. Already among the Shasta the shaman controls spirits as well as pains, but the name for the two is identical. With the Achomawi and Maidu the pain and the spirit are differently designated. Here, the doctor's concern in practice is more largely with the pains, but his control of them rests definitely upon his relation to the spirits as such. The doctor dance persists among all these tribes. It is practiced also by the northerly Wintun and the Yuki. The Yuki shamans possess and acquire spirits very much like the central Californians, and these are sometimes animals. The pain is still of some importance among them, however, and they and the Wintun agree in calling it "arrowhead." A line running across the state south of the Yuki, and probably through Wintun and Maidu territory about its middle, marks the farthest extension of remnants of the northwestern type of shamanism.

Among the Pomo there is no mention of the doctor dance, while indications of a considerable use of amulets or fetishes suggest that entirely different sets of concepts obtain. The Miwok and Yokuts also knew of nothing like a doctor dance, and with them it would seem that the Maidu of the south may have to be included, although here direct evidence is not available.

It may be added that central and southern California are a unit in regarding shamanistic power as indifferently beneficent or malevolent. Whether a given shaman causes death or prevents it is merely a matter of his inclination. His power is equal in both directions. Much disease, if not the greater part, is caused by hostile or spiteful shamans. Witchcraft and the power of the doctor are therefore indissolubly bound up together. The unsuccessful shaman, particularly if repeatedly so, was thought to be giving prima facie evidence of evil intent, and earnest attempts to kill him almost invariably followed. In other cases individuals in a neighboring group were blamed. This was perhaps the most frequent cause of the feuds or so-called wars of the central and southern Californian tribes.

In the northwest this intertwining of the two aspects of supernatural power was slighter. Shamans were less frequently killed, and then rather for refusal to give treatment or for unwillingness to return pay tendered in treatment, than for outright witchcraft. A person who wished to destroy another had recourse to magical practice. This northwestern limitation of shamanism is probably connected with the fact that among the tribes where it was most marked the shaman was almost invariably a woman. In these matters, too, tribes as far as the Maidu shared in some measure in the beliefs which attained their most clear-cut form among the Yurok and Hupa.

The use of supernatural spirit power was on the whole perhaps more largely restricted to the treatment or production of disease in California than in most other parts of aboriginal North America. There is comparatively little reference to men seeking association with spirits for success in warfare, hunting, or love, although it is natural that ideas of this kind crop out now and then. There are however three specialties which in the greater part of the state lead to the recognition of as many particular kinds of shamans or doctors, as they are usually known in local usage. These are rain or weather doctors, rattlesnake doctors, and bear doctors.

The rain doctor seems generally to have exercised his control over the weather in addition to possessing the abilities of an ordinary shaman. Very largely he used his particular faculty, like Samuel, to make impression by demonstrations. All through the southern half of the state there were men who were famous as rain doctors, and the greatest development of the idea appears to have been in the region where central and southern California meet. Control of the weather by shamans was however believed in to the northern limit of the state, though considerably less was made of it there. The groups within the intensive northwestern culture are again in negative exception.

The rattlesnake doctor is also not northwestern, although tribes as close to the focus of this culture as the Shasta knew him. His business of course was to cure snake bites; in some cases also to prevent them. Among the Yokuts a fairly elaborate ceremony, which included the juggling of rattlesnakes, was an outgrowth of these beliefs. Less important or conspicuous demonstrations of the same sort seem also to have been made among a number of other tribes, since we know that the northern Maidu of the valley had some kind of a public rattlesnake ceremony conducted by their shamans. There appears to have been some inclination to regard the sun as the spirit to which rattlesnake doctors particularly looked.

The bear doctor was recognized over the entire state from the Shasta to the Diegueño. The Colorado River tribes, those of the extreme northwest, and possibly those of the farthest northeastern corner of the state, are the only ones among whom this impressive institution was apparently lacking. The bear shaman had the power to turn himself into a grizzly bear. In this form he destroyed enemies. The most general belief, particularly in the San Joaquin Valley and southern California, was that he became actually transmuted. In the region of the Wintun, Pomo, and Yuki, however, it seems to have been believed that the bear doctor, although he possessed undoubted supernatural power, operated by means of a bearskin and other paraphernalia in which he encased himself. Generally bear shamans were thought invulnerable, or at least to possess the power of returning to life. They inspired an extraordinary fear and yet seem to have been encouraged.

It is not unlikely that they were often looked upon as benefactors to the group to which they belonged and as exercising their destructive faculties chiefly against its foes. In some tribes they gave exhibitions of their power; in others, as among the Pomo, the use of their faculties was carefully guarded from all observation. Naturally enough, their power was considered to be derived from bears, particularly the grizzly. It is the ferocity and tenacity of life of this species that clearly impressed the imagination of the Indians, and a more accurately descriptive name of the caste would be grizzly-bear shamans.

Throughout northern California a distinction is made between the shaman who sings, dances, and smokes in order to diagnose, in other words, is a clairvoyant, and a second class endowed with the executive power of sucking out disease objects, that is, curing sickness. This grouping of shamans has been reported from the Hupa, Wiyot, Nongatl, Yuki, Pomo, and Maidu. It has not been mentioned among more southerly peoples. It thus coincides in its distribution with the concept of the pain as a more or less animate and self-impelled thing, and the two ideas can scarcely be interpreted as other than connected. The sucking shaman seems to be rated higher than the one that only sings; as is only natural, since his power in some measure presupposes and includes that of his rival. It is not unlikely, however, that certain singing shamans were believed to possess a special diagnostic power over illness, and no doubt all such matters as finding lost objects and foretelling the future were their particular province.

Cult Religions

The cults or definitely formulated religions of California are too intricate to be described here, so that the following discussion is confined to their interrelations and certain questions of broader aspect. The respective ranges of the four cults are plotted on map 4.

It appears from this map that the specific northwestern cultus is separated from that of north central California by a belt of tribes that participate in neither.

The religions of north central and southern California, or Kuksu and "toloache" cults, on the other hand, seem to have overlapped in the region of the northern Yokuts and Salinans. It is unlikely that the two cults existed side by side with undiminished vigor among the same peoples; one was probably much abbreviated and reduced to subsidiary rank while the other maintained itself in flourishing or at least substantially full status. Unfortunately the tribes that seem to have shared the two religions are the very ones whose culture has long since melted away, so that data are exceedingly elusive. It is not improbable that fuller knowledge would show that the religions reacted toward each other like the basketry complexes that have been discussed: namely, that they were only partially preserved but without mixture.

This seems on the whole to be what has happened in southern California, where the jimson-weed or toloache religion emanating from the Gabrielino and the system of song-myth cycles issuing from the Colorado River tribes existed side by side to only a limited extent among the Diegueño and perhaps some of the Cahuilla and Serrano. Even in these cases of partial mixture it is possible that the condition is not ancient. A recent wave of propaganda for the jimson-weed cult radiated southward and perhaps eastward from the Gabrielino during mission times—may in fact have succeeded in then gaining for the first time a foothold, particularly when Christian civilization had sapped the strength of the older cults in regions where these had previously been of sufficient vitality to keep out this toloache religion.

In any event there are certain ceremonies of wide distribution in California which must be considered as belonging to a more generalized and presumably older stratum of native civilization than any of the four cults here referred to. Most prominent among these simpler rituals is the adolescence ceremony for girls. The dance of war or victory occupies second place. To this must be added in northwestern and north central California the shamans' dance for instruction of the novice, and in north and south central California various exhibitions by classes or bodies of shamans. Generally speaking, all these rites are dwarfed among each people in proportion as it adheres to one of the four organized cults; but they rarely disappear wholly. They are usually somewhat but rather lightly colored by ritualistic ideas developed in the greater cults. Thus the adolescence rites of the Hupa, the Maidu, and the Luiseño are by no means uniform. And yet, with the partial exception of the latter, they have not been very profoundly shaped by the cults with which they are in contact, and can certainly not be described as having been incorporated in these cults. In short, these old or presumably ancient rites—which are all animated by essentially individual motives as opposed to communal or world purposes—evince a surprising vitality which has enabled them to retain certain salient traits during periods when it may be supposed that the more highly florescent great religions grew or were replaced by others.

The mourning anniversary belongs to neither class and is best considered separately.

The Kuksu and toloache systems shared the idea of initiation into a society. This organization was always communal. The aim normally was to include all adult males, and even where some attempt at discrimination was made, as perhaps among the Wintun, the proportion of those left out of membership seems to have been small. Nowhere was there the institu-

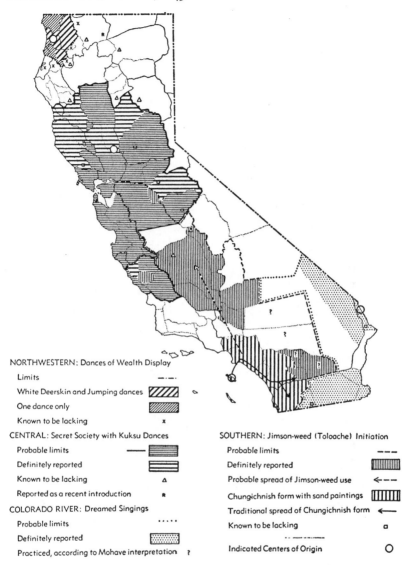

NORTHWESTERN: Dances of Wealth Display

Limits	—·—·—
White Deerskin and Jumping dances	
One dance only	
Known to be lacking	x

CENTRAL: Secret Society with Kuksu Dances

Probable limits	
Definitely reported	
Known to be lacking	△
Reported as a recent introduction	℞

COLORADO RIVER: Dreamed Singings

Probable limits	·····
Definitely reported	
Practiced, according to Mohave interpretation	?

SOUTHERN: Jimson-weed (Toloache) Initiation

Probable limits	---
Definitely reported	
Probable spread of Jimson-weed use	←--
Chungichnish form with sand paintings	
Traditional spread of Chungichnish form	←
Known to be lacking	◻
Indicated Centers of Origin	◯

Map 4. Distribution of Ritual Cults.

tion of distinct but parallel or equivalent fraternal religious bodies. The organization of the society was of very simple character, particularly in the south. In the Kuksu society two grades of initiates were recognized, besides the old men of special knowledge who acted as directors.

The Kuksu cult was the only one in California which directly impersonated spirits and had developed a fair wealth of distinctive paraphernalia and disguises for several mythic characters. This is a feature which probably grew up on the spot. It cannot well have reached central California from either the Southwestern or the North Pacific coast areas, since the intervening nations for long distances do not organize themselves into societies; not to mention that the quite diverse northwestern and toloache religions are present as evidences of growths that would have served to block the transmission of such influences as disguises.

To compensate for the simplicity of organization in the Kuksu and toloache religions, initiation looms up largely, according to some reports almost as if it were the chief function of the bodies. Novices were often given a formal and prolonged education. Witness the woknam, the "lie dance" or "school," of the Yuki; the orations of the Maidu and Wintun; the long moral lectures to Luiseño boys and girls. That these pedagogical inclinations are an inherent part of the idea of the religious society, is shown by the fact that the Yurok and Mohave, who lack societies, do not manifest these inclinations, at least not in any formal way. In the Southwest, education is much less important than in California, relatively to the whole scheme of the religious institution; and for the Plains the difference is still greater. It appears that these two aspects, initiation and organization, tend to stand in inverse ratio of importance in North American cult societies.

Police and military functions of religious societies are very strongly marked among the Plains tribes; are definitely exercised by the bow or warrior societies of the Southwest; and perhaps stand out larger in native consciousness than in our own, since ethnologists have often approached the religious bodies of the area from the side of cult rather than social influence. But such functions are exceedingly vague and feeble in California. There may have been some regulation of profane affairs by the body of initiates; but the chiefs and other civil functionaries are the ones usually mentioned in such matters in California. There certainly was no connection of the cult societies with warfare. The first traces of a connection between war and ritual appear on the Colorado River, where societies do not exist. The negativeness of the California religious bodies in regard to police functions is to be construed as an expression of their lack of development of the organization factor.

In spite of their performance of communal and often public rituals, American religious societies are never wholly divorced from shamanism, that is, the exercise of individual religious power, and one of their permanent foundations or roots must be sought in shamanism. On the Plains, there is a complete transition from societies based on voluntary affiliation, purchase, age, war record, or other nonreligious factors, to such as are clearly nothing but more or less fluctuating groups of individuals endowed with similar shamanistic powers. Farther east, the Midewiwin is little more than an attempt at formal organization of shamanism. In the Southwest, among the Pueblos, the fraternal as opposed to the communal religious bodies can be looked upon, not indeed as shamans' associations, but as societies one of whose avowed purposes—perhaps the primary one—is curative, and which have largely replaced the shaman acting as an individual. Among the Navaho, the greatest ceremonies seem to be curative. In California we have the similarity of name between the Luiseño shaman and initiates—pul-a and pu-pl-em; and the lit or doctoring of the Yuki societies is practically their only function besides that of perpetuating themselves by initiation. In spite of their loose structure and comparative poverty of ritual, it cannot however be maintained that the societies of California are more inclined to be shamanistic than those of the other two regions; and they are less shamanistic in character than the North Pacific coast societies.

Perhaps the most distinctive single trait of the two Californian cult societies is their freedom from any tendency to break up into, or to be accompanied by, smaller and equivalent but diverse societies as in the Plains, Southwest, and North Pacific coast regions.

The cults of the Colorado River tribes are bare of any inclination toward the formation of associations or bodies of members. They rest on dreams, or on imitations of other practitioners which are fused with inward experiences and construed as dreams. These dreams invariably have a mythological cast. Ritually the cults consist essentially of long series of songs; but most singers know a corresponding narrative. Dancing is minimal, and essentially an adjunct for pleasure. Concretely expressed symbolism is scarcely known: disguises, ground paintings, altars, religious edifices, drums or paraphernalia, and costumes are all dispensed with.

The northwestern cults adhere minutely to certain traditional forms, but these forms per se have no meaning. There is no trace of any cult organizations. The esoteric basis of every ceremony is the recitation of a formula, which is a myth in dialogue. The formulas are jealously guarded as private property. Major rites always serve a generic communal or even world-renewing purpose, and may well be described as new year rites. Dance costumes and equipments are splendid but wholly unsymbolic. All performances are very rigorously attached to precise localities and spots.

It appears that as these four cults are followed from northwestern California southeastward to the lower Colorado there is a successive weakening of the dance and all other external forms, of physical apparatus, of association with particular place or edifice; and an increase of personal psychic participation, of symbolism and mysticism, of speculation or emotion about human life and death, and of intrinsic interweaving of ritualistic expression with myth. The development of these respective qualities has nothing to do with the development of principles of organization, initiation, and impersonation or enactment; since the latter principles are adhered to in the middle of our area and unknown at the extremities.

The Mourning Anniversary

The anniversary or annual ceremony in memory of the dead bulks so large in the life of many California tribes as to produce a first impression of being one of the most typical elements of Californian culture. As a matter of fact, the institution was in force over only about half of the state: southern California and the Sierra Nevada region. There can be little doubt that its origin is southern. The distribution itself so suggests. The greatest development of mourning practices is found among the Gabrielino, Luiseño, and Diegueño. It is not that their anniversary is much more elaborate than that of other groups—the use of images representing the dead is common to the great majority of tribes—but these southerners have a greater number of mourning rites. Thus the Luiseño first wash the clothes of the dead, then burn them, and finally make the image ceremony. Of this they know two distinct forms, and in addition there are special mourning rites for religious initiates, and the Eagle Dance which is also a funerary ceremony. Another circumstance that points to southern origin is the fact that the anniversary is held by nearly all tribes in a circular brush enclosure, such as is not used by the Miwok and Maidu for other purposes, whereas in southern California it is the only and universal religious structure. Finally, there are no known connections between the anniversary and the Kuksu cult of the Miwok and Maidu, whereas the toloache religion of southern California presents a number of contacts with the mourning ceremony.

It is a fair inference that the anniversary received its principal development among the same people that chiefly shaped the toloache cult, namely, the Gabrielino or some of their immediate neighbors. It is even possible that the two sets of rites flowed northward in conjunction, and that the anniversary outreached its mate because the absence or rarity of the jimsonweed plant north of the Yokuts checked the invasion of the rites based specifically upon it.

The Mohave and Yuma follow an aberrant form of mourning which is characteristic of their isolated cultural position. Their ceremony is held in honor of distinguished individual warriors, not for the memory of all the dead of the year. The mourners and singers sit under a shade, in front of which young men engage in mimic battle and war exploits. There are no images among the Mohave and no brush enclosure. The shade is burned at the conclusion, but there is no considerable destruction of property such as is so important an element of the rite elsewhere in California.

An undoubted influence of the anniversary is to be recognized in a practice shared by a number of tribes just outside its sphere of distribution: the Southern Wintun, Pomo, Yuki, Lassik, and perhaps others. These groups burn a large amount of property for the dead at the time of the funeral.

Some faint traces, not of the mourning anniversary itself indeed, but rather of the point of view which it expresses, are found even among the typical northwestern tribes. Among the Yurok and Hupa custom has established a certain time and place in every major dance as the occasion for an outburst of weeping. The old people in particular remember the presence of their departed kinsmen at former presentations of this part of the ceremony, and seem to express their grief almost spontaneously.

On the question of the time of the commemoration, more information is needed. It appears rather more often not to fall on the actual anniversary. Among some of the southern tribes it may be deferred some years; with the Mohave it seems to be held within a few weeks or months after death; the Sierra tribes mostly limit it to a fixed season—early autumn.

Girls' Adolescence Ceremony

Probably every people in California observed some rite for girls at the verge of womanhood: the vast majority celebrated it with a dance of some duration. The endless fluctuations in the conduct of the ceremony are indicated in table 1. It appears that in spite of a general basic similarity of the rite, and the comparatively narrow scope imposed on its main outlines by the physiological event to which it has reference, there are very few features that are universal. These few, among which the use of a head scratcher and the abstention from flesh are prominent, are of a specifically magical nature. The wealth of particular features restricted to single nations, and therefore evidently developed by them, is rather remarkable, and argues that the native Californians were not so much deficient in imagination and originality as in the ability to develop these qualities with emotional intensity to the point of impressiveness. There is every reason to believe that this inference applies with equal force to most phases of Californian civilization. It merely happens that an unusually full series of details is available for comparison on the rite for girls.

Poor and rude tribes make much more of the adolescence ceremony than those possessed of considerable substance and of institutions of some specialization. In this connection it is only necessary to cite the Yurok as contrasted with the Sinkyone, the Pomo as against the Yuki, the valley Maidu against those of the mountains, the Yokuts against the Washo, the Mohave against the Diegueño. Precedence in general elaboration of culture must in every instance be given to the former people of each pair: and yet it is the second that makes, and the first that does not make, a public adolescence dance. This condition warrants the inference that the puberty rite belongs to the generic or basic stratum of native culture, and that it has decayed among those nations that succeeded in definitely evolving or establishing ceremonials whose associations are less intimately personal and of a more broadly dignified import.

In the northern half of the state the idea is deeprooted that the potential influence for evil of a girl at the acme of her adolescence is very great. Even her sight blasts, and she is therefore covered or concealed as much as possible. Everything malignant in what is specifically female in physiology is thought to be thoroughly intensified at its first appearance. So far as known, all the languages of this portion of California possess one word for a woman in her periodic illness; and an entirely distinct term for a girl who is at the precise incipiency of womanhood.

A second concept is also magical: that the girl's behavior at this period of intensification is extremely critical for her nature and conduct forever after. Hence the innumerable prescriptions for gathering firewood, industry, modest deportment, and the like.

This concept pervades also the reasoning of the tribes in the southern end of the state, but is rather overshadowed there by a more special conviction that direct physiological treatment is necessary to ensure future health. Warmth appears to be considered the first requisite in the south. Cold water must not be drunk under any circumstances, bathing must be in heated water; and in the sphere of Gabrielino-Luiseño influence, the girl is cooked or roasted, as it were, in a pit, which is clearly modeled on the earth oven. The idea of her essential malignancy is by comparison weak.

The southern concepts have penetrated in diluted form into the San Joaquin Valley region, along with so many other elements of culture. On the other hand the Mohave, and with them presumably the Yuma, practice a type of ceremony that at most points differs from that of the other southern Californians, and provides an excellent exemplification of the considerable aloofness of the civilization of these agricultural tribes of the Colorado River.

The deer-hoof rattle is consciously associated with the girls' ceremony over all northern California. Since there is a deep-seated antithesis of taboo between everything sexual on the one hand, and everything referring to the hunt, the deer as the distinctive game animal, and flesh on the other, the use of this particular rattle can hardly be a meaningless accident. But the basis of the inverting association has not become clear, and no native explanations seem to have been recorded.

A few Athabascan tribes replace the deer-hoof rattle by a special form

TABLE I

THE ADOLESCENCE CEREMONY FOR GIRLS

Present, X   Absent, O

	Singing	Dancing	Women Dance	Men Dance	Girl Dances	Dance in Circle	Dance Abreast	Dance Outdoors	Dance Indoors	Deer-hoof Rattle	Eye Shade	Girl Covered	"Roasting" in Pit	Girl Runs	Girl Carries Wood	Girl Works	Girl Bathes	Head Scratcher	Fasts from Meat	Fasts from Salt	Drinks no Water	Ears Pierced	Tattooed	General License	Duration: Nights	Repetitions of Cerem'y	Special Features
Yurok	X	O	X		X	X		O	O	X	X			O	O	X	X	X	X		X				10	3	Leaps toward morning star.
Karok	X	X	X		O	O		X	X	O	X	X		X	X	X	X	X	X		X				10	3	Pared stick rattle; painted boards; girl peers into haliotis shells.
Hupa	X	X	X							X															10		
Tolowa	X	X	X	X		X	X			X	X							X	X					X	10		10 or 5 nights; concluding dance by women in water.
Wiyot	X	X	X	X	X				X	O		X													5	2	Pared stick rattle; girl keeps awake; hair over her eyes.
Sinkyone	X	X	X	X	X	X						X															
Yuki	X	O	X	X	X	X		X								X											
Pomo	O	X	O	O	X	X	X	X		X															5	3	
Modoc	X	X	X		X	X									X			X	X	X				X	10	3	
Shasta	X	X	X		X	X				X	X						X	X	X				X	X	10	3	Girl keeps awake; does not look about; east is symbolic direction.
Achomawi	X	X	X	X	X	X						X		X	X	X	X	X	X					X	5	3	Girl in ring of fire.
Mountain Maidu	X	X	X	X	X	X				X	X	X		X	X	X	X	X	X					X	10	2	
Hill Maidu	X	X	X	O	X	X		X	O			X	X	X	X	X		X	X						5		Girl in trench in house.
Valley Maidu	X	O	X		O	O		X					X												4		
Central Miwok	X	X	X	X					X		X		X				X	X	X			X					Girl in trench in house.
Washo	X	O	O		X	X				O			X					X	X		X						Girl uses no cold water.
Yokuts												X	X						X		X						Girl in pit; roasting not sure.
Tübatulabal	X	X	X	X		O		X	O			X	X	X	X	O	O	X	X	X	X	X	X		3	2	Girl forbidden all work; tobacco drunk.
Cahuilla	X	X	X	X	O			X	X	O		X	X	O	O	O	O	X	X	X	X	X	X		3?		Sand painting; tobacco eating ordeal; rocks painted; girl forbidden all work.
Luiseño	X	X	X		X					O		X		O	O	O	O	X	X	X	X						
Diegueño	X	O	O	X	X			O	O	O		X	[X]	O	O	O	O	X	X	X		X	X				Crescentic stone applied; girl forbidden all work; tobacco drunk; period in pit indefinite.
Mohave	X	O	O							O				X	X	X	X		X	X					6		Girl washes 40 days with warm water; drinks no cold water; loused by mother; lies in hot sand.

of the clap stick which provides the general dance accompaniment throughout central California, but which is not otherwise used in the northwestern habitat. In southern California the deer-hoof rattle is known, but is employed by hunters among the Luiseño, by mourners among the Yumans.

The scarcity of the ritualistic number four in table 1 may be an accident of tribal representation in the available data, but gives the impression of having some foundation in actuality and therefore a historical significance.

Boys' Initiations

The description which has sometimes been made of Californian religion as characterized by initiation and mourning rites is not wholly accurate. Mourning customs, so far as they are crystallized into formal and important ceremonies, are confined to a single wave of southern origin and definitely limited distribution—the mourning anniversary. The girls' adolescence rite on the other hand is universal, and clearly one of the ancient constituents of the religion of all California as well as considerable tracts outside.

Boys were initiated into the two great organized religions of the state, the Kuksu and the toloache cult. Important as the initiation ceremonies were in these cults, it would however be misleading to regard them as primary: the cult has logical precedence, the initiation is a part of it. When therefore we subtract these two religions, there is left almost nothing in the nature of initiation for boys parallel to the girls' adolescence ceremony.

The only clear instance is in the northeastern corner of the state among the Achomawi and Shasta, primarily the former. These people practice an adolescence rite for boys comparable to the more widespread one for girls. Among each of them a characteristic feature is the whipping of the boy with a bowstring. The Achomawi also pierce the boy's ears and make him fast, besides which he performs practices very similar to the deliberate seeking after supernatural power indulged in by the tribes of the Plains. The entire affair is very clearly an adolescence rather than an initiation rite, an induction into a status of life, and not into an organized group. It may be looked upon as a local extension to boys of concepts that are universal in regard to girls.

In southern California there is sometimes a partial assimilation of the boys' toloache initiation and of the girls' adolescence ceremony. Thus the Luiseño construct ground paintings for both, deliver analogous orations of advice to both, and put both sexes under similar restrictions. The Kawaiisu are said to give toloache to both boys and girls.

But these local and incomplete developments are very far from equating the initiations for the two sexes; and neither balances with mourning ceremonies. The girls' adolescence, the boys' initiation into a society, and the mourning anniversary clearly have distinct origins so far as California is concerned, and represent cultural planes.

New Year Observances

A first-salmon ceremony was shared by an array of tribes in northern California. The central act was usually the catching and eating of the first salmon of the season; after which fishing was open to all. These features make the ceremony one of public magic. The tribes from which a ritual of this kind has been reported are the Tolowa, Yurok, Hupa, Karok, Shasta, Achomawi, and northern mountain Maidu. The list is probably not complete; but it may be significant that all the groups included in it are situated in the extreme north of the state, whereas salmon run in abundance as far south as San Francisco Bay. It thus seems possible that the distribution of the rite was limited not by the occurrence of the fish but by purely cultural associations. Its range, for example, is substantially identical with that of the northern type of overlaid basketry.

The first-salmon ceremony is clearly a ritual of the new year's type, but is the only widely spread instance of this kind yet found in California. The idea of ceremonial reference to the opening of the year or season seems not to have been wholly wanting in north and central California, especially where the Kuksu religion followed a calendar; but there is no record of this idea having been worked out into a definite ritual concept. In the narrower northwest, it is true, there were first-acorn and world-renewing ceremonies as well as the first-salmon rite, and among the Karok the super-added feature of new-fire making; all with associated dances. This, however, is an essentially local development among the small group of tribes that have advanced the northwestern culture to its most intense status.

In other words, an annual salmon producing or propitiating act of magical nature and of public rather than individual reference is usual in the northern part of the state and is therefore presumably an ancient institution. Among the specifically northwestern tribes this act has become associated with a ritualistic spectacle, the Deerskin or the Jumping Dance, which probably had no original connection with the magical performance; after which the combination of magic act and dance has been applied, within the same narrow region, to other occasions of a first-fruits or new year's character.

Offerings

Offerings of feather wands are reported from the Chumash, the Costanoans, and the Maidu, and may therefore be assumed to have had a considerably wider distribution. The idea is that of the feather stick or prayer plume of the Southwest, and there is probably a historical connection between the practices of the two regions; although this connection may be psychological, that is, indirectly cultural, rather than due to outright transmission. This inference is supported by the fact that there is no reference to anything like the offering of feather wands in southern California proper. In fact the practice of setting out offerings of any kind is so sparsely mentioned for southern California that it must be concluded to have been but slightly developed. The Californian feather wand was of somewhat different shape from the Southwestern feather stick. It appears usually to have been a stick of some length from which single feathers or at most small groups of feathers were hung at one or two places. The northwestern tribes are free from the practice.

Another ultimate connection with the Southwest is found in offerings or sprinklings of meal. These have been recorded for the Pomo, the Maidu, the Costanoans, and the Serrano. In some instances it is not clear whether whole seeds or flour ground from them was used, and it is even possible that the meal was sometimes replaced by entire acorns. The southern California tribes should perhaps be included, since the use of meal or seeds in the ground painting might be construed as an offering. The custom seems, however, to have been more or less hesitating wherever it has been reported. It certainly lacks the full symbolic implications and the ritualistic vigor which mark it in the Southwest. Among the Yokuts and probably their mountain neighbors, offerings of eagle down appear to have been more characteristic than those of seeds or meal. The northwestern tribes can be set down as not participating in the custom of meal offerings. They blew tobacco, or dropped incense on the fire.

The Ghost Dance

The Ghost Dance which swept northern California with some vehemence from about 1870 to 1872 is of interest because of its undoubted connection with the much more extensive and better known wave of religious excitement that penetrated to the Indians of half of the United States about 1889, and which left most of the Californians untouched. Both movements had their origin among the Northern Paiute of Nevada, and from individuals in the same family. The author of the early prophecies may have been the father, and was at any rate an older kinsman, of Wovoka or Jack Wilson, the later messiah. The ideas of the two movements and their ritual were substantially identical. There is thus little doubt that even their songs were similar, although unfortunately these were not recorded for the earlier movement until after its fusion with other cults.

The question arises why the religious infection which originated twice in the same spot in an interval of fifteen or twenty years should at the first occasion have obtained a powerful foothold in northern California alone, and on its recrudescence should have penetrated to the Canadian boundary and the Mississippi River. That the Californians remained passive toward the second wave is intelligible on the ground of immunity acquired by having passed through the first. But that a religion which showed its inherent potentiality by spreading to wholly foreign tribes should in 1870 have been unable to make any eastward progress and in 1890 sweep like wildfire more than a thousand miles to the east, is remarkable. The explanation seems to be that the bulk of the Indian tribes in the United States in 1870 had not been reduced to the necessary condition of cultural decay for a revivalistic influence to impress them. In other words, the native civilization of northern California appears to have suffered as great a disintegration by 1870, twenty or twenty-five years after its first serious contact with the whites, as the average tribe of the central United States had undergone by 1890, or from fifty years to a century after similar contact began. As regards the Plains tribes, among whom the second Ghost Dance reached its culmination, the same influence on the breaking up of their old life may be ascribed to the destruction of the buffalo as the sudden overwhelming swamping of the California natives by the gold seekers. In each case an interval of from ten to twenty years elapsed from the dealing of the substantial death blow to the native civilization until the realization of the change was sufficiently profound to provide a fruitful soil for a doctrine of restoration.

Individual tribes had of course been subject to quite various fortunes at the hands of the whites when either Ghost Dance reached them. But it is also known that they accorded the movement many locally diverse receptions. Some threw themselves into it with an almost unlimited enthusiasm of hope; others were only slightly touched or remained aloof. This is very clear from Mooney's classical account of the greater Ghost Dance, and it can be conjectured that an intensive study would reveal the skeptical or negative tribes to have been so situated that their old life did not yet appear to themselves as irrevocably gone, or as so thoroughly subject to the influences of Caucasian civilization that they had accepted the change as final. Then, too, it must be remembered that the wave, as it spread, developed a certain psychological momentum of its own, so that tribes which, if left to themselves or restricted to direct intercourse with the originators of the movement, might have remained passive, were infected by the frenzy of differently circumstanced tribes with whom they were in affiliation.

Similar phenomena can be traced in the history of the California Ghost Dance, imperfect as our information concerning it is. The Karok and Tolowa seem to have thrown themselves into the cult with greater abandonment than the Yurok. The Hupa, at least to all intents, refused to participate. This is perhaps to be ascribed to the fact that they were the only tribe in the region leading a stable and regulated reservation life. But it is not clear whether this circumstance had already led them to a conscious though reluctant acceptance of the new order of things, or whether some other specific cause must be sought.

On many of the northernmost tribes the effect of the Ghost Dance was transient, and left no traces whatever. It was perhaps already decadent when the Modoc War broke out. At any rate it is no longer heard of after the termination of that conflict. How far the Modoc War may have been indirectly fanned by the doctrine, remains to be ascertained. Its immediate occasion seems not to have been religious.

Somewhat farther south, the Ghost Dance took firmer root among tribes like the Pomo and Southern Wintun, who were beyond the most northerly missions but who had been more or less under mission influence and had also been partly invaded by Mexicans in the period between the secularization and the Americanization of California. The old Kuksu ceremonies were now not only revived but made over. A new type of songs, paraphernalia, and ritual actions came into existence; and these have maintained themselves in some measure until today—more strongly than the aboriginal form of religion. The Wintun at least, and presumably the Pomo also, are still conscious, however, of the two elements in their present cults, and distinguish them by name. Saltu are the spirits that instituted the ancient rites, boli those with whom the modern dances are associated.

This amalgamation, strangely enough, resulted in the carrying of the Kuksu religion, at a time when it was essentially moribund, to tribes which in the days of its vitality had not come under its influence. Evidently the Ghost Dance element acted as a penetrating solvent and carrier. The Central Wintun took the mixed cult over from the Southern Wintun, and the use since 1872 of typical Kuksu paraphernalia as far north as the Shasta of Shasta Valley evidences the extent of this movement.

None of the tribes within the mission area seems to have been in the least affected by the Ghost Dance. This is probably not owing to their being Catholics or nominal Catholics, but rather to the fact that their life had long since been definitely made over. Groups like the Yokuts, of whom only portions had been missionized, and these rather superficially, also did not take up the Ghost Dance. The cause in their instance presumably lay between their geographical remoteness and the fact that most of their intercourse was with missionized tribes.

The Modoc were probably the first California people to receive the early Ghost Dance from the Northern Paiute (map 5). It is hard to conceive that the Achomawi should have been exempt, but unfortunately there appear

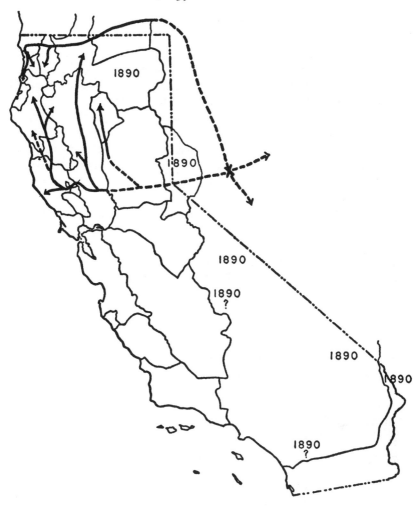

←----   Course of cult of 1869–1873

1890   Tribes affected by cult of 1889–1892

X   Source of both cults

Map 5. Diffusion of Ghost Dances.

to be no records concerning them on this point. The same may be said of the mountain Maidu. From the Modoc, at any rate, the cult was carried to the Shasta. These transmitted it still farther down the Klamath to the Karok. From there it leaped the Siskiyou Mountains to the Tolowa, from whom the lower Yurok of the river and of the coast took their beliefs. The upper Yurok were less affected and the Hupa scarcely at all. Here we lose track of the spread of the dance. Probably all the Athabascan tribes between the Whilkut and the Wailaki, at least those that survived in sufficient numbers, came under Ghost Dance influence, but the direction in which this influence progressed is not certain. It is more likely, however, to have been from the south northward, since the dance appears to have been associated with the erection of large round dance houses of central Californian type. This indicates an approximate Pomo or Southern Wintun source. It has already been mentioned how in the Sacramento Valley the Ghost Dance spread from south to north. To this it may be added that the Yana received the cult from the valley Maidu to the south of them. The question then arises how the dance reached the Pomo and Southern Wintun. There is no known information on this point. It may have traveled directly westward from the northern Paiute through the Washo and Southern Maidu. On the other hand, the entry into California may have been at a single point: that is, through the Modoc and Klamath River tribes, from whom the cult spread southward until, reaching its extreme limit among the Southern Wintun, it recrystallized and then flowed back northward. Inquiry among the Southern Maidu and Northern Miwok would probably determine this issue.

It is not known whether any of the Miwok took up the Ghost Dance. In a number of localities they have during the last generation or so erected circular or octagonal dance houses of wood and without earth covering. These look very much like Ghost Dance modifications of the old semi-subterranean dance house of the Kuksu cults. About fifty years ago, that is, at or near the time of the Ghost Dance, the hill Miwok received a number of dances, including some of the Kuksu series, that were new to them. These came from Costanoan territory to the west, but probably represent not so much a persistence of ancient Costanoan ritual as a cult revival among the less thoroughly missionized northern Valley Yokuts or possibly Plains Miwok domiciled at the Costanoan missions, who were original neighbors of the hill Miwok.

The 1890 Ghost Dance is reported by Mooney, specifically or by implication, for the Achomawi, Washo, Mono, Panamint, Yokuts of Tule River, Luiseño or other "Mission" groups, Chemehuevi, and Mohave. The Washo, Eastern Mono, Chemehuevi, and perhaps Panamint could hardly have escaped participation. The Achomawi may have been rendered susceptible by a failure to take part in 1872. The Mohave were never seriously affected. The Yokuts and Luiseño were no doubt interested, but seem never to have practiced the cult. No tribe in California retained for more than a very short time any phase of this second Ghost Dance religion.

Calendar

The California Indian did not record the passage of long intervals of time. No one knew his own age nor how remote an event was that had happened more than half a dozen years ago. Tallies seem not to have been kept, and no sticks notched annually have been reported. Most groups had not even a word for "year," but employed "world," "summer," or "winter" instead. Where there appear to be words meaning "year," they seem to denote "season," that is, a half-year.

Probably every tribe, however, had a system of measuring time within the year. This was by the universally known method of naming and reckoning lunations within the round of the seasons. The point of interest in this method to the historian of culture rests in the means taken to adjust the eternally varying and essentially irreconcilable lunar and solar phenomena. Half a dozen such calendars are known from California. These clearly belong to three types.

The Maidu, or rather some of them, knew twelve moons, named after seasonal occurrences. The series began in spring, and appears not to have been controlled by any solar phenomenon. There can accordingly scarcely have been a consistent method, however rude, of adjusting the moon count to the year. When the discrepancy became too insistent, something was presumably stretched or the reckoning simply suspended until matters tallied again. The whole scheme is essentially descriptive of terrestrial events, and has as little reference to astronomical events as a system can have and still be called a calendar. In line with this attitude of the Maidu is the fact that they made definite recognition of the seasons as such, as shown by a neat nomenclature. It should also be added that some of the upland Maidu counted only the winter moons, those of the summer being left unnamed.

The few other central Californian calendars known do not differ in plan from those of the Maidu.

The Yurok calendar had a more astronomical basis, although simple enough; and the descriptive element was almost lacking. The moons were numbered, not named, at least up to the tenth; the remaining ones had descriptive appellations. The year began definitely at the winter solstice. The summer solstice may have been noted also, but did not enter into the system. There was a clear recognition of the essential problem of a year calendar, some individuals counting twelve moons and others thirteen. The solution must have been less clearly formulated, since it is stated that disputes often took place as to the proper designation of the current moon. Yet the recognition of the solstice as a primary point, however inaccurately it may have been determined by offhand appearances without mechanically aided observations, would prevent any excessively gross errors or long continued conflict of opinion.

The Yurok system is undoubtedly connected with that of the North Pacific coast, where the moons are also frequently numbered and fitted into the frame afforded by the solstices.

The Modoc calendar seems to be a weakening of the Yurok one. Basically, the moons are numbered, although their actual names are those of the fingers of the hand. But the beginning of the round is in summer and is determined by a seasonal harvest; there is no mention of the solstices; and none of an intercalary thirteenth month.

In southern California, the moon names are probably descriptive, but the fixed points of the calendar, and the means of its more or less automatic correction, are the two solstices. The Diegueño have only six month names; which means that the second year-half repeats and balances the first, and presumably that the two solstices are pivotal. The Juaneño and Luiseño do not repeat month designations within the year, but the former name only five and the latter but four lunations in each year-half. This scheme makes the nonlunar periods that include the solstices long and somewhat variable, but also accentuates them as primary. All three varieties of this calendar must at times have been productive of difficulty within the year-half, but as a perpetual system the scheme is obviously self-correcting. Whether any of the southern California tribes took actual observations of the solstices is not known.

This southern calendar is clearly allied to that of the tribes of the southwestern states, who also deal in solstices but describe their moons. The Diegueño six-name plan is that of the Zuñi. The Pueblos definitely determined the solstices with fair accuracy by observations made on the horizon from established spots. It is possible that they were led to this procedure by their permanent residences. These would at least afford an advantage and perhaps a stimulus in this direction.

Astronomical knowledge not directly used in time reckoning was slight in northern and central California. The planets were too difficult to trouble with, except for Venus when it was the morning star. The Pleiades are the constellation most frequently mentioned, and seem to have had a designation among every tribe. Myths usually make them dancing girls, as in so many parts of the world. This may prove to be one of the concepts of independent or directly psychological origin which have so often been sought but are so difficult to establish positively. Orion's belt is probably recognized with the next greatest frequency, and then possibly Ursa Major. There are some references to Polaris as the immovable star. The Milky Way is known everywhere, and quite generally called the ghosts' road. In southern California stellar symbolism begins to be of some consequence, and a half-dozen constellations are named in addition to those recognized farther north. They are mostly those of the southern summer sky.

Numeration

The round numbers familiar to the Californians in ritual and myth are low, as among all American Indians. In the north, from the Tolowa and Sinkyone to the Achomawi and mountain Maidu, five or its multiple ten is in universal use in such connections (table 2). In the region of the well defined Kuksu cult, four takes its place, although the Pomo evince some inclination to supplement it by six. To the south, there is enough uncertainty to suggest that no one number stood strongly in the foreground. The Yokuts favor six, but without much emphasis. The Gabrielino employed five, six, and seven in addition to four; among the Juaneño, five is most commonly mentioned; for the Luiseño, probably three; among the Diegueño, three is clearly prevalent in ritual action, four in myth. For a group of American nations with a definite ceremonial cult, and that comprising sacred paintings of the world, this is an unusually vague condition. Only the Colorado River tribes are positive: four is as inevitably significant to them as to all the Indians of the Southwest.

Directional reference of the ritualistic number is manifest in the Kuksu tribes, but everywhere else is wanting or at least insignificant, except with the Yuman groups. Here there is some tendency to balance opposite directions; single pairs are even mentioned alone. North or east has the precedence. In the Kuksu region, there is a definite sequence of directions in sinistral circuit; but the starting point varies from tribe to tribe. Association of colors with the directions has been reported only from the Diegueño. Its general absence is an instance of the comparatively low development of ritualistic symbolism in California.

The same table (2) shows also the distribution in California of methods of counting—the basis of all mathematical science. Mankind as a whole, even when most advanced, counts as its fingers determine. But it is obvious that the unit or basis of numeration can be one hand, or two, or the fingers plus the toes, that is "one man." This gives a choice between quinary, decimal, and vigesimal systems. Whether from an inherent cause or because of a historical accident, practically all highly civilized nations count by tens, with hundred as the next higher unit. Peoples less advanced in culture are however fairly equally divided between a decimal numeration and one which operates somewhat more concretely or personally with fives and twenties. So too with the Californians. But to judge correctly their inclinations as between these two possibilities, it is necessary to distinguish between their use of low and high numbers.

For the first ten numerals, the majority of the Californians have stems only for one to five. The words for six to nine are formed from those for one to four. This system is replaced by a truly decimal one, in which the word for seven, for instance, bears no relation to that for two, chiefly in three regions. The first of these regions holds the two Algonkin divisions of California, the Wiyot and Yurok; and a few immediately adjacent Athabascan groups, notably the Hupa and Tolowa. The second area comprises the Yokuts, Miwok, and most of the Costanoans—in short, the southern half of the Penutian family. In the third area are the Plateau Shoshoneans east of the Sierra Nevada.

These distributions reflect geographical positions rather than linguistic affinities. The northern Penutians, southern Athabascans, and southern California Shoshoneans count by fives. The map makes it look as if decimal numeration had been taken over by the Hupa and Tolowa in imitation of the method of their Algonkin neighbors; but the difficulty in this connection is that the great mass of eastern Algonkins count by fives instead of straight to ten.

For the higher numbers, the corresponding choice is between a system based on twenty and four hundred, or on ten and one hundred. In this domain the decimal system prevails, showing that the quinary and vigesimal methods, even if inherently associated, are not inseparable. The situation may be summed up by saying that from twenty up, all California counts decimally except the people of two areas. The first comprises half or more of the Pomo, most of the Southern Wintun, in general the western Maidu, and the northerly divisions of the interior Miwok. This is precisely the region of intensive development of the Kuksu cults. Here the count is by twenties. The second area (although in this the count is, strictly speaking, by a multiplication of fives rather than by twenties) is that of the Gabrielino and Luiseño, with whom the Fernandeño, Juaneño, and perhaps Cupeño must be included, but no others. Now this, strangely enough, is precisely the tract over which the Chungichnish form of the jimsonweed religion had penetrated in its full form. The connection between a system of religious institutions and a method of numeration in daily life is difficult to understand, and the bonds must be indirect and subtle. That they exist, however, and that it is more than an empty coincidence that we are envisaging, is made almost indisputable by the fact that the northern tract of decimal counting for low numbers coincides very nearly with the

TABLE 2

RITUAL NUMBERS AND METHODS OF NUMERATION

Group	Ritual Number	Units of Count 1-10	11-19	20-
Yurok	5, 10	10	10	10
Wiyot	5, 10	10	10	10
Karok	5, 10	5	10	10
Chimariko		5	10	10
Tolowa		10	10	10
Hupa, Chilula	5, 10	10	10	10
Sinkyone	5	5		10
Wailaki		5		10
Kato		5	5	10
Coast Yuki		5	5	10
Yuki	4* (6)	8	8	64
Wappo		5	10	10
Pomo	4* (6*)	5¹	5²	10, 20
Coast Miwok		10	10	10
Shasta	5, 10	5	10	10
Modoc	5	5	10	10
Achomawi	(5)	5	10	10
Yana	(5)	5	10	10
Wintun, Northern		5	10	
Wintun, Central		5	5	
Wintun, Southern	4*	5	5, 10	20, 10
Maidu, Mountain	5*	5	10	10
Maidu, Hill	4 5	5	5, 10	20, 10
Maidu, Valley	4* (5)	5	5	20
Maidu, Southern		5	5	10
Miwok, Northern		10	5	20
Miwok, Central	4	10	5	20
Miwok, Southern		10	10	10
Yokuts, Central	6	10	10	10
Yokuts, Southerly	3 6, 12	10	10	10
Costanoan	(5)	10³	10	10
Esselen		5		
Salinan		4	16	16
Chumash		4	16	16
Washo		5	10	10
Eastern Mono	4	10		
Tübatulabal		10		
Chemehuevi		10		
Serrano		5	10	10
Gabrielino	4, 8 (10) 6 (7)	5	5	5
Cahuilla		5	10	10
Luiseño	(3) (4)*	5	5	5
Diegueño	3 4*	5		10
Yuma		5	10	10
Mohave	4*	5	10	10

* Referred to cardinal directions.
1 10 among Northeastern Pomo.
2 10 among Northeastern and Southern Pomo.
3 5 among Southern Costanoans.

area of the northwestern culture in its purest form as exemplified by new year rites and the Deerskin Dance.

That the basing of the vigesimal on a quinary count, although usual, is by no means necessary, is also shown by the Northern and Central Miwok, who count the first ten numbers decimally, but proceed from ten to twenty by adding units of five, and beyond with units of twenty. That a people should count first five and then another five and then proceed to operate systematically with the higher unit of ten, is not so very foreign to our way of thinking. But that our own psychic processes are by no means necessarily binding is proved by this curious Miwok practice of counting successively by tens, fives, and twenties.

Two other, totally divergent methods of counting are found in California. The Chumash and Salinans count by fours, with sixteen as higher unit, the Yuki by eights and sixty-fours. The latter operate by laying pairs of twigs into the spaces between the fingers. Thus the anomaly is presented of an octonary system based on the hand. The Yuki operate quite skillfully by this method: when they are asked to count on the fingers as such, like their neighbors, they work slowly and with frequent errors. Both these aberrant systems run contrary to speech affinity: the Chumash and Salinans are the only Hokans that count by fours; and the Coast Yuki, Huchnom, and Wappo related to the Yuki know nothing of the system of eights.

Every count that can progress beyond one hand involves arithmetical operations of some sort, usually addition. But other processes crop out with fair frequency in California. Nine, fourteen, and nineteen are sometimes formed from the unit next above. The word for four is often a reduplicated or expanded two; or eight a similar formation from four. Two-three for six, three-four for twelve, and three-five for fifteen all occur here and there; and the Luiseño count by an indefinitely repeated system of multiplication, as, "four times five times five."

The degree to which mathematical operations were conducted, other than in the counts themselves, has been very little examined. The Pomo speak of beads by ten and forty thousands. Every group in the state, apparently, knew how to count into the hundreds; how often its members actually used these higher numbers, and on what occasions, is less clear. Rapid and extended enumeration argues some sense of the value of numbers, and it is likely that people like the Pomo and Wintun developed such a faculty by their counting of beads. Of direct mathematical operations there is less evidence. An untutored Yuki can express offhand in his octonary nomenclature how many fingers he has; he evidently cannot multiply ten by two: for he finds it necessary to count his hands twice over to enable him to answer. An old Mohave knows at once that four times four is sixteen;

but four times eight presents a problem to be solved only by a sorting and adding up of counters. No Californian language is known to have any expression for fractions. There is always a word for half, but it seems to mean part or division rather than the exact mathematical ratio.

THE ABORIGINAL
POPULATION OF UPPER
CALIFORNIA

by

Sherburne F. Cook

After extensive travel in the area Stephen Powers (*Tribes of California*, 1877) stated the presettlement population of Alta California to be approximately 750,000, a figure which ethnographers ever since have regarded as a gross overestimate. Thirty years later C. Hart Merriam (*American Anthropologist* 7:594-606, 1905) using a combination of wide personal observation and mission records put the value at 250,000. In the *Handbook of the Indians of California*, Alfred L. Kroeber adopted an extremely conservative attitude and would allow no more than 125,000 aboriginal natives. Subsequently I reexamined the data (*Ibero-Americana*, No. 21, 1942) as presented by Kroeber and revised his figure upward slightly to 133,550. Further study through the past twenty years has led me to believe that both Kroeber and I were too low in our estimates and a much more realistic figure is that of Merriam. This opinion is based upon three intensive studies of population in restricted portions of California: the San Joaquin Valley (*Univ. Calif. Anthrop. Record*, Vol. 16, No. 2, 1955), the north coast (*Univ. Calif. Anthrop. Records*, Vol. 16, No. 3, 1956), and Alameda and Contra Costa counties (*Univ. Calif. Anthrop. Records*, Vol. 16, No. 4, 1957). In all three regions the new values turned out to be nearly twice as great as those previously accepted by Kroeber and by myself.

The physical and biotic environment, the density and cultural status of the inhabitants, and the social contact with invading races all show a very great diversity from one end of California to the other. As a result widely different methods must be employed in different areas for the computation of native population.

In general the demographic data can be allocated to three categories of native social organization, not all of which existed at any single place

Pp. 397–402 of Sherburne F. Cook, *The Aboriginal Population of Upper California*, Actas y Memorias del XXXV Congreso Internacional de Americanistas, Mexico, 1962 (1964), 2:397–403. By permission of the author. A recent examination of the question of how many Indians occupied the New World in 1492 (H. Dobyns, "Estimating Aboriginal American Population," *Current Anthropology*, Vol. 7, No. 4, 1966) concludes that there were about 90,000,000 Indians. Dobyns' figure is slightly over 11 times as great as that computed by Kroeber in 1919. The larger hemispheric figure encourages acceptance of Cook's calculation of California Indian numbers.

or time: (1) the linguistic major group (Pomo, Yokuts); (2) the tribe, or better tribelet, embracing usually several hundred persons and sometimes coextensive with a habitation unit; (3) the rancheria, or village, large or small, but bringing to a focus the family and community life. To these native entities must be added the mission, as introduced by the Franciscans in 1769; for the mission in a wide territory came to form the primary demographic unit.

The materials for estimating population are manifold. First, there are visible in the field, or have been in the recent past, hundreds of villages or other permanent habitation sites which were occupied at the time of the first white contact, or had been occupied not long prior thereto. The population of most of these is unknown, but for quite representative samples information is available and is valid statistically. In many instances remains of family living units have been found, such as house pits, which enable one to make a close estimate of the number of inhabitants.

The second primary source of knowledge concerning not only village but tribal populations is the body of information obtained from living informants by ethnographers during the past half century. In certain areas this constitutes our only clue to aboriginal conditions and as such is of the greatest value. On the other hand such ethnographic data suffer from two possible defects. One is the tendency of informants to remember qualitative facts, such as customs, beliefs, and ceremonies, with great clarity, but to forget or be very inaccurate in matters involving quantities. This tendency is manifest in the repetition of relative expressions such as "large" or "small" rather than in terms of absolute numbers. The other difficulty is that of time. The school of California anthropologists led by Kroeber operated in the field from approximately 1900 to 1940. An old man in 1900 could not remember with distinctness conditions much prior to 1850. With the aid of parental tradition, in the nonmissionized portions of the state, he could recall certain events and certain facts with reasonable accuracy, but numerical data were clouded by extreme vagueness. In the missionized areas it is safe to say that no descendant of the original stock had the slightest real knowledge of aboriginal habitation groupings. Furthermore, in view of the great decline of population and disturbance of living patterns which occurred prior to the advent of the North Americans in 1845–1850, all statements of informants to modern ethnographers are very likely to furnish a drastic underestimate of actual presettlement populations.

The third and fourth sources of information consist of the written diaries, reports, and letters of pioneer explorers, soldiers, or settlers and of established officials, clergy, and civilians. Between the two groups there is little real distinction, since the original pioneers very often settled down to become the later immigrant population; and conversely, inhabitants of long standing frequently undertook new expeditions of exploration and conquest. This was particularly true along the mission frontier where numerous forays and incursions into "wild Indian" territory continued until the discovery of gold accomplished the final destruction of native society.

These accounts, whether in the form of journals or official correspondence, whether by Spaniards, Mexicans, or Americans, are of the greatest importance, since they repeatedly make statements of numbers. The primary criticism which has been directed against this source of demographic material is that it is subject to extreme exaggeration — a criticism which has not been confined to the study of California. The basic tenet of this doctrine is that observers, either through carelessness, or, for a variety of reasons, through deliberate mendacity, overrate the numbers of foreign groups with which they came in contact. This position is arguable. Not all men are careless or mendacious, in particular among responsible officials and clergy. On numerous occasions there is not the slightest personal advantage to be gained from exaggeration. In any specific case critical evaluation is necessary, but the verdict need not always be decided in advance against the informant. In California we have examples of all sorts of population estimates, some of which are unquestionably sober, accurate, and reliable. We may use these with confidence and ignore those of dubious value.

The fifth source of information consists of the baptism and death records of the twenty-one Alta California missions, together with the very complete reports sent annually back to Mexico. Concerning the veracity and accuracy of these records there can be no question. The only problems associated with their use concern interpretation of the data and the application of mission statistics to areas outside the sphere of direct mission control.

For assessing the population of California we follow the political boundaries of the present state except that the Washo, Paiute, and Shoshoneans directly east of the Sierra Nevada are omitted, as are the Mojave and Yuma. The first group is considered as being affiliated with the Great Basin province and the latter group as being ethnically and politically distinct from California. The remainder of the state may be segregated for convenience into eight areas. Of two of these the population has been determined as carefully as the data permit in publications previously mentioned. A restricted portion of a third area has also been investigated with care. The population of the remaining regions has been provisionally estimated partly by analogy with the known areas and partly from independent data.

Area 1: The north coast and interior as far as the inner coast ranges. Includes linguistic groups: Coast Miwok, Wappo, Pomo, Athabascans, Yuki, Wiyot, Tolowa, Yurok, Hupa, Karok. This area was the subject of a special study using the methods of village sites, informants' memories, a few early explorations, and, for the southern portion, mission records. The final total found was 70,440 persons.

Area 2: The northeastern corner of California covering the headwaters of the Sacramento River, the Pit River basin, and Modoc County. It includes (1) the Shastan tribes, (2) the Achomawi and the Atsugewi, and (3) the Modoc. The information is derived mostly from a few ethnographers, in particular Kroeber and Kniffen. Their informants indicate approximately 3,000 for each of the three principal stocks.

In the coastal area (of Area 1) which corresponds in latitude to Area 2, there are five tribes, Wiyot, Yurok, Tolowa, Hupa, Harok, with a population of 13,500, and embracing a territory somewhat smaller than Area 2. However, if we allow for the much poorer subsistence resources of Area 2, the population estimate of 9,000 appears wholly reasonable.

Area 3: The San Joaquin Valley, or that portion of the Great Central Valley reaching from the crest of the Sierra Nevada to the eastward slopes of the coast ranges and northward from the Tehachapi Mountains to the latitude of the Cosumnes River and the north shore of San Francisco Bay. It includes the Yokuts, the Plains and Sierra Miwok, the Western Mono, together with the Tubatulabal and a few other minor groups. The population of this entire region was found to be approximately 83,800.

Area 4: The Sacramento Valley, north of the Cosumnes, embracing the basin of the Sacramento River south of the Pit River with the mountain slopes to both east and west. The linguistic stocks include the Wintun, Maidu, Yahi, and Yana. Kroeber placed the population of these tribes at 20,750. Later, in 1943, I raised the estimate to 25,650 but now feel that it is far too low. Two reasons conduce to this conclusion. First, we have learned a good deal about the tremendous epidemics (probably malaria) that swept the Sacramento Valley in the 1830's and destroyed most of the inhabitants. The informants upon whom Kroeber depended for his calculations could not remember conditions prior to 1850, or at the most 1840. Hence their figures are all post-epidemic, and depict a scattered, depleted population. Second, the Sacramento ecologically closely resembles the San Joaquin Valley, and indeed in some respects surpasses it as a habitat for primitive man. Hence a direct area comparison is permissible. The approximate territorial ratio of the San Joaquin Valley to the Sacramento Valley (as the two are here outlined) is 8/5. Hence the population of the latter may be put in round numbers at 50,000, twice as much as the figure obtained from the memory of modern informants.

Area 5: The Central Coast ranges from San Francisco Bay to San Luis Obispo. This was the home of the linguistic stocks known as the Costanoans, the Salinans, and the Esselen. It was rapidly and completely brought under the control of the missions between 1770 and 1790. For data concerning aboriginal population, therefore, we are dependent exclusively upon the accounts of early explorers and upon the mission records.

An intensive survey was undertaken of these two types of source material as they pertained to a restricted portion of Area 5, i.e. Alameda and Contra Costa counties on the east shore of San Francisco Bay. The "Contra Costa," as it was then known, was thoroughly explored by three full-scale expeditions in 1772, 1775, and 1776. Thereafter it was repeatedly visited by soldiers and priests who rendered numerous reports. At the same time and later the inhabitants were Christianized and incorporated into the missions of San Francisco, Santa Clara, and San Jose. The localities of their origin are clearly indicated in the respective baptism books. Hence the contemporary information is unusually complete and reliable.

The Fages and the Anza expeditions of 1772 and 1776 gave population values of 2,400 and 2,150 respectively, based upon village counts. The total gentile baptisms which could be attributed to the two counties were 2,248. The village counts were low because the voyagers did not see all the villages nor count all the inhabitants of those they did see. The baptisms were carried out over a period of twenty years during which the residual native population was declining rapidly due to disease, massacre, and fugitivism. For these reasons I have put the minimal aboriginal value at 3,000 and the maximum possible at 4,500.

Now it will be noted that the baptism figure is probably only 50 to 70 percent of the actual original number of the inhabitants, assuming the low value of 3,000 for the latter. Consequently this relationship may be used to estimate the remainder of Area 5 using baptisms as the point of departure.

The records of the nine missions from San Francisco to San Antonio inclusive show by village names 15,500 gentile baptisms which may be assigned with reasonable confidence to the Costanoans, Salinans, and Esselen, the total meanwhile being 27,300. The difference, 11,800 baptisms, represent neophytes brought in from the North Bay (Area 1) and the San Joaquin Valley (Area 3). Using, therefore, a ratio of 2/3 for the relation between baptisms and aboriginal inhabitants, we get a pre-mission population of 23,250.

Area 6: The Santa Barbara channel coast, with interior hill country and off-shore islands, from San Luis Obispo to the Los Angeles County line. This territory was held only by the Chumash.

Along the coast itself Kroeber, from an examination of all sources known to him, listed 41 villages. Of these, 15 can be identified in the baptism books of Santa Barbara and San Buenaventura missions and show an average of 93 gentile baptisms each. The total would be 3,813. If we apply the 2/3 ratio the result is 5,720 as the pre-occupation population of the coastal strip. Now this narrow stretch of land corresponds very precisely to the route taken by the expedition of Portola in 1769 which was recorded by the diary of Father Fray Crespi. This missionary carefully noted the number of persons found in all inhabited places. The total is 5,500, a value which agrees very well with the corrected figures of Kroeber and constitutes justification for the use of the 2/3 ratio for the Chumash.

For the inland portion of the Chumash territory, Kroeber listed 25 villages, of which 8 can be identified in the mission books, with a mean of 96 gentile baptisms. This would yield a total of 2,400, or after applying the 2/3 ratio, 3,600. A similar treatment applied to the channel islands gives 1,570 persons. The total population for the Chumash would then be 10,890, according to the corrected lists of Kroeber.

Turning again to the mission records, it is found that the total number of gentile baptisms performed at the five missions—San Buenaventura, Santa Barbara, La Purisima, Santa Ynez, and San Luis Obispo—was 9,105. Almost all of these were Chumash. With the ratio of 2/3 the aboriginal population would be 13,650, somewhat higher than is obtained by the adjustment of Kroeber's village lists. The discrepancy is undoubtedly referable to the islands, the natives of which were seriously depleted before they could be brought to the missions of the mainland, not only by introduced diseases but by the depredations of the Russian and other sea otter hunters who infested the California coast in the late eighteenth century. The figure 13,650 will therefore be accepted for Area 6.

Area 7: The southern coast ranges from Los Angeles to the border of Baja California and inland to the edge of the desert. This region was from 1769 completely dominated by the five southern missions: San Fernando, San Gabriel, San Juan Capistrano, San Luis Rey, and San Diego. The converts were drawn almost entirely from the tribes inhabiting the coast ranges themselves, not from the desert or the Colorado River Valley. Therefore the gentile baptisms constitute an adequate basis for a population estimate. Of these there was an aggregate of 15,181 or, say, 15,200.

It is a well-recognized fact that south of the Santa Barbara channel and the Tehachapi mountains the natives withstood the impact of occupation by European civilization much better than did the Indians to the north. The causes are obscure but there is much evidence to show that the death rates were lower and the survival greater than elsewhere in Alta California. Therefore the ratio of 2/3 should be increased, certainly to 3/4 and perhaps to 4/5. Using the latter ratio, the estimate for pre-mission population becomes approximately 19,000.

Area 8: The interior desert extending to, but not including, the Colorado River tribes. The territory embraces therefore the Cahuilla and the small groups south and southeast of the southern Sierra Nevada. These Indians remained in their native homes, although they adopted the Christian religion and tended toward a relatively mobile existence, rather than a sedentary village life. The result has been that neither classical ethnographic data nor mission records are of much help. Actually a new and exhaustive study of this area is needed. A good many years ago Kroeber allowed about 5,000 for all the desert tribes east of the missions and I have never seen any reason to revise his figure.

If the estimates for each of the eight areas of California are now added, the total appears as 274,140. This may be rounded to 275,000, or, if one wishes a range rather than a fixed number, 250,000 to 300,000. My own opinion is that the upper figure more closely represents the real value than the lower.

A NEW ECOLOGICAL TYPOLOGY OF THE CALIFORNIA INDIANS

by
Ralph L. Beals and
Joseph A. Hester, Jr.

Anthropologists have long been aware of the importance of ecology, particularly among peoples of relatively simple technology, but only rarely has it been possible to demonstrate ecological relationships satisfactorily in much detail. Birdsell recently has shown a very high correlation between population distribution and rainfall in Australia. Steward in several papers has suggested relations between ecology and social organization. The problem has long been of interest to workers in California, particularly in various publications of C. Hart Merriam and in the work of A. L. Kroeber. The most ambitious undertaking in this field undoubtedly is Kroeber's *Cultural and Natural Areas of Native North America (1940)*.

A major difficulty in most anthropological attempts to deal with ecology has been the unsatisfactory state of data concerning the environment. Few anthropologists have either the time or the skills necessary to obtain sufficiently detailed raw data where these are not already ·available. In California the wide variation in elevations, soil types, climatic factors, and flora and fauna has precluded the possibility of simple ecological correlations such as Birdsell secured in Australia, and has made any broad-scale analysis difficult. In recent years marked improvement in the data for California on climates, soil types, and floral and faunal distributions permit an attempt at a more fine-grained analysis than that provided by Kroeber.

Reexamination of the data for California has led us to the provisional formulation of six major ecological types and several subtypes. This typology is based upon the fact that separate regions in California differ markedly from one another in the amount and kinds of food resources they offered the California Indians and upon the similarity of economic adaptations of the various groups within each region. As is the case with many typologies, our types are abstractions, and dividing lines are not clear cut. In some cases food resources differed not so much in kind as in amount. In such cases the differences between types depend upon the

Pp. 411–418 of Ralph L. Beals and Joseph A. Hester, Jr., "A New Ecological Typology of the California Indians," *Selected Papers of the Fifth International Congress of Anthropological and Ethnological Sciences, Philadelphia, September 1–9, 1956*, ed. A. F. C. Wallace (University of Pennsylvania Press, 1960). By permission of the authors.

relative importance of various food resources. Particular local groups of California Indians in some cases had easy access to more than one type of environment and hence sometimes are not readily assignable to a single ecologic type.

ECOLOGIC TYPE IA. COASTAL TIDELANDS GATHERERS

Tidelands gatherers inhabited the coast from about Estero Bay to the Oregon border. Their economy was characterized by extensive use of shell-fish and surf fish, with acorns and game playing a secondary role in the diet. They possessed only balsas (raft-like boats of tules) or relatively small dugout canoes, both specialized for inland waters; hence they seldom ventured off shore. Usually, or perhaps always, they were closely related to neighboring inland groups.

In the south this subtype tended to intergrade with the sea hunters and fishers. Where rivers are sizable, they blended into the riverine ecologic type. And insofar as they used acorns and other land foods, they showed some aspects of the foothill type, differing markedly, however, in emphasis on food supply. In general, the degree of variation within the subtype depends on the size and usefulness of rivers or on the accessibility of inland foods.

The tidelands gatherers were closely limited to the cool, humid, coastal fog climate with some possible exceptions among the long-vanished peoples about San Francisco Bay. This climate exists as a narrow coastal

SUMMARY TABLE OF ECOLOGICAL TYPES

Ecologic type	Subsistence staples
	(In order of decreasing importance; all use seeds, bulbs, and greens in varying amounts as supplements to the staples.)
I. Coastal	
A. Tidelands gatherers	Shellfish, surf fish, acorns, game
B. Sea hunters and fishers	Sea fish, shellfish, game, acorns
II. Riverine (salmon cultures)	Fish, acorns/tule, game
III. Lake	Fish, tule/acorns, waterfowl, game
IV. Valley or plains (a mixed type)	Acorns/tule, game, fish
V. Foothill	Acorns, game, fish
VI. Desert	
A. Hunters and gatherers	Pinyon/mesquite, game
B. Farmers	Farm produce, mesquite, fish

belt from Estero Bay to the Oregon border, an airline distance of more than 500 miles. The belt is often as little as five miles wide and its greatest inland penetration is some 21 or 22 miles along the Eel River from the sea. The total area occupied by tidelands gatherers may have been around 3,000 square miles, but by far the most important dimensions for this group was not area but the number of miles of productive seacoast, estuary shores, and river banks available.

Some inland areas undoubtedly fall within the range of most tidelands gatherers, but most of the coast is rugged with intervening bays and beaches. In places, for many miles the coast-range mountains drop abruptly to the sea or rise steeply behind a narrow coastal shelf. Hence, most of the accessible inland range is relatively poor in resources. North of Marin County, areas adjacent to the coast are mainly dense redwood forest, sometimes mixed with other conifers, or poor grasslands. To the south, redwoods occur in groves of diminishing extent almost to Estero Bay, but the country in places is more open. Nevertheless, oaks are rare near the coast, the unproductive laurel being a much more common tree; and dense chaparral covered extensive areas, impeding travel but supporting sizable deer herds. The interior demand for seashells likewise permitted many of the tidelands gatherers to secure inland products through trade.

Coastal dwelling groups of Indians speaking the following languages were tidelands gatherers:

Tolowa	Sinkyone	Costanoan
Yurok	Yuki	Esselen
Mattole	Pomo	Salinan
Wiyot	Miwok	

Coastal dwelling groups of Diegueño, Luiseño, Juaneño and Gabrielino in southern California probably belonged to a similar type, but they vanished too early to permit definite assignment. Moreover, the greater proportion of sand beaches in the south not only supplied few shellfish but were poor surf fishing areas with aboriginal technology.

ECOLOGIC TYPE IB. HUNTERS AND FISHERS

Sea hunters and fishers were found from about Estero Bay southward to just beyond Santa Monica Bay and on the Channel Islands. They took large sea fish and sea mammals (on land), and exploited the shellfish along the coast and on the islands. Although they used the same basic economic adaptation as the tidelands gatherers, the technological addition of the ocean-going canoe and deep-sea fishing techniques tapped a rich source of food unavailable to the latter.

It is probably no coincidence that the distribution of the seaworthy plank canoe begins at the southern terminus of the coastal fog belt. Southeast of Point Conception the Santa Barbara coast is relatively sheltered from strong westerly winds. This, plus greater visibility and the proximity of the Channel Islands, facilitated the most successful marine adaptation found in California. Peoples of this ecologic subtype were the coastal and island-dwelling groups speaking various languages of the Chumash and Gabrielino families. Linguistically related groups living inland belonged to a different ecologic type.

Most groups belonging to this ecologic subtype were found along approximately 70 to 100 miles of sheltered shoreline (70 miles from Point Conception to Ventura, perhaps 20 miles of Santa Monica Bay, and an additional 10 miles at San Pedro Bay), and on the Channel Islands, plus a few at canyon mouths along the abrupt coast between Point Mugu and Point Dume. They undoubtedly ranged inland a moderate distance but, except for a few valleys, the coast range either rises abruptly from the sea or from a narrow coastal plain only two or three miles wide to crests averaging 2500 to 3500 feet elevation. Except for narrow strips of poor grassland, coastal chaparral and coastal sagebrush constituted the dominant vegetation near the coast. None are highly productive of vegetable foods. Inland and at higher elevations some oaks, and in places pine, existed, but game (including sea mammals along the shore) appears to have been the most important food derived from the land. Acorns, although the major vegetable food, apparently were of much less importance than animal foods. Because of early disruption of these peoples by the missions, it is impossible to know how closely their economies were integrated with those of the related inland groups belonging to a different ecologic type. It is unlikely that they often ranged inland beyond the crest of the coastal ranges and then only for specific resources.

ECOLOGIC TYPE II. RIVERINE

Riverine groups occurred chiefly along the main streams and certain tributaries of the Klamath, Eel, and Sacramento rivers. Groups of this type based a major part of their subsistence upon the annual runs of the large king salmon. (Species of smaller salmon entered some of the short coastal rivers but only the large king salmon was sufficiently important to have modified Indian economy to a significant extent along California streams.)

Despite occasional failure of the annual salmon run, groups of river type possessed marked economic stability. Further characteristics were compact settlement patterns (including large villages in the Sacramento Valley region), incomplete exploitation of vegetable resources, and some degree of social and economic dominance over neighboring hunting and gathering groups.

Groups of riverine type usually had their settlements on or near rivers and their major subsistence came from the streams and the immediately nearby valley bottoms and hills, with occasional visits to more remote spots. Except for the groups in the Sacramento River drainage, all other groups lived in rugged and heavily forested Coast Range areas. The forests there are predominantly coniferous, mostly redwood, Douglas fir, or mixed types, providing few food resources except along the streams and in and near unforested areas. Although the most numerous and preferred oak in northwestern California, the tan-bark (*Lithocarpus*), flourishes best in partial shade, it does not tolerate the heavy shade within dense mature coniferous forests. The same is true of most plants affording browse for deer or food for other animals, including birds.

In California there are about 650 miles of rivers and major streams in which king salmon are found, or were found before irrigation and the damming of streams began. Where these supported sufficiently large runs of salmon and advantageous fishing conditions, salmon provided a substantial portion of the staple diet. Acorns were the most important vegetable food while game was a poor third as a food source. It is important to note that salmon apparently were not usually taken in the ocean, in San Francisco Bay, or in the slack waters of the system of sloughs in the interior valley. In the upper reaches of many streams, salmon runs apparently diminished in size and were of minor importance to many peoples with good acorn and game resources who consequently fell into a different ecologic type.

People in whose habitat important salmon streams occurred included groups speaking the following languages:

Hupa	Okwanuchu
Tolowa	Pomo
Yurok	Yana
Chimariko	Miwok
Wiyot	Yokuts
Bear River	Wintun (River Wintun)
Karok	Patwin (River Patwin)
Shasta	Maidu (River Maidu)
Achomawi	Nisenan (River Nisenan)

Riverine groups of the last six named languages will be considered with the valley ecological type. Other groups, basically coastal or foothill in ecological type but with a partly riverine economy, included some speakers of each of the following languages:

Wilkut	Wailaki
Chilula	Yuki
Mattole	Huchnom
Lassik	Sinkyone

ECOLOGIC TYPE III. LAKE

Peoples of the lake type lived on islands or lake shores and gained the bulk of their subsistence from the water and its immediate vicinity. The major locations were Tulare, Kern, and Buena Vista lakes in the San Joaquin Valley and Clear Lake north of San Francisco Bay. Other smaller lakes and tideland marshes may have supported groups of similar ecologic type but none are reported in the literature.

Lake-type groups exploited primarily fish, waterfowl, and other lake foods. The San Joaquin Valley lake-type people also made extensive use of the bulrush or tule for food, clothing, and housing and had easy access only to relatively barren plains in a desert-type environment. The Clear Lake groups, on the other hand, had foothill-type environment readily accessible to them and utilized land products to a greater extent.

People belonging to this type included groups speaking languages of the Pomo and Yokuts families.

Owing to marked differences in the area of the shallow lakes in the San Joaquin Valley from year to year, it is difficult to estimate the area of primary subsistence. The secondary range included the few fertile areas with water supplies in a large area of the southern part of the west side of the San Joaquin Valley. The lake-dwelling Pomo, on the other hand, often had small but well-defined mainland territories in which they hunted and gathered.

ECOLOGIC TYPE IV. VALLEY

Valley-type ecologies are found among people in the Central Valley who occupied neither the lake nor tule areas of the southern San Joaquin nor areas of woodland-grass about the edges of the valley.

Settlements tended to be larger and more permanent than in many parts of California; and sometimes, in areas subjected to flooding, they were on artificially raised elevations. Most groups lived along the edges of permanent streams or water courses and gained much of their livelihood from fish (salmon, sturgeon, and lesser fish) and gathered fresh or brackish water shellfish. For groups in the central region, tule was of considerable importance. Most groups also had access to some oak groves, especially in the Sacramento Valley. The economy thus was of mixed type, and groups along the Sacramento River north of the delta were essentially riverine in their economy, while those with access to sizable oak groves approached the foothill type of ecologic adjustment.

The western part of the Central Valley was a region of relatively low rainfall and scanty resources. This is especially true of the southern part, and the account of the earliest Spanish expedition (Fages) along the west side of the San Joaquin Valley from Suisun Bay to about Pacheco Pass speaks of it as barren and virtually devoid of human occupation outside the tule swamps. The east side supported more vegetation but extensive areas between rivers are described as containing only the California poppy (*Eschscholtzia*) and members of the geranium family. Neither was a significant food source.

Except for the important salmon streams (the Sacramento above the American River junction and the clear-water sections of the San Joaquin and its larger tributaries) and the occasional groves of valley oaks (most common in the eastern part), the most important subsistence areas were the hundreds of miles of stream, slough, and tule-swamp borders. Especially in the so-called delta region and the lower San Joaquin, the basic economy for many groups possibly differed little from the southern San Joaquin Valley version of the lake ecologic type. If this was true, then our valley type disappears, divided between riverine and lake types (the latter perhaps better identified as tule-swamp type) with a few marginal intermediate groups who either had nearby oak groves on the valley floor (as in the Lodi-Stockton area) or periodically crossed the twenty or thirty miles of relatively barren plains to reach foothill oak groves. Unfortunately the very early disappearance of most groups in this area and the unusually meager descriptions of the early Spanish visitors make a choice of these alternatives difficult if not impossible.

Groups belonging to the valley type included speakers of the following languages:

River Wintun	Valley Nisenan
Valley Patwin	Valley Miwok
Valley Maidu	Valley Yokuts

ECOLOGIC TYPE V. FOOTHILL

Peoples of the foothill type lived in foothill or mountain regions with a variety of vegetable resources, of which the acorn usually was the most important. They are the "classic" type of the California Indian. They may have been the most numerous, and because of their generally mountainous and more interior habitat, more groups survived to yield at least memories to the ethnographer. Their primary subsistence came from those parts of the upper Sonoran and lower transition life zones occupied by a combination of woodland, woodland-grass, grassland, or chaparral vegetation types. Fish and/or game quantitatively were a minor part of the diet. The primary areas of occupation were the western slopes of the Sierra Nevada below the limit of winter snows, the Transverse ranges, a substantial part of the Coast ranges, including some of the intermontane valleys, and coastal plains and valleys back from the sea in southern California.

Depending upon the terrain, foothill type people lived either along streams in valleys or, especially in parts of the Sierra Nevada, on the ridges between streams. Settlements in most places tended to be relatively small, with a restricted "home range" often extending over two or more life zones and providing the bulk of the food supply, and a somewhat wider hunting and occasional gathering range. Within the life zones occupied, because of local soil and climatic conditions as well as the preferred adaptations of specific plants, most plant foods occurred in scattered locations rather than being distributed equally throughout the territory. As this was true of forage for many kinds of game, animal life likewise was unevenly distributed. At higher elevations groups of foothill type bordered on the heavily forested Sierra upper transition zone, an area of deep winter snows and relatively poor resources.

In general, the peoples of foothill type occupied the most favorable areas for Indian life in California (except the better river and coastal localities) and showed the highest general population density. With few or no exceptions, peoples of foothill ecologic type occupied relatively permanent settlements most of the year, but with either brief trips away or seasonal movements of varying magnitude and duration. Known settlements tended to be concentrated in areas of woodland and woodland-grass vegetation cover in which occur the great majority of oaks in California. The density of population within these zones varied primarily with rainfall and soil conditions, while the extent and duration of movement from permanent settlements was related to both richness of resources near the home village and the accessibility of alternative environments. Thus some groups visited the sea coast and some the desert, while yet others penetrated even into the boreal zones of the high Sierras in summer, although this often was a "food deficit" area requiring carrying in supplies. For many, however, movements took place within fairly short distances following the seasonal availability of supplementary foods occurring in scattered and restricted areas. Groups of foothill type included speakers of the following languages:

Foothill Miwok	Nisenan (Foothill)
Foothill Yokuts	Maidu (Foothill)
Tübatulabal	Yana
Western Mono	Wintu
Kitanemuk	Shasta
Alliklik	Fernandeño
Kawaiisu	Serrano (except Vanyume)
Nomlaki	Hill Patwin
Pomo (except Lake and Coast)	Yuki
Some Athabascans perhaps	Inland Costanoan
Inland Esselen	Pass and Mountain Cahuilla
Inland Salinan	Inland Chumash
Inland Gabrielino	Inland Luiseño
Inland Diegueño	Juaneño
Cupeño	

ECOLOGIC TYPE VIA. DESERT HUNTERS AND GATHERERS

Desert hunters and gatherers were found in the Colorado and Mohave deserts. Except in the most favored spots, the type may be considered an impoverished extension of the Great Basin cultures, with whom the California desert hunters and gatherers were all related linguistically and historically. These were the only people in California for whom the pinyon nut was the most important single item of food. The mesquite apparently replaced pinyon in importance for some groups, and it is possible that further analysis may permit establishment of low desert and high desert subtypes. In most areas use of the meager resources was further limited by the absence of water, and life centered as much about permanent or seasonal springs and the occasional stream as it did about supplies of food. The type is characterized by extremely low population densities, use of a wide variety of vegetable foods, and extreme simplicity of culture.

The best part of the area was in Owen's Valley, the east slope of the Sierra Nevada, and along the Mohave River. Here some permanence of settlement apparently was possible. In the remainder of the area frequent seasonal movement occurred with the individual family commonly the unit.

Peoples of this ecologic type included all or part of the groups speaking the following languages:

Desert Shoshoni	Washo
Northern Paiute	Vanyume Serrano
Southern Paiute	Desert Cahuilla

In addition to these, some groups primarily of foothill ecologic type occasionally ranged into the desert, for example, Kawaiisu, Kitanemuk, and some of the Serrano. However, they had little incentive to do so.

ECOLOGIC TYPE VIB. DESERT FARMERS

These included the Yuma and Mohave along the bottom lands of the Colorado River and the Kamia (or "Farming Eastern Diegueno") of the overflow lands at the south end of the Imperial Valley. At an indeterminately late date a few Chemehuevi also farmed along the Colorado River in Chemehuevi Valley. The desert farmers cultivated corn, pumpkins, and beans on lands flooded by the Colorado River during high water, usually in June. The Yuma and Mohave apparently obtained around 50 to 60 percent of their food from farming, the Kamia much less. The second most important food source was the mesquite which grew densely along the river wherever the water table was within 50 to 70 feet of the surface. It also grows in the Imperial and Coachella valleys where ground water is sufficiently near the surface.

Away from the river and a few overflow or seepage areas from the mountains, the land accessible to the farmers was as inhospitable as any part of the Colorado Desert and was used mainly by the scattered desert hunters and gatherers. The fertile lands subject to flooding or supporting mesquite constituted a small fraction of the state, perhaps not exceeding 1000 square miles. The Yuma and Mohave also utilized lands on the Arizona side of the Colorado River.

DISCUSSION

In a general sense our data suggest that within each of these ecological types there are characteristic manners of resource exploitation, settlement patterns, population densities and distributions, and cycles of seasonal movements. To some extent there is a relation between the size of social units and the total habitat area, but a closer fit appears between the size of social units and the abundance and distribution of the major sources of subsistence. We believe a substantial part of the variance of individual groups from the patterns characteristic of each ecological type will be explainable in terms either of intermediate locations between ecological zones, or through local modifications of habitat and resources.

Cultural correlates of the ecological types are still to be worked out in detail. It is reasonably clear that the different ecological types place differential emphasis upon various widespread technological skills and require some specialized developments. There is some variation in the relative economic importance of the sex roles in different ecological types. It is also evident that in some cases rather strikingly different ecological relationships could provide the conditions for rather similar social organizations. It is equally clear that conversely a single ecological type can provide the sufficient conditions for two alternative types of social organization. At present we have only promising leads for investigation rather than conclusive results. Neither can we at present estimate the extent to which variance from our ecological types may be influenced by cultural and social factors. Given the nature of the data on the California Indians, it is unlikely that we will be able to provide the kind of quantitative validation used by Birdsell in Australia. On the other hand the new possibilities for an ecological approach provide suggestive and fruitful new ways of examining the California Indian data. We believe the ecological typology presented will be helpful to this end.

SOME REGIONAL ASPECTS
OF NATIVE CALIFORNIA

by
S. J. Jones

There can be little doubt that the study of regional geography has been stunted in its development by a tendency to limit the analysis of human activity within a given set of physical circumstances to the developments of recent times. This is particularly clear in regional studies of non-European lands where, too often though not always, discussion is confined to the results of the later phases of European migration and settlement overseas. Regional assessments of such settlement are of great value in themselves, but attempts to draw from them academic conclusions concerning regional geography may give rise to many fallacies. To obtain a complete picture of regional processes, it is clearly necessary to weigh all the evidence and, in terms of non-European lands, to give careful consideration to the regional aspects of non-European settlement. In addition to increasing the body of available data, such consideration would widen our knowledge of regional possibilities through the opportunities afforded for the comparative study both of non-European and European settlement of the same areas and of the human uses made of similar physical circumstances in different parts of the world. Further, the study of non-European activities strengthens adherence to time sequences which, in turn, should ultimately make possible the environmental study of growth and change, and should produce a dynamic geography able to cope with the question of the potency of environmental elements. California may be taken as one specific example of an area from which material of considerable importance to the regional geographer may be gleaned in a study of non-European, or native, settlement. It yields regional knowledge concerning the relationship between non-European groups and the physical circumstances in which they live; in the non-European settlement of its areas of Mediterranean climate it provides provoking contrasts with the compar-

Pp. 19–29 of S. J. Jones, "Some Regional Aspects of Native California," *Scottish Geographical Magazine* (1951), 67:19–30. By permission of the Secretary, Scottish Geographical Society. For further discussion of why agriculture was absent in California, see R. F. Heizer, "Prehistoric Central California: A Problem in Historical Development Classification," *Univ. Calif. Archaeol. Survey Report* (1958), No. 41:19–26; and on the unusual lake culture of the southern San Joaquin Valley see R. L. Beals and J. A. Hester, "A Lacustrine Economy in California," in *Miscellanea Paul Rivet Octogenario Dicata* (Mexico, 1958), 1:211–217.

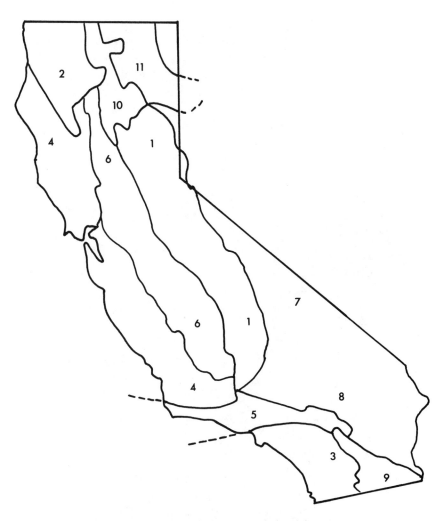

Map. 6. Geomorphic Provinces of California.

1. Sierra Nevada
2. Klamath Mountains
3. Peninsular Ranges
4. Coast Ranges
5. Transverse Ranges
6. Great Valley
7. Basin Ranges
8. Mojave Desert
9. Colorado Desert
10. Cascade Range
11. Modoc Plateau

able areas of Europe. Further, a closer examination of its Mediterranean climatic areas reveals certain facts that must be added to our present knowledge if a full assessment of such areas in the world is ultimately to be made. These aspects will be borne in mind in this brief exposition.

The first portion of this discussion is largely based on three maps. Those showing the geomorphological and climatic regions of California (maps 6 and 7) illustrate the regional pattern of two significant elements of physical environment. Reference to other elements not shown in maps will be made in supplementation where necessary. Vegetation, for example,

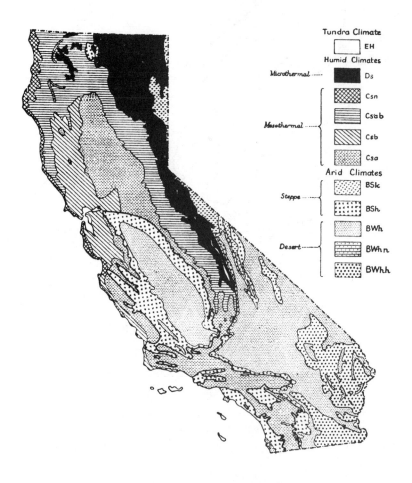

Map 7. Climates of California.

must play an important part in the argument, but it is difficult to present a completely satisfactory vegetation map suited to the present purpose. This is partly due to the need for more study of human interference with natural vegetation, and partly to the difficulty of showing concisely the relevant material. The importance of the acorn in the collecting economy of the Californian Indians focusses attention upon the distribution of the oak, and it soon becomes clear that the oak occurs in many regions which may be named, on a vegetation map, after some more dominant member of the vegetation complex. Similarly, a soil map has not been included because, despite the constant importance of this element, soils are not a major consideration in the present discussion of these nonagricultural peoples. On the human side, the map showing the distribution of Californian tribes (map 8) is one compiled by Kroeber. It is an attempt to reconstruct the distribution prevalent during the early stages of European entry into the area. As a reconstruction, it cannot claim complete accuracy, but there is little ground for thinking that it does not depict the essential features of the picture. The argument will not stray from the time element in this reconstruction and the question of the age of the distribution pattern will affect a later stage of the discussion.

The relative absence of agriculture and the complete absence of true pastoralism provide a major economic contrast between native and European California. Flood-plain cultivation of maize is found in the lower Colorado Valley. Some cultivation of tobacco occurred among the Yuroks of the northwest coast, and the practice of burning vegetation for the production of better wild crops, as recorded among some Pomo groups, is a reminder of the many transition stages which may occur between collecting and cultivating. The dog was the only domesticated animal: cattle, sheep, and horses are European introductions. Thus in terms of food supplies, native life was predominantly based on collecting and hunting, and it is important to remember that the California of to-day is, in the economic sense, the product of European settlement starting, in a major way, with the Spanish settlement of the late eighteenth century. Several reasons contribute toward an understanding of the great absence of cultivated food plants but do not provide an absolute answer to the problem. Agricultural development in the Americas centered largely, though not exclusively, around the cultivation of maize. Whether the native habitat of maize be in the grassland surrounds of the Amazon forests or in Asia, it would appear from current available evidence that a northward spread of the plant's cultivation into North America took place. Such a spread would certainly face the obstacle of the desert and semidesert areas of New Mexico, Arizona, and Southern California. That the obstacle was not insurmountable, however, is proved by the discovery of the extensive irrigation canals associated with the Hohokam cultures of the Gila Valley in Arizona and by the occurrence of the flood-plain agriculture of the lower Colorado valley.

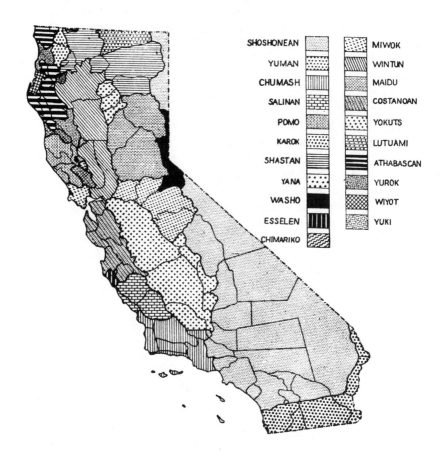

Map 8. Indians of California.

What is important for the present discussion is the fact that food plant cultivation did not spread, as it possibly might have done, into the area of Mediterranean climate in California. Fundamentally, the reason for this must be the failure of irrigation methods to extend beyond the Colorado. Without irrigation, there was, in this particular case, a further climatic obstacle. The Mediterranean climate is characterized by winter rain and summer drought; maize thrives on summer rain. Thus the combination of climatic regime and the requirements of a particular plant made a seemingly favorable environment one of limited agricultural possibilities. This situation gains added significance when one contrasts it with the association of winter wheat with the Mediterranean climate in southern Europe, an association contributing to the agricultural basis of the great early developments in that area. Such assessment needs, however, one qualification. The absence of agriculture in the greater part of California may be linked with the efficiency of the collecting and hunting economy. Available equipment often limited early cultivation to lighter and poorer soils, and it has been estimated that California had a denser population than several of the areas of native agriculture.

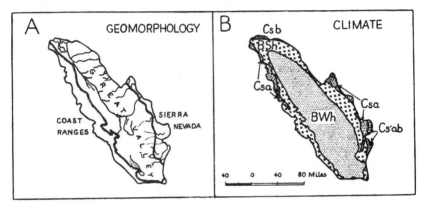

Map 9. Yokuts Territory.

Within the economy of California the acorn played a basic part. It was subjected to many preparation processes, including the leaching of its tannin with hot water. The oak is prominent in the areas of the Mediterranean climate but is not limited to them. It has a wide distribution within the several vegetation types and seems to be absent only at higher altitudes, in areas of great aridity, and in certain coastal spots. Despite the importance of the acorn, however, the efficiency of the economy rested largely on the wide use of the flora and fauna rendered possible by the application of certain techniques. This fundamental point has been well demonstrated by Kroeber and one cannot do better than summarize briefly his main conclusions. The collecting and preparation methods applied to the acorn could be applied to the pine nut, to the buckeye nut, and to small hard seeds. Further, the securing of plant foods was not separated by any gap of distinctive processes from that of obtaining grasshoppers, caterpillars, maggots, snails, or other molluscs. Similarly, weirs, nets, traps, and other devices for capturing fish were made with the same technique of basketry as were the beaters, carriers, and winnowers for seed. Hunting of wild fowl and rabbits also consisted quite largely of snaring and netting. The great part played by basketry in the provision of collecting and hunting equipment should be noted, as it affects a later stage of the discussion.

Within this composite picture of the food economy of the Californian Indians a good deal of local variation occurs. A comparative study of maps 6, 7, and 8 would reveal recognizable correlations between tribal areas and both geomorphological and climatic units. Reference to the Yokuts will suffice to illustrate this aspect. In maps 9A and 9B the relative material from the previous maps has been abstracted so that the degree of correlation may be more clearly seen. In both maps, the outer boundary is that of the territory of the Yokuts. In map 9A are indicated the geomorphological divisions within this territory; in map 9B the climatic divisions are similarly shown. It will be seen that the home of the Yokuts, of whom there may have been as many as 50 tribes, was essentially the San Joaquin Valley and its southerly continuation in the Tulare Lake and Buena Vista Lake basins. To the east, it includes, south of the Fresno River, a section of the Sierra Nevada foothills, while to the west there is some extension into the coast ranges. Climatically, the bulk of their territory was either desert (BWh) or steppe (BSh), but the extensions to the hills both to east and west gave some contact with the Mediterranean (Csa and Cs'ab) climates. The prevalence of desert climate in the San Joaquin Valley, now a major center of irrigation farming, emphasizes the contrast with the contemporary economic scene. At first glance, the desert-valley floor would seem to offer very limited food resources. Oaks extend some little way into the valley along the deltas of its eastern tributaries, but a large part of the valley is treeless. It is not known how many species of shrubs and grasses produced edible seeds, but probably sage seeds were eaten. The barrenness of the desert landscape was, however, counteracted to some degree by the flora and fauna of the narrow wetter belts bordering rivers and lakes. Swampy land along the San Joaquin and bordering the lakes to the south was covered by a dense growth of marsh grass and tule, the latter being the common bulrush of California. Tules from 10 to 12 feet high and 1 to 2 inches in diameter formed a belt two to three miles wide along the river. Tule seeds and roots were eaten, and tule stems used for the construction of huts, balsas, and rafts. Rivers, lakes, and marshes provided the habitat for a great variety of waterfowl, including pelican, cormorant, avocet, plover, gull, heron, tern, duck, grebe, bittern, geese, curlew, and snipe. From the rivers came also mussels and species of suckers and minnows. In summer, however, the marshes were almost certainly insect ridden and disease infested. Climate and economic need, therefore, combined to emphasize the advantages of the transition zone of valley edge and foothill margin, particularly towards the better-watered Sierra slopes to the east. This is demonstrated by the denser populations south of the Fresno River, where, as previously indicated, Yokuts territory spread into the bordering hills. Here pine nuts and acorns could be collected or obtained by trading, and the contacts promoted by slight seasonal migration could result in such resources being carried into the valley proper. Thus marsh and foothill counteracted desert handicaps and the economic basis of Yokuts life accords well with the possibilities of physical circumstances.

It must be remembered that the above discussion is based upon the probable extent of Yokuts territory at a relatively late date and also upon a relatively recent expression of Yokuts economy. In terms of a dynamic study, therefore, it is not yet possible to decide whether the accordance noted is fundamentally old or new. Referring to some of their reconnaissance work in the southern part of the San Joaquin Valley, Gifford and Schenck were forced to conclude that the material recovered by them would seem to be as readily assignable to the last century as to the last millennium. In some more recent work near Buena Vista Lake, Wedel hazards a guess that some of the older material found by him may be from 1200 to 1500 years old. It is not, however, possible to state definitely that this older material specifically represents an earlier phase of Yokuts settlement. There are some correlations but they are not absolute. It is true, however, that the location and nature of the sites excavated indicate a subsistence economy very similar to that of the Yokuts, and it is likely that the geographical concordance is an old-established feature. Further, there seem to be no grounds for postulating a change in the group occupation of the area; and consequently it is a reasonable assumption, though not a proved fact, that the Yokuts economy represents an adjustment to physical environment which has its origins considerably back in the past.

While correlations between tribal economy and tribal terrain, as exemplified by the Yokuts, are of significance and value in regional assessments, they do, if regarded as being purely static, leave many problems unsolved. Fundamental among such problems is the question of the potency of the interrelations between economy, social institutions, and physical environment. The answer to such a question may come eventually if geographical attention is increasingly focussed on the dynamic study of the growth of human economies and institutions against the relevant physical background. The greatest advances will obviously come from the study of the regional associations of emergent new economies, but an illustration of the significance of such study occurs in the regional pattern of native California. An important feature of this discussion has been the inability of the Californian Indian to break through the confines of a collecting and hunting economy even within areas comparable with the potent Mediterranean lands of Europe. To return to this aspect, it is obviously necessary to find out whether the areas of more favorable physical circumstances in California are or are not associated with some enrichment of economic and social life within the general pattern.

In seeking an answer to this question the geographer is helped by Kroeber and Klimek's studies of cultural climax in native California. The term "climax" is used in the sense of the culmination of a culture in relation to the culture's content and systemization; it includes also consideration of the area in which this culmination occurs. Its geographical significance can be judged from Kroeber's statement that "the very concept of climax, or, if one will, culture center, involves not only the focus of an area but also a culmination in time. Through the climax, accordingly, geography and history are brought into relation; or, at any rate, the areal and temporal aspects of culture cannot be really related unless consideration is accorded to climax." In his earlier work, Kroeber suggested that climaxes were distinguishable in northwestern, in southern, and in central California. The first two were considered as centers deriving many of their characteristics from areas outside California. By contrast, the climax in central California is a relatively independent and localized development and is, therefore, the one which can most suitably be discussed. Recognition of this climax was further helped by the statistical work of Klimek, the material for his analysis consisting of "411 elements of economic, social, and spiritual culture of California Indians." Knowledge of both the positive and negative distributions of these elements was available. Klimek's work substantiated the distinctiveness of the central area, and suggested a division into eastern and western subprovinces; the eastern represented by the Sierra and Plains Miwok and by the Washo, the western by the Pomo (see map 8). Returning to this problem, Kroeber analyzed 806 traits and concluded that culture foci or climaxes could now be territorially expressed in terms of groups or tribes instead of merely by tentative points on maps. He recognized two foci, or climaxes, within the central area. Climax I is represented by the Pomo of Clear Lake and Russian River; Climax II by the Patwin, the Maidu, and the Nisenan of the Sacramento Valley. As the Patwin are the southern Wintun and the term "Nisenan" applies to some of the southern Maidu, a preliminary location of the climax areas can be made by reference to map 8. These central area climaxes are relatively feeble when compared with those of northwestern or southern California. Of the 806 traits considered, Climax I has only 32 traits peculiar to it, and Climax II only 17; the two climaxes having in common a further 7 traits. The feebleness of these climaxes is understandable when one remembers that they occur within the limits of a general collecting and hunting economy, and the fact that such slight differences are definable gives them additional significance. In terms of material culture, the peculiar traits are mainly, though not exclusively, associated with basketry. If the part played by basketry in collecting and fishing is remembered, it is clear that skill in basketry had economic as well as artistic value. In terms of social culture, the distinctive traits arise mainly from the cults of Kuksu society type. These cults are based on a secret society and characterized by the Kuksu or "big-head" dances. Discussion of the nature and purpose of these cults is not necessary here, but their general significance may be appreciated from Kroeber's comment that to the natives any cessation of the Kuksu ceremonial organization "would have seemed equivalent to a general catastrophe, perhaps directly productive of a disintegration of the physical world." The cults reached their most elaborate forms among the Valley Maidu and the River Patwin, and among the Pomo of Clear Lake and Russian River. That material and social traits should thus blend to give distinctiveness to a climax is a fact of considerable importance and lends emphasis to the view that the geographer should be constantly alert to the part played by social organization as the medium through which adjustment to changes in the use of the physical environment may be fostered or retarded.

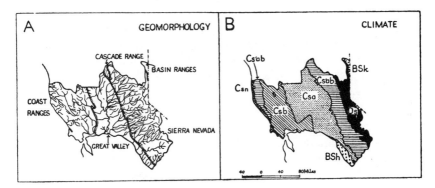

Map 10. The Climax Area of Central California.

It remains to note the geographical circumstances in which the identified climaxes developed. The boundaries of maps 10A and 10B are the territorial limits of all the groups associated by either Kroeber or Klimek with the climaxes. The maps have been drawn from the base maps in the same manner as were maps 9A and 9B. They require brief comment and some amplification. Climatically, it is clear that the climaxes occur within an area experiencing a Mediterranean climate, the symbols on map 10B denoting variants of the Mediterranean climatic type. This factor, however, is not peculiar to the climaxes, because considerable areas of similar climate lie outside the climax limits. Nevertheless, it should be noted that the small extension of Mediterranean conditions to the north is in the area where the southern boundary of northwestern cultural influence can be traced, while the Mediterranean portions of southern California are similarly placed in relation to other extraneous cultural elements. Climatic conditions are reflected vegetationally in the wide distribution of the oak, which occurs frequently in the "parkland" vegetation of the lower Sacramento Valley and is found on the slopes of both the coast ranges and the lower foothills of the Sierra Nevada. In drier portions of the Mediterranean area, manzanita and other seed-bearing brush are typical vegetational elements.

Geomorphologically, the main subdivisions are the coast ranges, the lower Sacramento Valley, and the western slopes of the Sierra Nevada (see map 10A). The Russian River, flowing through the coast ranges, is closely associated with Pomo development. Its series of small, enclosed valleys, separated by gorges, helps to explain the division of the Pomo into some 50 groups; its salmon made fishing an important complement to collecting. Also within the coast ranges, Clear Lake was the other major focus of Pomo settlement. One of the few large bodies of fresh water in California, Clear Lake has been described as "one of the ideal spots for Indian residence in the State." It drains by Cache Creek into the tule marshes of the lower Sacramento Valley, but was more accessible from the Russian River. Its fish and waterfowl adequately explain its significance.

The western portion of the lower Sacramento Valley and the tule marshes bordering the river were occupied by the Patwin (southern Wintun), who settled also along the northern shore of Suisun Bay and along part of the northern shore of San Pablo Bay, probably as far west as the divide between the Sonoma and Napa valleys. The tule marshes have much the same significance as they have in the San Joaquin Valley. Knoll sites near the Sacramento provided good winter bases for fishing and for the snaring of ducks and geese. In summer, they were largely abandoned for the drier hillslopes with their acorns and seeds. The importance of the marsh belt, with its dominant tule or bulrush, will no doubt recall the early physical setting of the lower Nile Valley. The eastern portion of the Sacramento Valley and the adjoining foothills of the Sierra Nevada were held by the Nisenan or southern Maidu. This territory is essentially the drainage basins of the American, Bear, and Yuba rivers. With their settlements mainly on the river divides, above the gorge valleys, the Nisenan could command much the same food resources as the other climax groups.

It would seem, therefore, that two aspects of the physical environment are important in the climax areas in terms of an assured food supply. Within the variations of Mediterranean vegetation there occurred a goodly supply of acorns and seeds; within the variety of terrain, rivers, lakes, and marshes provided good fishing and an abundance of waterfowl. Ultimately, to achieve a regional assessment in a dynamic sense, it will be necessary to attempt to resolve the relative importance of seed-collecting, linked with vegetation and climate, and of fishing and snaring, so closely linked with drainage and terrain. For the present purpose, however, the strong development of both in the climax area must suffice.

The identification of a cultural climax, however feeble it may be, which can be studied in relation to its physical setting does give some clue to the potency of environmental elements. Further light on the problem would be shed if the emergence of significant culture traits could be approximately dated. Unfortunately, this cannot be done in California, but one or two points bearing on this matter should be noted. On the balance of available evidence, it seems likely that in this specific case the climax is relatively old; it would certainly not seem to be a recent development. In terms of recent changes, however, Heizer has rightly pointed out that the period 1780–1850 was one of cultural change and adjustment among the coastal and interior valley tribes of California, consequent upon Spanish penetration and mission building. He suggests that there are archaeological grounds for identifying in this period significant developments in material culture in a natural refuge area such as the delta region of the Sacramento River. He would, therefore, postulate a "culture hearth" in the delta region, to some extent in opposition to Kroeber's climax among the Patwin of the lower Sacramento Valley. To avoid ambiguity, it should be noted that the shift of center suggested by Heizer falls within the climax area which has been discussed and that there is no ground for thinking that the degree of change and movement was sufficient to invalidate Kroeber's map of tribal distributions. While future work may substantiate Heizer's opinions concerning the period of cultural change, it seems most likely that the climaxes referred to in this paper are older than the centers of relatively late change noted by him. One is influenced in this decision by the strong development of the Kuksu cult among the Patwin which, quite rightly, is not considered by Heizer in his assessment of purely material culture.

Also pertinent to this discussion is the relative absence of long-distance communication among the climax groups. These peoples show in an emphasized form the contrast between North America and Europe in the evolution of means of transportation. The horse and wheeled vehicles were absent. Further, California was beyond the limit of dog-travois travel in North America. Between Cape Mendocino and Cape Concepcion true seagoing craft were not used, and water communication was largely limited to tule balsas on river and lake. Heizer rightly suggests the acceleration of change with the Spanish introduction of the horse, but prior to this, movement and culture contacts must have been limited. In this respect, Kroeber is probably right in judging Pomo communities to have been "at once narrowly localized and highly sessile. . . ." In such circumstances, the climax may have been long established, but the period of its growth cannot as yet be fully identified.

The most important conclusion of this study is that the Mediterranean area of California, while lacking the vigorous growth of material and social culture found in the Mediterranean lands of Europe, did nevertheless produce a climax within a collecting and hunting economy. The climax was feeble largely because there was no emergence of new economies, but its occurrence will be important in a final analysis of regional elements in Mediterranean lands. It must be clear, from the many aspects of the problem introduced in this paper, that no direct comparison between Mediterranean California and Mediterranean Europe is possible. Nevertheless, it is hoped that the assembling of such "case-histories" will eventually provide the data from which conclusions may be drawn. Regional studies of non-European peoples must provide an important body of the data from which sound premises concerning regional geography may be derived. Wherever possible, such studies should be dynamic in character, should note the rate of growth and change, and so add to our knowledge of the operative power of environmental elements.

CALIFORNIAN INDIAN PHYSICAL TYPES

by
E. W. Gifford

There are more families of languages spoken in California by the Indian tribes than in any other region of equal size. In habits and customs also, these Indians differ greatly among themselves. The tribes in the northwestern part of California have a mode of life reminding one of the totem-pole makers of British Columbia and Alaska; again, the tribes of southern California are much like the Indians of Arizona and New Mexico; but when one turns to central California, he notes that the native culture is unique, thus justifying the notion that central California is one of the primary aboriginal culture areas of North America.

With such variety in language and culture it is not surprising to find that California is quite as diverse in the matter of racial types. In the living Indian population of today (totaling about 16,000 souls) five types and subtypes are distinguishable. Although it is customary to regard the American Indian race as quite homogeneous, as indeed it is when compared with the Caucasian race, we find that in California there are distinctive types in stature, and in the form of the head, face, and nose, to name only four principal characteristics.

As the Indians in the more thickly settled parts of California became extinct before anthropologists had opportunity to gather data from them, it is necessary to rely upon skeletal material to determine the physical type of the aborigines in these parts. There seems to be no clear and indisputable evidence, however, even in those regions where Indians still dwell, that the physical type has changed during the long course of the Indian occupation of California. Generally speaking, in those regions where narrow-headed people live today, crania of similar type are forthcoming; and in other regions inhabited by broad-headed peoples, the cranial evidence reveals ancient peoples of the same type. This stability of population has its parallel in material culture, for the evidence of the shellmounds reveals no change

---

E. W. Gifford, "Californian Indian Types," *Natural History* (1926), 26:50–60.

There is a full analysis of California physical anthropology in *idem, Californian Anthropometry,* Univ. Calif. Publ. Am. Arch. Ethn. (1926), 22:217–390. For a bibliography of the subject see sec. 23 of *A Bibliography of the Archaeology of California,* Reports of the University of California Archaeological Survey (cited hereafter as Repts. UCAS), No. 4 (1949).

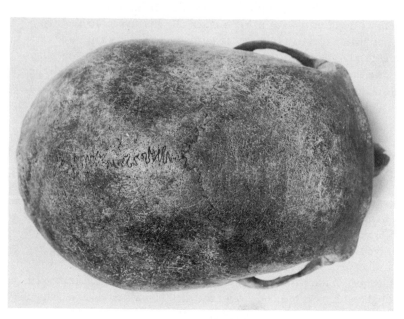

Range of Head Form of California Indians. *Left*, narrow skull of the Western Mono type from Santa Catalina Island, with a cephalic index of 70.4; *right*, a broad skull from the San Joaquin Valley, with a cephalic index of 90.6.

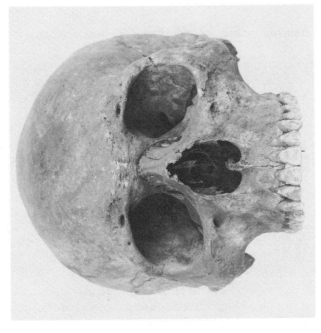

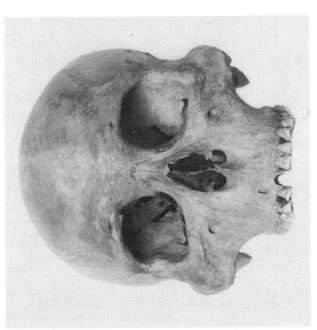

Two Types of Face Form of California Indians. *Left*, Buena Vista type, with high face and narrow nose; *right*, San Joaquin type, with low face and broad nose.

in culture from the remote past down to the time of Caucasian settlement.

California has among its living tribes examples of the shortest and tallest peoples of the whole American continent. The Yuki Indians, of Mendocino County, have an average stature for men of 157 centimeters. The Mohave, of the Colorado River region in southeastern California, have an average stature, for men, of 171 centimeters, making a difference between the averages of more than five inches. The difference is about equivalent to that between the average statures of the Nordic and Mediterranean branches of the white race. The stature of the greater number of Californians lies between the two extremes.

The head form likewise shows a considerable range. Some groups have narrow heads, like the short Yuki, with a cephalic index averaging 76, or like the extinct Santa Catalina islanders, with an average index of 74. Others, like the tall Mohave, have a cephalic index averaging 89, which is, however, due in part to deformation. It is not to be doubted, however, that the Mohave are normally broadheaded. Again, we may compare the Californian Indians with certain of the European races in this matter of head form, the difference between the averages being comparable to the difference between the averages of the Alpine and Nordic branches of the white race in Europe.

Nose form in California also reveals a considerable range, some groups having noses which are not very much broader than those of Europeans, other groups having noses that are almost negroid in their breadth. The short-statured Yuki, already referred to, belong to the latter class, and have an average nasal index of 87. In other words, the breadth of the nose is 87 per cent of the length. At the other extreme are such peoples as the Achomawi of Shasta County and the Karok of Humboldt County with average nasal indices of 73 and 72, respectively.

One feature of narrow noses is that the longer axis of the opening of the nostril usually runs from front to back. Very broad noses like those of many negro peoples have nostrils with the long axis running transversely. Most Californians fall into the intermediate class in this regard, having the axis of the nostrils oblique, that is to say, intermediate between the two extremes just described. The narrowest-nosed groups tend toward the anterior-posterior long axis; the broad-nosed groups toward the transverse long axis.

The profile of the nose in the majority of Californians may be characterized as straight, though there are a certain number of convex or aquiline noses and a certain number of concave noses. Concave noses seem to be particularly prevalent among the Yuki. The nose bridge is usually intermediate in height between that of Caucasians and Mongolians, that is to say, it is not as low as the bridges which are frequent with Mongolians, nor as high as the bridges which are frequent with Caucasians.

The glabella, the lower part of the forehead above the bridge of the nose, is frequently fairly prominent among Californian Indians, although not nearly so prominent as it is among the Australian aborigines. It is more marked, though, than in average Caucasians and Mongolians. This character has its most pronounced development in males, and serves often as a means of distinguishing the skulls of adult males from those of females.

An important character that divides the Californian Indians into two distinct classes is face form. The Yuki and certain of their neighbors have low faces, as expressed by the average facial index of about 76, while the majority of the Californian tribes have high faces with an average index of about 85.

Although it is possible to distinguish the different types by stature, head form, nose form, and face form, it is not possible to separate them upon the basis of complexion, eye color, hair color, and hair texture. All are uniformly pale brown in complexion on the unexposed parts of the body. All have straight, coarse, lank, black hair. Face and body hair is scanty, as in all Mongoloid peoples. The eye color is dark brown. With exposure to the sun the Californian Indian becomes dark brown in complexion, matching some of the paler Negroes in this respect. When the clothes are removed, the contrast between the dark brown face and the pale brown body is very striking.

Although the characters of the hair are among the most prominent of those suggesting relationship to the Mongolian peoples of Asia, the complete epicanthic eyefold (so conspicuous in Chinese and Japanese) is absent in adults, so far as observations go, although there are among adults occasional instances of partial or medium epicanthus. Another Mongolian trait, that of the shovel-shaped upper incisors, is very common, however.

Chins on the whole are less prominent than Caucasian chins, though their true character is often partly concealed under a heavy pad of flesh. The lips of the California Indians may be characterized as medium in thickness, occupying in this respect a position halfway between the lips of whites and of Negroes. In the matter of facial projection or prognathism they represent the opposite extreme to the Negroes, there being practically no facial projection in aboriginal Californians.

The foreheads of the Californian Indians are either vertical or very slightly sloped, but true low foreheads are lacking. A curious feature of hair growth frequently gives the impression of a low forehead. The feature consists of the hair growing exceptionally low on the forehead, and quite close to the outer ends of the eyebrows.

The slight protuberance on the upper edge of the ear, known as Darwin's point, is far less prevalent among Californian Indians than among whites, in fact its occurrence may be characterized as very rare. The ear lobe is generally medium in size, though a certain number of examples have been recorded as small, and a certain number as large. Only two individuals out of several hundred examined were without ear lobes, thus approaching in this regard the characteristic condition of the Bushmen of South Africa.

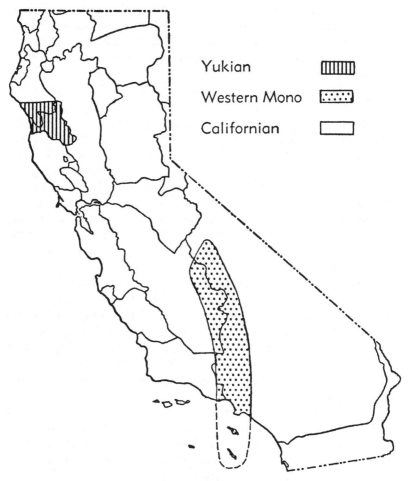

Map 11. Probable Distribution of California Physical Types.

The fact has been mentioned that the Californians fall into five types and subtypes. The three main types are the Yuki type, the Western Mono type, and the Californian type, the range of which is shown on the map. The Yuki type centers in Mendocino County in north-central California, while the Western Mono type is represented by living peoples in the southern Sierra Nevada and probably by the extinct inhabitants of the Los Angeles coast and of Santa Catalina and San Clemente islands. The Californian type may be regarded as the one truly typical of the state, for in its three subtypes it occurs throughout the length and breadth of the state, except for the relatively small regions occupied by the Yuki and Western Mono types.

The Yuki type embraces not only the Yuki and their linguistic relatives, the Huchnom, but also the Athabascan Wailaki and Kato, all of Mendocino County. It is of interest to note that the Athabascan Hupa are quite different in type from their linguistic relatives, the Wailaki. Here we have an excellent example of the fundamental distinctness of language and physical type. The Wailaki and Hupa tongues are but dialects of a single language, yet physically the Wailaki and Hupa peoples are very different, the short-statured, low-faced, narrow-headed, broad-nosed Wailaki contrasting with the medium-statured, high-faced, broad-headed, narrow-nosed Hupa. The Hupa are of the Californian type. This is a case in which either language or physical type would seem to have traveled, leaving the other behind; that is, either a people of Yuki type adopted an Athabascan language from neighbors, or an Athabascan-speaking people in contact with people of Yuki type had their physical type swamped and obliterated through marriage and replacement by their Yuki-type neighbors. The case perhaps parallels that of the Burgundians, in whom original blondness and blue eyes have been replaced through intermarriage by brunetteness and brown eyes.

Apparently similar to the Wailaki case is that of the Eastern Mono who live on the east side of the Sierra Nevada in Inyo County. Although speaking a language only slightly different from that of the physically distinctive Western Mono, the Eastern Mono are unlike them in physical type and belong instead to the widespread Californian type to which their other neighbors, the Washo and Miwok, also belong.

The Yuki type is characterized primarily by short stature (average for men, 157 cm.) and low face; and secondarily by a relatively narrow head and broad nose.

The Western Mono type is medium in stature (average for men, 165 cm.), high-faced, relatively narrow-headed, and medium-nosed. Although similar to the Yuki type in head form, it differs in the other characters.

The widespread Californian type is at once recognizable by its broad head and high face. The stature of men varies from medium (161 cm.) to tall (172 cm.). The nose form is variable, too, ranging from relatively narrow to relatively broad. The three subtypes distinguished are designated as narrow-nosed, broad-nosed, and tall.

As to the physical relationships of the Californians to other North American Indians little can be said at present. The Yuki type suggests one of the types described by Boas from the coast of British Columbia, while the broad-headed Californian type seems to resemble the broad-headed type of the Northwest, as represented by the Kwakiutl and the Shuswap. In the south, the Californian type appears to have relatives in Mexico. Hrdlička writes [Univ. Calif. Publ. Am. Arch. and Ethn. (1906), 4:64]:

Ancient crania from the California Peninsula are also of a different type. Arizona and Sonora show no population, recent or ancient, allied physically to the Californians. In Mexico, however, are several great Indian peoples who in many features approach the Californians to such a degree that an original identity must be held as probable. One of these is the Otomi, of the States of Hidalgo and Mexico. A large group of peoples in the States of Puebla, Michoacan, and farther south, even including the Aztecs, and finally the Tarahumare, in Chihuahua, are all physically related to the Otomi as well as to the Californians.

It seems clear then that two of the three outstanding Californian types are not peculiar to the state. The third type, the Western Mono type, will probably be found to have relatives elsewhere also.

LINGUISTIC FAMILIES
OF CALIFORNIA

by
R. B. Dixon and
A. L. Kroeber

Powell's classification and map of the linguistic families of America allotted twenty-two families or parts of families to California. For a number of years this reckoning stood unaltered; for many years it was unchallenged even to its details. In 1905 one of the present authors showed the relationship of the Shastan dialects to Palaihnihan (Achomawi and Atsugewi), and his combination, first under the name of Shasta-Achomawi and then of Shastan, came into general acceptance through its recognition by the Bureau of American Ethnology. This fixed the number of families in California at twenty-one.

A few years later the same writer suggested, on the basis of some preliminary but fairly considerable body of material, that Chimariko and Shasta were sprung from a single stock; and his colleague supported the view that Miwok and Costanoan must probably be considered akin—as, in fact, had been the custom before their separation by Powell. Neither of these consolidations, which would have reduced the families represented in the state to nineteen, was, however, advanced without reserve, and they failed of general acceptance.

Several other possible cases of kinship presented themselves to the writers at various times, as between Wintun and Maidu, Maidu and Yokuts, Chumash and Salinan, and even Yuman and Esselen, and several brief lists of similarities were compiled by them. Once or twice allusions to these possibilities found their way into print. But, on the whole, the resemblances seemed scant and best interpretable as due either to coincidence or borrowing.

By 1903 at least a slight body of information had been secured on the grammar of representative dialects of each of the twenty-two families then recognized in California, and the present writers published a brief monograph classifying these families into several types and subtypes on the basis of structure. They expressly emphasized that this classification was not

Pp. 48–54 of R. B. Dixon and A. L. Kroeber, *Linguistic Families of California,* Univ. Calif. Publ. Am. Arch. and Ethn. (1919), 16:47–118.

genetic, and assumed that while the structural resemblances were undoubtedly actual, they must be interpreted as due to secondary influences exerted
on each other by languages of distinct origin. In the main, or at least at several important points, the nongenetic type classification then advanced
coincides with the genetic classification presented in the present paper. That
it is different in several cases is due to the scant knowledge then extant as
to most of the languages, a paucity that necessitated the basing of comparisons on a small number of comparatively outward features of structure,
such as the presence and absence of pronominal affixation and a plural in
nouns. That the suggestions as to genetic relationship which this classification obviously bore were not adopted or even followed out by the authors
was due to an essentially conservative attitude, a reflection of the views
generally current for some twenty years after the publication of Powell's
basic classification, views not yet wholly deprived of vitality, and certainly
in the main justified by the sense of order and fixity which Powell's work
introduced as against the hesitations and random irresponsibilities of previous less systematic attempts.

This conservative attitude was adhered to by the writers for a number
of years—maintained, in fact, to a point that now seems to them to have
been unnecessarily belated. As evidences of similarities between this and
that language accumulated, they were indeed noted, but were consistently
interpreted as instances of one unrelated language borrowing either material or machinery from another.

Finally, it seemed desirable to bring together all the readily available
data and determine the exact degree and nature of the similarities. About
two hundred and twenty-five English words were selected on which material was most likely to be accessible in reasonably accurate and comparable
form, and the known native equivalents in sixty-seven dialects of the
twenty-one stocks were entered in columns. Comparisons were then instituted to determine all interstock similarities that seemed too close or too
numerous to be ascribed to coincidence. The purpose of the study was three-
fold: first, to ascertain the nature and degree of borrowing between unrelated languages; second, to trace through these borrowings any former contacts or movements of language groups not now in contact; third, in the
event of any relationship existing between languages then considered unrelated, to determine this fact.

Some similarities were soon apparent between nearly all the twenty-one
stocks, and with the completion of the comparative vocabularies the number of resemblances had become considerable. They seemed to show little,
however. Families some distance apart on the map often had more stems
in common than those in juxtaposition; if the remote group was regarded
as once in contact with the one with which it shared most words, it must

have been in contact also with others with which it shared but few words. Stems of the most diverse and scattering types of meaning showed similarities in distinct stocks: beyond onomatopoetic names of birds there was no one class of words that seemed more or less given than others to transference by loan. The results, in short, appeared completely meaningless.

Finally, in a mood rather of baffled impotence, an interpretation of the cases of most abundant resemblance as due to genetic relationship was applied. At once difficulties yielded, and arrangement emerged from the chaos.

The appended table 1 shows the first results. This table gives the number of stem resemblances common to every two of the twenty-one stocks, or to any dialects of every two of the twenty-one. It is evident that the highest numbers occurred in two groups, both of which are marked in the table by enclosing frames or boxes. One group contained the interrelations of Karok, Shasta, Chimariko, Yana, and Pomo; the other of Wintun, Maidu, Miwok, Costanoan, and Yokuts. Every instance of two stocks sharing twenty or more words was found to be included in these two groups, as were the majority of instances of two stocks sharing ten or more stems.

In other instances the number of words common to two stocks was absolutely small, but distinctly higher than the number shared by either with any other stock. Thus, apparently common to Chumash and Salinan, 12; to Chumash and any other language, 8; to Salinan and any other language, 6. Again, Yurok and Wiyot, as per the table, 4; Yurok and any other, 0 to 1; Wiyot and any other, 0 to 3. In both these instances the hint was reinforced by the fact of unquestioned structural similarity; and in the latter of the two, at least, a renewed search prompted by the growing suspicion quickly revealed an additional group of shared stems that had either not entered into the comparative vocabularies or whose resemblance had been overlooked.

An arrangement of the highest numbers of table 1 in order, as in table 2, also proved significant. The first sixteen pairs comprised eight belonging wholly to one of the groups (A) marked off in table 1; five belonging wholly to the other group (B); one (X) consisting of an A language and a B language in territorial contact; and two (Y) consisting of a language—Yuki, included neither in group A nor in group B—with respectively an A and a B language, between which it lies wedged geographically.

Again, Shasta and Chimariko had previously seemed related; but Shasta and Pomo presented more apparently common stems (21) than Shasta and Chimariko. So with Miwok and Costanoan: their similarities (27 in

TABLE 1

	Athabascan	Yurok	Wiyot	Lutuami	Karok	Shasta	Chimariko	Yana	Pomo	Yuki	Washo	Wintun	Maidu	Miwok	Costanoan	Yokuts	Esselen	Salinan	Chumash	Shoshonean	Yuman	Aggregate	Stems represented
Athabascan	—	0	0	0	0	0	0	0	1	0	0	0	0	0	0	0	0	0	0	1	0	2	1
Yurok	0	—	4	1	1	0	1	0	1	1	0	1	0	0	0	0	0	0	1	1	1	13	8
Wiyot	0	4	—	1	3	1	2	2	3	0	1	1	1	2	0	1	1	0	1	1	1	28	9
Lutuami	0	1	1	—	1	11	4	2	6	4	0	4	7	2	2	6	1	0	2	1	0	54	21
Karok	0	1	3	1	—	9	9	4	6	2	3	2	2	2	2	2	3	1	5	0	4	61	13
Shasta	0	0	1	11	9	—	19	13	21	5	2	12	8	5	5	9	4	5	5	0	7	141	49
Chimariko	0	1	2	4	9	19	—	9	13	6	2	8	4	2	5	4	7	2	5	1	6	109	30
Yana	0	0	2	2	4	13	9	—	15	2	3	7	3	4	7	7	6	2	3	3	5	97	27
Pomo	1	1	3	6	6	21	13	15	—	14	4	17	8	11	7	8	8	1	2	3	5	151	57
Yuki	0	1	0	4	2	5	6	2	14	—	4	14	12	12	9	8	4	0	2	3	5	105	34
Washo	0	0	1	0	3	2	2	3	4	4	—	3	4	3	2	3	2	2	3	3	4	45	8
Wintun	0	1	1	4	2	12	8	7	17	14	3	—	23	27	10	17	5	2	5	3	4	164	62
Maidu	0	0	1	7	2	8	4	3	8	12	4	23	—	18	6	24	3	3	4	2	2	136	58
Miwok	0	0	2	2	2	5	2	4	11	12	3	27	18	—	27	18	5	6	5	4	3	158	64
Costanoan	0	0	2	2	2	5	5	7	7	9	2	10	6	27	—	19	8	4	5	6	2	127	43
Yokuts	0	0	1	6	2	9	4	7	5	8	3	17	24	18	19	—	4	2	8	5	2	148	57
Esselen	0	0	1	1	3	4	7	6	8	4	2	5	3	5	8	4	—	4	8	9	4	78	16
Salinan	0	0	0	0	1	5	2	2	1	0	1	2	3	6	4	2	4	—	12	1	3	51	19
Chumash	0	1	1	2	5	5	5	3	2	2	4	5	4	5	5	8	8	12	—	4	6	87	23
Shoshonean	1	1	1	1	0	0	0	1	3	5	3	3	2	4	6	5	9	1	4	—	5	57	24
Yuman	0	1	1	0	4	7	6	5	5	3	3	4	2	3	2	2	4	3	6	5	—	66	15
Aggregate	2	13	28	54	61	141	109	97	151	105	45	164	136	158	127	148	78	51	87	57	66	—	—

number), were equaled by those of Wintun and Miwok, and nearly equaled
by those of Maidu and Yokuts (24) and Maidu and Wintun (23).

TABLE 2

Order	Families	Resemblances	Group
1	Miwok and Costanoan	27	A
2	Miwok and Wintun	27	A
3	Maidu and Yokuts	24	A
4	Maidu and Wintun	23	A
5	Shasta and Pomo	21	B
6	Shasta and Chimariko	19	B
7	Yokuts and Costanoan	19	A
8	Yokuts and Miwok	18	A
9	Maidu and Miwok	18	A
10	Yokuts and Wintun	17	A
11	Wintun and Pomo	17	X
12	Yana and Pomo	15	B
13	Wintun and Yuki	14	Y
14	Pomo and Yuki	14	Y
15	Chimariko and Pomo	13	B
16	Shasta and Yana	13	B

In short, only two attitudes seemed consistent. One was the old one of
regarding each of the twenty-one stocks as totally unrelated; the other, to
unite some of them as per the groups outlined.

In one respect the figures in tables 1 and 2 were quickly found unfavorably misleading. They might or might not be considered as including radi-
cal words due to a common origin: they certainly included words not due
to such common origin but derived by loan. This element must obscure
the incisiveness of the conclusions derivable from table 1. Further, the
comparisons used being avowedly superficial, that is, not based on analysis,
a certain number of false coincidences were bound to have crept in. For
instance, the writers never supposed that the nine stems apparently common to Yokuts and Shoshonean indicated any degree of genetic unity.
Several of the nine were obvious cases of borrowing; the remainder were
so few that they could scarcely be regarded as due to anything but accidental
outward resemblances such as are bound to arise on the probability of
chance. Now Yokuts, in the table, is credited with twenty-four stems shared
with Maidu, with which it is thrown into a new family, and nine with
Shoshonean, to which it is unrelated; a proportion which certainly seems
unconvincing. But on elimination of the nine Shoshonean cases as not
indicative of kinship and subtraction of an equal number from the Maidu-
Yokuts total of twenty-four as probably also due to loan or coincidence, the
proportion becomes 15 to 0; which is distinctly more positive, particularly
in view of the comparative paucity of the material examined and the neces-

sarily somewhat mechanical nature of the comparisons instituted on a first survey. Actually, in this case, the proportion would be stronger than 15 to 0, because Shoshonean is in geographical contact with Yokuts and Maidu is not, so that the probabilities of borrowing would be less in the latter case and the figure properly subtractable from the gross twenty-four would presumably be less than nine.

Another factor tended to obscure the first results. Table 1 deals only with stocks as units. Actually many of them were represented by data from several dialects or languages. To have included all these dialects in the table would have been exceedingly laborious and rendered the table rather unwieldy as a basis for reference. As drawn up, a stem common to only two dialects of different stocks was, therefore, entered exactly like a stem common to all the dialects of the two stocks: each counted as a case. For example, when the Tübatulabal dialect of Shoshonean, which is spoken in contact with Yokuts, has obviously borrowed the Yokuts word for "elk," the same weight attached to this instance, in the table, as to the fact that the identical stem for "two" runs through all dialects of Yokuts and of Maidu. Now the comparatively high number of Wintun-Pomo (A-B), Yuki-Wintun (Y-A), and Yuki-Pomo (Y-B) resemblances, which alone break the uniformity of table 2, is clearly due in considerable measure to this source of error of the tabulations. The Wintun-Pomo similarities were largely between dialects of these stocks, not between the stocks as wholes; and about half of the Yuki-Wintun and Yuki-Pomo cases held only for a small detached offshoot of Yuki, the Wappo, which is flanked on the map by Wintun on one side and Pomo on the other.

These considerations, accordingly, strengthened the authors in the conviction that the soundness of their inferences was greater than a merely cursory inspection of their results, as summarized in table 1, would indicate; and they proceeded to announce their findings, at first in mere abstract, and soon after with some slight indication of the nature of their evidence.

It was necessary to find names for the new groups or families. To extend the designation of one member of each group to the entire group would have been as misleading, in the end, as it would have been to name the tongues of Europe "Sanskritan." Binary designations of the type of Indo-Germanic, Ural-Altaic, and Uto-Aztekan were likely to prove unrepresentative, and certain to be clumsy. There seemed no recourse, accordingly, but to new and therefore arbitrary designations of the types of "Semitic"; and genealogical as well as national appellations being wanting in the native Californian field, and none of a geographical character applicable, the family names proposed were based on forms of the numeral "two" in the families of speech involved.

The result, then, of the investigations up to this point was the setting up of four larger families: [1]

Penutian, consisting of the Wintun, Maidu, Yokuts, Miwok, and Costanoan families as previously recognized.

Hokan, including Karok, Chimariko, Shastan, Pomo, Yana, and, by subsequent addition, Esselen and Yuman.

Iskoman, namely, Chumash and Salinan.

Ritwan, or Yurok and Wiyot.

---

[1] At present seven main language families in California are recognized: the Athabascan, Algonkian, Yukian, Lutuamian, Hokan (includes the former Iskoman), Penutian, and Uto-Aztekan (sometimes called Shoshonean). Their location may be seen in map 1 (see end-papers). — Eds.

THE HISTORY OF NATIVE
CULTURE IN CALIFORNIA

by
A. L. Kroeber

Now and then it seems permissible for the student to leave off his daily
association with specific facts and rise above them on the gyroscope of his
imagination to discover if a broader view may not give him new insights
into their relations, or alter his conception of their setting in the larger landscape of nature as a whole. Such flights indeed appear almost incumbent on
him at intervals if his occupation with his materials is close and unremitting.
The requirement which integrity imposes on these ventures is that knowledge and fancy, fact and fabrication, be kept as distinct as possible, lest one
come to pass for the other. The present essay is such a soaring of hypothesis.
While it starts from the solid ground of twenty years of inquiry into the
culture and speech of the Californian aborigines, it pretends to no greater
validity than any summary, undocumented, historical reconstruction may
claim.

FORMER CHARACTERIZATIONS

A number of early travelers and residents have left pictures of the Californian tribes they knew, without having come into contact with the inhabitants of any larger portion of the area. The first broader description, the
well-known *Tribes of California* of Stephen Powers, deals with nearly all
of the groups north of the Tehachapi Mountains. Powers wrote from observation and possessed to a high degree the journalist's faculty of rapid
perception and vivid presentation. In spite of some overdrawing, his work
remains unsurpassed as a delineation of California Indian psychology.
Some of his characterizations of groups are unusually felicitous. His survey
was however too rapid to allow of the assemblage of a sufficient number of
exact ethnic data for systematic study.

Several years after the foundation of the Department of Anthropology
at the University by Mrs. Phoebe Apperson Hearst, I attempted, in volume
two of this series [Univ. Calif. Publ. Am. Arch. and Ethn.] a review en-

Univ. Calif. Publ. Am. Arch. and Ethn. (1923), 20:125–142.

titled *Types of Indian Culture in California*. In its outlines this classification seems to have been generally accepted, although accumulating knowledge has resulted in some revisions and considerable shifts of emphasis.

Sixteen years later, in the seventeenth volume of the present series, I returned to the subject with an essay on the culture provinces of California. By this time, enough information had become available through studies of members of the University and others to make possible not only a fairly accurate delimitation of the areas of distinctive culture within California, but an appraisal of the relation of these areas to the generally recognized larger culture areas of America and an indication of the focal centers within the areas. The findings were embodied in two maps, the principal features of which are consolidated and embodied in the map herewith.

All this has been a labor first of accumulation, and then of classification. The unraveling of sequential developments in California has heretofore been attempted chiefly for restricted areas or limited aspects of culture. Yet every natural classification contains within itself, so far as it is sound, genetic indications. Recognition, for instance, of the affinity between the culture of northwestern California and that of the North Pacific Coast, or again between those of southern California and the Southwest, long ago forced the inference of a flow of cultural elements or stimuli from these more remote regions into the affected parts of what is now California.

At the same time, there would be something summary and short-circuiting in viewing these Californian tracts as mere reflections or extensions of extraneous culture developments. They are actually in juxtaposition to other local culture types which have been little affected by the remote centers, or at least not so specifically; and which have undergone their own growth on the spot. Local interrelations may not be lost sight of because of the presence of foreign influences—should, in fact, be the first to be accurately determined.

PROBLEMS OF DEVELOPMENTAL SEQUENCE

It seems worth while therefore to endeavor to discover how far it is possible to go in the direction of tracing the development of culture in the Californian area on the basis primarily of its own data. Such a limitation would be arbitrary if regarded as leading to final conclusions. The attempt has, however, the advantage of operating intensively; and such distortions of perspective as ensue will readily enough correct themselves on being brought into relation with the interpretations of our knowledge of other areas.

As a first step toward the conversion of the local ethnic data from their merely spatial relations into temporal ones, I have assembled a number of facts in the appended diagram. The idea of this diagram is to suggest geographical relations by horizontal arrangement, temporal relations by vertical disposition. Of course, the arrangement in both directions is necessarily somewhat rough. Also, the number of culture traits selected is only a fraction of those that might have been chosen; but it includes those whose nature or distribution seems most significant. Data for whose placement in this diagram no warrant is found in previous publications are discussed in more detail in a recent essay on *Elements of Culture in Native California,* in volume 13 of this series [Univ. Calif. Publ. Am. Arch. and Ethn.], and in a handbook on the Indians of California in press with the Bureau of American Ethnology.[1]

The genetic assumption which underlies the arrangement of elements in the diagram is that, other things equal, widely distributed traits are likely to be ancient; locally limited ones, of more recent origin. Obviously, this assumption may not be adhered to too rigidly: other things never are equal, or we often cannot be sure that they are.

For instance, had the Ghost Dance of fifty years ago been included in the tabulation, its place therein, on the basis of its fairly wide occurrence, would have been below the two peaks representing the culminations of the northwestern and central cultures; but on the basis of its known recency, overlying them. It is conceivable that a similar influence, institutional, mechanical, or religious, might have been only a very few centuries older than the Ghost Dance, just far enough in the past to be undocumented by history, and have left permanent residua in the culture of the same two provinces. In that event, it might have been entered, according to the plan followed, in a fairly low portion in the table, at a point representing an antiquity of perhaps several thousand instead of only a few hundred years.

Another factor which is likely to vitiate conclusions drawn too mechanically from a diagram like this one is the origination of elements wholly outside the Californian sphere. The sinew-backed bow is a case in point. It is now generally accepted that this bow is only an abbreviated form of the composite Asiatic bow, which is built up of layers of sinew, wood, and horn. In the eastern hemisphere, the composite bow is at least three to four thousand years old. There is little doubt of its having been carried into America and applied there in simpler form. It must then have been used first in the northwest of the continent and been diffused southward and eastward. Its Californian distribution represents only a minute fraction of its total distribution. Clearly, the history of the sinew-backed bow could not possibly be solved from a consideration of the facts of its occurrence

---

[1] Since published as *Handbook of the Indians of California* (1925).

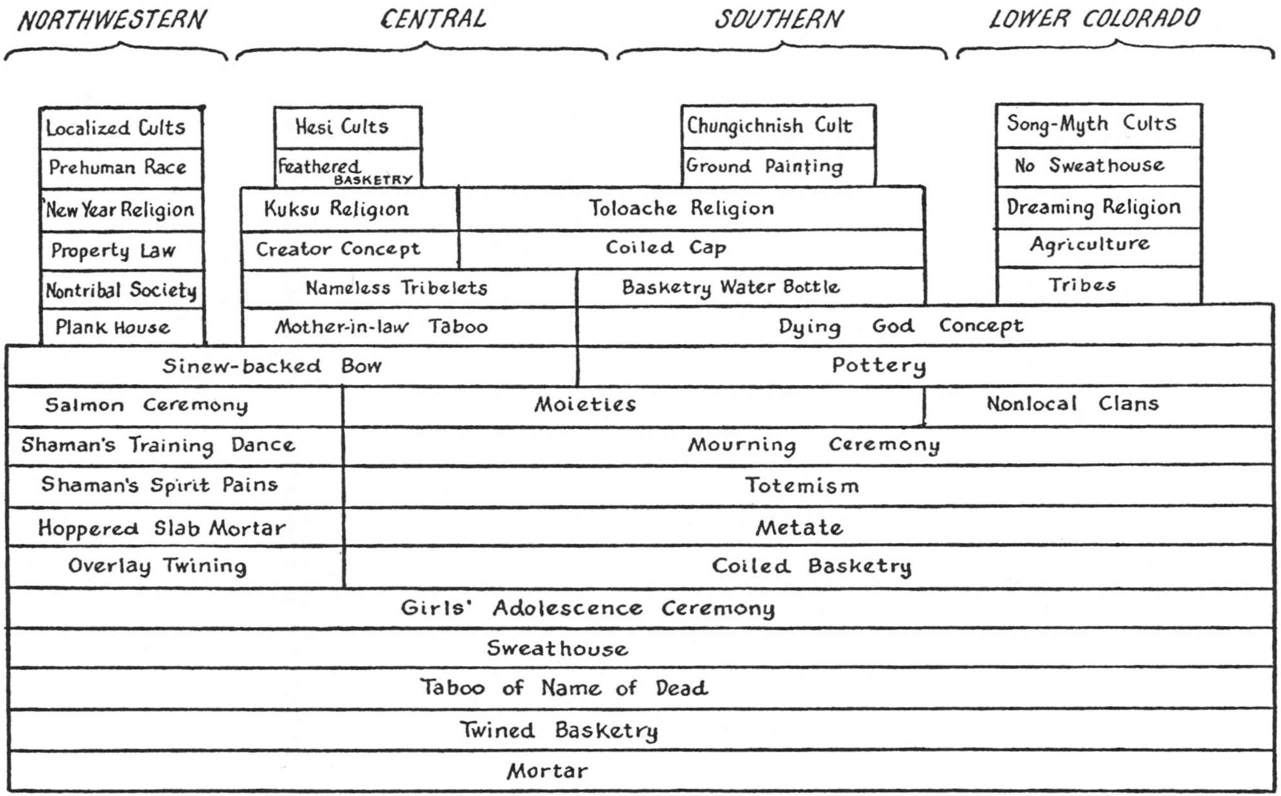

NORTHWESTERN   CENTRAL   SOUTHERN   LOWER COLORADO

Localized Cults
Prehuman Race
New Year Religion
Property Law
Nontribal Society
Plank House

Hesi Cults
Feathered Basketry
Kuksu Religion
Creator Concept
Nameless Tribelets
Mother-in-law Taboo

Chungichnish Cult
Ground Painting
Toloache Religion
Coiled Cap
Basketry Water Bottle

Song-Myth Cults
No Sweathouse
Dreaming Religion
Agriculture
Tribes

Sinew-backed Bow

Dying God Concept

Pottery

Moieties

Nonlocal Clans

Mourning Ceremony

Totemism

Metate

Salmon Ceremony

Shaman's Training Dance

Shaman's Spirit Pains

Hoppered Slab Mortar

Overlay Twining

Girls' Adolescence Ceremony

Coiled Basketry

Sweathouse

Taboo of Name of Dead

Twined Basketry

Mortar

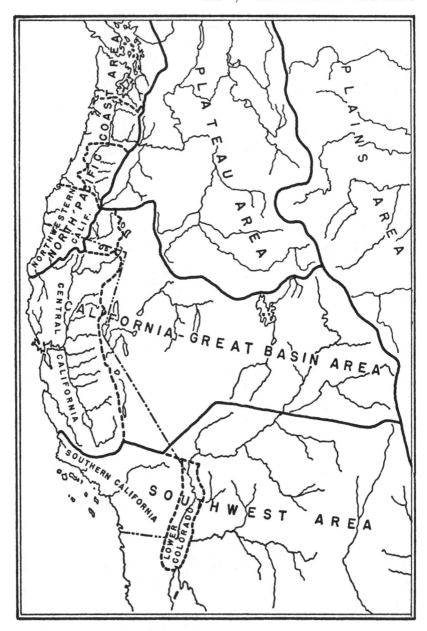

Map 12. Areas and Subareas of Culture in and about California.

within this limited region. The answer to the question of when it was first used in California depends in part on evidence that ranges from California through Alaska and Asia to Egypt.

Still, the facts of the bow's distribution within California have their significance, however abridged; and set by the side of facts concerning culture traits of less sweeping range, and still others which are wholly limited locally, a synthesis can result which will yield at least a tentative set of conclusions available for matching against the broader but less intensive syntheses built up on the consideration of data involving whole continents.

In any event, the diagram is valid so far as it presents the facts. Their meaning is another story.

With a clear realization, then, that at this point we abandon indubitable record for speculative interpretation, let us proceed in the reconstruction of the development of native civilization.

This civilization may be conceived as having run a course in four distinctive stages. The first period recognizable would be one of a simple culture with scant regional differentiation. In the second era, influences from the coast farther north and from the Southwestern plateau began to creep in, and the culture took on one color in the northern third and another in the southern two-thirds of California. A third period was that of the differentiation of the four cultures known to us. In the last period, which continued down to the time of Caucasian settlement, these local cultures attained their historic forms.

FIRST PERIOD: RELATIVELY SIMPLE AND UNIFORM CULTURE

The people of this era almost certainly comprised the ancestors of tne modern Hokans, perhaps of the Penutians. Algonkins and Athabascans are more doubtful; Shoshoneans had not yet entered. Among the Hokans, the Yuman division may still have been in touch with its congeners of the central Californian district; at any rate its habitat was scarcely that of the present. The northern Hokan divisions—the ancestors of the Chimariko, Karok, Shastan groups, Yana, Washo—were more widely spread than now.

The culture of all these peoples rested essentially on a food supply of seeds, especially the acorn, helped out by mollusks on the coast, fish, small game, and deer in the interior. The plant foods were crushed with stone pestles in stone mortars, stored, prepared, and cooked in baskets of twined weave, much as now. Wickerware, which is little used at present, may have been made then. Weirs, traps, and nets were worked in textile and cordage processes. The nets ran to rather large seines, weighted by stones. The fishing harpoon with detachable head, and the rush balsa, may have been already known. Wood was worked, at least split, with horn wedges; implements made of it must have comprised self-bows, and perhaps clubs, tubular tobacco pipes, and food stirrers.

The sweathouse is likely to have been in use much as we know it: a permanent structure, fire heated, entered nightly. To have served its purpose adequately, it could scarcely have been other than earth-roofed. The construction may therefore have been applied also to dwellings; but in the main, houses were probably of bark slabs or thatch on a frame of light poles.

The dead were buried, perhaps cremated here and there. They were feared more for their physical contacts than as spirits. Their names were not uttered. There was also a prejudice against the free use of the names of the living. Birth taboos were observed.

The principal dance, besides one of triumph over the heads of fallen foes, was that held for every adolescent girl, who endured a series of restrictions during the rite. For instance, she might not scratch her head nor eat meat. Religion was influenced largely by shamans who derived their power from actual or fabulous animals or celestial phenomena. They may have possessed stone charms. Besides curing and causing disease, they attempted to produce abundance of food, for the community as well as themselves; but these efforts were as yet unaccompanied by communal rituals.

The people lived without exogamic divisions, under chiefs who headed groups of kinsmen or small bodies united by coresidence. So far as descent was weighted at all, which was not often, it ran in the male line. Polygyny was tolerated and practiced. A man married his wife's sister or kinswoman, before or after her death; the widow married her husband's kinsman.

SECOND PERIOD: NORTHERN AND SOUTHERN INFLUENCES

Culture elements from the coast to the north and the interior highland to the southeast of California now began to penetrate. In each case they were worked into the existing culture. The northern influences seem to have been earlier and more effective, so far as they reached; but they scarcely affected more than the northern third of the area. Over this third, culture was comparatively uniform.

The northern house in this period commenced to be of frame construction, though still rudely made of bark slabs rather than planks. Some form of canoe must have been in use. Along with it, skill in woodworking developed. Basketry was commencing to refine on its old basis of twining. Possibly ornamentation in overlaying was practiced. At any rate, basketry was being put to special uses—cradles, caps, and the like. A woven hopper on a slab replaced the mortar. Shamanism was taking on a character of its own. The shaman's power was no longer derived so much from animals as from intangible spirits of localities. The novice in the art was aided by older men in a shaman-making dance. Shamanistic food–supply rites were slowly being elaborated, especially in connection with the salmon run. Society remained as unorganized as before, but possession of property and public influence were beginning to be correlated, and marriage was by purchase.

The Athabascans or Algonkins or both are likely to have entered northern California in this era; perhaps the Penutians were spreading along the Sacramento drainage. As a result of these movements, the Hokans were shifted and separated. The Athabascans came from the north; but, moving more slowly, or at least more intermittently, to judge by the preponderance of precedent, than knowledge and institutions diffused, they were not, in all likelihood, so much the carriers of the new elements of culture that were pervading northern California, as newcomers who found themselves in familiar social environment. The Algonkin ancestors of the Yurok and Wiyot are likely to have come down the Klamath. This movement would bring them out of a hinterland at a time when lapse and remoteness had deprived them of eastern Algonkin culture. Thus they too could not well have contributed much of novelty to the life of the region they were entering.

In the larger southern two-thirds of California the populational movements were less intricate. The Shoshoneans were probably spreading out of the Great Basin across the deserts toward the coast. They may have reached the ocean toward the close of the period. Here and there bodies of them that had come into intimate advance guard contacts with aliens were specializing their speech to become the ancestors of groups like the Tübatulabal or Cupeño. Culturally the Shoshoneans carried little into California: they could have had but little in the Basin. They did separate the southern from the central Hokans; and the break between the central and northern Hokan groups by Penutians may also have been effected during this period.

Most of the new civilizational elements in south and central California that can be assigned to the second era have Southwestern affiliations. They were of course not specific Pueblo elements. Pueblo culture was only beginning to organize; and even when organized it has never evinced a power of radiation equal to the degree of its development. Southern and central California at this time may be assumed to have used the unshaped metate alongside the mortar, and to have sewn coiled basketry. On the southern coast, shell beads began to be made in variety, and canoes were employed. Soon after the islands were reached and settled, the steatite industry may have had its inception, both as regards the manufacture of vessels and possibly also of ceremonial objects and ornaments. The beginnings of totemic sib organization perhaps fall in this period. Whether this took the form of moieties or clans, and whether these were exogamic or localized or not, is difficult to say. The emphasis is likely to have been on the totemic rather than on the organizational aspects of the system. In such groups as recognized descent, this was patrilineal. Shamanism had reached a stage of loose associations or public performances of coöperating individuals of the type of the rattlesnake ceremonies and shamans' contests of the San Joaquin Valley in the historic period. Rattlesnake and grizzly-bear shamans were commencing to be differentiated. The public mourning anniversary took form in this era and may have begun to creep northward. With it there is likely to have gone an accentuation of death taboos and perhaps a greater inclination to cremate corpses.

THIRD PERIOD: DIFFERENTIATION OF LOCALIZED CULTURES

Population movements on a large scale cannot be established for the third era. The Shoshoneans no doubt continued to press southwestward, and many minor shifts must have taken place in the welter of groups in the north. In the main, though, the territories of the greater linguistic blocks were commencing to approximate their present configuration. Culturally, the flow from the North Pacific Coast and Southwestern areas continued; but its effects remained more restricted geographically than before; because the imported elements now reached local cultures of some activity both in the north and south, and were there worked over before being passed on; and also because an independent culture was beginning to arise in the middle region.

In the northwest this local differentiation seems to have been most rapidly consummated, and to have become quickly established and correspondingly limited in geography. Consequently it is difficult to distinguish this period and the next in northwestern California. The pure type of plank house, the high esteem of property, exact valuations and laws connected with property, the use of compulsive formulas in religion, the attachment of rites to particular spots, the belief in a prehuman race in place of a creator, all must have evolved to an appreciable degree during the third period.

In central California, especially its northern portion in and about the Sacramento drainage, the vague shamans' associations began in this period to grow into the Kuksu organization: a formal initiation was instituted and spirits began to be impersonated. More or less connected was a development of mythology, in which increased coherence in accounting for beginnings was attained and the concept of a supreme creator began to grow clearer. On the side of arts, the culture failed to progress perceptibly, except in basketry; which was being made with added refinement and in techniques and styles that varied somewhat from region to region. Totemism, accompanied by a moiety system and more or less cross-cousin or other special forms of marriage, and here and there affecting rites, names, honors, or chieftainship, prevailed chiefly but not exclusively in the southern part of the central area. The mother-in-law taboo spread over the whole of it in this period.

South of Tehachapi, the narcotic jimson weed or toloache (*Datura*) was beginning to be worked more significantly into religion, especially in connection with an initiating organization which was becoming too inclusive to be strictly shamanistic any longer. The ritual came to include in time the idea of the ground painting—the basic element of the altar concept of the Southwest. For some unknown reason—perhaps the barrier interposed by the lower Colorado tribes—the elaborate ritual costuming of the Southwest was not carried into California, or if so only feebly and soon to be lost. A simple standardized costume of feather skirt and head topknot came into use, to continue century after century with practically no modification. The developing jimson-weed ritual and existing mourning commemoration commenced to influence each other, the toloache cult concerning itself more and more with problems of human life and death and spirituality, and instituting special mourning rites for its members. From the Southwest, too, were derived tendencies to reckon the year calendar about the solstices; and to weld the bulk of each tribal mythology into a long, complex whole, beginning with the first male and female principles and continuing through a series of births of beings and a sort of national migration legend. The most conspicuous episode in this cosmogony was that of the death of a great god. This concept seems to have originated in Mexico and either to have passed by the ancestors of the Pueblos or to have been discarded by them because unconsonant with their ritual system.

The scheme of society fluctuated locally between recognition of moieties, clans, and totemism, without ever freeing itself from association with the idea of chieftainship. In material culture, the influence of the Shoshonean Great Basin began to be perceptible at this or that point. The water bottle of basketry, the cap, perhaps the carrying net, emanated from this quarter. Pottery making, which was perhaps not introduced until later, had its source farther south: the region of the Gila and Sonora rather than of the Pueblos is indicated.

Along the Colorado, the bottomlands proved to be capable of sustaining a fairly large population as soon as agriculture was introduced from the Pueblos or more likely from Sonora; and agriculture remained thereafter the permanent basis of civilization. Physiography and climate, however, confined farming to the immediate river, thus concentrating the population into a uniform belt and marking it off sharply in customs from the inhabitants of the surrounding deserts and mountains. The narrowly localized and particularizing attitude characteristic of the remainder of California being effaced within the farmed tracts, settlements became fluid and lost their significance within true tribes. Had the civilization of these tribes been rich enough to support a real political organization, still further coalescence into a great nation might have ensued. As it was, they wasted one another in habitually sought wars, which absorbed much of their energy.

This growing emphasis on warlike undertakings did not interfere with the Colorado River tribes taking over from the New Mexican or Sonoran peoples such cultural elements as pottery, clan system, and prolix cosmogony, and passing them on to the groups nearer the ocean. For some reason, however, their military spirit and the civilizational distinctiveness enforced by their environment conflicted with other elements that came to them from the same source: the ground painting, for instance. These therefore traversed them without being able to make serious impression. Dreaming was evidently already established as the central idea and act in the religion of the river tribes. Why this should have been, we cannot see clearly. But the fact accounts for such elements as the altar, the dance, the recognized priest, not fitting in and therefore never taking firm root.

On the whole, then, the lower Colorado culture was the result of Sonoran influences being remodeled in a special environment. The product, compactly restricted within its physiographic confines, remained from an early date comparatively unreceptive to New Mexican influences, though without forming an impervious barrier to their spread.

FOURTH PERIOD: CONSUMMATION OF THE HISTORIC CULTURES

In this period North Pacific and Southwestern influences continued to enter California. But as they reached cultures of ever increasingly integrated organization, these influences were absorbed less and less directly. The characteristic event in Californian civilization in this era accordingly was the growth of its specializations.

The duration of this final period should not be underestimated. In the sixteenth century Alarcon, Cabrillo, and Drake sketched the native life that they found in portions of the lower Colorado, southern California, and central areas. They did not of course describe with minuteness nor enter upon intricacies or matters of organization. Consequently we cannot be sure how many of their more subtle and elaborate modern traits the groups in question possessed when visited by these explorers. But the picture for each locality tallies so perfectly, so far as it goes, with that presented by the historic cultures of the same spots, as to force the conviction that rather little development occurred in the three to four centuries that followed their visits. Twice that duration thus seems a conservative estimate for the length of this period.

In the northwest, these were the times in which finish in everything technological attained its modern degree. Forms remained less developed: the distance from the center of North Pacific Coast artistic achievement was too great, and central California had no examples to contribute. But the boat was refined with gunwales, seat, and prow ornament of local design; and polished horn was increasingly employed for objects whose material at an earlier time was presumably wood. The caste system hardened, debt slavery began to exist, marriage purchases became more splendid and more formally negotiated, a greater number of possessions and activities were given economic valuations. Treasures or money as such assumed a larger part in life, as compared with merely useful things: dentalium shells from the north, obsidian from the east, ornaments of woodpecker crests obtained at home. The dances, whose esoteric part remained formulistic, afforded opportunities for the display of much of this wealth, thus rendering unnecessary a potlatch or credit system and perhaps preventing an introduction of this northern institution which might otherwise have taken place. The wealth in turn gave an added dignity to the festivals and enabled them to take on more definitely their ultimate character of world renewing or new year rites. The intensive localization of ritual, myth, magic, and custom was no doubt fostered in some measure by the assignment of economic and legal values to fishing places and nearly all tracts or spots that were specially productive. Fighting wholly lost the character of war and became a system of economically regulated murder for revenge. Any remaining vestiges of scalping or the victory dance disappeared, and the war dance of incitement and negotiation of settlement prevailed exclusively. The idea of spirits as guardians diminished to the vanishing point; disease and cure were thought to be concerned mainly with self-animate pain objects; and shamans of importance were now always women.

In the central area, totemic sib organization perhaps began to decay. If it developed locally, it was without vigor. In religion, the movement of the two preceding eras toward cult organization gained in momentum. The rather widely spread Kuksu impersonations grew more elaborate, their combinations into great dances more numerous and spectacular, the earth-covered dance houses larger. Initiation into membership now was twofold: preliminary and full. The foot drum, split-stick rattle, and other paraphernalia, or such of them as did not go back to an earlier time, were introduced or at least associated with the Kuksu rites. In the heart of the area, about the lower Sacramento, a superstructure was reared on the Kuksu organization: the Hesi cult. The upper San Joaquin Valley was scarcely influenced in religion. Its southward remoteness preserved more ancient forms of ritual, or exposed it to partial permeation by the southern California toloache religion. Throughout the central province, in fact, the hill and mountain tribes took over only patches of the valley culture. Elements of civilization were accepted by them rather freely, organization of elements scarcely at all. Even in the active hearth of the culture, progress was mainly along the line of organization, elaboration, and integration. Aspects of civilization that did not lend themselves readily to making over in this manner—shamanism, for instance, adolescence rites, and many arts—remained primitive.

In basketry alone must we assume a notable progress per se. But this occurred independently in several parts. The effect thus was, as it were, centrifugal. The Pomo, the Maidu, the Washo, the Yokuts, each developed their own styles, technically and aesthetically. Single-rod coiling, lattice twining, feathering, bottleneck shapes are concrete examples among many slighter indications.

In southern California there was also a differentiation. At least as far back as the preceding era the Chumash seem to have begun to develop a special technological expertness, the Shoshoneans an interest in mysticism. The islanders, who in historic time were of both stocks, participated in both movements. Santa Catalina held the principal steatite quarries and was in close touch with the most favorably situated of the mainland Shoshoneans. It became therefore a radiant point. From it emanated the Chungichnish religion, superposed upon the basic toloache cults much like Hesi upon Kuksu, though its stress was laid more upon the meaning of symbols than their form. This religion had something of a propagandist spirit, which did not spend itself until after the introduction of Christianity, in fact was probably stimulated and possibly even induced by Christianity. World, birth, death, and soul mysticism flourished in belief and ritual. The basic world myth became more and more inclusive, the sacred ground painting took on its special features that mark it off from the Southwestern altar painting. As in the central province, shamanism, adolescence customs, and the like ancient institutions were little affected by these developments; only mourning rites grew ever more elaborate.

In the island and Chumash district the finest of the ornamental and ceremonial manufactures of steatite, hard stone, shell, and wood, as recovered by excavations, must probably be attributed to this late period. An increased refinement in the arts of basket making, feather working, and canoe carpentering seems also to have occurred.

Along the lower Colorado, two main events happened. The dream idea got such a hold on the culture as to associate itself with everything religious. Myth, song, shamanism, dance were all stamped deeply with its pattern. They assimilated increasingly. Everyone dreamed similar narratives and songs and sang the latter almost indiscriminately for a festival or a mourning, to cure the sick or to celebrate a victory. Secondly, the rather meager culture became so fixed as no longer to digest what might flow in from the pure Southwestern tribes. The dream concept in particular was again influential in this civilizational self-sufficiency and introversion. Being essentially an emphasizing of individual experience obtained in a certain way, dreaming engulfed shamanism as a separate activity; prevented associations or organizations; forbade the adoption of ritual apparatus or even curtailed such as existed; and thus caused the river tribes to do without masks, significant dance costumes, symbols, priests, sweathouses, or general use of jimson weed. Even the mourning commemoration became or remained abbreviated.

CHRONOLOGY AND ARCHAEOLOGY

The least sound portion of a reconstruction like the foregoing is likely to be the dates assigned to it; yet the human mind hankers after the specific. The problem may therefore be considered. Ultimately, of course, the chronology of native Californian culture must be worked out largely in connection with the prehistoric chronologies that are gradually being built up for other parts of the world. There are two sources of local information which will contribute something.

One of these is the descriptions of the earliest Caucasian visitors to California, which, as already mentioned, extend back to between three and four hundred years and suggest that the local culture types of the present were already well established then, making it a fair inference that the fourth period has endured perhaps twice as long. Approximate as this fact necessarily is, it seems conservative, and furnishes some basis for estimating the length of preceding periods.

The second line of local evidence is furnished by archaeology. On the whole, this has yielded much more slender results as to sequences in California than in most parts of North America. In part this paucity of inferences is the result of the absence of pottery from the greater portion of the state, and its late introduction and lack of variety in the remainder. Retardation of insight is also due to the fact that while prehistoric objects are abundant in California, there is little evidence of stratification; in fact, practically no indication of different cultural types being represented within the same area. It is true that portable mortars, for instance, are found everywhere in the state and that many of the tribes in the historical period no longer used them. But the very universality of the prehistoric distribution renders it difficult to interpret this change in terms of time. Most of the archaeological material, further, has been collected without much attention to depth, position, or collocation. It is almost inconceivable, for instance, that the fairly high types of stone and shell work of the Santa Barbara region could have been made in their full development from the time of the first settlement of the islands. One cannot rid himself of the feeling that the data for distinguishing two or more phases of local culture sequences could have been obtained. Yet it is clear that either the collections formed were assembled without recognition of the historical problems which they might help solve, or that the conditions of their deposition have been exceptionally unfavorable for science. It is still possible that some of the few remaining larger sites in the Santa Barbara region may yield the key of stratification. If not, it will be necessary for the future to attempt to sift out something from the available data by an intensive study of types and the consideration of such information as is available as to their association.

In the San Francisco Bay region, certain of the shellmounds had a very considerable depth—thirty and more feet—and have been partly excavated under methodical supervision. The first exploration of this sort, reported by Uhle, does indeed emphasize a considerable developmental sequence within the mound. The total quantity of objects, however, is small; and I have repeatedly gone over the collection without being able to satisfy myself of any marked cultural changes having occurred in the long period during which the mound accumulated. There is no question that the finer and better made pieces came from the later strata. But it is quality and finish that are involved, rather than new types.

The authority best fitted to pronounce a verdict on this point is Nelson, who excavated several of the larger mounds and has had by far the fullest experience in examining both large and small ones along the ramified shores of San Francisco Bay. He has been extremely hesitant in formulating an opinion as to the degree of change indicated by the remains. This hesitation may in itself be taken as an indication that the changes are rather slight. If there were obtrusive ones, he would unquestionably have long since set them forth. I have access to Nelson's data, including his preliminary tabulations of types of artifacts classified according to depth, and am in charge of the mound collections made by him and others. I am unable to see any important alterations in the culture from the earliest to the latest shellmound period. There are indeed distinctions, and there is no question but that the upper strata are by far the richest culturally. But the principal types—whether they be pestles or specialized forms like charmstones or imported materials like obsidian—occur in all strata.

Another consideration of importance in this connection is that artifacts characteristic of a region have been discovered only within that region. There are well marked types found respectively around Humboldt Bay, San Francisco Bay, the San Joaquin delta, the Santa Barbara Channel: they do not extend beyond these areas. If these idiomatic types, if such an expression may be pardoned, are of comparatively late origin, say during the third and fourth of the periods that have here been outlined, this local restriction becomes not only intelligible but significant. We should however in that event expect to find in these areas separate depositions of earlier objects different from the later specialized ones and perhaps fairly resembling those of the other areas. But here is where the evidence leaves us in the lurch. And it seems impossible even to say whether the evidence is actually nonexistent or is merely unknown to us because of lack of discrimination in exploration.

One help, however, can be derived from archaeology: an estimate of absolute age. Nelson, following a method of computation which it is not necessary to recount here but which seems at least reasonable, has arrived at the conclusion that some of the deeper San Francisco Bay mounds must have begun to be inhabited from 3,500 to 4,000 years ago. Gifford, in a subsequent examination of the mound constituents, with special reference to the ash content, came to a conclusion that approximately corroborated Nelson's finding, or at least presented no obstacles to its acceptance. Here then is a datum, however tentative, which may help us out for our beginnings, as the discoverers' voyages aid us for the last period. If we assume Nelson's 3,500 or more years, and take for granted further that, in accord with precedent elsewhere, Californian culture tended to develop somewhat faster as it grew more advanced, the first of the four culture phases might be set roughly in the time between 2000–1500 B.C. and 500 B.C.; the second as continuing from about 500 B.C. to 500 A.D.; the third until approximately 1200 A.D.; and the fourth from then on.

This does not of course place the beginning of all culture in the area as late as 4,000 years ago. The first occupation by man may well have occurred more than twice as long ago. In other words, our "first" period is almost certainly not the original one. It is the first that is fairly recognizable in the present state of knowledge.

What seems to be especially needed, not only for the firmer dating of these eras but for their more accurate and reliable recognition, is further archaeological evidence. The actual facts on the prehistory of California must be much more intensively studied and integrated than they have been, and very likely supplemented by future exploration, before they will be of much use either in corroborating or in correcting the sort of hypothetical reconstruction of prehistoric culture which has been attempted here mainly on the basis of ethnology.

---

[2] The reader is referred to the articles in the next section and to the reference bibliography at the end of this volume for more recent publications on the archaeology of California and the radiocarbon age dating of sites and cultures.

archaeology

THE WESTERN COAST
OF NORTH AMERICA

by
Robert F. Heizer

The Pacific Coast of North America north of Mexico may be defined phys-
iographically as a narrow coastal plain bounded by a more or less continuous series of mountain ranges running closely parallel to the shore.
From Prince William Sound in the north (lat. 60° N.) to Los Angeles in the
south (lat. 34° N.), the coast could be reached from the continental interior
only by crossing substantial mountain barriers. Free access along this
coastal border was available to boat-using groups, but the main population
accretions of the past were presumably provided by small contingents
moving westward across the mountains. The distribution of boat types
along the Pacific Coast does not encourage the view that they served to
transport migrating groups. Level access to the Pacific rim from the east
was provided only in the south through the Basin-and-Range province
across what is now southern Nevada, southern Arizona, and the southern
California desert, or from the south out of Mexico by way of the west-coast
corridor known as the Sonoran Desert.

The western continental fringe clearly has not been an area into which
massive population movements or major culture complexes have flowed
and spread out as they have east of the Rockies, but rather has been a
marginal area, generally difficult of access, into which many small groups
have been pushed or found their way over a long period of time, with the
result that an extraordinarily complex series of local cultures have taken
root, developed, and interinfluenced their neighbors over the past several
thousand years.

Lest this statement appear to imply flatly that no external influences
have helped modify and shape California cultures, the reader is reminded
that southwestern ("Pueblo") influences in southern and central California
were fairly strong, that the northwest coast proper significantly shaped
the basic features of northwestern California, and that California and Great
Basin peoples share a basic cultural substratum. Oceanian elements also
may have been received, but conclusions on this score depend upon

Revision by the author of a portion of a chapter in *Prehistoric Man in the New World*,
eds. J. D. Jennings and E. Norbeck (University of Chicago Press, 1963), pp. 117–148.

whether such features as curved shell and bone fishhooks, the plank canoe, and Polynesian-style cosmogonic myths noted in southern California are ultimately proved to be independent parallels or due to trans-Pacific diffusion.

Although Kroeber once warned against too easy acceptance of the "fish-trap theory, according to which the multiplicity of languages in California is due to the successive crowding into this more desirable habitat of waves or bands of unrelated immigrants from less favorable territories, to which none of them were ever willing to return," a considerable body of evidence and opinion indicates that acceptance of the fish-trap theory helps to account for some of the considerable linguistic, cultural, and somatic variability on both the ethnographic and the prehistoric time levels of the west coast region. Only in this way can we reasonably account for the high degree of linguistic diversity and cultural fractionation exhibited anciently, as well as ethnographically, along the Pacific Coast.

In recent years we have been presented with a number of claims of the finding of evidence of man's presence in California at a time so early, and with proofs so vague, that most American archaeologists have taken the position that they would wait to see more evidence before they accepted the proposals. I refer here to G. Carter's claims and to their critical assessment by Haury, Johnson and Miller, and Krieger. Carter's "artifacts" have been judged by nearly all archaeologists who have examined them to be natural forms and not man-made implements.

In this same vein, I wish to state here my opinion that the several bone fragments from Potter Creek Cave, believed by F. W. Putnam to be tools made by man, are *not* artifacts. A few bone scraps that have features (grooves and holes) suggesting artificial modification, found in the midst of thousands of bone fragments that are clearly not artifacts, make their fortuitous production the most probable explanation. Nature can, on occasion, cause certain features in bone pieces that make them appear to be the result of the hand of man, and in these instances our usually workable — but not infallible — test criteria give us the wrong answer. If we were to accept Sellard's proposition that the earliest men in the New World were so poorly equipped that stone tools were rare or lacking, we should be coming very close to the concept of a Prelithic, or Protolithic, or Eolithic, or possibly Osteodontokeratic culture level, for none of which I see any support at all.

A series of alleged ancient evidences of man has been proposed by P. C. Orr on the basis of his findings on Santa Rosa Island. It is not possible to accept these claims as they are stated, because we are not given the detailed evidence of occurrence. Orr may be correct in stating that he has found evidence of man's presence on Santa Rosa Island dating back to

30,000 or more years ago, but until his findings are published in detail the claims cannot even be judged, much less accepted.

A similar degree of obscurity, which necessitates withholding acceptance, surrounds the age of artifacts associated with former beach lines in southern California lake basins such as Lake Mohave and Lake Manix. A radiocarbon age (LJ-200)* for freshwater mussel shells from the high shore line of Lake Mohave of 9640 years may indeed date the lake stand, but it does not answer the problem of whether the stone artifacts occurring on the surface of that beach are the same age as the molluscan remains imbedded in the beach deposit. The same hazard in applying the date for some event in nature to an assumed contemporaneity of surface artifacts obtains also in the radiocarbon age of Lake Manix tufa (UCLA-121) of 19,300 years. In view of the known fact that in the very brief historic period some of these lakes have repeatedly filled with water which has remained for many months, we may assume that a number of these temporary fillings have occurred in the last 10,000 years and would have attracted aboriginal settlement. In 1938, for example, Lake Mohave filled in a 13-day period and formed a body of water 16 miles long, 2.5 miles wide, and 10 feet deep. Thus, artifacts lying on the surface of these beaches may or may not date from the time the beaches were formed. Regardless of how persuasive and detailed the reasoning, it is not possible to be convinced that the dry lake basins of southern California have produced datable evidence of early man or that the "cultures" or "complexes" that have been proposed are probably contemporaneous aggregates of artifacts (i.e. industries). If one wishes to argue that water is necessary in the southern California desert for Indians to be present, he might first ponder Julian Steward's observation:

In the southern end of Eureka Valley, near the northern end of Death Valley, California, there is a site bordering a playa and extending several miles. Thousands of flint flakes with relatively few artifacts mark it as predominantly a workshop, though the source of the flints is several miles distant in the mountains. The nearest water is a spring 3 to 5 miles away. There is no apparent reason why anyone should choose a place lacking water, having virtually no vegetation, and in fact, devoid of anything of apparent use to man or beast, for a workshop or other purpose. Nevertheless the presence here of large spherical stone mortars of the type used by Death Valley Shoshoni, and at least one arrow point of the Shoshonean type, is presumptive evidence that the Shoshoni visited the site, though it does not, of course, prove that they used it as a workshop. . . . The writer has repeatedly received accounts from Shoshoni and Paiute informants of camps maintained by entire

---

* Radiocarbon sample numbers are indicated here in parentheses. For lists and comments see reference bibliography at the end of this volume.

families and groups of families for days at a time, 10 or even 20 miles from water, when seeds, salt, flint, edible insects, or other important supplies made it worthwhile to do so. Water is used sparingly, and when the ollas in which it is transported are empty one or two persons make the long trip to replenish them. Remoteness from present water, then, is not *per se* the slightest proof that a site dates from the pluvial period.

While the Santa Rosa Island, Lake Mohave, and Lake Manix materials may be ancient, they have not been adequately demonstrated to be so. The most persuasive indication to date that the Lake Mohave materials may predate 7000 years ago come from the excavation of the Harris site near San Diego. The lower levels of the site, which was excavated earlier by D. B. Rogers, produce materials of the San Dieguito culture, named by Rogers and equated by him on the basis of shared traits with the Lake Mohave-Playa cultures of the interior lake basins of southern California.* The San Dieguito culture inventory is limited to chipped stone forms, including scraper planes, a wide variety of scrapers (keeled, flake, snubnose, side, end, etc.), heavy bipointed blades or knives, eared "crescents," leaf-shaped projectile points, choppers, pebble hammerstones, and hammerstones made from cores or nuclei. Radiocarbon dates for the site range from 6540 to 7080 B.C. (A-724, A-725, A-722A). If we accept the Harris site materials from the bottom level as providing an adequate sample of material culture of the San Dieguito II and III culture phases, the absence of grinding tools is worthy of comment. W. Wallace has discussed the lack of seed-grinding tools in the Death Valley I culture and points out that it appears to be a non-seed-using culture whose primary economy rested upon hunting, and that these characteristics do not permit its classification in the "Desert Culture" tradition. Warren and True suggest that the San Dieguito culture may represent evidence of an early "Western Hunting Culture," different from and older than the Desert Culture, and that the Lake Mohave–Playa cultures of the interior lake basins are manifestations of this hunting culture. Although a few manos were found on the Lake Mohave beach terraces they incline to accept Amsden's explanation that these are attributable to the later Pinto Basin culture. Absence of portable

---

* M. J. Rogers' chronology proposed in 1939 is much too short. He has revised this several times, most notably in Haury's report on Ventana Cave, to give it a greater time range. The revision is critically discussed by Warren and True. The complicated terminology is summarized in the following table.

Rogers 1929	Rogers 1939	Rogers 1958 Haury 1950	Warren and True 1961
Shell Midden	Playa II	San Dieguito III	Yuman
Scraper-Maker	Playa I	San Dieguito II	La Jolla
	Malpais	San Dieguito I	San Dieguito

stone mortars or metates at camp or village sites does not necessarily prove that a group did not grind seeds, since the site may have been occupied for reasons, or at times, when seed-grinding was impossible or inappropriate. Alternatively, the wooden mortar in wide use in recent as well as ancient times, if used, would leave no archaeological vestiges. Clearly, we should be careful not to decide too hastily that we are dealing only with hunters when we fail to find, in a very small series of sites producing very few material objects, familiar forms of seed-grinding implements. Indeed, to prove that a prehistoric culture group shunned seeds as food and subsisted solely on hunting requires direct and positive evidence of exclusive economic reliance on the latter pursuit.

For the period of about 7000 to 4000 years ago, we have a number of radiocarbon-dated sites from the southern California coast region extending from Santa Barbara to San Diego. From Santa Rosa Island an age determination (M-1133) of midden shell gave an age of 7350 years for what is apparently the Dune Dweller culture, and for the later Highland culture on Santa Rosa Island there are two age determinations, 5370 (LJ-446B) and 4790 (UCLA-105) years old. On the mainland there is the Topanga site, as yet undated; Zuma Creek site, dated 4950 years old (LJ-77); Malaga Cove site at Redondo Beach, with an age of 6510 years (LJ-3); the undated Little Sycamore site; the undated Oak Grove culture; the "Pauma complex"; and the Scripps Estate site, which is radiocarbon dated as occupied between 5460 and 7370 years ago (samples LJ-79, LJ-109, LJ-110, LJ-221). All or most of these sites can be construed as manifestations of the La Jolla culture, which is more generally subsumed under what Wallace has called the "Milling Stone Horizon." The trait inventory of the sites listed varies somewhat and may thus reflect regional subphases of a fairly simple and uncomplex culture type. The culture is generally characterized by the following: abundance of deep-basined metates, manos, scraper planes, flake scrapers, choppers, pebble hammerstones, pitted hammerstones, rarity of bone tools (awls, punches), cogstones, flexed burials (at Little Sycamore site, Scripps Estate site), prone extended burial usually covered with a cairn of metates (Oak Grove sites, Topanga site), and reburial (Little Sycamore site, Topanga site). The economy was based on seed-gathering, which was supplemented with hunting and shellfish-collecting. The Milling Stone Horizon sites lack cremation, pottery, and C-shaped shell fishhooks. Use of ocean resources is limited and marine foods are apparently secondary to economic pursuits of the terrestrial hunting-catching-gathering order.

The abundant presence of stone mortars on the ocean bottom off La Jolla is difficult to explain. No means of firmly dating these have been found, and it may be that they are evidence of a marked change in sea level which occurred after the shore had been occupied by man, although one has the impression that the artifacts are of later, rather than earlier, types, and that geological changes of this magnitude should involve older types of artifacts. Only more investigation will help explain these ocean-floor concentrations of artifacts.

Curved shell fishhooks are radiocarbon dated on San Nicolas Island at 400 years old (UCLA-164), but they must be rather older in the general channel area. The oldest archaeological dates for the Channel Islands (omitting Santa Rosa) are 3300 (UCLA-165), 3980 (UCLA-147), and 5070 (W-981) years for San Nicolas Island; 3880 years (M-434) for Santa Catalina Island; 450 years (LJ-259) for San Clemente Island; 2120 (LJ-218) and 1750 years (LJ-25) for San Miguel Island. These dates do not, of course, necessarily mark the earliest occupation of any of the islands.

For the southern California coastal area, a series of what Wallace terms "Intermediate Cultures" occupies the two millenniums between 2000 B.C. and the beginning of the Christian Era (or perhaps to A.D. 500). These are little known in detail and include the poorly defined "Hunting Culture" of the Santa Barbara region and the La Jolla II phase in the San Diego region. The basket or hopper mortar makes its appearance, perhaps indicating the institution of the widespread California Indian acorn preparation process (hulling, grinding, winnowing, warm water leaching, and stone-boiling in baskets), a greater variety of flaked implements occurs, flexed primary burial is the standard method of disposal of the dead, and hunting and shellfish gathering are the main economic pursuits. Larger villages and more sedentary patterns indicate this period as developmental and anticipatory to the appearance of the late prehistoric period of cultural climax, which ends with the appearance of the Spanish explorers and missionaries in the mid-sixteenth century.

The late prehistoric period in southern California is marked by the clear emergence of local culture varieties as a result of large population numbers, and their separation is registered culturally through local ecological accommodations and political independence. This is clearest in the Santa Barbara region where local mainland-shore culture subtypes are apparent, as well as accentuated mainland-island differentiations. The bow and arrow is by now the dominant weapon. Steatite is a common material for cooking vessels except where pottery is the alternative for direct fire cooking. The essentially exclusive distribution of steatite and pottery indicates the latter as a recent acquisition in desert and coastal southern California, the source apparently lying to the east across the Colorado River in Arizona. The circular shell fishhook, while it may make its appearance in the Intermediate culture period, so far as is known is most characteristic of the later period, and by this time an undoubted maritime orientation of the coastal peoples has been effected. The plank canoe of the Chumash is in use and used for fishing and mainland-island communication. An abundance of stone and shell bead and shell ornament types, bone artifacts, burins and bladelets presumably used in woodworking, circular thatch-covered houses, complicated painted pictographs, and flexed burial or cremation are characteristic. Wallace has summarized the site inventories for the southern coast for this period.

The desert interior of southern California is, culturally speaking, an extension of the Great Basin area toward the Pacific. Artifact materials associated with shore-line features of extinct lakes (Lake Mohave, Pinto Basin, Lake Manix) have been mentioned earlier. The cultural adaptation to the rather confining way of life imposed by a water-deficient land has prevailed from the earliest times. An uncomplicated technology, which manifests material expression in seed-grinding tools, flaked knives, points and scrapers, and little else in open sites, with the addition of some perishables in the form of basketry and cordage in cave or shelter sites, provides us with a picture of the so-called Desert Culture that has endured in relatively stable form for several thousand years. Petroglyphs are abundant and are of several styles that are widely distributed throughout the Great Basin, serving as a ritual accompaniment to hunting.

Central California, defined here as the region lying between Tehachapi (where the Sierra Nevada joins with the Coast Range) in the south to the head of the Sacramento Valley in the north, and the ocean coast on the west to the Sierra Nevada crest on the east, may be divided into three zones: (1) coastal (shore plus Coast Range section); (2) interior valley (the combined Sacramento and San Joaquin valleys); and (3) Sierran (western slopes of the Sierra Nevada).

The most carefully worked out sequence is for the lower Sacramento Valley region. Here occur sites of the Early Horizon characterized by rigid adherence to disposal of the corpse lying on the face and fully extended (i.e. prone); "charm stones" of various forms (including phallic shapes), almost invariably drilled at one end; large, heavy projectile points; shell beads and ornaments of several types; flat slab metates and stone bowl mortars and pestles; fiber tempered baked-clay balls (surrogates for rocks used in cooking by stone-boiling); rare bone awls; twined (but not coiled) basketry (evidenced by impressions in baked clay); the atlatl as the chief weapon; fairly clear indications that strong development of individual accumulation of wealth did not exist; and apparent evidence that warfare was uncommon. The age of the Early Horizon, which is now known from seven sites, derives from a series of radiocarbon dates based on charcoal from site SJo-68 which lies about 20 miles north of Stockton. These are

4052, 4100, and 4350 years old (samples C-440, C-552, M-645, M-646, and M-647).

The Oak Grove-Topanga-La Jolla-Milling Stone Horizon is probably related to the culture disclosed in the lowest levels of the sites reported on by Wedel at Buena Vista Lake in the southern San Joaquin Valley, where mullers are associated with extended burials, and the connection may be traced farther north to the Cosumnes Valley near Sacramento in the Early Horizon sites. The Tranquillity site in the San Joaquin Valley appears to be ancient on the grounds of fossilization of animal and human bone, but the uncertainly associated cultural materials are puzzling because they seem to be of fairly recent types.

The Middle Horizon, which follows in time and is in part an outgrowth of the Early Horizon culture, falls in the time period from about 2000 B.C. to A.D. 300. Emphasis on materials and type has changed from the earlier period. Burial position is now regularly tightly flexed; cremation occurs (though rare, and usually with a rich accompaniment of grave foods); offerings with primary interments are minimal or absent; and bones are fairly frequently found with weapon points imbedded — an indication that warfare (or at least violent death) has become more common since the preceding period. Sparing use of grave offerings may indicate emphasis on wealth accumulation and reluctance of heirs, through greed, to "waste" such goods, a situation having an ethnographic parallel among the Yurok of northwestern California. Coiled basketry (as indicated by an abundance of bone awls) was manufactured; a large variety of abalone shell bead and ornament types is present; and bone is now used more as an industrial material (for making sweat-scrapers, punches, whistles, and tubes). The slab metate carries over, but the deep wooden mortar (with stone pestle) is the most important seed-grinding tool. Charmstones or plummets continue to be made, though in forms different from earlier types; and the phallic form is lacking. Barbed harpoons and a peculiar blunt-tipped bone or antler point, probably used for taking fish, appear in this period. The bow, as well as the atlatl, was apparently in use. Sites are larger and the population was obviously greater than in the Early period.

The Late Horizon, which is dated from A.D. 300 to the opening of the historic period in the eighteenth century, can be almost certainly identified as the prehistoric culture of the Penutian-speaking tribes of central California. The Middle Horizon culture carries over in essence, but again, specific material forms are distinctive. Thus this period is characterized by a new set of varieties of shell beads; a bewildering array of ornaments made of abalone shell; small obsidian arrowpoints (often with deep edge-serration) for use with the bow and arrow; large stone mortars (bowl as well as slab form with basketry hopper attached); long, tubular steatite smoking pipes; bird-bone tubes with extremely detailed and complicated fine-line incised decoration; and increased use of cremation and sacrifice by burning grave offerings in the grave prior to placing the corpse in the grave. Based upon both archaeological and ethnographical evidence, central California seems to have come under fairly strong influence from the Southwest over the last millennium, the line marked by the territories of the Pomo, Wintun, and Maidu tribes appearing to represent the northwestern frontier of the "greater Southwest."

In the southern San Joaquin Valley there is evidence for a long sequence of cultures that go back to the same period as the Early Horizon culture and continue into the historic period. The late period shows strong influence from the Santa Barbara coast, as well as from the Colorado River region.

On the coast of central California south of San Francisco Bay, shellmounds are the characteristic type of site. At the mouth of Willow Creek in Monterey County, the base of a shoreline midden has been dated by radiocarbon as 1879 and 1840 years old (C-628, C-695). Curved shell fishhooks in this level help to date this form, which is more abundant in the Santa Barbara region to the south. At this time level a fully developed coastal culture was operating, as indicated by evidence of fishing, mollusk collecting, and taking of shore-frequenting sea mammals (seal, sea lion), as well as oceanic forms (sea otter). On the shores of San Francisco Bay a number of large shellmounds have been excavated. The antiquity of these mounds has been estimated by rate-of-accumulation and most recently by the radiocarbon method. The bottom levels of these shellmounds cluster around the age of 3000 years; for example, site Ala-328 on the Southern Alameda County shore with an age of 2588 years (C-690), site SMa-77 with dates of 2700 and 3150 years old (L-187A, L-187B), site Ala-307 with a series of inconsistent radiocarbon dates whose maximum for the mound base probably should read about 3500 to 4000 years old, and the base of the Emeryville shellmound site (Ala-309) with an age of 2310 years (LJ-199).

Thus far large-scale occupation of the well favored shore of San Francisco Bay seems to have occurred in early Middle Horizon times; substantial Early Horizon sites, if ever present, have either escaped detection or were situated in locations where subsidence of the shore of the bay has led to their encroachment by water. There is some evidence though it is not as abundant or clear as would be desirable, in the bottom of site Ala-307 (West Berkeley shellmound) of Early Horizon occupation. Generally speaking, allowing for local ecologic adjustments to tidal shore (as against valley riverine locale), the Middle and Late sequences on the bay conform to that already sketched for the interior valley.

The general picture of the coast and valley sections of central California is, in summary, one of a change from peaceful egalitarianism in Early Horizon times to warlike wealth-consciousness in the following Middle Horizon. One can read the Late archaeological evidences as conformable to the political units reported for central California tribes by ethnographers. Beardsley has perceptively characterized the cultures by the industrial materials upon which greatest attention was lavished — Early Horizon on stone, Middle Horizon on bone, and Late Horizon on shell. The major shoreline occupation of the central California coast seems to have occurred from 3000 to 3500 years ago, although traces of earlier settlement almost certainly remain to be discovered. The first clear indication of dense populations goes back to Middle Horizon times, and with improving economic exploitative techniques, the population numbers increased until, by the opening of the historic period, California is believed to have held about 275,000 Indians. California, with roughly 1 percent of the land area of North America north of Mexico, held about 3.5 percent of the total population, if we accept Dobyns' figure of 9,800,000 Indians for North America. This density of population led to very large villages in some districts (actual counts run as high as 1400 persons), and there was a notable development of craft specialization. Willey and Phillips class California as Formative in their system of developmental stages; Meighan calls California an area of Archaic cultures; and Heizer has argued that late prehistoric California can be ranked in climax locations (southern San Joaquin Valley, Sacramento River, and Santa Barbara Channel) as "Preformative" or "Incipiently Formative" in the revised classification system of Willey and Phillips. The failure of California Indians to accept agriculture is ascribed primarily to cultural resistance based on the well-established and complicated technology of the acorn economic complex; although as Jones and others have suggested, the dry summer climate may have required irrigation for corn growing in some areas, and the failure of irrigation to diffuse may have in some areas prevented the acceptance of farming.

In the Coast Ranges and along the coast north of San Francisco Bay, there was substantial inhabitation in Middle Horizon times, the cultural materials being similar to those found farther east in the interior valley. On an earlier time level is site Nap-131 which produced flaked basalt and obsidian implements similar to some from the Borax Lake site in Lake County, whose proper position in time has never been satisfactorily agreed upon, even though it has yielded a number of Clovis fluted points. The recently developed method of age determination by amount of obsidian hydration indicates the Borax Lake fluted points as quite old, estimated at 9000 years. Surveys carried out since 1949 have led to the location of eight additional sites, characterized by manos; heavy, short, concave base projectile points with basal-thinning flakes; and heavy flake scrapers and scraper planes, which are coming to light in the Coast Range valleys north of San Francisco Bay. It is tempting to lump these together as evidence of an old seed-using–hunting culture that is coeval with, or possibly antedates, the Early Horizon culture of the lower Sacramento Valley, whose age is 4000 and more years old. What are called the Mendocino and Borax Lake complexes are probably both to be included in this proposed category, as well as some sites to the north in Shasta County. A definite tendency to use flint and basalt rather than obsidian for flaked implements appears to be characteristic of this time level. However, until more investigation is carried out and some dating of these sites can be secured, this suggestion of an early hunting-collecting culture can be considered only a hypothesis. Late Horizon sites in the northern Coast Ranges are abundant, although little archaeology has been carried out in the region. Just west of the head of the Sacramento Valley, in the Coast Range section, salvage archaeology in reservoir areas has yielded an abundance of late materials that are basically central Californian in type, but which were modified by influences reaching southeast from the area of distinctive culture development of northwestern California.

In the Sierra Nevada Mountains which rise to the east of the Sacramento and San Joaquin valleys, the history of human occupation probably begins with the same metate-using collectors and hunters whose presence has been dimly perceived in the northern Coast Ranges. This possibility derives from numerous discoveries in the last half of the nineteenth century of artifacts in the auriferous gravel deposits. Evaluation of these older finds cannot be done at this date, nor can Holmes's critical review of 1901 be improved upon. Dating of the artifacts recovered from the gravels in the past century is not possible at this remove, and the best that can be said is that some finds probably date from middle postglacial times — say 5000 to 6000 years ago. It was thought that similar materials were found *in situ* at the Farmington site about thirty miles east of Stockton, but radiocarbon ages of 1660 and 1170 years old (UCLA-132, UCLA-133) from the gravels at Farmington seems effectively to dispose of this site as ancient. However, the Farmington gravels may be much older than the radiocarbon dates secured, and further age determinations should be made before a final decision is reached on the antiquity of the implements that are incorporated in the lower gravels. Middle Horizon materials (dated by comparison with the valley area) occur in the Sierran limestone caverns, usually in association with human bones, this association resulting from the practice of throwing corpses and burial offerings down the natural shafts. Some of the bones have thick incrustations of travertine, which led one archaeologist to compute their age at 12,000 years, but this has now been reduced by radiocarbon tests to 1400 years (L-530A, L-530C). Probably equivalent in time to the limestone cavern ossuaries is the Martis complex of the High Sierra in the Lake Tahoe region, which is characterized by heavy basalt points (stemmed and side-notched forms), scrapers and drills, "boat-stones" (atlatl weight?), slab metate and portable mortar, and economic emphasis directed to seed-collecting and hunting. The Martis complex is succeeded in this region by the Kings Beach complex, which is late in time and is believed to refer to the late prehistoric Washo tribe. It is character-ized by the use of obsidian, bedrock mortars, small light Desert Side-notched projectile points (used with the bow and arrow), and economic emphasis on fishing and seed-collecting. That this same general sequence of cultures occurs through the central and southern Sierra is indicated by the more recent work of Bennyhoff, Elsasser, and Hindes. Northeast California has been unduly neglected by archaeologists, but what little investigation has been done shows that the Pit River area is a transition cultural zone between central California and the Great Basin. Smith and Weymouth have described the Late period archaeology in the Shasta Dam area; Treganza found Late period sites in the Redbank Reservoir area in Tehama County; and Baumhoff, on the basis of excavations in Payne's and Kingsley caves in Tehama County, identifies two archaeological com-plexes: (1) Mill Creek, which is similar to the Late Horizon of the Sacra-mento Valley area; and (2) Kingsley, which seems to have a close similarity to the Martis complex. In the southeastern Sierra, Owens Valley Brown Ware pottery was introduced about A.D. 1300 by diffusion across the Great Basin through Shoshonean-speaking peoples, its source perhaps being in the Woodland pottery of the western Great Plains.

Northwestern California north of Cape Mendocino and the southern coast of Oregon south of the Coquille River are believed to form an identi-fiable prehistoric cultural subarea. This conclusion is supported by the relatively small amount of work done in this coastal area, at Chetco, the lower Coquille River, Pistol River, and other sites on the south Oregon coast and at a limited number of sites on the northernmost coast of Cali-fornia. Most of the sites excavated thus far are shellmound deposits which appear to be fairly late in time. Few radiocarbon dates have been secured. A site (Cs-23) on the lower Coquille River (Oregon) was occupied 350 years ago (L-189B); there are radiocarbon ages of 1050 and 1070 years (M-938; I-2352) for the base of the Gunther Island site in Humboldt Bay. Radiocarbon ages of 545 and 640 years (GX-0181, GX-0182) for the bottom of the Patrick's Point shellmound; a radiocarbon age of 2260 years (I-4006) for the base of the Point St. George site (CA-DNo-11) near Crescent City; and a date of A.D. 1620 calculated as the initial settlement date of the Tsurai site at Trinidad Bay. Some cultural change has occurred in northwestern California in the last thousand years, evidenced mainly by small variations in projectile point forms and bone harpoons and the late appearance of the wooden smoking pipe with inset steatite bowl. The archaeological practice, evidenced in the lower levels of the Gunther Island site, of lavish burning of grave goods in the grave pit with the corpse laid on top of the still-burning embers, was succeeded in late prehistoric times by extended primary interment without burned offerings, which is the ethnographic mode of disposal of the dead. Also in the Gunther Island site were curved bone fishhooks, grooved clay balls (sinkers?), pottery female figurines, and slate zooform clubs inaptly labeled "slavekillers" by Loud, which were clearly a distinctive form of wealth object whose vogue had passed before the opening of the historic period.

Surveys on the southern Oregon coast have failed to produce evidence of occupation older than 500 years ago, and the roster of archaeological traits is interpreted as late prehistoric manifestations of the cultures of the ethnographic people (Tututni). About the same situation, though perhaps with a slightly longer period of settlement, obtains in northwestern California where we are obviously dealing with the archaeological manifestations of historic tribes (Tolowa, Yurok, and Wiyot). Whether the origin of these coastal peoples lies farther north along the shore or in the interior from which they came down river is not known; as a guess, a southward coastal drift seems most likely.

In northeastern California only the beginnings of tracing the sequence of prehistoric occupation have been made. In Surprise Valley, J. O'Connell has identified an early phase which seems to have strong affiliations with the Plateau area to the north and a later phase whose connections lie to the west with the Great Basin. The earlier occupation is not yet radiocarbon dated but must be older than the later phase which goes back about 2100 years (I-3209).

SAN FRANCISCO BAY SHELLMOUNDS

by
N. C. Nelson

DISTRIBUTION OF THE SHELLMOUNDS

Present Number

The group of shellmounds examined in the San Francisco Bay region . . . numbers 425 separate accumulations. It is not to be supposed, however, that this figure exhausts the evidences of aboriginal occupation to be found within the given territorial limits, because the shellmounds are confined to a narrow belt around the open waters of the bay and grade off landwards into earth mounds of a more or less artificial character. In fact, some of the deposits occurring both at the northern and southern extremities, specifically those on Sonoma Creek and on the Napa and Guadalupe rivers, contain a larger percentage of earth and ashes than of shell. According to reports, moreover, earth mounds and old Indian rancherias are situated on the banks of the Alameda and San Francisquito creeks, above the alluvial plain in the foothills; and it is hardly to be doubted that sites of this character could be found in great numbers by following up any other of the minor streams. As it is, several more or less obliterated camp and village sites of late and ancient date are definitely known in the region, some of them even on the University campus in Berkeley; and the publication of news items relating to discoveries here and there of relics and skeletal material is no uncommon occurrence.

The now known list of genuine refuse heaps certainly falls short also of the number that originally existed in the region. Many of the deposits appear to have been either obliterated or destroyed by natural causes. Thus there were discovered, quite by accident, four shell heaps of unknown lateral extent, but from one to three feet deep, that were completely covered by natural deposits, ranging in thickness from one to two and a half feet. Of these four, no. 6 [1] lies at the bottom of Elk Canyon, northwest of Sausalito, and its covering is simply a light sandy alluvium; but nos. 4 and 15,

Pp. 322–331, 335–341 of N. C. Nelson, *Shellmounds of the San Francisco Bay Region*, Univ. Calif. Publ. Am. Arch. and Ethn. (1909), 7:309–356.
[1] Site numbers in this paper refer to the insert map which accompanied original publication (*ibid.*, opp. p. 348).

below Mill Valley, lie on hillsides and the covering here is a hard clay or adobe that could have washed from the slope above only very slowly. The last, no. 96, situated west of Point San Pedro, lies in the edge of a reclaimed salt marsh, and was discovered only through the presence of a ditch lately dug across the area containing the buried deposit.

Another point worthy of note is the fact that there are at the present time no less than thirty relatively large mounds so situated by the shores, central on the bay, that they are subject to wave action. Some of these mounds have their foundation below sea level while others are raised on high bluffs and cliffs; but they are all alike disappearing, though necessarily at very different rates. One such mound, no. 266, situated on the bay shore north of San Pablo Creek, has been washed away within the last three or four years, the only signs of its former presence being certain fragments of worked stone and a few human bones that lie scattered over the muddy beach.

The suggestion that some of the deposits examined have their bases below sea level is of special significance and will be considered in detail later; it will be enough to state here that the subsidence appears to have affected the entire San Francisco Bay region, and that it is of such magnitude as to make it seem probable that a large number of mounds may have sunk entirely out of sight.

In addition to these natural forces, acting in the capacity of destroyers, there are to be taken into account several artificial agencies. Thus agriculture has been practiced more or less intensively in the region for over one hundred and twenty-five years; and, judging from reports as well as from conditions at the present time, it is not improbable that many of the mounds have been either plowed down or literally removed. In a number of cases where mounds have evidently disappeared in recent years, reliable information was not to be obtained. The majority of the country population, especially around the northern end of the Bay, are Portuguese ranchers, mostly of the first generation, who know little or nothing about the recent history of the region. A little experience made it evident that negative information was not to be implicitly relied upon. All the more suitable places, such as springs and streams and canyons, were visited; but very often mounds of comparatively large size were found by chance in what appeared to be most unnatural situations.

All the foregoing circumstances clearly confirm the opinion that the original number of shell heaps on the San Francisco Bay shores may have been much larger than the figure now given, and that indeed this figure may not even include all the deposits existing at the present time. As to the latter point, however, it is fairly certain that no mounds of any considerable size or special importance are left unnumbered.

Appearance, Size, and State of Preservation

To detect the presence of a shell heap, even if inconsiderable in size, is not as a rule a very difficult task. During the dry season, and especially after the crops have been removed or the natural vegetation has died down, a slightly bluish tinge, imparted by the mussel shells, distinguishes these places often at a considerable distance. So also, immediately after the first heavy rains, the mound material being unusually rich and vegetation quick to respond, the sites lie revealed here and there before the observer as richly green spots in the generally barren, dull-colored landscape. Another fact which drew attention to the deposits was a frequently accompanying growth of buckeyes (*Aesculus californica*). Indeed, after the relation once became apparent, the discovery of a group of these trees often became an irresistible argument for making long detours into parts otherwise judged unsuitable for mound sites. As a rule trees do not grow directly on the mounds, unless there happens to be a good deal of earth mixed up with the shell and ashes; and the presence of the buckeyes immediately about the deposits is somewhat of a puzzle. It is well known that the Indians of recent times prepared the large, bitter nuts of this tree for food. They are said, moreover, to have used its soft wood for making fire and to have believed in the medicinal virtues of its bark. There can be no doubt, therefore, that at least the latest of the shellmound people also used some of the products of this tree; but it is impossible to say whether they planted the trees about their camps or whether the sites were originally chosen because of the presence of the trees. The latter alternative seems hardly tenable however; and neither may be correct, as the trees in many instances (i.e., where they grow on top of the mounds), must have developed from seeds scattered perhaps accidentally at the time of the departure of the inhabitants.

Certain definite physical conditions, such as the presence of fresh water, timber, shelter from the wind, and easy access to the seashore, appear to have controlled the location of most of the camps; and the presence of these elements, singly or in combination, in turn yields valuable guidance. Fresh water was probably one of the first essentials, and it is often today a matter of superstitious conviction with the old settlers that "wherever you find an Indian mound, there you'll find water—if you look long enough." Generally the connection holds, but not invariably, and this partly by reason of the geological changes which have taken place in the region since the shellmounds were begun.

The size and form of the shell heaps, while often much altered by one cause or another, are still in most cases approximately determinable. For instance, if a mound has been partly hauled away, abundance of material made economy unnecessary, and the thinner peripheral portion is usually left undisturbed. Actual dimensions vary greatly. Thus the basal diameters range from thirty to six hundred feet, and the height runs from a few inches up to nearly thirty feet. Curiously enough, the famous mound referred to the San Francisco Bay region by Southall and De Roo, and probably the same that Marquis Nadaillac locates at San Pablo, was not found; and in spite of the fact that it is definitely described as measuring one mile by a half-mile across and as having a height of over twenty feet, it appears never to have existed. There are, however, three mounds of more than average size in the vicinity of the old Spanish town, and the circumstance that these lie within the area of half a square mile may possibly have given rise to the error.

The typical shell heap of the San Francisco Bay region is oval or oblong in outline, with smooth slopes, steepest of course on the short transverse diameter; and the longer axis is generally parallel to the shore line or stream to which the pile may be contiguous.

A remarkable fact about the accumulations is that though they are made up of comparatively loose material they do not appear to weather appreciably. This may be due partly to the resisting quality of the shells and partly also to the binding power of the broken fragments which, when laid down horizontally, may in some degree resemble loess in structure, and, like loess, cave less readily than ordinary soil. To illustrate this binding power may be cited the fact that it has been found safe and practicable to sink a vertical shaft, six feet square, through twenty-five feet of the material without the provision of a curbing. In one instance such a shaft was carried about twelve feet below sea level, but even the strong head of water failed to break down the walls. At the surface, the shell disintegrates somewhat, but probably more in consequence of vegetal processes than those of weathering. It would appear therefore that under perfectly natural conditions the configuration of the mounds would have remained perhaps almost unchanged for many decades, if not for centuries; and they might in that condition have told a valuable story. As it is, on account of recent artificial disturbances, it is generally uncertain precisely in what state the mounds were left. Nevertheless, a few of the larger and better preserved examples present roughly flattened tops and in two instances these surfaces are dotted with distinct saucer-like depressions, as of house pits.

The state of preservation of the mounds, just touched upon, is a matter of some consequence. It so happens that the majority of the larger accumulations lie precisely in the places since found suitable for habitation by the modern invaders, and therefore have to give way to the requirements of civilization. Towns are growing up in the principal valleys favored by the shellmound peoples; and in the canyons, as well as on the plains, ranch houses often cluster about, and not infrequently occupy the summits of these ancient dwelling sites. The accumulated refuse has also been found useful in many ways. For example, the composition will sometimes yield splendid crops of potatoes and other vegetables; and this fact, as it has become known, has generally led to reduction and cultivation of the mounds. In addition to this source of destruction, the material is removed to serve a variety of purposes, such as ballast for roads and sidewalks, as garden fertilizer, and even as chicken feed. It is said that the mound material, mixed with rock salt, produces tennis courts that for combined firmness and elasticity are unexcelled. The result is that while there is still ample opportunity for the investigator, not a single mound of any size is left in its absolutely pristine condition.

Many of the accumulations, as indicated on the map, have disappeared in recent years, leaving only the faint traces that lead to inquiries, and usually only to very general results. The artifacts from these obliterated deposits have as a rule been scattered broadcast among individual curio seekers; and even when found in more or less representative groups, there are no accompanying data. It is said that a good share of the archaeological material from the two large mounds formerly in the town of San Rafael found its way to the British Museum in London; but, according to the informant who claims to have culled the deposits for the one-time English consul at San Francisco, no detailed records went with it. From only two more of the destroyed sites is any collection known to be extant. The Golden Gate Park Museum of San Francisco obtained some years ago a small but quite complete culture exhibit from mound no. 276, at one time in the yards of the Standard Oil Company at Richmond; and only recently the city of Alameda collected a small group of implements from no. 316, a large shell heap formerly near the intersection of High Street and Santa Clara Avenue.

Exclusive of the results obtained in the systematic work carried on during the last six years by the University of California, there are only a few minor collections from mounds still partially intact. The Stanford University Museum is in possession of several pieces from no. 356, near Mayfield; the owner of no. 3, at Sausalito, shares with the public school of that place a collection of skulls and stone implements; and from no. 199, at Lakeville, a small exhibit has found its way to the Dime Museum in Petaluma. All of these collections, while taken from scattered sites, are numerically small and probably in no case fully representative of the given culture, and cannot therefore furnish an entirely safe basis for comparison and generalization. Enough is known to warrant the statement that a general similarity in culture obtains for the entire region; but the differences, if any, remain to be brought out clearly.

Situation with Respect to Shore Line and Sea Level

The shell heaps under consideration are situated in a great variety of places; but, on the whole, the positions may be characterized as convenient rather than in any sense strategic. Many of the largest mounds are located at the head of the sheltered coves, yet not a few deposits lie in thoroughly exposed places, out on the bluffs and higher headlands. Occasionally a hillside, with or without any accommodating shelf or hollow, has been chosen, doubtless on account of some small spring issuing in the vicinity. Good illustrations are furnished by no. 65, at Corte Madera, and no. 379, near South San Francisco. From San Rafael northward nearly every ravine and every gully appears to have offered attractions. But the great majority of the mounds are situated on or near the small streams, though with considerable indifference, it seems, as to whether the surrounding country is barren plain or timbered hills. Wherever a group of separate deposits line a stream it is usual to find the largest accumulations at the lower end of the series. Lastly, some mounds are found in apparently unnatural situations, such as on the plain where no streams pass, or out in the salt marsh where fresh water could not be had; and a few deposits are to be seen also on the small islands, both those immediately surrounded by marsh and those which are completely insulated by deep and swift currents.

Normally the shell heaps lie quite close to the open waters. The only general variation from this rule occurs on the north and northwest, where some of the deposits are situated four or five miles back from the present shore. But it seems legitimate to assume in explanation of this fact that at least the larger and older of the accumulations in this locality were begun, if not actually abandoned, before the building up of the now broad belt of reclaimable marsh, away from which they do not in any case extend very far. A more singular and striking exception occurs on the east, between Rodeo Creek and Carquinez Strait, where two neighboring mounds are situated comparatively far inland and at unusual elevations. Thus no. 254, directly east of the town of Rodeo, is nearly one and one-fourth miles back from the shore, at an approximate elevation of two hundred and twenty-five feet; and south of this mound, on Rodeo Creek, lies no. 259, which is over two miles inland and about one hundred and twenty-five feet above sea level. Both were extra large mounds and probably of relatively great age. The unusual situation of the two deposits mentioned above, while suggestive perhaps of a local rise, may after all be perfectly normal. The barren hills close to the shore offer little attraction, while back in the canyons, where the mounds lie, the laurel and the oak find existence possible on the shaded slopes, about the springs and along the wet-weather gullies. There is also the further argument against a recent upward movement, namely, that within two or three miles on either side of the elevated deposits several shell heaps of more than average dimensions are situated at sea level, with indications of having been lowered into their present position. Among these apparently lowered deposits may be specified no. 236, at the head of Glen Cove on Carquinez Strait, and no. 262, on the San Pablo Bay shores, southwest of Pinole. But, whatever may have taken place in this particular locality, there can be no doubt about the subsidence of the Bay region as a whole or concerning the fact that however ancient or slow this movement, the latter portion of it was witnessed by man.

As a natural consequence of favoring proximity to the open shore, the shell heaps tend to keep close to sea level. The fact is that nearly all the mounds lie within fifty feet of the surface of the Bay waters, and this may be termed the normal zone. But exceptions occur on either side of this zone; and these, because of their numerical scarcity, are perhaps all the more significant. We have already seen that two mounds lie very far above the normal zone, and there remains only to state that at least ten of the known deposits extend below sea level. Most of these sunken accumulations, it is true, occur in the central part of the region, about Berkeley and Richmond, and also on the opposite shore, near Tiburon; but good examples are not entirely wanting at either extremity. Thus to the north one large mound lies well out in the Petaluma Creek marsh, off Lakeville; while to the south there remains at least one small shell heap, scarcely noticeable any longer, out on the reclaimed flood lands on the north bank of the Coyote River; and there is evidence that two additional deposits once lay on the marshy shore near the south end of the Coyote Hills. Besides these ten or twelve partially submerged accumulations, there are also the scattered deposits previously mentioned as giving indication of having been lowered to their present position within reach of the waves.

The foundations upon which the submerged refuse heaps rest are generally of firm material, excluding the possibility of the accumulated weight of the mound having forced the mass below sea level. Several of these unique deposits lie on the alluvial slopes; but others, such as those on Brooks Island and at Tiburon, rest on older formations, even upon solid rock. Up to the present time only three of the ten submerged deposits have been carefully tested for depth, and these show a subsidence ranging from three to eighteen feet.

Geographical Distribution and Its Control

A glance at the map will show the relative frequency of the shell heaps along the Bay shore to vary somewhat locally. It is uncertain, of course, what the original geographical distribution may have been, on account of the disturbing factors, more or less active, all around the Bay. At the same time, it is hardly to be doubted that economy was in some sense a primitive trait, or that these rude savages had intelligence enough to take advantage of a combination of favorable circumstances. At any rate, judging from present conditions, the general scarcity of mounds at the extremities of the region under consideration does not seem inexplicable. The southern arm of San Francisco Bay cannot now be regarded as entirely suitable, even if mollusks were abundant; and there is no indication of any very recent change from a better to a worse condition. To be near the main source of animal food would often mean to be several miles distant from the foot-hills which yielded wood, acorns, berries and the like. And granted even that the alluvial slope was covered with live oak, which is not at all probable, the water supply close to the shore line would still be a very uncertain quantity during the dry season. Finally, to judge from the nature of the shell heaps now remaining about the southern end of the bay, mollusks then, as now, were not plentiful or were not easily obtained. Central on the Bay, however, and especially on the west side from San Mateo to Petaluma, the more or less wooded hills, charged with springs and streams, come in many places directly to the open water and here, consequently, as might be expected, the mounds are relatively numerous. On the east side, from Alameda to Carquinez Strait, the deposits are also at intervals quite well represented both as to number and size; and this fact can hardly escape relation to another fact, namely, the comparative narrowness or entire absence of the alluvial plain, which brings the small wooded canyons within easy reach of the shore. There is one exception to this generalization in the case of the mounds located on or near the Potrero Hills in the vicinity of Richmond; for here, at the present time at least, both water and wood are practically absent. It may be assumed, however, that recent changes have removed these necessities or else that an extraordinary abundance of shellfish was the compensating element.

Reasonable proof of the suggestion that the presence of shellfish was the first essential to a camp is furnished by the ocean shore. Conditions have been closely studied here for about two hundred miles adjacent to San Francisco Bay, that is, from Halfmoon Bay to the mouth of the Russian River; and the results are not without interest. Water and shelter are easily obtained and timber also is fairly abundant north of the Golden Gate; but the nature of the beach is either unfavorable for a molluscan fauna or is too steep and difficult of approach. Consequently, within the mapped limits, mounds are scarce except at the head of Halfmoon Bay, where shelter is good though timber is lacking. The few deposits indicated along the coast northward are often not even near any of the predisposing elements, but lie exposed on high barren rocks and sand dunes. But along the coast immediately to the north of the map, shell heaps, though usually small, are very numerous, particularly on Tomales and Bodega bays where all the favorable conditions obtain. . . .

COMPOSITION AND INTERNAL STRUCTURE

The San Francisco Bay shell heaps contain, besides molluscan remains, a large percentage of ashes and charcoal, together with varying quantities of broken rock and waterworn pebbles. Occasionally there seems also to have been added more or less of ordinary earth or dirt, until in some of the mounds—and usually those farthest from the shore—the shells become an almost negligible element. The presence of the pebbles in some of the deposits is difficult to explain, unless they were brought with the earth; and this seems not always to have been the case because the pebbles are often most abundant in the accumulations containing little but shell and ashes. Furthermore, it is to be observed that some of the mounds containing the pebbles are situated on the marsh and in other places near which pebbles are not now to be obtained.

The cracked and broken rocks, which were supposedly brought together chiefly for hearth and cooking stones, vary in kind locally, but foreign specimens are everywhere present and some of these must have been brought long distances.

The internal structure of the mounds has been studied with some minuteness in three places, and has besides been observed in several other widely separated localities where either natural or artificial agencies have exposed the interior to view. To speak of definite structure in a promiscuous mixture of more or less broken shell and other matter may be unwarrantable; nevertheless, bedding planes or lines of deposition are often made visible by sudden changes in the shell species or may be inferred from streaks of ashes running through the mass. In the Emeryville mound distinct strata are in fact produced by alternating depositions of raw and calcined shells. But this is an exceptional occurrence. The burnt shells and ashes, always most apparent in the upper levels of the deposits, occur usually in streaks and sometimes in large pockets, mixed with rock, as if marking individual fireplaces. It is a noteworthy fact, however, that, unlike the shell heaps in the Aleutian Islands, these show unmistakable evidences of the use of fire from the very beginning. Thus, while actual fireplaces are not readily detectable in the lower levels, charcoal is abundant at the bottoms of two thirty-foot mounds and has been brought up repeatedly from points twelve to eighteen feet below high tide level. In one of the mounds, however, a shade of doubt is cast on this point owing to the fact that the material at the bottom seems to have been disturbed or at any rate does not truly represent the center, that is, the oldest part of the accumulation.

In general, the vertical section of a mound begins at the top with a foot or two of somewhat finely disintegrated material; grows loose, coarse, and distinct in structure for some distance; and, finally, the lower end of the column becomes a compact and practically homogeneous mass in which nearly all the shells are crushed. At first, such a condition seems perfectly natural. But the rule does not hold in all cases. That the disintegration at the surface is the normal result of weathering and vegetal processes need not be doubted; but the finely broken shells of the lower half or two-thirds of the pile do not represent a clear case of disintegration. It is true that the lower levels of the mounds in question are made up largely of mussel shells, the bits of which are somewhat softened and fragile, though they still retain their luster; and it might be argued that the mere weight had crushed the mass and reduced it to its present consistency. However, there is a small admixture of clam and oyster shells, nearly always crushed to the same fineness as the mussels, but sometimes scattered about entirely unbroken. The clam and oyster fragments are still quite as firm as the shells of the present day; and if weight or disintegrating processes reduced some, why not all? Again, if the weight could crush the mussel shells in some of the mounds, why not in the rest? It would seem that the lower, compact portions of some of the mounds were laid down under different conditions from those on the top. In two mounds the line dividing the finer and the coarser depositions is very sharp and distinct, but whether it represents a long interval of time or corresponds to a change of inhabitants is made clear neither by the remains of the higher animals nor by the cultural evidences.

Molluscan Remains

Of the molluscan remains the "soft-shelled" clam, *Macoma nasuta,* and the "soft-shelled" mussel, *Mytilus edulis,* are common to all the mounds, and usually make up the bulk of the material. The only marked exception to this rule occurs in the mounds at Point Isabel, West Berkeley, Alameda, and San Mateo, where the oyster, *Ostrea lurida*—practically absent in the sites bordering the extremities of the bay—is found in great quantities. Other species such as the large "hard-shelled" clam, *Tapes staminea;* the long "hard-shelled" mussel, *Mytilus californianus;* the cockle, *Cardium corbis;* the abalone, *Haliotis rufescens,* and three small univalves, *Purpura crispata, Cerithidea californica,* and *Acmaea patina* are only sparsely represented. Of these, the two first-named univalves and the mussel may have had restricted habitats in the bay; while the clam, the cockle, and the abalone probably were brought from the ocean shore.

Some changes appear to have affected the species and their habitats in the bay since the shellmound people arrived. The native oyster, for example, no longer breeds in the Bay, except possibly off San Mateo; the "hard-shelled" mussel has been observed only on the ocean shore where the rough surf plays; and none of the univalves mentioned above have been noticed anywhere about the Bay. A particular species of clam, *Mya arenaria* Linn., observed only in one mound, central in the region, seems now to thrive wonderfully in most parts of the Bay. A new mussel, *Modiola* sp., is said to have been imported from the Atlantic Coast within historic times and samples of its shell have been found on the surface of one or two of the mounds. Oysters from the Atlantic Coast have been planted in the bay in recent times and these appear to thrive fully as well as any of the native mollusks, though at the present time all of them are threatened by crude petroleum which escapes in the form of waste from the various oil works on the bay shore.

Of all the mollusks represented in the shellmounds only the common clam and mussel seem to have persisted since the middens began to accumulate; and these are still found in sufficient quantities in the Bay to supply the markets of all the bordering cities. Certain mounds do nevertheless furnish indication of probable local changes in the preponderating species; and wherever these changes are marked, it is the mussel which is most abundant in the lower strata while the clam becomes suddenly quite excessive in the upper horizons. It is impossible to say whether these changes are due to biological or geological causes. Probably the rate of sedimentation has been a vital factor; in any case, the sinking of the region and the disappearance of rock-bound shores would have seriously affected the life of the mussel. It is interesting also in this connection to learn from the fishermen that the last twenty years have witnessed some very marked fluctuations both in the quantity and the habitat of the shellfish.

Following is a list of mollusks known to occur in the shellmounds:

Oyster, *Ostrea lurida*
Mussels, *Mytilus edulis* and *M. californianus*
Modiola, sp.
Soft-shelled clams, *Macoma nasuta* (and *M. edulis?*)
Myra arenaria
Hard-shelled clams, *Tapes staminea* and *T. tenerrima*
Cockle, *Cardium corbis*
Abalone, *Haliotis rufescens*
Purpura crispata and *P. caniculata*
Cerithidea californica
Olivella biplicata
Acmea patina

Standella, sp.
Land snails, *Helix,* two species

Vertebrate Fauna

While the indicated change in the preponderating shell species is of no particular cultural significance, it is otherwise with the remains of the vertebrates represented. There are no sharp changes from invertebrates to vertebrates and from fishes to mammals, such as Dall appeared to find in the Aleutian Island shell heaps. But progress is here. Mammalian bones seem to occur at all levels in some of the largest mounds; yet it is safe to say that more than 95 per cent, quantitatively measured, are confined to the upper six or eight feet. The doubt implied is again due to the uncertainty as to whether or not the excavations reached the oldest part of the mounds. But in any case, the occasional surprise or accidental capture in earliest times of big game, marine or terrestrial, counts little against the successful slaughter of a great variety of animals in later days.

Fishing may or may not have been an important industry. There happen to be very few fishbones in the mound material, although the grooved stones, usually held to have been net sinkers, occur at all levels in some of the deposits. It is of course possible that fish may have been cured for consumption elsewhere.

Bird bones, apparently of ducks and waders, are rather numerous, especially in the upper strata. Their presence suggests two things: first, that at least the latest mound people lived on the Bay shore during the winter time, when ducks were present; and, second, that these peoples possessed no domestic dog. The latter inference is based simply on the fact that no half savage, hungry dog would have left the bird bones in the condition in which they are often found.

The identified animal bones include the following species:

Deer, *Cervus,* sp.
Elk, *Cervus canadensis*
Sea otter, *Enhydra lutris*
Beaver, *Castor canadensis*
Squirrel, *Spermophilus,* sp.
Rabbit, *Lepus,* sp.
Gopher, *Thomomys talpoides*
Raccoon, *Procyon lotor*
Badger, *Taxidea,* sp.
Skunk, *Memphitis occidentalis*
Wildcat, *Lynx,* sp.
Bear, *Ursus,* sp.

Dog, *Canis familiaris* (?)
Seal, *Phoca*, sp.
Sea lion, *Zalophus californianus* (?)
Porpoise, *Phocaena communis*
Whale
Canvasback Duck, *Aythya vallisneria*
Goose (?)
Cormorant, *Phlaeocorax*, sp.
Waders, or some large birds
Turtle
Skates, Thornbacks, and other fish
Wolf, *Canis*, sp.

CULTURE AND HISTORY OF THE SHELLMOUND PEOPLE

Material Culture

The augmenting capacity of the shellmound people, implied in a measure by their more and more successful hunting, is made sufficiently evident by a study of the artifacts. As with the animal bones, while some of the preserved suggestions of industrial life occur from the bottom of the accumulations to the top, they are after all relatively abundant only in the upper levels. But this fact would of itself prove little did not the implements of later times also show much greater variety and specialization as well as perfected workmanship. Viewing the culture as presented in its entirety however, the change or progress is not perhaps so clear and marked as might have been expected. These people, rude as they may have been, from the start employed fire; used prepared vegetable foods; satisfied their hunting instinct; and fished, supposedly with seines—if they ever fished at all. They also used body paint and they buried their dead. In other words, they were from the beginning quite above the stage in which savage man may be supposed to have struggled for his mere existence alone. The later mound occupants may have brought, or, if they were direct descendants of the first inhabitants, may have originated activities along other fundamental lines; though the clear proof of such seems wanting. For instance, it is tolerably certain that skin-dressing and basketry were practiced in late times, but with our present knowledge it would be unsafe to say when these arts began or even that they did not arrive with the first appearance of the mound people. More evident seems the relatively recent development of certain luxurious habits and tastes such as are implied by the presence of pipes, musical devices, and decorative objects. Finally, it may be well to add that there appears to be no form of artifact found at the bottom of the accumulations that does not also occur near the top.

The culture as observed, were one to describe it in terms of the present system of archaeological classification, is neolithic. Some roughly chipped flint and chert flakes were indeed found in the lower horizons of one of the shell heaps, but these pieces may hardly be considered paleolithic in the true sense. As would be expected, only such effects as are made of bone and stone and shell have resisted disintegration, and these remnants include weapons, household utensils, working tools, ornaments, and possibly ceremonial objects. Such fundamental things as spear and arrow points, mortars and pestles, hammerstones, and roughly grooved sinkers occur at all levels in many of the deposits; but the shapely and sometimes highly polished bone awls, the graceful "charmstones," the delicately worked stone pipes, the bone whistles, the stone labrets, and certain shell beads and pendants, all appear to be confined to the upper horizons in at least some of the very largest mounds. The record, apparently so clear and simple, is nevertheless difficult to interpret with certainty, and even if it be accepted at face value, there still remains a legitimate doubt whether the cumulative nature of the culture is due to the natural development of a fixed population or is the result of substitution by conquest or migration.

CULTURE SEQUENCES IN CENTRAL CALIFORNIA ARCHAEOLOGY

by
Richard K. Beardsley

An analysis of the archaeology of two coastal areas of Central California gives strong support to the sequence of three culture periods proposed in 1939 for the prehistoric archaeology of the lower and middle Sacramento River Valley. For one area, the ocean coast of Marin County just north of San Francisco Bay, the first intensive excavations were made by archaeological field parties from the University of California during the summers of 1940 and 1941; the data and conclusions have not been published previously. For the second area, around the shores of San Francisco Bay, few additions have been made to the artifact collections and field data since the latest full site report was made in 1926. However, the interpretation presented here comes from reappraisal of the original artifacts and notes from the limited number of published sites, and from study of museum collections from a greater number of smaller sites which have not yet been described in print. The culture sequences revealed in the study of these two coastal areas agree closely with those outlined for the near-by Sacramento Valley, and present the coast of Central California in a new light. Further, these offer additional perspective on the archaeology of the interior region.

For many years, the fundamental theme of California archaeology was its lack of recognizable change. The most frequently cited examples of this cultural stagnation were the shellmounds around San Francisco Bay. These were first examined almost half a century ago for evidence of evolution in culture. Since artifacts of excellent workmanship frequently appeared in the lowest levels, it was properly insisted that no site showed convincing evidence of local cultural evolution. But the opinion that evolutionary change was unproven changed imperceptibly into the reiterated thesis that all cultural change was lacking. Not until new fields were entered was this dogma shaken. David Banks Rogers' volume on the archaeology of the Santa Barbara region, published in 1929, and Ronald L. Olson's preliminary report, which appeared the next year, concurred in the view that successive cultures occupied the mainland and offshore islands. The suggestion of

Pp. 1–21 of Richard K. Beardsley, "Culture Sequences in Central California Archaeology," *American Antiquity* (1948), 14:1–28.

culture change was echoed in the Stockton-Lodi area by W. Egbert Schenck and E. J. Dawson in their report on the northern San Joaquin Valley. It remained for summary reports of the intensive work done in close collaboration by the University of California and the Sacramento Junior College in the lower Sacramento Valley to substantiate, with detailed tabulations, the view that Central California prehistory had not been endlessly static and unchanging after all, but instead had several distinctly recognizable stages of development. Finally, culture changes defined by Waldo Wedel in his report on the extensive excavations conducted by the Smithsonian Institution under Civil Works Administration in the southern San Joaquin Valley gave greater body to the new outlook on California archaeology and left the coastal regions of Central and extreme Northern California as the only excavated areas in which cultural succession has been consistently denied.

For the present paper, consideration has been somewhat arbitrarily limited to the three excavated areas within about a one-hundred-mile radius of San Francisco Bay, collectively referred to as Central California (map 13). The problem apparent at the outset was whether it was true that clearly marked culture changes might occur in the inland zone of this region without recognizably affecting the coastal population. In the years that had passed since excavation of the San Francisco Bay mounds, techniques had progressed beyond the application of an unrefined stratigraphic principle, just as anthropological theory had outgrown the stage at which evolutionary development of culture in the classical sense was a primary concern. In the first place, as hints of culture sequence appeared, those who were digging in the Sacramento Valley sought small sites in order to isolate pure manifestations of each culture, as well as continuing to probe the problems of stratigraphy in large and complex sites. Of equal importance was the development of a sharper analytic technique which exploited the potentialities offered by the abundant burials of Central California middens. Each burial, with its associated artifacts and traits, was treated as a unit in stratigraphic analysis, in contrast to the former procedure of plotting the depth of each individual artifact without regard to its associations. Another methodological advance was the recognition of a class of burial artifacts in potteryless California which is able to serve the important function filled by ceramic analysis in other areas. Shell bead and ornament types supply such a class, combining frequent occurrence and comparability of form with relatively sensitive variation. These techniques of burial analysis were first applied to interior sites of the Sacramento Valley, and the reports, which are frankly presentations of burial complexes rather than of prehistoric cultures in the full sense, carry their evidence in terms of itemized burial tabulations. The same procedure has now proven successful as a method of working out the culture sequences of the coastal areas.

The principal periods, or culture horizons, thus outlined in the lower Sacramento Valley area were named Early, Transitional, and Late. The same scheme is used as the basic frame of the cultural sequences presented in this paper, but with the following changes and additions. The Transitional Horizon (or Period) is now called Middle Horizon, to avoid un-

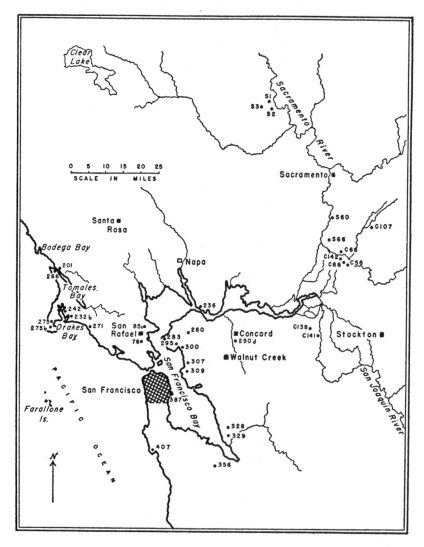

Map 13. Archaeological Sites in Central California.

warranted implications. Each horizon of the sequence is split into provinces, which are areas of cultural similarity that also show a certain geographic consistency. Because the provincial configurations differ in various time levels, separate province names have been used for each horizon. The cultural units in each province are called facies, and are groups of intimately related settlements or components (table 1).

TABLE 1

CULTURE SEQUENCES IN CENTRAL CALIFORNIA ARCHAEOLOGY

(Lower case names are components. Classificational terms are capitalized.)

		LITTORAL ZONE		INTERIOR VALLEY ZONE					
		MARIN PROVINCE	ALAMEDA PROVINCE	COSUMNES PROVINCE		COLUSA PROVINCE			
LATE HORIZON	PHASE 2	ESTERO FACIES — Estero A, McClure A, Cauley A, Toms Pt.	FERNANDEZ FACIES — Fernandez A, Newark #1 A	MOSHER FACIES — Mosher, Johnson, Goethe, Nicolaus #4, Nicolaus #5, Hotchkiss A, Hicks A		MILLER FACIES — Miller A, Howells Point A			
	PHASE 1	MENDOZA FACIES — Mendoza, Cauley A	EMERYVILLE FACIES — Emeryville A, Greenbrae B, Bayshore A, Ponce A, Maltby, Glen Cove	HOLLISTER FACIES — Hollister, Brazil A, Hotchkiss B, Hicks B		SANDHILL FACIES — Sandhill, Miller B			
		COASTAL PROVINCE		INTERIOR PROVINCE					
MIDDLE HORIZON		McLURE FACIES — McClure B, Estero B, Cauley B	ELLIS LANDING FACIES — Emeryville B, Greenbrae B, Bayshore B, Ponce B, Ellis Landing, Stege, Potrero, W. Berkeley, San Rafael B, Newark #1 B, Fernandez B?, Monument ?, Princeton	MORSE FACIES — Morse, Van Loben-Sels, McGilli-vray A, Calquhoun, Koontz, Hicks C	DETERDING FACIES — Deterding, Wamser	BRAZIL FACIES — Brazil B	NEED FACIES — Need, Vail	ORWOOD FACIES — Orwood #2	
EARLY HORIZON		(Unknown)		WINDMILLER FACIES	(Province Unnamed) — Windmiller C, Blossom, McGillivray B, Phelps				

The concept of a component, as the archaeological record of human occupancy of a single locality at a specific time, is borrowed without change from the Midwestern Taxonomic System; the components described in this paper are essentially full settlements or communities which have evidence of the various living activities together with the remains of the dead at the same spot. The term "facies" similarly corresponds to the "focus" of the Midwestern Taxonomic System and has been used instead to avoid the erroneous implication that the whole Midwestern system is duplicated here. Thus, the original sequence of culture horizons has been further divided into provinces, facies, and components to embrace the archaeology of the littoral zone as well as the interior zone of Central California.

TABLE 2

CENTRAL CALIFORNIA MORTUARY DATA USED IN MAKING PRESENT CULTURAL ANALYSIS

	Sacramento Valley* (13 sites)		San Francisco Bay** (13 sites)		Marin County (7 sites)	
	Bur.	Cremat.	Bur.	Cremat.	Bur.	Cremat.
Late Horizon	249	30	76	20	64	34
Middle Horizon	261	18	150	..	35	..
Early Horizon	197	..	(2)	..	..	..
Totals	707	48	228	20	99	34

* Total in this column is from Lillard, Heizer, and Fenenga, 1939. For various reasons many of their reported burials are not included.

** This column shows a selection from a potential total of more than 1,060 burials in the 13 sites considered. At Emeryville and Ellis Landing sites, 705 and 106 burials, respectively, were counted during excavation or while the mounds were being leveled by steam shovel. Only a part of these have any fuller record than the simple notation of their presence. The selection shown here was limited to burials having a definite record of accompanying artifacts, or having clear notation of their location relative to such burials.

Since, as noted above, burial information is of paramount importance to the problem of determining cultural relations in Central California, it is methodologically sound to treat mortuary data as a rough index of the quality of the sample from each area. . . .

It may be added that the burials here are distributed more evenly among the sites than on the coast, where some sites produced fewer than ten burials despite quite extensive excavations. As a general rule, moreover, a higher percentage of burials with artifacts is encountered in the interior than along the coast. Nonetheless, the sample from all three areas is large enough to make fairly reliable the definition of culture complexes presented here.

Legend:

| ■ Trait first appears in this horizon. | ▨ Trait persists in same form from earlier horizon. | ▨ Trait persists in same and in variant forms | or | ▨ Trait persists but in variant forms. | Width of column shows abundance between horizons. |

HISTORIC

LATE

MIDDLE

EARLY

Vegetal foods
Fishing
Hunting
Interest in stone
Interest in bone
Interest in shell
Extended burial
Flexed burial
Cremation
% Westerly orientation
Red ocher
Haliotis ornaments
Haliotis beads
Olivella beads
Stone beads
Clamshell beads
Percussion flaking
Pressure flaking
Points more than 5 gms.
Points less than 5 gms.
Charmstones
Quartz crystals
Stone pipes
Metates
Mortars
Bone awls
Baked clay objects

Culture Development in Central California (compiled jointly by R. F. Heizer, F. Fenenga, and R. K. Beardsley).
Note: The Sacramento Valley area is most accurately represented in the selection of traits shown; coastal areas are weakly represented or have somewhat different development of certain traits, and lack evidence for Early Horizon traits.

Of all these classificational divisions the most clear-cut is the cleavage between horizons. In other words, within this hundred-mile area temporal differences are sharper than changes from one area to another. There are, however, trait uniformities running from one end of the archaeological record to the other, though with variable emphases, as a glance at the accompanying chart of culture development will show. Firmly settled village residence and lack of agriculture are two obvious examples; also the use of charmstones, beads, and ornaments made from ocean shells; primary burial of the dead; and other traits. The evolutionary point of view may find comfort in an apparent development through increasing complexity of the seed-grinding complex and, more certainly, in the use of baked-clay objects in the Sacramento Valley. Many Early Horizon traits gradually become extinct in the Middle Horizon, while new traits are introduced which finally flower in the Late Horizon. Yet the cultural configurations of each horizon are essentially distinctive. The earlier term used for the Middle Horizon, namely, "Transitional Horizon," recognized the overlapping traits but underrated, or at least did not sharply delineate, the distinctive configurations.

Traits unique to each period will be mentioned below. At this point, however, an attempt may be made to characterize the distinctive flavor of each. In concrete terms, one can point to the predominating interest of the Early Horizon in stone materials, of the Middle Horizon in bone, and of the Late Horizon in shell. Working with the collections, however, one acquires a stronger sense of differences which can be described only impressionistically at this point. The Early Horizon burials are disposed in such rigorously predictable fashion and accompanied by such a surprising amount and variety of carefully made and ritually treated artifacts as to imply keen and personal concern with the ceremonialism of death. Unfortunately, we know relatively little of the other aspects of life. There is no doubt, however, that the people of the Middle Horizon took comparatively little account of the death of any but a few select individuals. Most burials have few or none of the array of grave goods which accompany a small honored number of their dead. Strife is emphasized by the number of Middle Horizon burials found with projectiles embedded in the bone or with other marks of violence. For the Late Horizon, we seem to discern still different orientations; domestic arts find more favor than before. The people of the Late Horizon lavish artistic care on mortars, pestles, and similar household implements, or improve their own beauty with personal ornaments of bone, feather, or shell. Impressive reserves of shell beads and ornaments, which served also as wealth in historic times, were buried with the dead or destroyed together with their ornate basketry in cremation fires. Thus, each horizon has its distinctive flavor and varying foci of interests as reflected particularly in burial customs.

THE NATURAL SETTING

In this paper the Interior Zone includes the middle and lower drainage of the Sacramento River. This river and the San Joaquin River run from opposite ends of the Great Central Valley of California and meet near San Francisco Bay in a confusion of deltaic tidal channels (map 13). The extremely flat, low-lying valleys of each merge at this point without perceptible topographic break. A network of meanders and sloughs made a reed marsh wilderness of the lower river reaches east of San Francisco Bay and left very little permanently dry ground, until recent drainage and flood control turned it into rich farmland. Farther up the Sacramento on either side lie great overflow basins which are still subject to periodic inundations. Although grassland and oak groves sheltered abundant animal life and provided lush plant harvests, Indian habitation was concentrated along the river banks, where natural levees or rare elevations provided flood-free locations for the villages of successive generations of Indians. The limited number of unflooded spots thus partly accounts for an abundance of stratified village remains.

The Interior and Littoral zones are separated by the much-dissected, steep-sided hills of the Coast Ranges, which, though habitable, form a real barrier except where the San Joaquin and Sacramento rivers join and flow westward through Carquinez Strait into San Francisco Bay. The topography of the Littoral Zone shows an abundance of rocky cliffs along the ocean front, broken by rare inlets where the ocean has invaded the mouths of a few short streams. A lone arm of land projects from the uniform coastline at Marin County and hooks southward to provide sheltered water in Drakes Bay. This arm is all but cut off from the mainland by a gash from the northwest known as Tomales Bay. Archaeological excavation of the Marin County coast has been confined to the triangle of land thus bounded by Tomales Bay, Drakes Bay, and the ocean, where sheltered waters and less rugged cliffs invited the Indians to seashore habitation (map 13).

The landlocked salt waters of San Francisco Bay intensified the attractions which brought settlement to the Marin County coast. Stretches of broad beach and shallow water alternating with rocky peninsulas reaching into the Bay permitted various types of fishing, waterfowl hunting, and shellfish collecting, while hills that surrounded the Bay furnished grasses and oak groves for plant food. The quiet waters of the Bay were easily crossed on the double-ended reed balsas used by the Costanoan Indians of historic times. It might be thought that communication with the Indians of the Sacramento and San Joaquin rivers by means of these same balsas via the Carquinez Strait gap in the Coast Ranges would be easier than liaison across the rough encircling hills with Indians of the coast. But the archaeological remains suggest strongly that a common littoral economy gave more binding ties along the coast than between the Bay and the interior, although the physiographic boundaries were not sharp enough to isolate any of the three areas from the others.

Climatic conditions reinforce this division with surprising sharpness. Though the famed climate of California is shared by both the Littoral and Interior zones, which have warm dry summers and cool rainy winters, with temperatures consistently above freezing, the Sacramento Valley has less moisture and much more extreme fluctuations of temperature. On the coast only 7 degrees difference exists between the hottest and coldest average monthly temperatures. This results principally from the prevailing summer fogs, which keep the coastal summer temperatures from 30 to 40 degrees below averages for the interior valley. The unbroken barrier of hills, by blocking sea winds, preserves these inequalities in climate.

THE EARLY HORIZON: WINDMILLER FACIES

Four sites in the Mokelumne River region of the lower Sacramento Valley, yielding almost 200 burials, give us our knowledge of the Early Horizon. A complete report on the Early Horizon by Robert F. Heizer is in preparation.[1] Since in the present paper our interest is focused on the cultural manifestations shared by coast and interior, and the Early Horizon is not yet certainly located in the Littoral Zone, only a very brief summary of this extremely interesting period need be given to indicate the possible coastal relations.

The physiographic situation and site conditions alone suggest very considerable antiquity. The sites are on subsurface clay knolls which barely protrude through silts accumulated on the flat valley floor; the deposit mass is extremely indurated; stones and bones alike are incrusted with mineral deposit; and chemical alteration of the bone has occurred. Absolute age of this period is entirely conjectural, but Heizer's considered estimate is between 4,000 and 5,000 years. Relative position in the sequence is securely fixed at the type site, the Windmiller site, where the Early Horizon component is the basal member of an Early, Middle, Late stratigraphic se-

---

[1] Since published: R. F. Heizer, *The Archaeology of Central California I: The Early Horizon,* Univ. Calif. Publ. Anthro. Rec., 12:1 (1949).

quence. This and the McGillivray component may be burial knolls more than true settlements, since little occupational refuse was found in excavation.

Most knowledge of the Windmiller Facies comes from burials, 70 per cent of which are associated with artifacts. Excellently preserved skeletons show a large-boned, rugged population with long, high heads and broad noses. Most striking among cultural traits is the burial position and orientation. Over 90 per cent are buried face down in extended position, arms at the sides and legs together as though tied, the head oriented strictly to the west. Associated artifacts are outstanding for their variety as much as for their careful workmanship. Most commonly represented classes are *Olivella* and *Haliotis* shell beads, large flaked projectile points, and clear quartz crystals. Although utilitarian items are scarce in burial association or deposit, the materials in hand suggest that hunting received more emphasis than fishing or the gathering of roots and seeds. Small, light projectile points are rare or absent; the commonest large forms have slanting shoulders and straight or contracting stems. Curved bone hooks, straight "gorge" hooks, and fish spears with trident points were used in fishing; weighted nets may have been used, if a few miniature, biconoid, baked-clay objects, among other artifacts, are correctly interpreted as net sinkers.

The scarce bone tools include no slim-pointed awls characteristically associated with the manufacture of coiled basketry. Coiled basketry is presumed absent for lack of evidence, but twined basketry impressions are found on several of the limited number of hand-molded, baked-clay objects. One or a few specimens each is known of bone splinter awls, cylindrically eyed needles, flat-shafted thatching needles, blunt-ended split bone implements, and bird-bone tubes. Characteristic Middle Horizon implement types are foreshadowed in long, spatulate forms with rounded or concave ends, certain ones of which are described as sweat scrapers.

Ceremonial implements are numerous and varied. Human bone is utilized to make a skull "cup," a fibula dagger, and a radius whistle. Charmstones, the polished plummet-like stone objects of uncertain use famous in California archaeology, are commonly found with Early Horizon burials, in several unusual or unique forms. They are made from ornamental materials such as alabaster, mottled granite, and blue schist, in flattened or cylindrical forms tapering to either end from a central bulge. On occasion shell beads are affixed with asphaltum to one flattened face. Early Horizon charmstones almost invariably have a biconically drilled suspension hole near one end. Almost one-quarter of the burials have whole or fragmentary quartz crystals, sometimes in large numbers. A few short tubular stone pipes are known, but none shows evidence of having been smoked.

The shell beads which help to define the Early Horizon include a large, rectangular *Olivella* bead with ground surfaces; a small, rectangular *Haliotis* bead perforated once or twice; and a small, whole *Olivella* bead. Beads occur at the neck or are scattered as though used as sequins, and are also asphalted on various objects such as charmstones or shell ornaments. Distinctive *Haliotis* ornament types include a disk with one or two central perforations (sometimes used as facings on wooden earplugs, the holes plugged with asphaltum) and a concave-sided rectangular form. The only decoration of shell ornaments is made by radially incised lines near the edges.

Powdered red ocher, found with about 10 per cent of the burials, may have been ground on palettes. The one example known is of ocher-coated sandstone and is strongly reminiscent of Hohokam palettes of slate with rectangular outline and rectangular central basin. Special ornamental features of the Middle Horizon are foreshadowed by ornaments of biotite mica, perforated ground slate pendants, and slender obsidian cores which may have been tinklers or bangles, as well as by the ocher scattered in the burial fill.

No components comparable to the Windmiller Facies have yet been identified in sites of the Littoral Zone, yet specific trait resemblances to the Windmiller Facies have sporadically appeared. These include prone, extended burials at or near the base of the Ponce B (N356), Newark #1 B (N328), and Ellis Landing (N295) sites; [rectangular] *Haliotis* beads in the Emeryville (N309) and West Berkeley (N307) sites; and *Haliotis* disk ornaments with twin central perforations at the West Berkeley site. When we turn to the Interior Valley Zone, we find there centrally perforated shell ornaments whose central perforations apparently were considered useless and were plugged with asphaltum. The postulation that these ornaments were traded ready-made from the coast presupposes a shellworking population in or near the Littoral Zone contemporaneous with and trading to the Windmiller Facies. The coast combines land and sea food resources which might well have attracted settlement by an ancient hunting-gathering culture. But components as ancient as Early Horizon might be rare or unusually difficult to find because of subsequent shore erosion and subsidence or burial beneath deep deposits of later periods. It is just such rare remains, however, which have the best chance of surviving the destruction of sites that has accompanied industrialization of the San Francisco Bay area. Even Middle Horizon coastal deposits have been found to extend below present ground and water level; antecedent Early Horizon components underlying these may still lie undisturbed for ultimate discovery and excavation.

MIDDLE HORIZON: INTERIOR AND COASTAL PROVINCES

There is no doubt that Central California was well populated during the Middle Horizon. Sites are plentiful in the interior and, on the coast, are at least as numerous as Late Horizon components. Broad cultural similarities link all components of the horizon, but the Coastal Province is clearly distinguishable from the Interior Province by various trait differences, not least of which is reliance on different food sources. Components on the ocean coast and bay shores are generally shellmounds, whereas those of the interior have only random fragments of river mussel shell scattered through the deposit of camp refuse.

Interior Province components are divided into five facies in recognition of the differences among more than twenty components excavated in the low-lying river delta and in higher ground along stream courses to the north and east. These are the Morse, Deterding, Brazil, Need, and Orwood B Facies, of which the Morse Facies is best represented. The two facies of the Coastal Province are Ellis Landing, with twelve components around the shores of San Francisco Bay and on the ocean coast south of the Golden Gate, and McClure, with three sites on Drakes Bay and Tomales Bay north of the San Francisco Bay entrance. (See table 1.)

The refuse accumulations of Interior Province components are tough and indurated, though by no means compacted and solidified by calcareous cementation to the extreme degree of Early Horizon components. These settlements differ from Early components also in the fact that each site was intensively occupied, as shown by the abundance of fire-cracked stones, fish, bird, and animal bones, and the ash and charcoal which contribute a perceptibly "greasy" texture to the soil of the deposits. Depth of deposit varies from 48 to over 100 inches. Occasional stream alluviation, however, contributed nonoccupational deposition to the deepest of these sites (S99, Deterding Component). Although, in the Coastal Province, field observations of Ellis Landing Facies deposits are not consistent, more compact deposit and more complete maceration of shell than in Late components is noted for the type site at least. McClure Facies components also have compact deposit, in which shell is relatively sparse and finely ground. Ample evidence of regular habitation, nonetheless, is present in the form of burned stones, bones, ash, and the like. Depth of deposit in Coastal Province components has the surprising range of 2 to 24 feet. Much of this variation undoubtedly is due to more permanent habitation, greater percentage of thick-shelled mollusks in the diet of certain localities, or similar factors having no invariable relation to length of occupation. It is quite patent that depth of accumulated deposit alone cannot serve as a simple yardstick to measure the relative age of any of the Central California archaeological sites, because of the importance of factors unrelated to time lapse.

Limited measurements of crania from Middle Horizon components in the Interior Province show relationship to the physical type of the Early Horizon. A departure from the long and high-headed, broad-nosed standard of the Early Horizon in the direction of the Late Horizon is indicated, however. It remains for future skeletal analysis to demonstrate how accurate is this apparent distinction, and whether it was gradual mixture or actual population replacement that produced the changes suggested slightly in Middle Horizon, more strongly in Late Horizon. Crania identifiable with the Ellis Landing Facies of the Coastal Province are consistently mesocephalic, and may represent a different genetic group from that of the Interior Province, where the range of metrical variation is greater. Crania of the McClure Facies are not completely studied so that no statement on these is possible at present.

Burial customs of the Interior Province are much different from those of Early Horizon. Extremely tight flexure of primary burials is most characteristic, although semiflexure and extension, both prone as in Early Horizon and supine, are present. Loose flexure, resembling a relaxed sleeping posture, is more common in all components of the Coastal Province. In both provinces disposition may be on either side, back, or front; orientation is almost as variable, but a modal tendency is exhibited toward orientation in the western or southern quarters of the compass or, on the coast, toward the nearest body of water. Group burials and contorted burials are known especially from the Coastal Province. The Interior Province of the Middle Horizon is distinguished by the introduction of cremation. Although cremation became more popular and spread throughout the Central California area in Late Horizon times, it remained a relatively minor practice restricted to components of the interior throughout the Middle Horizon.

With virtually every one of the few (18) cremations, artifacts of some sort are included, whereas less than half of the burials of the Interior Province have any grave goods. The same restriction is true of burials from the Ellis Landing Facies of the Coastal Province. Although up to 70 per cent of the McClure Facies burials are accompanied by some form of grave goods, this frequently consists of no more than red ocher, an abundance of cut or unworked animal bones, or a few shell beads. These same items are the ones most frequently found with all burials of the horizon. When other artifacts do occur, they are frequently numerous and highly varied. In other words, considering only the uncremated burials, all settlements of the Middle Horizon strongly tend to distinguish a few select individuals

by loading them with grave furniture and mortuary ornament, a necro-
logic practice that may reflect social privileges among the living.

From the viewpoint of archaeological classification, Middle Horizon
traits known from burials or from the mound mass can be most conveniently divided into categories such as: traits unique to either province or
to facies within a province; traits common to both provinces but limited
to the Middle Horizon; traits shared with the Early or Late Horizon or
both. Each of these categories would comprise a group of traits of significant
size. However, in order to furnish a coherent picture of the life patterns
of the Middle Horizon, its traits will be described instead as they throw
light on the economic and social, ornamental, and ceremonial aspects of
life. The attempt will be made in the course of this account to point out
features relevant to the problems of classification.

Mortars and pestles are much more common than in the Early Horizon,
though not abundant. The prominence of vegetal ash and charcoal in the
midden deposits confirms the suggestion offered by the mortars that seeds,
nuts, and other plant foods were more important to Middle Horizon than
to Early Horizon diet. Pestles with polished chisel-shaped points, combined with rarity of large stone mortars in the stone-poor areas of the Interior Province, suggest the use of wooden mortars. Large stone mortars
with round-pecked base and sides or with unshaped exterior are most
common in the Ellis Landing Facies components, where they are upended
over the heads or feet of burials. These also occur in the McClure Facies.
Flat grinding slabs and grinding stones are known also from the Interior
Province and from the Ellis Landing Facies of the coast. Miniature mortars,
for use in grinding pigments or for macerating small rodents or birds, link
the facies of both provinces.

Numerous hammerstones occur in Coastal Province components. These
tend to be globular in the Ellis Landing Facies, ovate in the McClure
Facies. Hammerstones with a pit in one or both faces, which may be anvils
for acorn cracking, occasionally occur, especially in ocean shore locations.
A series of crude picks and blunt choppers made of cryptocrystalline rocks
comes from the McClure Facies.

Projectile points are related to those of the Early Horizon in size, since
only a very few weigh less than 5 grams. Middle Horizon point makers,
however, use obsidian more regularly, with minor percentages of chert,
slate, and other materials, and tend to prefer stemless or even hollow-based
points. Diagonal ripple-flaking on long blades is a special mark of the
Interior Province, which also displays a larger variety of well-defined
shapes; simple willow-leaf or laurel-leaf shapes characterize the Coastal
Province. A broad, single-shouldered point may represent a special McClure
Facies knife form. Small projectile points definitely made for arrows are

absent, or at least not typical of the horizon as now known, although a series with long barbs is reported in association with Middle Horizon traits from two little-explored Sacramento Valley sites. Use of the hand spear or casting lance is strongly indicated for Middle Horizon patterns of warfare, as well as for hunting, by the numerous blades or large points embedded in crania or body skeletons of burials, and many more in presumably lethal position within the body cavity. Although burials without skulls, as evidence of head taking, occur in the Early and Late Horizons as well as in the Middle Horizon, the high percentage of indisputably violent deaths indicated by embedded projectile points seems distinctive of the Middle Horizon at present accounting.

Fishing techniques are understandably more abundant in Coastal Province components, where the most common artifacts are notched or grooved stones which probably served as sinkers on nets. That these are much more common in certain coast components than in others is unexplained, unless net fishing might have been more appropriate in those localities. Both line fishing and spear fishing probably were known in the Coastal Province, but were less favored, since only a few straight bipointed gorges and unilaterally barbed bone fish spear points for use in compound arrangement are known. Identical compound fish spear points and similar bipointed bones for gorges occur in greater numbers in Interior Province components, which, conversely, lack stone sinkers except for a single find of three very large grooved stones at Miller B (Site S1). Rectangular bone "mesh gauges" are known from both provinces and suggest use of nets. Clam baking with hot stones and seaweed is suggested by basins of baked earth found singly in this Ellis Landing Facies and in united clusters in the McClure B Component.

The abundance of sharp bone awls, in the face of their near absence during the Early Horizon, implies that coiled basketry either may have been introduced or first became well developed in the Middle Horizon. The awls characteristically have cleanly trimmed butts. Bone and antler implements of various shapes and uses become numerous: perforated needles, flat thatching needles, flakers, fleshers, knives, wedges, and deer scapulae with notched or scalloped blades.

Typical of the Middle Horizon are confusing assortments of bone and antler objects of ornamental, ceremonial, or conjectural use, of which each component produces new types as well as previously known ones. A small, bead-like antler tip, bullet shaped and notched transversely near the squared end, links the Ellis Landing Facies with the Interior Province. Socketed antler tools which may be knife handles form a similar link. Various facies exhibit elongate triangular spatulae of antler. Limited to Coastal Province components, however, are long, pointed, spatulate bone implements sometimes occurring in large numbers near the head of a burial. Some of these have fork-tined bases and may have been head scratchers; others have a ring at the base made by hollowing out the epiphysis of a split cannon bone; most, however, have rounded bases and only wrapping stains on the shaft to suggest a parallel to the feather-tufted hairpins of ethnographic times. The closest parallel from the Interior Province to the few perforated examples of these pointed bones are long pendants, incised and perforated with two holes near the nonpointed end. Undecorated bird-bone beads and tubes, and grooved or perforated animal teeth are generally prevalent. Unique antler adzes and three small marked dice of bone are known from the Interior Province.

Ornamental artifacts, especially shell-bead and ornament forms, furnish the most unequivocal identification of Middle Horizon interments, as they do likewise of Early and Late Horizons. Small and large *Olivella* shell beads of saucer, elongate-saucer ("saddle"), and rounded rectangular shapes; circular or rounded rectangular beads of *Haliotis* shell are diagnostic. These occur as strings or sequins scattered over the burial. Large whole *Olivella* shell beads carry over from the Early Horizon (where small beads are far more usual) and survive into the Late Horizon. Distinctive *Haliotis* ornaments are circular with twin central perforations or with a large central orifice ("ring" shape). These may have radial incisions, as in the Early Horizon, or, most commonly, scalloped or notched rims. Concentric incised grooves mark the faces of some disk ornaments. Roughly rectangular and triangular forms, which are not distinctive, also occur. Changing trade relations may account for the Middle Horizon switch to a high percentage of green-backed *Haliotis* (*H. cracherodii*). This species is absent in Early and Late Horizons, at least in the Interior Zone, whereas it comprises one-half and one-third, respectively, of the specimens from the Interior and Coastal Provinces of the Middle Horizon.

Although the Coastal Province equals or surpasses the Interior Province in number, though not variety, of bone implements, there is no question of its inferiority in shell ornaments. Only the Emeryville Component (Site N309), largest of the San Francisco Bay settlements, compares favorably with any Interior Province community in number or variety of ornaments. Particularly common from this component is the coastal trait of beads ornamentally affixed with asphaltum mastic on shell and stone ornaments, mortars, and other objects.

Ring-shaped ornaments and elongate, spatula-like, perforated ornaments of slate are more numerous in the Interior Province, though known also on the coast. Small, round-edged, steatite beads are limited to the Interior Province, which also utilizes steatite for spool-type earplugs; the latter, when found in coastal components, are generally of sandstone, available in the vicinity. Most distinctive of the Coastal Province, on the other hand, are roughly pentagonal ornaments of perforated mica and the prismatic obsidian splinters known as tinklers. Only one occurrence of the former is noted in the Interior Province. The tinklers are absent from the Interior Province during the Middle Horizon, although they occur in the same area in both Early and Late Horizons. On the coast, tinklers are found sometimes in large numbers near the skulls of burials. A related form, thoroughly retouched (to eliminate the dull surface produced by burning?), is noted in one ceremonial burial of the McClure Component, in which over 100 were grouped with some 60 of the problematical spatulate bone implements described above, quantities of red-ocher and mica ornaments, eccentric forms of chipped obsidian, and shell beads. Ocher is most abundant in Coastal Province graves, but is noted in "beds" under Interior Province burials as well; its presence in graves becomes much rarer after the Middle Horizon.

Charmstones continue as ceremonial objects in the Interior Province, where the so-called "fishtail" form, a plummet shape with one terminus flattened, is distinctive. On the coast, however, most are found in the deposits without association and many are badly scarred or battered, as though put to rough practical uses. Lack of clear associations makes difficult the isolation of forms unique to the horizon, although a pyriform shape with short stem is of common occurrence. The position of a single phallic charmstone from the Ellis Landing site on San Francisco Bay is somewhat questionable; it was found without association near the upper limit of a Middle Horizon deposit, and may more properly be grouped with phallic charmstones from the coastal components of the Late Horizon.

Ceremonial traits of the two Middle Horizon provinces frequently do not coincide. Shared traits include cup-shaped stone pipes or pipe-bowl inserts, bird-bone (occasionally terrestrial mammal-bone) tubular whistles, and unworked animal bones or teeth plentifully scattered through the burial fill. Polished, elongated, bird-bone tubes may have been used as drinking tubes or by shamans as sucking tubes. From Interior Province components are noted cracked quartz crystals and whole quartz crystals; cobblestone platforms laid below or above burials; red-ocher painting of small boulders, shell ornaments, or parts of the corpse; intentional breakage of various articles of grave furniture; and ceremonial burials of animals. These traits are very rare or lacking in coastal components. Various Coastal Province traits mentioned above, such as the variety of spatulate bone implements (especially the forked "head scratcher"), retouched obsidian prismatic splinters, or quartz crystals and stone rings bearing asphalted appliqué of shell beads, may possibly have been part of the ceremonial dress or equipment. Most notable, however, are human figurines of baked clay unique to Coastal Province components, where baked clay in any other form is almost completely lacking.

Baked clay in ball shapes, sometimes with grass or fiber impressions, definitely increases in use during the Middle Horizon in the Interior Province, where the balls appear to have been substituted for stones for basket boiling and similar uses in the stone-poor delta land. More elaborate examples occur in spool and discoidal shapes. Only fragmentary lumps and balls are known from the coast, although there are occasional bits of clay which apparently were used for wall or smoke-hole chinking or perhaps as plaster on stick and grass house coverings.

The above summary shows that traits of all phases of Middle Horizon culture have frequent parallels on both sides of the Coast Ranges. Altogether, the Interior Province is somewhat richer in number of artifact types and the artifacts are better made or more frequently ornamented than those of the Coastal Province. The Coastal Province is not, however, simply a paler reflection of a dominant interior area, but has a consequential body of distinctive traits of its own. It is interesting to note that a few Early traits which disappear from the interior during the Middle Horizon but reappear in the Late Horizon, are present on the coast during the intervening time. These include the use of burned obsidian prisms as tinklers, attachment of beads to ornaments or other objects with asphaltum, and possibly phallic charmstones.

It should be emphasized that the Middle and Late Horizon components near San Francisco Bay have been defined by reanalysis of published reports and field data, and not by any recent excavations undertaken with this problem in view. The method of analysis, which emphasizes burial associations, has been briefly described above. It has not been possible to correlate the analysis based upon burial typology with stratigraphic levels in the San Francisco Bay mounds. Most field notes have no observations on stratification and one report denies any significance to the layers of shell in the mounds. This has perhaps been some handicap to the analysis of the few sites in which clear stratification is present. On the other hand, comparison of stratification and burials by inch levels in the Marin County coast sites having both Middle and Late components shows that Middle Horizon burials, as defined typologically, occur at slightly higher levels than the most obvious stratigraphic break in deposit. This phenomenon remains unexplained, but indicates that a clean correspondence is not to be anticipated between typological groupings and stratigraphic divisions.

For this and other reasons, it has been necessary to use double caution in dealing with all artifacts except those in burial association. When plotted by depth, however, the typological groupings of burials do show unmistakably the break between horizons.

A check of this burial-depth grouping from published reports is at present possible only in the case of the Emeryville site (N309). This shellmound was situated at the mouth of Temescal Creek on the east shore of San Francisco Bay. Its precise shape before the top was scraped level for a dance pavilion is unknown; maximum depth from this artificial surface was 32 feet, greatest of any known site in the Bay area. The sides sloped steeply to make a truncated conical profile. Max Uhle excavated a broad trench on the west side and pushed a tunnel toward the center, finding ten burials. W. Egbert Schenck and others salvaged what they could when the mound was leveled in 1924, recording 651 burials seen or recovered, then obtaining 34 more burials from trenches they dug in the deposit remaining below the modern ground surface. Of these nearly 700 burials, only 83 have records of associated grave goods.

Forty-eight of the 83 burials may be used to determine the components represented in the site. All have depth data and one or more link traits are in each case specifically mentioned (4 by Uhle, 44 by Schenck). The remaining burials cannot be used because of lack of depth data or of diagnostic artifact affiliation, but they do not in any way contradict the indications of the selected 48.

The schematic site profile, on which burial locations are superimposed, shows the apparent line of cleavage, running from about 10 feet deep near the northwest side to about 14 feet near the southeast section of the mound. The two components represented belong with the Ellis Landing Facies of the Middle Horizon (below the line of cleavage; 31 burials) and the Emeryville Facies of the Late Horizon (above the line of cleavage; 17 burials). Comparison of the artifacts known to have been found with these burials and the trait lists given in the present paper indicates that the most complete consistency appears in the frequently recurrent shell bead and ornament types.

Some attempt at estimating the antiquity of San Francisco Bay shellmounds has been made in the past. With the identification of their lower components as Middle Horizon settlements, these dates may be taken as estimates of the antiquity of the Middle Horizon. N. C. Nelson and E. W. Gifford, in independent studies of shellmound contents, made total mass a measure of total age. They computed the daily accumulation of deposit per individual and multiplied that figure by the estimated number of inhabitants. Nelson's estimate was made in terms of volume, for Ellis Landing; and Gifford's, in terms of weight for such a site as Emeryville. The two estimates harmonize with each other and with the more recent work of S. F. Cook, who brings a physiologist's point of view to the question of daily dietary intake of shellfish for the average Bay mound resident. All three, when considering the total age of such a deposit as the Emeryville site, arrive at estimates which overlap at about the 4,000 year mark.

In 1946, the discovery of burials at the base of a swimming pool excavation north of the town of Walnut Creek, 10 miles inland from San Francisco Bay, was reported to the University of California. Investigation of the report showed that indurated midden deposit lay buried 4 feet beneath the sterile estuarine (?) sediments of the valley floor. A field party from the university under the direction of R. F. Heizer succeeded in recovering ten burials, of which three were accompanied by artifacts of Middle Horizon affiliation. A report on the finds at this locality, which bears the name Monument site, is in preparation.[2] The subsurface location of this and three similarly buried midden deposits discovered subsequently within a 5-mile radius was of extreme interest, and led to pedologic examination of the soil overlying the sites. The preliminary report gives an estimated period of 4,000 to 8,000 years as indispensable to the development of a mature ("Tierra") profile in the sterile sediments.

Quite different approaches thus coincide in estimating separate Middle Horizon components to be somewhere around 4,000 years old. If one inclines toward accepting minimal dating of American cultures, this figure seems to exceed what would be expected in relation to other areas. But the common figure offered by these dating methods is not to be lightly brushed aside. While they are only estimated dates, presented tentatively, they point the way to a possibly fruitful approach toward chronological ordering of the older sites.

LATE HORIZON: COLUSA, COSUMNES, ALAMEDA, AND MARIN PROVINCES

Population changes in Central California seem, in the main, to have ceased by the opening of the Late Horizon. In major respects the culture of the Indians inhabiting the coast and interior in ethnographic times runs in full continuity from the earliest phase of this latest period. But even within the Late Horizon no claim of a static and changeless culture can be made. Instead of two provinces, four are distinguishable, each with two sequential facies. The Colusa Province, represented by the Sandhill Facies followed by the Miller Facies, occupies the Sacramento Valley north of the town of Knight's Landing. The Cosumnes Province, with the Hollister followed by the Mosher Facies, stretches through the delta region southward from the city of Sacramento. The Alameda Province, with the Emeryville followed by the Fernandez Facies, encompasses San Francisco Bay. The

---

[2] Since published: R. F. Heizer, *Archaeology of CCo–137, the "Concord Man" Site*, Repts. UCAS, No. 9, Paper No. 7 (1950).

Marin County coast to the north has the Mendoza followed by the Estero Facies. (See table 1.)

The earlier facies in all four provinces are linked together as Phase 1 of the Late Horizon, which is entirely prehistoric. The later facies, which constitute Phase 2 of the Late Horizon, are of protohistoric date and include contact materials dating to 1595 on the Marin County coast. The full historic period following this, marked by association of trade beads, iron objects, shovel-dug graves, bottle-glass arrow points, and the like, has sometimes been called Phase 3. In the classification used in this paper it is not segregated from the facies of Phase 2 because the Indian elements of culture were not greatly altered before their eventual disappearance.

Interior sites are uniformly located along stream banks or overflow areas and have very slight or no trace of lime cementing of the deposits. Ash, charcoal, and bone fragments are abundant in the black "greasy" soil of the Interior Zone middens. Shell is mixed in large fragments with blackish soil in the Coastal Zone shellmounds. Most coastal settlements overlie Middle Horizon components at stream mouths or in sheltered coves. Many sites in both zones have only thin deposits, but certain ones extend to depths of 12 feet or more, not only along the coast where the shells pile up rapidly but also in the interior where ashy dirt is the principal element.

Mesocephaly perseveres without definable change in Alameda Province according to measurements available at present. In Cosumnes Province, however, a change toward brachycephaly appears to be a continuation of trends observed in Middle Horizon skeletal materials. Studies now in progress on Marin coast crania and Sacramento Valley skeletons should throw welcome light on some of the problems of archaeological and ethnic relationships.

A good many traits are close parallels to those of Middle Horizon: flexed primary burial, bone basketry awls, bone whistles, bipointed gorges, simple shapes and radial incision of shell ornaments, whole *Olivella* shell beads, and occasional large stone projectile points. Cosumnes Province, in particular, carries over cremation, baked-clay objects, animal burials, perforated stone discoidals, chisel-pointed pestles, and possibly cylindrical earplugs, as well as the trait of "killing" objects included in burials. Certain traits, indeed, go clear back to the Early Horizon, though with variations: awls, gorges, radial incision of *Haliotis* ornaments, whole *Olivella* beads, large points, and "killed" grave goods.

It may be seen from the greater number of provinces that areal differentiation is more evident in the Late Horizon than during former periods. However, from the beginning of Late Horizon times certain important changes link together all of the provinces. Small obsidian arrow points, weighing less than 5 grams, appear for the first time and abound in most components. These are triangular, stemmed, and often serrated. Mortars become numerous and large. Long, tubular, steatite pipes appear. Increased use of shell ornaments is coupled with greater variety of decoration; and it is new types of shell beads again, with associated ornamental traits, that particularly distinguish the phases of the horizon.

LATE HORIZON: PHASE 1

Burial position and orientation in the two coastal provinces carry over without notable change from the Middle Horizon, except that semiflexure is rare and semiextension is apparently absent. Cremation is introduced into Marin Province, perhaps coming from the interior, where it now continues from the Middle Horizon. Flexed burial in a general westerly orientation, however, continues to be most important in both areas. Artifacts accompany a high percentage of the cremations, but only 50 to 65 per cent of the unburned dead. Especially in Cosumnes Province, burials are found which have charred basketry, fibers, acorns, and other remains below the skeleton, indicating preinterment burning of offerings in the grave pit.

Shell ornaments and beads are included with interments in greater number and variety, especially in Cosumnes Province. The diagnostic Phase 1 bead type is a small rectangular *Olivella* bead, drilled at the center or at one end and frequently laid in shingled rows on the skull or on carbonized textile. These are often accompanied in burials by whole *Olivella* beads (used continuously since Early times). New *Haliotis* ornament shapes include the "banjo," which may represent the important Big Head dancer of the Kuksu cult; only simple versions of this shape occur on the coast. Incisions forming a split V appear around the edges of ornaments. Additional decorative objects are tubular bird-bone ear or hair ornaments covered from end to end with repetitive geometric patterns in fine line incision; the focus of this art form is clearly in Cosumnes Province, although crude specimens appear elsewhere and become more frequent in Phase 2. Bone beads sometimes have constricted waists. Red ocher is infrequent and in lumps more often than in powdered form. Thus in ornament as in burial customs, the reinterpretation of Middle Horizon habits is noteworthy.

Late Horizon objects which are "killed" in graves are more frequently domestic utensils than ceremonial or ornamental objects as previously. These domestic implements show full emphasis on techniques of preparing seeds and acorns, that is, charred baskets, mortars, and pestles. In Cosumnes, Alameda, and Marin provinces there appears a large, artistically proportioned mortar with flat bottom, straight or flared sides, and beveled rim.

Cosumnes Province pestles may be elongated and have flanges or knobs near the hand grip.

In the Cosumnes Province fishing implements include bilaterally barbed one-piece spears as well as the gorge hooks of the Middle Horizon. The use of stone sinkers seems to be restricted in the interior and limited or absent in the coastal provinces, especially Marin County. Spool-shaped or other baked-clay forms may have supplemented flat notched stones in this capacity in the Cosumnes Province. In all areas, the bow and arrow with small point is the dominant hunting device. Although large points still occur, some of gigantic size suggest that they were made for ceremony or display as well as for actual use.

Charmstones remain an important ceremonial item to the last. Although shapes differ, in all periods in the Sacramento Valley charmstones are well made and artistically finished. In Alameda Province the same is true only of Late Horizon charmstones which are long, tapered forms resembling those from the Interior. Phallic charmstones appear in both coastal and interior components. Other ceremonial objects include: quartz crystals, paired bird-bone whistles (with stops medially placed on outside curve), the biconically drilled tubular pipes of schist or steatite mentioned above, and clusters of bird-wing bones found with burials of Alameda Province components.

Only one Phase 1 component of the Late Horizon is known in the Marin Province, where excavation has been limited. Phase 1 settlements of the Late Horizon are found in all parts of the San Francisco Bay area, as well as being well represented in interior provinces. At least seven Alameda Province sites contain Phase 1 remains. One of these sites (Glen Cove, Site N326) is a single-component site and closest culturally as well as geographically to the Phase 1 settlements of the Cosumnes Province. The remainder are superimposed on Middle Horizon components, and have been segregated through typological analysis of burials as described above.

LATE HORIZON: PHASE 2

Only two Phase 2 components are known in the San Francisco Bay area, although settlements of the same period are numerous in other areas. These two components, Newark (N328) and Fernandez (N260), are at some distance from each other and not close to the Bay shore (map 13). It is not yet clear why so few Phase 2 remains should be known from Alameda Province. In Marin Province, at least, this phase was in progress almost two centuries before Spanish colonization of San Francisco Bay in 1776; Chinese porcelain and iron spikes taken from Phase 2 components near

Drakes Bay date from the wreck of the Manila galleon *San Agustín* on that shore in 1595. It may be that San Francisco Bay Indians during these two centuries failed to acquire the new ornament styles developed elsewhere. Or, on the other hand, additional Phase 2 sites may actually exist undiscovered on the now industrialized shores of the bay. Heizer's argument that the Phase 2 remains in the Sacramento Valley do not antedate 1790 supports the first of these possibilities. The dating problem cannot be solved with present information, but it should be observed that the recognition of Late Horizon phases in coastal sites, whereas only interior sites had been known before, brings the problem into clearer perspective.

The most common marker trait for Phase 2 is a disk bead made from clam (*Saxidomus nuttalli*), in late times a monopoly of the Pomo and Coast Miwok north of Marin County. Other ornamental traits are linked with clam disk beads in a complex which recurs in all four provinces: small, cupped *Olivella* beads, steatite disk beads, and tubular beads made from magnesite, steatite, and the shell of a more southerly clam (*Tivela stultorum*). Clam disk beads were used and traded very widely through California in historic times as articles of standard value, creating a generally recognized form of currency. In coastal archaeological components they occur in no greater quantities than other grave goods, but in the richer interior settlements, where their value is perhaps increased by distance from the source, they are found piled in lengthy strings on burials of all sexes and ages.

Cosumnes Province in the Sacramento River delta is not only rich in traded items. Its status of superiority in material goods is enhanced by the appearance of several unique traits: dentate semilunar "Stockton curves" of obsidian, wooden fishhooks, whistles of incised bird bone, and bird effigies of baked clay. Three additional items—turquoise disk beads, flat, ovoid *Tivela* clam beads, and three-quarter grooved axes—signal relations set up also with the south.

In Cosumnes Province, thus, we find throughout the Late Horizon a culture climax which moved only slightly north to the territory of the Patwin in ethnographic times, according to Kroeber's estimate. Cosumnes Province is notable for the development in Phase 1 (Hollister Facies) of many special traits which only gradually and selectively spread to other areas. Exchanges in return seem relatively rare. This interchange of elements operated more along an east-west axis than along the north-south axis, affecting Alameda Province somewhat less extensively than Marin Province. Colusa Province, for example, is excluded from the following traits which link the other areas within Phase 1: cremation, preinterment burning of offerings in the grave pit, flat-based mortars with straight or flaring sides, flat-based pestles (some with knobbed or flanged grip), banjo-shaped *Haliotis* ornaments, bone tubes with constricted waists, and bilaterally barbed one-piece fish spears. Traits which are exclusive to the Hollister Facies of Phase 1, but which had spread west or north by Phase 2, include: square serration of projectile points, fine-line incising on bird-bone tubes, and variously elaborated baked-clay forms (limited to the interior provinces throughout).

It is essentially the unchanged cultural assemblage of Phase 2, including elements of the clam disk complex, into which materials of European manufacture are introduced during the historic period. Glass trade beads from Spanish and Hudson's Bay Company sources, metal knives, files, and other evidence of continuous contact with the whites are found. Within a very short time after the truly historic period began in each area, native culture was disrupted as some groups were missionized and others fled from the vicinity of the Spanish missions, founded at San Francisco in 1776, at San Jose in 1797, and at San Rafael in 1818. Heizer has presented evidence of the widespread and important repercussions which the Spanish soldier-missionary culture brought to the interior tribes during a protohistoric period, initiated before close or permanent contact had been established. These repercussions entailed disruption of established patterns and migration of total communities. The time period is too short, however, to permit archaeological evaluation, at this point, of changes wrought in the aboriginal culture by actual contact. Only a few shifts are suggested: increase in the frequency of cremation, wider use of clam disk beads, and the dissemination of a few other ornamental, cult-connected items. These are but continuations of trends which had begun during prehistoric times. The Indian culture was not long in vanishing: probably shortly after 1776 on San Francisco Bay, by 1830 at the latest in the Sacramento Valley, and probably after 1860 on the Marin County coast.

SUMMARY

Important changes are discernible in the prehistoric culture of Central California. Three sequential culture horizons stand out, with close and explicit relationships in each of three separate physiographic areas for which we have adequate data: the Sacramento River Valley, San Francisco Bay, and the ocean coast of Marin County (map 13). A systematic arrangement of culturally defined facies into provinces under each of these culture horizons has been presented (table 1).

The longest record of human habitation is in the Sacramento Valley, where the Windmiller Facies of the Early Horizon exists under circumstances suggesting very considerable antiquity. On the coast, except for traces at the base of certain sites near San Francisco Bay, the remains of this hunting and gathering culture, with its elaborately ritualized burial practices, are yet undiscovered.

After an interval of unknown duration, the Early Horizon is replaced by the Middle Horizon, a culture of different orientations and interests. Its presence is attested not only in the Sacramento Valley, where five separate facies are discernible, but also on the coast, where littoral adaptations of culture link two facies into the Coastal Province, presumably synchronous with the Interior Province. Underneath much variation from site to site and area to area is a broad uniformity in the techniques which Middle Horizon people employed to gather and prepare their food, the weapons they used, the sociological rating they gave to warfare, the ornaments with which they adorned themselves, and the conventions with which they approached death. They are not simply intruders independent of earlier inhabitants and divorced from those who replaced them; they carry traits over from the Early Horizon and likewise preserve or add some for transmission to the Late Horizon.

In the Late Horizon the acorn-gathering patterns are consolidated still more thoroughly, and traits regarded as fundamental to the ethnographic Indian tribes of California are either added to the culture (such as the bow and small pointed arrow) or developed to their final proportions (such as shell ornaments). In each of the four provinces of Marin, Alameda, Cosumnes, and Colusa, two sequential facies can be delineated. Although the basic patterns of Late Horizon are established in the earliest of these facies and continue with few rejections to historic times, specific trait parallels link the earliest facies of all the provinces into what has been termed Phase 1, and all the later facies into Phase 2 of the Late Horizon.

We have a clearer idea of the nature of the later archaeological periods than of the earlier ones, but even for the latest times unsolved problems of extreme interest are more clearly defined by the extension of archaeological perspective to include the coast. The dynamics of culture change in Central California are but poorly understood. The dominance of valley over coast is expressed in greater quantities of shared items and higher frequencies of unique traits in the valley; however, the role of initiator versus receptor is less sharply defined in the Middle than in the Late Horizon. The Interior Province of the Middle Horizon achieves superior rank less through groups of peculiar traits than through frequent display of traits which are common to both provinces. The culture climax area of the Late Horizon is clearly in Cosumnes Province of the lower Sacramento Valley, somewhat south of the Patwin climax of ethnographic times, in territory lacking recorded ethnographic detail. This sort of qualitative areal relationship, together with problems of direction of cultural exchange, will be much more readily evaluated when excavation has revealed the standing of intervening areas.

CALIFORNIA AND NORTH AMERICA

The cultural horizons of Central California, as described in this paper, show interesting parallels not only to other areas in California but to wider areas in North America as well. In California programs of excavation near Santa Barbara on the coast of south central California and in the southern San Joaquin Valley have revealed culture sequences which bear quite recognizable resemblances to the cultural horizons of Central California. Referring to the resemblances of these sequences with the lower Sacramento Valley, Heizer and Fenenga wrote: "Cultural development in certain California areas has apparently not been autochthonous, but in at least the three areas outlined above there has been a parallel succession, thus making it a general California phenomenon, further evidence of which we may expect when additional areas are investigated carefully." More detailed comparative analysis than theirs has not since been made, but increasing information supports their conclusion. Their tentative table of cultural synchronisms places the Santa Barbara Oak Grove culture of the mainland at an earlier position than the Sacramento Valley Early Horizon, and brackets successively later Santa Barbara periods with the Early, Transitional (now Middle), and Late Horizons. The Oak Grove culture thereby becomes a contender with the San Dieguito Plateau lithic industry of Southern California for the earliest position in the definitely post-Pleistocene series of cultural developments in the state.

The southern San Joaquin Valley sequence near Buena Vista Lake, now known from final reports, begins with very scant evidence of an Early period which may be coeval with either the Early or Middle Horizons of Central California. Small, triangular projectile points, perforated steatite discoidals, multiple perforation of *Haliotis* ornaments, and shell-bead types suggest that the Buena Vista Intermediate is at least partly on the level of the Central California Late Horizon, Phase 1, although artifact types reminiscent of the Middle Horizon also appear. Buena Vista Late has bead types, including clamshell-disk beads, as links with the Late Horizon, Phase 2. The historic cemetery at Elk Hills in the same area shows many of the Buena Vista Late traits occurring in association with European goods. Thus the trait linkages from this area, added to those of Santa Barbara, justify confidence that the cultural horizons defined in Central California are much more than local phenomena.

Attempts to relate these harmonizing culture sequences of California with archaeological periods elsewhere must be made solely on the basis of trait comparisons, until such time as internal dating makes absolute chronologies more reliable for comparing separate areas. Any list of parallels, of course, may be met with the reminder that correspondences between distantly separated areas do not guarantee contemporaneity; nor, in the case of simple traits, do they even guarantee derivation from a single source. These qualifications have made it all the easier for parallels outside California to be swallowed up in the abundance of evidence for the isolated marginal development of native culture within the state. Yet it has never been denied that the West Coast must have participated to some degree in the cultural history of North America as a whole. On the contrary, specific traces of common cultural heritage have been singled out by several investigators.

A SUGGESTED CHRONOLOGY FOR SOUTHERN CALIFORNIA COASTAL ARCHAEOLOGY

by
William J. Wallace

Southern California prehistory has never occupied a prominent place in North American archaeological researches, and literature on the subject is not very imposing. This is true despite the fact that much archaeological work has been done by local educational institutions, museums, and interested amateurs. Many localities have been searched for evidence of human occupation and a fair number of sites have been dug, some with a degree of completeness; but publication has lagged far behind survey and excavation. As a consequence, the characteristics of the prehistoric cultures and their sequences in time are but vaguely known. Enough information exists, however, to provide a basis for a few tentative statements concerning cultural development.

Southern California, which includes approximately one-third of the state, can be separated into a western or coastal province and an eastern or desert zone. These subareas are distinct geographically and, in the light of present archaeological knowledge, culturally, though there is some overlapping. Only the coastal region, including Santa Barbara, Ventura, Orange, and the nondesert portions of Los Angeles and San Diego counties, will be discussed here.

THE COASTAL PROVINCE

Stretching from Point Conception southward to the Mexican border, the coastal province comprises a broad strip of broken land along the sea and inland for some miles. A complex network of mountain ranges, 5000 to 7000 feet high with peaks much higher, separates it from the deserts of the interior. The year-round climate is mild with small daily and annual ranges because sea breezes and fogs tend to stabilize the temperatures, without extremes. Year averages are from 65 degrees in January to 70 degrees in July, with a greater range in the intermediate and interior val-

Pp. 214–228 of William J. Wallace, "A Suggested Chronology for Southern California Coastal Archaeology," *Southwestern Journal of Anthropology* (1955), 11:214–230. By permission of the author.

leys. The year divides in general into two seasons — wet and dry — with nearly all the rain falling in the months from October to May. Annual precipitation varies from eighteen inches at Santa Barbara to about ten inches at San Diego. Summer is a period of drought.

The streams and rivers of Southern California carry little or no water during most of the year. Large flows come only during heavy winter rains and taper off soon afterward. Springs and small perennial streams in the canyons provide the water supplies.

The dominant woody vegetation is not trees but the almost impenetrable chaparral. Foothills, interior valleys, and canyons are characterized by groves of oaks, while sycamores and willows grow along the stream beds. Large areas are grass- and shrub-covered, particularly in the inland valleys behind the coastal hills. A real forest growth occurs only in the dividing mountains where pines, firs, and cedars are found.

Large land mammals are not abundant, being represented only by the California mule deer and in some localities by the American antelope. Small mammals are numerous, however, with several species of rabbits and many of squirrels, rats, and mice. Carnivores include foxes, coyotes, raccoons, skunks, and badgers. Wild cats and mountain lions are occasionally seen. In the coastal waters are various sea mammals — seals, sea lions, dolphins, and the like. Sea otters formerly abounded. Bird life is varied and profuse with many land and marine species. There are ample resources of fishes and shellfish.

The coastal strip, with its pleasant climate and more than adequate plant and animal food resources, was favorable for aboriginal occupation and contained a heavy population estimated at over 20,000. Most of the native peoples — collectively referred to as the Mission Indians because they were quickly taken to the Franciscan missions by the Spaniards and Christianized — spoke languages of the Shoshonean family. Included were the following groups: Gabrielino, Cupeño, Nicoleño, Juaneño, Luiseño, most of the Fernandeño, and some of the Cahuilla. Non-Shoshoneans were the Hokan-speaking Chumash or Canalino of the Santa Barbara region and the Yuman Diegueño in the southwestern section of the state. The Mission Indians shared essentially one basic culture though there were some regional differences. Most of the coastal tribes are now extinct or nearly so. Abundant traces of the former presence of the historic peoples and their predecessors survive, however, in the numerous and easily discernible habitation sites.

Archaeological evidence now suggests a classification of these remains into four broad temporal divisions or horizons: an initial period of "early man" finds; a long "milling stone" phase; a little known intermediate period; and a late manifestation including historical materials and what appear to be their immediate prehistoric antecedents. These wide and rather vague divisions do not reflect detailed cultural-historical changes with accuracy but they do provide a framework in which to discuss the data.

HORIZON I. EARLY MAN

There is little positive evidence concerning the earliest peopling of the Southern California coast. Quite recently claims have been made for a Third Interglacial occupation. These are based upon the recovery of fractured stones from the silts and gravels of river and ocean terraces in the San Diego area. There is no convincing proof that these random finds are artifacts. True, they all show percussion flaking but natural forces can produce chipped edges on rock as well as man. Until supporting evidence is offered, these stones cannot be accepted as conclusive evidence of man's presence in this remote period.

Three finds of human skeletal material have been made in the city of Los Angeles under conditions which suggest some antiquity. During the construction of a storm drain in the Ballona Creek area in 1936, human bones were recovered twelve to thirteen feet below ground surface in a geological stratum attributed to the Pleistocene. In the same layer, but not in direct association, were bones and two teeth of a mammoth (*Archidiskodon imperator* Leidy). The remains of "Los Angeles" man consisted of a cranium and seven fragments of other bones, all heavily fossilized. The fluorine content of the human and elephant bones is quite similar, presumably indicating contemporaneity.

At least six human skeletons were uncovered nineteen to twenty-three feet below the surface, during construction in the Angeles Mesa district in 1924. The osseous material was not scattered, all coming from an area of not more than twelve square feet. Some bones show considerable mineralization; in other cases the replacement is not so great. The deep occurrence of the skeletons and a lack of evidence of disturbance of the overlying deposits precludes the possibility of recent burial. Presumably the remains were deposited before the nineteen to twenty-three foot overburden was laid down. No bones of Pleistocene or Recent mammals were secured from the sand and sandy silt in which the human material lay. A quartzite boulder, regarded as an implement, and a small awl-like object were recovered, however.

The famed asphalt deposits of Rancho La Brea, containing a record of life extending from a stage somewhere in the Pleistocene (probably Last Interglacial) into Recent times, has also yielded human remains. An almost entire skull and some other portions of the skeleton were encountered in Pit 10 at depths extending from approximately six to nine feet. The associated mammals and birds were for the most part more characteristic of the present time than of the Pleistocene, though some Ice Age forms were included. Judging from the accompanying faunal remains the human skeleton would belong to the early Recent epoch or not earlier than the very latest portions of the Ice Age. Purely geological evidences of age are generally exceedingly difficult to obtain in asphalt deposits, owing to the peculiar manner of their accumulation and the possibility of movement in the deposit after they are formed.

These finds have received little consideration, primarily because they were made during a period when skepticism of all "early man" discoveries still prevailed. The skeletal remains and the circumstances of their recovery should be reexamined. Careful cranial reconstructions and measurements need to be made. It would be of great interest, for example, to see how the skulls compare morphologically with types believed to be very early arrivals in the New World. With the possible exception of Los Angeles Man, the present evidences do not point unequivocally to Pleistocene age. They do indicate, however, that they considerably antedate the present and that, if not of Ice Age antiquity, they at least fall in an early phase of the Recent epoch.

There are also a few artifacts which point to man's living along the coast of Southern California in remote times. Traces of man's presence at Rancho La Brea are not limited to the skeleton from Pit 10. Scattered objects of human manufacture have been recovered in another pit from which a more ancient fauna has come. A series of fifteen artifacts of bone, stone, and shell were found in excavation unit 61-67 (which began as two separate pits but merged into one) at depths of from eight to eighteen feet. Most of the items are of types which have no known diagnostic significance. Four, however, all apparently from the same general depth and area, appear to be of old forms unknown in late coastal sites. Three are broken sections of heavy wooden dart foreshafts. The fourth is a more complete specimen, a wooden bunt foreshaft, again presumably for a dart. It is quite possible that these belonged to Late Pleistocene or Early Postglacial hunters who preyed upon animals trapped in the sticky asphalt.

Also attributed to Late Pleistocene or Early Post-Glacial times are archaeological remains from Level 1 at Malaga Cove and from San Dieguito campsites. Malaga Cove is a large site on a high cliff overlooking Redondo Beach in Los Angeles County. Four physical and cultural levels have been distinguished. In the bottommost (Level 1), a compact yellow stratum, was found an unusual and simple assemblage in which the distinguishing items were microliths. Included also were flake knives, convex-based projectile points (two only), flake scrapers, chipped core and pebble hammerstones, abalone shells with openings plugged with asphaltum, spire-lopped Olivella shell beads, clamshell disk beads (rare), scored and incised stones, bone points, bone harpoon barbs (projectile tips?), bone spatulae, and bone beads. The uniqueness of this assemblage is emphasized by the apparent absence of seed-grinding implements so characteristic of Californian archaeological sites. The early people subsisted largely by shellfish-gathering, supplemented by some hunting and fishing. There is no concrete evidence of plant-collecting. No human skeletal remains were uncovered, so that information on disposal of the dead is lacking. Level 1 materials lie in the upper three feet of a 25-foot, nonmarine Pleistocene terrace. If humans lived at Malaga Cove during the deposition of this last three feet, presumably they were there during the late Pleistocene. The associated fauna, however, includes only one extinct species, a diving goose. The archaeological sampling is such a meager one that additional excavation is needed before any certain conclusions can be drawn concerning this occupation.

San Dieguito represents a distinctive and widespread chipped stone industry distributed from the Pacific shores to the Colorado River and beyond. Typically sites are situated on mesas or hilltops and contain no occupation refuse other than stone objects. All of the lithic material occurs upon the surface or slightly below. The fundamental elements of this assemblage are: numerous scrapers and scraper planes, choppers, "amulets" or "ceremonial stones" (small chipped and notched crescents), large blades, and points. The last three are far from abundant. There is some question whether milling stones and mullers form part of the complex.

An age of 1200 B.C. (or Little Pluvial) was originally assigned to the San Dieguito complex. A greater antiquity has been suggested because of the occurrence of remains on ancient land forms such as elevated marine terraces and inland around the margins of extinct lakes. The general simplicity of the materials has also been taken as a criterion for an earlier placement in time. Dating has recently been confused by a revision downward of the cultural sequence for the Colorado River basin where several phases of San Dieguito are recognized. This was done on the basis of a review of collections from the occupational layers in Ventana Cave. Early San Dieguito remains are now recognized in the Ventana complex, which brings them into chronological agreement with Folsom. This cultural and temporal equation rests on the common possession of a relatively few classes of simple percussion tools and needs to be demonstrated more convincingly. If the dating is accepted, it would push the beginnings of the coastal manifestation farther back in time. The San Dieguito complex is assumed to have endured much longer in the west than in the arid interior and to have passed through several distinct phases with the last (San Dieguito IV) persisting in Baja California until about 900 A.D.

HORIZON II. MILLING STONE ASSEMBLAGES

A fairly adequate archaeological record exists for a group of lithic assemblages which appear to follow the above in time. These are characterized by the extensive use of milling stones and mullers. There is also a general lack of well-made projectile points. The few points which have been found are often leaf-shaped and of a size to suggest that they were used to tip darts propelled with the throwing stick. Bone tools and shell items are scarce or absent. No containers for storing and cooking food have been recovered. It is probable that these were of basketry and have left no traces in the archaeological deposit. The early people were primarily food collectors, with hunting and fishing definitely in a secondary role. Mammal, bird, and fish bone refuse is scarce in the deposits. These early coastal inhabitants appear to have been more or less sedentary, as the size and depth of some of the sites suggests a long-continued occupancy of the same locality.

The Oak Grove culture of the Santa Barbara region is the best-known representative of this horizon. Similar assemblages have also been unearthed at the Little Sycamore shellmound in southwestern Ventura county, at Topanga Canyon just north of the city of Los Angeles, in Level 2 at Malaga Cove, and in the La Jollan shellmounds of San Diego County. Distinctive traits are summarized in Table 1.

In addition, the Porter Ranch site at San Fernando probably should be included in this horizon. Here a vast concentration of milling stones was uncovered along with a few handstones. The remaining artifacts consisted of a flaked stone knife blade with a convex base, two large projectile points — one leaf-shaped and the other stemmed and corner-notched — a stone discoidal, one mortar, and several "problematical stones." A few burned mammal bones and a single human reburial were also found. The deposit did not give evidence of the existence of a village and is assumed to represent a ceremonial site.

Comparable milling stone assemblages have also been unearthed at Point Dume (Zuma Creek, Site A) on the Los Angeles County coast, and at Encino (LAn 111) in the San Fernando Valley. None has yet been unearthed in Orange County though the lower level (Culture 1) of the Goff Island site may represent this horizon.

There is some diversity in the local expressions as, for example, in the nonutilization of shellfish resources by the Oak Grove and Topanga

TABLE 1
MILLING STONE HORIZON CULTURAL ASSEMBLAGES

	Oak Grove	Little Sycamore	Topanga	Malaga Cove (Level 2)	La Jolla
Subsistence	Seed-collecting	Shellfish and seed-collecting	Seed-collecting	Shellfish and seed-collecting	Shellfish and seed-collecting
House type	Circular pit-house	Unknown	Unknown	Unknown	Unknown
Grinding implements	Mullers-milling stones, few mortars pestles	Mullers-milling stones, few mortars pestles	Mullers-milling stones, few mortars pestles	Mullers-milling stones, few mortars pestles	Mullers-milling stones
Stone projectile points	Few, large and crude	Few, large and crude, mainly leaf-shaped	Few, large and crude	Absent?	Few, large and crude
Other chipped stone tools	Large blades (leaf-shaped rounded base), retouched flakes	Retouched flakes, few core tools	Abundance of flake and core tools	Knife blades	Retouched flakes, beach cobble choppers
Bone objects	Rare or absent	Few in number	Few in number	Present (no description)	
Ornaments	Absent	Few spire-lopped Olivella beads	Few clamshell disk beads, slate pendants	Shell ornaments, bone beads	Few spire-lopped Olivella beads
Mortuary complex	Extended burial, rock cairns over corpses, few grave offerings, red ocher abundant	Flexed burial, re-burial, rock cairns over corpses, few grave offerings, little red ocher	Extended burial, reburial, rock cairns over corpses, few grave offerings	Reburial, rock cairns over corpses	Flexed burial, rock cairns over corpses, few grave offerings
Special features		Stone discoidals, pitted hammerstone	Stone discoidals and cores, pitted hammerstones	Stone discoidals, steatite objects	

peoples. Also the multitude of forms of rude flake and core tools from Topanga is not duplicated elsewhere. The resemblances overweigh the differences, however, and seem to indicate that the assemblages constitute a basic cultural stratum. Actually the similarities may be greater than indicated as the data are not very complete. Various authors have pointed out possible relationships with similar assemblages in the interior of California and to the Cochise culture and other early lithic complexes in the southwest.

The antiquity of the milling stone assemblages cannot be expressed in exact dates as no radiocarbon analyses have been made. Although the remains are definitely post-Pleistocene, none having been found with convincing evidences of a climate, fauna, or flora demonstrably different from that of the present, they do give indications of respectable antiquity. Signs pointing to an early dating are: the metamorphosed nature of the archaeological deposits; the semimineralization of human skeletal material; and the general simplicity of the remains. Estimates of time are hard to make in the absence of specific dates, yet to allow 4500–5000 years for the beginning of these simple cultures and 2000–3000 years for their duration does not seem excessive.

HORIZON III. INTERMEDIATE CULTURES

An impressive gap lies between the milling stone assemblages and the rich and elaborate artifact inventories of the late prehistoric period. This "gap" does not imply that the Southern Californian coast was uninhabited for some hundreds or thousands of years, rather it indicates a lack of knowledge of what occurred during the intervening years. Archaeological remains dating from this period have either not been recognized or described. The paucity of well-stratified sites has been a handicap here.

In the Santa Barbara region the Hunting Culture lies intermediate in time but seems to show few specific relations either to the preceding or following cultures. The Hunting people introduced the basket-hopper mortar, mortar, and pestle. Chipped stone implements are more diverse and plentiful, with broad leaf-shaped blades and heavy, often stemmed, projectile points being characteristic. Bone and antler objects though present are far less numerous and varied in form than in subsequent phases. Personal ornaments are few, consisting of massive beads of bone and shell. Asphalt and steatite were occasionally used. No traces of dwellings have been observed. The Hunting people customarily interred their dead in a flexed posture, face down, with the head to the west. Red ocher was spread over corpses, and rocks were heaped up over them.

In contrast to their predecessors, the Hunting people, as their name implies, were primarily dependent on wild game. Land mammal bones are plentiful in their village refuse. There is also a fair proportion of sea mammal remains but only a few fish bones. Quantities of sea shells scattered through the debris give an indication that shellfish contributed heavily to this people's diet.

The Sand Dune site (USC-Ven 2), just across a small creek from the Little Sycamore "milling stone" site, yielded evidences of a rather simple complex characterized by numerous pestles and a few mortars. These may have been the only seed-grinding devices employed as there was an apparent absence of milling stones and mullers. Projectile points are heavy and characteristically stemless, though a few small specimens are included. Bone implements, mainly awls, were present in some numbers. Articles of personal adornment were disk-shaped and spire-lopped Olivella beads. No information on mortuary practices was obtained. The prehistoric population maintained itself by collecting shellfish and wild vegetable foods, supplementing their diet quite often with fish and wild game.

An archaeological site at Big Tujunga Wash in the San Fernando valley may also be included in this horizon. Many hundreds of fragments of stone bowls were turned up. Mortars, pestles, and handstones were also obtained. Also present were several forms of large projectile points, flaked stone blades, bone awls, and beads of Olivella shells. These items are roughly analogous to the classes of artifacts from Hunting settlements and the Sand Dune site. Included in the Big Tujunga inventory were a series of objects generally regarded as somewhat more recent, namely containers, tobacco pipes, and beads made from steatite, mortars with flat bases and flaring sides, and a few small points. None of the latter, however, are typical late forms. Two separate methods of disposal of the dead appear to have been practiced by the Tujunga population: reburial under stone cairns and cremation. About forty Hohokam sherds, apparently all from a single vessel, have been dated between the seventh and ninth centuries A.D.

For San Diego County the La Jolla culture is assumed to have persisted with little change. During a later phase (La Jolla II), chipped stone tools increased in quantity and variety but the mortar and pestle grinding assemblage is not reported. La Jolla II is assumed to have merged with Diegueño, the last prehistoric phase.

Excluding San Diego County, the major cultural change during this period, aside from an increased dependence upon hunting, was the shift in grinding implements from the milling and hand-stone combination to the mortar and pestle, though the former continued in use on a reduced scale. This may signify a change in food habits or emphasis from hard-shelled seeds to larger fleshier fruits such as the acorn, the great staple of the historic California Indians. Mortars and pestles are regarded as being more efficient for pulverizing and grinding oily and fleshy acorns preparatory to leaching out their tannic acid content. This superseding of one set of grinding tools by another is duplicated elsewhere in California. The milling stone and muller apparently were kept because they filled a special need.

The prehistoric peoples seem to have used the bow and arrow, at least occasionally. Judging from the size and weight of the majority of their projectile points, they continued to cast darts with the throwing board. The fair number of bone awls suggests the manufacture of coiled basketry, though the sharp-tipped bone implements may conceivably have served some other purpose.

For the present these "intermediate" complexes cannot be arranged in a chronological sequence one to the other, though age differences between them seem apparent. For instance, the Tujunga materials appear to be somewhat more recent. All that can safely be said is that they fall in time somewhere between the milling stone and later horizons. Any attempt to set definite temporal boundaries is entirely guesswork, but a span of time between 1000 B.C.–0 A.D. and 1000 A.D. appears to be well within the bounds of probability. As in the preceding phase, cultural growth progressed at a slow rate. Information is badly needed for this chronological period.

HORIZON IV. LATE PREHISTORIC CULTURES

The Late pattern of life along the Southern California coast is more complex, with many more classes of artifacts present which in general show a high order of workmanship. There appear to be a number of distinctive local complexes but all share certain traits, most of which were known to have been present at the time of European penetration. Important new developments include increased use of the bow and arrow (as inferred from the abundant presence of small finely chipped projectile points), stone projectile tips characteristically stemless with either a concave or convex base, steatite containers, pottery vessels (in the south), circular shell fishhooks, perforated stones, generous use of asphalt as an adhesive, bone tools many and varied, numerous personal ornaments of shell, bone, and stone, and elaborate mortuary customs with abundant grave goods. The population seems to have increased as settlements are more extensive or perhaps small local groups joined together to form larger villages. There was a greater utilization of available food resources with more land

TABLE 2
LATE HORIZON CULTURAL ASSEMBLAGES

	Canalino	Malaga Cove (Level 4)	San Luis Rey I Complex (S.D. 132)	San Vicente Creek	Fallbrook Area (Site 7)
Subsistence	Shellfish- and seed-collecting, hunting, fishing	Shellfish- and seed-collecting, hunting, fishing	Seed-collecting, some hunting	Seed-collecting and hunting	Seed-collecting, some hunting
House form	Circular	Unknown	Unknown	Circular	Circular, rock-paved area
Grinding implements	Mortars-pestles	Mortar-pestle, basket-hopper mortar	Bedrock mortars-pestles, milling stones-mullers rare portable mortars and bedrock milling stones	Bedrock mortars, milling stones, mullers	Bedrock mortars, pestles, milling stones, mullers
Stone projectile points	Small, stemless concave and convex-base	Small, stemless concave and convex base	Small, stemless, concave base dominant	Small, stemless, concave base	Small, stemless, concave base

TABLE 2 (continued)

	Canalino	Malaga Cove (Level 4)	San Luis Rey I Complex (S.D. 132)	San Vicente Creek	Fallbrook Area (Site 7)
Other chipped stone tools	Drills, knife blades	Drills, knife blades, scrapers	Drills, scrapers	Flake scrapers	Drills, flake scrapers
Bone objects	Numerous, awls, ornaments	Numerous	Fairly numerous, awls, flakers	Not numerous, awls	Not numerous, awls, scrapers (?)
Ornaments	Numerous shell and stone beads, pendants	Numerous shell beads, bone beads	Shell beads (disk and spire-lopped Olivella), stone pendants	Shell beads (spire-lopped Olivella), disk (Olivella?)	Shell beads, spire-lopped Olivella
Mortuary complex	Flexed burial	Flexed burial, rare cremation		Cremation, bones often placed in pottery vessels	Cremation
Special features	Charmstones, steatite vessels, extensive use of asphalt, shell fishhooks	Steatite vessels, extensive use of asphalt, shell fishhooks, glass trade beads, painted pebbles		Pottery vessels and pipes	Pottery vessels and pipes, steatite arrow-straightener

and sea mammal hunting and fishing, along with a continued interest in collecting.

The Canalino culture of the Santa Barbara channel region, divided into three developmental phases, was the most elaborate of the late coastal manifestations and marks the peak of California Indian culture. It is evident that material culture in practically all of its phases underwent an independent, special, and uncommon development here, which is displayed in an unusual wealth and variety of industrial and artistic forms. The Channel Islands offshore may have received their first occupation at this time, though there is no agreement on this point. The Canalino culture extended southward into Ventura County (Point Mugu site) and into western Los Angeles County (Arroyo Sequit site), localities well within the boundaries of the territory of the historic Chumash or Canalino. Material culture was no respecter of linguistic and ethnic boundaries, however, as quite similar materials have been uncovered farther south in territory occupied in the historic period by Shoshonean-speaking peoples. A like complex is present in Malaga Cove in Level 4 and probably also in Level 3. Although these two strata are separated and regarded as distinct cultural entities, they appear to have much the same content. Except for the lack of a few classes of traits (arrow points, painted pebbles, basket-hopper mortars, flexed burials), Level 3 is much like the overlying area. These absences may well be due to chance circumstances of excavation. A site at Long Beach (Los Altos 1) and several on or near the coast of Orange County have also produced this type of culture. A rock shelter in the Simi Valley, Los Angeles County, gave evidence of late occupation. The number of artifact classes here was small, as this was a temporary stopping place rather than a permanent settlement.

Farther south in San Diego County late manifestations have been reported from a number of localities: Diegueño sites on the coast, Site 7 on the north bank of the Santa Margarita River in the Fallbrook region, the San Vicente Creek site, four miles north of the village of Lakeside, and at SD-132, just west of Pala and a few miles inland from the Pacific Coast.

Table 2 lists the characteristic items occurring in some late sites. Although all share basic traits, a distinction is noticeable between the northern and southern (San Diego County) sections in grinding implements, containers, mortuary practices, and to a lesser extent in the form of projectile points. Portable stone mortars and pestles, along with the basket-hopper slab, continue to be the dominant grinding implements in the north, whereas bedrock mortars and a more extensive employment of the milling stone appears at the San Diego County sites. Pottery vessels are few in number north of the Orange County line. Competition with steatite containers, which are equal to pottery in every respect and can be used directly over the fire in cooking, may have hampered the spread of the potter's art northward, though knowledge of the craft may still have been spreading at the time of Caucasian entry. Whereas the predominant mortuary practice in the northern section remained flexed burial, cremation was practiced in the south at least during the closing phase of the prehistoric period. Both the knowledge of ceramics and cremation appear to have diffused into the San Diego area from the arid interior. The convex-based point, though not unknown in the south, occurs in reduced numbers. Curved shell fishhooks have not been reported beyond the Orange County line, though at least occasional specimens have been recovered much farther south.

The late period sites are not all chronological equivalents but they can be placed within a time span from about 1000 A.D. to contact times. Throughout this period there appears to have been a definite cultural lag in the southern part of the region, despite such innovations as pottery and cremation. The present dating of late sites appears to be a little conservative. The placing of the first appearance of the Diegueño culture in the fifteenth century and San Luis Rey I, regarded as essentially pre-ceramic, in the period between 1400 and 1750 A.D. seems too moderate and does not allow enough time for subsequent cultural-historical developments.

The coming of the Spaniards to the California coast during the last third of the eighteenth and the first third of the nineteenth century and the removal of the native peoples to the missions brought the aboriginal period to a close. The Indians suffered greatly from missionization and their cultures quickly collapsed. As a consequence there are few sites in the coastal strip belonging to the period of contact with Western civilization when Indian and white lived side by side.

SUMMARY AND CONCLUSIONS

Regional sequences as now conceived for the Southern California coast are summarized in Table 3. Correlation between the various localities is replete with difficulties, and the chronological placement of sites and complexes has been arrived at by rather broad typological comparisons and guesswork, only occasionally from archaeological stratigraphy. The whole scheme suffers from a lack of reliable dates, so that the complexes included in the same level can be regarded only as approximate time equivalents.

Though the primary concern is with sequence, estimates of age and duration are included. These are admittedly estimates which probably will change radically with new evidence. As regards more reliable dates

TABLE 3
REGIONAL SEQUENCES IN SOUTHERN CALIFORNIA ARCHAEOLOGY

Date	Santa Barbara County (northernmost)	Ventura County	Los Angeles County	San Diego County (southernmost) Inland	Coastal
	III Canalino II I	Canalino (Point Mugu)	Canalino (Arroyo Sequit) Malaga Cove IV (Probably also III)	San Luis Rey I San Vicente Creek Fallbrook	Diegueño
1000					
AD BC	Hunting	Sand Dune	Big Tujunga	La Jolla II	
	Oak Grove	Little Sycamore	Malaga Cove II Topanga	La Jolla I	
3000			Malaga Cove I La Brea Angeles Mesa Los Angeles Man	San Dieguito	

nothing constructive can be offered as none has yet been provided by carbon-14 samples.

A broad interpretation of the archaeological record indicates a more or less parallel development in the several localities. Following a scantily-represented and ill-defined early phase, there was a period in which the peoples lived primarily by gathering and made use of milling stones and mullers. The remainder of their material equipment was meager and crude. They were replaced in time by populations preferring the mortar and pestle for grinding and who added to their diet through more hunting and fishing, though collecting continued to be extremely important. The final phase shows a marked elaboration of culture and probably a rise in population. Fishing and sea-mammal hunting assumed more significance.

The picture is one of slow progress with simple cultures persisting for long periods. Part of this can be explained by the marginal, isolated position of the Southern California coast in relation to the main centers of cultural development in native North America. Also the habitat did not make numerous and rigorous demands on the people settling in it, so that cultural adaptation to the geographical environment was fairly easy. Once established, the pattern of life was maintained relatively unaltered for many centuries.

There are many critical problems which remain to be solved before a detailed and connected history of human occupation in Southern California can be written. The development of detailed local sequences constitutes a basic need. The rareness of stratified deposits, combined with the general simplicity of form and manufacture of the artifacts and the absence of sensitive time-makers, makes accomplishment of this task difficult. Once reliable local chronologies are set up, the problem of synchronizing regional sequences can be attacked with more assurances of success. Another critical question involves the relationship of the coastal assemblages to those of the interior desert province. For the present only tenuous relationships can be noted. Finally, the Southern California sequence needs to be fitted into a wider western North American or continental perspective.

A contribution toward an answering of many critical questions can be made by an ordering, publication, and interpretation of data already secured. But further field investigations and site reports are badly needed. Also some absolute datings are necessary. There is an ever-growing interest in Southern Californian prehistory and a considerable amount of archaeological research is being carried on; so in the near future, at least, some of the gaps in present knowledge will be filled.

ANTIQUITY OF SAN FRANCISCO BAY SHELLMOUNDS

by
S. F. Cook

A good many years ago N. C. Nelson and E. W. Gifford made a careful and extensive survey of the shellmounds of San Francisco Bay, in the course of which they utilized quantitative methods of analysis to determine the probable age of cultures represented.[1] In the years since their publications, new deposits have come to light in various parts of the Americas to which their methods might be applied, and a great deal more knowledge is now available which is applicable to the field of primitive dietetics.

There are two possible methods of attacking the problem of the relationships of quantity of shell to population and age: volume and weight. Nelson used the first, Gifford the second.

Nelson calculated the volume of the mound at Ellis Landing, near Richmond, California, as 1,260,000 cubic feet. He then assumed that the mean daily consumption per person was fifty mollusks, in this case the Bay mussel, *Mytilus edulis*. From house pits and other evidence the population was placed at 100. Hence the total daily consumption was 5,000 animals. He then proceeds: "Actual trial shows that the volume yielded by the total 5,000 shells, crushed down to their present consistency would be about 1,200 cubic inches. To this amount should be added a quantity of ashes, broken rock and such extra debris as may collect about a camp— possibly sufficient to make up one cubic foot for the daily average. Calculated on this basis it would apparently have required about 3,500 years to accumulate the pile."

The methodological difficulty lies in Nelson's value for the volume of 5,000 crushed shells. He evidently thought in terms of the pieces having been crushed; embedded in a matrix of ash, refuse, and soil; and packed in by years of pressure so that the interstices were filled with air or soil water, as the case might be. But the over-all volume of pure crushed shell in the laboratory is not the same as under field conditions. Moreover, it is difficult

Pp. 51–52 of S. F. Cook, "A Reconsideration of Shellmounds with respect to Population and Nutrition," *American Antiquity* (1946), 12:51–53.

[1] N. C. Nelson, *San Francisco Bay Shellmounds*, Univ. Calif. Publ. Am. Arch. and Ethn. (1901), 7:345–346; E. W. Gifford, *Composition of California Shellmounds, ibid.* (1916), 12:1–29.

to see how he derived the value of 1,200 cubic inches. In order to make a check, the present writer secured forty fresh specimens of *Mytilus edulis* from San Francisco Bay. The shells were cleaned of meat, freed of organic matter by treatment for twenty-four hours with 20 per cent NaOH at 60°C., and dried in an oven. The volume was determined by direct water displacement. The mean volume per shell (both valves) was 0.948 cc. That of 5,000 shells is therefore 4,740 cc., which is 289 cubic inches. Nelson assumes a ratio of shell to matrix of 1,200 to 1,728. Applying this ratio with 289 cubic inches and retaining Nelson's other constants we get an age for the mound of 14,500 years.

Since Nelson apparently used, not the actual volume of 5,000 shells, but the space occupied by them in the crushed state, including air, it might be possible to utilize specific gravity. Gifford found that the specific gravity of mound material was 1.3. The determinations in the laboratory for both mussel and clam yield a value of 2.7 for shell itself. Since Gifford found that the content of the Ellis Landing mound was 69.43 per cent shell, the volume of the latter would be 9,500 cubic centimeters and the number of shells 10,000. Assuming Nelson's rate of consumption the age would be calculated at 6,900 years.

It is clear that the attempt to utilize volume, either of the actual shell substance or of the space it might occupy in the ground, is beset with difficulties owing to uncontrollable variables, which render a reasonable result highly uncertain. A simpler, more consistent approach is through measurements of weight.

Gifford determined the quantity of shell by screening the mound material through meshwork of different sizes, and by chemical analysis. His data appear highly reliable and may be accepted without qualification. From the known dimensions of the mound and its mean specific gravity he estimated its total weight as 51,085 short tons. The shell comprised 69.43 per cent of the total by weight: 35,468 tons, or 32,169,476 kilos. However, he then arrived at the rate of deposition from Nelson's time estimate of 3,500 years and concluded that it was fifty-six pounds (25.4 kg.) per day. He adds that "this amount of shell seems reasonable enough, if we accept one hundred people as the average population of the mound throughout its growth." Nevertheless, some further analysis of the situation is desirable.

In his table 13, Gifford shows that of the total shell at Ellis Landing approximately 62 per cent was *Mytilus* and 38 per cent *Macoma nasuta* (clam). Therefore the former contributed 19,945,075 kg. and the latter 12,224,401 kg. All of Nelson's calculations were predicated upon consumption of mussels, but obviously the consumption of clams must also be considered. It has been suggested that twenty clams be regarded as equivalent to fifty mussels, but this seems to me too high. The gathering of clams, which must be dug individually, involves much greater labor and time than does the gathering of mussels, which may be scraped in masses off the rocks. Moreover, experiments performed in the laboratory show that the meat of a clam weighs on the average about eight times as much as that of a mussel. Hence, to obtain the equivalent in food value of fifty mussels only six clams would be needed. In the course of the same experiments, however, it was found that the mean weight of a clean dry mussel shell is 2.5 gm.; that of a clam shell (both valves), 29.75 gm. Therefore, by Gifford's weight data and direct division the mound contained the remains of 7,879,-000,000 mussels and 410,942,000 clams. This is in a ratio of 2.57 clams per fifty mussels, somewhat less than the estimate based on diet.

If we now use Nelson's assumption that the inhabitants of Ellis Landing consumed fifty mussels per person per day (neglecting clams) and that the mean population was 100 persons, then the age of the mound is 7,879,000,000 $\div$ (5,000 $\times$ 365), or 4,370 years. When clams are included, it becomes necessary to use weight rather than number of shells. Since Nelson's figure of fifty shellfish gathered per person per day is a pure guess, it will not seriously modify his statement to presume that in addition to fifty mussels each person gathered 2.57 clams. Then the weight of shell gathered per person per day is 125 gm. for mussels and 76.5 gm. for clams, a total of 201.5 gm. This means 7,342,750 gm. per year for the village. The age of the mound then becomes 4,380 years.

In recent years we have learned that throughout prehistoric time the coast natives exported large amounts of shellfish to the interior, in particular to the lower San Joaquin and Sacramento valleys. Some of the mollusks were shipped in the shell, but the far more economical and efficient method was to export only the dried meats. The exact extent of this trade is unknown, but certain facts are pertinent. The mean wet weight of the meat of one mussel, as determined recently from fresh material, is 1.065 gm. The dry weight is, like that of most soft tissue, about 20 per cent of the wet weight, or about 0.2 gm. Then one kilogram of dried meats would represent 5,000 animals and, in terms of Nelson's assumption, would correspond to one day's labor on the part of the entire village population. One hundred kilos of dried mussels a year for export does not seem excessive, since this would require only one trip annually to the interior for four men, each carrying 25 kilos. If export was of this order of magnitude, then actually from one-quarter to one-third of the shellmound, say 30 per cent, represents export. On the other hand, there is no reason to modify Nelson's original idea that 5,000 mussels, plus 200–300 clams, were gathered daily for home consumption. If such was the case, the gross rate of gathering was a good deal greater than Nelson thought. How much his value should be increased is a matter of conjecture.

If 30 per cent of the deposit represented export, then the gathering rate must be set at seventy-two mussels per person per day and the age becomes 3,070 years. If it can be conceived that 50 per cent was export, then the age would be 2,190 years. To assume higher values and still retain Nelson's rate of home consumption would, it appears to me, call for improbably great effectiveness and industry in the actual gathering. To reduce the basic rate of consumption—fifty mussels per person per day—would mean again extending the age of the mound. With regard to age, it must be admitted that this reëxamination of the data, even allowing for commerce in shellfish, cannot permit a duration of less than 2,000 years. More satisfactory is at least 3,000, thus in general confirming the original supposition of Nelson and Gifford.

For purposes of discussion, let us assume a home consumption of fifty mussels and 2.5 clams per person per day. In terms of meat this is $53 + 21$, or 74 grams. The chief dietary value of such food is in the animal protein and, hence, essential amino acids thereby furnished, since the vitamin content is negligible. According to Rose's table 1, 100 grams of clams furnish about 7.5 grams of protein. Presumably the protein content of mussels is of the same order. Therefore, the aboriginal daily intake would have been about 5.5 grams. This is far below the minimal maintenance intake of 25 to 30 grams. But it must be remembered that the natives were eating many types of food, particularly plant material, which furnished considerable protein. The latter may have been of low biological value, although adequate in quantity. It has been repeatedly shown that under such circumstances the addition of very small amounts of high value animal protein is sufficient to supplement the low-value protein and produce an adequate diet. There can be no doubt that in this respect the presence of shellfish was of major importance.

As a more or less speculative check upon the validity of the procedures and calculations developed for the California shellmounds, it is of interest to attempt their application to an entirely different geographical and cultural background. If the results were in general conformity with those obtained by quite different methods, then there would be justification for pursuing an intensive investigation and analysis at the site in the hope of achieving a fairly high degree of precision with respect to population, age, and dietary conditions.

PREHISTORY OF THE
SANTA BARBARA AREA

by
R. L. Olson

INTRODUCTION

This account of two summers' archaeological work in the vicinity of Santa Barbara and on Santa Cruz Island is intended as a brief résumé of some of the more important general findings. For this reason it deals, in the main, with stratigraphic work and with site differences based upon the relative frequency of occurrence of various types of objects. A detailed, systematic account of the excavations made, of general geography and site location, and of the objects found, grave by grave, is reserved for a future publication.

In 1927 two weeks were spent in work on the Mainland, eleven on Santa Cruz Island; in 1928 seven weeks were spent on the Mainland, six on the Island. The sketch map indicates the sites at which excavations were made. On the Mainland fairly extensive work was done at four sites (nos. 1, 2, 6, and 10), and casual excavations made at the others. Island sites, 3, 83, 100, 122, 131, 135, 138, 147, 159, and 162 were each worked for a week or more. A number of other sites were given some slight attention. Sites 1 and 2 proved to be the only Mainland sites whose cemeteries had not been rifled by previous investigators or by vandal amateurs. The result is that it was impossible to verify the apparent site and depth differences by means of excavations in the relevant cemeteries. The sites on the Island's northern shore have for the most part suffered the same fate as those of the Mainland, and it was only with difficulty that sites were found which had not been plundered by relic hunters.

The sites of the area which lie near the ocean front are, for the most part, of the familiar shellmound or kitchen-midden type, and do not differ

R. L. Olson, *Chumash Prehistory,* Univ. Calif. Publ. Am. Arch. and Ethn. (1930), 28:1–21.

The only other general survey of Santa Barbara archaeology is that of D. B. Rogers, *Prehistoric Man on the Santa Barbara Coast* (Santa Barbara, 1929). A bibliography of the archaeology of this region may be found in sec. 20 of Repts. UCAS, No. 4 (1949). The plank canoe mentioned by Olson is fully discussed in R. F. Heizer, "The Plank Canoe of the Santa Barbara Region," *Ethnological Studies* (1938), 7:193–229. Data on the curved shell fishhooks are presented in R. F. Heizer, "Curved Single-Piece Fishhooks of Shell and Bone in California," *American Antiquity* (1949), 15:89–97.

materially in composition from their counterparts in other parts of California. In size the middens vary from an insignificant scattering of a few thousand shell fragments to deposits nearly twenty feet in depth. The area covered varies just as greatly: a site half a mile in length may average but a few inches in depth, while other sites which may be no more than two hundred feet long may be many feet in depth. Site 3 on Santa Cruz Island is probably the largest of the entire region in respect to cubic content. It measures some 600 by 700 feet and averages about 6 feet in depth, giving about 2,500,000 cubic feet (93,000 cubic yards). The shell content, however, is unusually low, so that these figures give a somewhat exaggerated idea of its actual size. Probably the average of the more important middens on the island is under 300,000 cubic feet. Sites on the Mainland would average considerably less.

Without any systematic effort or sacrifice of time, 120 sites were located on the Island in addition to the 86 mapped by Mr. Leonard Outhwaite in 1918. Of these 206 about 10 per cent have been touched by the archaeologist's spade, but the treasures of more than double that number have been looted by trophy hunters. While considerable collections could still be obtained, the more promising sites have all been more or less systematically excavated.

The usual plan followed in the excavation of large sites was first to sink a stratigraphic pit about three by thirty feet in the deepest part of the mound, using 6- or 12-inch intervals. Following this the cemetery or cemeteries were worked by series of pits. In the smaller mounds the same procedure was used, except that small stratigraphic pits were dug and the materials from them were not screened. In the stratigraphic pits all objects, fragments of objects, and animal bones were saved and segregated according to depth. Materials from the cemeteries were segregated according to burials. Whenever possible, skulls, pelves, and long bones were saved.

In all about 725 burials were unearthed, but in only about one-half of these were the bones firm enough to permit handling, and not more than 100 were sufficiently well preserved to allow the entire skeleton to be saved. A feature which greatly hampered operations was the occurrence of large numbers of burials in restricted areas. Within a space 75 feet square as many as 150 burials were found. The natives had a sophisticated attitude toward earlier interments and the digging of a new grave was often, even usually, accompanied by displacement of the remains of several previous burials. In most such cases little could be done with the disturbed bones in the way of allocating them with the proper skulls. Out of perhaps 300 individuals who at one time or another had been buried in cemetery 1 of site 83, only 107 were found in an undisturbed condition. In view of this state of affairs it hardly need be added that the depths at which bodies and objects are found in the cemeteries is seldom a criterion of relative antiquity.

GEOGRAPHY

Kroeber, in his *Handbook of the Indians of California,* outlines the territory occupied by the Chumash as follows:

They held the three northern large islands of the Santa Barbara archipelago—Anacapa does not appear to have been inhabited permanently. They clustered thickly along the calm shore from Malibu Canyon westward to Point Concepcion and from there extended northward along the more boisterous and chillier coast as far as Estero Bay. Inland, in general, they reached to the range that divides the direct ocean drainage from that of the great valley; except that in the west their frontier was the watershed between the Salinas and the Santa Maria and short coast streams; and in the east, some small fragments had spilled into part of the most southerly drainage of the San Joaquin–Kern system. The Carrizo plains are doubtful as between Chumash and Salinan and may not have contained any permanent villages.

The mountainous nature of the mainland portion is relieved only by the valleys of the Santa Maria, Santa Ynez, Ventura, and Santa Clara rivers, a few smaller valleys, and the narrow intermittent coastal plain between Point Concepcion and Point Mugu. Most of the river valleys begin as narrow defiles which gradually widen as they approach the coast. The coastal region, moistened by more abundant rains and by frequent fogs, contrasts with the semidesert of the interior, where only the mountain slopes give relief from the monotony of chaparral, cactus, and random oaks by presenting a generous clothing of conifers. Most of the small watercourses are dry the greater part of the year; and even the rivers fail to maintain a continuous flow all the way to the sea.

The islands, like the mainland, are cut by deep narrow valleys, though here and there fairly gentle slopes stretch from the higher peaks to the ocean. Sandy, surf-pounded beaches alternate with forbidding cliffs. The groves of large oaks, common on the mainland, are restricted to the wider and more sheltered valleys.

The flora and land fauna of the hinterland occupied by the Chumash offered no exceptional inducements to the native. It was otherwise along the coast, where sea mammals, fish, and shellfish are abundant. Accordingly we find a concentration of population along the coast, especially along the more favored ocean frontage between Point Concepcion and the Ventura River. The islands were in some ways even more favorable than the mainland coast—at any rate the sites are here both larger and more abundant. Higher winds and frequent fogs, especially at the western ends of the islands, are compensated for by the abundance of sea life.

Along the coast from Estero Bay to Malibu Canyon as well as on the islands, shell heaps which mark the old camp and village sites are found at the mouth of nearly every canyon, and frequently near springs as well.

Obviously a supply of fresh water was a potent factor in the determination of village and camp locations. It seems certain that many, perhaps the majority, of these sites were not inhabited the year round. The acorn harvest, seasonal presence of game, and an intermittent water supply were probably the major features which influenced occupancy in such cases. It was along these shores where the population was concentrated that all our archaeological work was done. In the remainder of Chumash territory nothing was attempted beyond the briefest reconnaissance.

STRATIGRAPHIC EXCAVATIONS

While exploratory pits to determine composition and depth, as well as to locate cemeteries, were dug in a great many sites, careful stratigraphic work was done at only seven sites, and in only five cases were the mound materials screened. Ordinary gravel screens with 3 or 4 meshes to the inch were employed. In most cases a sufficient portion of the comminuted shell passed through the mesh with the ash and soil to render the artifacts visible in the residue of rocks and coarse shell. In most instances the mound material was removed in 6-inch layers, but at Mainland site 1 and Santa Cruz Island site 147, 12-inch intervals were substituted.

Table 1 lists the commonest objects and their frequency in intervals of two feet. For the sake of brevity the smaller intervals which were actually employed have been grouped into these larger strata. Certain types of objects which occurred too rarely to be tabulated here have been included in table 4. It should be borne in mind that in all the tabulations fragments of objects, unless obviously from the same original, are counted as if they were complete artifacts.

Site and Depth Differences

In all the mounds there is a decided tendency in the direction of progressive diminution in number of objects as the bottom of the mound material is approached. This is especially noticeable in the bottom two feet. At first glance this might be taken to imply a certain amount of "progress" through the centuries, of cultural development and enrichment. Actually the differences are more apparent than real. They are almost certainly due for the most part to a decrease in the shell and bone in the lower levels. Intensity of occupation is no doubt indicated very largely by shell and bone proportions. Artifacts, shells, and bones undoubtedly find their way below the original surface of the site and since the trenches were consistently carried to the extreme limit of the shell, the tabulations cannot but indicate discrepancies between levels which are in all probability determined by

TABLE I

Stratigraphic Excavations

Sites	Depths	Mortars	Pestles	Metates	Mullers	Pseudo-metates	Flint points	Basket pebbles	Bone tools	Straight fishhooks	Circular type fishhooks	Ornaments, beads, etc.	Steatite objects	Presence of asphaltum	Animal bones (lbs.)	Totals
Mainland site 6, trench 47'×5', screened	0–2'	15	11	1	0	0	13	39	38	3	0	0	0	×	20	119
	2'–4'	11	6	3	8	0	6	45	42	6	0	1	1	×	36	129
	4'–6'	3	1	15	67	0	5	42	42	3	0	3	0	×	16	181
	6'–6'8″	0	0	2	28	0	7	6	37	1	0	4	1	×	1	87
Totals..................		28	18	21	103	0	31	132	159	13	0	8	2		73	
Mainland site 10, trench 30'×3', screened	0–2'......	2	1	0	0	0	14	39	35	2	10	22	1	×	11	126
	2'–4'	2	1	0	0	0	27	41	73	0	16	20	0	×	14	180
	4'–6'	4	3	0	0	0	20	78	55	1	4	5	0	×	20	170
	6'–8'	0	0	0	0	0	12	47	23	3	2	10	0	×	15	95
	8'–10'6″	0	0	0	1	0	1	5	0	0	0	2	1	×	2	10
Totals..................		8	5	0	1	0	74	210	186	6	30	59	2		62	
Mainland site 1, trench 30'×3', screened	0–2'	3	4	0	0	2	9	9	10	2	0	3	2	×	4	44
	2'–4'	2	2	0	0	3	1	3	5	1	0	0	0	×	12	20
	4'–5'	1	1	0	0	1	4	7	11	1	1	3	0	×	7	30
Totals		6	7	0	0	6	14	19	26	4	1	6	2		23	
Sta. Cruz Island, site 100, trench 30'×3', screened	0–2'	0	0	0	0	1	14	17	15	7	3	11	0	×	8	68
	2'–4'	0	2	0	0	8	11	40	20	7	14	12	0	×	38	114
	4'–6'	5	4	0	0	3	6	105	14	4	10	5	1	×	33	157
	6'–6'8″	6	0	0	0	3	2	75	10	3	1	6	0	×	13	96
Totals		11	6	0	0	15	33	237	59	21	28	34	1		92	
Sta. Cruz Island, site 147, trench 40'×3' to 6', then 10'×3', Items below 6' multiplied by 4.	0–2'	10	3	0	0	6	22	99	57	11	9	36	0	×	40	253
	2'–4'	26	2	0	0	19	8	182	33	12	9	64	3	×	40	358
	4'–6'	20	6	0	0	4	20	220	55	16	13	18	0	×	48	372
	6'–8'	0	0	0	0	0	36	200	36	20	4	16	4	×	36	316
	8'–10'	0	0	0	0	8	8	68	16	4	4	0	0	×	20	108
	10'–12'*	0	0	0	0	0	0	4	8	4	0	0	0	×	16	16
	12'–14'†	0	8	0	0	0	0	0	4	0	0	0	0	×	16	12
Totals		56	19	0	0	37	94	773	209	67	39	134	7		216	

* Not screened below 10'.

† Shell ends at 16'6″. Mid-tide level at about 15'9″.

natural forces rather than cultural factors. In harmony with this interpretation is the obvious positive correlation between frequency of animal bones and frequency of artifacts. The same relationship will be found to hold for percentage of shell and frequency of artifacts.

Differences in pattern or style of the same objects are almost nonexistent as we pass from the lower to the upper levels of any one site. Nowhere was a definite or significant change observable. Mortars and pestles, metates and mullers, flint work, fishhooks and barbs, ornaments—all these, if present at the various levels, show a drab uniformity throughout.

In comparing site with site, however, a few seemingly significant differences come to light. Mainland sites 1 and 10 and Island sites 100 and 147 are alike in nearly all particulars. With the exception of the absence of "pseudo-metates" from site 10, all of the classes of objects occur in all these sites. Mainland site 6 alone stands out as differing from the others in some respects. Genuine metates and mullers, except for a single muller from the lower stratum of site 10, are absent in the other four sites but are present in considerable numbers in site 6. Furthermore the proportion of metates-mullers to mortars-pestles changes very materially as we proceed from the lower to the upper levels of site 6. In the lower 4½ feet of pits A and B, 112 metates and mullers were found while only 4 mortars and pestles appeared. The relative frequency is reversed in the upper 4 feet, which yielded 42 mortars and pestles but only 12 metates and mullers. The excavations at this site make it appear that while both the mortar-pestle and metate-muller modes of grinding were present almost throughout, there was a real change in the prevailing method. The metate and muller were used almost exclusively during the period when the lower strata were laid down, but gave way to the mortar and pestle in the later period. The very definite type of both metates and mullers found at this site (see figure below) makes it extremely unlikely that their absence from other sites should be an error of observation.

Oval Metate, Santa Barbara. Type found in site 6. Muller used with metates of this type; length 134 mm.

Site 6 also shows variation from the other sites in the absence throughout of the circular type of fishhooks. These are consistently present at virtually all levels of the other shellmounds. The straight type of hook seems to be present throughout in all mounds (figure below, *c, d*).

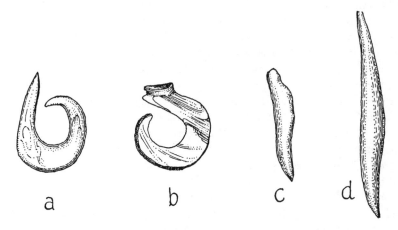

Shell and Bone Fishhooks, Santa Barbara. *a, b,* circular type fishhooks of mussel and *Haliotis rufescens* shell; *c, d,* straight type fishhooks of bone.

Relative Age of Sites

Of the 5 mounds under discussion, post-European objects were found in 3 (sites 1, 10, and 147). Sites 83 and 100, judging by the preservation of perishable objects, are also relatively recent. Site 6, on the other hand, gave every indication of being considerably the oldest. Here the soil, shell, and ash have settled into a mass so compact that picks had to be employed before the shovel could be used.

The differences in texture of mound material, like the differences in types of objects, are not to be ascribed to local conditions, for sites 6 and 10 are only a few hundred yards apart and both have their seaward margins washed by the surf.

Furthermore, site differences in types of objects have been noted by other investigators. In 1877 at a site near Guadalupe, Stephen Bowers found more than 200 mullers as well as spearpoints, arrowpoints, and charmstones. In 1900 Dr. Philip Mills Jones visited the same site. I have gone over his materials from this site in the University of California Museum of Anthropology and find that, exclusive of flint objects, he collected 51 oval metates, 199 mullers, 11 mortars, and 3 pestles. Mr. David Rogers of the Santa Barbara Museum of Natural History has told me that he finds these definite types of mullers and oval metates restricted to certain sites. Mr. Malcolm Rogers of the San Diego Museum has written a paper in which he has stated that he believed the shell heaps which yield metates and mullers are the oldest sites in the San Diego region. This is substantially in harmony with the hypothesis of Mr. Rogers of the Santa Barbara Museum.

TABLE 2

TIME RELATIONS OF TWO SITES AT RINCON

					Site 6								Site 10									
Depths	Pounds animal bones	Presence of asphaltum	Ornaments	Basket pebbles	Flint points	Bone tools	Circular hooks	Straight hooks	Mortars and pestles	Metates and mullers	Metates and mullers	Mortars and pestles	Straight hooks	Circular hooks	Bone tools	Flint points	Basket pebbles	Ornaments	Presence of asphaltum	Pounds animal bones	Depths
											0	3	2	10	35	14	39	22	X	11	0–2'
											0	3	0	16	73	27	41	20	X	14	2'–4'
											0	7	1	4	55	20	78	5	X	20	4'–6'
											0	0	3	2	23	12	47	10	X	15	6'–8'
											1	0	0	0	0	1	5	2	X	2	8'–10'6"
0–2'	20	X	0	39	13	38	0	3	25	1											
2'–4'	36	X	1	45	6	42	0	6	17	11											
4'–6'	16	X	3	42	5	42	0	3	4	82											
6'–8'6"	1	X	4	6	7	37	0	1	0	30											

My own work in the Santa Barbara region bears out these findings in a more positive way, my proof being based on stratigraphy rather than on site differences alone. In site 6 the metate was the most common grinding tool during its earlier period, the mortar during the later. In adjacent site 10 no metates were found, and but one muller—and that in the bottom stratum. The recency of site 10 is proved by the presence of a Spanish coin (dated 1790) in the 2-feet to 2-feet-6-inch stratum. It therefore seems likely that all, or most, of site 10 was laid down after site 6 was abandoned.

Table 2 represents what is probably the approximate time sequence of these two sites.

It is apparent from this tabulation that metates and mullers persist throughout the period of site 6 and into the beginning of the period when site 10 was being laid down. Circular fishhooks were unknown to the inhabitants of site 6 but were used during all but the earliest period of site 10. All other classes of objects were employed throughout the entire combined period.

TABLE 3

STRATIGRAPHIC EXCAVATIONS: FREQUENCIES PER 1,000 CUBIC FEET

Site	Depths	Actual cubic feet	Mortars and pestles	Metates and mullers	Pseudo-metates	Straight fishhooks	Circular fishhooks	All other objects	Total objects	Average per 1000 cu. ft.
Mainland	0 –4′	940	45	13	0	10	0	205	264	294
site 6	4′–8′6″	828	5	135	0	5	0	182	323	
Mainland	0 –6′	540	11	0	0	4	48	857	920	616
site 10	6′–10′6″	405	0	2	0	10	10	289	311	
Mainland site 1	0–5′	450	29	0	13	9	2	149	201	201
Sta. Cruz Island	0–4′	360	6	0	25	39	47	447	564	616
site 100	4′–8′6″	405	37	0	17	17	27	598	669	
Sta. Cruz Island	0–6′	720	93	0	40	54	43	1232	1462	980
site 147	6′–14′	240	8	0	8	29	17	436	498	

Table 3 presents the same data as table 1 in a different form. Mortars are combined with pestles and metates with mullers. By calculations of the frequency of types of objects per 1,000 cubic feet, the figures are made directly comparable, and differences in frequency which may be dependent on size of excavation are eliminated.

The significant differences between frequencies of metates-mullers and mortar-pestles and of the two types of fishhooks stand out more clearly than in table 1. Table 3 shows more plainly than table 1 that Island sites are definitely richer in artifacts than those of the Mainland. Site 6 (early) exceeds site 1 (late) in number of artifacts per cubic foot but falls far below all other late sites. In average number of artifacts the mounds of the Santa Barbara region are much richer than those of San Francisco Bay. Five Santa Barbara sites yielded an average of 14.6 artifacts per cubic yard; three San Francisco Bay mounds, 0.9 artifacts; a single mound on Humboldt Bay, 3.0.

It is evident from the foregoing data that, so far as Chumash territory is concerned, the metate and muller precede the mortar and pestle as the type grinding implements; and that the circular (shell) fishhook was unknown until about the middle of the period represented by the sites excavated. In other respects few evidences of change in culture based on stratigraphic work are to be seen. Flint work, ornamental objects (beads, etc.), and bone tools show no marked differences in type or frequency; and asphaltum, steatite, and basket pebbles, in spite of their specialized characters, seem to have been used during the entire period covered by the sites investigated.

The inferences drawn from the stratigraphic work are borne out by findings at other sites. Surface collections from site 8 (Mainland) yielded 15 metates and mullers, and but 5 mortars and pestles; Mainland site 3 produced 48 metates and mullers, only 2 mortars and pestles; at Mainland site 5 were found 25 metates and mullers, no mortars or pestles. The site near Guadalupe where Jones collected 150 metates and mullers and but 14 mortars and pestles has already been mentioned. At none of these sites were human remains located, and at none were European objects found.

On the other hand, the Mainland sites which were occupied until European times give reversed ratios of these objects: site 1, mortars-pestles 42, metates-mullers less than 10; site 10, mortars-pestles 13, metates-mullers 1. Santa Cruz Island sites yielded mortars and pestles numbering hundreds, but not more than a half-dozen genuine metates and not one muller. A number of these Island sites were occupied until European times. It seems to be definitely established, therefore, that so far as the Santa Barbara region is concerned, metates and mullers constitute the typical grinding tool of the "early" period, while mortars and pestles virtually displaced them in the later periods. There is good evidence that the circular fishhook (commonly of shell, rarely of bone) came in at a relatively late period. It is nowhere associated in time with metates and mullers. In Island sites it occurs in all but 2 sites; on the Mainland only in sites which are definitely late.

EXCAVATIONS IN CEMETERIES

Table 4 presents the majority of classes of objects found and their frequency in various sites. The assignment of sites to tentative periods is based on a number of considerations: cemeteries which yielded European objects are in all cases classed as "late"; Mainland cemeteries which contain objects typical of the early period exemplified by site 6 are classed as "early"; Mainland sites which lack the types of objects found in site 6 as well as European objects are classed as "intermediate." Island sites which yielded European objects are classed as "late." The "early" Island sites are less objectively classified. Thus, charmstones are wholly absent from late sites and accordingly their presence has been used as one of the criteria of the early Island period. Similarly, bone pendants are not found in late Island sites, but do

TABLE 4

CLASSIFICATION OF ARTIFACTS WITH BURIALS

Tentative period	Materials from Cemeteries*															Materials from Stratigraphic Excavations				
	Early Mainland		Intermediate Mainland		Early Island				Intermediate to Late Island						Late Mainland	Early Mainland	Intermediate to Late Mainland		Intermediate to Late Island	
Site number	2	11	1	1	159	162	3	83	83	81	100	82	135	138	1	6	10	1	100	147
Cemetery or pit numbers	1	…	1	2	19	…	…	…	1	…	…	…	…	…	3	A, B	A	A	H	A
Total burials	49	4	26	37	19	25	107	72	88	5	161	9	19	48	56	4' 4'6"	6' 4'6"	5'	4' 4'6"	6' 8'
Mortars	17[13]	6[3]	12[8]	3[3]	0	1[1]	10[10]	12[8]	77	6[4]	4[4]	0	3[3]	0	14[10]	25	8	0	0	56
Pestles	12[6]	0	7[7]	3[2]	5[3]	6[5]	9[6]	2[2]	6[4]	0	6[6]	0	0	2[1]	3[2]	17	5	7	11	11
Metates	0	4[3]	0	0	0	0	0	1[1]	0	0	1[1]	0	0	0	0	4	0	0	0	8
Mullers	1	4[2]	2	0	0	0	0	0	0	0	1[1]	0	0	0	0	8	0	0	0	0
Pseudo-metates	21[12]	0	0	0	6[2]	4[1]	2	0	4[4]	2	2	5	1[1]	7[3]	2[2]	0	0	6	9	29
Flint points	7[2]	0	2[2]	26[11]	4[1]	4[1]	14[10]	7[4]	40[18]	21	53[23]	…	8[3]	6[5]	14[7]	19[12]	61	14	25	50
Drills and picks	0	0	1[1]	0	1[1]	4[3]	2	0	15[7]	13[13]	13[13]	…	1[1]	7[7]	1[1]	0	7	0	12	79
Perforated stones	0	0	0	0	2[1]	14[7]	21[18]	16[14]	9[9]	11[9]	11[9]	…	1[1]	5[1]	1[1]	…	0	0	0	3
Charmstones	9[4]	0	0	0	4[2]	2	1[1]	0	0	0	0	0	0	0	0	0	0	0	0	4
Steatite pans	0	0	0	0	0	0	0	0	0	1[1]	0	0	0	0	5[4]	0	0	0	0	0
Steatite ollas	0	0	5[5]	0	0	0	0	0	0	1[1]	0	0	2[1]	3[2]	15[9]	0	0	0	0	0
Steatite bowls	3[3]	0	5[4]	3[3]	0	0	3[3]	0	0	1[1]	1[1]	0	0	0	7[4]	0	0	0	0	0
Steatite beads, etc.	1	0	11[6]	17[9]	2[1]	2[1]	2[1]	1	14	10+	10+	0	1[1]	1[1]	6[4]	0	1	2	0	1
Pipes	9[3]	0	0	18[5]	1[1]	1[1]	1[1]	2[1]	2[2]	2	6[5]	0	1[1]	0	1[1]	1[1]	0	0	1	3
Whistles	0	0	0	0	1[1]	2[2]	38[5]	1[1]	8[8]	6[6]	13[13]	0	0	5[4]	8[5]	0	0	0	0	0
Basketry	0	0	0	0	0	3[3]	0	0	3[3]	3[1]	42[15]	0	8[3]	14[9]	3[3]	0	1	0	2	42
Bone tools	2[2]	2[2]	9[3]	9[5]	12[8]	33	89[38]	18[16]	57[21]	20[1]	55[6]	0	1[1]	1[1]	3[3]	80[79]	163	26	35	145
Circular hooks	0	0	1[1]	1[1]	0	0	0	0	4[2]	4[1]	4[3]	0	0	0	1[1]	0	23	4	17	31
Straight hooks	0	0	0	0	11[5]	11[5]	0	0	13[7]	1[1]	17[15]	0	3[1]	0	12[7]	9	30	1	14	39
Haliotis shell dishes	5[5]	0	3[2]	2[1]	3[3]	7	19	11	2	1	25	0	4	11	6	0	3	0	0	6
Haliotis beads, etc.	1[2]	0	1	…	1	6	31	8	7	0	8	0	0	…	0	0	0	0	1	7
Limpet shell beads	0	0	0	0	0	10	18	14	8	2	46	1	0	14	0	1	2	3	1	3
Pismo clam beads	1[1]	0	0	0	10	9	52	23	17	0	2	0	4	…	0	3	3	0	2	12
Other shell beads	0	0	0	12[6]	5	1	2	24	19	17	46	1	4	14	0	0	22	0	8	108
Bone beads and tubes	0	0	3	2[1]	1	0	19	…	6	0	5	0	0	0	1[1]	0	7	0	1	11
Bone pendants	0	0	0	0	0	8	35	17	0	1	27	3	0	0	4	0	2	0	0	0
Inlay work	0	0	0	…	6	8	35	17	6	1	5	0	…	0	1[1]	0	5	0	0	4
Ochre	11[2]	2	3[1]	2[14]	6	8	35	17	12	1	27	3	0	8	4	0	6	2	3	0
Quartz crystals	2[1]	0	3[1]	3[1]	0	0	0	11	0	0	5[5]	0	2[1]	4[2]	1[1]	0	0	0	0	1

* Large figures denote number of objects or fragments of objects, small superior figures the number of burials in which such objects were found.

TABLE 5

Frequencies of Various Objects per 100 Burials

Site number	2	11	1	1	159	162	3	83	83	100	135	138	1
Cemetery number			1	2				2	1				3
Tentative period	Early Mainland		Intermediate Mainland		Early Island				Intermediate to Late Island				Late Mainland
Number of burials*	100 (49×25)	100 (4×25)	100 (26×4)	100 (37×2.7)	100 (19×5)	100 (25×4)	100 (107×0.9)	100 (72×1.3)	100 (88×1.1)	100 (161×0.6)	100 (19×5)	100 (48×2)	100 (56×1.8)
Mortars and pestles	58	150	76	16	25	28	17	18	14	6	15	4	31
Metates and mullers	2	200	8	0	0	0	0	1	1	1	0	0	0
Pseudo-metates	2	0	0	0	0	0	2	0	4	2	5	14	4
Drills	0	0	4	0	0	16	2	0	16	8	5	14	2
Perforated stones	0	0	0	0	10	56	19	27	10	7	5	10	0
Charmstones	18	0	0	0	20	0	1	0	0	0	0	0	0
Steatite ollas and pans	0	0	20	0	0	0	0	0	0	0	10	8	36
Stone pipes	18	0	0	0	5	0	0	3	2	2	5	2	10
Circular hooks	0	0	4	4	0	0	0	0	46	33	0	6	5
Straight hooks	0	0	0	0	10	4	10	0	14	3	0	2	2
Bone pendants	0	0	0	2	5	4	2	25	0	0	0	0	0
Inlay work	0	0	28	16	0	0	5	0	5	3	0	0	2

* Figures in parentheses show basis of calculations.

occur in a number of others. The occurrence of circular fishhooks has been used as a fourth criterion in temporal determinations.

To a certain extent my impressions of the relative antiquity of a site, based on density or hardness of the mound materials, on degree of patination of objects, and on preservation of bones and artifacts, have also been used in the placing of sites chronologically. Such general impressions have in most cases been in harmony with the less subjective determination by similarities in types or occurrences of classes of objects.

The stratigraphic materials presented in table 1 are in part duplicated on the right-hand side of table 4. In addition a number of objects obtained in stratigraphic work which could not be conveniently shown in table 1 are also indicated.

Table 5 presents some of the data of table 4 in a different manner. Types of artifacts which do not seem to be of chronological significance have been omitted, and the frequencies have been made equivalent by presenting the frequency per 100 graves rather than actual numbers found. Island sites 81 and 82 have been omitted. As in other tabulations, fragments of objects, unless from the same original, are counted the same as complete artifacts.

CULTURAL CHANGES AND DEVELOPMENTS

The data presented in tables 1 to 5 allow us to draw certain conclusions as to the changes, rather minor to be sure but perceptible, which came about in the course of time in the region under discussion.

The Early Mainland Period

The stratigraphic work at site 6 and the minor investigations made at sites 3, 5, 8, 9, and 11 enable us to characterize the period, though in an inadequate way. More complete results should be forthcoming with the excavations of cemeteries which have an equal antiquity. At the beginning of the period covered by these sites there was already a certain amount of local specialization—as is evidenced by work in steatite and by the use of hot pebbles and asphaltum in coating baskets. It seems reasonable, therefore, to infer a previous period during which these techniques were unknown.

The main sources of food were shellfish, fish, land and sea mammals, and probably acorns and other seeds. Perhaps the high frequency of metates and mullers denotes a specialization in vegetable foods. At any rate such an interpretation fits in well with the relatively small amount of shell in sites of this period. On the other hand low shell content may in itself be a correlate of the greater time factor, though this seems unlikely.

Mortars (both the basket mortar and deep types) and pestles were used, but to a minor extent. The bow and arrow, spear, flint scraper, chipped flint drill, and flint knife were expectably present. The ubiquitous bone awl and a fishhook (see fig., p. 212) with a straight, double-pointed bone barb are the only bone tools recovered. Ornamental objects consisted of steatite and shell beads and ocher. Evidence of basketry rests on the occurrence of basket pebbles, and these permit us to infer that baskets were given a coating of asphaltum to render them watertight. Charmstones complete the list of objects from site 6.

Site 2 is rather difficult to place chronologically, but it seems likely that it represents a late phase of this early period. The metate-muller has by this time all but gone out of use, to be replaced by the mortar and pestle. To the list of objects known in site 6 have been added small steatite bowls, steatite pipes, abalone-shell dishes, and quartz crystals. Sites 9 and 11 add nothing new in the way of artifacts, but the presence of metates and mullers stamps them as of this period. Sites 3, 5, and 8 also represent this early period.

The Intermediate Mainland Period

With the exception of the metate and muller the elements of material culture known in the earlier period have persisted into this. New elements are steatite ollas (nearly globular urns or bowls, 5 to 18 inches in diameter, usually with small mouths), inlay work of shell beads set in asphaltum, whistles, circular fishhooks, a variety of shell beads, and bone beads and tubes. Steatite beads have become more common.

Late Mainland Period

Culturally there is little to distinguish this period from the preceding. It is represented by only one of the three cemeteries of Mainland site 1. Only one new element is added, steatite pans (large slightly concave slabs of steatite, evidently used as frying or baking pans). The higher frequency of steatite ollas is probably explainable on the basis of Spanish-introduced horses and larger boats which made communication with Catalina Island and the Mainland to the south easier. The late period culminates in the brief post-European phase of Chumash culture.

The Early Island Period

In point of time this period, represented by sites 159, 162, 3, and cemetery 2 of site 83, is probably equivalent to the last phase of the early Mainland and the beginning of intermediate Mainland. Mortars and pestles are known but are not so common as on the Mainland—probably owing to the paucity of acorn-bearing oaks. Metates and mullers are rare or unknown. The presence of charmstones and of bone pendants, and the absence of steatite ollas, cooking pans, and circular fishhooks set this off from later Island periods.

The Late Island Period

The "late" sites designate those in which European objects were found or in which other factors indicate recency. The charmstone has now passed out of vogue and bone pendants have followed suit. There has been a decided development of work in shell and nearly every grave of this period yields some sort of pendants, beads, and various other types of shell ornaments. By far the most common are those of haliotis shell and these occur in a bewildering array of shapes and sizes. Ornamental objects in other types of shell are more stereotyped in pattern. As on the Mainland the steatite pan and the steatite olla come in late. The low frequency of these objects on the islands seems to indicate that most of the traffic in them was between Catalina Island (which seems the most likely source) and the Mainland rather than between Catalina and the other islands.

MISCELLANEOUS ITEMS

Canoes

Several fragments from canoes were found, but only one of sufficient size to warrant any interpretation as to form and type. Seven short pieces, evidently from the two top planks, average about two feet in length, four inches in width, and one inch or less in thickness. They were lashed together by means of cord or sinew which was passed through holes bored about one inch from the edge. There are no indications that ribs were used in construction. If no ribs were employed, it seems likely that the lower part of the hull was of the dugout type, since planks of the type found would not provide a strong enough hull if used exclusively. The lack of rib marks on our bits of plank, however, cannot be considered conclusive evidence that ribs were not used, or that the bottom of the hull was of dugout type.

Perforated Stones

No definite evidences of the use of these objects was obtained. Some show the marks of use as polishing implements, and were probably used in finishing arrow, spear, and harpoon shafts. There is some evidence that they were used as the hoop in the hoop and pole game. A number of considerations point to a purely ceremonial use, perhaps replacing the earlier charmstones. Only a small percentage of the specimens have perforations large enough to permit use as digging-stick weights, and their occurrence in the graves of males also indicates other uses than that of auxiliaries to the digging stick.

Basketry

The majority of our basketry remains consists of the asphaltum lining of water baskets. The fibers have decayed, leaving the imprint of the texture and weave. That nearly all the specimens are from Island site 3 is undoubtedly to be explained by the fact that a supply of fresh water is some one and one-half miles distant in summer, hence a need for a considerable number of water receptacles. Wicker, twined, and coiled forms occur but the wicker type seems to be the most numerous at this site. Wicker basketry seems to be rare or unknown in southern California in recent times. Since site 3 is early, it is likely that wicker weaves were more common in the early period and that the coiled and twined types came to be almost the only weaves used in the late period. A few bits of basketry from late sites show a preference for the use of surf grass in open twined work. A few fragments of the coiled type were also found in late sites, but wicker weaves seem to be absent. Mats which probably served for wraps and bedding were common, with surf grass in twining the prevailing form.

Fetish Bundles

The identification of wrapped ceremonial objects as fetish bundles is based on comparable objects described by living Indians in southern California. Groups of objects with remains of the bundle or wrapping were rare; in most cases the mat or basket wrapping had probably disappeared. Of the contents of such bundles one example will suffice: painted fabric or basketry containing 2 perforated stones, 5 awl or spatula-like batons with quartz crystals set into the open ends, 3 loose quartz crystals, 2 steatite pipes, a small incised steatite dish, and a number of beads, pendants, curious shells, etc.

Pottery

The Chumash did not manufacture pottery but now and then stray pieces were acquired by trade. Not more than a half-dozen sherds were found, and these were all found within three feet of the surface of the mounds or in post-European cemeteries. All the fragments are the rough, reddish ware common in southern California.

Houses

It is noteworthy that not more than a half-dozen definite floor surfaces were encountered in all our work. Even pits dug in hut circles often failed to locate the floor levels. This may mean that the same spots were seldom occupied by houses for long periods of time or it may simply indicate that the debris of the shellmounds packs little and that the floor stratum does not become appreciably harder than the normal refuse.

One hut circle was completely excavated. The house was circular, 16 feet 8 inches in diameter, the floor rising a bit near the walls. The entire structure was evidently a hemisphere. The frame was of poles which were supported by 4 or 5 posts near the center. The door was formed by 2 whale ribs so placed as to form an arch. The roof was thatched with surf grass laid 2 or 3 inches thick. The fireplace was a slight depression at the center flanked by a rough circle of cobbles and flat stones. We can infer a smoke hole at the crest of the dome. The entire floor was covered with a layer of clean beach sand. The door was to the north, in this instance the land and leeward side.

CULTURAL DEVELOPMENT

In the foregoing pages I have tried to indicate the evidences of culture changes from the early to the late periods. The culture of the region was already somewhat specialized during the earliest times of which we have information. This is indicated by the use of asphaltum and steatite. The capture of sea mammals and the gathering of shellfish indicate a culture already more or less maritime in its outlook. The mortar and pestle are gradually substituted for the metate and muller at what is perhaps the middle period. We can suppose that about this time the islands were populated. A little later the charmstone passed out of vogue and the circular shell hook was developed. Bone and whale-tooth pendants, often decorated with designs in dot depressions filled with black or red paint, seem to be a special development and are limited to the earlier Island culture. Perforated stones are of very rare occurrence in Mainland sites but are common enough in both early and late Island sites. Fishhooks of both types are much more numerous in Island sites—an indication that the Island culture was more maritime in nature than that of the Mainland. This inference is borne out by the lower frequency of mortars and pestles.

The changes in culture which the materials indicate are rather minor in nature and for the most part gradual. There are no indications of sudden or major shifts in pattern of culture. The tribal or linguistic groups may have changed a number of times in the several thousand years probably involved, but if so the newcomers must have taken over the culture of their predecessors substantially *in toto*. The material culture represented throughout gives evidence of no remarkable developments beyond the bare needs for a rather drab existence, and here, as elsewhere where this is true, there is long adherence to primitive uniformity in the few objects needed to secure a livelihood.

The stable character of the culture, the few new developments, and the regional differences are diagrammatically represented in the figure below. Relative frequencies are based on tables 3 and 5.

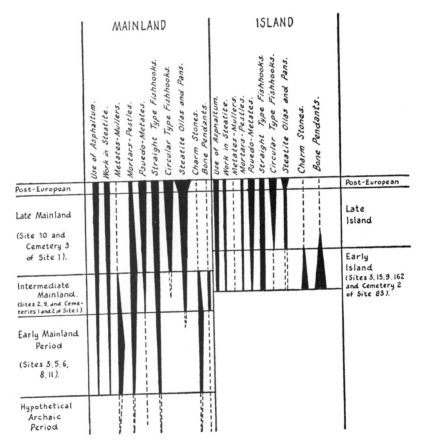

Reconstruction of Prehistoric Cultural Changes, Chumash (Santa Barbara) Area.

Possible Oceanic Affiliations

Southern California exhibits a number of traits in both material and social culture which have provided cause for the suspicion of Oceanic influences. But until some bit of definite evidence comes to light the safest attitude is one of cautious acceptance of the possibility of such affiliation. Our investigations yielded no such definite evidence. The late appearance of the circular shell hook, the perforated stone (which is a faint reminder of the club heads of Oceania), and, by inference, the plank canoe—all reminiscent of Oceanic culture—provide little grist for the mill of those who believe in these historical contacts. On the other hand, Oceanic provenience is not ruled out by any hoary antiquity for these artifacts, which are all relatively recent.

SPECULATIONS ON THE PREHISTORY OF NORTHWESTERN CALIFORNIA

by
Albert B. Elsasser and
Robert F. Heizer

On July 1, 1948, which date marked the establishment of the California Archaeological Survey, there became available to the Department of Anthropology at Berkeley for the first time substantial funds to execute a program of systematic exploration of California prehistory. Among the several separate field parties working during the summer of 1948, one took the form of a regular summer session field training course in archaeology and involved the excavation of site Hum-118, located in Patrick's Point State Park.

In 1949 a field party financed by the California Archaeological Survey worked during the summer exploring the refuse deposits of site Hum-169 at Trinidad Bay, which is also known as the historic coastal Yurok village of Tsurai.

Northwestern California was, in 1948, as little known archaeologically as any region in California. The only archaeological investigation which had been carried out and reported before 1949 was by L. L. Loud, who, in 1915 dug a trench in a large site (Hum-67) located on Gunther Island in Humboldt Bay.

Beyond these three investigations, the only other excavation worthy of mention conducted in the northwestern corner of the state was the exploration of site DNo-11, near Crescent City, which was carried out under the supervision of Dr. Richard A. Gould in the summer of 1964.

It will thus be seen that in the extreme northwestern corner of California, in the present area of Humboldt and Del Norte counties, which was occupied at the beginning of the historic period by the Wiyot, Yurok, Karok, and Tolowa tribes, very little is known about the prehistoric period. At Berkeley in the Archaeological Research Facility site files, are records of twenty-four sites in Del Norte County and two hundred and six sites in Humboldt County.

In the penumbra of the two-county area mentioned, we have some archaeological information from A. E. Treganza's excavation of sites on

Pp. 1–6 of A. B. Elsasser and R. F. Heizer, *Excavation of Two Northwestern California Coastal Sites*, Repts. UCAS, No. 67 (1966), pp. 1–149.

the Trinity River about sixty miles east of Eureka; bits of information from the Chetco and Pistol rivers on the southern Oregon coast; the interior riverine sites at Gold Hill on the Rogue River in Takelma territory excavated by L. S. Cressman; and the Iron Gate Reservoir site excavated by F. C. Leonhardy. All in all, we lack any substantial body of controlled archaeological information from the coast of northwestern California since we are limited to four excavated sites. No significant body of excavation data for the area remains unanalyzed. One can say that nearly everything yet remains to be done to secure even the most rudimentary understanding of the history of human occupation of the northwestern section of the state.

It has been suggested, though without much evidence to support the proposition, that the northwestern coast of California was the last area of the state to be permanently settled. This may be true, but it may also be wrong. The few radiocarbon dates for site levels can be taken as indicating that the sites of historic villages were first occupied within the last 1000 years. Peat from the base of the Gunther Island site is dated at about 900 A.D., and the lowest levels of the Patrick's Point shellmound date from about 1300 A.D. These are both situated in attractive locations and if more ancient evidence of occupation does not occur here, it may be because there are older sites as yet not recognized, excavated, and dated, or because there was in fact no sedentary occupation of the coastal edge before a thousand years ago. Newman's review of the prehistory of the Oregon coast led him to remark on the lateness of all known archaeological sites, indicating that the same apparent lack of time depth prevails along the coast to the north as far as the mouth of the Columbia River. On present evidence, though this is admittedly slender, there is general agreement that all of the presently known archaeological sites from Eureka northward along the Oregon coast are very late in time, and that they contain evidence of a technology and economy which are, with few exceptions, directly comparable with ethnographic forms. The presumption is, therefore, that these sites (exception is reserved, of course, for significantly earlier sites which may be found in the future) are settlement spots of village groups of the same linguistic units or tribes that held the area at the opening of this historic period. We are on fairly firm ground, therefore, in concluding that site Hum-67 on Gunther Island is a Wiyot site first occupied about 1000 years ago, and that the Patrick's Point site (Hum-118) is a Coast Yurok village first occupied about 700 years ago. The Hupa are estimated, by the lexicostatistic method, to have been resident on the lower Trinity River for about 1000 years, and W. R. Goldschmidt argues positively for the late crystallization of Hupa and Yurok culture. While he makes no age estimates, we judge that Goldschmidt would perhaps admit as much time as a millennium for this process to have occurred. The Athabascan-speaking Kato are suggested as having linguistically separated from the Hupa about a thousand years ago. The Kato are of special interest since they are physically of the distinctive Yuki type. Such a shift, presumably one of a Yuki group acquiring a new language, ought to be traceable archaeologically, and with reasonable success in such an effort a new linguistic time depth datum could be secured.

Another culture historical problem can be suggested for the north-western corner of the state. This pertains to the broad problem of im-mediate origins of the several Athabascan, Hokan, and Algonkian tribes who live in fairly small territories, crowded up against each other, and all sharing to a remarkable degree the same material and social culture but each retaining its special language forms. While general culture forms are shared, there are specific differences whose analysis (especially if carried out diachronically and comparatively) should tell us a great deal about the details of intertribal culture diffusion. Where and in what way the distinctive northwestern California culture pattern took specific form can only be answered by archaeological data, and in the attempt to unravel these little tribal histories the prehistorian can test several hypotheses which have been advanced.

The boat-, harpoon-, and dugout canoe-using, gabled plank-dwelling, salmon and sea mammal eating culture pattern of northwestern California must have had its origin farther north in the Northwest Coast culture area proper; and the southward diffusion of that pattern, which changed as it spread, may have been along the Pacific shoreline, probably by river-by-river steps or southward from the Columbia River by way of the Willa-mette Valley. There may have been some leap-frogging along the long coast route as suggested by the fact of small and relatively stabilized terri-torial holdings of linguistically differentiated tribes, strung out like beads on a chain and running south from the Makah along the Washington and Oregon coasts. M. Jacobs suggests an alternative to large scale and rela-tively rapid migrations to account for the Athabascans in the southern Oregon-northwestern California region in the form of "processes of village intermarriage and intercommunication with consequent gradual speech boundary shifts." While Jacobs admits the possibility of "occasional more rapid populational movements," it does not seem to us very probable that the score or so of Athabascan groups settled on the southern Oregon coast and in northwestern California south of the extended block of Penu-tian tribes on the Oregon coast — who in turn are backed up in the interior by the Penutian Kalapuya of the Willamette Valley — have got to their present locations at the slow speed which we might call the "Jacobs intermarriage rate." The first Athabascans, however many there were, probably came as a unit, speaking Athabascan and moving through western Oregon before it became Penutian territory. Jacobs proposes that the Coos-Siuslaw-Alsea Penutian-speakers have lived in their present territories "during many hundreds if not thousands of years." We are sure Jacobs did not intend these words to be taken, thirty years later, as estimated dates, but do assume that he at least meant to indicate his belief that the Penutian tribes had long been residents of the central Oregon coast. The special distinctiveness of the northwestern California culture type is a local subcultural specialization which has existed long enough to flow northward, as H. G. Barnett says, "in an everfading overlay as far as the Coos [tribe on the central Oregon coast], there to blend with the more precise manifestations of North Pacific Coast features." This dispersion from what Kroeber calls the northwestern "hearth" also apparently diffused upstream into the interior, if we may judge from the ethnographic culture of the Karok, the archaeological manifestation at the late prehistoric site in Shasta territory in the Iron Gate Reservoir area which is radiocarbon dated at 1400–1500 A.D., and the prehistoric site in Takelma territory on the Rogue River at Gold Hill (these last two sites lying some 88 and 82 airline miles east or northeast of the mouth of the Klamath River). All these sites produce material culture forms which are practically indistinguishable from those we know from the Yurok of recent times as well as from prehistoric sites in Yurok territory.

P. Drucker comments on the distinctive manifestation of northwestern California culture in the following words: "The whys and wherefores of this northwestern Californian culture focus, from the standpoint of areal culture history, remain to be discovered. Many distinctive features of [Northwest Coast] areal culture were lacking, such as the potlatch, masked dances, representative art, and the like. But the local pattern cannot be regarded as a marginal, watered-down manifestation in the process of diffusion from a higher center far to the north."

It is not clear whether the Oregon and northwestern California tribes exhibit a maritime culture which has been secondarily adapted to riverine environments or whether these are originally river-oriented cultures which have adjusted to the ocean coast. Although the Wiyot, Yurok, and Tolowa seasonally hunted sea lions on offshore rocks, they were apparently not maritime in the sense that they ventured into the ocean at will. G. Nomland and A. L. Kroeber discuss this situation and state that "the Wiyot had made the pattern of their life attach to still water and its shores." The Coast Yurok concentrated their settlements on the shores of the several freshwater lagoons which lay just behind the sand bars; otherwise they were mainly riverine in their outlook and economic dependence. Kroeber argued that the Yurok canoe and paddle are designed for river rather than ocean use.

T. T. Waterman characterized the Yurok dugout canoe as "exactly what we would expect to find, if a knowledge of navigation and a specialized industry in canoe-making had become gradually diffused southward from a center somewhere north of the Columbia River." From the map one would guess that Humboldt Bay and the lower Klamath River are the most favored areas of the northwest, and that they may have been settled first and held longest. A hint that this is so comes from Kroeber's discussion of types of kinship nomenclature of the Yurok, Wiyot, Tolowa, Hupa, and Karok, where he differentiates the Wiyot and Yurok from the other three. Since the "separation date" for Yurok and Wiyot languages is placed by lexicostatistics at slightly over 2000 years ago, and similar data for the California Athabascans indicate more recent separations, the Wiyot and Yurok may be argued as being older residents in the area, a conclusion which Kroeber reached — though with the proviso that it was pure inference — from his analysis of kin term systems in northwestern California. Jacobs makes a similar proposition on relative age of Algonkians and Athabascans in California but on different grounds. It must be due to more than mere accident that the Wiyot and Yurok, who are both Algonkian in speech-family affiliation and who live next to each other, jointly held the most attractive economic locales in northwestern California; they seem, in short, to be the groups which arrived first and staked out the best living areas.

From this welter of opinion one can extract two useful and apparently sound conclusions: first, migrations of Algonkian and Athabascan-speaking peoples into northwestern California have occurred, a point made obvious by their geographical separation from the main bodies of speakers; and second, the two Algonkian-speaking tribes can be viewed as having entered the area either at the same time or serially but at not too great an interval. They were then followed by the Athabascan-speaking group or groups who were forced to take up residence either in unoccupied territories or, at least, in localities not occupied by the Wiyot and Yurok.

To bring the several points discussed here together with reference to suggested procedures to be followed in a program aimed at defining the prehistory of northwestern California, we propose the following:

1. Concentration of site survey and test excavation on the lower courses of the several rivers which in most cases were held by separate groups. These would include, from north to south, the Smith and Klamath rivers; Redwood Creek; and the Mad, Eel, Bear, and Mattole rivers. In addition, the lower Trinity and middle course of the Klamath should be surveyed.

For each stream we have locations of named ethnographic village sites and these total, as a guess, 500 locations.

2. After this initial survey and excavation results from, say, twenty sites, the larger drainage areas of each stream could be examined. This should not require as much time as the initial survey of lower stream courses, since settlement patterns would by now be understood and some judgments of cultural affiliation of sites could be made on the basis of the information then in hand. Also, by this time the archaeologist should quite easily recognize anomalous sites, either as to location or material remains, and such abnormalities should be a reflection of age differences.

3. Once these two surveys were accomplished, further excavation for the purpose of throwing light upon duration of occupation, skeletal types, time of appearance in the sequence of specific artifact forms, and the like could proceed at selected spots with the aim of providing necessary data to determine the exact nature of intra-area diffusion and, ultimately, to throw light upon extraregional origins.

ROCK ART IN CALIFORNIA

by
Campbell Grant

The existence of aboriginal rock paintings and petroglyphs in California has been known for a long time. The colored drawings of Painted Cave near Santa Barbara were sketched by the Reverend Stephen Bowers about 1875, several years before the first discovery of the Paleolithic cave paintings at Altamira, Spain. At about the same time, the early settlers in the lower San Joaquin Valley first saw the elaborate Yokuts paintings on the granite boulders of the Sierra foothills.

Over the years, information on the location of such sites was collected at the University of California, Berkeley, until in 1929, Julian Steward, using the accumulated records, published his classic study *Petroglyphs of California and Adjoining States*. This work attempted for the first time to classify design elements. Steward mapped the distribution of forty-three design elements that occurred frequently at a number of sites to determine the relationships of one area to another. He omitted elements that occurred rarely or in only a single area.

Since 1929, a great deal more information has been collected, particularly in the decade of the 1960s. Many articles and books have been published and some investigators have used Steward's system of design classification. As specialized studies of particular regions were made, it became obvious that the occurrence of such basic designs as spirals, wavy lines, bi-sected circles, etc., over a very wide range did not necessarily mean that there was any connection either direct or indirect between the various areas but might simply indicate that certain similar designs may occur to primitive artists in complete isolation from one another. It is only when extremely complex patterns or a sizable assemblage of almost identical designs are found in widely separated regions that a connection can be proved. Not only designs but techniques must be considered in a search for relationships. Ethnological studies have shown that identical motifs often have completely different meanings in widely separated regions.

Article contributed by the author and adapted by him from Chap. 14 of his *Rock Art of the North American Indian* (Crowell, 1967). The editors thank Mr. Grant and Thomas Y. Crowell Co.

The two basic techniques are painting (with finger or fiber brush) and pecking or incising. Where the rock is light colored and natural caves or rock shelters occur, paintings predominate. The exception to this is in the forests and foothills of northern California where incising and pecking on light-colored rocks is the favored technique. Where the basic rock is basaltic (confined to the desert regions bordering Nevada and Oregon), the designs are pecked into the dark patinated surfaces.

All the evidence to date based on ethnographic information and subject matter indicates that most of the drawings were made for ceremonial purposes probably by the shamans or under their direction. Precise dating of both paintings and petroglyphs is difficult or impossible, though comparative dating through superimposition of designs can be made. Other methods to determine comparative or approximate dating are through degree of repatination of pecked surfaces, radiocarbon tests on associated artifacts, ethnographic identification by living Indians who made such drawings, and datable subject matter (such as the horse).

California Rock Drawing Styles

Style	Method	Major Concentrations
Great Basin abstract	pecked	Desert ranges of eastern California from Oregon to Mexico
Great Basin representational	pecked	Coso and Argus ranges, Inyo County
Abstract curvilinear	incised	Forests and foothills of northern California
Pit-and-groove	pecked	fornia
Abstract polychrome	painted	Coastal ranges (Santa Barbara area); Sierra foothills (Kern-Tulare Counties)
Abstract rectilinear	painted	Coastal ranges and desert, southwestern California

PRINCIPAL STYLE AREAS

Great Basin Abstract (pecked)

There are great concentrations of petroglyphs pecked shallowly into the dark brown or black patinated surfaces of basaltic rocks in that part of California that drains into the Great Basin. The pecking stone, breaking through the patina or "desert varnish" to the lighter original rock color, leaves an image of high contrast that will remain fresh-looking for many hundreds of years. The desert ranges are subject to great summer heat accompanied by thunder showers — ideal conditions for the formation of patina.

The Painted Cave near Santa Barbara. This site has been protected with an iron grille for many years and is the best preserved of the California paintings accessible to the public. The large wheel, top right, is 18 inches in diameter.

Elaborate Figures Pecked on Basalt; Big Petroglyph Canyon, Coso Range, Inyo County (photo Donald Martin).

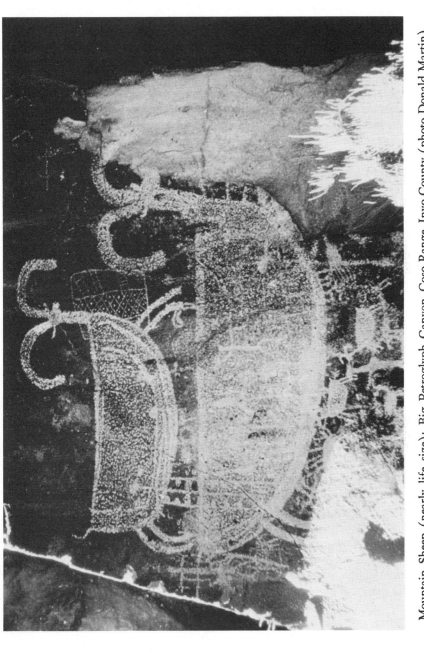

Mountain Sheep (nearly life size); Big Petroglyph Canyon, Coso Range, Inyo County (photo Donald Martin).

Chumash Polychrome Painting from the Carrizo Plains, San Luis Obispo County. Colors: red, black, white. The photograph was taken in 1894 by von Petersdorff. This panel and adjoining sections, over 100 feet long, have since

The subject matter is predominately abstract; spirals, concentric circles, meandering lines, rayed circles, and the like with an occasional group of sheep, deer, or crude anthropomorphic figures. They occur mainly on isolated boulders or cliff surfaces. This style is found throughout the Great Basin and is mainly the work of the Shoshonean-speaking people who with their Desert culture, dominated the Basin until the coming of the whites.

Heizer and Baumhoff in 1962 postulated a hunting magic motivation for most of these Great Basin abstract petroglyphs based on their location near known game trails and in narrow draws leading to water. They noted the almost total absence of rock pictures in areas unsuitable for the taking of game. It is known that among recent Great Basin tribes, a hunt shaman often directed the communal hunt; and it seems likely that many of the pictures were pecked by the shaman or under his direction prior to the hunt.

There are a few painted sites widely scattered through eastern California with a notable concentration in the Tule Lake–Lava Beds National Monument region of extreme northeastern California. These are simply painted renditions of typical Great Basin motifs. The oddest site, Fern Cave, is deep in a lava tube, with the paintings (black on white and white on black) continually wet from water seeps but still bright and sharp.

Great Basin Representational (pecked)

This style is concentrated in a remarkably small area — the Coso Range at the extreme northern edge of the Mojave Desert. Here at an average height of 5,000 feet, there is what may be the greatest concentration of petroglyphs in the country. Over 14,000 designs were tallied at 18 sites in an area of roughly 36 square miles. If the immediately adjacent areas are included, the number would be at least doubled. More than 10,000 of these pecked designs are naturalistic in style and most represent the bighorn sheep. Other recognizable motifs are elaborately costumed anthropomorphs, dogs, deer, quail, eagles, bows and arrows, weighted atlatls and medicine bags. Many panels depict the shooting of sheep and sheep impaled with arrows or darts. Dogs are frequently shown attacking the sheep.

The petroglyphs are located mainly at the entrances to canyons formed by the faulting of the lava flows that overlay the basic granitic rocks of the region. Here where the basaltic rock has weathered to an intense brown-black, the drawings occur in bewildering profusion on isolated boulders and on cliff faces. There are many stone hunting blinds located near the petroglyphs, and the conclusion is inevitable that we are dealing with a people completely preoccupied with the hunting of bighorn sheep and who killed them in great numbers by driving them past ambush points. The drawings reinforce the conclusions of Heizer and Baumhoff that the rock drawings in southeastern California were mainly connected with hunting magic. In the Coso and Argus ranges, the immense number of sheep drawings indicate that somehow a picture of the sheep near the scene of the hunt would aid the hunter. The great number of elaborately dressed anthropomorphs in conjunction with the sheep (some even wearing sheep horn headdresses) strongly suggests that here we are dealing with a sheep-hunting cult.

Of particular interest is the transition of weapons shown by the petroglyphs. The oldest-appearing pictures show the weighted spear-thrower, or atlatl. Great numbers of panels depict the atlatl and the bow and arrow. The freshest-looking panels show the bow and arrow but no atlatls.

Linguists have theorized that the Shoshoneans who dominated the Great Basin and much of the Colorado Plateau at the start of the historic period originated in southeastern California, centering in the region of Death Valley and the Coso-Argus ranges. This theory is backed by the new evidence of the petroglyphs. Many panels in the canyon country of Arizona, Utah, and New Mexico have figures remarkably like those from the Coso area, with sheep, complicated anthropomorphs, weighted atlatls, etc.

Dating this area is difficult, but based on patination and subject matter (sequence of weaponry), the oldest petroglyphs were probably made 3,000 or more years ago and the most recent as late as 500 to 1,000 years ago.

Abstract Curvilinear (incised)
Pit-and-Groove (pecked)

The abstract curvilinear is confined to the foothills of the coastal ranges, the Cascade Range, and the Sierra Nevada in northern California. Usually found along streams, the sites may be on isolated boulders or on horizontally bedded rock. The basic technique is the deep incising of patterns in soft rocks such as sandstone, steatite, and schist. These rocks are not subject to the deep patination of the desert basalt, and the motifs must be deeply carved to have any definition. The motifs are very simple — meandering lines, rows of dots, concentric circles, rakes, bear and bird tracks, and various abstract patterns.

The heaviest rainfall in the state is recorded from northern California, and it is not surprising to find the designs at many of the sites covered with a heavy lichen growth, making photography impossible until the surface has been cleaned.

The major concentration of the curious pit-and-groove rocks is in this

same region. Almost invariably located on isolated boulders, the petroglyphs consist of deeply pecked cups (up to an inch in depth and usually
about 2 inches in diameter) that may completely cover the upper surface
of the rock. They may be arranged at random or in patterned lines and
groups. Often there are accompanying deeply incised grooves. In the
Sierra foothills these occur on granite boulders.

In the Pomo territory they were known as "baby rocks" and were used
by women wanting children. Among the Hupa, Karok, Tolowa, and Shasta
Indians in northwestern California, such rocks were important in ceremonies to control the weather.

This type of petroglyph occurs sparingly in California but is found in
all the rock art regions. Identical rocks are found in many parts of the
world and the style may well be the oldest in California.

Abstract Polychrome (painted)

The most spectacular rock art in California is found in the coastal ranges
of the Santa Barbara area (mainly Chumash country) and in the Sierra
Nevada foothills of Kern and Tulare Counties (chiefly Yokuts territory).
The benign climate of these two areas and the abundant food supplies
supported two of the three largest Indian groups in California, and allowed
abundant spare time for ceremonial development.

The paintings in the Chumash area are never located near the large
permanent coastal villages, but occur in the mountains, often in very remote and inaccessible spots. The coastal ranges are made up of ancient
sedimentary rocks and most of the sites are in shallow, wind-sculptured,
sandstone caves.

The paintings do not seem to be very old. This belief is based on the
lack of superimposition of styles, on the known rate of paint erosion at
certain sites recorded in the 1880s, and on the association of datable artifacts with painted caves.

The Chumash artists worked in as many as six colors, though the usual
range was red, black, and white, with many of the sites in red alone.
Besides the dominant abstract polychrome style, there is a considerable
amount of abstract linear. With both styles, bizarre and striking anthropomorphic and zoomorphic beings occur with an endless variety of purely
abstract shapes. A constantly recurring theme is the circle, with every
conceivable variation of spokes, rays, cogs, and curious appendages.
The polychrome paintings often have circular designs with multiple outlines of contrasting colors to give great richness to basically simple
shapes. In all instances, the craftsmanship is excellent.

The most elaborate paintings are found in the innermost mountain

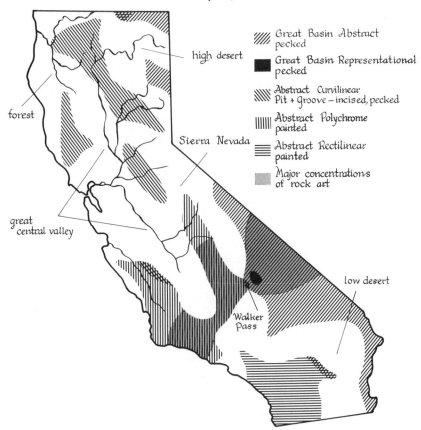

Map 14. The Rock Art Style Areas of California (main sources: University of California; Santa Barbara Museum of Natural History; San Diego Museum; John Cawley and Donald Martin).

ranges and close to the western edge of the San Joaquin Valley. The crudest paintings are located on Santa Cruz Island 30 miles off Santa Barbara, and consist of a number of parallel red lines and dots, daubed on the conglomerate walls of caves.

Most of the Chumash paintings are unvandalized, thanks to their location in extremely rough, brush-covered mountain country where a survey was made in 1961–1963. The examples in open country and near public roads have been destroyed.

To the northeast of the Chumash territory, in San Luis Obispo and Monterey counties, there are a number of sites having paintings that are markedly inferior in quality; many are abstract linear. The most interesting is a smoke-blackened cave in the Big Sur region with hundreds of impressions of white hands. San Nicolas Island, 60 miles off the southern California coast, was inhabited by Shoshonean-speaking Indians sharing many cultural traits with the Chumash. There are incised drawings of porpoises and killer whales on the walls of a sea cave, indicating the importance of these large marine mammals in the life of the people.

The Yokuts, a large Indian nation with many affinities with the Chumash, were located on the east side of the San Joaquin Valley. There was much trade between the two peoples, and it is not surprising that there is a great similarity in their paintings. The design motifs, reflecting regional concepts, are different; but the techniques in both areas are very much the same. In the Sierra foothill country, however, the paintings are found on the undersides of the huge granite rocks that strew the grass-covered hillsides. At some of the sites near Porterville and Exeter, the paintings are carefully executed and considerable imagination is shown in the designs.

In the Chumash region, there is only one site depicting horsemen (drawn side view as opposed to the traditional spread-eagle or pelt method). In the Yokuts area, animals are often shown this way, and the occasional drawings of horses or cows would indicate that many of these paintings are of the historic period.

Adjoining the Yokuts territory to the southeast were the Shoshonean Tubatulabal of the Kern River and the Shoshonean Kawaiisu of the Techachapi Mountains. Both of these peoples sporadically occupied country on the Great Basin side of the Sierra divide. Their paintings basically follow the Yokuts tradition, though some motifs are similar to those of the desert Indians east of Walker Pass. This pass, the most southerly in the Sierra Nevada, must have been used for thousands of years by men and ideas entering and leaving the Great Central Valley. In the Coso Range east of Walker Pass, there are a few late appearing paintings near the petroglyphs; and west of Walker Pass on the Kern River, there are some very old petroglyphs near the paintings. See Map 14 for areas of maximum rock art, east and west of Walker Pass.

Abstract Rectilinear (painted)

The main concentration of this painting technique was in the coastal ranges of southwestern California and in the fringing desert to the northeast where there was a certain overlap with Great Basin pecked styles.

The motifs are quite similar over a large area and consist of red linear designs of diamonds, zigzags, parallel lines, cross-hatching, and hand prints. They are painted on the country rock, granite, usually on an overhanging surface where there was a measure of protection from the weather, though many of them are on exposed rock surfaces and are rapidly being destroyed through erosion. That they have lasted as long as they have is due to the ability of the red iron oxide pigment to penetrate the grainy surface of the granite and to leave a red stain actually under the surface of the rock.

We know from ethnographic evidence that, among the Juaneño and Luiseño (Shoshonean tribes that shared many ceremonial practices with the Chumash), such paintings were made by young women during puberty rites. Many southern California Indians used the narcotic jimsonweed in their ceremonies, and it has been suggested that many of the paintings were made while under narcotic influence.

This area, mainly in western Riverside County, was occupied by Shoshonean groups that had migrated westward from the Great Basin, and their rock paintings probably derived from the Great Basin abstract pecked designs. Such designs are found in the desert region just to the east of the coastal ranges, notably in Joshua Tree National Monument where both pecked and painted techniques appear in close proximity.

The Diegueño Indians, members of the scattered Hokan language family that included the Chumash, were located to the south, in San Diego County. The only concentration of paintings in this region is in Green Valley near Poway. Here many huge granite boulders were painted with elaborate fret and maze-like patterns, very carefully executed in thin red lines. Unfortunately the paintings are completely exposed to the weather and are rapidly weathering away. In addition, suburbs are overwhelming the valley and the bulldozers are assuring the speedy and total destruction of these interesting paintings. There are a few examples in the valley of typical Great Basin style pecked designs — dotted patterns and curvilinear meanders and circles.

In conclusion it can be said that the type of rock dictated the sort of rock art that is found in California. The motivation was apparently mainly ceremonial, for puberty and fertility rites, hunting magic, weather control, and possibly healing ceremonies. The oldest petroglyphs appear to be the pit-and-groove or the Great Basin abstract and representational. The latest rock art is almost certainly the southern California polychrome and rectilinear paintings, and many of these may have been made in conjunction with the use of jimsonweed.

The great mass of Californian rock drawings — perhaps 90 percent or more — are located south of the latitude of San Francisco. Our knowledge of California rock art has increased enormously since Steward's pioneering study of 1929. He describes the 130 sites known to the University of California at that time. Today we have records for nearly 800. The number of sites actually gives no clue to the density of rock drawings. A site may consist of a single pit-and-groove boulder in northern California, while some sites in the Coso range of Injo County are a half-mile or more in length with thousands of individual figures.

historical accounts of
native californians

THE COLORADO
YUMANS IN 1775

by
Pedro Font

[*The reader is reminded that this and the three accounts that follow were written by persons untrained in ethnology. Most of the facts recorded are correct, but the inferences drawn from them are not. Each account should be compared to a recent ethnography as a check on the reliability of the interpretations made by the original authors.*]

The Yumas dwell on the bottom lands of the Colorado River and on both of its banks. Its waters, although always more or less turbid, are fresh and good, and are not salty like those of the Gila River, but this stream, on account of the Rio de la Assumpción, has muddy waters, and this makes the Colorado River somewhat impure after the Gila joins it. The bottom lands extend on one side of the river and the other for about two leagues, and in some places more. In them there are many cottonwoods, and also mesquites and other scrubby trees; and the cottonwoods, although very tall, are usually very slender because they grow so close together. Of these and of the willows there are many that are dry, for they die because the Indians strip off the bark and use it to make the little skirts of the women, as I said.

The river appears to have only a small amount of fish, and these are bony. Each year the river spreads out for a long distance through the bottom lands in the season of the floods, which come from the melting of the snow in summer in the mountains to the north and far in the interior. For this reason it does not rise suddenly but gradually. Indeed it rises and falls nearly all the year, for it begins to rise in March and April and from that time each day it gets larger until July, when it begins to go down, and then every day it gets smaller until the end of the year. The lands which it waters are generally good, and since the water spreads over them so gently it does not injure them. On the contrary, from this irrigation they are greatly fertilized and have moisture for the crops which the Indians plant in them when the water recedes, and for the abundant harvests which they get. In a word,

---

Pp. 97–112 of Herbert Eugene Bolton, ed., *Font's Complete Diary* (1931).

The Yuma are discussed in an excellent monograph, C. D. Forde, *Ethnology of the Yuma Indians*, Univ. Calif. Publ. Am. Arch. and Ethn. (1931), 28:83–278.

this Colorado River appears to me very much like the Yaqui, both in its floods and in other circumstances, as well as in the nature of the Indians who inhabit it, although in everything this river excels the other, especially in the cottonwood groves, which the Yaqui River lacks.

The climate in winter is very cold, and in the mornings there are ice and very heavy frosts, this weather lasting three or four months, from November to February inclusive. The rest of the year the climate is very hot, with excessive heat in the height of the summer, when it usually rains a little, as it also does in the winter. The crops raised by the Indians are wheat, maize, which they call Apache maize and which matures in a very short time, orimuni beans, tepari beans, cantaloupes, watermelons, and very large calabashes of which they make dried strips, which in Sinaloa they call bichicore, and seeds of grasses. With these things they have plenty to eat. They likewise gather a great quantity of tornillo and péchita, although this is more for variety than for necessity.

The territory which the Yumas occupy must be about twenty leagues long. Its center is the Puerto de la Concepción, which is the best place that I saw, and near which Captain Palma has his dwelling and his village. This captain, as I said, is at present the one of greatest authority amongst the Yumas; and although Captain Pablo is chief of more people and of a larger village, he also recognizes Captain Palma, doubtless because he sees that he is so much favored by the Spaniards, by Captain Urrea, by Captain Ansa, and even by the viceroy. Captain Palma succeeded to the command through the death of another chief whom they formerly acknowledged, and of whom the Indian called by us the Prince was the son, as I said above. According to what I was able to ascertain, his dominion was not acquired through descent (for he is not the son, nor, as I believe, is he even a relative of the former captain), but through aggressiveness, valor, and eloquence, for it usually happens among the Indians that the one who talks and boasts most makes himself captain or ruler and is recognized by the rest. Proof of this is the fact that the lands which Captain Palma formerly had inherited from his ancestors are on this side of the river and near the Gila before it joins the Colorado (Palma himself pointed them out to us when with us as we passed through them on the twenty-eighth of November, and they are not very good), whereas those which he at present possesses on the other side of the river in his village, and which are better, were ceded by the Indians just a few years ago.

Palma's rule and authority should not be understood as very rigorous; for since the Indians are so free and live so like animals and without civilization, sometimes they pay no attention to their chief, even though he may give them orders, as I noticed on several occasions. Indeed, I think they recognize him principally in order that he may avenge any injury or lead them to war on other tribes, their neighbors, the Jalchedunes, the Cajuenches and others, who are in no manner subject to Captain Palma, and do not recognize him, for they regard themselves as quite as valiant as the Yumas.

These Yumas, and likewise the Cajuenches and the rest, are well formed, tall, robust, not very ugly, and have good bodies. Generally they are nearly eight spans high and even more, and many are nine and some even above nine, according to our measurements. The women are not so tall, but they also are quite corpulent and of very good stature.

Their customs, according to what I was able to learn, are the following: In religion they recognize no special idolatrous cult, although it appears that there are some wizards, or humbugs, and doctors among them, who exercise their offices by yelling, blowing, and gestures. They say that there is a god, and that they know this because the Pimas have told them so; and that these Pimas and Pápagos, with whom they maintain peace and have some commerce, have told them that above, in the heavens, there are good people, and that under the ground there are dogs, and other animals that are very fierce. They say they do not know anything else because they are ignorant, and for this reason they will gladly learn what we may teach them, in order that they may be intelligent. And since the basis of a well-ordered monarchy, government, or republic is religion, even though it may be false, and since none is found among these Indians, they consequently live very disorderly and beastlike, without any civilization and with such slight discipline as I have previously said, each one governing himself according to his whim, like a vagabond people.

Their wars and campaigns usually last for only a few days, and they reduce themselves to this: Many of them assemble with the captain or some one who commands them; they go to a village of their enemies; they give the yell or war cry, in order that their opponents may flee or become terrified if taken by surprise. They usually kill some woman, or someone who has been careless, and try to capture a few children in order to take them out to sell in the lands of the Spaniards. These captives are called Nixoras by us in Sonora, no matter where they come from, and this commerce in Nixoras, so unjust, is the reason why they have been so bloody in their wars. Their arms are a bow, taller than themselves, badly tempered, and a few arrows, of which generally they carry only two or three, as I saw, and these somewhat long, bad, and weak. Very few carry quivers, if indeed they carry any at all, for I did not see a single one.

Their houses are huts of rather long poles, covered with earth on the roofs and on the sides, and somewhat excavated in the ground like a rabbit burrow; and in each one twenty or thirty or more live like hogs. These houses are not close together in the form of towns, but are scattered about the bottom lands, forming rancherías of three or four, or more, or less.

The clothing of the men is nothing, although as a result of the peace treaties which they have been able to establish since the first expedition, it is noticed that they have had some commerce with the other tribes, so that now we saw some Indians wearing blankets of cotton, and black ones of wool which come from El Moqui [Hopi], which they have been able to acquire through the Cocomaricopas and Jalchedunes. . . .

In the matter of incontinence they are so shameless and excessive that I do not believe that in all the world there is another tribe that is worse. The women, it might almost be said, are common, and the hospitality which they show their guests is to provide them with companions. And although among the old people there seems to be a sort of natural matrimony, recognizing as legitimate some one of the many women they have or had in their youth, yet among the young men I believe there is no such thing as matrimony, because they live with anyone they desire and leave them whenever they please—or at least polygamy is very common among them.

All the females, even though they may be small, and even infants at the breast, wear little skirts made from the inner bark of the willow and the cottonwood. This they soften a little, tear it into strips, enlace or interweave them, and make a sort of apron of them which they tie around the waist with a hair rope, one piece in front and the other behind, the one behind being somewhat longer than the one in front and reaching clear to the knees. Since they are made of so many strips or narrow ribbons the thickness of a finger, and hang loose, with the shaking which they are given on walking they make quite a noise. Among the women I saw some men dressed like women, with whom they go about regularly, never joining the men. The commander called them amaricados, perhaps because the Yumas call effeminate men maricas. I asked who these men were, and they replied that they were not men like the rest, and for this reason they went around covered this way. From this I inferred they must be hermaphrodites, but from what I learned later I understood that they were sodomites, dedicated to nefarious practices. From all the foregoing I conclude that in this matter of incontinence there will be much to do when the Holy Faith and the Christian religion are established among them. Likewise, some women, although not many, are accustomed to cover the back with a kind of cape or capotillo which they make from the skins of rabbits or of beaver, cutting the skin into strips and weaving it with threads of bark; but generally they go around with all the body uncovered except for what the skirts conceal.

On cold nights, and especially in the winter, they make a fire and crouch round it, lying down huddled together and even buried in the sand like hogs. In the daytime they are accustomed to go around with a burning brand or tizón in the hand, bringing it close to the part of the body where they feel the coldest, now behind, now in front, now at the breast, now at the shoulders, and now at the stomach. These are their blankets, and when the fire goes out they throw the brand away, and seek another one that is burning.

The men are much given to painting themselves red with hematite, and black with shiny black lead-colored earth, whereby they make themselves look like something infernal, especially at night. They use also white and other colors, and they daub not only the face but all the body as well, rubbing it in with marrow fat or other substances, in such a way that even though they jump in the river and bathe themselves frequently, as they are accustomed to do, they cannot remove the paint easily. And those who have nothing else, stain themselves with charcoal from the top down with various stripes and figures, making themselves look like the Devil; and this is their gala dress. The women use only red paint, which is very common among them, for I saw only one large girl who, in addition to the red hematite, had some white round spots in two rows up and down the face.

The men have their ears pierced with three or four large holes (the women not so many), in which they hang strings of wool or *chomite* and other pendants. Likewise they wear around the neck good-sized strings of the dried heads of animals that look like tumble bugs, which are found here. They are very fond of cuentas or glass beads, for which they bartered their few blankets, with which some members of the expedition provided themselves. They likewise traded their grain and other things which they brought, so that yesterday about five hundred watermelons and great quantities of calabashes, maize, and beans were sold at the camp, and today more than twice as much. Besides this, nearly all the men have the middle cartilage of the nose pierced (I did not notice this among the women), from which the richest men, such as Captain Palma, hang a little blue-green stone, others a little white stone, half round, like ivory or bone, such as Captain Pablo wore. Others wear beads or other gewgaws in the nose, and although I saw several with nothing, on the other hand I saw some who were contented to wear a little stick thrust through the cartilage.

The coiffure of the men is unique. Most of them wear the hair banged in front at the eyes, and some have it cut at the neck, others wearing it quite long. They are accustomed to make their coiffure or dress their hair by daubing it with white mud and other paints, in order that it may be stiff. They usually do this on the banks of the water and with great care. They raise the front hair up and fix it like a crown, or like horns, and the rest they make very slick with the paints and mud, and they are accustomed also to decorate it with figures in other colors. The women do not make use of all this, their ordinary coiffure being to press the hair together and fix it with mud as in Europe the women use flour paste. Their usual custom is to wear the front hair cut off even with the eyebrows, wearing the rest somewhat long, hanging down the shoulders and back.

They are very fond of smoking, and are very lazy, and if this were not so they would reap much larger harvests; but they are content with what is sufficient to provide themselves with plenty to eat, which, since the soil is so fertile from the watering by the river, they obtain with little trouble. This consists solely in the following: before the river rises they clear a piece of land which they wish to plant, leaving the rubbish there. The river rises and carries off the rubbish, and as soon as the water goes down and recedes, with a stick they make holes in the earth, plant their seeds, and do nothing else to it. They are likewise very thievish, a quality common to all Indians. Their language is not so harsh as that of the Pimas, and to me it appeared to be less difficult to pronounce; for there is a pause like an interrogation at the end of each clause or thing which is said.

As a result of our persuasion the Yuma tribe at present is at peace with all of its neighbors, except the Indians at the mouth of the river, who are still hostile because of a war which Palma made on them a short time ago, in which he killed about twenty of their people. But this breach has now been composed by Father Garcés during his journey there, as he says in his diary. In virtue of this peace some Jalchedunes came down to the junction of the rivers, bringing their Moqui blankets and other things to barter with the people of the expedition. They did not find us there, but Father Thomás, who remained there, received them well and gave them presents.

Finally, these people as a rule are gentle, gay, and happy. Like simpletons who have never seen anything, they marveled as if everything they saw was a wonder to them, and with their impertinent curiosity they made themselves troublesome and tiresome, and even nuisances, for they wearied us by coming to the tents and examining everything. They liked to hear the mules bray, and especially some burros which came in the expedition, for before the other expedition they had never seen any of these animals. Since the burros sing and bray longer and harder than the mules, when they heard them they imitated them in their way with great noise and hulla-baloo.

As a conclusion to all that I have said, since I have been somewhat prolix in speaking of the Yumas and their customs, I wish to note down a question or reflection which many times came to me in this journey, in view of the ignorance, infelicity, and misery in which live the Indians whom I saw on all the journey as far as the port of San Fráncisco. For it is true that the Yumas undoubtedly may be reputed as the most fortunate, rich, and prosperous of them all, since at least they have plenty to eat, and live on their lands, and suffer fewer inconveniences. But the rest, whom I saw farther inland, are in constant warfare between the different villages, as a consequence of which they live in continual alarm, and go about like Cain, fugitive and wandering, possessed by fear and in dread at every step. Moreover, it seems as if they have hanging over them the curse which God put upon Nebuchadnezzar, like beasts eating the grass of the fields, and living on herbs and grass seeds, with a little game from deer, hare, ground squirrels, mice and other vermin. On this assumption, and since the Apostles asked Christ that question concerning the man who was blind from his birth: *Rabbi quis peccavit, hic aut parentes ejus, ut caecus nasceretur?* (John, chap. 9), I might inquire what sin was committed by these Indians and their ancestors that they should grow up in those remote lands of the north with such infelicity and unhappiness, in such nakedness and misery, and above all with such blind ignorance of everything that they do not even know the transitory conveniences of the earth in order to obtain them; nor much less, as it appeared to me from what I was able to learn from them, do they have any knowledge of the existence of God, but live like beasts, without making use of reason or discourse, and being distinguished from beasts only by possessing the bodily or human form, but not by their deeds.

And this same question, and all the rest which I have said, is applicable to many other tribes who inhabit the unknown lands of the Arctic and Antarctic regions and other parts of the earth. But I know that the answer is *Neque hic peccavit, neque parentes ejus, sed ut manifestentur opera dei in illo.* And so, since God created them, His Divine Majesty knows the high purposes for which He wished them to be born to such misery, or that they should live so blind, and it does not belong to us to try to inquire into such high secrets, for *Judicia Dei abyssus multa.*

But, considering that the mercy of God is infinite, and that so far as it is His part, He wishes that all men should be saved, and should come to the knowledge of the eternal truths, as says the Apostle St. Paul, *Qui omnes homines vult salvos fieri, et ad agnitionem veritatis venire* (Ep. I ad Timoth, cap. 2); therefore, I cannot do less than piously surmise, in favor of those poor Indians, that God must have some special providence hidden from our curiosity, to the end that they may be saved, and that not all of them shall be damned. For, as the theologians say, if there should be a man in the forest without knowledge of God and entirely remote from possibility of acquiring the necessary instruction, God would make use of His angels to give him the necessary knowledge for eternal salvation. And that man *in sylvis* whom the theologians assume as a hypothesis, is typified without doubt by some of the Indians whom I saw, and by others who must be farther inland and whom I have not seen. For if God has permitted those people to live for so many hundreds and even thousands of years in such ignorance and blindness that they hardly know themselves, or, as I believe, that they are rational beings, what can we infer, especially in view of a God so merciful that *Misericordia ejus superexaltat judicium?*

THE CHUMASH INDIANS
OF SANTA BARBARA

by
Pedro Fages

At the mission of San Luís Obispo and for a radius of about twelve leagues around it, I have observed the following: The natives are well appearing, of good disposition, affable, liberal, and friendly toward the Spaniard. As to their government, it is by captaincies over villages, as in the others; the captains here also have many wives, with the right of putting them away and taking maidens only; here also the other Indian men have not this privilege, for they have only one wife, and do not marry a second time, until they are widowed. They have cemeteries set apart for the burial of their dead. The god whom they adore, and to whom they offer their seeds, fruits, and all that they possess, is the sun. They are addicted to the unspeakable vice of sinning against nature, and maintain village joyas for common use.

Their houses, shaped like half-globes, are neatly built; each one is capable of sheltering four or five families which, being kin, are accustomed to live together. The houses have one door on the east, and one on the west, with a skylight in the roof, halfway between. Their beds are built up high on bedsteads, which are here called tapextles, of heavy sticks; a reed mat serves as a mattress, and four others as curtains, forming a bedroom. Beneath the bedsteads are the beds of the little Indians, commodiously arranged. The men do not often sleep in their houses at night; but, carrying with them their arms, bow and quiver, they are accustomed to congregate in numbers in great subterranean caves, where they pass the nights in sheer terror; [if they stayed at home] they might be surprised in their beds by the enemy whilst defenseless on account of the presence of their wives and children. They also congregate thus in order to keep watch, spy upon, set traps for and surprise those who may be taken off their guard, for they are a warlike people, always roaming from village to village at odds with everyone.

Their dress and clothing are like those of the Indians of San Gabriel, except that here one sees the hair oftener worn flowing, and of fine texture. The women wear toupés made by burning, and their coiffure is of shells, as I said in a previous chapter. On their cloaks or skirts, stained a hand-

Pp. 47–53, 31–36 of H. I. Priestley, ed., *A Historical, Political and Natural Description of California by Pedro Fages* (1937).

some red, they put as a trimming or decoration various fabrications made from tips of shells and small snail shells, leaving numerous pendants hanging from the margins, after the style of the trinkets of our children. For an ornament and as a protection from the sun, they cover their heads with little woven trays or baskets, decorated with handsome patterns and shaped like the crown of a hat. Both men and women like to go painted with various colors, the former especially when they go on a campaign, and the latter when they are having a festal occasion, to give a dance.

When an Indian woman is in childbirth, she makes a small hole wherever she may be when her labor begins, even though it be in the open field; she digs out the soil, puts in a little hay or grass neatly arranged, warms the hole with fire, of which she always carries a supply ready, and composes herself tranquilly to give birth. She removes from her child the envelope and adhesions bestowed by nature, strokes it, and deforms the cartilaginous part of the nose by flattening; then she goes without delay to bathe herself with cold water, whereupon the entire operation is completed without further ceremony. The child is then swaddled from the feet to the shoulders with a band to shape its body; thus enveloped, it is fastened against a coffin-shaped board, which the Indian woman carries suspended from her shoulders by cords; she takes the child in her arms without removing it from the frame every time she needs to give it milk, or to soothe it if it cries. Thus the Indian women are left unencumbered for all their duties and occupations without on account of them having to leave off caring for and nursing their children, a very natural course of procedure.

It is not to be denied that this land exceeds all the preceding territory in fertility and abundance of things necessary for sustenance. All the seeds and fruits which these natives use, and which have been previously mentioned, grow here and in the vicinity in native profusion. There is a great deal of century plant of the species which the Mexicans call mescali. The mode of using it is as follows: They make a hole in the ground, fill it in compactly with large firewood which they set on fire, and then throw on top a number of stones until the entire fire is covered but smothered. When the stones are red hot, they place among them the bud of the plant; this they protect with grass or moistened hay, throwing on top a large quantity of earth, leaving it so for the space of twenty-four hours. The next day they take out their century plant roasted, or tlatemado as they say. It is juicy, sweet, and of a certain vinous flavor; indeed, very good wine can be made from it.

They use the root of a kind of reed of which they have a great abundance; cleansing the earth from it, and crushing it in their mortars, they then spread it in the sun to dry; when it is dry they again moisten it, removing all the fibrous part until only the flour is left. From this they make a gruel and a very sweet, nourishing flour. At the beginning of the rainy season, which, as in Spain, occurs in the months of November and December, they gather a quantity of cresses, celery, and amaranth. They also eat a kind of sweet flower similar to the wild rose although smaller, of which the bears are also very fond; it grows in swampy humid places in canyons. The cubs of this kind of bear, which the Indians hunt, stealing them from their mothers, are raised and fattened for eating when they are ready, as is done with pigs.

I will omit repetition of the land animals, birds, and amphibians, of which I have made mention in other chapters. Among reptiles and insects, here are seen the tarantula, the starred lizard, and a kind of small but extremely poisonous viper. Among the sea fish there are many sea bream, crabs, whitefish, curbina, sardines of three kinds, cochinillo, and tunny; in the streams and rivers there are trout, spinebacks, machuros (an Indian name), and turtles. The fishing canoes are finely described in the public accounts published in October of the year 1770. The tridents they use are of bone; the barb is well shaped and well adapted to its use. The fishhooks are made of pieces of shell fashioned with great skill and art. For catching sardines, they use large baskets, into which they throw the bait which these fish like, which is the ground-up leaves of cactus, so that they come in great numbers; the Indians then make their cast and catch great numbers of the sardines.

In their manufactures, these Indians, men and women alike, are more finished and artistic than those of the mission of San Gabriel. They know how to make very beautiful inlaid work of mother-of-pearl on the rims and sides of stone mortars, and various other utensils. The women weave nearly all their baskets, pitchers, trays, and jars for various uses, interweaving with the reeds or willows, or embroidering upon them, long, flexible, fibrous roots, which keep their natural color, white, black, or red. They also do the same with shells, and small stones of the same three colors for decorating their cloaks and embroidering the bands of their headgear. The tools of these skillful artisans are only two, the most simple ones in the world, the knife and the punch. This latter, used by the women, is a piece of bone as sharp as an awl, from the foreleg, next to the shinbone, of the deer. The other is more particularly a tool for the men. They usually carry it across the head, fastened to the hair. It is a flint cut tongue-shaped, with very sharp edges; they affix it to a very small handle of straight polished wood inlaid with mother-of-pearl. These knives are made, as is perhaps natural, by rubbing and rubbing away the stone (or natural glass) in contact with harder ones, with water and fine sand. With these knives they supply their lack of iron and steel by dint of much labor and industry.

For starting a fire, which can be communicated to, and made to inflame, other materials, they use the only means they have—since they lack steel, as has been said, or instruments for focusing the rays of the sun—namely, that of rubbing one stick forcibly against another.

These natives always carry their means of making fire in the shape of two small sticks attached to the net with which they are accustomed to gird themselves; one stick is like a spindle, and the other is oblong, or it might properly be called a parallelopiped; in it there is a hole in the middle, in which the end of the other stick may be rotated. When they want to make fire, they secure the square stick firmly on the ground between the feet, and the round one, stuck into the hole, they rotate rapidly between the hands. It begins to smoke instantly, and both sticks are burned a little.

Concluding the chapter, I will say that at a distance of two leagues from this mission there are as many as eight springs of a bitumen or thick black resin which they call chapopote; it is used chiefly by these natives for calking their small water craft, and to pitch the vases and pitchers which the women make for holding water. This black liquid springs from the ground and runs amid the water of the streams without commingling with it or giving it a bad flavor; I observed that, on the contrary, the water of such supplies was most excellent. The source or spring of this bitumen is four leagues farther up, in a canyon which runs east and west, in which it is seen collected in pools arising from different sources and running together with the water, like that of the springs farther down. . . .

In the preceding account of the habits and customs of the natives, and of the products of those countries, I have already included all that pertains to [the territory] from San Diego, not only as far as the Cañada de Santa Clara, as was proposed in Article II with reference to day's marches, but as far as the place called La Carpintería, which is included in this third stage. It only remains to recount here, then, those observations which concern the interval between La Capintería and the Punta de los Pedernales. They are as follows:

The Indians of all these villages are of good disposition and average figure; they are inclined to work, and much more to self-interest. They show with great covetousness a certain inclination to traffic and barter, and it may be said in a way that they are the Chinese of California. In matters concerning their possessions, they will not yield or concede the smallest point. They receive the Spaniards well, and make them welcome; but they are very warlike among themselves, living at almost incessant war, village against village.

In each of these villages (which are very populous here, each one containing on an estimate about six hundred men capable of bearing arms) there is a captain, as has been said of the previous territory. This chief has hardly any other function than that of military command; they always choose the most conspicuous and intrepid one in the village. The position is for life, and [the incumbent enjoys] an absolute, total independence in the government.

The men go clothed with a large cloak made of skins of cony, hare, fox, or sea otter; the garment reaches to the waist, the captain only being allowed to wear it reaching to the ankle, without other mark of distinction. The women wear skirts, made and fitted uncouthly of antelope hide, either colored or white, which do not extend below the knees. Most of them are decorated with various trinkets chosen from the smaller sea shells and stones of various colors. They wear the hair tightly bound and gathered at the back, forming a short, heavy queue, with a very handsome adornment of shells; they also wear collars and bracelets of snail shells and little sea shells. The few men who desire to cut their beards accomplish it, not without great pain, by using a pair of shells of the clam or large oyster, which, being fastened together on one side by nature, can be given a kind of opening and shutting motion on the other. With these they extract the hairs one at a time by the root, as though pulling with nippers. Those who like to wear the hair short, do so by burning it close to their pates—an uncomfortable and fatiguing operation, but necessary on account of their lack of any iron instrument.

They are idolators like the rest. Their idols are placed near the village, with some here and there about the fields, to protect, they say, the seeds and crops. These idols are nothing but sticks, or stone figurines painted with colors and surmounted with plumage. Their ordinary height is three hands, and they place them in the cleanest, most highly embellished place they can find, whither they go frequently to worship them and offer their food, and whatever they have.

Although in this district the captains commonly enjoy the privilege of taking two or three wives, and putting them away at will, the ordinary men have only one, and may abandon her only in case of adultery. The Indians of either sex who wish to marry a second time, may do so only with another widow or widower—a custom which seems not at all irrational if we consider what result such a practice should have in favor of the population.

I have substantial evidence that those Indian men who, both here and farther inland, are observed in the dress, clothing, and character of women —there being two or three such in each village—pass as sodomites by profession (it being confirmed that all these Indians are much addicted to this abominable vice) and permit the heathen to practice the execrable, unnatural abuse of their bodies. They are called joyas, and are held in great esteem. Let this mention suffice for a matter which could not be omitted,— on account of the bearing it may have on the discussion of the reduction of these natives,—with a promise to revert in another place to an excess so criminal that it seems even forbidden to speak its name. Let us go on, then, to describe the ceremony of their funerals and burials.

When any Indian dies, they carry the body to the adoratory, or place near the village dedicated to their idols. There they celebrate the mortuary ceremony, and watch all the following night, some of them gathered about a huge fire until daybreak; then come all the rest (men and women), and four of them begin the ceremony in this wise. One Indian, smoking tobacco in a large stone pipe, goes first; he is followed by the other three, all passing thrice around the body; but each time he passes the head, his companions lift the skin with which it is covered, that the priest may blow upon it three mouthfuls of smoke. On arriving at the feet, they all four together stop to sing I know not what manner of laudation. Then come the near and remote relatives of the deceased, each one giving to the chief celebrant a string of beads, something over a span in length. Then immediately there is raised a sorrowful outcry and lamentation from all the mourners. When this sort of solemn response is ended, the four ministers take up the body, and all the Indians follow them, singing, to the cemetery which they have prepared for the purpose, where it is given sepulture; with the body are buried some little things made by the deceased person himself; some other objects are deposited round about the spot where the body rests, and over it, thrust into the earth, is raised a spear or very long rod, painted in various colors. At the foot of this rod are left a few relics, which naturally represent the ability and kind of occupation which the man had while he was living. If the deceased is a woman, they leave strung on the rod some of the boxes and baskets which she was accustomed to weave.

The occupations and ordinary pursuits of these people are limited; some of them follow fishing, others engage in their small carpentry jobs; some make strings of beads, others grind red, white, and blue paint clays, and a certain kind of plumbiferous stones, which serve for the men to paint themselves with when they are celebrating and dancing or when they go to war, and which are used by the women for their usual adornment. They make variously shaped plates from the roots of the oak and the alder trees, and also mortars, crocks, and plates of black stone, all of which they cut out with flint, certainly with great skill and dexterity. They make an infinite number of arrows. The women go about their seed-sowing, bringing the wood for the use of the house, the water, and other provisions. They skillfully weave trays, baskets, and pitchers for various purposes; these are well made with thread of grass roots of various colors.

There is abundance of all seeds needed for their use, and many acorns. There are birds and land animals of the same species as above mentioned, besides many additional ones. The fishing is so good, and so great is the variety of fish, known in other seas, that this industry alone would suffice to provide sustenance to all the settlers which this vast stretch of country could receive. In the mountains there are seen many pines like those of Spain, *mollares,* and oaks and live oaks upon the slopes and in certain spots on level ground. On the rivers and streams there are many white and black poplars, willows, alders, elms, small poplars, some laurels, and canes. The soil is very good; it is black, well grassed, and mellow; and the fields are thickly dotted with shrubs. Almost every half-league one encounters a stream more or less sizable which flows to the sea, besides headwaters and springs of excellent water, so that there are many places having all the advantages necessary for establishing missions; such are: first, San Luís Obispo, one league inside the canyon of the stream; second, the Ranchería dela Isla; third, the village of La Carpintería, also within another canyon into which another stream empties.

Finally, that nothing may be omitted in the narrative, I will tell [the customs] which these Indians observe in their dances. The women go to them well painted, and dressed as has been described, carrying in both hands bundles of feathers of various colors. The men go entirely naked, but very much painted. Only two pairs from each sex are chosen to perform the dance, and two musicians, who play their flutes. Nearly all the others who are present increase the noise with their rattles made of cane dried and split, at the same time singing, very displeasingly for us, who are not accustomed to distressing the ear with this kind of composition.

THE YUROK OF
TRINIDAD BAY, 1851

by
Carl Meyer

The Allequas or Wood Indians strike me as being the finest looking and most intelligent of all the Indians of California. They are strong and muscular, with a build similar to our own. Their skin is slightly cinnamon colored, or rather bleached, like that of the ancient Incas. The cheeks of the young men and women frequently show a delicate red coloring. The head (homaschkwa) is slightly flattened, the brow vaulted, the facial angle is approximately eighty degrees, the nose (ellek) has a Roman curve, the eye (mellin) is large and intelligent, with a slightly angular cavity, the lips (matella) are not everted, the chin (schtalas) is oval, and the hands and feet (metzk) are small. All their features are less angular and broad than the southern Indians'. It is possible to detect in their faces the distinguishing features of each human race and to designate them as the facial traits of the original man. The Allequas have thick, rather smooth hair; that of the men (woa) and of the children (papusch) is burned off to a uniform length of one inch, which gives them the appearance of having Titans' heads. Sometimes the men wear rather long, upright braids, stiffened with some resinous fluid. These are considered an ornament, and upon festive occasions or in war are adorned with red and white feathers like a hoopoe's crest.

Like all North American Indians they have but little beard (liptasch). The chin hairs are ordinarily plucked out and only allowed to grow as a sign of mourning. The women (squa) and girls (wintscha) wear their hair smoothly combed and unplaited. It falls over their shoulders in gentle waves and is fastened at the forehead with chains of shells and beads (agählalä). The Allequas wear jewels in their ears; these they sometimes obtain from the whites, and sometimes they copy them in wood. At other times these ornaments are replaced by small stones which are supposed to have a talismanic property. Only those Indians who inhabit the distant mountains wear wooden or iron rings in their nostrils.

Pp. 196–236 of Carl Meyer, *Nach dem Sacramento; Reisebilder der eines Heimgekehrten* (Vaaren, 1855).

Additional data on the Yurok of this locality are presented in a collection of documents compiled and edited by R. F. Heizer and J. E. Mills, *The Four Ages of Tsurai* (Berkeley and Los Angeles: University of California Press, 1952).

When five years of age the girls are tattooed with a black stripe extending from both corners of the mouth to below the chin. To this line is added every five years another parallel line, by which means it becomes easy to determine the age of every Indian woman. These daughters of the wilderness are totally unlearned in the fine art practiced by ladies of the civilized world of counting—or concealing—their age. On special occasions the men paint their faces with a varnish derived from the pine tree, and they draw all manner of mysterious figures and ornaments on their cheeks, noses, and foreheads, by removing the varnish while yet soft with a small stick, leaving individual portions of the skin bare. When dry the varnish is of a deep red brown color, while the bare portions retain the natural tint of the skin. This decoration is done in such a way that the face is not disfigured, but the elliptical lines running symmetrically from the forehead across the temples and cheeks give a fuller and quite pleasing appearance to the face. This in itself serves to demonstrate the skilled hand of the Allequas and their appreciation of more complete and beautiful human contours.

In the summer the men go quite naked; in winter they wear over their shoulders wraps of tanned stag or doe leather. They are always provided with bows and arrows, which they carry either in their hand ready for use or in a quiver made of fox or beaver skin which is slung over the shoulder. The bow (smotah) is made of the strong, elastic root of the fir tree; it is about three and one-half feet long and is covered on the back surface with a bear's sinew, which serves to give it greater elasticity and strength. The Allequa draws his bow with the greatest ease. He also has larger bows which are used for long distance shooting. These are six feet long and when using them, the Indian lies on the ground, pushes his right knee firmly against the bow when spanning, and reinforces with both arms.

The arrows (nekwetsch) are skillfully constructed, partly of reeds, partly of cedar wood. The upper part is furnished with two rows of feathers, drawn crosswise through the shaft. Some tips are made of volcanic glass, some of a fine kind of delicate pebble; frequently also they are of iron or ivory. The glass arrows are the most dangerous. Their points are from one to one and a half inches long, three-cornered and jagged. They are fastened to the arrow by means of a firm mass of resin. If they penetrate a human body the glass generally splinters on the bones, the wound promptly festering with fatal results. The iron tips, which are supplied with strong barbs are only lightly fastened to the arrow, with the result that when the latter is withdrawn they remain in the body. The ivory tips usually bore through the body completely. Sometimes the arrows are poisoned with the juice of the sumac tree, but these are only used to slay wild beasts.

Other weapons of the Allequas are the following: the obsidian hatchet or tomahawk, the club, the lance, and the javelin. The Indians are usually also provided with knives (tschalisch) resembling cutlasses, made of iron which they pick up on the beach or obtain by means of barter or purchase from the whites. On one occasion on the banks of the Klamath I received the offer of a fine boat (yatsch) and several beaver skins, as well as of a bow and quiver full of arrows for my hunting knife. The Indian who made the offer and who would have been only too glad to barter or exchange (tschikwatsch) with me was a chief, and I would have accepted his offer, had not a hardened American who was present warned me that trouble would ensue if I were to accede to the request of the Indian warrior.

The Indians' whoops of the hunt, war, and triumph are very penetrating, and their shrill cry for help rises even above the raging of a stormy sea. When running at full speed they resemble a flying stag, and as a proof of their accuracy in shooting I may mention that I once witnessed them strike a ten-cent piece at a distance of twenty paces, six times out of ten. The gun (bakschoss) of the whites will never equal their own bows, in their estimation, as long as they can succeed thereby in filling the whites with amazement and admiration in their prowess. This flatters them and fills them with pride—a characteristic peculiar to all Indians, which is easily comprehended when one becomes familiar with their tremendous self-confidence, which is based on character and strength of will. The Indian assuages all his trials and tribulations by means of this invulnerable self confidence, and therefore never feels consciously unhappy. Sometimes when I was in the presence of a group of Allequas, lost in the contemplation of the conditions peculiar to the mode of life of these naked men, which from a superficial point of view afford so much occasion for pity, I would suddenly be surprised by a derisive laugh, and the group would disperse as though shamed or insulted at being pitied by a white. "Don't weep about us, weep about yourself," seems to be the native's answer to the sympathy of the whites, and I cannot blame them for this.

In the summer the Allequa women wear aprons extending to the knees made of laced bast or strips of deerskin; for winter use they are made of fur or goose down. Ornamental bracelets, wampum, and colored feathers, rings, and buttons (tschämah), for which they have a special weakness, are priceless treasures in their eyes.

What the calabaza [calabash] is for the native of Central America, the haihox is for them; this is a small basket woven out of finest bark. A mother of the Wood Indians considers a group of children her most beautiful adornment. She carries the smallest child on her back in a rush basket and the older children in her arms or on her hips. A mother so adorned worthily symbolizes ever-productive Nature, under whose protection every living thing derives nourishment from the strength of the sun and the milk of the planets, and withers only in the presence of shade or drought.

The huts (mahlämath) of the Allequas are constructed of planks, obtained either from ships which have stranded on the seashore, or made by themselves of split fir [redwood] trees. The floor dimensions of the huts are approximately sixteen by twenty feet, the height of the walls is four to six feet, and the height of the gable ten to fifteen feet. In one corner is the door, if the two-feet wide oval hole through which the inhabitants crawl in and out can be so designated. This opening is smeared over with the blood of their sacrificial animals; it serves as a magic sign to keep off evil and to "ward off the destroying angel."

In the middle of the floor, which is dug out several feet is the fireplace, over which in the roof is a hole that can be closed by means of a cover, which serves the double purpose of a flue and a window. The fire (metsch) is never permitted to go out. Over it are suspended pieces of resinous wood which when dry serve the purpose of matches and from which the Allequa bites off splinters as they are needed. The fire is the surest sign of undisturbed family life and recalls the sacred or eternal flame of the Catholics and Jews. The Allequas sit and sleep around the fire, always with the seniors nearest to the fire, whilst the younger members range themselves around them according to their ages. The space in front of the hut is kept very clean and the courtyard is sometimes paved with pebbles. If the settlement constitutes a village, the mählamath stand in straight lines next to each other two to four feet apart, surrounded by a mound of earth. The graves are located in the middle of the settlement, carefully fenced in and kept sacred. No woaki [white man] can venture closer than a distance of three paces, for they are always guarded by women who, should any bold person overstep the limit, immediately cry out for help and scold the intruder with the words "Qui malla" [bad]!

At daybreak (ahwoak) all the year round the Allequa betakes himself to the neighboring spring, where he washes himself all over, drying himself by the rays of the rising sun. The father of the family is the first one to leave the hut. He opens the chimney flue, stirs up the fire, and after apportioning the daily tasks to the various members of his family, goes off either to hunt or to gather wood (nakoh) in the forest (thebbah). At low tide the women go to the seashore to look for sea creatures of various kinds, while the children go off to hunt for acorns, roots, edible berries (nekbrah) and wild potatoes (lokala). The food is never preserved but always prepared immediately before the meals. Acorns constitute the main food article of the Allequas and they are prepared in the form of a stiff mush. This is placed in a haihox, rubbed on to the sides of the vessel and then quickly baked until hard by placing hot pebbles in the container. Sometimes, instead of a haihox, a rounded cavity in the floor, lined with clean sand, is utilized for this purpose, and glowing embers are piled on the top and the mush is left until cooked. Oysters [mussels or clams] too, are a favorite article of food.

These the Allequas consume in such large quantities that it is a common sight to find great mounds of oyster shells in Indian settlements, and in devastated Indian villages these finds have even provoked geologic investigations. Without the acorn, which also serves to nourish seventy different species of insects, the Indian would lead a pitiable existence. It is his chief source of fat supply and also chiefly contributes to keeping him healthy. Nevertheless, it is undeniable that in order to render satisfying a diet of acorns it is necessary to lead the existence of a red skin, with its alternations of cold and heat as supplied by the rain and sun. The Allequa's only drink is water (pahha). Civilization has not approached closely enough to give them other drinks in accordance with the Christian teaching of Solomon's proverb, "Give strong drink to those who should be killed, and wine to the sad souls, that they drink and forget their misery and think no more of their misfortune."

The Allequas lead a solitary, quiet and contented existence; it might be called a close-knit family life, although the family is never united for long. The man is often away hunting, the wife remains at home with her children or at the graves of her loved ones. The chief (mauhemi) is very greatly respected; he has control over the actions and customs, life and death of his subjects, and his power is passed on to his first born. Polygamy is permitted the chief; frequently he is the father of a very large family.

After an Allequa has chosen his future mate from among the belles of his tribe and wishes to marry her, he must show the mauhemi a chain of shells of an arm's length. This consists of large, long, black shells, the size of a thumb, furnished with a natural hole. These shells (hiaquay) are only found in the extreme north and are obtained from other Indian tribes through trade or war. On account of their rarity these shells also represent in the eyes of the Allequas the highest form of money (tschikh). In addition to this chain of shells a bridegroom must be the possessor of several red feathers like those formerly part of the costly mantle worn by King Kamehameha and the one owned by the present monarch of the Sandwich Islands. If the chief thinks that the purchase price is sufficient, the Allequa is permitted to take home his bride and the young wife receives the jewels as her dowry, together with other ornaments. The chain of shells and the costly feathers thereafter become the hereditary property of the first-born son, so that at a later time he will be able to marry without difficulty, whereas his younger brothers will be compelled to struggle in order to obtain the costly purchase price.

The conjugal life of the Allequas is very chaste. Like all other wild creatures, they mate only in the spring, and from this union regularly spring strong, healthy children, who are nourished at their mother's breast.

Although unfamiliar with the abstract conception of morals, the Allequa faithfully observes and practices its precepts, and although only dimly conscious of his superiority to the white man in this respect, he instinctively realizes the latter's moral shortcomings and calls him "pale-face" or "weak-ling." He and his wife treat with contempt the bold, lewd "pale-face"; the young girls blush with shame and shrink back in horror when a white man jests about their nakedness or stares lustfully at them. . . . The Indians of North California are on a higher moral level than are their tribal relatives of the east or of the softer south. But foreign customs which have been im-pressed upon them, concepts of society and religion, which when brought into sudden contact with a primitive form of human life are bound to be both misunderstood and misapplied, have served rather to ruin than to elevate the wild inhabitants of the forests and plains.

The Allequas harden their children at an early age and inspire them with profound respect for the Divinity, old age, and the mauhemi. Their customs are wild, but in their own untamed manner they respect that which is honorable. The father trains his son to be a hunter and a warrior; the mother teaches her daughter to be a diligent housewife, although she is also taught the use of the bow. The children are trained to be merry and alert. . . . The boys are not permitted to indulge in sexual intercourse until they have attained complete manhood. They are taught to vent their energies in manly occupations and must make the acquaintance of the Muses of Nature before they are permitted any intimacy with the Graces.

The various tribes of the Allequas which inhabit the northern regions of Upper California do not always live on mutually amicable terms; they have frequent disputes, a condition which is readily understood when one considers that with them, as with all Nature's children, it is not law, but might, which is held to be right. Therefore they fight in every way, in the open and in ambush. During my stay in Trinidad the son of the mauhemi was killed while hunting by the Wood Indians on the Klamath River (Rhäkwa). This caused a terrific commotion among the Allequas of Trini-dad (Tschura) and they swore bloody revenge on their enemies (ihnek). Twenty well-armed archers hastened into the mountains along hidden paths (layapp), led by the unhappy father, their sixty-year-old chief. They roamed all over the region for several days, killed some of their enemies and burned down their dwellings. They found the corpse of their relative fearfully mutilated and scalped, and brought it back to their burial place, together with the blood-soaked earth on which the body had lain. Here the whole tribe gathered every morning for a whole week, mourning for the dead and weeping and lamenting in a monotonous dirge. The corpse was not buried until heavy decomposition had set in. The mourners brought all the possessions of the dead man to the grave, which they encircled with small baskets and shells, strewing flowers over all.

After a time these little baskets frequently become converted into dainty flower vases for the bases, when brought into contact with the moist earth, rot away and plants sprout up through the opening in great profusion. A flower sprouting out of a basket is a lucky omen, indicating that the deceased has reached Paradise. This profound veneration for grave flowers is a marked characteristic of the Allequas. Often the maidens of the village go to pick the flowers growing on the graves of their dead relatives. They look at them with the greatest respect and, obeying an innate impulse for grace and beauty, place them in their hair as an adornment.

The religion of the Allequa teaches him to "love his relatives even after death, so that they may think of you when they reach the realm of eternal life, whence they have come and whither all men return." The origin of this religion appears to be the longing for the long-lost state which preceded this earthly existence. For the Allequa, as with all primitive peoples, the hereafter is only a more glorious repetition of this world, from which all trouble will have vanished; it is the happy hunting grounds where are assembled the shades of the departed. But he also believes in the transmigration of souls who, when weakened through an evil life on earth, assume after death some animal form, varying in type according as they were more or less good or bad, strong or weak. Only after a long period of such atonement can these beings enter the celestial paradise. In particular, the Allequa believes that his favorite "prairie dogs" and their mongrels are the incarnations of these souls. He hopes by constant association with these animals, or by eating them, to absorb their souls into his own. He thinks that by degrees a soul can pass from a lower animal form to a higher and that when in a state of complete perfection it may reënter a woman's fertilized womb. These transmigration beliefs of the Indians are very involved, and it is very difficult, in the absence of an exact knowledge of their language, to investigate their real significance, as well as the real meaning of the other esoteric religious customs of the Allequas; for they strive to conceal them even from their most trusted alien friends.

Certain animals and fruits possess religious significance in the eyes of the Allequa and, in the same manner as the Sandwich Islander's taboo, he is forbidden to partake of them. He is permitted to eat of the flesh of the stags (mauwitsch), of the sea lions (swega), the hedgehogs (kahwin), salmon (wuimosla), geese (kwakwa), ducks (nayamed), and all scaly fish. Pork and fat bear's flesh (negwitsch) is forbidden and only permitted to old women.[1]

---

[1] I was astounded at the repulsion and hatred aroused in these Indians by the sight of the donkey. Every time it appeared to them as a fresh misfortune when a white arrived in their midst with one of these animals. I was unable to discover whether this had a basis in religious superstition or not, but the suggestion forced itself upon me that the Allequas

According to the strictest interpretation of anthropophagy the Allequas are cannibalistic and partake of human flesh or blood, namely, when they eat their own lice, for they are of the opinion that by absorbing this parasite they are able to take to themselves some portion of a departed soul which has entered into some particular form of transmigration, or at least to be able to absorb that individual's character. An example of this is found in certain other Indian races who for the same reason drink the ashes of their departed ones with water.

The Allequa worships the sun (woanuschla) and moon as symbols of subordinate divinities, and he prays to them aloud and in a singsong manner when he is walking, running, or dancing. This occurs on the occasion of festivals, and is accompanied by such a state of excitement that one is justified in comparing this religious practice with the modern revivals occurring in certain sects among civilized races, where consciousness is completely deadened and the religious ideas become confused, serving to show what an indispensable factor the sensual element is in religion.

The evil spirit (magäschkwa), on whom the Allequa has bestowed the color white, rules in the air and manifests his terrible anger in the storm; the good spirit he worships in the luxuriant meadows and groves, identifying him with the spirit of Nature, in whose presence alone he is happy. That is the reason he is always out of doors where he feels happy.

As with many of his tribal relatives, the Allequa holds the northwest trade wind in religious veneration. It indicates to him the direction whence, according to his own opinion and mythical hearsay, all the white races as well as his own have come. Because, as this appears to indicate, he believes in a common descent of all human beings, he shows a disposition to live with the whites on a peaceable footing and is willing to be friends with them if their attitude toward him is kind. He takes delight in the good customs of the white man, in his skill and manner of dress, and sometimes is even glad to imitate him in the latter particular. He has already given distinctive names to the various articles of clothing (woa-Kaẏa). So, for instance, akah is hat; kahlin, cover; släkwa, coat; tschäkwa, trousers; noahai, shoes. With his very simple but flexible language, so rich in onomatopoeia, the Allequa readily finds expressions for new ideas. Inflection and gestures greatly help to supplement his conversation, in which he is very animated. His sibilants are particularly effective, produced by pressing the tongue against the teeth of the lower jaw and pressing the air between this and the hollow cheek, which is easily done, thanks to the Indian's agile tongue. Nevertheless, the language of the Allequa is limited and inadequate

hereby appeared to demonstrate a bond of union with the Phoenicians and the Egyptians, for these races, as is known, symbolize in the donkey, as in the pig, the universal conflict or typhoon, which also corresponds with their conception of evil.

to his need of expression, considering that he is usually endowed at birth with no inconsiderable mental powers.

I soon learned some words of the Allequa language, and conversed with my wild friends to the extent of my powers. Certainly a good deal of patience was needed for this, but I luckily possessed considerably more than do the Americans, who are quite indifferent to the Indians and think that they are not human. For this reason the Indian hates the American—to be correct, he despises him. Although he recognizes no national difference other than that of color, and simply divides men into good and bad (skuya and quimalla), nevertheless he has already discovered that the Americans are worse, because more hard-hearted. No wonder! Have I not with my own eyes seen Americans steal Indian women and girls for slaves, and compel the men to serve them as guides and burden bearers?

The Allequas possess a developed form of phonetic hieroglyphics, but they draw their concepts in symbolic, or more frequently in kyriological, pictures. I would often ask the chief the name of some object or other (tennäschä), whereupon he would draw illustrations in my pocket note-book with a pencil with which he was always wanting to scribble. This and many other striking examples made me remark the Allequas' intelligence and acquisitiveness. The first thing they ask their white friends to tell them is their name. 'Kaluschkwa?' ("What is your name?"). They, too, are willing to give their names, which usually refer to some external or internal characteristic of a person and do not sound bad. Thus, for example, the following are some of the men's names: Tetawa, Neeschak, Tschimma, Schenna, Mawema, Tenna; and women's names: Negawa, Homika, Tschäkscha, Mirza, Seinna, Peyakwa.

Very acceptable as presents in the eyes of the Allequas are sugar and bread (papschu), which they greatly enjoy, but usually not without paying the price of this unfamiliar food in internal pain. Then they get angry with the donors and "Cigana Papschu!" ("Give me bread!") is followed by, "Quimalla woaki!" ("Bad white man!"). I sometimes cured the Allequas of these and other troubles, for which reason they venerated me as a doctor —an individual, by the way, upon whom not very flatteringly they bestow the same name (mahgäschkwa) as that given to their devil or magician. Thus, mahgäschkw' with them means medicine; whilst mahgäschkwa is the source of disease and at the same time its healer, a power equally feared and venerated. Their knowledge of medicine is limited to an acquaintance with very few substances, considered panaceas and subject to combination according to certain prescriptions, like the magnetic Baquet. These serve as charms, but the Allequas' idea of medicine is so inadequate and confused that it is surely not to be wondered at that the doctor and the devil convey the same idea to them.

Though the Allequas lack art, nature serves them the more. Animal magnetism, although not recognized as such, seems to play an important role in the lives of these and other Indians. Think of the hypnotic influence on wild animals of a sharp look, like the snake fixing his eye on the frog which he wishes to devour; of the gentle stroking of a sensitive person, then confusing him with tobacco, touching his body and breathing on it so as to impart to him prophetic ability; and then think of the wild, stormy religious dances in which the dancers change partners, embracing each other while looking sharply into each other's eyes. It is not astonishing that the miracles springing from such experiments based on the phenomena of animal magnetism often gave rise to religious theories among the Indians just as in recent times the same thing occurred among the Christians with their "somnambulistic table" about which another Galileo could say: *e ppur si muove!*

When I took leave of the Tschura-Allequas there was no end to their "Ayaque!" ("Greeting!") and "Tschohho!" ("Farewell!"). The old mauhemi told me to come again soon, and in the meanwhile offered to sell me his daughter, negawa, who, he declared, already belonged to me in part, as I had made a sketch of her. However, even if I had been able to contemplate that felicity, like a happy Endymion, by what means would I have been able to obtain the costly price of purchase, in particular the chain of shells?

I took my departure, not without a secret feeling of anger at the reflection that, instead of [the white man's] trying to win these good people to a sensible form of civilization, they were being subjected to a continually increasing persecution, nay, a systematic war of extermination.

THE LONE WOMAN OF SAN NICOLAS ISLAND

by

Emma Hardacre

Of the group commonly called the Santa Barbara Islands, so near the mainland that on the map they seem mere crumbs of the Pacific coast, little is known even by Californians. Scarcely an American has not read of the tropical islands where the mythical Robinson Crusoe was wrecked, yet few persons know that over the desolate steeps of a nearer island of the same vast sea hang the mystery, the horror, and the pathos of a story of a captive woman — a story, if it could be fully told, more thrilling than that of Crusoe, inasmuch as one is fiction, the other fact; one, the supposed exploits of a hardy man, the other, the real desolation of a suffering woman; one the tale of a mariner whom the waters flung against his will into a summerland, the other, of one who voluntarily breasted the waves, and fought death, in response to the highest love of which the human heart is capable.

The Santa Barbara Islands, on one of which this strange romance was enacted, lie to the southward of Santa Barbara channel, the nearest of the group being about twenty-five miles distant from the mainland. The names of the islands are Anacapa, Santa Rosa, San Miguel, Santa Cruz, Santa Catalina, San Clemente, Santa Barbara, and San Nicolas. They are now uninhabited, and have been so for years. The islands nearer the coast are used for sheep-grazing; a sailboat carries over the shearers and brings back the wool. The more distant are known to trappers as fine beds of otter and seal. The sea lions and sea elephants in the Centennial Exposition, New York Aquarium, and Cincinnati Zoological Gardens were lassoed off the outlying islands of the Santa Barbara group. Boats visit the beaches for abalones, the meat of which is dried and shipped to China for food, while the shells (*Haliotis splendens, Haliotis rufescens,* and *Haliotis cracherodii*), sold at an average price of fifty dollars per ton at the San Francisco wharf, are bought by dealers in marine shells, cut into jewelry

Pp. 23–27 (Document 2A) of R. F. Heizer and A. B. Elsasser (eds.), *Original Accounts of the Lone Woman of San Nicolas Island*, Reports of the Univ. of Calif. Archaeol. Survey (1961), No. 55. Reprinted there from the original article entitled "Eighteen Years Alone: A Tale of the Pacific" which appeared in *Scribner's Monthly* (1880), 20:657–664. The San Nicolas Island woman was the stimulus for the children's book *Island of the Blue Dolphins* by S. O'Dell (Houghton Mifflin, 1960).

to be sold to tourists or shipped to Europe to be manufactured into buttons and other pearl ornaments. Excepting the occasional camps of shearers, seal hunters and abalone packers, the islands are totally deserted.

Yet, wild and desolate as they now are, Cabrillo says that in the sixteenth century they were densely peopled by a superior race, and that the mainland was dotted by villages. The children of the islanders are described by early navigators as being "white, with light hair and ruddy cheeks," and the women as having "fine forms, beautiful eyes, and a modest demeanor." The men wore loose cloaks, the women dressed in petticoats and capes of seal skin, heavily fringed and handsomely ornamented. The more industrious and wealthy embroidered their garments with pearl and small pink shells. Necklaces of sparkling stones and carven ivory were worn by the higher caste, and earrings of iris-hued abalone were not uncommon. They cooked their food in soapstone vessels or in water heated by dropping hot stones into watertight baskets. Bancroft, in his "Native Races," mentions, among articles of their manufacture, needles, awls, and fishhooks of bone or shell; water-tight baskets; ollas of stone; and canoes, deep and long, with both stem and stern equally elevated above the water. Fletcher wrote of the coast when he visited it with Sir Francis Drake in 1579.

In the year 1542, Cabrillo landed at what is now known as San Miguel, and christened it *Ysla de Posesion*. He died on the island in 1543 and is buried in its sands.

Going back still further in our search, we find that before the Spanish fleet, Sir Francis Drake, or Cabrillo ever visited the coast, the villages thereon were thrifty and populous and the isles of the sea swarming cities of the period.

Of San Nicolas, on which the scenes of this wild romance are laid, very little has been known until a recent date. It is the outermost of the group, distant seventy miles from the coast, and thirty miles away from its nearest neighbor. It is thought to have been at one time the abode of a people differing in manners, habits, and mode of life from the inhabitants both of the mainland and the neighboring islands. Mons. De Cessac, a gentleman engaged in collecting archaeological specimens for the French government, says that the relics found by him on San Nicolas are more elaborate in form and finish and show a superiority of workmanship. This testimony tends to confirm the story of the early voyagers concerning the cultivation and remarkable taste of the handsome dwellers in Gha-las-hat, centuries ago. Mons. De Cessac has found also upon San Nicolas articles of warfare and domestic use, evidently belonging to a northern tribe, similar to those picked up by him on the borders of Alaska. Hence, he infers that the place was at one time the dwelling of north country tribes.

Corroborating Mons. De Cessac's opinion, search through ancient manuscripts has brought to light the fact that, many years ago, a ship belonging to Pope and Boardman, of Boston, and commanded by one Captain Whitmore, brought down from Sitka a lot of Kodiaks for the purpose of otterhunting on San Nicolas Island. They were left upon the island, and years of feud resulted in a massacre, in which every grown male islander was killed by the powerful and well-armed Kodiaks. The women were taken by the victors, lived with them as wives and bore children to the murderers of their husbands and fathers. The fact is recorded that the inhabitants of San Nicolas faded away strangely and rapidly, so that in 1830, less than two score men, women, and children remained of the once dense population.

Meantime, Franciscan zealots poured from the south of Europe into America, and under lead of Father Junipero Serra found their way up the coast, building churches beside the sea, planting gardens of olive and palm, making aqueducts and altars, founding a kingdom of temporal and spiritual splendor, which leaves to Protestant America the names of saints set indelibly on every stream, headland, and island along the southern slope of the Pacific. It was the dawn of a temporary civilization, imposing and wonderful, a civilization whose ruins are most artistic and fascinating.

The missionaries pressed the Indians into service. They set them to tilling the soil, herding the flocks, and quarrying the rock. The coast Indians having been put to labor, the thrifty padres turned their gaze to the islands in the offing, and brought to the mainland the people from Santa Rosa, San Miguel, Santa Cruz, and Santa Catalina. The more distant island of San Nicolas was left awhile to repose in its heathen darkness. How affairs progressed during that time on the island we have no account. At this day the queen isle of Gha-las-hat lies bare and silent as a tomb amidst the sea.

In this deserted spot, for eighteen years, a human being lived alone. Here she was found at last by fishermen who are living, and whose affidavits, properly witnessed, stamp as true every detail of the remarkable incident.

In the year 1835, Isaac Sparks and Lewis L. Burton, Americans, chartered a schooner of twenty tons burthen, for otter-hunting on the lower California coast. The vessel was owned by a rich Spaniard of Monterey and was commanded by Captain Charley Hubbard. The schooner bore the name *Peor es Nada*, and she started out of Santa Barbara harbor, on a fine April morning, followed by the eyes of the entire population. In those times, the sight of a sailing vessel was not an everyday occurrence. It drew the men to the beach, the women to the casements, and attracted the friars from their usual meditative gaze on ground or book. For hours previous to the departure of the schooner, the curving stretch of sand had been alive with racing horsemen and lazy pedestrians, exchanging in Spanish words of praise concerning their visitor.

After a successful cruise, the *Peor es Nada* came three months later into the more southerly harbor of San Pedro, unloaded her pelts, and immediately, under direction of Captain Williams, collector of the port, set sail for San Nicolas to bring the islanders to the mainland, in accordance with the will of the church fathers. Before they reached their destination a sudden gale came up, rising almost to the severity of a tempest. The winds — which by the Santa Ynez mountains are deflected from the valleys of the southern coast — struck with full force upon the upper end of San Nicolas, lashing the shoal waters into fury and shooting the spray in volleys through the picturesque carvings of the low cliffs. The landing was effected with difficulty. The wind increased in violence. The weather became so boisterous as to endanger the safety of the vessel. No time was wasted. The islanders, some twenty in number, were hurried into the boats and all speed was made to reach the schooner.

In the excitement and confusion of the final abandonment of their home, it was not known until they were on the ship that a child had been left behind. The mother supposed it to have been carried aboard in the arms of an old sailor. She frantically implored the men to return. The captain replied that they must get to a place of safety; after the storm — tomorrow, perhaps — they could come back for the baby. Finding that they were going out to sea, the young mother became desperate and, despite all efforts to detain her, jumped overboard and struck out through the kelpy waters for the shore. She was a widow, between twenty and thirty years of age, of medium height and fine form; her complexion was light, and her hair of a dark, rich brown. No attempt was made to rescue her, and in a moment she was lost in the seething waves. The ship, already under headway, staggered through the storm; the affrighted islanders huddled together on deck, and fear shut every other emotion for the time from their hearts.

After an adventurous voyage, the *Peor es Nada* eventually reached San Pedro, where the exiles were landed. Some of them were sent to Los Angeles, fifteen miles back from the coast; some were put to work in the neighboring mission of San Gabriel; two of the women were soon married to wealthy men of Los Angeles.

It was the intention of Captain Hubbard to return to San Nicolas immediately to see if the woman or child were living. But the schooner had orders to come directly to Santa Barbara, to take George Nidiver and a party of otter-hunters to Santa Rosa Island and, afterward, to carry from Monterey a cargo of timber to San Francisco. The boat was in urgent demand along the coast, and these two trips were imperative before a second visit could be made to San Nicolas. Delaying their errand of humanity and justice a few weeks, they lost it forever; for on that very trip the *Peor es Nada* capsized at the entrance to the Golden Gate. The men were washed ashore in an almost exhausted condition, and the schooner drifted out to sea. It was reported long after, though without confirmation, to have been picked up by a Russian ship.

After the loss of the Monterey schooner, there was no craft of any kind larger than the canoes and fishing boats on the lower coast. No one cared to attempt a passage of seventy miles to San Nicolas in an open boat, and after a time the excitement and interest faded out. Those who at first had been most solicitous that assistance should be sent, settled into the belief that the couple had perished during the days of waiting; the remainder of the community, never having believed that the woman had reached shore through the storm, were indifferent, supposing that the child had died soon after the tragic death of the mother.

Their uncertain fate lay heavy on the more tender hearted of the Mission fathers; but it was not until 1850 that Father Gonzales found an emissary to search for the lost. Thomas Jeffries had come into possession of a small schooner, and was offered $200 should he find and bring the woman or child to Santa Barbara alive. Fifteen years having passed since the abandonment of the island and no one having visited the spot during that time, the probability of the death of the parties was universally accepted, although no actual proof of death had been sought or found.

But when Thomas Jeffries's boat was seen, at the close of a balmy day of midwinter, coming up the bay without the signal he was to have displayed provided his search had been successful, the matter was settled. Groups of persons congregated on the sands. Some watched from shore the small craft fold her wings and settle to rest on the mirror-like water; others put off in canoes to meet the boatmen. Jeffries had found no trace of living beings on the island, and whether the woman had been beaten to death in the surf or died after gaining land would probably never be known. The schooner was left idly rocking close to shore; sailors and landsmen strolled slowly up to the town. Night mantled the moaning waters, and the great deep was left in possession of another secret.

The return of Jeffries brought up afresh the incident which by some had been almost forgotten. For a few hours, little was talked of save the heroic young mother and her child in the sea-girt isle.

Time passed swiftly on, and in the dreamy full contentment of the land the dead woman of San Nicolas slipped from mind, and thought, and speech.

Tom Jeffries's visit to San Nicolas was the theme of more than one day's gossip. The island he described as seven or eight miles long, by three or four in width; the body of the land near six hundred feet above the beach, the plateau falling in steep gulches to the sea. There were quantities of small lark inland, but no other fowl, save seagulls, pelicans, and shags. Numbers of red foxes were seen in the hills, and droves of curious wild dogs, tall and slender, with coarse, long hair and human eyes. On a flat near the upper end of the island and half hidden by sand dunes, he found the remains of a curious hut, made of whales' ribs planted in a circle, and so adjusted as to form the proper curve of a wigwam-shaped shelter. This he judged to have been formerly either the residence of the chief or a place of worship where sacrifices were offered. He had picked up several ollas, or vessels of stone, and one particularly handsome cup of clouded green serpentine. But of all the wonders of the island, the features on which Jeffries liked best to dwell were the fine beds of otter and seal in the vicinity of San Nicolas. So fabulous were his yarns, that the interest of the other hunters was aroused; early the following year a boat was fitted out, and George Nidiver, accompanied by Thomas Jeffries and a crew of Indians, started on an otter hunt to the wonderful otter beds seventy miles away.

A landing was effected near the southern end of the island; and climbing the cliffs to see where the otter lay, they had a magnificent view of the islands to the north and east. On the southwest the Pacific rolled out its azure breadth, unspecked by shore, or raft, or spot of any kind. The island on which they stood seemed a quiet, calm, deserted spot, in the sunshine that then enfolded it. Butterflies hovered over the wild sage upon the knolls; soft breezes rocked lazily the scant grass about their feet; thickets of chaparral dotted the hills; cactus held out waxen trays, where, on burnished mats of thorns, reposed fringed yellow satin flowers; a trailing sand plant, with thick, doughy leaves, wafted from its pink clusters a most delicious odor — an odor that had in it the haunting sweetness of the arbutus and the freshness of the salt sea wind.

The otter hunters did not linger long on the cliff, for on one side they found the rocks swarming with black seal, thousands of them mingling their sharp bark with the heavy roar of sea lions. The otter were thick on the reefs, and a stranded whale lay in the edge of the crinkling surf.

The party remained six weeks in camp on the beach. Oars stuck upright in the sand, covered by canvas, composed their shelter; a spring was found midway up the cliff, so that during their stay no one had occasion to go inland or wander far from the otter beds, which were on the side of the island where their tents were pitched. The seal is caught asleep on the rocks, lassoed or knocked in the head; incisions are made in the flippers, lower jaw, lip, and tail, and about four minutes are required for a good workman to skin an ordinary seal. The hides are salted, and after a week or two, bundled and packed. The otter, most timid of the animals of the sea, is caught in nets spread upon swaying beds of seaweed or is shot while lying with head buried in kelp to shut out the sound of a storm. It is very sensitive to noise, and so shy that it takes alarm at every unusual sight. The loose hide is taken from the body with one cut, turned wrong side out, stretched and dried.

Before the schooner left the vicinity of San Nicolas, a terrible storm arose, lasting for eight days, carrying away a mast and dragging the anchor, so that another had to be improvised of a bag filled with stone. During the tempest, a sailor fancied he saw a human figure on the headland of the island. Through the washes of spray it seemed to be running up and down the edge of the plateau, beckoning and shouting. The captain was called, but the apparition had vanished. On the eighth day, the schooner was enabled to run over to San Miguel, and from there to Santa Barbara, where the sailor's story of the beckoning ghost of San Nicolas haunted for a long time the dreams of the superstitious on shore.

A second cruise of the otter hunters failed to bring any additional news of the phantom of the sea. Everything on land was just as before; not a leaf had been disturbed, not a track was found.

In July, 1853, the otter men made a third trip to San Nicolas, anchored off the northeast side, and established a camp on shore. The party consisted of Captain Nidiver, a fisherman named Carl Detman, who went among sailors by the *sobriquet* of Charlie Brown, an Irish cook and a crew of Mission Indians.

The evening after their arrival, Nidiver and Brown strolled several miles down the beach, enjoying their pipes and discussing plans for work. It was one of those limpid nights, such as California knows — a night when the stars shine large and warm from the low sky, when the moon burns with an amber blaze, and fragrance is in the air.

As the comrades were about to retrace their steps, Nidiver stopped, looked quickly about him, then stopped and closely examined something on the ground. In the weird moonlight, plainly outlined on the lonely shore, was the print of a slender, naked foot.

"The woman of San Nicolas! My God, she is living!"

He lifted his voice, and shouted in Spanish that friends were come to rescue her. Overcome by the conviction that the lost woman must have been near when he was in camp two years before — that it was not a creation of fancy, but a living being, they had seen in the storm — the captain ran to and fro, calling, looking, and swearing by turns. Hours were spent by the two men in search, but in vain.

The next day, Nidiver found a basket of rushes hanging in a tree. It contained bone needles, thread made of sinews, shell fishhooks, ornaments, and a partially completed robe of birds' plumage, made of small squares neatly matched and sewed together. Nidiver proposed replacing the things, but Brown scattered them about, saying that, if they were picked up, it would be proof that the owner had visited the spot. Inland they discovered several circular, roofless inclosures, made of woven brush. Near these shelters were poles, with dried meat hanging from elevated crosspieces. The grass was growing in the pens, and nothing indicated their recent habitation. In fissures of perpendicular rocks near the springs were wedged dried fish and seals' blubber; but no sign of the near presence of the hermitess.

After several days, the men abandoned the chase. There was no doubt that someone had been on the island very lately. Either the woman, or the child grown to womanhood, had lived there, or, perhaps both mother and child had survived until recently. But they must have been dead months at least. The footprint was older than at first supposed. The robe had not been replaced in the tree. The captive perchance died of despair after they left her beckoning in the storm.

After that, the fishing went on for weeks; and they were about returning home, when Nidiver said he believed a person was hiding on the island. If she was living he was bound to find her. If dead, he would find her body if he had to scrape the island inch by inch. This provoked a laugh of derision. Of course the wild dogs had devoured her remains. But Nidiver was convinced that the woman was afraid; had concealed herself, possibly on the opposite side of the island, where the shore was precipitous, difficult of access, containing perhaps gulches and caves unknown to them. The men murmured at the delay, were incredulous as to the success of the raid, rebelled at the long tramps over a wild country.

The old captain was firm; suitable preparations were made, and the entire force of otter men started on their final hunt for a ghost. Near the head of the island they came across the bone house Jeffries had described. Rushes were skillfully interlaced in the rib framework; an olla and old basket were near the door. It stood amidst untrampled weeds. After several days' march, a dangerous climb over slippery rocks brought Brown to a spot where there were fresh footprints. He followed them up the cliffs until they were lost in the thick moss that covered the ground. Walking further, he found a piece of driftwood, from which he concluded the person had been to the beach for firewood, and dropped the faggot on her way home. From a high point on the ridge he saw the men moving about below. Then his eye caught a small object a long way off on the hills. It appeared like a crow at first glance, but it moved about in a singular manner. Advancing toward it stealthily, he was dumbfounded to find that it was the head of a woman, barely visible above the low woven-brush sides of her roofless retreat in the bushes.

As Brown drew nearer, a pack of dogs reclining close to the woman growled; but without looking around the woman uttered a peculiar cry which silenced them, and they ran away to the hills. Brown halted within a few yards of her and, himself unseen, watched every movement within the hut. Inside the inclosure was a mound of grass, woven baskets full of things, and a rude knife made of a piece of iron hoop thrust into a wooden handle. A fire smouldered near, and a pile of bones lay in the ashes. The complexion of the woman was much fairer than the ordinary Indian, her personal appearance pleasing, features regular, her hair, thick and brown, falling about her shoulders in a tangled mat. From the time Brown arrived within hearing, she kept up a continual talking to herself. She was leaning forward, shading her eyes with her hand, watching the men crossing the flat below her dwelling. After looking at them with an anxiety impossible to be depicted, she crouched in terror, but immediately started up as if to run. The men on the flat had not seen her; and Brown, putting his hat on the ramrod of his gun, alternately lifted and lowered it to attract their attention; then by signs he intimated that the woman was found, and they should spread out so as to catch her if she tried to escape. Before the men reached the knoll, Brown stepped around in sight and spoke, She gave a frightened look into his face, ran a few steps, but, instantly controlling herself, stood still, and addressed him in an unknown tongue. She seemed to be between forty and fifty years of age, in fine physical condition, erect, with well-shaped neck and arms and unwrinkled face. She was dressed in a tunic-shaped garment made of birds' plumage, low in the neck, sleeveless, and reaching to the ankle. The dress was similar to the one found in the trees. As the men came up, she greeted them each in the way she had met Brown, and with a simple dignity, not without its effect on both Indians and white men, made them welcome and set about preparing food for them from her scanty store. The meal consisted of roasted roots, called by Californians *carcomites;* but when was there a more touching hospitality?

Among the Indian crew, there were several dialects spoken, but none of the party were able to converse with their hostess, or understand a word she uttered, and they were forced to try and make her know by signs that she was expected to go with them. Brown went through the motion of packing her things in baskets, shouldering them, and walking toward the beach. She comprehended instantly, and made preparations to depart. Her effects were neatly placed in pack baskets, one of which she swung over her back; and taking a burning stick from the fire, she started with a firm tread after the Indians to the shore. Beside the load the female Crusoe carried,

Nidiver and Brown had their arms full. Upon reaching the boat, she entered without hesitation, going forward to the bow, kneeling and holding to either side. When the schooner was reached, she went aboard without any trouble, sat down near the stove in the cabin, and quietly watched the men in their work on board. To replace her feather dress, which he wished to preserve, Brown made her a petticoat of ticking; and with a man's cotton shirt and gay neckerchief, her semicivilized dress was complete. While Brown was sewing she watched him closely, and laughed at his manner of using a needle. She showed him that her way was to puncture the cloth with her bone needle or awl, and then put the thread through the perforations. She signified that she wished to try a threaded needle, and Brown good naturedly gave her sewing materials; but she could not thread the needle. Brown prepared it, and gave her an old cloak of Nidiver's to mend; and while she took her first lesson in sewing, she told her teacher on shipboard, by signs, portions of her life on the island.

She had from time to time seen ships pass, but none came to take her off. She watched as long as she could see them; and after they were out of sight, she threw herself on the ground and cried; but after a time she walked over the island until she forgot about it and could smile again. She had also seen people on the beach several times. She was afraid and hid until they were gone, and then wept because she had not made herself known. She said that he had taken her by surprise and she could not run, and she was glad because he would take her to her people; her people had gone away with white men in a ship. Brown understood by her signs that at the time of the desertion of the island she had a nursing baby, which she represented by sucking her finger, and placing her arm in position of holding an infant at the breast; she waved her hand over the sea, to indicate that the ship sailed away, calling back *manana* (tomorrow); then she could not find her child, and wept until she was very ill and lay prostrate for days, in a bed of plants resembling cabbage, and called by Californians *Sola Santa*. She had nothing to eat but the leaves. When she revived somewhat, she crawled to a spring; and after a time, as her strength returned, she made fire by rapidly rubbing a pointed stick along the groove of a flat stick until a spark was struck. It was a difficult task, and she was careful not to let her fire go out; she took brands with her on her trips, and covered the home fire with ashes to preserve it.

She lived during her captivity on fish, seals' blubber, roots, and shellfish; and the birds, whose skins she secured for clothing, were seabirds, which she caught at night off their roosts in the seams of the crags. The bush inclosures she made for a screen from the winds, and as a protection while asleep from wild animals. She made frequent excursions over the island from her main dwelling, which was a large cave on the north end of San Nicolas. She kept dried meat at each camping station; the food in the crevices by the springs was for the time when, from sickness or old age, she would only be able to crawl to the water and live on what she had there stored out of reach of the dogs.

That the woman had faith in a supreme power was evinced soon after the schooner set sail from the fishing grounds. A gale overtook them, and the passenger made signs that she would stop the wind. With her face turned in the direction from which the storm came, she muttered words of prayer until the wind had abated, then turned with a beaming countenance and motioned that her petition had been answered. They anchored under the lee of Santa Cruz, where the woman was highly interested in seeing an island other than her own. When they approached the shores of Santa Barbara, an ox team passed along the beach. The stranger was completely bewildered. Captain Nidiver's son, who had been on the lookout for his father's sail, rode down to the landing on a handsome little bronco. The islander, who had just stepped ashore, was wild with delight. She touched the horse and examined the lad, talking rapidly, and if the sailors turned away, calling them to come back and look. Then she tried to represent the novel sight by putting two fingers of her right hand over the thumb of her left, moving them to imitate the horse walking.

Captain Nidiver conducted the woman to his home and put her in charge of his Spanish wife. The news spreading, Father Gonzales, of Santa Barbara Mission, came to see her; many persons gathered from the ranches round about, and the house was crowded constantly. The brig *Fremont* came into port soon after, and the captain offered Nidiver the half of what he would make, if he would allow her to be exhibited in San Francisco. This offer was refused, and also another from a Captain Trussil. Mrs. Nidiver would not hear of the friendless creature being made a show for the curious.

The bereft mother evinced the greatest fondness for Mrs. Nidiver's children, caressing and playing with them by the hour, and telling the lady, by signs, that when she swam back to the shore her baby was gone, and she believed the dogs had eaten it. She went over, again and again, her grief at its loss; her frantic search for it, even after it had been gone a long time; her dread of being alone, her hope, for years, of rescue, and at last the despair that in time became resignation.

The visitors sometimes gave her presents, which she put aside until the donors had departed, seeming to know by intuition that they would be offended if she refused to accept them; but as soon as the guests were gone she called the little children and distributed her gifts among them, laughing if they were pleased, and happy in their joy.

A few days after her arrival, Father Antonio Jimeno sent for Indians from the missions of San Fernando and Santa Ynez, in hope of finding some one who could converse with the islander. At that time there were Indians living in Los Angeles County belonging to the Pepimaros, who, it was said, had in former years communication with the San Nicolas Indians. But neither these, nor those from San Buena Ventura, or Santa Barbara, could understand her, or make themselves understood. In less than two decades after the little band had left San Nicolas, their whereabouts could not be discovered. They were a mere drop in the stream of serfs known by the general name of Mission Indians. Beyond a few words, nothing was ever known of her tongue. A hide she called *to-co* (*to*-kay); a man, *nache* (nah-chey); the sky, *te*-gua (tay-gwah); the body, *pinche* (pin-oo-chey). She learned a few Spanish words: *pan* (bread), *papas* (potatoes), *caballo* (horse). Sometimes she called Captain Nidiver, in Spanish, *tata* (father), sometimes *nana* (mother).

The gentleness, modesty, and tact of the untutored wild woman of the Pacific were so foreign to ideas of the savage nature that some parties believed that she was not an Indian, but a person of distinction cast away by shipwreck, and adopted by the islanders before their removal from their home. Others were certain from her evident refinement that she had not been long alone, but had drifted to San Nicolas after the Indian woman perished in the surf and had by mistake been taken for the original savage. The old sailors who rescued her affirm that she was an Indian, the same who jumped from the schooner to save her child. The representative of a lost tribe, she stands out from the Indians of the coast, the possessor of noble and distinctive traits; provident, cleanly, tasteful, amiable, imitative, considerate, and with a maternal devotion which civilization never surpassed.

She was greatly disappointed when none of her kindred were found. She drooped under civilization; she missed the outdoor life of her island camp. After a few weeks she became too weak to walk; she was carried on to the porch every day in a chair. She dozed in the sunshine while the children played around her. She was patient and cheerful, looking eagerly into every new face for recognition, and sometimes singing softly to herself. Mrs. Nidiver hoped a return to her old diet would help her. She procured seals' meat, and roasted it in ashes. When the sick woman saw it, she patted her nurse's hands affectionately, but could not eat the food. She fell from her chair one morning, and remained insensible for hours. Seeing the approach of death, Mrs. Nidiver sent for a priest to baptize her protégé. At first he refused, not knowing but that she had been baptized previously, although the burden of proof was against it. At length, heeding the kind Catholic lady's distress, he consented to administer the rite, conditionally. As she was breathing her last, the sign of the cross was pressed on her cold brow, and the unknown nameless creature was christened by Father Sanchez, in the beautiful Spanish "Juana Maria." In a walled cemetery, from whose portals gleam ghastly skull and crossbones, close to the Santa Barbara Mission, under the shelter of the tower, is the neglected grave of a devoted mother, the heroine of San Nicolas.

The abandonment of San Nicolas occurred forty-six years ago. The survivor of eighteen years' solitary captivity arrived in Santa Barbara September 8, 1853. Captain Nidiver's house, where the stranger died, stands in sight of the ocean and can be pointed out by any schoolboy in the town. Nidiver and his wife are living, and their son George follows the sea, as his father before him. Carl Detman, or Charlie Brown, as he is called by old sailors, may be found any day where the retired boatmen congregate. Thomas Jeffries walks the streets in blouse, wide hat, and flowing gray hair. Dr. Brinkerhoff, who attended the woman of San Nicolas, is a well-known physician of the city. Father Gonzales died a few years ago, after a continuous residence of a more than a quarter of a century in the mission. For a long time he was partially paralyzed and was carried about in a chair. I remember him as a little dark man, with eyes that blazed unnaturally from sunken sockets, his appearance rendered more startling by a white turban bound around his head. He is buried under the floor of the old chapel. The rambling mansion on State Street, known as the Park Hotel, may have sheltered tourists who read this account. It was the first brick house built in Santa Barbara and was the private residence of Isaac Sparks, the lessee of the sailboat from which, in 1835, the woman jumped overboard. "Burton's Mound," a picturesque knoll, threaded by rows of olive trees, belongs to Lewis L. Burton, another lessee of the *Peor es Nada*. A lady in San Francisco has some of the islander's needles. Nidiver and Brown retain her curious watertight baskets. The mission fathers sent her feather robes to Rome. They were made of the satiny plumage of the green cormorant, the feathers pointing downward, and so skillfully matched as to seem one continuous sheen of changeful luster.

The record of baptism is in the church register. Her grave will be pointed out to any one by the Franciscan brothers on the hill.

ISHI, THE LAST YAHI

by
T. T. Waterman

I often feel that it is hard to tell the story of Ishi in such a way as to convince people of its reality. He has been described as the last survivor of a tribe that remained in the Stone Age until the twentieth century. I should like to tell enough of the history of his little group to explain how it was possible for them to remain "primitive." In spite of the fact that in 1910 he was still living in the age of stone, he was himself a rare character, with a mind of unusual caliber.

First of all I should like to tell you something about his tribe. It is the old story of an Indian people being crowded by the whites. In this case, however, the Indians most concerned were already a small group surrounded by enemies when the whites came into the country. They called themselves simply Yahi (people) as Indian tribes mostly do, and this has come to be used as their tribal name. The Yahi were not numerically as strong as the surrounding peoples, and had for some generations been driven to follow a prowling life. They frequented a very wild area along Mill and Deer creeks, east of the Sacramento River in northern California. Their fastnesses lay in the hills just to the east of the great level stretches of the Sacramento Valley. The country here is an old lava formation and is accordingly a region of cliffs and wild gorges, with numerous dusky glens and duskier caves, the canyon floors and slopes of the hills overgrown with a perfect tangle of scrub.

In this wild region the Yahi roved about safe from intrusion, and lived securely in their own empire except for the fact that at infrequent intervals snow and heavy weather brought them to the verge of starvation. Under such circumstances they were forced to pay flying visits to the sunny lands of their richer neighbors in the valley. The memory of old scores still unsettled on each side always made these trips an occasion for violence. Long before the coming of the whites the Yahi had learned one principle very

The Southern Workman (Hampton Normal and Agricultural Institute, 1917), 46:528–537.

There have been many accounts of the Yahi and of Ishi himself. See papers by S. T. Pope, T. T. Waterman, and E. Sapir in Univ. Calif. Publ. Am. Arch. and Ethn., vol. 13 (1918–1922); and T. T. Waterman, "The Last Wild Tribe of California," *Popular Science Monthly* (March, 1915), pp. 233–244.

thoroughly. It was, in plain language, this: "When outnumbered, scoot for Deer Creek." Consequently, when the white invasion began, the Yahi escaped the fate of the other Indian tribes. The valley Indians became hangers-on of civilization and lost in some cases even the memory of their old life. The Yahi followed their time-honored rule and took refuge in their foothill fastnesses. As the Indian tribes of the valley were replaced by white settlers, the Yahi transferred to the white "valley people" the bitter hostility they had already learned to feel. So they remained a "wild" tribe.

The history of this wild tribe has in it a good deal of the pathetic. The whites were not satisfied to let them alone. It grew to be the custom to blame every miscarriage of plans to the presence of these "wild" Indians. If sheep strayed or were eaten by pumas, the settlers preferred in most cases to believe that the Indians had made way with them. If provisions were taken from outlying camps, Indians could always be conjured up to take the blame. Even if freshets drowned the onion patches, or if potato bugs got away with the "spuds," it was felt in some dim way that Indians were probably at the bottom of it. In more tragic cases, where murders were committed in out-of-the-way places, nothing could convince the settlers of the Indians' innocence. By 1860 there came to be a sort of war between the whites and the Indians, in which most of the aggression was on the part of the whites. The rest is a story I almost hate to tell.

The men into whose hands fell the adjusting of relations between the whites and the Yahi Indians showed at times a ferocity that is almost incredible. It was of course unavoidable that there should be friction. In a general way, and sentiment aside, the old Indian way of life had in every case to be done away with. When Columbus landed on San Salvador, there was only one Indian to each twenty-four square miles of North America (speaking in general averages). The outlook for humanity as a whole demanded that this Indian population be displaced and crowded together. It was inevitable that intensive farming should replace the haphazard husbandry and roving hunting habits of the Indians. The pity was that this "displacing" was never done systematically, nor was it ever done by the recognized agents of government. Recognized government took a hand in every case only after the displacing had already been made an accomplished fact by traders and trappers along the frontier. The "frontiersman" is not quite so romantic and Homeric a figure as the novelists would make us believe. The truth is that he is always irresponsible, usually indifferent, frequently ignorant, and in some cases thoroughly brutalized. I might cite three or four instances in connection with the Yahi.

A party of whites, in April 1871, pursued a band of Indians with dogs. They located them in a cave across a narrow gulch, and shot a number of them, finally entering the cave itself. Here they found a lot of dried meat, and some small children. The hero of the occasion, being a humane man, a person of fine sensibilities and delicacy of feeling, could not bear to kill these babies—at any rate, not with the heavy 56-calibre Spencer rifle he was carrying. "It tore them up too bad." *So he shot them with his 38-calibre Smith and Wesson revolver.* The names of several men who were in this party are in my notes. The bodies later disappeared. Another informant, referring to an occasion some years later, told me of finding a cave with marks of occupation, ashes, and human teeth. From his description of the locality I gathered that he was describing the same cave. Apparently the survivors had returned and cremated the dead, according to their tribal custom.

In the fall of 1865 a party of whites looking for scalps (the whites did the scalping then in California, not the Indians) spied a party of Yahi encamped. There were men, women, children, babies, and dogs—a whole tribe, or what was left of one. Just before daybreak the whites separated into two parties and closed in on the Indians from two sides. The stage was set for one act in the drama of the Yahi tribe. When the firing began the startled Indians, avoiding one party, ran into the other. An informant of mine who visited the scene of the "skirmish" some time later counted forty-three skeletons. Only a few Indians escaped.

On good authority I can report the case of an old prospector-pioneer-miner-trapper of this region who had on his bed even in recent years a blanket lined with Indian scalps. These he had taken years before. He had never been a Government scout, soldier, or officer of the law. The Indians he had killed he had killed purely on his own account. No reckoning was at any time demanded of him.

It is important to note these facts, for they explain what would otherwise be almost incredible. By 1870 or soon after, the Yahi tribe had been reduced to a few individuals. They disappeared from sight, and for forty years we have practically no account of them. I say practically, for as a matter of fact they were seen on at least half a dozen occasions during this time. I might cite one or two. A good man and true, who is now well known to me, was deer hunting as a lad, about twenty-five years ago, on Big Antelope Creek. The following curious incident happened. In working about a buck-eye thicket, he heard noises. He sent his dog in to rout out whatever was in there. The dog came out frightened, so he went in himself. The plain fact was that he had run on to a party of the wild Indians, though all he could see at first were objects moving through the brush trying to get away from him. They finally began to shoot at him with bows. Three arrows were fired at him. One went through his hatbrim, grazing his face, and broke off on a boulder in front of him. He has the arrow yet, and showed it to me. In trying to get away, they dropped among other things a complete arrow-making outfit. This outfit is now in our Museum. On other occasions they were more clearly seen, so that it is not true that they totally disappeared. It is a very curious fact that when individuals at rare intervals reported such incidents as the one I have mentioned it created no interest, for they were simply put down as liars. So the presence of "wild" Indians persisted through a long period as a sort of local tradition or myth. The incidents when they were seen were not even reported in the papers.

It seems almost impossible that in a thickly settled region like California, this group could go on living their own primitive life. Yet they did so. It is perfectly certain that they had nothing to do with the whites directly. They carried on an independent existence. They profited, however, by picking up certain property around abandoned camps, as they naturally would. Thus they got bits of metal which they used for tools, and some cloth. They also preferred to make arrow points out of bottle glass, rather than out of the native obsidian rock. They hunted with the bow and arrow, for two reasons. In the first place they did not understand fire-arms, and seemingly never had had any in their possession. In the second place the bow was silent. In the river they speared fish in the primitive way, smoking it over a fire and storing it away for winter. I have seen the framework of the brush hut they used for this purpose. In the summer they slipped out of their retreat, and went to the eastward as far as Mount Lassen and on its upper slopes they hunted in peace until the snow drove them down. We know this peak now as California's only active volcano but in those days it was silent and still. Most of their time they spent in Deer Creek canyon, within a few miles of the valley, in the midst of its thickest jungles of scrub oak and brush. Here they fished and hunted, gathered acorns and seeds, and managed an independent existence. That they were not discovered is due to their experience with the whites, and to the fact that there were only a few of them. This, in connection with the character of their country, enabled them to keep out of sight for more than a generation.

Fifteen miles in an air line from their foothill stronghold, trains on the Southern Pacific Railroad passed daily back and forth. Yet in their rugged canyon, where the scrub oak and poison oak are so thick that the explorer can make only two miles a day through it (I speak from experience) they passed long years safe from detection. The story of how the small remnants of a tribe were finally discovered and became scattered, I have told in another place. I merely want to insist here that the last survivor, who fell into my hands in 1910, was still a stone-age Indian, as unaccustomed to the ways of civilization as could well be imagined.

I should like to tell something of my acquaintance with Ishi, especially those incidents which illustrate the character of the man and shed light on his peculiar viewpoint. I may begin by speaking of railroad trains. Our friendship started at Oroville, California, where loneliness and hunger had driven Ishi to come into a slaughterhouse near town. In bringing him

A. L. Kroeber and Ishi (1916)

Ishi, the Last Yahi Indian

down to the University, where his home was to be for the rest of his life, it was necessary to take the train. Behold Ishi and myself, an attendant Indian, and some hundreds of interested palefaces, waiting on the platform for the train to come in. As Number Five appeared in the distance and came whistling and smoking down the humming rails in a cloud of dust, Ishi wanted to get behind something. We were standing some distance from the track as it was, for I felt that he might be afraid of the engine. My charge however wanted to hide *behind* something. He had often seen trains. Later he told us in his own language that he had in his wanderings seen trains go by in the distance. But he did not know they ran on tracks. When he saw them he always lay down in the grass or behind a bush until they were out of sight. He visualized a train as some devil-driven, inhuman prodigy. Security lay not in keeping off of the right-of-way, but in keeping out of its sight.

Here is another fact that illustrates his personal attitude. To a primitive man, what ought to prove most astonishing in a modern city? I would have said at once, the height of the buildings. For Ishi, the overwhelming thing about San Francisco was the number of people. That he never got over. Until he came into civilization, the largest number of people he had ever seen together at any one time was five! At first a crowd gathered around him alarmed him and made him uneasy. He never entirely got over his feeling of awe, even when he learned that everybody meant well. The big buildings he was interested in. He found them edifying, but he distinctly was not greatly impressed. The reason, as far as I could understand it, was this. He mentally compared a towering twelve-story building not with his hut in Deer Creek, which was only four feet high, but with the cliffs and crags of his native mountains. He had something in some way analogous stored up in his experience. And to see five thousand people at once was something undreamed of, and it upset him.

Which is to be considered more interesting and surprising, per se, an ordinary trolley car or an automobile? For Ishi, the trolley car, every time. I stupidly expected him to grow excited over his first automobile, as I did over mine, in the year 1898. For Ishi, of course, both were plain miracles. Both the auto and the streetcar were agitated and driven about by some supernatural power—one as much as the other. The street car, however, was the bigger of the two, it had a gong which rang loudly at times, and moreover was provided with an attachment which went "shoo!" and blew the dust away when the airbrakes were released. Ishi would watch trolley cars by the hour.

Airplanes, by the way, he took quite philosophically. We took him down to Golden Gate Park to see Harry Fowler start to fly across the continent. When the plane was trundled out and the engines started, the Indian was surprised and amused at the uproar they created. The machine was finally launched, and after a long circuit, soared back above our heads. As it came overhead we particularly called his notice to it. He was mildly interested. "Saltu?" he said interrogatively, nodding toward the plane a thousand feet skyward, "White man up there?" When we said yes he laughed a bit, apparently at the white man's funny ways, and let it pass. Either he was ready to expect anything by that time, or else his amazement was too deep for any outward expression. Like most "nature-people," he was inclined to preserve his dignity in the face of the unfamiliar or the overwhelming, giving very little sign. Under equivalent stimulation of course the paleface dances about and squeals.

Ishi was however jarred completely out of his equanimity, amazed past speech or movement, by a window shade. On the morning of his second day at the Museum, I found him trying to raise the shade to let the sunlight in. It gave me a queer feeling to realize that never in his experience, either in his canyon home or in the Oroville jail (the first thirty hours of civilization he spent as an honored guest at Butte County's penal establishment) had he encountered the common roller shade. He tried to push it to one side and it would not go. He tried pushing it up and it would not stay. I showed him how to give it a little jerk and let it run up. The subsequent five minutes he utilized for reflection. When I came back at the end of that time, he was still trying to figure out where the shade had gone.

Concerning foods he had certain prejudices which he was never able to overcome. For example he politely asked to be excused from gravies and sauces. He did not take at all kindly to the notion of boiling food. Fried, baked, roasted, broiled, or raw he could understand. He did not like those processes which lead to semiliquids. No milk if you please for Ishi, and no eggs unless they were hard boiled. All such things, he said, lead to colds in the head! The real basis of his dislike seemed to be their aesthetic effect. I have often wondered since just how far our eating habits may be considered messy. He wanted his food dry and clean appearing. For drink he liked only transparent beverages, that could not have anything concealed about them. Tea was his idea of the proper drink.

I should like to say that in all his personal habits he was extraordinarily neat. At his first dinner he behaved as many another man has done under similar circumstances. He waited patiently until someone let him know, by setting the example, whether a given dish was to be consumed with the aid of a spoon, a knife, some kind of a fork, or with the plain fingers. Then he calmly did likewise. His actions were always in perfectly good taste. Even during his first days in civilization, he could be taken comfortably into any company. He had a certain fastidiousness which extended to all his belongings. His effects were kept carefully in order. Not only his apparel, but his arrow-making appliances, his bow, and his other impediments, were always in perfect array. During the time he lived at my home a certain member of my family constantly urged me to model my own behavior in such respects after the Indian's shining example.

Ishi, moreover, was remarkably clever with his hands. In his own way he was a fine workman. He made bows of perfect finish. He could chip arrow-points to perfection out of any of the materials which give a conchoidal fracture—obsidian, flint, agate, or bottle glass. Some of his handsomest specimens were made out of bromo-seltzer bottles. No more beautiful arrow-points exist than the ones he made. His finished arrow—point, shaft, and feathering—is a model of exquisite workmanship.

On the whole he took very kindly to civilization. He seemed apprehensive at times that we would send him back ultimately to his wilderness. Once when we were planning with much enthusiasm to take him on a camping trip, to revisit with him his foothill home, he filed a number of objections. One was that in the hills there were no chairs. A second was, that there were no houses or beds. A third was, that there was very little to eat. He had been cold and gone empty so often, in the hills, that he had few illusions left. In camp, however, he proved to be a fine companion. He could swim and wash dishes and skylark with anybody, and outwalk everybody.

He convinced me that there is such a thing as a gentlemanliness which lies outside of all training, and is an expression purely of an inward spirit. It has nothing to do with artificially acquired tricks of behavior. Ishi was slow to acquire the tricks of social contact. He never learned to shake hands but he had an innate regard for the other fellow's existence, and an inborn considerateness, that surpassed in fineness most of the civilized breeding with which I am familiar. His life came to a close as the result of an over susceptibility to tuberculosis, to which he was at some time or other exposed, and to which he never developed the slightest immunity. He contributed to science the best account he could give of the life of his people, as it was before the whites came in. To know him was a rare personal privilege, not merely an ethnological privilege. I feel myself that in many ways he was perhaps the most remarkable personality of his century.

ethnology: material culture and economy

THE FOOD PROBLEM IN CALIFORNIA

by
A. L. Kroeber

The California Indians are perhaps the most omnivorous group of tribes on the continent. The corn, salmon, buffalo, reindeer, or seal which formed the predominant staple in other regions, did indeed have a parallel in the acorn of California; but the parallel is striking rather than intrinsic.

To begin with, the oak is absent from many tracts. It does not grow in the higher mountains, in the desert, on most of the immediate coast; and it is at best rare in districts like the baked plains inhabited by the southern Yokuts valley tribes, a fact that may help to explain the permanent association and commingling of the majority of these tribes with their foothill neighbors. It is true that at worst it is rarely a far journey to an abundant growth of acorn-bearing trees anywhere in California; but the availability of such supplies was greatly diminished by the habits of intense adherence to their limited soil followed by the great majority of divisions.

Then, where the acorn abounded, the practices both of collecting and of treating it led directly to the utilization also of other sources of nourishment. The farmer may and does hunt, or fish, or gather wild growths; but these activities, being of a different order, are a distraction from his regular pursuits, and an adjustment is necessary. Either the pursuit of wild foods becomes a subsidiary activity, indulged in intermittently as leisure affords, and from the motive of variety rather than need, or a sexual or seasonal division becomes established, which makes the same people in part, or for part of the year, farmers and in part hunters. An inclination of this sort is not wanting in many districts of California. The dry and hot summer makes an outdoor life in the hills, near the heads of the vanishing streams, a convenience and a pleasure which coincide almost exactly with the opportunity to hunt and to gather the various natural crops as they become available from month to month. The wet winter renders house life in the permanent settlement in a valley or on a river correspondingly attractive, and combines residence there with the easiest chance to fish the now en-

Pp. 523–526 of A. L. Kroeber, *Handbook of the Indians of California* (1925).

For a discussion of the modern diet of the California Indians see S. F. Cook, *The Mechanism and Extent of Dietary Adaptation among Certain Groups of California and Nevada Indians,* Ibero-Americana: 18 (1941).

larged streams on an extensive scale, or to pursue the swarms of arrived water fowl.

But this division was not momentous. The distances ranged over were minute. Fishing was not excluded among the hills. Deer, rabbits, and gophers could be hunted in the mild winter as well as in summer. And while acorns and other plant foods might be garnered each only over a brief season, it was an essential part of their use that much of their preparation as well as consumption should be spread through the cycle of the calendar.

Further, the food resources of California were bountiful in their variety rather than in their overwhelming abundance along special lines. If one supply failed, there were a hundred others to fall back upon. If a drought withered the corn shoots, if the buffalo unaccountably shifted, or the salmon failed to run, the very existence of peoples in other regions was shaken to its foundations. But the manifold distribution of available foods in California and the working out of corresponding means of reclaiming them prevented a failure of the acorn crop from producing similar effects. It might produce short rations and racking hunger, but scarcely starvation. It may be that it is chiefly our astounding ignorance of all the more intimate and basal phases of their lives that makes it seem as if downright mortal famine had been less often the portion of the Californian tribes than of those in most other regions of the continent. Yet, with all allowance for this potential factor of ignorance in our understanding, it does appear that such catastrophes were less deep and less regularly recurring. Both formulated and experiential tradition are nearly silent on actual famines, or refer to them with rationalizing abstraction. The only definite cases that have come to cognizance, other than for a few truly desert hordes whose slender subsistence permanently hung by a thread, are among the Mohave, an agricultural community in an oasis, and among the Indians of the lower Klamath, whose habits, in their primal dependence on the salmon, approximated those of the tribes of the coasts north of California.

The gathering of the acorn is like that of the pine nut; its leaching has led to the recognition of the serviceability of the buckeye once its poison is dissolved out; the grinding has stimulated the use of small hard seeds, which become edible only in pulverized form. The securing of plant foods in general is not separated by any gap of distinctive process from that of obtaining grasshoppers, caterpillars, maggots, snails, mollusks, crawfish, or turtles, which can be got in masses or are practically immobile: a woman's digging stick will procure worms as readily as bulbs. Again, it is only a step to the taking of minnows in brooks, of gophers, or lizards, or small birds: the simplest of snares, a long stick, a thrown stone even, suffice with patience, and a boy can help out his grandmother. The fish pot is not very different from the acorn receptacle, and weirs, traps, stiff nets, and other devices for capturing fish are made in the same technique of basketry as the beaters, carriers, and winnowers for seeds. Even hunting was but occasionally the open, outright affair we are likely to think. Ducks were snared and netted, rabbits driven into nets, even deer caught in nooses and with similar devices. There is nothing in all this like the difference between riding down buffalo and gathering wild rice, like the break from whale hunting to berry picking, from farming to stalking deer.

The California Indian, then, secured his variety of foods by techniques that were closely interrelated, or, where diverse, connected by innumerable transitions. Few of the processes involved high skill or long experience for their successful application; none entailed serious danger, material exposure, or even strenuous effort. A little modification, and each process was capable of successful employment on some other class of food objects. Thus the activities called upon were distinguished by patience, simplicity, and crude adaptability rather than by intense endeavor and accurate specialization; and their outcome tended to manifold distribution and approximate balance in place of high yields or concentration along particular but detached lines.

The human food production of aboriginal California will accordingly not be well understood until a really thorough study has been made of all the activities of this kind among at least one people. The substances and the means are both so numerous that a recapitulation of such data as are available is always only a random, scattering selection.

Observers have mentioned what appealed to their sense of novelty or ingenuity, what they happened to see at a given moment, or what their native informants were interested in. But we rarely know whether such and such a device is peculiar to a locality or widespread, and if the former, why; whether it was a sporadic means or one that was seriously depended on; and what analogous ones it replaced. Statements that this tribe used a salmon harpoon, another a scoop net, a third a seine, a fourth poison, and that another built weirs, give us in their totality some approximation to a picture of the set of activities that underlie fishing in California as a whole: but for each individual group the statement is of little significance, for it is likely that those who used the nets used the spear and poison also, but under distinctive conditions; and when they did not, the question is whether the lack of one device is due to a more productive specialization of another, or to natural circumstances which made the employment of this or that method from the common stock of knowledge impracticable for certain localities.

There is, however, one point where neither experience nor environment is a factor, and in which pure custom reigns supreme: the animals chosen for the list of those not eaten. Myth, magic, totemism, or other beliefs may be at the bottom; but every tribe has such an index, which is totally unconnected with its abilities, cultural or physical, to take food.

Among the Yokuts, one animal stands out as edible that everywhere in northern California is absolute taboo and deadly poison: the dog. The Yurok give as their formal reason for not drinking river water that a large stream might contain human foetuses or a dead dog. The Yokuts did not shrink from eating dogs.

Coyote flesh was generally avoided, whether from religious reverence or magical fear is not clear. Grizzly-bear meat was also viewed askance. The bear might have devoured human flesh, which would be near to making its eater a cannibal. Besides, in all probability, there was a lurking suspicion that a grizzly might not be a real one, but a transformed bear doctor. The disposition of the animal showed itself in the muscular fibers bristling erect when the flesh was cut, the Yokuts say. Brown bears had fewer plays of the imagination directed upon them, but even their meat was sometimes avoided. Birds of prey and carrion from the eagle down to the crow were not eaten. Their flesh, of course, is far from palatable; but it is these very birds that are central in Yokuts totemism, and the rigid abstinence may have this religious motivation. All reptiles were unclean to the southern Yokuts, as to the Tübatulabal; but the northern tribes exercised a peculiar discrimination. The gopher snake, water snakes, and frogs were rejected, but lizards, turtles, and, what is strangest of all, the rattlesnake, were fit food to the Chukchansi. There is a likely alien influence in this, for the neighboring Miwok probably, and the Salinans to the west certainly, ate snakes, lizards, and even frogs. On the other hand, the southern Yokuts relished the skunk, which when smoked to death in its hole was without offensive odor; while to the Miwok and Salinans it was abomination.

CALIFORNIAN
BALANOPHAGY

by
E. W. Gifford

Balanophagy, or acorn eating, was probably the most characteristic feature of the domestic economy of the Californian Indians. In fact, the habit extended from Lower California northward through the Pacific states practically wherever oaks grew. The northern limit of abundant oaks was the Umpqua divide in Oregon. Beyond that they were relatively rare and played a correspondingly small part in the native dietary. A few grew in the Willamette Valley and in the Puget Sound region.

Wherever hard seeds or grains are eaten, some sort of pulverizing or grinding device is employed, in order to render the food assimilable. Acorns do not belong in this class of foods. The nuts can be masticated as readily as walnuts or almonds. The universal use of grinding or pulverizing implements on the one hand and the limited distribution of acorn pulverizing on the other hand, point to the likelihood that the former is exceedingly ancient and the latter far less so, and that the acorn industry has here and there taken over the grinding process, not because of the hardness of the food, but for the sake of reducing it to meal, or to aid in leaching it. In California this is further apparent when it is noted that the same species of acorns which were pulverized were sometimes treated by immersion or burial and eaten without pulverizing.

The crux of the Californian acorn industry is the removal of the objectionable tannic acid from the nuts. The discovery of the relatively rapid process of leaching pulverized acorns made available a vast new food supply of high nutritive value. It is likely that once this discovery was made it spread rapidly and resulted in a greatly increased consumption of acorns. It is probable that the cruder method of rendering acorns edible by immersing them in water or mud, without pulverizing, was the antecedent of leaching the pulverized nuts in a sand basin or basket. The immersion or burial method, sometimes accompanied by boiling or roasting of the nuts, was employed to some extent among the Yurok, Hupa, Shasta, Pomo, and Yuki, the last-named burying the acorns in a sandy place with grass, charcoal, and ashes, and then soaking them in water from time to time until

Pp. 87–98 of *Essays in Anthropology presented to A. L. Kroeber* (1936).

they became sweet. Gunther mentions burial or immersion for the Klallam, Nisqually, and Snohomish, and Spier and Sapir describe burial in mud by the Wishram. It should be emphasized that the immersion method dispenses entirely with the mortar and pestle.

Certain species of acorns apparently have less tannic acid than others. Among the Shasta, *Quercus chrysolepis* acorns were sometimes roasted in ashes and eaten without any preliminary burying or boiling. However, burial whole in mud for several weeks was the customary treatment for these acorns.

The striking thing about the acorn eating of the American Pacific Coast is the well-nigh universal knowledge of leaching, attributable no doubt to diffusion rather than separate inventions. Leaching of pulverized meal had the advantage of rendering edible at once the acorns which otherwise had to undergo months of immersion in mud and water. The time necessary for the spread of the leaching process throughout the oak districts of California was probably brief. Judged by the rapidity of the spread of maize and tobacco cultivation among primitive peoples in the Old World in post-Columbian times, it seems likely that two or three centuries would be ample for the spread of so important a discovery as the leaching of acorn meal over so small an area as California. However, as to when it spread—whether 1,000 years ago or 10,000 years ago—there is as yet no clue.

The uniformity of the Californian acorn-meal leaching process, either in a sand basin or in a basket, contrasts with the multiplicity of pulverizing devices and seems to indicate that leaching carried with it no special pulverizing device, but rather superimposed itself on the local varieties of pulverizing devices which had already developed. Possibly some methods of pulverizing developed after leaching was introduced, but no method is wholly limited to acorns.

Cabrillo's expedition was the first to record the use of acorns in California, but the account, which refers to the Santa Barbara region in 1542, makes no mention of leaching.

Removal of tannic acid by immersion or burial of the nuts is obviously a simple process which might be arrived at through testing the qualities of accidentally immersed acorns. Pulverizing and leaching are more complicated and involved processes, and appear as inventions to improve and hasten the tannic acid removal. The overlapping distribution of the two methods seems to indicate their genetic relationship. Reason dictates that immersion was the earlier process.

However, if leaching is a process which formed part of the original stock of culture of the ancestors of the American Indians, and not an independent Californian invention, we may look upon manioc leaching in South America and acorn and buckeye leaching in California as based upon this early knowledge. But, that leaching is such an ancient invention is by no means assured. The absence of leaching for acorns in the southeastern area of the United States makes the case dubious. However, there the interest in extracting oils and the development of agriculture may have obliterated an earlier leaching complex. With the development of agricultural products a people would hardly resort to leaching acorns, except in time of famine.

If there was no widespread fundamental concept of leaching, then California would appear to be a region in which the leaching process was independently invented. The only clue, and that uncertain, as to the part of California in which the invention might have been made, is offered by the number of plants treated by leaching. Nevertheless, this criterion is dubious, as a people learning to leach acorns may have been enterprising enough to test the method for other likely foods. However, the opposite case is offered by the Yavapai of Arizona, who leach ironwood seeds by boiling, but have not applied the method to acorns.

In regard to the acorn industry on the Pacific Coast, California seems central, Washington marginal. At least, this view is dictated by the methods of tannin removal. For Oregon it is to be noted that the Takelma leached.

Leaching in a sandy shallow depression or basin seems characteristic of the northwestern Californian culture area and most of the central Californian culture area. The Luiseño and Cahuilla were the only southerners reported to employ this method, but they also employed the southern method of leaching in a basket. The Costanoan and Sierra Miwok of central California also employed both methods. Peoples reported using the sand basin only were the Yokuts, Western Mono, Eastern Mono, Patwin, Southern Maidu, Northern Maidu, Pomo, Chimariko, Hupa, and Yurok. Beals reports leaching on bare hard ground for the Southern Maidu, which may be a degeneration from the sand basin reported by Powers. Reported to employ only the basket leacher were the Salinan, Gabrielino, and Southern Diegueño. The Shasta employed a device which seems to have been sort of a compromise between the sand-basin leacher and the basket leacher. The Kamia used a sand basin covered with a layer of foliage. Some Eastern Mono lined the leaching basin with bark.

Coniferous twigs used to break the fall of the water in leaching acorn meal are recorded for the Miwok, Nisenan, Northern Maidu, Pomo, and Yuki, but probably are used by other tribes, too.

None of the Californian peoples extracted the oil of acorns, as was done in the southeastern area, where it was used in preparing food and to anoint the body. Chesnut states that the oil was extracted by boiling the nuts in water containing the ash of maple wood.

As might be expected among pottery-using peoples, acorn meal was boiled in pots among some Eastern Mono, the Southern Diegueño, the Luiseño, and the Kamia, and in steatite vessels among the Gabrielino. Probably other pottery-using peoples did likewise, but there is no record. Stone boiling of the meal in baskets was the customary central and northwestern practice. However, so far as the published record goes it has been mentioned specifically only for the Pomo of Ukiah and the Yuki, the Southwestern Pomo, Patwin, Southern Maidu, Northern Maidu, Salinan, Hupa, Yurok, Chimariko, Shasta, Miwok, Western Mono, and some Eastern Mono.

According to Powers, the Yurok slightly parched their acorns before grinding. He also records that they cooked the meal in the leaching basin, which seems a most unlikely procedure.

Of additional methods of cooking we find the Shasta roasting the moistened meal, and the Pomo, Lake Miwok, Patwin, Central Wintun, Plains and Northern Miwok, and Salinan baking it in the earth oven. The Pomo, Lake Miwok, and Central Wintun mixed red (presumably ferruginous) earth with the meal, a custom also followed in Sardinia. The Plains and Northern Miwok sometimes mixed ashes of *Quercus douglasii* bark with the dough.

Wherever tan oak acorns (*Pasania* [formerly *Quercus*] *densiflora*) were obtainable they seem to have been preferred. This is essentially a northern coast species. Among the other species, the preference varied: *Quercus kelloggii* (*californica*) with the Southern Maidu or Nisenan, Miwok, Shasta, Luiseño; *Quercus dumosa* with the Cahuilla; *Quercus gambeli* with the Southern Maidu (although Beals mentions black oak, presumably *Quercus kelloggii*); *Quercus kelloggii*, *Quercus chrysolepis*, and *Quercus wislizenii* with the Northern Maidu; and *Quercus agrifolia* with the Pomo. The distribution of the various species of oaks was largely the determining factor as to the species most highly regarded by each tribe and as to the number of species used by each tribe. After *Pasania densiflora*, *Quercus kelloggii* seems to have been the favorite. The Klamath of southern Oregon did not eat the acorns which grow near Klamath Falls in their territory. This lack of interest may be due to scarcity of oaks and to specialization in other foods, notably water-lily seeds.

The leaching out of the tannic acid after the nut meats had been reduced to meal seems to have been limited to the Pacific Coast. In central Arizona only sweet acorns were eaten by the Yavapai, and the bitter ones neglected. The acorns of *Quercus oblongifolia* were obtained by the Pima from the Papago by trade. After the hulls had been removed they were parched and ground into meal. Consequently, in Arizona a vast supply of bitter acorns was neglected as food. In southern California, the Diegueño, close linguistic relatives of the Yavapai, were thoroughly familiar with leaching. It would seem that the separation of these two groups took place before leaching of acorns was invented, or at least before it had become known to them. It is entirely possible, of course, that the Diegueño, moving into California, came in touch with people already familiar with leaching. Between the Yavapai and Diegueño lies a 200–300-mile stretch of oakless desert country.

Thus, a more or less concentric distribution appears for the methods of acorn utilization in the western United States—a highly specialized leaching process bordered by an area in which only sweet acorns, unleached, were utilized. To the southward, in the highlands of Mexico, lies the peripheral area of complete neglect of acorns. This concentric distribution in western America seems to indicate complete separation from the acorn-boiling area of the Eastern Woodlands.

[Note.—Some analyses of the food value of acorns have been made. Acorn meal before cooking contains 21.3 per cent fat; 5.1 per cent protein; 62.2 per cent carbohydrate; water, ash, and fiber making up the remainder. Cooked meal contains only about one-half these amounts of oil, protein, and carbohydrate, the difference being made up of contained water. Compare the food value of acorns with maize and wheat, which contain approximately 1.5 per cent fat, 10.3 per cent protein, and 75 per cent carbohydrate.—Eds.]

DESERT PLANT FOODS
OF THE COAHUILLA

by
David Prescott
Barrows

To the unsophisticated it would seem that the dry and rocky slopes of the desert's sides, with their curious and repellent plant forms, could yield nothing possible for food, but in reality the severe competition and struggle with aridity have operated to invest desert plants with remarkable nutritive elements. The very hoarding of strength and moisture that goes on in many plants is a promise of hidden nutrition. And, while many plants protect their growth against destruction by animals through the secretion of poisonous or noxious elements, the cunning of the savage woman has taught her how to remove these. Beside every Coahuilla home there stands ever ready the wide pá-cha-ka-vel, or leaching basket. The results prove far more than the expectation would warrant.

I cannot pretend to have exhausted the food supply of these Indians, but I have discovered not less than sixty distinct products for nutrition, and at least twenty-eight more utilized for narcotics, stimulants, or medicines, all derived from desert or semidesert localities, in use among these Indians. . . .

On the desert the main reliance of the Coahuilla Indians is the algaroba or mesquite. This remarkable tree is well known to any one who has traversed the sandy Southwest. Its range is wide, from the desert slopes of the California mountains, eastward in southern latitudes to Texas. Of the Colorado basin it is the characteristic tree. It grows to a height of from thirty to forty feet. Its wood is close grained and hard; its leaves small but abundant, and its branches well armored with spines. . . .

The fruit of the algaroba or honey mesquite (*Prosopis juliflora*) is a beautiful legumen, four to seven inches long, which hangs in splendid clusters. A good crop will bend each branch almost to the ground, and as the fruit falls, pile the ground beneath the tree with a thick carpet of straw-colored pods. These are pulpy, sweet, and nutritious, affording food to stock as well as to man.

Everywhere in the Colorado country, to the Mojave, Yuma, and Cocopah,

Pp. 54–70 of David Prescott Barrows, *The Ethno-Botany of the Coahuilla Indians of Southern California* (1900).

as well as to the Coahuilla, they are the staple of life. The Coahuillas gather them in July and August in great quantities, drying them thoroughly and then packing them away in the basket granaries. The beans are never husked, but pod and all are pounded up into an imperfect meal in the wooden mortar. This meal is then placed in earthen dishes and thoroughly soaked. It is then ready to be eaten, and is called by the Coahuillas, pé-chi-ta, or mén-yi-kish, according as it is, or is not, sifted. A light fermentation, which shortly results, improves it. The mass itself, while requiring vigorous mastication, is sweet and wholesome. It is sometimes rolled into compact balls and carried for food on a journey.

According to Dr. Harvard, this pulp contains "more than half its weight of assimilative principles, of which the most important is sugar, in the proportion of 25 to 30 per cent."

The "screwbean" or tornillo (*Prosopis pubescens,* Benth.) is less abundant than the algaroba. Its fruit is a cluster of little yellow spirals united at one point. It contains even more saccharine matter than the algaroba, and may be eaten with relish as plucked from the tree. A fermented beverage can be made from this meal and was once much drunk by the Indians of the Colorado River. Major Heinzleman described its use among the Yumas: "The pod mesquite begins to ripen in June, the screwbean a little later. Both contain a great deal of saccharine matter; the latter is so full it furnishes by boiling a palatable molasses, and from the former, by boiling and fermentation, a tolerably good drink may be made."

Along the overflowed banks of the New River, and elsewhere about the desert's edge, where cloudbursts or freshets send their sudden streams of muddy water out over the sand, there grows up luxuriantly an enormous species of Chenopodium. In the New River country I have seen the growth higher than a man's head as he sat on horseback. The stalks are sometimes six inches in diameter. The leaves are eaten readily by horses, and the plant is of much value to parties crossing the desert and to stockmen. Its local name is "careless weed." The seeds are eaten by the Indians and the leaves used for greens. Northward, in the Cabeson and Coyote, a smaller and probably distinct species, identified by Professor Jepson as *Chenopodium fremontii,* flourishes after freshets. Its dry branches are covered with seeds which are gathered by the Indians in large quantities, and ground into flour which is baked into little cakes. The Coahuillas call the plant kit or ke-et. After a good harvest of this Chenopodium the edge of the Coyote Cañon will be fringed with granaries holding stores of this food. . . .

The most varied stores of food, however, do not come from the fluviatile plain of the Colorado, but from the forbidding mountains that rise high and abruptly on the westward. . . .

Most remarkable of all the plants that flourish in these wastes is the agave, perhaps the most unique and interesting plant of all America. It ranges widely throughout southwestern United States and Mexico with a large number of species, perhaps one hundred in all; and outside of Mexico, where it furnishes "pulque" and "vino mescale," it is used for food by Apaches, the Pah Ute family, and desert tribes in general. By all these Indians it is prepared for food in much the same way. Several species have become familiar, as the "century plants" of California gardens, but they are not handsome plants except when in bloom, though they give themselves most beautifully to the wants of the Indian.

The life history of all these species is much the same. They come up in little round heads or cabbages. For years this head enlarges, throwing out fibrous leaves armed with a spine at the point. Even in the hot air of the desert it is twelve to fifteen years before the period of flowering is reached. Then from the center of the plant there starts up a stalk, growing with great rapidity. In the larger species this stalk may be twenty to thirty feet high and eighteen inches through at the base. From this stalk clusters of pale yellow blossoms, thousands in number, open in the hot, quivering sunshine. This supreme act ends the life of the plant.

Within the territory of the Coahuillas there is but a single species, the *Agave deserti,* Engelm., which grows abundantly along the eastern base of the coast ranges in San Diego County, and southward into Baja California. It was first discovered by Lieutenant W. H. Emory, of the Mexican Boundary Survey, in 1846. It is a small species with leaves densely clustered, thick and deeply concave, only six to twelve inches long. The scape or stalk is from ten to twelve feet high and slender. The flowers are a bright yellow. From April on, the cabbages and stalks are full of sap and are then roasted. Parties go down from the mountain villages into Coyote Cañon for the purpose. Great fire pits or ovens, called na-chish-em, are dug in the sands and lined with stones. Fire is kept up in the pit until the stones are thoroughly heated; the mescal heads are then placed in the hole and covered over with grass and earth and left to roast for a day or two. Mescal heads thus cooked consist of fibrous, molasses-colored layers, sweet and delicious to the taste and wonderfully nutritious. Pieces will keep for many years. The agave is called a-mul, the sections of the stalk, u-a-sil, which are also roasted and, though fibrous, are sweet and good, and the short leaves about the head, ya-mil. The yellow blossoms, amu-sal-em, are boiled and dried for preservation, and then boiled anew when ready to be eaten. The fibers from the leaves of the agave, amu-pa-la, are exceedingly important in manufactures. . . .

The *Yucca mohavensis* (Coahuilla hú-nu-vút) grows abundantly on various hillsides and sandy cañons of the southern exposure of the San Jacinto Range, as well as near the summits of the cañons on the desert slopes.

The species is quite different in appearance from the *Yucca whipplei,* Torr., which grows so abundantly nearer the coast and in the vicinity of Pasadena, and is known as the "Spanish bayonet" or *quijotes.* In the *Yucca mohavensis* the clusters of spines are very dense about its foot, and its short, thick stump or caudex rises to a height sometimes of six feet from the ground. Its flower stalk or scape is short and thick, but clustered with the delicate waxy flowers of the yucca kind. The fruit, nin-yil, appears as plump, sticky, green pods, three or five inches long with big, black seeds filling the center in four rows. These are picked when green and roasted among the coals. They have a sweet, not unpleasant taste, slightly suggestive of roasted green apples. When ripe, the pods are eaten uncooked and are sweet and pleasant, though slightly puckering to the taste. . . .

Higher up on the mountains grow two species of wild plum or cherry. One, the *Prunus ilicifolia,* Walp., has an extensive range along the California coast and had a wide use among the California Indians. It is called by the Mexicans "yslay" and by the Coahuillas chá-mish. It grows abundantly in all the cañons of the San Jacinto Mountains, its dark, handsome foliage crowding many a pass and hillside. Its fruit is of a reddish-yellow color, and resembles very small gage plums. The pulp is, however, very thin and puckery and the pit preposterously large. It is the kernel of the latter and not the pulp that is mostly utilized. These plums are gathered in very large quantities in August and are spread in the sun until the pulp is thoroughly shrunken and dried. The thin shells of the pits are then easily broken open and the kernels extracted. These are crushed in the mortar, leached in the sand basket, and boiled into the usual atole. The other plum tree has with some question been identified by Professor Jepson as the *Prunus andersonii,* Gray. I found it growing along the eastern summits of the San Jacinto Range. Its fruit somewhat resembles the *Zizyphus* and was formerly eaten by the Coahuillas, who called it cha-wa-kal. . . .

Before dismissing the truly desert plants that yield food, a word is merited by the palms. These have been referred to above. They grow in long, waving lines along the gorges leading into the desert wherever water stands in pools or seeps through the sandy bottoms. Beneath the wide fronds the dates grow in great clusters, supported by a strong but drooping stalk. These dates are very small and the seeds are disproportionately large, but early in the fall, when they ripen, the Coahuillas lasso the clusters and draw them down for food. Swarms of bees surround the fruit as it ripens, and in the fronds of the palms are multitudes of yellow jackets' nests. The Indians of Lower California cut out the heart or center of the top of young palms and eat them with great relish. I have not known the Coahuillas to indulge in these "palmitos."

In the valleys near the summit of the range and especially in the Piñon

Flats are groves of the *Juniperus occidentalis,* Hook., low evergreen trees, with thin, shreddy bark. The fruit, a bluish-black drupe the size of a small marble, is eaten by the Coahuillas and called by them is-wut.

The acorn was one of the most generally used foods of the Indians of the Pacific Coast. Its use was noticed by Cabrillo, the first white explorer to navigate these waters. "They eat acorns and a grain which is as large as maize and is white, of which they make dumplings. It is good food." Certain parts of the coast, the Upper San Joaquin Valley and the mountains of the Coast Range are thickly covered with forests of this stately tree. There are no less than fourteen species of oaks in the whole of California and about eight are found in the southern part of the state. Their fruit contains "starch, fixed oil, citric acid, and sugar, as well as astringent and bitter principles." The largest and most palatable acorn is that of the white oak, or Mexican "roble" (*Quercus lobata*), "common throughout the state, on the plains and in the foothills, in the southern part of the state somewhat higher in the mountains." It was mostly from this tree that the Indians of the past supplied themselves. . . .

The *Quercus dumosa,* Nutt., which has a thick, large fruit, grows on the Coahuilla Mountain and is gathered in considerable quantities by the Indians of Coahuilla Valley. This acorn is called by them kwín-yil. It is ground in the mortar and leached in the sand basket. Dr. Harvard reports that the sand mixed with the meal by washing has "a decided effect upon the teeth. My informant, a medical officer, tells me that he has seen an Indian forty-five years old with the crowns of his otherwise healthy teeth half gone, while in Indians sixty years old it is not uncommon to see all the teeth worn down even with the gums." Although the sand basket as a means for preparing food is in constant use among the Coahuilla Indians, I have never myself noticed any such effects.

The piñon or pine nut is a very important article of food. The lower limit of the pineries, in southern California, is, of course, high, being almost everywhere about 5,000 feet, and it is only by reason of the fact that the Coahuillas have penetrated into the mountains from the desert that this source of food is available to them at all. The summits of Torres and Coahuilla mountains and the higher San Jacinto peaks are covered with pines of several species; the gigantic sugar pine of the Pacific slope (*Pinus lambertiana,* Dougl.) with a cone a foot and a half in length, the Mexican nut pine (*P. sembroides*), and (*P. parryana,* Eng.), and also the single-leafed or Nevada nut pine (*P. monophylla*), so precious to the Indians of the Great Basin. These nuts are gathered in large quantities, generally in the late fall of the year. B. H. Dutcher, of the Death Valley Expedition of 1891, has given a careful account of piñon gathering among the Panamints on the west side of Death Valley. The tree was the *P. mono-*

phylla, which has a small cone three inches long. These were pulled and beaten from the trees with a pronged stick and collected in light packing baskets while still sticky with gum. They were then piled on a heap of brush and roasted, which dried the pitch and spread the leaves of the cone. The nuts were then jarred out by a heavy blow from a stone on the apex of the cone. The nuts were winnowed from the chaff by tossing them from a flat basket in the breeze. The Coahuillas harvest the nuts in precisely the same manner. Sometimes in mid-summer the cones are beaten from the trees, before the ripened harvest time, thoroughly roasted in a fire, split open with a hatchet and the nuts extracted. Piñons are called by the Coahuillas te-wat-em; the cones te-vat, and the little almond-like cavities in which the nuts lie and which are exposed in section when the cone is split open are called he-push or the "eyes" of the te-vat. The pine most used is the *Pinus monophylla.* . . .

Perhaps the most important of the seed foods used by the Indians is the justly famed "chia" (*Salvia columbariæ,* Benth.), called by the Coahuillas pá-sal. The plant is one of the smallest of the sage family. It grows up from an annual root with a slender branching stem, terminated by several curious whorls containing the seeds. These are dark, round, flat bodies, that have a slippery, uncertain feeling to the touch. The genus Salvia has an exceedingly wide range and use as a food plant. According to Dr. Harvard the *Salvia polystarchia,* Ort., is largely cultivated in northern and central Mexico. These seeds are rich in mucilage and oil. "After careful roasting they are ground into meal, which, when thrown into water, expands to several times its bulk, the mucilage rapidly dissolving. By adding lemon and sweetening a very popular Mexican beverage is produced."

Chia was a staple food with the Indians of the Pacific Coast. Large quantities, already parched, have been taken from graves on the Santa Barbara Channel. The seeds are gathered by the Coahuillas with the seed fan and flat basket, and are parched and ground. The meal is then mixed with about three times as much wheat flour and the whole pounded up together. It makes a dark looking meal. This is "pinole," called by the Coahuillas to-at. It is an old and famous preparation. . . .

Pinole, by the Coahuillas, is sometimes baked into little cakes or biscuits. Either way chia is used, it is very good; has a pleasant, nutty flavor, and is exceedingly wholesome. . . .

Among the fruits most important to the Indian inhabitants of the Southwest stand those of the cactus family. There are over fifty species in the United States and a majority of these are found in California.

The Mexican prickly pear or "tuna" (*Opuntia tuna,* Mill) is said by Dr. Harvard to have been brought to the Pacific Coast from Mexico, where it had been cultivated from time immemorial. It was planted in hedges about the missions and ranch houses, where it thrives still in picturesque clusters and is now thoroughly naturalized. Its fruit is the well-known "Indian fig." While it has not been planted anywhere on the reservations of the Coahuillas, they sometimes obtain the fruit from other Indians of the valleys. The cactus plant is called by the Coahuillas na-vit and the little bud-like fruit na-vit-yu-lu-ku or "the little heads of the cactus."

There are numerous species of cactus throughout the mountains down to the desert level. About a dozen yield fruit products utilized by the Coahuillas. In most cases it is the ripened fruit or "fig" that is eaten. In several cases it is the abundant seeds, in others, the buds and succulent joints of stalk. Except in a few instances I can do no more in the way of identification of these species than to give a description of the plant and state its uses and Indian name.

The *Opuntia basilaris* is an especially valuable cactus plant of the Coahuillas. It is one of the small varieties and has a tender slate-colored stem in flat joints. The young fruit in early summer is full of sweetness. These buds are collected in baskets, being easily broken off with a stick. The short, sparse spines are wholly brushed off with a bunch of grass or a handful of brush twigs. The buds are then cooked or steamed with hot stones in a pit for twelve hours or more. This cactus is called má-nal. Coville describes exactly the same use of this plant by the Panamints. This cooked cactus is, he says, called nä-vo. I would call attention to the similarity of this word to the general Coahuilla word for cactus fruit, na-vit. No vocabulary of the Panamints has ever been published, but they are undoubtedly of the same great stock as the Coahuillas and such verbal similarities are to be expected.

Mu-tal is another of the opuntia, with flat, ugly jointed stems, growing low and spreading over the ground in the most arid stretches of the valleys. The flat joints, the size of one's palm, are crowded along their edges with buds as big as the last joint of a man's thumb. They are gathered in large quantities, brushed, and dried. They are often stored for subsequent use, and when needed for food are prepared by boiling in water with a little salt and lard. Very frequently also the fruit is allowed to ripen for its seeds. The figs, after being dried, are spread out on a hard, smooth, dirt floor and then the woman sits down beside the pile of cactus heads and with a flail, made from the leaf stem of the desert palm, thoroughly threshes out the seeds. These are then winnowed from the chaff and stored for winter use. Along through the winter, as needed for food, they are pounded into meal and cooked into an atole. These seeds are called wi-al and they are obtained from several species of cactus besides the mu-tal. . . .

Ko-pash is the famed "nigger head," the *Echinocactus cylindricis*. It appears above the sand simply as a round fluted globe, a little larger than a man's head. It is covered with spines and bears a small edible fig. But its chief value does not lie in its fruit, but in its succulent and thirst-relieving interior. No plant could be more admirably contrived as a reservoir, and the thick tough rind and protective spines enclose an interior that is full of water. This plant is often resorted to by thirsty travelers and, according to the stories told over the desert, frequently saves life.

A review of the food supply of these Indians forces in upon us some general reflections or conclusions. First, it seems certain that the diet was a much more diversified one than fell to the lot of most North American Indians. Roaming from the desert, through the mountains to the coast plains, they drew upon three quite dissimilar botanical zones. There was no single staple, on the production of which depended the chances of sufficiency or want. Any one of several much used products might be gathered in sufficient quantities to carry the entire tribe through a year of subsistence. There was really an abundant supply of wild food, far more than adequate, at nearly all times of the year, for the needs of the several thousand Indian inhabitants of former times, although hardly a score of white families will find a living here after all the Indians are gone. And the secret of this anomaly lies in the fact that the Indian drew his stores of food from hillsides and cañons, where the white man looks for nothing and can produce nothing. The territory is a very large one, perhaps 4,000 square miles of cañons and mountains, rough plains, and sandy deserts. In all of it, as we have seen, there are few spots of beauty; only the valleys of pines, the wonderful cañons of palms, and the green potreros about the springs; while over most broods the hot, throbbing silence of the desert. And yet this habitat, dreary and forbidding as it appears to most, is after all a generous one. It bears some of the most remarkable food plants of any continent. Nature did not pour out her gifts lavishly here, but the patient toiler and wise seeker she rewarded well. The main staples of diet were, indeed, furnished in most lavish abundance. Let us notice a few instances. The crops of legumens, that annually fall from the splendid mesquite groves of the Cabeson or the New River country, could not be wholly utilized by a population that numbered a hundred thousand souls. I have seen the mesquite beans fallen so heavily beneath the trees in the vicinity of Martinez as to carpet the sand for miles. Centals could be gathered about every tree. Hundreds of horses and cattle that ranged the valley, to say nothing of the busy women that had crowded their granaries full, effected no visible diminution of the supply. . . .

The road from Coahuilla Valley down to Ahuanga Creek descends along the bottom of a gorge. The sides of this cañon are covered with *Yucca mohavensis*. In July or early August these palm-like trees, for so they almost are, are all crowded with stalks hung with heavy pods, more fruit drying in the sun than the entire tribe could devour. The groves of oaks and pines in the higher valleys of San Jacinto; the abundant crops of chia and other seed plants; the elder berry, so greatly enjoyed, that frequently families will live for weeks on little else; all of these can be found in inexhaustible quantities. Another fact very favorable to the Indians is the long season over which the gathering of these staples is distributed. The harvest time opens in April, with the budding out of agave and yucca stalks, and from this time until late fall there is no month without its especial product. The chia and other seed plants are ready for the fan in May and June, the wild plums in June and July, the mesquite and sambucus in August, and the piñons and acorns from September on. For only about four months of winter was it necessary to hoard food. The ollas and basket granaries were sufficient storehouses.

THE VALUE OF
INSECTS TO THE
CALIFORNIA INDIANS

by
E. O. Essig

Indians probably knew a great deal more about certain facts concerning the natural instincts and habits of insects than the white race will ever know. The aborigines of California literally lived with their tiny six-legged brothers and liked them in more ways than one. Apparently there were no feelings of rivalry on the part of the red men as is so often expressed today by the entomological economists who class insects as man's greatest rivals on this earth. The Indians accepted nature as it was without carrying out any ambitious schemes to replace the forests and the prairies with cultivated fields and great cities. Theirs was the lot to live with and enjoy the bountifulness and beauty of the natural paradise from which they exacted only the barest necessities of immediate life. That they had an intimate knowledge concerning the intricate life habits of insects may be inferred from the meager bits of information gathered by anthropologists in entirely different fields of science. Unfortunately the interest in Indian entomology came too late to communicate directly with these aboriginal seers of nature, and what they may have gleaned by sharp-eyed and patient diligence throughout the ages has forever perished with them. The few entomological scraps which have fallen from the tables of anthropology are meager indeed, but they may serve to stimulate our imaginations of what might have been.

Insects played a conspicuous part in the legends of the California Indians. The Mohave had a story concerning termites which indicates that they knew the subterranean and aerial as well as the wood-destroying habits of these rather obscure white ants. The coastal tribes of northwestern California looked upon the sand cricket with almost human regard. This insect was supposed to have brought mortality to man, when he might otherwise have remained immortal. Flies are said to have first taught the savages how to mourn and cicadas how to wail.

Lice enter into a number of Indian legends. In one case the common hero coyote, after the earth emerged from the primeval flood, failing to find mankind, married a louse from whose eggs sprang many tribes.

E. O. Essig, "The Value of Insects to the California Indians," *Scientific Monthly* (1934), 38:181–186.

There is a Yokut myth concerning the origin of the Pleiades. It is a little story of a flea and five girls whom the insect married and subsequently followed into the sky. "That is why there are five stars now in the Pleiades and one at the side. That one is he, the flea."

In spite of the ancestral beliefs and legends concerning lice and fleas the Indians were somewhat annoyed by them. I say somewhat because, as a matter of fact, the savages were apparently hardened to these pestiferous foes of mankind and actually gave them little thought or attention. However, they did try to dislodge them from the hair on the head. The Mohave Indians plastered their scalps with mud to kill the vermin. Among all the natives, the sweat houses and frequent plunges into the streams and lakes were also resorted to as a means of shifting the parasites. But at best only the active forms were removed and the eggs remained to furnish a new supply of tormentors in a very short time. By firing their huts countless numbers of the pests were killed, but the Indians overlooked those which were carried on their own bodies into the new abodes.

In ritualistic ceremonies and for musical instruments, many tribes in middle and northern California used the cocoons of the giant wild silkworm moths for rattles. These cocoons were split open, the chrysalids removed, a few pebbles inserted, and then bound singly or in numbers to the end of a stick often further ornamented with feathers.

Few arts were to be found among our west coast aborigines. There was little or no pottery, but basket weaving attained a high state of perfection. The baskets in which they cooked were made watertight by coating them with wax obtained from several species of coccids, or scale insects closely related to the famous lac insect of India, from which commercial shellac is produced. Insect wax was also used for fastening the sinew backing of bows and even for chewing gum.

Fashionable Mohave Indian women painted their faces in butterfly patterns in red and yellow with artistic ability.

Insects appear to have been most useful to the California Indians as a source of food. When we remember that these red men ate very little real meat and that many tribes were poor hunters, it is not to be wondered that they ate everything that came their way. Professor Kroeber, of the University of California, states that the "California Indians are perhaps the most omnivorous group of tribes on the continent." Along the coast and streams fish, eels and shellfish were conspicuous articles of diet. But in the valleys acorns formed, by far, the most important item. Then came seeds, bulbs, roots, berries and other vegetable products. Small animals, chiefly rodents and insects, supplied most of the proteins and fats. A great number and wide variety of insects were eaten, either raw, dried, roasted, or otherwise prepared.

The young fat larvae of bees, wasps, ants, and wood-boring beetles were a delicious relish not often overlooked by the ever-hungry boys and girls. White grubs from the sod, termites from decaying wood, crane fly larvae or leatherjackets from the wet earth, and maggots from many sources were similarly sought as ready-to-eat commodities of the diet.

Aside from that obtained in the native fruits and berries, sweets were available in the form of the so-called Indian honey or honeydew, the excrement of plant lice, coccids, and a few other homopterous insects. Small quantities of honey were to be found only in the nests of bumblebees and some other wild bees, since the honeybee was unknown in California until it was introduced by the American settlers only eighty years ago.

Grasshoppers were universally eaten wherever available, and in the large interior valleys and along the foothills of the Sierras they often occurred in immense swarms. Then it was that the entire Indian populace turned out to gather a large part of the winter's food supply. Several methods were employed to capture the insects, but usually a fire was first built on level ground or in a pit, and when reduced to coals the drive began from afar. In an ever-contracting circle the Indians beat the ground and vegetation with bushes and finally forced the bewildered grasshoppers into the masses of coals, where they were quickly roasted and subsequently stored away in bulk or impaled or strung on sticks to be eaten as we might dispose of roasted peanuts, or to be ground into a meal and mixed with pinole, or acorn meal, and boiled in baskets with hot stones. Literally tons of hoppers were thus consumed, but the annual supply never seemed to diminish, for locusts were among the most serious pests which devastated the fields, orchards, and gardens of the early white settlers throughout the state.

Yet another interesting insect food, still collected by the Indians in the Mono Lake region, is the pupa of a small fly which breeds in unbelievable numbers in certain portions of the brackish waters of Mono Lake and other saline lakes in eastern California and western Nevada. In late summer the pupae of the fly are washed upon the shores of these lakes in great windrows. The edible part consists of a small fat body about the size of a kernel of wheat, which is readily separated from the protective outer skin by rubbing the pupae between the hands. Nor were the squaws too particular to separate the kernels from the chaff. The material thus collected was called kootsabe and, in addition to becoming rancid and odorous, would keep for months and could be eaten without further preparation like raisins or popcorn. Very great quantities have been collected even to the present time.

Another astonishing food product still utilized by the western Indians is the large caterpillar of the pandora moth, which feeds on the needles of the yellow pines of the Sierra and Cascade mountains. The full-fed caterpillars are from 2 to 2.5 inches long, or almost as large as your index finger. They live in the pine trees far out of reach — and only descend to the ground to enter the soil to pass into the chrysalis or pupal stage. Therefore the Indians were either compelled to await their natural descent or to resort to some means of forcing them to drop off. This they did by building a fire under the infested trees and making a smoke smudge to stupify the caterpillars which rained to the ground. These were gathered in baskets by the women, children, and old men; killed and dried in a bed of hot ashes, coals, and sand; and stored away for future consumption. After boiling in water, without any seasoning whatever, the resulting pabulum was called pe-ag-gie and was fished out by the none-too-clean fingers as serving implements. Hungry whites, who tasted the food, claimed that boarding with the early Californians on the "American plan was not so good."

Other caterpillars, both hairy and smooth, were parched before an open fire by the Pomo Indians of the San Francisco Bay region and served hot or cold, or, if preferred, with less trouble, like oysters on the half-shell.

It might be thought by some of my readers that such insect food is unwholesome. While it might be admitted that most of us would not care to eat grasshoppers, maggots, and caterpillars, the fact remains that they are perfectly harmless and wholesome and, if prepared in more modern ways, might even be palatable. Let me suggest that if you are ever lost and unable to secure the customary foods, you need never suffer hunger if insects are available. Even a fire would be unnecessary to prepare a meal under such circumstances.

Regardless of what we may think about the bill of fare of our California predecessors, it must be remembered that all aborigines ate insects; and even today the abundance of grasshoppers in many old world countries may be ascertained by noting the prices in the local markets.

CALIFORNIA BASKETRY
AND THE POMO

by
A. L. Kroeber

A recent account of the basketry of the Pomo Indians of California by Dr. S. A. Barrett is perhaps the most complete study of the basketry of any North American tribe yet published. It both offers opportunity to examine the relations existing between the Pomo and other tribes as regards this art, and supplements and illustrates the conclusions that can be drawn from other studies.

MATERIALS

The materials used by the Pomo in basket making number ten or twelve, but the majority of these are used rarely or for special purposes or in restricted districts. The materials whose use is at all common or of general consequence are five. Of these only one is used as warp in either twined or coiled ware. This is willow. The woof materials are four: the root of a sedge, *Carex*, the bark of the redbud, *Cercis*, the root of the bulrush, *Scirpus*, and the root of the digger pine. Of these the sedge is the most important, furnishing, as willow does for the warp, woof of both coiled and twined baskets. The redbud furnishes red patterns and is employed chiefly in twined weaves. The bulrush root, after being dyed, provides patterns in black and is used almost entirely in coiling. Digger-pine root fibers are employed principally for the woof of coarse twined baskets.

It shows the influence of convention and habit on technique, that practically all the basketry of the Pomo is made in these five materials, although an occasional different use shows that they possess knowledge of other plants and although their habitat produces many other species which would be serviceable, as demonstrated by the employment of these in regions

American Anthropologist n.s. (1909), 11:233–249.

For additional information on California Indian basketry see O. T. Mason, "Aboriginal American Basketry," *Report of the U.S. National Museum for 1902* (1904), pp. 171–548; S. E. Barrett, *Pomo Indian Basketry*, Univ. Calif. Publ. Am. Arch. and Ethn. (1908), 7:133–308; L. M. O'Neale, *Yurok-Karok Basket Weavers*, ibid. (1932), 32:1–184; F. H. Douglas, *The Main Divisions of California Basketry*, Denver Art Museum Leaflets, No. 83 (1937), pp. 130–136.

where different technical habits prevail. The other Indians of California evince a similar restriction, voluntary it might be called, of their choice of basket materials.

In northernmost California, where only twining is practiced, the warp is almost universally hazel, and the woof is root fibers of conifers—pine, redwood, spruce, or other species being used according to local distribution. The ornamentation of this basketry consists of a glossy white overlay, which is the shining grass, *Xerophyllum tenax*. For patterns in black the stems of the five-fingered fern, *Adiantum*, are used, and for patterns in red, alder-dyed fibers from the stem of a large fern, *Woodwardia*.

A description given by Dr. Dixon of the materials used by the northern Maidu also shows characteristic limitation. The northern Maidu make large carrying baskets in the twined technique of northern California, and use for this purpose the same materials. The great bulk of their basketry is coiled, and only two principal materials, willow and redbud, are used. Both of these are employed for both foundation and wrapping. The outer bark of the redbud gives red patterns.

Among the Cahuilla, Luiseño, and Diegueño of southern California the ordinary materials are only three. For the foundation a grass, *Epicampes rigens*, is used. The wrapping consists of either a reed, *Juncus*, or of sumach, *Rhus*. Twined basketry, which is subsidiary, is made entirely of reed.

Information from other tribes is incomplete, but as there is nowhere any indication of a greater variety of materials used, it appears that the specialization followed by the Pomo is the rule and not exceptional.

TECHNIQUES

In the matter of weaves it appears that the Pomo are anomalous in California in practicing an unusual variety of technical processes. The total number of distinct processes is perhaps not greater among the Pomo, but whereas other tribes employ regularly and frequently only one or two of the techniques with which they are acquainted, the Pomo practice five processes abundantly and often make baskets of one kind in several weaves.

The California Indians belong to two groups according as they follow twining or coiling processes of making baskets. There are very few tribes that use both types of technique. The narrow limitation in the employment of materials is therefore paralleled by a limitation of technical processes.

All the Indians of northernmost California, the Tolowa, Yurok, Karok, Hupa, Wiyot, the Athabascan tribes of the middle drainage of Eel River, the Shasta, Northern Wintun, Achomawi, Atsugewi, and Modoc, make only twined work. Generally speaking all tribes to the south of these may be characterized as makers of coiled basketry. There is however a distinction. While the tribes using twining know nothing of coiling, the tribes that employ coiling also twine to some extent. This difference is inherent in the nature of the two processes. The coiled basket is stiffer, closer, and requires much more labor. It lends itself with difficulty to the construction of openwork textiles, such as are desirable or necessary for many purposes. A fish trap in coiled basketry is practically impossible. A conical carrying basket can be made as well in coiling as in twining; but such a basket being intended for firewood and similar loads, an openwork construction is in every way as serviceable as a close coiled one, besides being much lighter and readily made in one tenth the time. Even among tribes inclined toward coiling, twining is therefore employed for many implements of household usage and for those in which either an open or a ready construction is desired. Carrying baskets, weirs and traps, seed beaters, winnowers, and baby carriers are usually twined by tribes whose more characteristic basketry, such as vessels for water, food, storage, and cooking, is coiled. In short, twined weaves are adequate for most forms and purposes, so that tribes whose cultural circumstances have led them to lean toward twining usually employ no other process. Coiling is not applicable to all purposes, and tribes with a specific bent toward this technique are therefore compelled to use also twining, or other processes, for certain implements.

The tribes of whom coiling is characteristic held all of southern and central and part of northern California, much the larger part of the state. The line of separation from the northern region of twining is as follows: In the east it is the boundary between the Maidu and the Achomawi and Atsugewi of the Pit River Valley. The Yana employed both processes, their twined ware being of the northern type, their coiling resembling that of the Maidu, but with greater coarseness and crudeness. The majority of Yana baskets that have been collected, and the best made, are twined, so that this is likely to be the typical and best acculturated Yana technique. The northernmost Wintun twine, the southern Wintun coil, but the boundary is not precisely known. In the Coast Range the line of division separates the Yuki, who are distinctly a coiling tribe, from the Wailaki. The Wailaki make a crude form of the typical basketry of northern California. Occasional coiled pieces of Yuki character occur among them, but are in great minority and clearly due to Yuki influence.

It is of particular interest that the Pomo, who fall well within the limits of the southern group, hold the two techniques in balance. They cannot be included among the border tribes subject to two influences, for to the north of them are the Yuki, who are as clearly a coiling tribe as any. The twined basketry of the Pomo is also entirely different from the twined basketry of northern California. It must therefore be set down as an independent development, which has flourished side by side with the development among the same people of coiled techniques, without either process greatly influencing the other.

According to Dr. Barrett, the coiled basketry of the Pomo is about equally divided between one-rod and three-rod foundations. Single-rod foundations are rare in California, being otherwise found only among the Miwok and Washo. A few pieces have also been obtained among the Yokuts and Shoshoneans adjacent to the Miwok. The Maidu, most commonly the Miwok and Washo, and probably the Wintun where uninfluenced by the Pomo, employ three-rod foundations. The Yokuts and the tribes of Southern California use a multiple foundation. The Yuki use a rod and welt foundation. Neither the rod and welt nor a multiple foundation ordinarily occur among the Pomo.

Five twined weaves are practiced by the Pomo: plain twining, diagonal twining, lattice twining, three-strand twining, and three-strand braiding. The two three-strand weaves are not used to make entire baskets, except occasionally in openwork. The characteristic twined weaves therefore are the plain, diagonal, and lattice. Of these plain twining is most frequent, but the two other processes are by no means rare, and, especially in well-finished baskets, dispute the palm with the simpler technique. Lattice twining—which is almost a combination of coiling and twining—seems to be confined entirely to the Pomo, if we except one or two small adjacent groups, such as the Huchnom, of unrelated linguistic origin but of Pomo culture. Diagonal twining, which is a characteristic Shoshonean process, is of secondary importance in California outside of the Pomo. A sporadic Yurok basket made entirely in this weave has been described. The University of California museum contains also one or more pieces each from the Wiyot, Athabascans of southern Humboldt County, Yana, Chumash, and Mohave, though the normal weave of all these tribes, except possibly the last, is simple twining. The Chemehuevi, who are Shoshoneans, make caps and carrying baskets; and the Shoshonean Mono, with their neighbors the Miwok, Yokuts, and probably Washo, make many or most of their winnowers, beaters, carriers, and cradles in openwork and half-openwork diagonal twining. Among all these tribes, however, diagonal twining is not employed for ordinary baskets as by the Pomo. The Pomo have developed a distinctive type of pattern for their diagonal-twined baskets, which in its general diagonal arrangement differs from the usually horizontal arrangement on plain-twined baskets.

The plain-twined Pomo basket differs radically from the twined basket of northern California. It is either nearly flat or quite deep. The typical basket of northwestern California, while its walls are vertical, is comparatively shallow. The Pomo never use the overlaying which is the sole means of producing patterns in northern California. Pomo designs are normally in redbud. Designs in northern California are in white on a neutral background, or in black or red or both on a background of overlaid white. The texture of the two wares is thoroughly different. The distinction is apparent even in details, such as that the northern people trim their warp ends off flush with the upper course of woof twining, whereas the Pomo habitually allow them to project evenly for a short distance. On the whole Pomo twining is firmer and more closely set than that practiced in northern California, a difference which may perhaps be ascribed to the experience which every Pomo woman has in the necessarily close technique of coiling.

As illustrating the Pomo balance between different weaves, and the apparent desire to maintain one beside the other instead of permitting one process to develop to the exclusion of others, it appears that conical carrying baskets are made both in plain twining and in diagonal twining; storage baskets in plain twining, lattice twining, and diagonal twining; various baskets of the same shape and use in both one-rod and three-rod coiling; and cooking baskets and flat baskets in plain twining, diagonal twining, and lattice twining.

Dr. Barrett describes also Pomo wickerwork. The use of this is confined to handled seed beaters of circular form. Wickerwork is comparatively rare in North America, though there are well-known forms in the Southwest. A wickerwork seed beater from the northwestern Maidu is described by Dr. Dixon. This piece is from Butte county, in the original habitat of the Maidu. A number of Maidu from this region have long lived on Round Valley reservation, in close association with Pomo of the northern and eastern dialectic divisions, and some of these Maidu have returned to their old home. It is therefore possible that the specimen in question is due to modern Pomo influence even though collected on Maidu soil. If, however, as seems more likely, it is an old Maidu type, the practical identity of the Maidu and Pomo wickerwork forms makes it highly probable that the Wintun in the intervening territory also employed this technique in the seed beater. In that case wickerwork would have a wider distribution in California than heretofore believed. The Mohave and Diegueño use soft-warped stiff-woofed wickerwork in the hoods of cradles.

Direction of Progress in Manufacture

In twined Pomo baskets the general course of the woof turns from right to left, as one looks at the basket from above. Dr. Barrett's explanation is illuminating. In twining, the long projecting warp rods at the top render it necessary for the weaver to hold the bottom of the basket toward her. The left hand firmly grasps the warp and keeps in place the just inserted woof strands, while the right hand manipulates the twining of the pliable woof. The progression is therefore to the weaver's right, which corresponds to the left as one looks into the basket.

The same direction of the twining woof is followed practically all over California, as by the Yurok, Karok, Hupa, Tolowa, Wiyot, Wailaki, Modoc, Wintun, Yana, Achomawi, Yuki, Wappo, Miwok, Yokuts, Mono, Cheme-huevi, Chumash, Cahuilla, and Luiseño. The only exceptions found are the rude openwork Diegueño baskets, which twine in the opposite direction from the identical Cahuilla and Luiseño pieces; the close-woven flat baskets of the Yurok-Hupa territory; part of the baskets of this type made by the Modoc; and certain flat coarse openwork baskets of the Wappo. It is evident that if a basket is held reversed while in manufacture, with the bottom up or turned away from the weaver, the course of the twining when it is finished will be the reverse of the usual while the process of manipulation remains the same. The flatter the basket, the less difference does it make, in working on it, which side is held above, and the less reason is there, when it is finished, to regard one surface as specifically the inner one. In fact an essentially flat basket with a certain amount of curvature can be held and worked like others, and when finished turned inside out by a thrust in the middle. This is actually done by the Yurok. With the exception of a few unexplained Diegueño pieces, the twining of California therefore always turns from right to left, as one looks into the basket, or progresses from the maker's left to right, and contrary cases are only nominally or apparently such.

Outside of California, the direction of twining seems to be usually the same, as among the Apache and in the Puget Sound region. The baskets of the Alaska Eskimo, the majority from the Aleutian Islands, and a minority among the Haida and Tlingit, however, turn abnormally or clock-wise. A number of baskets from the Haida-Tlingit area turn one way on their flat bottom, and in the opposite direction on their sides. It is interest-ing to note that Aleut baskets are described as habitually, and Haida baskets sometimes, suspended bottom up in manufacture; so that the abnormal or reverse direction of twining in this northern region seems to be the result merely of a reversed position of the basket, the weaver following the usual manipulation in her work. It follows that Dr. Barrett's explanation of the direction of twining is to be accepted as of general application. It also follows that the absolute uniformity of this direction among most tribes argues for a very rare or weak natural development of left-handedness, or its almost total suppression by right-handed custom. No apparatus being required in weaving, and the product being identical whatever the direc-tion of the twining, there is every inducement for a left-handed woman to work as is natural to her. It seems as if tribal habit or blind imitation influenced the Indian basket maker as much and as unreasonably as it influences us in writing, sewing, riding, and shooting.

The direction of Pomo coiling is the reverse of that obtaining in twining. Dr. Barrett explains this fact as also due to the process of manipulation, the left hand being engaged in holding the loose end of the warp, toward which the right advances the woof. His suggestion as to the reason for the direction of coiling is however perhaps less compelling, since the nature and position of the single projecting warp are such as to allow the worker more readily to hold the bottom of the basket either toward her or away from her. The former is perhaps the more natural position, especially in baskets approaching a spherical shape, and the corresponding direction of the coil is the prevalent one in California. Nevertheless nearly all tribes except the Pomo coil at least some ware in the opposite direction, and in some regions outside of California this opposite direction is the rule. The position of the basket while in manufacture is probably the sole cause of the difference in coil direction; yet it is evident that if such is the case mere industrial habit or tribal invention must largely determine this position, since with the Maidu and Miwok only flat baskets, with the tribes of central and southern California only spherical or constricted baskets, with the Yuki all baskets of whatever shape, and with the Pomo no baskets, progress contraclockwise.

DECORATION

The general scheme of pattern arrangement followed in Pomo baskets seems to depend in the main on the weave employed. In twined baskets a horizontal or banded arrangement is by far the most common, while a diagonal arrangement occurs in a minority. Dr. Barrett estimates the average frequency of horizontal, parallel diagonal, and crossing diagonal arrangement at 70, 25, and 5 per cent. As has been said, the horizontal arrangement occurs usually in plain twining and lattice twining, while the diagonal arrangement is characteristic of the diagonal-twined weave.

In coiled baskets there is a much greater variety of arrangement. Dr. Barrett gives the following proportions: horizontal, 40; parallel diagonal, 30; crossing diagonal, 10; vertical, 15; individual or separate groups of patterns, 5. It is apparent that these proportions are not at all related to those obtaining in twined basketry. Considering the parallel diagonal and crossing diagonal arrangements as fundamentally the same, it may be said that diagonal and horizontal dispositions of designs are of about equal frequency in Pomo coiling, and that a vertical or individual arrangement, while less common than either, is also characteristic.

The typical Maidu pattern arrangement is diagonal, either parallel, crossing, or zigzag. In southern and central California the prevailing arrangement is horizontal, a secondary one vertical, a diagonal arrangement of any sort being uncommon. As these are regions of coiling, it appears that pattern arrangement is not altogether dependent on technical motives. The shape of ware is undoubtedly a potent factor. In the case of twining this is evident. In northwestern California, where baskets are mostly low, a diagonal arrangement would not be effective, and a horizontal arrangement prevails; in northeastern California, where technique and materials are the same, baskets are normally higher, and a diagonal disposition is customary. Nevertheless there are many instances where the arrangement of patterns is clearly the outcome of neither technique nor shape, but of esthetic convention.

As regards the Pomo, it is almost certain that independently of technical influences and of the factor of decorative area as determined by shape of the basket, a greater variety of pattern arrangements is found than with other tribes.

In several other respects Pomo basketry shows specialization. According to Dr. Barrett the Pomo were in aboriginal days the only California people to attempt the complete ornamentation of baskets with feathers. Feather decoration is found as far south as the Yokuts, but the feathers occur only on part of the surface of the basket. Some of the tribes immediately adjacent to the Pomo, such as the Wappo, Yuki, southern Wintun, and coast Miwok, used feathers, but never covered entire baskets. Owing to trade demands they have now in some cases learned to do so, but their work is still inferior to that of the Pomo.

The Pomo are perhaps also unique in never completely encircling a basket with a design. If the pattern is a horizontal band, a break called dau, ham, or hwa must be left in it. If this is not done it is believed that the maker will be afflicted with blindness. This break in the encircling pattern is familiar from the Southwest, but has not been reported from any other California tribes, many of whom, such as the Hupa, Yurok, Yokuts, and Cahuilla, frequently employ continuous and uniform bands of design. Most flat Yuki baskets with a pattern of simple encircling bands, but usually no others, show a break in the design, but its significance has not been reported, and it does not seem to have been the same as that of the dau.

A peculiar practice of the Pomo is also to insert in a coiled basket a few wrappings of the orange-colored quills of the yellowhammer, as a preventive charm, in all cases in which a woman works on a basket during her menstrual period.

Finally may be mentioned the shaiyoi or initial design, the introduction of which is also connected with religious beliefs.

So far as known, the Pomo and the adjacent tribes of the same culture are the only ones among whom any basketry is made by men. Men make fish traps and weirs, baby carriers, coarse openwork baskets for carrying and storage, and shallow openwork forms. In general most openwork is made by men. Dr. Barrett notes that all close-woven baskets are made with a downward turn of the woof-strands, and most openwork baskets are made with an upward turn. As the men make no close-woven baskets, and the women few in openwork, it may be said in general terms that the men employ one direction and the women another in turning the woof in twining.

Names of Designs

In the matter of interpretations of names attached to designs, Dr. Barrett's work is particularly full. He obtained explanations of more than eight hundred designs, appearing on some three hundred baskets. As most of these patterns were explained by a number of informants, the total number of interpretations was several thousand. Such a mass of information on this phase of basketry has probably never before been gathered among one group of people, so that the conclusions become of unusual significance. If anyone still cherishes the belief that patterns were put upon baskets by the California Indians from religious or symbolic motives, or that their significance is ceremonial or poetical, the idea will be dispelled by a glance at Dr. Barrett's data, in which the thousands of monotonously commonplace and concordant names are unbroken by even a single instance of symbolic interpretation.

Among Pomo speaking three different dialects or languages, Dr. Barrett encountered 54 different names of designs. Omitting 2 that are doubtful and 6 that are representations of objects introduced by Europeans, there remain 46. Ten of these are pairs, deer-back, for instance, being the name in one dialect of a design which in another dialect is called wild-potato-forehead. Of the 46 undoubted aboriginal design names only 33 occur in the northern dialect, 24 in the central, and 22 in the eastern. Twenty of the 46 names are however rare. Of the 26 in common use, 20 are found in the northern dialect, 17 in the central, and 14 in the eastern. The number of common elementary design names among any one group of Pomo people is therefore about 15 to 20.

This result agrees with determinations made among other tribes of California. Among the Yurok there are only about 18 names in customary use, though the addition of designations that are rarely employed brings the total to about 30. These rare names are perhaps in part individual interpretations, in part survivals of obsolete names, and in part introductions of terms which belong to neighboring tribes and have not yet taken firm root.

Among the Hupa and Karok the number of names appears to be about the same. The total of design names, common and rare, found among the three northwestern tribes, is about 45, or practically identical with Dr. Barrett's total for the three Pomo groups. The Yurok, Karok, and Hupa speak languages that are entirely unrelated, but their territory is more restricted than that of the three Pomo divisions, and their culture is at least as uniform. Conditions are therefore comparable.

Dr. Dixon encountered about 40 different design names among the Maidu, who belong to three divisions which are linguistically about as divergent as the three Pomo groups. Their territory is more extensive and their environment and culture at least as diverse. Dr. Dixon's total therefore also agrees well with Dr. Barrett's. It seems probable that if only the design names in ordinary use among one division of the Maidu had been listed by him, the number would have fallen between 15 and 20.

Dr. Barrett classifies the 26 common names of Pomo design elements as follows: names of animals and parts of the body, 12; plants, 2; inanimate objects, natural and artificial, 4; geometrical, 4; miscellaneous, 4. It should be observed that in many cases names of animals and parts of the body are combined. *Deer-back, turtle-neck,* and *quail-plume* occur, but neither *deer, turtle,* and *quail,* nor *back, neck,* and *feather* alone are found. This is in accord with the nonrealistic and unsymbolic interpretation of the designs. Apparently names suggested by the designs have been applied to them. If there had been an original attempt at representation it is almost certain that deer, birds, turtles, horns, or feathers would have been shown and so named. No one, civilized or uncivilized, could have any motive for picturing the back of a deer or the neck of a turtle.

The relative frequency of these classes of names is about the same among the Pomo as among other California tribes. Almost everywhere names denoting animals or parts of the body are most numerous. The principal divergence occurs in northwestern California, where spatial and dynamical ideas, corresponding to Dr. Barrett's geometrical names, are relatively more frequent, and among the Maidu, where names derived from plants are most numerous after names of animals and body parts. Spatial or geometrical terms, such as *zigzag, striped,* and *spotted,* occur among all tribes, and are often of frequent usage. That they are not proportionately as numerous with the Pomo as among the northwestern Indians, is probably due to the fact that by the Pomo most conceptions of space and position are expressed by qualifying additions to the elementary design names.

Characteristic animal design names among the Pomo are *deer-back, deer-teeth, turtle-neck, turtle-back, goose-excrement, grasshopper-elbow, killdeer-eyebrow, quail-plume, crow-foot, bear-foot, bat-wing,* and *sunfish-rib.* Names of animals not connected with parts of the body are much less numerous and describe only small animals: *ant, butterfly, mosquito, star-*

fish, water-snake. Characteristic geometrical terms are *zigzag* or *crooked, wavy, spotted, dot, small figures, little pieces.* Typical names of objects are *arrowhead, string, stretcher,* and *tattoo.*

In usage, however, such names of designs are rarely employed alone. They are almost always combined with a descriptive or qualifying term, such as *barbed, pointed, short, round, large, downward, bulging, blank, white, half, both, single, imperfect, resembling.* These qualifying terms are nearly as numerous as the elemental design names. Dr. Barrett classifies them according as they relate to form, direction, position, size, color, number, and quality.

The design name of the Pomo, whether qualified or used alone, however describes only the unit or element of a pattern. It is a simple figure of a certain shape. The pattern may consist of a repetition of this element, or of combinations of two or more elements. The pattern and the design element must be sharply distinguished. In exact usage the Pomo always distinguish them. The names that have been discussed designate elements. Pattern names are almost always longer and more complex. This is not only because of the qualifiers of names of design elements, but because in many cases the interrelation of several elements in a pattern is made clear. There is therefore a third class of terms which may be described as qualifiers of pattern names. Of these Dr. Barrett has found 44, though a number of these occur in only one or two dialects of the three examined. Among the most common are: *crossing, meeting, collected, on both sides, connected, close in a row, and, near, on, among, along, in the middle, tied, scattered, separated, leading, following.*

The typical pattern name among the Pomo is therefore quite complex, and at the same time exactly descriptive of the pattern to anyone acquainted with the significance of the names of design elements, qualifiers of design elements, and qualifiers of patterns. Typical names are:

Arrowheads in-the-middle zigzags stripe
Design empty in-the-middle ants close-in-a-row
Deer-back arrowhead crossing
Arrowhead-slender band
Water-snake and arrowhead-barbed
Ants arrowhead crossing in-the-middle
Spotted in-the-middle string stripe
Wild-potato-forehead on-both-sides arrowhead

It is evident that, allowing for convention in the use of the terms designating elements and their relations, these pattern names are sufficient to convey an accurate description of any pattern. A Pomo woman fairly conversant with the art of basket making, and who like every member of her tribe sees baskets in daily use in every household, could make or duplicate any native pattern described to her. Such a practical purpose, and not any religious or symbolic motive, and not even to any considerable degree an artistic impulse, seems to be at the base of these design and pattern names. In other words they are conventional names of conventional figures, corresponding to our diamond, horseshoe, cross, star, crescent, fleur-de-lis, meander, and egg-and-dart. If there is a difference between the Pomo and ourselves, it is that among the Pomo, so far as can be observed, these conventional figures give no evidence of having or of ever having had a symbolic significance. Among ourselves heraldry and religion have in some cases read deep significance into simple figures, and in other instances have given to symbols a popularity which in turn has led to their being employed for purely decorative purposes. It is however to be observed that the designations even of conventional symbolic figures are not symbolic but descriptive. The fleur-de-lis is named for the flower, not after the dynasty of which it is the emblem. The horseshoe itself, not the good luck which it typifies, gives name to the figure. The Pomo in their basket decoration are less inclined to symbolic or religious interpretation than we are in the ornamentation of our architecture, implements for household use or display, and dress. But in both cases there is no evidence that any decorative figure originated directly from a creative symbolic impulse. Symbolism can only interpret what is already given.

The development of subsidiary qualifying terms was probably carried farther by the Pomo than by other California Indians. It is not possible to speak with certainty on this point, no inquiries even approximately as extended as those of Dr. Barrett having been made elsewhere. To a casual inquirer Pomo women give only the name of the most conspicuous element in a pattern, and in comparison with Dr. Barrett's painstaking effort inquiries among other tribes have been casual. It is not unlikely that an equally thorough investigation elsewhere would reveal something of the same system of descriptive adjuncts as among the Pomo. At least some approaches are found in northwestern California, where several subsidiary qualifying terms have been recorded, such as Yurok, Karok, and Hupa *small-in-the-middle, large sharp-teeth, sitting-in-the-middle, sharp different, together, it-encircles, tataktak ascending, snake-noses on-top-of-each-other, they come together, worm goes-round, one-on-the-other-its-scratches.* It is, however, in any case likely that descriptive qualifiers are more developed among the Pomo than among other tribes because Pomo patterns are in the main more complex.

GENERAL CONCLUSIONS

All in all it appears from Dr. Barrett's careful study that the basketry of the Pomo is unique in many aspects. It shows no connection with the basketry of northernmost California and Oregon. It possesses very little relation with the basketry of the Yuki immediately to the north. It is quite different from the basketry of the Maidu to the east. Nor does it show any direct contact with the industries of the tribes of central and southern California. The Pomo are the only California people among whom the arts of twining and coiling basketry are approximately in balance. They are nearly the only people among whom different forms either of coiling or of twining are employed side by side for similar or even identical purposes and with about equal frequency. They regularly and abundantly practise a greater number of radically distinct technical processes of basket-making than any other tribe. They are the only people in the state among whom men have a share in the making of baskets, among whom the symbolic break in the design and symbolic insertion of yellowhammer feathers were practiced, or the symbolic initial design was used. They carried the art of ornamenting baskets with shell beads and feathers to a much higher perfection than any other group. They were either alone in using wickerwork, or shared the technique with but a few tribes. Their general disposition of patterns on the surface of baskets displays a greater variety than is found elsewhere, both in respect to the relation of such arrangement to technical processes and irrespective of it. They show a wealth of subsidiary terms descriptive of the form, position, and relation of design elements and their combination in patterns, to which but scant parallels have as yet been found elsewhere, and which it is unlikely any other California people possess in the same degree. In short, it is evident that the art of basketry in all its phases underwent an independent, special, and uncommon development among the Pomo, which is displayed in an unusual wealth and variety of industrial, technical, and artistic functions.

On the other hand it appears that certain traits are common to the art of basketry among all the tribes of California. Among the most conspicuous of these features are the use of only a small proportion of available materials; a selective specialization in certain types of technique to the exclusion of others; a system of ornamental pattern arrangement determined by esthetic convention or artistic history as well as by technique and shape of the decorative field; a close restriction of the number of names for pattern elements; and a complete absence of religious or symbolic significance from the decorative designs. The conclusion which these facts perhaps most impress, is the tremendous predominance of unmotived custom and habit over conscious utilitarian, artistic, or religious purpose.

MIWOK HOUSES

by
S. A. Barrett and
E. W. Gifford

Shelter

After food, house materials perhaps reflect the physical environment more than any other feature of Miwok material culture. Miwok structures were of several kinds: (1) the conical dwelling house wholly above the ground, (2) the sun shelter, (3) the semisubterranean conical dwelling house, (4) the semisubterranean assembly house, (5) the sudatory or sweathouse, (6) the ceremonial circular structure of brush, (7) the ceremonial rectangular structure of brush, (8) the grinding booth, and (9) the acorn granary.

Dwellings

Difficulty was encountered in determining the exact scope of the terms applied to houses, especially since purely aboriginal structures are completely lacking and intermediate types common. Apparently, too, there is considerable doubt in the native mind as to just how the terms were applied formerly. The following seem to be the several types of dwellings:

Umū′tca (P, N, C) [1] seems to be the specific term for a conical bark house, sometimes with an inner layer of pine needles and an outer layer of earth heaped against its lower parts.

Kŏ′dja (P), and ko′tca (N, C) apparently designate a semisubterranean earth-covered dwelling.

Ū′tcū (C, S) apparently designates a modern board house.

Wo′lle (P), ko′llī (N), and mole (C) designate a simple conical framework of poles covered with a thatch of brush, grass, or tule (wallakayu, C) bound on, in overlapping courses, with grapevine withes. In the hot, dry, rainless summer,

Pp. 198–208 of S. A. Barrett and E. W. Gifford, "Miwok Material Culture," *Bulletin of the Public Museum of the City of Milwaukee* (1933), 2:117–376.

For further information on native California houses see F. Krause, *Die Kultur der kalifornischen Indianer in ihrer Bedeutung für die Ethnologie und die nordamerikanischen Völkerkunde*, Institut für Völkerkunde, Ser. 1 (Leipzig, 1921), 4:1–98; S. A. Barrett, "Pomo Buildings," *Holmes Anniversary Volume* (Washington, 1916), pp. 1–17; W. C. McKern, *Patwin Houses*, Univ. Calif. Publ. Am. Arch. and Ethn. (1923), 20:159–171.

[1] P, N, C, and S, after native words, indicate the dialectic groups: Plains, Northern, Central, and Southern.

the thatch was put on loosely, so as to allow free passage of air, thus making a shade or sun shelter. The terms also apply to shades or sun shelters more or less rectangular and flat-topped in form. Such easily constructed shades were erected on summer camping trips. The flat-topped shade, in particular, served as a pleasant working or resting place by day, for the women and children, and as a sleeping place by night. Often thistle stems (*Carduus californicus*), sawala (C), were laid about such a sleeping place to keep away rattlesnakes, king snakes, and a large lizard called metubu (C), which was reputed to bite and not let go, thus causing the victim's death and subsequent cremation with the lizard still attached. Herpetologists state that the only reptile to be feared was the Pacific rattlesnake (*Crotalus oregonus*).

Tcaama (C) was a portable conical house with tule mat covering and tule mat door. All of the mats were fastened to sticks, for rolling and ready transport. This type was employed below 1,500 feet elevation in Central Miwok territory.

Sitcma (C) was a very small conical hut, covered with either bark or tule. An aged person or a newly menstruating girl was relegated to it. Apparently the special designation refers to use rather than to any structural peculiarity.

In the mountains the preferred covering for conical dwellings, which ranged from 8 to 15 feet in diameter, was slabs of incense cedar bark (ene'na, N, C, S), but bark from other conifers was also used. This was stripped only from dead trees, and the digger pine was especially mentioned for the Upper Sonoran zone; the western yellow pine and big tree (*Sequoia gigantea*), pusine (C), for the Transition zone. No framework or center post was necessary: the bark slabs were leaned together and supported one another. No binding was required. Weather tightness was secured by overlaying the cracks with other slabs until there were three or four thicknesses. The entrance was an opening left in the sloping side. There was no built-out framework or doorway. The opening was closed with a large bark slab, kept leaning against the house when not in place.

Large earth-covered semisubterranean dwellings, in which a dozen people could live, were constructed at times, in the plains, hills, and mountains. The pit of such a one was examined at the site of the former village of Eyeyaku, near Tuolumne, at about 2,500 feet elevation. This type of dwelling was similar in construction, but smaller than, an assembly house (hañi, C), to be described below; it was, however, entered by a ladder through the roof. There was no dancing in this type of house. The Plains Miwok describe this as a rather rare type of winter house, built by men of importance.

In the center of a dwelling was a fireplace, a shallow depression. The fire furnished warmth, and light at night. Here some of the cooking was done. Beside the fire was the earth oven, a simple pit a foot or 18 inches deep by a foot or more across. In it, by means of hot stones, acorn bread, greens, bulbs, corms, meat, and fish were baked or steamed.

The inmates slept on and under mats or skins (usually deerskins, talka,

C) spread upon digger or western yellow pine needles on the earthen floor. A chief used bear hides for bed and seat. Occasionally a well-to-do man had a sleeping bench (etcī′nnī, P; ya′ña, N) or bed of willow or other poles, raised 15 to 18 inches off the floor. Sometimes a small stump or block of wood served as a stool. Leaves of a species of *Cyperus* (kistsi, C) were used for a seat outdoors as well as indoors. Pine needles were piled up for a pillow, or sometimes a rolled coyote (aseli, C) skin was used.

In the dwellings of poor people there might be a scarcity of bed covers, so that a person would have to sleep between fires to keep warm. A man might lie facing the main fire with a small fire of oak bark behind him. Oak bark was selected because the coals retained heat for a long time. The man's back might become purple from the heat.

Only one family occupied a house, though sometimes a newly married son or daughter might reside with the family for a time after marriage. The new relative-in-law did his share in providing for the whole family.

Earth Lodge

The large, semisubterranean assembly and dance house (hanē′pū, P; ha′ñī, N, C, S) characteristic of central California, was constructed by the Miwok. It was never used as a dwelling or even as sleeping quarters for the men, except sometimes when a ceremony was being held in the village. It was in charge of an official fire tender (wükü′ppe, P, N). The assembly house was for social and ceremonial gatherings. It was the place where gambling and dancing were conducted. Frequently when people cooked meat or acorns they took some to this house to distribute to other people.

A large pit, 40 or 50 feet in diameter, was dug to a depth of 3 or 4 feet. Over this was erected a roof in the form of a low cone, supported by heavy beams. These in turn were supported by means of four center posts (to′le, tco′ñe) and eight side posts (fig., p. 335). The edges of the cone rested on the edge of the pit. This cone was covered with thatch and earth, which made the roof air and water tight. In having four center posts the structure resembled that of the Southern Maidu, but resembled the Pomo structures in the eight additional posts and octagon of stringers.

One of its chief adjuncts was the large foot drum (tū′mma, P, N), 5 to 10 feet long, made from a section of a log. Various woods were used, though the accidentally hollowed trunk of a white oak was preferred. Further hollowing was by burning. Half of the log, forming a semicircle or less in cross section, was placed over a pit 2 or 3 feet deep, between two of the rear posts, and tangent to the rear wall of the house, but within it. The pit served as a resonance chamber, both ends of the drum being left open. The drum was stamped upon, the drummer at times steadying himself by means of an adjacent post. Drums were replaced only when rotten. The space around the drum is called adja (C) and, during ceremonies, is occupied by the singers. The floor where the spectators sat was covered with pine needles or sedge (*Carex*), kissi (C).

After the timbers for the building had been gathered it took only four or five days to erect the building, everyone in the village helping. The wood used was oak, usually obtained by burning down the trees. If only two or three men were employed in obtaining the timbers, it took them two months.

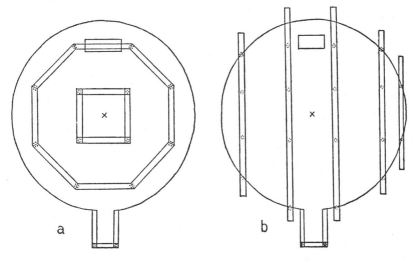

a   b

Roof Plans of Miwok Assembly Houses.

The first step in the actual construction of the house was the excavation. The size of the area to be excavated was carefully measured. The measure of the radius was called oyisa yaña, literally "four men." Four men actually stretched out on the ground, the head of one man touching the feet of the next man. If we consider the men as averaging $5\frac{1}{2}$ feet, the diameter would be 44 feet. The excavating was done with digging sticks.

Next the four center posts which supported the roof were put in place, forming the four corners of a square, each side being the reach of a man in length. Four horizontal pieces were tied with withes to the tops of these posts. From these, radial beams were laid sloping to the sides of the pit, but supported midway by an octagon of stringers resting upon the eight side posts. (See the diagram, *a*, above.) The four center posts were each about a foot in diameter, the eight side posts smaller. The stringers were about 6 inches, the radial roof beams about 5 inches, and the numerous horizontal closely laid cross sticks upon which the roofing material was laid about 3 inches, in diameter. The posts were of oak, the stringers and roof beams of buckeye or willow. The four center posts were imbedded 2 feet, the others a foot. The two rear center posts were treated with "medicine" and only dancers could approach them closely. Posts were either notched or naturally forked at the top to hold the stringers.

A thatch of brush, topped with digger or western yellow pine needles, never sugar pine needles, was next put on. This was followed by the final covering of earth. Altogether the roof was 1½ or 2 feet thick. The opening in the top of the conical roof served as the smoke hole, the fire being built directly under it. The entrance was on any side.

Certain niceties appear in placing brush and earth on the roof. The first layer of brush, which was laid radially over the numerous horizontal roof timbers, was of willow. On this another layer at right angles was placed. The third layer was of a shrub with many close parallel twigs that kept the earth covering from leaking through and resisted rot. The proper depth of the earth layer was 4 or 5 inches and was measured by thrusting in the hand. The proper depth came to the base of the thumb.

The digging of the fireplace in the center of a new assembly house took place at the celebration following its completion. A digging stick was the tool; the depth to which dug was about a foot; its diameter between 2 and 3 feet.

At Chakachino, a post-Caucasian village near Jamestown, there have been four assembly houses within the memory of the informant, Tom Williams. When one became old and rotten it was torn down, the occasion being one for merrymaking. Also, the death of a chief was followed on one occasion by the burning of the assembly house as a mourning observance, as was the usual Miwok custom. Following the construction of each new assembly house at Chakachino, Miwok from various villages came to the opening ceremonies.

The following notes refer to a semisubterranean assembly house (the figure, *b*, p. 335) at Jackson Valley, near Ione, Amador County, in Northern Miwok territory, as it appeared in 1917. It was built in 1913. In 1927 the roof had rotted and was replaced. Only the points in which it differs from the type described above are noted.

Diameter 36 feet. Depth of excavation 3½ feet to 4¾ feet, depending on slope of ground outside. Door on east side. The south side had been washed out and repaired with a stone wall, and mud mortar, a modern innovation. All of the posts are of white oak and water oak. The stringers are not radially arranged, but extend from front to back, overlapping the edge of the pit, in some cases over three feet. Where stringers overlap over a post they are beveled to make a snug joint, and spiked. The center posts are 8 feet 8 inches high, the posts at the walls 4 feet 6 inches, all others intermediate. The short roof beams across stringers are 5 to 3 inches in diameter, in five rows, and total 265 individual pieces. The center row is 9 feet wide, the two rows flanking it each 8 feet wide, and the two outside rows of varying width owing to the curvature of the side of the pit. This means that the two center lines of posts and stringers are 9 feet apart, and the two sides lines each 8 feet from these. The smoke hole is at the peak of the roof between the four center posts, as in Maidu assembly houses. The entrance passage is 6 feet 10 inches long, 5 feet 10 inches high, 5 feet 6 inches wide, and brush and earth-covered. It is closed by a modern, hinged, board door.

At Big Creek near Groveland two pits encircled by rings of earth indicate two former assembly houses. The present circular assembly house is the modern wooden substitute, without excavated floor and earth covering. It is called tapla utcu (C). The inside diameter is 31½ feet. The main radial rafters divide the roof into five sectors. These are crossed by five concentric sets of stringers resting on posts. A sloping ladder runs up the roof to a small platform, from which the chief or orator addressed the people.

No evidence was obtained among the Miwok to indicate that the smoke hole formerly was used as an entrance, or that the side entrance developed from an original draft opening. Whether this negative evidence means that this type of house reached the Miwok only after the smoke hole entrance had gone out of use, or whether the evolution of the features mentioned occurred too early to be remembered, we are unable to decide.

The distribution of semisubterranean earth-covered houses is wide, but only in California is the foot drum employed as an adjunct of the house in its ceremonial form. It seems likely that the original diffusion of the house to central California was as a dwelling. With its adaptation to the needs of the god-impersonating cult, came the introduction of the foot drum and the attribution of sanctity to certain of the posts of the house. Whether the foot drum is a central Californian invention or an importation from elsewhere is not evident. However, the possible connection of the pit and foot drum with the *sipapu* pit and board covering of the Hopi kiva suggests itself.

Sweathouse

The sweathouse (tcapu'ya. C, S) was not slept in, was not an habitual club, and was not used as a lounging place for men and boys. It was only a sudatory for men, for hunting and curative purposes, heated by fire and not by steam. It was a conical, earth-covered structure, 6 to 15 feet in diameter and of a height permitting only half erect posture. The largest would accommodate ten men. The house was built over a pit 2 or 3 feet deep. Brush, digger, or western yellow pine needles, bark (in the mountains cedar bark), and earth formed the successive layers of the roof. The smoke hole at the top was about 6 inches in diameter.

Each man who sweated had a little pile of wood to feed the fire. Whoever added most fuel, thus creating most heat, was regarded as the strongest. The fire was preferably of white oak. Often several men would sweat for two hours, then yield their places to a second group. Each man knelt and put his face on the ground, so as not to be smothered.

A deer hunter entered the sweathouse before sunrise and stayed from one to three hours. Then he jumped into a pool in the creek. He repeated the sweating and bathing once or twice, continuing until about 1:00 P.M. This was thought to purify him. Sometimes a man on leaving the sweathouse would faint before he reached the creek. Some men sweated before dancing, so as to "feel better" when dancing.

The sweathouse was used especially by men who had bad luck in deer hunting. It was supposed to make their legs strong, so that they could walk far without aching. The sick were not sucked in the sweathouse, but were simply sweated there. The sweathouse did not enter into shamanistic treatment.

When a chief announced a social or ceremonial gathering many men sweated to be successful in killing deer for the celebration. If a man was not sweated he would not get deer. Sweating was not necessary for rabbit hunting or mountain lion hunting.

It seems likely that the sweathouse was more regularly used for deer-hunt preparations than for curative purposes. However, men with rheumatism and headache, at least, made use of it. They sweated two or three hours, then bathed in a pool. The legs were also scratched with a sharp quartz crystal as a curative measure. Sometimes, in frosty weather, a family with a poor house would occupy the sweathouse.

Brush Assembly House

The circular brush assembly house, usually roofed with brush and pine needles, but without earth covering, was used in summer for mourning ceremonies. In the winter these were held in the semisubterranean assembly house. The name of the brush assembly house varied locally; at Jamestown it was lutcumte (C), north of the Stanislaus River it was tewate (C). At West Point it was kütca (N), and among the Southern Miwok it was sala. It was not ordinarily used for dances like kuksuyu, although this dance was once held in one at Knights Ferry. In July, 1927, a roofless example 30 feet in diameter, was seen at Chakachino, near Jamestown, Tuolumne County. It had been constructed some months before to hold the mourning ceremonies for a deceased resident of that place.

The brush assembly house was much smaller than the semisubterranean assembly house, and measured only two and one-half men (otega yaña homotani) in radius. The short men were used as measures at that. They lay down on the ground as for measuring the larger ceremonial structure. The "half" was measured by a third man lying on his back doubled up. The openwork nature of this structure allowed the breezes to blow through it.

Many of the ancient brush houses were rectangular, flat topped, and erected on the surface of the ground without excavation. These were designated as kutcala (C). There were large doorways on two opposite sides, with smaller doorways on the other two sides. The roof and sides were formed of green boughs. There was one center post, four corner posts, and one post in the middle of each side. This type of building, coupled with its use for mourning ceremonies, suggests a southern Californian derivation. It was erected by four or five men at the behest of the chief, who fed the builders. The chief's wife cooked for them. Ownership appears to have been vested in the chief and these men.

Grinding House

A small conical grinding or milling house of bark slabs or brush might be built over a bedrock mortar or an imbedded portable mortar as protection from sun and bad weather. . . . [There was a structure of this sort] at Railroad Flat, Calaveras County. It was made almost entirely of modern boards, with a few cedar bark slabs added. It was 6 feet in diameter by 7 feet in height. Its framework was six poles, each about 4 inches in diameter at the base. A simple grinding shelter was sometimes made of stones and brush. This served as a partial sun shade and windbreak. The grinding house seems to be merely a sun shelter applied to one specific purpose.

Acorn Granary

Acorns were stored whole in specially constructed caches. . . . A small one (he'sma, N), built in a low branching bush, was more or less of a makeshift. It was an inverted cone about 3½ feet high, and had a capacity of perhaps a bushel. Powers figures Miwok acorn granaries of the large type.

The large type of cache was constructed with care. Several vertical posts were set firmly into the ground. About these, heavy grapevine or other withes were bound to form hoops. Inside were bound small vertical poles forming the ribs of the cache. Within these was placed a horizontal layer of twigs and brush, inside of which was laid a lining of weeds and grass.

So tightly were these caches built, that they were used for the storage of grass seeds. There was no true weaving, but the inside of such a cache resembled a bird's nest in construction.

The smaller of two granaries seen at Railroad Flat, California, stood originally about 6 feet high. It had four grapevine hoops and a thick roof of weeds and twigs. A larger cache next to it was nearly 12 feet high, had six vertical posts and five grapevine hoops. The conical bottom rested on a block of wood about a foot high by 15 inches in diameter. Two grapevine hoops passed around an adjacent pine tree, which served as a support for both these caches. The larger cache was 5 feet in diameter and its conical bottom was about 3½ feet deep. Sometimes the bottom of such a cache was suspended two or three feet off the ground. The top of the cache was covered with layers of grass and brush so placed as to shed the rain. Over this was usually placed a final roof of cedar-bark or pine-bark slabs. Thus was produced a water-tight storehouse where a whole winter's supply of acorns or seeds could be kept. Nearly every family had at least one of these caches, and a man of importance who must provide for feasts required several.

No special opening was provided for removing the acorns or seeds. The construction made it possible to make a rent in the side from which the acorns would run into a basket held below. When a sufficient quantity had been secured, the weeds and grass of the side were readjusted to make it tight again.

According to Powers acorn granaries were sometimes miles from the villages where their owners dwelt.

FIRE-MAKING OF THE WINTU INDIANS

by
George H. H.
Redding

While angling for salmon and trout during a vacation, last summer, on the McCloud River, in Shasta County, I had an opportunity of seeing a Wintoon Indian make a fire by the friction of two pieces of wood. The process adopted by him differs in some particulars from that used by the savages of other countries. It will be of interest to the archaeologist who desires to preserve the evidence of all the habits and customs of man in his original savage condition, and may be of service in showing some ship-wrecked mariner how easily fire may be made where he can obtain two pieces of dry wood.

Word came to the United States Fishery that there was to be an Indian dance that evening at the upper rancheria, which is a beautiful spot on the right bank of the McCloud, about five miles above the fishery. Just before sunset, with two companions, I crossed the river in a dugout, where we found the trail. The weather was perfect. The sun had descended below the hills that guard the western bank of the river. The narrow valley and its cold, hurrying stream, fringed with alders and azaleas, were sinking into shade and seemed hushed to sudden silence, broken only in the still reaches and quiet pools by the occasional heavy splash of a salmon at play, or the sudden leap of the hungry trout intently busy in making entomological collections from among the ephemera, caddice, and other flies that spring into multitudinous and joyous existence under the magic wands of the long shadows creeping over the water. Our trail led along the east bank among the talus from Mount Persephone, whose gray limestone summits tower three thousand feet above the river. Our path was in the shadow of the opposite hills; but, a few hundred feet above us, the setting sun was bathing the somber rocks on our right in purple mist, while the loftier peaks stood out against the deep blue sky, like minarets burnished with refulgent gold.

After passing the cliffs, the trail led through groves of mingled oaks and pines self-planted on the benches above the river. How few Californians

George H. H. Redding, "An Evening with Wintoon Indians," *The Californian* (No. 12, Dec., 1880), 2:563–566.

know that the particular region of the foothills of the Sierra in which both oaks and pines intermingle, is blessed with a more delightful and health-giving climate than any other part of the State. The shadows now more rapidly darted up the mountain sides, and we were soon in the gloom of the forest, and found it difficult to keep our way. This trail is the only one near this bank used by the Indians in going up and down the river. Without doubt it has been used for thousands of years; yet in all this time it has never occurred to one of them to remove from it a fallen tree, or roll away a bowlder. I wondered, as we stumbled on in the dark, whether man, when first emerging from his original, savage state, commenced by the domestication of animals, cultivating the soil, or by clearing a path from his cave to the forest where he killed his game. The Wintoons have not yet arrived at any of these stages of civilization. They have no domestic animals other than the horse and dog, obtained originally from the Spaniards. The nearest approach to cultivation is not connected with a supply of food, but with intoxication. All of their camps are "kitchen middens," in a state of slow but constant accretion, and the soil about them becomes very rich.

Wild tobacco (*Nicotiana bigelovii*) grows sparsely in favored spots on the hills near the river. When, by accident, the seeds are carried to the rich and prolific soil of these kitchen middens, it grows with added vigor to increased size, and is much prized by the Indians for smoking. To the civilized smoker of tobacco it has an intensely vile flavor, and is exceedingly nauseating and stupefying. When the plant makes its appearance above the ground in the spring they frequently loosen the earth about it with a sharpened stick, and pile brush about each plant to prevent it being trodden upon or injured. It has not occurred to them that the seeds could be saved and planted. While cultivating no food plants, they guard with jealous care particular oaks of the species *Quercus chrysolepis, kellogii,* and *brewerii,* and all the prolific nut-pines (*Pinus sabiniana*), as these supply them a large amount of food. They are learning that the hog of the white man is their great enemy—that he eats the acorns as they drop from the trees, that he destroys the grass in the small valleys, the seeds of which they gather, and that he roots up and eats the camas (*Camassia esculenta*) and other bulbs that yield them food when the salmon have returned to the ocean.

Filled, as these people are, with the densest ignorance and the most weird and mythical superstitions, they yet have, in all that relates to their supply of food, a knowledge of the natural history of their immediate vicinity that seems wonderful. No fish or crustacean of the river, no reptile, no animal or bird, no tree or plant but has a name; and every child is taught these names, and given the knowledge of what can be used as food and what would be injurious.

In about an hour we arrived at the Government trout ponds, but found all the attendants had left for the dance, except an Indian with his canoe to ferry us again across the river. The village was about a mile above the crossing. On arriving we found a great many families had gathered, coming for many miles up and down the river. There were, probably, three hundred and fifty, of all ages. We learned that the dance and gathering was an annual meeting, partly religious, and that it is given as an expression of gratitude for the return of the salmon to the river.

The rancheria, or village, is on the right bank of the river, at a beautiful bend, where the water sweeps around the base of a mountain. From what could be seen at night, the spot had been occupied by the Indians for ages.

In the center of the rancheria was the temescal, or sweathouse. It was constructed by digging a large circular, basin-shaped hole in the ground, four or five feet deep. Around the edge of this hole large posts are sunk, about five feet apart, which extend upward to the top of the ground. In the center are planted four large trunks of trees, with the original limbs upon them, extending a few feet above the surface. From these four trees stout limbs of trees are laid, reaching to the posts at the edge. These limbs are fastened firmly by withes to the branches at the center trees. The whole is then thatched with pine and willow brush, and covered with a layer of earth about a foot in thickness. The entrance is a long, low passage, and is made by driving short, thin pine posts side by side, about three feet apart, and covered in the same manner as the house proper. To enter, one has to stoop quite low, and continue in this position until he comes into the sweathouse. We entered. All about us, crowded together, were the Indians, squatted on the earth, the males in the foreground, and the mahalas, or squaws, with their papooses, in the rear. In the center a low, small fire was burning, quite near to which sat the caller of the dances, smoking a pipe which looked like three large wooden thimbles placed inside of each other. This he held perpendicularly in the air, with his head thrown back so as to allow his lips to inclose the mouthpiece. After puffing three or four times, he passed it to others of the crowd. Some of the Indians had similar pipes, but, so far as I could see, this one was the largest and finest.

Directly opposite to the entrance, there had been a kind of fence erected, behind which the dancers were getting ready. We did not have long to wait, for soon the caller commenced yelling, and all the eyes of the audience were turned toward the dressing room. Out came the Indians—seven men and about fifteen mahalas. The men were naked, except for a girdle of eagle feathers about their loins and a narrow band of woodpecker feathers about the forehead. The latter is very handsome, and brings a good sum when sold. In their hands they carried long, thin reeds, covered with small, fine feathers, which they blew as they ran around the fire, stamping the ground. The women wore calico dresses of bright colors, and in their hands carried grasses, which they held up. As the men ran, the women formed a half-circle about them, turning from side to side, all singing in a monotonous, low tone. They were accompanied by the musicians, who consisted of three men—one blowing a reed, one pounding on an old tin pan, and the other striking a split stick against a piece of wood. The time was perfect, and it was astonishing with what rapidity the men dancers got over the ground. They put their whole strength into the dance, and keep it up for an hour at a time, only stopping at intervals to get breath and hear comments on their performance. When the dance is finished, the men cast off the feathers and run naked, reeking with perspiration, and plunge into the river, the water of which is rarely warmer than 45° Fahrenheit.

It is usually those who are sick who take part in the dance of this kind, and this treatment is supposed to cure; but, as a remedy or luxury, it seems to have been in universal use among all the California Indians.

While the monotonous dance was in progress, we left the sweathouse, and, meeting Sarah, the daughter of the old Chief Consolulu, I asked her to tell her father that I wanted him to have an Indian make a fire as it was made before white men came to the country. Sarah is one of the few members of the Wintoon tribe who have any knowledge of the English language. When a child, she was taken to live with a family at Shasta. In a few years she became homesick, and longed for the companionship of her own people, for their wild, free life, and for the mountains where she was born. So Sarah turned her back to civilization and its constraints, and joined her people, that she might live as they live, and share their joys and privations. She retains, apparently, but little evidence of the attempt at civilization except her Christian name and some knowledge of the English language.

After long negotiations, and the exercise of considerable diplomacy, an Indian came to me, bringing his beaver-skin quiver, filled with arrows. From among these he took a dried branch of buckeye (*Aesculus californica*) about as long as the shaft of an arrow, but much larger at one end. From his quiver he also produced a piece of cedar (*Librocedrus decurrens*). This was about eighteen inches in length, an inch thick, and two inches wide in the center, but tapering to a rough point at each end. Its general appearance might be described as boatshaped. In the center of this piece of cedar, on one side, he had made a circular hole a quarter of an inch deep, with a piece of obsidian, and from this hole he had cut a channel extending to the edge of the wood. He now gathered a handful of dry grass, and some fine, dry, powdered wood from a decayed pine. Each end of the boatshaped piece of cedar, with the side containing the hole and channel upper-most, was placed on a couple of flat stones and held firmly by another Indian. The dry grass was piled loosely under the center, and on it was scattered the fine powder of the decayed wood. The fine powder was also scattered in the channel leading to the hole in the center of the boat-shaped piece of cedar. He now took the branch of buckeye and placed the largest end in the circular hole, and, spitting on his hands, commenced revolving it back and forth rapidly between his palms, and at the same time bearing down with considerable force. This constant exercise of pressure, while revolving the buckeye, caused his hands to be rapidly shifted to the lower end of the stick, when he would remove them to the top again and renew the process. At the end of five minutes he was perspiring from the exercise, and no fire had been produced. He stopped a few seconds and said some-thing. I asked Sarah to translate his speech. Sarah told me he was saying, "Fire, why don't you come to me now as you did when I was a boy?"

This he repeated several times, and commenced work again. In another five minutes smoke made its appearance where the two woods were in con-tact. In a few seconds the powdered dust of the decayed wood took fire, and the fine coals communicated this fire to the dust in the channel, and rolled down to the dust scattered on the dry grass. He now took the bundle of grass in his hands, and, carefully blowing upon it, soon created a blaze. Meanwhile, a great many of the Indians came out where we were, and crowded about us, and seemed to take great interest in the proceedings. All manner of questions were asked of us, and translated by Sarah; among which were:

"Where you come from? Don't white man have any more matches?" or, "You like this way better than white man's way?"

The buckeye is very much harder than the cedar; and I find it is the invariable custom among savage people, in making fire by friction, to use woods of different texture and hardness.

As soon as the fire blazed the crowd went back into the sweathouse, and we with them, but only to remain a short time, as it was already midnight, and we had a long distance to travel. Soon we were on our way to the fish-ery. As we were crossing the river, the moon came over the mountains and shone down upon us. We made a weird looking picture in the canoes, with an Indian at each end, paddle in hand. As the first gray streaks of dawn appeared in the northeastern sky, we arrived at the fishery.

MINES AND QUARRIES
OF THE INDIANS OF
CALIFORNIA

by
R. F. Heizer and
A. E. Treganza

Prehistoric exploitation of mineral resources by the Indians of North America made no appreciable impression on the earth's supply. Few of the products (for the most part nonmetallics) quarried by the Indians are of much present-day economic importance. With one or two minor exceptions, none of the North American aborigines smelted ores to extract metals; indeed, the majority of tribes showed a surprising disregard and disinterest in metals which were obtainable in the native state. Instead, the Indian tribes north of Mexico lived in a technological Stone Age, their material possessions being made chiefly of stone, wood, bone, pottery, and skin. This is especially true for the 103 tribes (speaking 21 mutually unintelligible languages) who lived in the territory now within the boundaries of the State of California. The history of California might have been very different if the Indians had employed native gold and had tapped the rich placer deposits of the Sierra Nevada. The gold rush would have occurred several hundred years earlier, and under the flag of Spain. In sixteenth-century Mexico the rapid development of mining following the Spanish conquest was due largely to exploitation, by European methods and inducements, of mineral localities already known to the native population. . . .

THE INDIAN AS A MINERALOGIST AND CHEMIST

A large body of traditional physical and chemical knowledge belonged to the aboriginal inhabitants of California. It was rude, simple, and practical, and of the order which characterized the beginnings of our own tradition of science in the Old World in the Neolithic period 10,000 years ago. Familiarity with the physical properties (texture, hardness, cleavage, and color) of stones was a necessity to the Indians, and was gained through constant use. A tough dense rock was better suited for a pestle, drill, axe,

Pp. 292–303 of R. F. Heizer and A. E. Treganza, "Mines and Quarries of the Indians of California," *California Journal of Mines and Geology* (July, 1944) (Calif. Div. Mines), 40:291–359.

or hammer, than brittle, glassy obsidian, which, under skillful pressure, could be flaked into thin, sharp blades used as knives or arrowheads.

The collections of thousands of stone tools made and used by the primitive peoples of California demonstrate clearly that they always selected available stone materials which would make the most efficient and enduring implements. For example, steatite (soapstone) was the almost universal material from which smoking pipes were fashioned in California. Steatite, unlike most other rocks, has a low index of thermal expansion and therefore will not break when heated. In addition, it is soft, and the problem of drilling a hole through the long axis of the pipe was a comparatively easy one. To show that the discovery of steatite as a heat-tolerant material was exploited beyond its first application, we may note in the accompanying figure, thin-walled globular bowls of steatite from Santa Barbara in which food was boiled, and flat steatite plates used as drip pans for grease in the Klamath River country, and for frying pans in the Santa Barbara Channel area. The use of segmented cane (*Phragmites* sp.) for arrowshafts in southern California led to the employment of grooved steatite arrowshaft straighteners (d, fig., p. 349). The joints are crooked and must be straightened in order to produce an arrow of true flight. The stone is heated and the erratic cane joint set in the groove. The heat of the stone relaxes the bent joint, which is straightened by pressing down the ends of the cane. This technique depends basically upon the employment of a stone which can be heated. The Karok Indians of the Klamath River call soapstone (asaxusas), "soft rock," a term which reveals the tendency on the part of the natives to label rocks descriptively.

The Santa Catalina steatite was not all of the same quality. The softer, more micaceous variety was used for globular pots, while the harder, closer-grained (i.e., more dense) and darker variety was used for weights for digging sticks, pipes, and ornaments. No doubt the Gabrieleño Indians knew these two varieties by different names.

The Chukchansi subtribe of the Yokuts of the lower San Joaquin River "cooked" a newly made steatite pot overnight in a fire. This cooking process had the effect of hardening or tempering the pot so that its durability was increased.

The Pomo Indians of Clear Lake divide the local obsidian into two types: batixaga, "arrow obsidian," which comes from Lower Lake; and dupa xaga, "to cut obsidian," which comes from Cole Creek. The first type is used for arrow points; the second, which breaks cleanly with sharp edges, finds use as knives or razors. The specialized uses of each of these obsidians are thus recognized by the Indian equivalent of mineralogical terms.

Certain tribes of northern California warmed obsidian before flaking it. It is possible that the size, shape, or even ease of flaking, was affected by such warming. One hears stories of Indian arrow-point chippers who heated their raw material to a high temperature and flaked it by dropping water on it. There is no evidence at all to support these statements which may have a basis in the misinterpretation of the fairly widespread technique of gently warming the flint or obsidian prior to pressure or percussion chipping.

Further recognition of mineralogical alteration of rocks is found among the Wintu tribe of the northern Sacramento Valley, who say that they do not quarry obsidian which has been exposed to the sun; the exposed surface is weathered and altered so that it does not flake properly. The alteration, however, is probably caused by other factors in addition to exposure to the sun. Similarly, the Karok Indians recognize that the greenish serpentine from one deposit "is not much good for making pipe bowls since it will soon crack when it gets hot."

It was the practice among southern California Indian potters to add crushed grit temper (granite was commonly used) to the clay so that the pot would not crack when fired. The discovery of at least one clay deposit in the State that produces a clay to which no tempering material need be added, may be credited to the Indians.

The Indian, no doubt, was faced often with the problem (which we may liken to our own scientific curiosity) of explaining geological and mineralogical phenomena. Thus, the Clear Lake Pomo account for the exfoliated flakes of obsidian scattered on Mount Konocti by a myth in which "Obsidian Man" caught in the brush, fell in his struggles to free himself, and broke into thousands of pieces which are now represented by the scattered fragments of volcanic glass on the mountain slopes.

The religious attitude of the Indian must also be taken into account in assessing his knowledge of mineralogy. For example, although obsidian was very widely used in California, it was sometimes considered extremely poisonous. The origin of this belief is not known, but perhaps the effectiveness of obsidian as a material to tip war and hunting arrows accounts for its reputed lethal qualities. Among the Western Achomawi of Modoc County, the chips struck off a block of obsidian were carefully inspected by the arrowpoint maker, who judged whether or not they were poisonous. One chip he might consider poisonous and the next flake not poisonous. As he splits the flakes off he examines them and says "This for grizzly bear, this for coyote, this for war," and these pieces he keeps.

The peculiar optical qualities of quartz crystal were appreciated by the California Indians, and nearly every tribe believed the crystals had magical significance. The Yana Indians of Deer Creek used them as luck charms; elsewhere they were used in curing ceremonies.

The chemical processes employed by the California Indians appear to

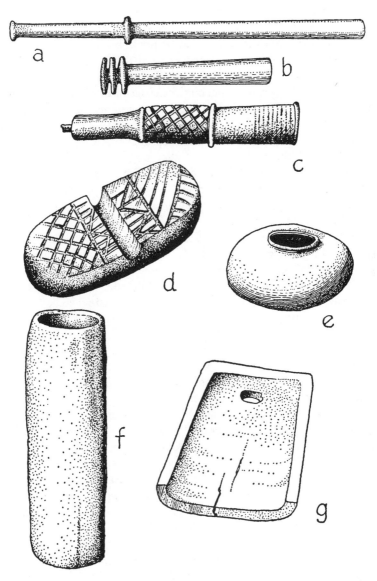

Prehistoric Steatite Artifacts. *a*, pipe, Modoc County; *b*, pipe, Sacramento Valley; *c*, pipe, Santa Barbara; *d*, arrowshaft straightener, San Bernardino County; *e*, small-mouthed, thin-walled olla, Santa Barbara; *f*, cylindrical jar, San Joaquin County; *g*, "comal," or frying pan, Santa Barbara.

have been largely limited to simple application of three techniques: evaporation by boiling, baking, or exposure to open air; leaching with water percolation; and oxidation through action of fire. The Kamia of the Imperial Valley leached the salt-impregnated earth of the Salton Sink and crystallized the salt out by boiling. The Stonyford salt seepage yields salt crystals which are left, after evaporation, on the surface of the ground. The Indians scraped up these crystals during the warm summer, stored them in the crude state, and later refined them by dissolving them in water, then recrystallizing by evaporation the decanted salt solution.

The Paiute Indians of Surprise Valley dug a soft brownish-tan chalk rock from a deposit on Bidwell Mountain. This was crushed, soaked in water, and drained, the soluble brown coloration being leached out in the soaking process. It then appeared white, and was used for face paint.

The Cocopa at their manganese quarry which they called Kwinyilwawa, or "black place," burned chunks of manganese, which could then be easily broken and pulverized into powder for black face paint. At their hematite quarry called Akwurawawa, "red place," a hole was dug in the quarry and a fire built in the hole. The fire altered the dull reddish hematite to a bright red product, which was dug out and put in a pot, where the salt was leached out and the mineral softened so it could be easily pulverized. A similar technique was employed by the Surprise Valley Paiute, who put dull red hematite in a hole in a rock and kindled a fire on top. After the coals were raked off and the ocher had cooled, it turned a brick red.

In the area north of San Francisco Bay and west of the Sierra Nevada, it was a common culinary practice to mix ferruginous clay with acorn meal to bake native bread. Acorns contain a high percentage of tannic acid which is generally leached out by water percolation before the acorn meal is boiled as mush and eaten. Chesnut cites one analysis of unleached acorn meal which contained 6.63 per cent tannic acid. The purpose of the clay mixture was to convert the tannic acid remaining in the meal into an insoluble compound formed at the baking temperature, under influence of air and moisture, by the action of the tannin of the acorn meal with the iron oxide contained in the clay. The Pomo Indians of Potter Valley call this red clay masil and translate the term as "Indian baking powder." A clay sample analyzed by V. K. Chesnut contained 10 per cent FeO_2 by weight.

Mineral springs were used by the California Indians as we use them today. The Eastern Pomo of Upper Clear Lake knew that Highland Springs, now a health resort, near the headwaters of Adobe Creek possessed medicinal qualities. Tribal members afflicted with certain ailments camped at places near the springs, and drank and bathed in the waters. Skaggs Springs, called Kahowani, "water hot," Calistoga Hot Springs, and Pluton Geysers in Sonoma County were used in the same way.

The following hot mineral springs were used by the Indians: Jacumba Hot Springs, San Diego County; Warner's Hot Springs, San Diego County; Slates Hot Springs, Monterey County; Tassajara Hot Springs, Monterey County; Casa Diablo Hot Springs, Mono County. Two carbonated springs were known: Witter Medical Springs, Lake County, and Mount Ida Spring, Butte County. Sulphur Springs in the Santa Susanna Mountains, Los Angeles County, were known to Indians, and four artesian springs in Riverside County (Toro, Alamo Bonito, Agua Dulce, and Figtree John Springs) were sites of Cahuilla Indian settlements.

The curious Indian custom of burying the dead in hot springs was practiced by the Paiute of northeastern California. In the collections of the University of California are human bones from a hot spring near Cedarville, Modoc County. These bones are heavily impregnated with lime and cinnabar, this last mineral apparently being in solution in the water. . . .

THE INDIAN AS A GEOLOGIST

The California Indian's explanation of such outstanding natural phenomena as earthquakes and of physiographic features like the Sierra Nevada, Yosemite Valley, Salton Sea, and San Francisco Bay, was traditional or mythical. He attributed present-day physiographic features to the actions and feats of mythical animals possessing unlimited powers and endowed with human thought and speech. The interesting point is, however, that the Indians, like ourselves, had an innate desire to explain how the world came to be as it is. Their explanation is to them as completely rational as ours is to us.

The Cahuilla Indians of southern California tell this story of the origin of ancient Lake Cahuilla:

Then the water from the south began to rise and all the people moved ahead of the water toward Palm Springs. They settled near Kavinic, where the water did not reach. Then the water began to go back, gradually at first and sometimes rising again.

This myth agrees fairly well with the accepted geologic history of ancient Lake Cahuilla, and may conceivably reflect some Indian memory in tradition of the terminal pluvial fluctuations of the water body; or, more probably, it may be simply a theoretic explanation for the clearly marked ancient beach lines in this desert area.

The Yokuts tribe of Kings River tell the following myth of the origin of the Sierra Nevada and Coast Ranges. Hawk and Crow gathered earth and began to build mountains, starting at Tehachapi Pass, Hawk making the

Sierras and Crow the Coast Ranges. After many years they met at Mt. Shasta, and, when they compared their labors, found Crow's mountains were the largest. Hawk claimed Crow had been stealing dirt from his beak, which was true; so Hawk chewed some tobacco and became very wise, and seized the mountains and turned them around. In this way the fact that the Sierra Nevada is larger than the Coast Ranges is explained.

California Indians all knew what earthquakes feel like, and had explanations for the terrifying manifestations, which they believed to be caused by giants dwelling within the earth. The Southern Diegueño believe a blind man causes quakes; that if he were to roll over quickly, the earth would turn over. But he rolls just a little, and so causes only tremors. The giant who moves in the earth is the common Indian explanation for earthquakes, as shown by the accounts of the 1906 earthquake collected by S. A. Barrett and A. L. Kroeber.

Other legends explaining natural phenomena are the Wintu Indian myth concerning the origins of Glass Mountain in Modoc County, and obsidian; the myth accounting for the origin of San Francisco Bay; and the Miwok legends concerning the origin of Yosemite Valley.

THE INDIAN AS A PROSPECTOR

The fact that at least 131 mine or quarry localities were known to the California Indians is sufficient proof of the efficiency of their prospecting.

The primitive California Indians were continually foraging over the countryside in search of food, firewood, and raw materials with which to form their tools and implements. Each tribe, as a rule, occupied a restricted territory whose boundaries were rarely trespassed by neighbors. To do so without permission was a certain cause for war. These limitations of exploitable area had a number of interesting effects; primarily this restriction led to the development of a system of conservation of natural resources.

Each local Indian group knew every rock outcrop within its territory, and if any stone was of a variety which lent itself to making implements, they used it. Actual prospecting, where the Indian would set out blindly on a search to locate a specific stone material, probably was unknown. Their prospecting was limited to accidental discovery of surface exposures while hunting, gathering food, or moving across country to another village. Mines and quarries seem universally to have belonged to the group and not to an individual, even though the individual discovered the site by himself. This is completely contrary to our own system of ownership, which stimulates, by expectation of economic gain, the discovery and development of ore deposits.

SOCIAL AND ECONOMIC ASPECTS OF ABORIGINAL MINES AND QUARRIES

Trade

The most important function of Indian mines and quarries was to supply materials for the implements and tools to be used to secure subsistence (stone points for war or hunting weapons, mortars or metates for grinding seeds, sling stones, chipped knives for meat cutting), or maintain life's necessities (housebuilding, skin dressing, clothing) or as luxuries (decorative or ceremonial objects).

It was only when the local group's needs were satisfied and a surplus of raw material was available that intertribal commodity exchange was possible. Although a certain stone may be used for implements or ornaments by an Indian tribe, or may turn up in an archaeological site, it need not necessarily be of local occurrence. Usually native manufactures are of local materials, but intertribal barter of goods and even long-range trading are not out of the ordinary. Stefansson noted that the Arctic Eskimo made boat trips of 400 miles to get flint from the quarries at Fort Good Hope. Catlinite (a red-clay stone) from Minnesota reached New York and Georgia through native trade channels, and the mound builders of the lower Mississippi drainage used quantities of obsidian which came from Yellowstone National Park, some 1,500 miles distant. Turquoise from New Mexico (and perhaps even from southern California localities) reached the Valley of Mexico, where it was used by the Aztecs. The Walla Walla Indians of the Columbia River came south to obtain the brilliant cinnabar from the New Almaden outcrop near San Jose. These are admittedly exceptional examples of far trade, and it was the rule for Indians to use materials which occurred within their own boundaries or within those of adjoining friendly tribes. Simple needs which were easily satisfied, cross-country transport limited to back packing, a simply developed economic system, and intertribal linguistic difficulties had the cumulative effect of discouraging the development of a true system of international trade. Barter of one type of goods for another between units of one tribe or between friendly neighboring tribes was common, and it was the exception in native California for a stone material to be traded farther than 100 or 150 miles from its source. The Masut group of the Pomo tribe living around Calpella made the 50-mile trip to Clear Lake to secure raw magnesite and obsidian from the quarries owned by the other Pomo groups. They had to ask permission to quarry the stone, but did not pay for the privilege. Groups that could not come in person to quarry the stone might secure obsidian, soapstone, chert, hematite, or other desired substances in exchange for food, tanned skins, or manufactured items like bows, arrows, baskets, or shell ornaments. Finished articles and implements such as magnesite cylinders, obsidian arrowheads, soapstone arrowshaft straighteners and cooking pots, and ground hematite paint, were often traded to neighboring tribes in exchange for unfinished raw materials or manufactured articles. In 1939 the University of California archaeological excavations at one site on Drakes Bay, Marin County, produced 20 vesicular basalt mortars of the type shown in the accompanying figure, *a*, which range in weight from 20 to 125 pounds. Each of these pieces must have been carried to the spot from not less than 25 miles away, no mean task for the slightly built, barefoot natives. Stone is completely lacking in the alluvial deposits of the valley floodplain of the Sacramento and San Joaquin delta region. Each stone found in the

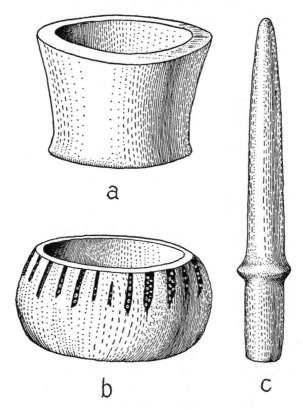

a

b   c

Prehistoric Stone Grinding Implements. *a*, basalt mortar from Drakes Bay shellmound; *b*, sandstone bowl decorated with shell beads inlaid with asphaltum, Santa Barbara; *c*, stone pestle, Klamath River.

habitation mounds has been imported from outside. Similarly, in the Gran Chaco of South America, stone was lacking and had to be imported by the natives. E. Nordenskiöld, the Swedish anthropologist, tells how the Chaco natives who accompanied him on a long trip outside the area began filling their pockets with the first stones they saw, deeming them valuable and unique because they were so rare in their home surroundings. The situation was hardly so special in the central California delta, since the Indians could visit the near-by Sierra Nevada or Coast Ranges, but even to these natives stone doubtless had a higher value than to Indians living in a region where rocks were abundant. At least two successful attempts to find substitutes for stone implements were made in the delta region: small balls of baked clay half the size of a fist, which were used for stone-boiling; and seed-grinding mortars made of wood instead of stone. Thus substitutes for stone eliminated the inconvenience and practical difficulty of securing distant, heavy stone mortars and stone cobbles for cooking.

Ownership

So far as we know there was no private, individual ownership of mine or quarry sites by the Indians. Rather these places were considered property of the group, in which everyone was allowed to share. The Indian's life, however, was not one of communal ownership, since such property as acorn-bearing trees, fishing spots, fish-spearing dams, grass-seed plots, and deer trails were often owned privately. The position of tribal chief normally did not carry with it special economic prerogatives, though a man might become chief because of his accumulated wealth. Mine and quarry sites in native California were national resources which were available to any or all tribal members who shared in possession of such sites. Advantage to the individual under such an organization would come through his special ability to produce finished or manufactured articles from a particular stone material.

Evidence of the rude beginnings of a special class, social as well as economic, is found in the artisans of the Pomo, who manufactured obsidian arrowpoints, wooden bows, shell wampum, and chert drills. Among the more highly advanced Chumash and Gabrieleño of the Santa Barbara–Los Angeles–Channel Islands region there was a similar development, for makers of plank canoes and soapstone bowls had become highly skilled artisans, whose livelihood was largely derived from their work.

Thus, economic advantage did not result from owning a quarry site itself, but rather from the manufacture of finished articles from the quarry product, since any individual in the tribe was free to make use of the raw material which he collected at the quarry. Rarely, if ever, did a tribe establish a rigid monopoly on a certain material, even though this could have been done by refusing access to the source. The Pomo who controlled the excellent Lake County obsidian quarries allowed any Pomo-speaking group and even alien tribes (the Long Valley Wintun and the Coyote Valley Miwok) to visit the quarries and secure implement material. The case is less clear for the Cache Creek magnesite deposit, over which the local Pomo apparently exercised rather strict monopolistic control.

When a neighboring group did not recognize the ownership of a salt or obsidian quarry and was apprehended in the attempt to steal, warfare was the result. The famed Pomo Salt Wars were caused by the unsuccessful attempt of the Potter Valley Pomo to take salt from the Stonyford people without asking permission or giving gifts for the privilege. Efforts of the San Joaquin Yokuts to take cinnabar from the New Almaden mine resulted in battles between the Costanoan owners and the valley tribe. Conflicting claims of ownership of quarries which lay near the boundary division of two tribes were also the cause of contention. The Kato and Yuki both claimed the Black Rock obsidian deposit, and the disagreement caused open warfare between the two tribes. The Modoc and Achomawi both claimed the Sugar Hill obsidian quarry, and war resulted when the two tribes came into contact.

Mining Laws

The Indians probably had no particular "mining code" as such, although one principle of Indian philosophy which ran through everything was applied to the use of mines and quarries; this principle is the conservation of natural resources. Thus the Maidu flint miner at Table Mountain was prohibited from taking away more flint than he could detach with one blow of his stone hammer.

In the eastern United States, certain quarry sites (for example the catlinite quarry of Minnesota and Wisconsin, the Yellowstone obsidian cliff locality, and the Flint Ridge quarries of Ohio) were recognized by all natives as neutral ground where tribes which were bitter enemies could meet but not fight. The concept and practice of neutral ground also obtained in California at the Stonyford salt seepage and the obsidian quarries of Clear Lake where any hostile group could meet another but trouble was forbidden. The theory of neutral ground, found widely throughout the world, is a very interesting one. It works in practice through common consent, for mutual benefit, since it is doubtful that any actual enforcement means guarantee its observance.

Mining Methods and Tools

Intensive mining operations, in which systematic, large-scale, and continuous exploitation of a localized mineral body or rock deposit was the sole aim, did not occur in Indian California in pre-Spanish times. The only possible exception is the turquoise mining area of San Bernardino County where very extensive workings are known. As there is no clear evidence of permanent occupation by the Pueblo peoples who came from the south to mine this turquoise, it is assumed that they worked seasonally and perhaps at intervals of several years. Many native mines and quarry sites in California seem to have been worked over a long period of time by different groups or individuals who needed the specific material at the moment. Examples of these sites are the soapstone quarries on Santa Catalina Island, the cinnabar paint mine of New Almaden, the Glass Mountain obsidian quarries in Modoc County, and the Stonyford salt seepage. There is no evidence that any tribe had evolved a special class of miners whose sole job was the production of raw material. The absence of such occupational groups can not be explained on the grounds that the California Indians were culturally incapable of such development. A relatively small Indian population (total for the State in 1770 estimated at 133,000, with a density of about 1 person per square mile) could not have overtaxed the abundant stone resources of the State. There is some evidence that in a few tribes there were specialists who devoted most of their time to the production of finished stone articles, but these were individual artists and not an economic group. The Pomo recognized flint drill makers, shell wampum drillers, and obsidian chippers, as artisans who were known as dawi xaga duyi gauk, "drill flint make person"; ghal dawi xale gauk, "wampum drill person"; and ce emai tsu donta, "bow arrow maker." Among the Santa Catalina Gabrieleño it seems probable that certain individuals devoted much of their time to making finished soapstone pots. There were no large-scale systematically organized, continuous mining or quarrying operations by the California Indians. The total amount of mining activity was large, but divided among a multitude of independent, small-scale mining and quarrying ventures.

Perhaps the most extensive aboriginal quarry workings in California are the turquoise mines of San Bernardino County. Since these mines were worked by Puebloan peoples from Arizona and New Mexico, who are known to have been excellent and industrious miners in their homeland, the San Bernardino County workings constitute a special case of aboriginal California mining. Exposed turquoise veins were followed to depth (12 ft. in some cases) in open pits by breaking and crushing the waste mass with hafted stone axes and hammers and throwing the muck out with a hand scoop made from a tortoise carapace or an animal shoulder blade shovel.

Heavy pointed stone picks weighing up to eight pounds were employed to break out the rock, and there is some indirect evidence that wedges were also used. No signs of the fire-and-water method of breaking rock was found here, but there is evidence of its use in the Arizona–New Mexico region from whence the miners journeyed. When the turquoise vein thinned out the pit was abandoned. If the pit got too deep and the amount of labor required to carry out the waste rock became inordinate, it was left for another more easily worked.

Steatite was quarried in considerable quantity at Pots Valley on Santa Catalina Island. This material served predominantly for globular vessels, and the Indians ingeniously worked out the exterior form while the base of the vessel was still attached to the bedrock. The mass was broken off at the base and was then ready for excavation of the interior and smoothing of the sides. This same technique was used at steatite quarries near Providence, Rhode Island, in Virginia, the District of Columbia, and on the Klamath River in northwestern California. Ball notes that this technique was also known to the Scandinavians of Norway and Sweden in Viking times, and to their northern neighbors, the Laplanders. Hard slate chisels, hafted hammers of stone, quartzite and granite(?) picks, and quartzite scrapers were used to quarry the Catalina soapstone. Some of the Indian workings are 15 feet in diameter and 5 feet deep. Schumacher states that at the southeastern end of Santa Catalina Island in an area of about 2 square miles he counted not less than 300 quarry pits.

Another steatite quarry of some size occurs near Lindsay, Tulare County. The outcrop consists of vertical tilted soapstone sheets which were broken down by heavy stone picks. Shallow depressions near the outcrop indicate that the Indian went to some depth in order to obtain unweathered chunks.

The New Almaden cinnabar deposit was the site of an Indian mine which, although a small-scale venture, had a fairly long tunnel, in which a man could work with comfort. We have two early accounts concerning this tunnel wherein estimates of its length are given as 100 feet and 50 or 60 feet. The deposit of cinnabar, which the Indians used for red paint, was being worked in 1800, and it is probable that the site was known centuries before this time. The presence of human skeletons and rude stone mining tools at the tunnel's working face suggest abandonment after a cave-in. Taylor's statement that as late as 1841 or 1842 the Santa Clara Mission Indians were collecting cinnabar here might roughly date the skeletons and cave-in. Rounded stream pebbles, which probably served as hammers, are mentioned as the mining tools, but there were undoubtedly other types used as well, such as picks and mauls. Torches, too, were probably used, since a small, long tunnel would be too dark inside to see to work.

The only statement on record of the use of fire for quarrying refers to the northern Sacramento Valley Wintu, who split off blocks of obsidian at Glass Mountain by building a fire against the rock. Probably other California tribes used the fire-breaking technique since it is a widely known method among North American Indians.

The flint mine of the Maidu Indians on or near Table Mountain is described as having a very small opening, but the interior was such that a man could stand upright. This working, like the New Almaden tunnel, may be classed as a mine in the specific sense of the word.

There are numerous instances of Indian operations to obtain subsurface, unweathered material, but these are for the most part only shallow pits.

Not always were massive deposits selected for quarrying, judging from the wide use of float material and gravel deposits. In the Mojave Desert, particularly between Barstow and Crucero where chert and jasper boulders are found, the entire exposed gravel strata show evidence of picking over by Indians, presumably over a long period of time.

It may be of interest to note here the practice of excavation of deep water wells by the natives of southern California. These data demonstrate that the Indians were capable of large-scale earth removal, and if they had so desired, could have applied the technique to mining operations. Wells were dug by means of a mesquite wood shovel and the earth removed by baskets. In form they consisted of a sloping trench with steps measuring 50 to 75 feet long and up to 25 feet in depth. At the end of the trench was the well, a circular pit some 15 feet in diameter and 25 to 30 feet deep, whose sides were funneled out toward the top so that the earth did not slide off the sides and fill the well. The Kamia of Imperial Valley and Cahuilla of Coachella Valley were the chief well excavators of southern California.

STONE-FLAKING OF THE KLAMATH RIVER YUROK

by
Paul Schumacher

The Manufacture of Stone Weapons

During my rambles among the remnants of our Pacific Coast aborigines I had an opportunity, among the Klamath Indians, of gaining information of the manufacture of stone weapons, for which my interest was not a little stimulated by extensive collections made by our party among the deserted hearths of the coast tribes. I had the good luck to meet the last arrow maker of the tribe, on the right bank and near the mouth of the Klamath River, who has since joined his forefathers in the happy hunting-ground. He showed me the mode of making stone weapons, of which the following is a description.

For the manufacture of arrow and spear points, knives, borers, adzes, etc., chert, chalcedony, jasper, agate, obsidian, and similar stones of conchoidal fracture are used. The rock is first exposed to fire, and, after a thorough heating, rapidly cooled off, when it flakes readily into sherds of different sizes under well directed blows at its cleavage. The fragments are assorted according to shape and size best corresponding to the weapons desired; the small ones, best fit in shape and thickness, are used for arrow heads; similar sherds, but larger in size, for spear points; the long narrow pieces for borers, and so on. To work the flakes into the desired forms, certain tools are required, one of which is represented (*a*) in the figure opposite. It consists of a stick, which is in form and thickness not unlike an arrow-shaft and about 1½ feet in length, to one end of which a point is fastened, of some tough material, as the tooth of the sea-lion, or the horn of elk, and even iron among the present Klamaths, although the rock does not work as well, and brittles where the edge ought to be sharp. The point (*b* of the figure) is represented in natural size to better illustrate its

---

Paul Schumacher, "Methods of Making Stone Weapons," U.S. Geographical and Geological Survey, Vol. III, *Bull.* 3 (1877), Art. 17, pp. 547–549. Translated by the author for the *Bulletin* from an earlier publication in *Archiv für Anthropologie* (7:263 *et seq.*). The article may be considered supplementary to Arts. 2 and 3 by the same author, in the first number of this journal [U.S.G. and G.S. *Bull.*]

Articles on the flint chipping of California Indians are listed in section 3 C of Repts. UCAS, No. 4 (1949).

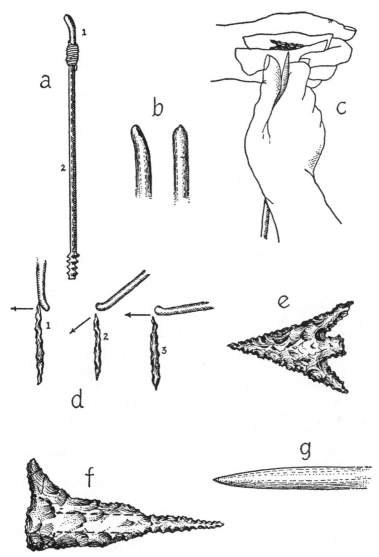

Yurok Method of Making Stone Weapons.

beveled curve, which form admits a gradual pressure to a limited space of the edge of the sherd. During the operation, the rock is partly inwrapped in a piece of buckskin for better manipulation, its flat side resting against the fleshy part of the thumb of the left hand, only the edge to be worked (*c*) being left exposed. The tool is worked with the right hand, while the lower part of the handle, usually ornamented, is held between the arm and the body so as to guide the instrument with a steady hand. The main movements are shown in the figure (*d*). With the first movement as illustrated, larger flakes are detached, and the rock is roughly shaped into the desired form; while with the second movement long flakes are broken, which frequently reach the middle of the sherd, producing the ridge of the points or knives; finally with the third movement the smaller chips of the cutting edge are worked. The work proceeds from the point, the more fragile part of the weapon toward the stronger end, as illustrated by the unfinished borer, the form of which, as frequently found, is shown by dotted lines. To work out the barbs and projections of the arrow or spear points (*e, f*), a bone needle (*g*) is used, as pictured in natural size in the figure, about 4 to 5 inches long, without a shaft.

Straightening the Arrow Shaft

On the coast of California and Oregon especially, the common willow was used for shafting the arrow of the aborigines, although any other tough straight twig may have supplied the want. The arrow of these tribes is usually about 2½ feet long; the shaft is worked round to a diameter of about ⁵⁄₁₆ of an inch, and tapers slightly toward the ends, to one of which is fastened the point, while the other one is winged with the guiding feathers. The aboriginal warrior was well aware of the advantage of a straight arrow-shaft over a crooked one, and when therefore nature did not provide the desired perfection, ingenuity was resorted to by which it was attained. The way it was accomplished I learned from living witnesses and by the many implements found which were used for the purpose of straightening the arrow-shaft.

The twigs were cut into the proper length, worked by scraping into the desired thickness, and were left to dry in the shade. When partly dry, such bends and crooked parts which resisted the common practice of straightening were subjected to the action of the arrow straightener. This utensil is made of steatite, a rock that well resists the destructive power of the fire to which it is subjected during the process of straightening the shafts, and retains the heat long. It is usually oval in shape, and slopes toward both ends and sides, ending in a flat base, upon which it rests when in use. Across its ridge passes a groove (sometimes two and even three), corresponding in its width to the thickness of the arrow-shaft, while the depth varies often to twice its width, according to the service it rendered, by which the grooves are deepened and at its edge even enlarged. The size varies from the one illustrated to about 5 inches in length and 2½ in width. Into the groove of the heated utensil, the crooked part of the shaft is pressed, and by heating or steaming the wood becomes very flexible, and is easily bent or straightened, which position it will retain when cooled off. It is the same principle now employed in the manufacture of furniture, wagon wheels, and so on of bent wood, brought into almost any shape by the process of steaming.

ethnology: social culture

THE TRIBE IN CALIFORNIA

by
A. L. Kroeber

THE YUKI

The distribution of the Yuki seems irregular. This is not because their location ran counter to natural topography but because it followed it. Their country lies wholly in the Coast Range mountains, which in this region are not, on the whole, very high, but are much broken. They contain some valleys, but the surface of the land in general is endlessly rugged. The Yuki habitat is, however, not defined, except incidentally, by limiting mountains and ranges, but is given in block by the drainage of such-and-such streams. The native did not think, like a modern civilized man, of his people owning an area circumscribed by a definite line, in which there might happen to be one or many watercourses. This would have been viewing the land through a map, whether drawn or mental; and such an attitude was foreign to his habit. What he did know was that the little town at which he was born and where he expected to die lay on a certain river or branch of a river; and that this stream, or a certain stretch of it, and all the creeks flowing into it, and all the land on or between these creeks, belonged to his people; whereas below, or above, or across certain hills, were other streams and tributaries, where other people lived, with whom he might be on visiting terms or intermarried, but who had proprietary rights of their own.

Yuki territory may be described as all the land lying in the drainage of Eel River above the North Fork, except for a stretch on South Eel River where the allied Huchnom were situated. This sounds and is simple enough. It is nature's fault, and not any intricacy of the Yuki mind or subtlety of Yuki institutions, if this extraordinarily compact and unitary fact takes form on our maps in the shape of a meaninglessly curved, indented, and irregular border.

The same basic simplicity of topography applies to the habitat of the larger Yuki divisions. The Ta'no'm were on main Eel River, the farthest down. The Lilshikno'm or Lilshaino'm or Lilnuino'm were upstream from

Pp. 160–163, 474–475, 727, 228–230, 234–235, 3 of A. L. Kroeber, *Handbook of the Indians of California* (1925). For further discussion see *Univ. Calif. Arch. Survey*, Report No. 56 (1962).

them. Still farther up, where the river forks into the South Eel and the Middle Eel, were the Utitno'm. Each branch can be followed up in the same way. On the South Eel, nearly to its forks, were the Huchnom; from the forks up, the Onkolukomno'm. Along Middle Eel, there were, first, on the south side, especially on the tributaries, the Witukomno'm. Eden Valley was the largest piece of level land in this section. Opposite, where a number of creeks flow into the river from the north and west, mostly through Round Valley—the largest flat tract not only in this area but in the whole Yuki habitat—were the Ukomno'm. Farther up, the Middle Eel also divides. On its South Fork were the Huititno'm, on the North Fork the Sukshaltatano'm.

It would be entirely erroneous, however, to regard these eight or nine groups as being in any way tribes. They were each merely an aggregation of smaller units that happened to live together in a natural area. Among themselves, they probably did not use the designations just mentioned, and thought of themselves as the people of villages A, B, and C, or the people of chiefs X and Y. The broad names were those used by outsiders when they wanted to generalize, just as we, for convenience, speak of the Balkan peoples or the Indo-Chinese, while well aware that Serbia is not Bulgaria and that a Burman does not dream of considering himself of one nationality with an Anamese.

A distinction which has not always been observed must be drawn with scrupulous exactness between the village as a town or physical settlement and the village as a group or community.

The community always might and usually did embrace several settlements. This seems simple enough. What has caused confusion and makes the acquisition of accurate information so difficult, now that the old organization is gone, is the fact that the community was nameless. If designated, it was referred to by the name of the principal village. This place name therefore denotes at one time a cluster of several little towns and on other occasions one of these towns. Even the addition of a term changing the reference from the spot to the inhabitants leaves the situation obscure: "X people" may mean either the residents at the particular settlement X or those of X, Y, and Z, which together are called X.

The word "tribe" cannot be extended to these communities without an entirely erroneous implication, since they possessed, as a rule, no group appellation, no separate dialect, and no distinctive customs. In the sense that the communities were the only political units they were tribes; but as they lacked all the traits of individualized nationality, which it is customary to attach to the meaning of the term "tribe," it is wisest to avoid its use.

The Yuki type of organization existed among the Pomo and the Maidu, with both of whom the village community and the village settlement can be definitely distinguished in certain areas. It is likely to have been the plan of political society followed by the majority of other Californian Indians, well into the southern part of the State; but, other than among the stocks cited, positive information fails us, except in a few areas where it is clear that a different organization prevailed.

These exceptions are, first, the Yuman peoples on the Colorado River, who were clearly constituted into tribes in the usual sense of the word, and thoroughly similar to the tribes of, for instance, the Plains region in the heart of the continent. This true tribal organization, however, clearly did not extend to the neighboring Chemehuevi, Cahuilla, and Diegueño.

Second, there were the tribes of northwestern California. Here . . . there were no groups other than the persons, often largely connected in blood, who lived in one spot. Except for their permanent occupation of one site, the Yurok town groups were accordingly in the political status of the primitive horde, as it is theoretically depicted.

The extent of the northwestern type of organization is not clearly known. Besides the Yurok, Hupa, and Karok, the Tolowa, Wiyot, and Chilula participated in it. The Shasta and Chimariko are in doubt. The southern Athabascans, at least the Wailaki and Kato, followed the Yuki plan, and there are indications that the Yukian scheme of organization may have prevailed as far north as the Sinkyone, if not beyond.

The third and last exception is provided by the Yokuts, but it is only a partial one. The Yokuts were divided into tribes, each named and each with a dialect. But, as set forth in the section dealing with these people, the Yokuts tribes in size, in relation to territory, and in their own consciousness were rather similar to the Yuki and Pomo community groups, so that their distinctive nature, however significant, was secondary rather than fundamental. Some of the Shoshoneans east of the Yokuts, on both sides of the Sierra Nevada, were organized somewhat like them. . . .

THE YOKUTS

The Yokuts are thus unique among the California natives in one respect. They are divided into true tribes. Each has a name, a dialect, and a territory. The first of these traits, the group name, is wanting in other Californians, who normally are able to designate themselves only by the appellation of the place they inhabit. The second feature, dialectic separateness, of course is an old story for California, but elsewhere in the State each idiom is usually common to a considerable number of tribelets or "village communities." Only in the third trait, their political independence and their ownership of a tract of land, are the ordinary Californian village communities and the Yokuts tribes similar.

Forty of these tribes are sufficiently known to be locatable. In the northern part of the Yokuts areas the map is, however, blank except for a few names of groups of uncertain situation and doubtful affinities. The total number of tribes may therefore have reached fifty. Such an array of dialects is unparalleled, and gives to the Yokuts alone nearly one-third of all the different forms of speech talked in the State. The differences of language from tribe to tribe were often rather limited; but they are marked enough to be readily perceptible to the interested Caucasian observer. Since the total length of the Yokuts area does not much exceed 250 miles and the breadth nowhere attains to 100, the individual geographical range of these little languages was exceedingly narrow. Their territory averaged perhaps 300 square miles—say a half day's foot journey in each direction from the center.

Some of the tribes occupied a single spot with sufficient permanence to become identified with it: thus the Wowol on Atwells Island in Tulare Lake, the Gawia and Yokod on opposite sides of Kaweah River where this leaves the hills, the Choinimni at the junction of Mill Creek and Kings River. Such groups, save for their distinctive speech, would be indistinguishable from the village communities of their neighbors if the purely local designations of the latter were replaced by appellations for the people themselves. Still fainter is the line of demarcation when the Choinimni, for instance, are called, as occasionally happens, Tishechuchi after their town Tishechu; but such terms are rare among the Yokuts.

For other tribes a principal and several subsidiary abodes are specified; thus the Paleuyami are identified with Altau and sometimes called Altinin, but lived also at Bekiu, Shikidapau, Holmiu, and other places. The Hometwoli lived at three principal sites, and the Chukchansi, Tachi, Yauelmani, and others dwelt from time to time, and perhaps simultaneously, at a number of places scattered over a considerable tract. These instances confirm the Yokuts divisions as true tribes.

Fully half the Yokuts tribal names end either in -amni, found also as -imni, -mina, -mani; or in -chi. The former suffix recurs added to place names among the Plains Miwok to designate the inhabitants of such and such spots, and among the Maidu as an ending of village names; the latter among the southern Miwok with the significance "people of." But the subtraction of either of these endings from the names of Yokuts tribes usually leaves only meaningless syllables; and in general the people themselves are well content to employ their little national designations without inquiring what they may denote. The few etymologies which they have ventured in response to inquiries are obviously naïve and unhistorical. . . .

THE MOHAVE

For every people hitherto mentioned a list of towns or villages has had some significance. When such information has not been given, ignorance has been the sole cause. The settlement is the political and social basis of life in California. The tribe, at least as a larger unit, exists hardly or not at all. The reverse is the case with the Mohave. They think in terms of themselves as a national entity, the Hamakhava. They think also of their land as a country, and of its numberless places. They do not think of its settlements. Where a man is born or lives is like the circumstance of a street number among ourselves, not part of the fabric of his career. The man stands in relation to the group as a whole, and this group owns a certain tract rich in associations; but the village does not enter into the scheme. In fact, the Mohave were the opposite of clannish in their inclinations. Their settlements were small, scattering, and perhaps often occupied only for short times; the people all mixed freely with one another.

With such proclivities, it is small wonder that the petty Californian feuds of locality and inherited revenge have given way among the Mohave to a military spirit, under which the tribe acted as a unit in offensive and defensive enterprise. Tribes hundreds of miles away were attacked and raided. Visits carried parties of Mohave as far as the Chumash and Yokuts. Sheer curiosity was their main motive; for the Mohave were little interested in trade. They liked to see lands; timidity did not discourage them; and they were as eager to know the manners of other peoples as they were careful to hold aloof from adopting them. . . .

THE POMO

The village community as a political unit comprising ordinarily several settlements, but with one principal village in which lived a chief recognized by all members of the group, had evidently the same form among Pomo and Yuki. Within the tract claimed by the community everyone belonging to it was at liberty to hunt, fish, or gather plant food, it would appear, without limitations of private ownership as among the northwestern tribes. At least, such restrictions have never been reported. The boundaries of the land owned by the group were, however, definite; and as regards other groups, the rights of property and utilization were clearly established. In case of amity and abundance these rights might be waived. Thus the Pomo of Shanel and Sedam and the Huchnom of Ukuknano'm in Potter Valley used each other's territory freely. The northeastern Pomo were welcome on Little Stony Creek of their Wintun neighbors, just as Coast Yuki and Kato insisted on no boundary. With such laxness between people of utterly alien speech, it is to be presumed that groups of identical language were even more liberally easygoing. But it seems that visitors were always visitors; that the confines of each body were always remembered; and that as soon as suspicion or ill feeling arose the crossing of the boundary was an offense.

As to the relation between the main and the subsidiary villages of a group, it is likely that the adjustment between them varied seasonally, winter bringing the maximum of concentration and summer of dispersal. Often a settlement split: a petty quarrel, a shortening supply of some food in the vicinity, a death, or mere indifferent instability would lead to a living apart without any sense of a division having taken place. Thus settlements of a few houses sprang up, decreased, or were totally abandoned; and then, after the passage of a few years or a generation or two, when the memory of the omen or disaster or feud that had caused their desertion had weakened, might come to be reoccupied. In themselves, the events involved in these little shiftings and recombinings were too trivial to be worth recording in full in even the most painstakingly minute history. But until some instances of such happenings can be concretely followed out as examples typical of the regions in question, our understanding of the motives that ran through and patterned the political and social fabric of the California Indians must remain hazily unsatisfactory.

An instance may make the relation clearer. The principal town of the already mentioned Kuhla-napo was Kashibadon; besides which, they had settlements, at one time or another, at Boomli, Kato-napo-ti, and Hadabutun. The Habe-napo metropolis was centered at Bidami-wina, their lesser settlements, not all contemporaneous, at No-napo-ti, Shabegok, Hmaragimo-wina, Hagasho-bagil, Sedileu, So'-bida-me, Haikalolise, Tsubahaputsum, Hadalam, Lishuikalehowa, Manatol, and Halibem. Further, there was an array of regular camp sites, without permanent houses, in each division.

The number of named and located Pomo settlements reported is 479, which does not exhaust the list of those recollectable by informants, without counting recognized camping places. The number of principal villages or political units was about seventy-five. In the northern, central, eastern and southeastern divisions these are determinable with fair accuracy from the available data; even the boundaries can generally be drawn with reasonable correctness. In the other three groups, matters are much less certain. . . .

Distribution of the Communities

It is clear that, assuming the communities to have averaged about the same in population, the members of the Pomo stock were quite unevenly distributed, both as regards the seven dialect groups and the three environmental regions. The fewness of the units on the coast is especially striking. Salt water can have had little attraction for this people. They got more to eat, it would seem, on a lake than along an ocean frontage of the same extent; and five or even three miles on an inland river, with a creek or two coming in and some miles of hill country on each side, would hold as large a population as ten miles on the ocean with an even greater extension inland.

It is also noticeable that where two or more communities abutted, their principal towns might be close together. From this center of population the hunting and camping districts then radiated out. Just so among the Yuki: the Ukomno'm villages of U'wit, Pomo, Titwa, and no doubt others, were all close together in Round Valley; the tracts of which they were the "capitals" reached far out over the hills and into smaller remote valleys. Evidently there existed no marked striations of highlanders and lowlanders, or poorly and unfavorably located groups, within these stocks. Each community had its bit of valley and its range of hill or mountain land.

This distribution is connected with the homogeneity of Pomo culture, as compared with that of the stocks of the great interior valley. Among the Maidu and the Yokuts, for instance, there were groups that held their territory entirely in the plains, others wholly in the foothills, and still others in the high mountains. Adjacent groups on different levels invariably evinced some divergence of speech. In the whole Penutian family, valley dialects stand off from hill dialects, either as the primary divisions of speech or as noticeable secondary modifications of other lines of linguistic cleavage. And so, in the Sacramento as well as the San Joaquin region, a civilizational distinction has constantly to be followed: the lowlanders are richer, possess more organization and specialization, and much more complex institutions than the hill people.

It may be that the large-scale topography of the great valley and Sierra Nevada region as compared with the broken character and little patches of level land in the Coast Range region lies at the bottom of this difference between the Penutians on the one hand and the Pomo and Yuki on the other. But whatever the ultimate reason provided by nature, the people of the two areas had adjusted their intercommunal lives in distinct ways.

A majority of the principal villages of the Pomo, in fact of all their settlements, lie on the north or east sides of streams. Not only was the sun grateful, or when too hot easily avoided, so that a southern or western exposure was the pleasanter; but the vegetation is invariably thickest, in all California, on the northern and eastern slopes of hills, where ground and foliage hold moisture better through the long rainless summer. The same inclination has already been noted among the Yurok, the Hupa, and the Chilula. It applies also to the Shasta. In the interior, conditions are scarcely comparable. In the treeless plains of the great valley the sun did not matter: elevation and other factors determined. In the Sierra the streams are usually too deep in canyons and bordered by too little level land to furnish suitable habitation. The villages are therefore on crests, or on the slopes of ridges. Here, too, open places, and that means sunny exposures, were sought; but they did not lie with direct reference to the streams. . . .

THE YUROK

Property and rights pertain to the realm of the individual, and the Yurok recognizes no public claim and the existence of no community. His world is wholly an aggregation of individuals. There being no society as such, there is no social organization. Clans, exogamic groups, chiefs or governors, political units, are unrepresented even by traces in northwestern California. The germinal, nameless political community that can be traced among the Indians of the greater part of the State is absent. Government being wanting, there is no authority, and without authority there can be no chief. The men so-called are individuals whose wealth, and their ability to retain and employ it, have clustered about them an aggregation of kinsmen, followers, and semidependents to whom they dispense assistance and protection. If a man usually marries outside the village in which he lives, the reason is that many of his coinhabitants normally happen to be blood relatives, not because custom or law or morality recognize the village as a unit concerned with marriage. The actual outcome among the Yurok may, in the majority of cases, be the same as among nations consciously organized on an exogamic plan. The point of view, the guiding principles both of the individual's action and of the shaping of the civilization, are wholly nonexogamic. Such familiar terms as "tribe," "village community," "chief," "government," "clan," can therefore be used with reference to the Yurok only after extreme care in previous definition—in their current senses they are wholly inapplicable.

MIWOK LINEAGES AND THE POLITICAL UNIT IN ABORIGINAL CALIFORNIA

by

E. W. Gifford

THE LINEAGE AS AN AUTONOMOUS POLITICAL UNIT

The Miwok of the Sierra Nevada region of Central California have, in addition to social organization on a moiety basis, organization upon the basis of the patrilineal joint family, or what I prefer to call the male lineage, which formerly was an independent autonomous political unit. The Miwok term for such a lineage is nena. The word nena has a twofold meaning. It means not only a male lineage or patrilineal joint family, but it also means the ancestral home in which the lineage is supposed to have arisen. The lineage name is always a place name. Few Miwok today live at their nena, but every Miwok knows his nena and can name the ancestral spot from which his patrilineal forefathers hailed. The nena is more than the birthplace, in fact today it usually is not the birthplace, yet it is always remembered. The nena had as its head a chief who was, so to speak, the patriarch of the lineage. The chieftainship normally descended in the direct male line, from father to eldest son. The lineage was a land-owning group, the limited real estate which was held by it being used in common by all members of the lineage.

Each nena is exogamous and belongs to one of the patrilineal exogamous moieties called respectively Land and Water. Were there no patrilineal moieties the nena would doubtless be exogamous nevertheless, for it is comprised of such a small group of closely related people that marriage within it is inconceivable. Both lineages and moieties are patrilineal. The fundamental thing about the Miwok lineages is that their members are bound together by genealogical relationship, although today, under the altered conditions of life among Caucasians, the members of the lineages are scattered. The exact relationship that each person bears to every other member of the lineage is usually remembered. Lineage membership, as

American Anthropologist (1926), 28:389–401.

The social organization of California tribes is also discussed in W. D. Strong, *Aboriginal Society in Southern California*, Univ. Calif. Publ. Am. Arch. and Ethn. (1929), Vol. 26; W. R. Goldschmidt, "Social Organization in Native California and the Origin of Clans," *American Anthropologist* (1948), 50:444–456.

indicated by the use of the term patrilineal, passes only through the father to the offspring. Children never belong to the lineage of their mother. . . .

From all of the information that can be gathered, the lineage was anciently among the Miwok a political group, each lineage dwelling at its ancestral home, with the men of the lineage normally bringing their wives to the hamlet to live and the women of the hamlet normally marrying out of the hamlet. Thus, aside from the marrying-in women, the hamlet at the ancestral home was comprised of the male members of the lineage, their male offspring, and their descendants through males. Thus what is today only a social group was anciently also an autonomous, political unit, maintaining, however, friendly relations with other nena, particularly those from which wives were drawn and those whose members attended ceremonial gatherings. Each nena held a small tract of land about its hamlet. There was always a spring or stream within the tract. The bulk of the country, however, was unclaimed by the nena and was regarded as "no-man's-land," or more correctly "every-man's-land," upon which people from any nena might seek vegetable foods and hunt animals. This rather unusual arrangement in which much of the land was unclaimed is better understood when it is realized that each summer the Miwok moved into the higher mountains, so that practically every Miwok nena had occasion to travel and had occasion to collect food and other materials away from its fixed place of habitation. It is quite possible that these periodic movements into the higher mountains on the part of all nena shaped the ideas as to land ownership and resulted in only limited holdings which were jealously guarded because of their proximity to the ancestral dwelling, while there was mutual recognition of the international rights of all nena to gather vegetable products and hunt animals in the remainder of the country.

Even before the coming of the Americans to Sierra Miwok territory in 1848 there had already been considerable pressure from the Spaniards and Mexicans resulting in the abandonment of certain of the nena which lay in the lowest hills close to the San Joaquin Valley. This seems to have been the beginning of the process of amalgamation of the nena into villages, resulting in the type of settlement represented by the village of Tcakatcino near Jamestown, or the village at Big Creek near Groveland, Tuolumne County. . . . In such villages there were brought together, through Caucasian pressure, people from many nena. The same story holds everywhere in Miwok territory. The Caucasian invaders drove the people from their ancestral nena sites to take refuge with other Miwok in less disturbed places and thus true village life arose and new territorial ties were created. Yet in spite of one hundred years of Caucasian pressure we find that every person today remembers the putative place of origin of his paternal ancestors. At rare intervals this memory is further refreshed by the performance of the pota ceremony.

As we have just seen, Caucasian pressure brought about true village life among the Miwok, in which a number of unrelated lineages, often of different moieties, came to form a new political body, the village community. Although it took Caucasian pressure to bring this about among the Miwok there would seem to be other groups in California which had achieved the village community, comprising several lineages, before the coming of the white man. Before I take up the discussion of such peoples, however, I wish to speak of other groups which appear to have lived like the Miwok in patrilineal joint families or lineages.

In southern California the Miwok situation seems exactly paralleled by the case of the Desert Cahuilla, a Shoshonean people, who are divided into at least forty-four male lineages which in an earlier paper I have called clans. Each of these Cahuilla lineages seems to have had a single spot which it claimed as its own, a location which always, of course, possessed the requisite supply of fresh water. Most of the names of Cahuilla lineages seem to refer to these ancestral dwelling places, as do the Miwok lineage names. The parallel between Cahuilla and Miwok organization is carried further when it is noted that the Cahuilla are also organized upon a moiety basis just as are the Miwok. As the moieties are patrilineal like the lineages, each lineage is definitely assigned to one moiety or the other. Like the Miwok lineage each Cahuilla lineage had a patriarchal chief who was usually the oldest son of the preceding chief. Like the Miwok lineages, too, each Cahuilla lineage seems anciently to have been an autonomous political unit, although a small one to be sure. Whether the Cahuilla lineages had only small land holdings like the Miwok lineages or divided all the country between them, I do not know.

The same interpretation should evidently be placed upon the organization of the neighboring Serrano, another Shoshonean people of southern California. The groups which I have called patrilineal clans among the Serrano were obviously similar in character and in political autonomy to the Miwok and Cahuilla lineages. The Serrano like the Cahuilla and Miwok have a moiety organization. The similarity between these three groups seems obtrusive, all possessing male lineages, lineage chiefs, ancestral homes, and full political autonomy. All comprised small groups of people, probably in most cases not exceeding fifty, exclusive of married-in females of other lineages.

Turning now to another southern Californian people, the Southern Diegueño, we find also localized patrilineal groups which I now prefer to call lineages instead of clans as I named them in an earlier paper, or gentes as Dr. Spier calls them. The Southern Diegueño lineages seem in every way comparable to the lineages of the Miwok, Cahuilla, and Serrano, except that they are not grouped into moieties. In chieftainship, landownership, and political autonomy they closely parallel the lineages of the three linguistic groups we have been discussing. Dr. Spier has plotted their territorial holdings. The Northern Diegueño lineages seem less localized and approximate more closely the condition of the Cupeño and Luiseño lineages discussed below, residing together in villages, a condition which may be due to Caucasian interference, however. They are not grouped in moieties.

Unpublished information concerning the Western Mono indicates the male lineage as the autonomous political unit. Again these are grouped in moieties.

The determination of whether or not the lineage and the political unit are coterminous can be achieved only by genealogical investigation. This method has not been applied to many of the Californian groups, so that it is impossible to say just how extensively lineages and autonomous political units coincided. From the small size of the settlements in the mountainous and desert portions of the state it would seem likely that each autonomous hamlet in most cases comprised but a single lineage.

THE LINEAGE AS AN INTEGRAL PART OF THE BODY POLITIC

Let us pass from the consideration of the lineage as an autonomous political unit to the consideration of it as an integral part of a larger political unit. I have already referred to amalgamation of lineages among the Miwok through Caucasian pressure, but there were doubtless many places in the state, particularly in the more fertile portions where the Indian villages were large, in which the dwelling together of two or more lineages to form a larger body politic had taken place long before the advent of the white man. A good example of such a village composed of distinct paternal lineages is Kupa, one of the two Cupeño villages of San Diego County reported by the Spanish explorers in the eighteenth century. In Kupa there were seven lineages which, although living in a single village and therefore bound by certain territorial ties, nevertheless maintained their distinctness, each lineage having its own land upon which wild products were gathered, each having its patriarchal chief, and each keeping fresh the story of its origin. A similar situation was to be found in the second Cupeño village of Wilakal. The Cupeño lineages were grouped into moieties like the lineages of the Cahuilla and Serrano. The only difference between the Cupeño lineages and those of the two tribes just mentioned was that the Cupeño lineages no longer lived in their reputed ancestral homes, but already at the time of the coming of the Spaniards had taken to living peaceably together in the two villages of Kupa and Wilakal. The factors that brought about this clustering of lineages are not known. Quite possibly the aggression of enemies, coupled with the favorable environment of the present Cupeño territory, were the factors that brought about the living together of these distinct lineages. The following paragraph summarizes my unpublished notes as to the affiliations of the several Cupeño lineages.

The Cupeño lineages were nine in number, seven residing at Kupa village, two at Wilakal village. Six of the nine lineages are of reputed non-Cupeño origin as the following tabulation shows. Under the heading "Origin" is given the name of the linguistic group from which the paternal ancestor of each lineage is said to have been derived. The table reveals the interesting point that the putative original Cupeño were all of the coyote moiety, but of three lineages. Before the entry, into the community, of foreign lineages of the wildcat moiety there could therefore have been no moieties among the Cupeño. That moieties thus originated by the settlement of "wildcat people" with the three original Cupeño lineages is, of course, open to doubt like many another native explanation of cultural features. Another point that the table reveals is the dependent position of the village of Wilakal, which having only "wildcat" lineages was thus forced into village exogamy; while Kupa, having a goodly representation of lineages of both moieties, was a self-sufficient political unit which could maintain itself without foreign marriage alliances. Wilakal was no better off than the autonomous single lineages of the Miwok, for its men, like the Miwok men, had to seek their wives elsewhere.

CUPEÑO LINEAGES

Name	Synonyms	Moiety	Village	"Origin"	Remarks
Kauval	Nauwilet Changalanga- lish Nukwa	Coyote	Kupa	Cupeño	
Potamatoligish	Pala'adim Pala'ut	Coyote	Kupa	Cupeño	
Tamakwanis		Coyote	Kupa	Cupeño	Extinct
Saubel		Coyote	Kupa	Cahuilla	
Sivimoat		Wildcat	Kupa	Diegueño	
Aulingawish	Auliot	Wildcat	Kupa	Diegueño	
Takanawish	Taka'at	Wildcat	Kupa	Luiseño	
Djutnikut		Wildcat	Wilakal	Diegueño	
Tashmukimaatim	Tuchil	Wildcat	Wilakal	Cahuilla	

The Cupeño also illustrate another process of amalgamation of lineages, in addition to the territorial bond created by their living together. I refer to the uniting of certain of the lineages for ceremonial purposes. In case a lineage has become chiefless it is customary for the people of the lineage to affiliate themselves with some more powerful lineage of the same moiety which still has a chief and to perform with this more powerful lineage its ceremonies. These ceremonial groups are called in English "parties." In Cupeño they are called "nout" which is also a word meaning chief, thus clearly indicating the extent to which the party centers in the chief. This is obviously an extension of the lineage-idea that the lineage focuses in the chief.

Passing to another southern California Shoshonean group, the Luiseño, we find a series of some eighty lineages recorded. In the paper just cited I hesitatingly call these lineages patrilinear clans or families. I think they may unhesitatingly be set down as lineages similar to those we have been describing. They have, however, a rather different type of designation, which as a rule has no reference, unless veiled, to an ancestral home place. The far greater number of lineages among the Luiseño as compared with the Cupeño is quite in keeping with the much larger territory which the Luiseño occupy. It is possible that we may regard the Luiseño as having gone a step further than the Cupeño in the matter of creating territorial ties which held the lineages together in the respective villages. The nonlocalization of the lineages among the Luiseño may be evidence of this and, if so, perhaps indicates that the lineages have so long lived together that the original home settlements have been forgotten. As with the Cupeño the breaking down of lineage barriers, as manifested by the chiefless lineages uniting for ceremonial purposes with those which still possessed chiefs, has taken place. In lacking moieties the Luiseño approximate rather closely to the condition of the Diegueño; but the Diegueño, so far as I know, lacked the so-called parties or combinations of lineages for ceremonial purposes which the Luiseño and Cupeño have.

Upon the basis of the concrete evidence from the Cupeño and Luiseño it seems reasonable to suppose that the villages of the other peoples of the western part of southern California, such as the Juaneño, Gabrieliño, and Chumash, may likewise have comprised a number of lineages. The possibility of determining this, however, has vanished. In the Chumash villages, which seem to have been exceptionally large as Californian villages go and to have maintained themselves for many centuries, it is not impossible that all trace of original localized lineages had disappeared by the time of discovery in 1542. The Luiseño evidence cited above seems to indicate some such condition for that people, and if such is admitted as probable with the Luiseño, it seems far more likely with the Chumash in their exceedingly favorable environment in which communities of probably several hundred persons developed without danger of food shortage.

Concerning the seminomadic Yokuts tribes of the San Joaquin Valley we have no evidence as to the extent to which originally localized lineages may have been modified and worked into the prevailing political unit, the named tribe of from 250 to 500 people.

The Eastern and Northern Pomo of the northern shores of Clear Lake, Lake County, give us further illustration of the sort of relationship which doubtless existed in considerable degree in California between the lineage and the political unit, the village. Certain of the villages of these peoples are composed of but a single lineage and have but a single chief each, to whom all members of the village, not married-in, are attached by blood ties. Unlike the people I have hitherto discussed, the blood tie among the Pomo which binds the average person to his chief is matrilineal and to a considerable extent the succession to chieftainship is likewise matrilineal. In certain respects the Pomo female lineages are comparable to the Cupeño and Luiseño male lineages. In the smaller Pomo villages, as I have already said, but a single lineage with its chief may be represented. In the larger villages, like Cigom on the northeastern shore of Clear Lake, there may be two or more lineages. In the case of Cigom there were three lineages without names and with no tradition as to a former place of residence. Each lineage, however, had its own chief so that in the village there were three chiefs apparently all equal in power, except in so far as the matter of constituents of each chief varied. Each person born in the village was bound by blood ties, usually matrilineal, to one of these three chiefs. It would seem that chieftainship is the most enduring feature of the lineage. Lineage name, ancestral home, and lineage real estate may all disappear, but the chief usually remains and serves as the focus for the activities of the lineage and as the central figure from which all relationships within the lineage radiate. The lack of lineage-owned land among the Pomo of Cigom village indicates that we may regard this village as having gone a step further than Kupa village in the matter of political amalgamation of the lineages. It is conceivable that the next step among the Pomo of Cigom might have been ascendancy of one chief over the other two with the obliteration of the lineages and the substitution of true political relationship of the chief to his followers.

From the examples I have given it seems not unlikely that lineages, either patrilineal or matrilineal, underlie the political organization of all of the Californian tribes. In favor of this possibility is to be noted the fact that wherever genealogical information has been gathered lineages have been found. This is true even among the Yurok, where Dr. T. T. Waterman has recorded extensive genealogies and censuses of villages. Among the Yurok, however, the wealth concept and the utter absence of chiefs in the usual sense of the word obscure the lineage idea. The wealthy man is the most important person in each village, there being no chiefs. As the possession of wealth is a variable matter and this world's goods have a tendency to slip out of the hands of one family into the hands of another, the wealthy man can hardly be regarded as the equivalent of the hereditary lineage chief of other parts of California. On the other hand this weakening of the lineage through the absence of a chief is offset by the strong patrilocal tendencies of the Yurok. If one may speculate as to possible history, it might be imagined that at one time the Yurok did possess well defined localized lineages with patriarchal chiefs like the Miwok and Cahuilla, that development of the wealth concept weakened the chiefly and local features of their lineages, and that to a certain extent the bonds of obligation created by the wealth concept subverted the bonds of lineage.

The wealth factor is not the only one which would tend to weaken the localized, autonomous lineage. A favorable living environment would indirectly operate against the continuance of localized autonomous lineages, inasmuch as it would make possible the living together of two or more lineages. Such coresidence carries with it naturally enough the corollary of a surrender of a certain amount of autonomy on the part of each lineage in the combination. Wherever two lineages dwell together it is obvious that certain territorial ties are present which must be regarded as over and above the kinship ties which operate within each lineage and serve to make each a compact, consanguineous group.

Two concepts which are particularly strong among the Miwok, the Cahuilla, and the Serrano tend to strengthen and perpetuate the lineage and to preserve at least a memory of past political autonomy on the part of each lineage. The two concepts I refer to are hereditary chieftainship and the belief in an ancestral home at which the forefathers of the lineage dwelt.

Professor Kroeber suggests that even among the Yuman tribes on the Colorado River, notably the Mohave, Yuma, and Cocopa that are today organized into strong coherent tribes with nonlocalized sibs, quite the opposite of the tiny, patrilineal, politically autonomous lineages I have been discussing, a localized lineage organization may once have existed, for when certain of the Mohave myths are stripped of their supernatural elements they appear to tell of the origin of localized paternal lineages which later settled in the present abode of the Mohave, became scattered over that abode, and were thus transformed into the nonlocalized sibs of the present-day Mohave nation. Mohave mythology, in short, presents a picture of organization that quite parallels that of the related Diegueño tribes, who until Caucasian invasion lived in politically autonomous, localized lineages. A problem of great interest among the Mohave, Yuma, and Cocopa would be to determine the factors that welded the hypothetical localized lineages into great warlike tribes and at the same time transformed these lineages into true father-sibs or gentes. It is not unlikely that movement from a former desert homeland, in which large aggregations of people were not possible, into the agriculturally fertile valley of the Colorado brought about a unification and commingling of formerly distinct, autonomous lineages.

A word as to the relation of lineages to moieties seems worth while. With the possible exception of the Yokuts for whom information is lacking, the peoples with moieties in California have also localized lineages. Moreover, there are a number of peoples such as the Diegueño who have the lineages but not the moieties. Owing to the wider distribution of the lineages it seems logical to assume that they are the earlier and that the moieties are the later. Without regarding the distribution it seems to me, however, that this same assumption would be arrived at on a priori grounds since the moiety embraces a large number of people, often several thousand as among the Sierra Miwok, whereas the lineage embraces only a very limited number of people who trace their relationship to one another genealogically. Of the two groupings it seems natural to suppose that the lineage is the earlier since really no organization is necessary, the facts of consanguinity serving as the bond and relationships being, as it were, automatically established with the advent of each individual into the world. The moiety, on the other hand, embracing as it does a large number of people appears to me to be conceivable only as a much later development than the lineage.

The limited family of father, mother, and offspring is, of course, a universal institution. The extended family which embraces relatives both through the father and the mother is equally a biological group like the limited family, but it is a group which, according to Rivers, seldom functions socially. In its unilateral form of the joint family of Rivers, or the lineage as I have designated it, the extended family does occupy an important place in primitive society. It is this unilateral aspect of the extended family which I have discussed for California, showing that it was in certain parts of the state an autonomous, political unit, the probable forerunner of the later village community.

A closer study of the Californian peoples will doubtless make clear the steps by which autonomous lineages combine to form political units of a higher order. In California, as I have demonstrated, the lineages existed both as autonomous political units and as integral parts of larger political units with their distinctness, however, more or less maintained within the body politic. A third stage, in which the lineages had completely lost their distinctness and become welded into a single body politic, perhaps existed in the Channel region of southern California, but all opportunity of obtaining evidence is gone. It is possible that we are justified in regarding the Colorado River tribes with their keen sense of national unity, as illustrating this third stage, in which the lineage completely disappears as a localized political unit.

YUROK NATIONAL CHARACTER

by
A. L. Kroeber

The Yurok were a small tribe or nationality of Indians in northwestern California along the lower Klamath River and adjoining sea coast. They numbered about 2,500 when first reached by Americans in 1850 and had had no previous Spanish contacts. They were surrounded by five tribes with similar customs and institutions, all somewhat less populous, aggregating perhaps 6,000 additional persons, by my estimates. Later computations by Cook increase the population of this little ethnic world somewhat short of doubling it. Tribes beyond the nuclear six possessed a simpler and less accentuated culture, and the Yurok had few contacts or relations with them.

In 1900, those Yurok who were 70 years old had been adults when the native culture was first impinged on. Their knowledge of that culture was therefore first hand. In fact, at many points, the cultural practices were still unchanged, which is why it was selected for study. At the same time, transformation of the Yurok into disadvantaged and second-class Americans was going on as the result of contact with our infinitely more massive society — a transformation that has been accelerated since 1900. This process proved traumatic for many Yurok. It is not gone into here.

The undisturbed, pre-1850 native culture seems to have been largely in static balance. It has been described in systematic ethnographic outline in the first four chapters of the *Handbook of Indians of California* and in special monographs. The pages that follow are an attempt to separate out and precipitate an ethnographer's impressions and his experiences with living or remembered Yurok who were still leading a predominantly native life, and to formulate these in personality terms. It is perhaps an unachievable task, but one that ethnographers will continue now and then to attempt, probably without ever satisfying psychologists.

This is a descriptive account, where Erickson's monograph of 1943 is explicative. The present tense must be construed as a narrative one, referring to a century or more ago.

Article No. 7 (pp. 236–240) of *Ethnographic Interpretations: 7–11*, Univ. Calif. Publs. Amer. Arch. and Ethn. (1959), 47:235–310.

The Yurok are an inwardly fearful people, cautious and placatory. Before other persons, pride often covers up their fear; but in the face of nature, taboo, or fate, they are timorous and propitiating. Moreover, they are suspicious of motives, quick to become jealous, and, by their own accounts, given to envy.

They are touchy to slight, sensitive to shaming, quickly angered. Their restraints of prudence break with a jerk, and they are then likely to explode into reckless violence of speech and anger. They hate wholeheartedly, persistently, often irreconcilably. They scarcely know forgiveness; their pride is too great. If unlimited acting-out of hostility is unfeasible, they take refuge in the negation of blotting out an opponent's existence by complete nonintercourse, within which they continue to nurse their hurt. Native law recognizes the perseverance of this by stipulating that settlement for injury include abrogation of the condition of nonintercourse, though common experience with one another has taught the Yurok to more than half expect continued hate after settlement and formal reconciliation.

They are acquisitive, but even more avaricious and retentive. They are particularly greedy for treasure, whose possession brings prestige and which is never given away gratis except in partial return of bride price. But they are not greedy for food; liberality with food brings credit, and restraint in one's own eating is an index of good breeding and success. Acquisition of property by tenacious production is recognized, but its actual rewards are probably modest. The largest transfers of property follow on misfortune; they consist of fees paid shamans for treating the sick and of compensation paid for death or injury of close kin. (The full marriage of daughters also brings wealth, which however is diminished by return of a partial unstipulated equivalent.) The greatest reliance for acquisition is on the supernatural and one's own will — a willing through abstinence and deprivation, and by sheer pertinacious wishing, weeping, insistence, and proclaiming — devices psychologically effective because they direct and focus volition. In short, the Yurok depend more on concentration of mind to acquire wealth than on extraverted activity.

That they are litigious, resourceful in finding and countering claims, and stubborn in maintaining rights follows from their sensitive pride, their defensive avarice and aggressive acquisitiveness, and the prestige they attach to wealth. The cultural counterpart is a complex and refined system of law almost wholly resolvable ultimately into claims for property.

Perseveration characterizes not only the hates of the Yurok but all their affects, and the strength of their perseverations tends to deepen with increasing age. They become intensely attached to places, to habits, to their property; the feeling is more one of longing, regret, and nostalgic remembrance than of active satisfaction. Affection and sadness intertwine with it. Serenity is rare in their lives; rooted attachment ever present. They recognize the danger of such concentration when it is misdirected, as toward a pet or supernatural animal; this brings its own tragedy in such consequent loss of normal love objects as death of one's children.

In terms of long-recognized temperaments the Yurok are most often melancholic, punctuated by choler. They look upon the sanguine man as a rash fool, the phlegmatic one as a sort of base clod.

Abstemiousness marks the Yurok attitude to life, verging at times on asceticism. They believe in the virtue and power of deprivation — strong restraint in eating, in sexual pleasure, in any indulgence. They do not urge limitation of intense wishing for wealth, for it is through punishment, through self-deprivation and self-pity, that fulfillment of such wishing is heightened. Money is believed to flee the house in which it is subjected to the indignity of witnessing the loosening of restraint on sexual pleasure; therefore proper intercourse takes place outdoors. As for the men's sweat house, a woman may not even enter it; when a woman shaman novice properly dances in it, she is in trance and therefore sexually clean, and the structure is partly dismantled for the occasion.

Puritanism in loving, in genital exposure, in decency of speech or gesture is as characteristic of the Yurok as is the puritanism of thrift and capitalism. Like puritans they feel sin as well as shame, expiating it by public confession on threat of loss by death of one of their loved ones — itself a puritan's ordeal of choice.

A multitude of specific, minute "don't" taboos of most miscellaneous and highly special character fill the interstices of the larger fundamental restrictions. These endless little restraints are relieved and illumined by the occasional contrasting flash of a traditional belief expressing a day-dream of extreme indulgence — such as eating a whole salmon in one ritual sitting, or cohabiting ten times in a night — but characteristically such feats are also regretfully thought of as unattainable.

With deprivation goes limitation. The Yurok love a small, snug, known, unchanging world, and in imagination often contract their universe, even short of the bounds of their actual knowledge. But they identify with this shrunken core of a universe intensely and passionately. It follows that they are incurious and really antipathetic toward what may lie beyond, toward all that is not of immediate and familiar affective concern. And they want their world stable; they dread its tilting and slipping, its shaking by earthquake, its flooding, its invasion by famine or by epidemics advancing like clouds. It is the warding off of these threats that is the formal motivation of their greatest rituals, the "World Renewals."

The Yurok like to fit and adapt themselves into their world. Their houses have the center sunk into the ground, the gables low, the eaves still lower;

the sweat houses fit in even deeper; both often nestle under a tree or crag or slip into a natural slope; there is no effort at all to make buildings stand out boldly. The dwellings are named, most often from their location — by the trail, at the elderberry or bay tree, in the middle, farthest uphill — and sometimes by function — where they dance or dress for it — but never in commemoration of a person or particular event. On the contrary, people derive their usual designations and appellations — their actual, individual names are private and are avoided rather than used — from their village settlement or from their particular house. Coupled with the house name is their marital status: married into, married to a woman born in, living with a woman of, divorced from, widowed in. This double device identifies persons socially as well as geographically; but it is the precise familiar society and the intimate location that are discriminated, not placement in any broad general scheme.

The lack of anything abstract or universal is evident also in the directions recognized by the Yurok, which are those of the flow of water at any given spot of the slope, to or away from water, whether this side or across stream. As the drainage of the area — including the main river — is tortuous, the directions, such as "upriver," sometimes happen to agree with solar or cardinal directions such as "east" but often disagree radically with them. The Yurok have not tried to compromise or reconcile the two possible systems but have simply discarded the abstract or cardinal method in favor of the localized, particular, and qualitatively more concrete one.

In manners, the Yurok, in spite of their aristocratizing values, make a show of democratic affability. They are perceptive, courteous, normally sensitive to the sensitivities of others, grave but able to smile, basically reserved — never telling all.

Individuals vary considerably in neatness. They bathe frequently, especially as part of the use of the sweat house, and for all major ritual purification. Among them tidiness with objects runs toward emptiness. The terrace before the house is swept clean; the formulist for some rituals is called "he who brushes it out," and in all ceremonies he keeps clear the dance strips and the incense hearth. Sweat houses are bare; and a well-brought-up, industrious housewife has enough baskets for orderly storage of her provisions and effects. But it is hard for them to throw away anything; in the less well-kept homes discarded utensils, worn-out baskets, and maggotty dried food tend to accumulate in heaps and clutter the space needed by persons. Lack of both axes and saws gives a ragged appearance to the eaves of houses, for the projecting plank-ends weather unevenly; and the indoor fuel sheds, in which the split and crooked limbs of broken firewood cannot easily be stacked, also look disorderly.

There is considerable sense of workmanship and technological standard. Texture of artifacts is highly appreciated, especially in such hard materials as stone and antler, less in wood, but again in baskets and dressed skins. Except for the caps which women wear and which are an index of their being well-dressed, basketry is definitely sober and unshowy, without feathers, shell, or other attachments, its patterning limited mostly to a single band, and that negative — a paler overlay on root-brown — but evenness and fineness of stitch, surface, and contour are prized. There is also an evident feeling for texture of fur and feathers in the treasured dance regalia; the feathers, and sometimes pieces of fur, lie flat and smooth rather than bristling or radiating. In the best of the highly valued large display flints and obsidians, even and ripple-like flaking is achieved.

With all their feeling for material and surface, the Yurok decorate very simply, chiefly with triangles and diagonal quadrilaterals, never representing anything; that impulse seems wholly lacking. Even for objects — elk-horn spoons and purses, cylindrical dance baskets which sometimes almost force a symbolic interpretation on us — the Yurok consistently deny any "meaning" of shape. Their ritual face-and-body paints, their dance postures are arbitrarily traditional, never mimetic.

Only in straight magic, usually practiced individually and often in secret, does a definite mimetic symbolism frequently enter. And verbal symbolism has some occurrence in myth and legend — image, metaphor, occasional brief similes.

The Yurok do not scalp, decapitate, or spoil the body of a slain enemy. In fact, on the beach they drag his body above the surf for his kinswomen to claim. This may be because if the corpse is injured or lost, the punitive damages to be paid are increased. But even so, this fact implies discrimination under strong passion. They concentrate the aim of their hate on actual hurt instead of diffusing it in a flood of expressive gestures. The wish to hurt the living man may become overpowering; but in spite of their perseveration of affects, the wish, once accomplished, does not continue to indignity toward the corpse. In fact, if any mutilation of the body is practiced, it is by the bereaved women, who may run arrows into the dead body of their kinsman hoping that their magic will bring the same fate on his killer; they will mutilate their own murdered sons or fathers to achieve revenge for them.

A somewhat reminiscent dignity is extended to women, in spite of the extreme defilement residing in menses and parturition and the generic impurity of sex. Women claim and tend with impunity the bodies of their slain kinsmen. The full-married mistress of a prosperous house is a person of importance. The bride price paid for her redounds to her credit as well as to her husband's, and she contributes equally to their children's social rank, which is definitely bilateral. She can inherit dance treasures, though she is disadvantaged in using and maintaining them. If of good family, she inherits from her mother a complete display dress outfit, and from one or both parents intangible property such as spells and formulae, of which even a widow cannot be robbed. And finally, with few and second-rate exceptions, it is only women who are eligible to become curing shamans. Therewith they have in their control perhaps the greatest opportunity in the Yurok world to regular, consistent acquisition of wealth.

I might add that among the only slightly acculturated aged Yurok I knew or met in the first decade of the century, the men often seemed to me bitter and withdrawn, and some were of terrifying mien; but the old women made an impression rather of serenity.

I have long thought and still believe that the Yurok adhere to the classical anal temperament first recognized by Freud. My friend Erikson diagnoses rather an oral type of personality; he is a psychoanalyst gifted with extraordinary perceptiveness and therefore perhaps more interested in the subtle and veiled nuances than in obvious qualities of character. His imaginative comparison of the Yurok concepts of the body, its orifices, and food; of houses and sweat houses and their doors; of river, salmon, and weir is stimulating and illuminating. These are findings in a dimension which it is not for an ethnographer or culture historian to believe or deny or to use, though he can recognize them as valuable, as I do. As for the oral constituents, there is no doubt that the Yurok wealth-acquiring behavior connected with the sweat house strongly enacts infantile attitude and behavior, and I have myths that emphasize the similarity even more. And a great deal of the thousand-headed traditional practices of magic is certainly at least puerile in the symbolic fusion of its concept and effect. I do not therefore see any quarrel between recognition of anal and oral components of Yurok personality; each is presumably true on its own level and degree.

As for the type of neurotic behavior among ourselves which customary Yurok personality most suggests to me, it is compulsion.

YUROK LAW AND CUSTOM

by
A. L. Kroeber

PRINCIPLES OF YUROK LAW

These are the standards by which the Yurok regulate their conduct toward
one another:

1. All rights, claims, possessions, and privileges are individual and personal, and all wrongs are against individuals. There is no offense against
the community, no duty owing it, no right or power of any sort inhering
in it.

2. There is no punishment, because a political state or social unit that
might punish does not exist, and because punishment by an individual
would constitute a new offense which might be morally justified but would
expose to a new and unweakened liability. An act of revenge therefore
causes two liabilities to lie where one lay before.

3. Every possession and privilege, and every injury and offense, can be
exactly valued in terms of property.

4. There is no distinction between material and nonmaterial ownership,
right, or damage, nor between property rights in persons and in things.

5. Every invasion of privilege or property must be exactly compensated.

6. Intent or ignorance, malice or negligence, are never a factor. The fact
and amount of damage are alone considered. The psychological attitude
is as if intent were always involved.

7. Directness or indirectness of cause of damage is not considered, except
in so far as a direct cause has precedence over an indirect one. If the agent
who is directly responsible can not satisfactorily be made amenable, liability
automatically attaches to the next agent or instrument in the chain of
causality, and so on indefinitely.

8. Settlement of compensation due is arrived at by negotiation of the
parties interested or their representatives, and by them alone.

Chap. 2 (pp. 20–52) of A. L. Kroeber, *Handbook of the Indians of California* (1925).

Additional notes on Yurok law may be found in A. L. Kroeber, "Yurok Law," *Proceedings*
of the International Congress of Americanists, 22d Session (Rome, 1926). A spirited account
of the Yurok by a member of the tribe is Lucy Thompson, *To the American Indian* (Eureka,
1916).

9. When compensation has been agreed upon and accepted for a claim, this claim is irrevocably and totally extinguished. Even the harboring of a sentiment of injury is thereafter improper, and if such sentiment can be indirectly connected with the commission of an injury, it establishes a valid counterliability. The known cherishing of resentment will even be alleged as prima facie evidence of responsibility in case an injury of undeterminable personal agency is suffered.

10. Sex, age, nationality, or record of previous wrongs or damage inflicted or suffered do not in any measure modify or diminish liability.

11. Property either possesses a value fixed by custom, or can be valued by consideration of payments made for it in previous changes of ownership. Persons possess valuations that differ, and the valuation of the same non-material property or privilege varies, according to the rating of the person owning it. The rating of persons depends partly upon the amount of property which they possess, partly upon the values which have previously passed in transfers or compensations concerning themselves or their ancestors.

One doubtful qualification must be admitted to the principle that the Yurok world of humanity recognizes only individuals: the claims of kinship. These are undoubtedly strong, not only as sentiments but in their influence on legal operations. Yet a group of kinsmen is not a circumscribed group, as a clan or village community or tribe would be. It shades out in all directions, and integrates into innumerable others. It is true that when descent is reckoned unilaterally, a body of kinsmen in the lineage of the proper sex tends to maintain identity for long periods and can easily become treated as a group. It is also conceivable that such patrilinear kin units exist in the consciousness of Yurok society, and have merely passed unnoticed because they bear no formal designations. Yet this seems unlikely. A rich man is always spoken of as the prominent person of a town, not of a body of people. In the case of a full and dignified marriage, the bond between brothers-in-law seems to be active as well as close. Women certainly identify themselves with their husbands' interests as heartily as with those of their parents and brothers on most occasions. These facts indicate that relationship through females is also regarded by the Yurok; and such being the case, it is impossible for a kin group not to have been sufficiently connected with other kin groups to prevent either being marked off as an integral unit. Then, a "half-married" man must have acted in common with the father-in-law in whose house he lived; and his children in turn would be linked, socially and probably legally, to the grandfather with whom they grew up as well as with their paternal grandfather and his descendant. So, too, it is clear that a married woman's kin as well as her husband retained an interest in her. If the latter beat her, her father had a claim against him. Were she killed, the father as well as the husband would therefore be injured; and there can be little doubt that something of this community of interest and claim would descend to her children. Kinship, accordingly, operated in at least some measure bilaterally and consequently diffusively; so that a definite unit of kinsmen acting as a group capable of constituted social action did not exist.

This attitude can also be justified juridically, if we construe every Yurok as having a reciprocal legal and property interest in every one of his kin, proportionate, of course, to the proximity of the relationship. A has an interest in his kinsmen X, Y, and Z similar to his interest in his own person, and they in him. If A is injured, the claim is his. If he is killed, his interest in himself passes to X, Y, Z—first, or most largely, to his sons, next to his brothers; in their default to his brothers' sons—much as his property interests pass, on his natural death, to the same individuals. The only difference is that the claim of blood is reciprocal, possession of goods or privilege absolute or nearly so.

It may be added that this interpretation of Yurok law fits very nicely the practices prevailing in regard to wife purchase. Here the interest in a person is at least largely ceded by her kinsmen for compensation received.

It is men that hold and press claims and receive damages for women and minors, but only as their natural guardians. The rights of a woman are in no sense curtailed by her sex, nor those of a child by its years; but both are in the hands of adult male trustees. Old women whose nearer male kin have died often have considerable property in their possession. The weakness of their status is merely that they are unable to press their just claims by the threat of force, not that their claim is less than that of a man.

It may be asked how the Yurok executed their law without political authority being in existence. The question is legitimate; but a profounder one is why we insist on thinking of law only as a function of the state when the example of the Yurok, and of many other nations, proves that there is no inherent connection between legal and political institutions. The Yurok procedure is simplicity itself. Each side to an issue presses and resists vigorously, exacts all it can, yields when it has to, continues the controversy when continuance promises to be profitable or settlement is clearly suicidal, and usually ends in compromising more or less. Power, resolution, and wealth give great advantages; justice is not always done; but what people can say otherwise of its practices? The Yurok, like all of us, accept the conditions of their world, physical and social; the individual lives along as best he may; and the institutions go on.

MONEY

The money of the Yurok was dentalium shells. Dentalia occur in California, the species *D. hexagonum* inhabiting the southern coast, and *D. indianorum* perhaps the northern. Both species, however, live in the sand in comparatively deep water, and seem not to have been taken alive by any of the California Indians. The Yurok certainly were not aware of the presence of the mollusk along their ocean shore, and received their supply of the "tusk" shells from the north. They knew of them as coming both along the coast and down the Klamath River. Since the direction of the first of these sources is "downstream" to them, they speak in their traditions of the shells living at the downstream and upstream ends of the world, where strange but enviable peoples live who suck the flesh of the univalves.

Dentalia are known to have been fished by the Indians of Vancouver Island, and were perhaps taken by some tribes farther south; but it is certain that every piece in Yurok possession had traveled many miles, probably hundreds, and passed through a series of mutually unknown nations.

The Yurok grade their shells very exactly according to length, on which alone the value depends. They are kept in strings that reach from the end of an average man's thumb to the point of his shoulder. Successive shells have the butt end in opposite direction so as not to slip into one another. The pieces on one string are as nearly as possible of one size. So far as they vary, they are arranged in order of their length. But shells of sufficiently different size to be designated by distinct names are never strung together, since this would make value reckoning as difficult as if we broke coins into pieces. The length of "strings" was not far from 27½ inches, but of course never exactly the same, since a string contained only an integral number of shells and these, like all organisms, varied. The cord itself measured a yard or more. This allowed the shells to be slid along it and separated for individual measurement without the necessity of unstringing. The sizes and names of the shells are as follows:

Length of shell in inches.	Yurok name of shell.	Hupa name of shell.	Yurok name of string.	Hupa name of string.	Shells to string of 27½ inches.
2½........	Kergerpitl.....	Dingket......	Kohtepis......	Moanatla......	11
2⁵⁄₁₆......	Tego'o.........	Kiketukut-hoi	Na'apis.......	Moananah.....	12
2⅛........	Wega.........	Chwolahit.....	Nahksepitl....	Moanatak.....	13
2—........	Hewiyem.....	Hostanhit	Ta'anepitl.....	Moanadingk...	14
1⅞—......	Merostan......	....	Tsepupitl.....	....	15

The Yurok further distinguish tsewosteu, which is a little shorter than mero-stan, though still money. Possibly tsewosteu was the name of the 15-to-the-string shells, and merostan—sometimes called "young man's money"—denoted a size of which 14½ measured a string. The Yurok further specify the length, both of pieces and of strings, by adding a number of qualifying terms, especially oweyemek and wohpekemek, which denote various degrees of shortness from standard.

Dentalia which go more than 15 or 15½ shells to the string are necklace beads. These come in three sizes, terkutem, skayuperwern, and wetskaku, the latter being the shortest. The value of all these was infinitely less than that of money, and they were strung in fathoms or half-fathoms, the grade being estimated by eye, not measured. Ten half-fathom strings of terkutem were equal to about one 13-string of money; making a rate of an American dollar or less per yard.

The Karok call dentalia ishpuk, the broken bead lengths apmananich. The largest size of money shells is pisiwawa, the next pisiwawa afishni, the third shisharetiropaop.

All sizes of dentalia have depreciated since first contact with the whites, so that valuations given today in terms of American money fluctuate; but the following appear to have been the approximate early ratings, which in recent years have become reduced about one-half:

To string.	Value of shell.	Value of string.
11	$5.00	$50.00
12	2.00	20.00
13	1.00	10.00
14	.50	5.00
15	.25	2.50

From this it is clear that an increase in length of shell sufficient to reduce by one the number of pieces required to fill a standard string about doubled its value.

Dentalia of the largest size were exceedingly scarce. A string of them might now and then be paid for a wife by a man of great prominence; but never two strings. Possession of a pair of such strings was sufficient to make a man well known.

Shells are often but not always incised with fine lines or angles, and frequently slipped into the skin of a minute black and red snake, or wound spirally with strips of this skin. The ends of the cord are usually knotted into a minute tuft of scarlet woodpecker down. All these little devices evince the loving attention with which this money was handled but do not enhance its value.

As might be expected, the value of dentalia was greater in California than among the northern tribes at the source of supply. In Washington or northern Oregon, as among the Yurok, a slave was rated at a string; but the northern string was a fathom long. Among the Nutka, money was still cheaper: it took 5 fathoms of it to buy a slave.

The size of the shells used in the north has, however, not been accurately determined. For the Oregon-Washington region, 40 shells were reckoned to the fathom, which gives an individual length averaging at the lowest limit of what the Yurok accepted as money, or even a little less. In British Columbia it is stated that 25 pieces must stretch a fathom. This would yield an average of considerably over 2½ inches, or more than the very longest shells known to the Yurok. It may be added that the fathom measure was in constant use among the Yurok for almost everything but money.

The actual valuing of dentalia was individual or in groups of fives, the length of men's arms being too variable and the size of shells too irregular to permit of exact appraisals by treating a string as a unit. The shells on a cord were therefore turned over and matched against each other, and then laid against the fingers from crease to crease of the joints. The largest size was gauged from the farther crease of the little finger to the fold in the palm below; according to some accounts, the measure was also taken on the index. Other sizes were matched against the middle finger. A shell from a full 13-piece string was supposed to extend precisely from the base of this finger to the last crease and was called wetlemek wega. A 12-to-the-string shell, of course, passed beyond.

Measurement was also by fives, from the end of the thumbnail to a series of lines tattooed across the forearm. These indelible marks were made from fives of known value, and served as a standard not dependent on bodily peculiarities.

The generic Yurok name for dentalium is tsik. Since the coming of the whites it has also been known as otl we-tsik, "human beings their dentalium," that is, "Indian money," in distinction from American coins. The early settlers corrupted this to "allicocheek," used the term to the Indians, and then came to believe that it was a native designation common to all the diverse languages of the region.

Dentalium is frequently personified by the Yurok. Pelin-tsiek, "Great Dentalium," enters frequently into their myths as if he were a man, and in some versions is almost a creator. Tego'o is also a character in legend.

All other shells were insignificant beside dentalia in Yurok consideration. Olivellas were strung and used for ornament, but did not rate as currency. Haliotis, which seems to have been imported from the coast to the south of Cape Mendocino, was liberally used on the fringe of Yurok women's dresses, on ear pendants, in the inlay of pipes, and the like. But it also never became money and did not nearly attain the value of good dentalia. Now and then a short length of disk beads from central California penetrated to the Yurok, but as a prized variety rather than an article of value.

A myth, told, it may be noted, by a Coast Yurok of Eshpeu married at Orekw, narrates how the dentalia journeyed by the shore from the north. At the mouth of the Klamath the small shells went south along the coast, but Pelintsiek and Tego'o continued up the river. At Ho'opeu and Serper Tego'o wished to enter, at Turip his larger companion; but in each case the other refused. At Ko'otep and Shreggon they went in. Pekwan they did not enter, but said that it would contain money. Nohtsku'm and Meta they passed by. At Murekw they entered, as at Sa'a and Wa'asei, and left money. At Kenek, Pelintsiek wished to leave money, but apparently did not do so. At Wahsekw and again at Weitspus they went in and left three shells. At Pekwututl also they entered, and there the story ends with Pelintsiek's saying that some money must continue upstream [to the Karok] and up the Trinity to the Hupa. The tale records the Yurok idea as to the situation of wealth; it illustrates their interest in money; and although a somewhat extreme example, is a characteristic representation of their peculiar mythology, with its minimum of plot interest, intense localization, and rationalizing accounting of particular human institutions.

TREASURE

Of articles other than shells, those that approach nearest to the character of money are woodpecker scalps. These are of two sizes, both of them scarlet and beautifully soft: those from the larger bird are slightly more brilliant. The two kinds of scalp are known as *kokoneu* (Karok: furah) and *terker'it*. The former are rated at $1 to $1.50 each, the latter variously at 10, 15, and 25 cents. The native ratio seems to have been 6 to 1. Woodpecker scalps differ from dentalia in that they have value as material, being worked into magnificent dance headdresses, and used as trimming on other regalia. They represent the Yurok idea of the acme of splendor. Dentalium currency is never worn or exhibited in display, and being entirely without intrinsic utility or ornamental possibility, is wholly and purely money.

Deerskins of rare colors and large blades of obsidian and flint possessed high values; in fact, all objects carried in dances represented wealth. But these articles varied so greatly according to color, size, fineness, or workmanship, that their civilized equivalents are jewels rather than money. At the same time, there was a strong tendency, as can be seen from the examples below, to make part of every payment of consequence in a variety of articles. When large sums changed ownership, as in the purchase of a high-class wife or settlement for the death of a rich man, not more than about half the total seems to have been in dentalia. In the same way strings paid over were of graduated sizes, not all of one value. These facts indicate that a proper variety and balance of wealth as well as quantity were desirable.

Even a common deerskin represented value when prepared for dance use. Besides the hide, there was the labor of stuffing the head, and woodpecker scalps were needed for eyes, ears, throat, and tongue. An unusually light or dark skin was worth more, and those that the Yurok call "gray" and "black" and "red" are estimated at $50 to $100. A pure albino skin, with transparent hoofs, is rated at $250 to $500. But this is a theoretic valuation given for the sake of comparison. The Yurok state that fine white skins did not change ownership. Their possession was known far and wide and to part with one on any consideration would have been equivalent to a king selling his crown.

Similarly with obsidians. The usual statement that these are worth $1 an inch of length is true for blades of half a foot to a foot. A 20-inch piece, however, would be held at about $50, and the few renowned giants that reach 30 and even 33 inches are, from the native point of view, inestimable. The above applies to black obsidian. The red, which is rarer and does not come in as large pieces, is worth considerably more. Most valuable of all are the blades of white flint, which can not be chipped quite as evenly as the obsidian, but can be worked broader and somewhat thinner. The largest of these run to about a foot and a half long.

VALUATIONS

The following are some Yurok valuations, apparently on the modern basis of a 12-dentalium string being worth 10 American dollars:

A large boat, that is, a capacious one—the length is uniform—was worth two 12-strings, one full and one short; or 10 large or 60 small woodpecker scalps.

A small boat: One 13-string or 3 large woodpecker heads.

A very small boat carrying two men: Five shells from a 13-string.

The Karok put a boat at two strings of small shells.

A blanket of two deerskins sewn together and painted is said to have been worth a small boat. This seems a high valuation; but the Karok say, 4 to 10 medium or short dentalia or a whole string of small ones, if the skins are ample.

A quiver of otter or fisher fur, with bow and 40 arrows, was the equivalent of a good-sized boat. The Karok reckon an otter skin worth 4 to 7 dentalia.

An entire eagle skin—the birds were shot with the bow at a bait of deer meat on mountain tops—was worth only one shell of smallest size.

A woman's capful of tobacco, one small shell.

A house, 3 strings.

A well-conditioned house of redwood planks, 5 strings.

A fishing place, 1 to 3 strings. Two instances are known of Karok fishing rights having been sold for $5. The value must have been very variable.

A tract bearing acorns, 1 to 5 strings.

The meat from a "small" section—perhaps a half fathom—of a whale, 1 string, presumably of short shells.

A "black," "red," or mottled deer skin, dressed for dance use, 5 strings.

A light gray skin, 6 strings.

A white skin, 10 strings.

Obsidian or flint blades, 2 to 10 strings.

A headband, sraisplegok, of 50 large woodpecker scalps, 10 strings. This seems too high a rating in comparison with the others. Small shells must be meant.

Doctors' fees were high: $10 to $20—that is, 1 to 2 strings of good money—are specified as the cost of a treatment.

A slave was rated at only 1 or 2 strings. Evidently the Yurok did not know how to exact full value from the labor of their bondsmen, not because the latter could not be held to work, but because industry was too little organized.

For a wife from a wealthy family 10 strings seem to have been expected, made up, perhaps, of one of 11 shells, one of 12, two of 12 short, and so on, with perhaps a headband of 50 woodpecker scalps, an obsidian, a boat, etc. One Yurok boasted of having paid 14 strings for his wife, plus as much more in other property, including two headbands, the whole representing $300 American at the lower valuation here followed.

For a poorer girl 8 strings and a boat might be given.

The Karok say that a wife was worth 5 to 10 strings. Among both tribes, therefore, a man's life came somewhat higher than what he would pay for a bride of his own rank; which rating, seeing that her relatives did not have to mourn her, is rather favorable to the woman.

For "half-marriage" the price actually paid seems to have been rather less than half.

For the killing of a man of standing the cost was 15 strings, plus, perhaps, a red obsidian, a woodpecker scalp headband, and other property, besides a daughter. The Karok also quote a man's price at 15 strings.

A common man was worth 10 strings, probably of somewhat shorter dentalia, plus, perhaps, 20 large scalps and a good boat.

For a bastard 5 to 6 strings, presumably of small shells, and a few loose woodpecker scalps, are mentioned as usual blood money.

Seduction and pregnancy were rated as calling for 5 strings, or perhaps 20 woodpecker scalps. For a second child the compensation would be less, about 3 strings. The Karok say 2 to 3 strings for seduction, but 4 to 7 if the father took his illegitimate child.

Adultery came at about the same figure.

Uttering the name of a dead man called for the payment of about 2 strings of 13 shells. For a rich man 3 strings of somewhat better money might be demanded.

For breaking a mourning necklace, whether by accident or in play, three or four pieces of money were given.

BLOOD MONEY

The principles of weregild are sufficiently clear from what has been said; an instance or two may be worth adding.

An American at Rekwoi engaged a number of Indians to transport stores from Crescent City. In the surf and rocks at the dangerous entrance to the Klamath a canoe was lost and four natives drowned. Compensation was of course demanded; when it was not forthcoming, the American was ambushed and killed by the brother of one of the dead men. According to one version, the goods were Government property, and the trader responsible only for their transport. The Indians' claims are said to have been forwarded to the Government, but while officials pondered or refused, the Indians, losing hope of a settlement, fell back on the revenge which alone remained to them.

In a Karok myth dealing with the establishment of institutions, it is said in so many words that "if they kill and do not pay, fighting will be perpetual. If a woman is not paid for, there will be bad repute; but if she is bought, everyone will know that so much was given for her, and she will have a good name."

A Yurok myth, which tells of five brothers who made the sky, instituted money and property, and provided for purification from corpse contamination, has them say: "If human beings own money and valuables they will be pleased and think of them. They will not be vindictive; and they will not kill readily, because they will not wish to pay away what they have and prize."

MARRIAGE LAWS

In marriage the rank of husband and wife and children depended on the amount paid for the woman. People's social status was determined not only by what they possessed, but by what had been given by their fathers for their mothers. Men of wealth made a point of paying large sums for their brides. They thereby enhanced their own standing and insured that of their children. A young man of repute preserved the tradition of his lineage and honored the person and family of his wife in proportion as he paid liberally for her. A poor man was despised not only for his lack of substance, but for the little that he gave for the mother of his children, and for the mean circumstances surrounding his own origin. A bastard was one whose birth had never been properly paid for, and he stood at the bottom of the social scale.

How far the wishes of girls were consulted it is difficult to say, but marriages in which they were unwilling partners are spoken of. We are likely to think in such cases of mercenary fathers intent on profit, when perhaps the main motive in the parents' minds was an honorable alliance and a secure and distinguished career for the daughter.

"Half-marriage" was not rare. The bridegroom paid what he could and worked out a reasonable balance in services to his father-in-law. Of course he lived in the old man's house and was dependent on him for some years, whereas the full-married man took his wife home at once—in fact had her brought to him. It is not certain how often half-marriage was the result of deliberate negotiations, and how frequently a device for decently patching up a love affair.

In a full marriage the groom was represented by two intermediaries, kinsmen, and the price was very exactly specified and carefully considered. A young man rarely possessed sufficient property in his own right, and received the purchase money from his father, or from the latter and his brothers. This was not a formal loan, the blood feeling being very strong among the Yurok. When the bride arrived, at least among the well bred, a considerable amount of property accompanied her. Ten baskets of dentalia, otter skins, and other compact valuables, a canoe or two, and several deerskin blankets seem to have passed in this way among the wealthy, without any previous bargaining or specification. In this way a rich father voluntarily returned part of the payment made him, the Yurok say. However, on a divorce taking place, these gifts must be returned as fully as the stipulated purchase price.

Sometimes two men traded their sisters to each other for wives; but in such case each nevertheless paid to the other the full amount of money, as if a single purchase were being transacted. In short, the formality of payment was indispensable to a marriage.

On the death of the father of a household, his sons would be entitled to the price received when their sisters were married. In default of sons, the dead man's brothers arranged the marriage of their nieces and received the pay for them. A man sometimes gave to his son part of the money he received at his daughter's wedding, or used the whole of it to buy his son a wife.

Pressing debt sometimes led to betrothal. An infant daughter might be sold to another man for his little boy, the children perhaps remaining in ignorance of their relation. As soon as the girl had passed her adolescence the marriage was consummated.

Sometimes an arrangement was entered into by which a youth received the sister of a sick or crippled man in return for labor or services rendered him.

Divorce was by wish of either party, and entailed only complete repayment. A woman could leave her husband at will, provided her kin were ready to refund; though this was not their usual disposition unless she had been abused. A man, it seems, was not expected to divorce his wife without cause, such as laziness. Probably if a reasonable allegation could not be produced, the woman's relatives would refuse to repay him, in which case the divorce, while still thoroughly open to him, would be an absurd loss.

An implied condition of purchase of a wife was that she bear children. Sterility therefore meant nonfulfillment of contract, and was perhaps the most frequent cause of divorce. If a couple with children separated, the woman could take them with her only on full repayment of her original price. On the other hand, each child left with the husband reduced the repayment, and several canceled it altogether. Theoretically, therefore, the average middle-aged or elderly woman with adult children was free to return to her parents' house, and remained with her husband from choice alone. This privilege is clear, but the Yurok do not seem to formulate it, perhaps because its exercise was not a normal occurrence.

Similarly, it might be inferred that a wife was bought for a natural span of life. If she died young a sister or kinswoman was due the husband. If he passed away first his equity did not lapse but remained in the family, and she was married by his brother. In either event, however, a payment, smaller than the original one, was made to her family. In case of the wife's death this might be interpreted as due to a desire to distribute the loss between the two families involved, since the furnishing of a marriageable and therefore valuable substitute, perhaps repeatedly, wholly gratis, would work hardship on the woman's kin. The payment by the dead man's brother, however, can not well be understood except on the basis that the woman's family retained an interest in her after her marriage. A more likely interpretation of both cases is that the Yurok did not operate on principles so legalistically defined, but held to a generic notion that no union could take place without a payment. The amount given appears to have been nearly half of the original price, although the Indians customarily speak of it as "a little."

It is said that even when a married woman of some age died her kinsmen were required to provide a substitute or repay her original purchase price unless she had borne three or four children. If she had had only one or two children, partial repayment was due.

It may be added that a full year elapsed before the widow's remarriage to her brother-in-law. During this time she kept her hair very short, did not go about much, cried considerably, lived on in her dead husband's house, and kept his property together.

The levirate, as it is called, and the corresponding custom of marrying the sister of the dead or living wife were universal in California, although among many tribes payment for the wife was slight or nominal and among some lacking. The particular legal ideas which the Yurok have connected with these customs can therefore not be regarded as causative of the customs. Historically it is extremely probable that priority must be granted to the levirate, the Yurok merely investing this with the economic considerations that shaped all their life. The foregoing interpretations of Yurok marriage laws must accordingly be construed only as an attempt to make precise a point of view, not as a genetic explanation. Ethnologically, the significance of the group of tribes represented by the Yurok lies largely in the fact that whereas their practices, when compared with those of the bulk of the Indians of California, are obviously closely similar at most points, or at least parallel, they nevertheless possess a distinctive aspect and value throughout.

If a man was jealous and beat his wife without due cause she was likely to return to her parents. Sometimes her father would then dissolve the marriage by returning the purchase price. Her maltreatment did not of itself nullify the marriage transaction. But it did cause a claim for liability, and her relatives seem to have been entitled to keep the woman until her husband had paid them damages for his abuse of her, whereupon he resumed full jurisdiction over her. This provision appeals to us perhaps primarily as one of humanity. Juridically it is of interest as indicating that a woman's kin retained a legal interest in her. Unfortunately we do not know how blood money for a married woman was distributed. It may be suspected that its amount was somewhat greater than her marriage price, the excess going to her relatives.

A curious practice was followed in the Wohtek Deerskin dance following the Kepel fish dam. Before this was finished on the hill at Plohkseu, they danced downstream from Wohkero at Helega'au. Here the old men made men tell what their fathers had paid for their mothers. Those of moderate ancestry were permitted to dance; the rich-born and the illegitimate were both excluded.

A Karok woman born at Ashipak about the time the Americans came had relatives among the Yurok of Rekwoi, the Hupa, and the Shasta. Her grandfather had had wives in or from five different places. For some of these he had paid only partially, the agreement being that the children should remain in the mother's house. It is likely that this is a case of a wealthy man's love affairs legalized after pregnancy set in, rather than of formally proposed marriage; and that the payments made, and the status of the father, were sufficient to remove serious stigma.

Adultery was of course paid for to the husband. From one to five strings are mentioned as the fine.

Constructive adultery also constituted an injury. Speech or communication between a woman and a former lover made the latter liable. If he met her on the trail he might have to pay a medium-sized string. If he came into a house in which she sat the husband was likely to charge that the visit was intentional, and on pressing his claim might succeed in obtaining double compensation.

Two reasons are given for the payment for seduction. A woman's first bearing is hard and she might die; also, her price to her future husband is spoiled; that is, reduced.

DEBT SLAVERY

Slavery was a recognized institution but scarcely an important one. The proportion of slave population was small, probably not over one-twentieth, certainly not over a tenth. One Yurok man had three slaves, but he was exceptionally rich, and may not have owned them simultaneously. Slaves entered their condition solely through debt, never through violence. Men were not taken prisoners in war, and women and children were invariably restored when settlement was made; solitary strangers that elsewhere might have been oppressed were suspected and killed by the Yurok. Debt arose from legal rather than economic vicissitudes, Yurok industry and finance being insufficiently developed for a man to fall gradually into arrears from lack of subsistence or excessive borrowing. The usual cause was an act of physical violence or destruction of property; striking a rich man's son, for instance, or speaking the name of a dead person of wealth. Slaves made string and nets, fished, and performed similar work. They were not killed in display of wealth, as farther north on the coast, the Yurok seeing no sense in the destruction of property except when carried away by spite. Slaves, however, were full property. An owner might buy his slave a wife to keep him contented; the children then belonged to the master. The institution seems to have been unknown in California except for the advanced northwestern tribes.

It appears that female relatives paid in blood settlement by poor people became slaves or of kindred status. It is said that if the man to whom such a woman was handed over wished to marry her, or to give her in marriage to a kinsman, he paid a small amount to her family. This indicates that the law accorded him a right to her services, not to her person, and the former was the only right in her which he could transfer on sale.

A bastard, in burning over a hillside, once set fire to certain valuables which a rich man of Sregon had concealed in the vicinity. He was unable to compensate and became the other's slave. Subsequently the Sregonite killed a Tolowa, and transferred the slave as part of the blood money. This was long after the American was in the land; but the slave knew that if he attempted to avail himself of the protection of the white man's law, he would be liable under the native code and probably ambushed and killed by his master. He therefore arranged with him to purchase his liberty, apparently with money earned by services to Americans.

The Yurok state that their slaves did not attempt to run off. A slave might evade a new master; in which case his old proprietor would be appealed to and would threaten him with instant death if he did not return to the service of his new owner. It must be remembered that enslavement of foreigners was not practiced. Among his own or known people, public sentiment would support the master and not the slave. If the latter fled to aliens, his status would at best remain the same, his condition would certainly be worse, and he was likely to be killed at once as an unprotected and unwelcome stranger.

Payment for a murdered slave was, of course, due his master, not his kinsmen. A rich owner would receive a high settlement. It is the old story of values being determined not only intrinsically but according to the value borne by the owner or claimant.

FISHING PRIVILEGES

If several men jointly owned a fishing place, which seems to have been the case with nearly all the most prolific eddies, they used it in rotation for one or more days according to their share, relieving each other about the middle of the afternoon for twenty-four-hour periods. Thus a famous Karok spot called Ishkeishahachip, formerly on the north side of the river at the foot of the Ashanamkarak fall, but subsequently obliterated or spoiled by the river, belonged for one day to an Ashanamkarak man; for one to a man from Ishipishi, a mile above; for one to the head man of the village opposite Orleans, a dozen miles downstream; and for two days to the rich man of the village at Red Cap Creek, still farther below. A successful fisherman usually gave liberally of his catch to all comers, so that it is no wonder that the Yurok have a fondness for stopping to chat with a fisherman whom they are passing. If a man allowed another to fish at his place, he received the bulk of the catch. If only one salmon was taken, the "tenant" kept merely the tail end.

A fishing place near Wahsekw was originally owned by two Weitspus men who were not kinsmen, or at any rate not closely related. One of them dying, his share passed to his son, who sold it to a Wahsekw man for $5 in American money. The new part owner also possessed a place at which he was entitled to put up a platform a short distance below.

It was forbidden to establish a new fishing place or to fish below a recognized one. This provision guaranteed the maintenance of the value of those in existence, and must have very closely restricted the total number to those established by tradition and inheritance.

If one man used another's fishing place, even without explicit permission of the owner, and fell and slipped there and cut his leg or was bruised, he would at once lay claim to the fishing place as damages. People would say to the owner: "It was your place and he was hurt; you should pay him."

Perhaps a compromise would be effected on the basis of the plaintiff receiving a half interest in the privilege of the spot.

OWNERSHIP OF LAND

Up to a mile or more from the river, all land of any value for hunting was privately owned; back of this, there were no claims, nor was there much hunting. It may be that deer were scarce away from the river; but more likely, the private tracts in the aggregate represented accessibility and convenience to the game rather than exhaustive control of its total supply. It may be added that the Yurok country, being well timbered, was poor in small game, deer and elk being the principal objects of the chase. Rich men often held three or four inherited tracts, poor people perhaps a single one, others none. Poachers were shot. A small creek near Weitspus is named Otl-amo, "person caught," because, according to tradition, a poacher was there taken in a deer snare. A wounded animal could be pursued anywhere. It belonged to the hunter, and the owner of the tract in which it fell had no claim upon it.

Certain prairies on the Bald Hills, valuable for seed gathering, belonged to Weitspus and Wahsekw families, who had bought them from the Chilula.

A Weitspus man who had killed a fellow resident of that village fled to the Coast Yurok, bought himself a small stream that flowed into the ocean not far from Osagon Creek, and made his home there. This case is doubly illuminating. It shows the personal heterogeneity of the larger villages, and demonstrates that land was bought and sold for abode and asylum—a rather unusual feature in American Indian society.

The ownership of house sites is discussed elsewhere.

LAW OF FERRIAGE

Free ferriage must at all times be rendered. At least in theory it is extended also to those who can not reciprocate because of being boatless or in chronic poverty. The underlying assumption of this custom seems to be that ferriage is a primal necessity to which everyone is at times subject and which everyone is also at times in position to relieve. The traveler accordingly has much the status which a guest enjoys as regards food, but his claims are crystallized into a definite privilege. The Yurok and their neighbors extend the right also to Americans resident among them, charging ferriage only to transient voyagers. In the old days even an enemy with whom one did not speak had to be taken as passenger. Such a man on arriving opposite a village shouted. If no one was about but the one who bore him a grudge, the latter nevertheless paddled over. The traveler sat in the boat with his back to the steersman, keeping silence. For a refusal to accord ferriage from three to six short dentalia could be claimed. If a traveler finds a settlement deserted, he takes any boat at the river's edge and puts himself across, without the least care or obligation as to its return.

The carrier being his passenger's agent, the latter becomes liable for any injury to him. A Yurok of Kenek had his house catch fire while ferrying an acquaintance. The latter was due to repay his entire loss: except for the service rendered the owner would have been at hand and might have extinguished the blaze, the Yurok said.

LEGAL STATUS OF THE SHAMAN

Shaman's fees for the treatment of disease were very high, as the examples previously given indicate. Shamans are said to have frequently urged their female relatives to try to acquire "pains"—shamanistic powers—because wealth was easily got thereby. The rule was for payment to be tendered with the invitation to cure. Usually some negotiation followed. The doctor held out for more; but being legally obliged to go was apt to plead indisposition or illness of her own. The offer was then increased, the pay being actually shown, it appears, and, reaching a satisfactory figure, was accepted, and the shaman went on her visit. Acceptance, however, implied cure, and if this was not attained the entire amount must be returned to the patient or his relatives. This was the old law; but the Karok state that American physicians' example has in recent years caused the practice to spring up of the shaman retaining a small part of her fee as compensation for her time and trouble.

Usually the patient felt improved and the doctor returned claiming a cure. If a relapse followed, she was summoned and came again, receiving a small fee. In strict logic, she should have served for nothing, the patient not having received the complete cure that was tacitly contracted for; but a new effort being involved, there seems to have been some concession to this. The principle is analogous to that which compels a widower to pay a small sum for his second wife, who replaces the first. It is as if the law recognized the equity of partially distributing the loss in cases that are in their nature beyond human agency. This is a mitigating influence that contrasts rather strangely and somewhat pleasingly with the remorseless rigor of the main tenor of Yurok law.

It is a common belief of the Yurok that some shamans would extract one of the pains from a sick person, thus effecting a temporary improvement in his condition, but deliberately leave another within him, in order to be paid for a second treatment. Other shamans sometimes accused them of such malpractice, declaring they could see the remaining pain. It is very characteristic that the Yurok and their northwestern neighbors think in such cases of the shaman's motives as greed, the other California Indians almost invariably as malice.

It is in accord with this diversity of point of view that one scarcely hears among the Yurok of shamans being killed for losing patients, one of the commonest of events elsewhere in California.

On the other hand, the law-spinning inclination of the Yurok is manifest in their absolute rule that a shaman who had declined to visit a patient was liable, in the event of his death, even after treatment by another shaman, for the full fee tendered her, or even a little more. Only a conflicting case, or genuine sickness of the shaman herself, was ground for an attempt on the shaman's part to evade this liability. The argument was that if the fee had been accepted and treatment extended, the sick person might not have died. Hence the liability was complete up to the amount which the patient's family were ready to offer in his behalf. A Karok shaman who had attained some reputation by once appearing to die and then returning to tell of her experiences in the other world, subsequently laid herself open to a claim for not attending a sick person and refused to settle it. The kinsmen of her prospective but deceased patient thereupon waylaid her in the brush and choked her to death. Many a central and south California doctor has met this fate: but his supposed misconduct was intent to kill, as evidenced by failure to cure. The northwesterners took satisfaction because a claim for damages was not met.

It is said that people were bewitched not only by shamans hungering for fees and by avowed foes, but sometimes by mere enviers, who hoped to see a rich man's wealth gradually pass from him to his physicians.

A Karok of Katimin began to suffer with headache, and accused a woman of having bewitched him. Doubtless there was ill feeling between them. He formally voiced his complaint to her brother. The family conferred and offered him three strings as damages. He refused the amount as insufficient, and they, feeling that a sincere effort at reparation had been slighted, announced that they would henceforth be inivashan, enemies. Since that time the families have not spoken.

MOURNERS' RIGHTS

As long as a corpse remained unburied, no one was allowed to pass the village in a boat. If a traveler attempted to go on, the kin of the dead person would lay hold of his canoe. If he succeeded nevertheless, he incurred liability to them. The motive of the prohibition seems to have been that it was a slight to mourners if others transacted ordinary business in their sight or vicinity.

It is, however, specifically stated that this statute did not apply if the dead person had been killed by violence. Similarly those slain were not included among the dead of the year whose kin must be paid before a village could undertake a dance. The reason is clear: if there is a killing, the mourners have been or will be paid, and no further compensation is necessary; while those who grieve for a relative dead from natural causes are enduring an irremediable loss, and their feelings must be assuaged.

If a man died away from home his body might be taken back or buried on the spot. In the latter case the right to interment was purchased. Once payment had been accepted for this privilege, subsequent protest at the inclusion of a stranger's body in a family graveyard subjected the critic to liability for a claim for damages.

Before a major dance could be held, the dead of the year had to be paid for. This was done by contributions of the residents of the village, or by the rich man of the locality. If a village did not hold a dance, the law nevertheless applied, no residents being entitled to visit a ceremony elsewhere until the home mourners were satisfied. This is an extremely characteristic Yurok provision. The dances were held by them to be absolutely necessary to the prosperity and preservation of the world: still, because they afforded entertainment and pleasure to those who assembled, the mourners resented the occasion, and prevented it, until tendered pay for the violation of their grief. In short, a private right is not in the least impaired by coming into conflict with a communal or universal necessity. Since the ceremony is desirable, let those interested in it extinguish the personal claim, rather than have the holder of the latter suffer, would be the Yurok point of view. To us, the legal sanctioning of the obtrusion of a private interest in the face of a general need seems monstrous. The native probably feels that the mourners are extremely reasonable in allowing the dance to be held at all, and that in proportion to the necessity thereof the community ought to be ready to make sacrifices. This is anarchy; but the Yurok are an anarchic people.

Before the Weitspus dance of 1901, four families were paid $2 each. The compensation thus amounts to only a very small percentage of the value of a man's life. The rich man of Pekwututl, across the river, demanded and received $3 because he was rich. Having the money in his possession, he demanded a second payment of like amount for a relative he had lost at Hupa. The Weitspus people demurred on the ground that he would be paid for this death by the

Hupa when they held their dance at Takimitlding; but he stood firm and received what he asked.

If a village did not make or visit a dance for a year the mourners' claim lapsed totally. There was the same limit to the prohibition against uttering a dead person's name.

According to a Karok informant the dead of the year were paid for by the rich men so far as the dead were relatives of those who contributed dance regalia, whereas even fellow townsmen who were too poor to help, or had been unwilling, were passed over.

The Yurok declare that the minor "brush dance" was not preceded by payments formerly, but that of late years small compensations have been exacted. The Hupa, they state, pay more heavily for the privilege of making this dance. The difference in custom may be due to an earlier abandonment of the great dances by the reservation Hupa, whereby the brush dance was exalted to a more significant position. But it seems more in accord with the spirit of Yurok institutions that the brush dance should also have been permitted only after compensation; mourners particularly resent hearing singing. The pay is, however, likely to have been small at all times, since the brush dance was instituted by an individual, who was at considerable expense apart from purchasing the privilege.

Compensation for utterances of the name of the dead went, of course, to the immediate kin—father, brother, or son. A brother might give part to the widow; but she acted only as custodian of her dead husband's wealth, and was herself still the property of his family, unless she had borne a number of surviving children. If it was she that was dead, payment is said to have gone to her husband, not to her kin. The Yurok state that the amount of compensation depended solely on the rank of the deceased; age or sex were not factors. After the name was bestowed on a child of the family, a year having elapsed, the taboo was of course thereby lifted. This makes it clear that the conscious motive of the custom is respect for the mourners' grief for a due season. If two men had the same name, the poorer, on the death of the richer, would "throw his away," so as to avoid occasion of giving offense. If the wealthy man was the survivor, he would pay his namesake's family, perhaps as much as five strings, satisfy them, and retain his name.

INHERITANCE

Only a small amount of property was buried with the dead, and none of this of great value. The bulk of the estate went to a man's sons, but the daughters received a share and something was given to all the nearer relatives—at least on the male side—or they would be angry. The kinsman who actually interred the corpse—or rather, the one who assumed defilement on behalf of the others—made a particular claim; no doubt for the restrictions to which his contamination subjected him. Moreover, if there was no one in the family who knew a formula for purification from a corpse, it was necessary for this voluntary scapegoat to hire some one to recite on his behalf; and the fee for this service was high. It is said that poor men were sometimes compelled to give one of their children into slavery in payment for this indispensable release from the excommunicating taboo.

For the building of a house, kinsmen were called upon. They were fed but not paid while they labored; and of course could expect reciprocation. If one of them possessed planks already cut, he furnished them, to be replaced at subsequent convenience. The house was inherited by the son. The brother is said to have received it only if there were neither adult sons nor daughters.

An old and sick Karok woman allowed her half-breed daughter to take possession of her property. Thereupon the sister with whom she lived at Kenek, no doubt in disappointed spite, said to her: "You have nothing. I do not want you," and the decrepit woman went to a more charitable relative at Rekwoi to end her few days.

RICH AND POOR

The Yurok are well aware of the difference in manners and character between rich and poor in their society. A well-brought-up man asked to step into a house sits with folded arms, they say, and talks little, chiefly in answers. If he is given food, he becomes conversational, to show that he is not famished, and eats very slowly. Should he gobble his meal and arise to go, his host would laugh and say to his children: "That is how I constantly tell you not to behave." If an obscure person commits a breach of etiquette, a well-to-do man passes the error with the remark that he comes from poor people and can not know how to conduct himself. Such a wealthy man exhorts his sons to accost visitors in a quiet and friendly manner and invite them to their house; thus they will have friends. A poor man, on the other hand, instructs his son not in policy but in means to acquire strength. He tells him where to bathe at night; then a being will draw him under the water and speak to him, and he will come away with powerful physique and courage.

Life was evidently so regulated that there was little opportunity for any one to improve his wealth and station in society materially.

The poor, therefore, accepted more or less gracefully the patronage of a man of means, or attempted to win for themselves a position of some kind not dependent on property. A savage temper, and physical prowess to support it, were perhaps the only avenue open in this direction; shamans were women, and priests those who had inherited knowledge of formulas.

The rich man is called si'atleu, or simply pegerk, "man." Similarly, a wealthy or "real" woman is a wentsauks or "woman." A poor person is wa'asoi. A slave is called uka'atl. A bastard is called either kamuks, or negenits, "mouse," because of his parasitic habits. Uwohpewek means "he is married"; winohpewek, "he is half-married."

Even a small village group was known as pegarhkes, "manly," if its members were determined, resentful, and wealthy enough to afford to take revenge.

The following Yurok statement is characteristic: "The beautiful skins or headdresses or obsidians displayed at a dance by one rich man excite the interest and envy of visitors of wealth, whereas poor men take notice but are not stirred. Such wealthy spectators return home determined to exhibit an even greater value of property the next year. Their effort, in turn, incites the first man to outdo all his competitors."

The Karok speak of a branching of the trail traversed by the dead. One path is followed by "poor men, who have no providence, and do not help [with regalia, payments, and entertainment] to make the dances." The other is the trail of people of worth.

When an honored guest was taken into the sweathouse he was assigned the tepolatl, the place of distinction, and the host offered him his own pipe. A common man was told to lie at legai, by the door, or nergernertl, opposite it. A bastard who entered was ordered out, the Yurok say. It is likely, however, that such unfortunates were more tolerantly treated by their maternal grandfather and uncles.

Food was sometimes sold by the Yurok: but no well-to-do man was guilty of the practice. "May he do it, he is half poor—tmenemi wa'asoi" would be the slighting remark passed; much as we might use the term *nouveau riche* or "climber."

PURSUIT OF WEALTH

The persistence with which the Yurok desire wealth is extraordinary. They are firmly convinced that persistent thinking of money will bring it. Particularly is this believed to be true while one is engaged in any sweathouse occupation. As a man climbs the hill to gather sweathouse wood—always a meritorious practice, in the sense that it tends to bring about fulfillment of wishes—he puts his mind on dentalia. He makes himself see them along the trail, or hanging from fir trees eating the leaves. When he sees a tree that is particularly full of these visioned dentalia, he climbs it to cut its branches just below the top. In the sweathouse he looks until he sees more money shells, perhaps peering in at him through the door. When he goes down to the river he stares into it, and at last may discern a shell as large as a salmon, with gills working like those of a fish. Young men were recommended to undergo these practices for ten days at a time, meanwhile fasting and exerting themselves with the utmost vigor, and not allowing their minds to be diverted by communication with other people, particularly women. They would then become rich in old age.

Direct willing, demanding, or asking of this sort are a large element in all the magic of the Yurok, whatever its purpose. Saying a thing with sufficient intensity and frequency was a means toward bringing it about. They state that at night, or when he was alone, a man often kept calling, "I want to be rich," or "I wish dentalia," perhaps weeping at the same time. The appeal seems to have been general, not to particular or named spirits. Magic is therefore at least as accurate a designation of the practice as prayer. How far the desires were spoken aloud is somewhat uncertain, the usual native words for "saying" and "thinking" something being the same; but it is very probable that the seeker uttered his words at least to himself. The practical efficacy of the custom is unquestionable. The man who constantly forced his mind and will into a state of concentration on money would be likely to allow no opportunity for acquisition to slip past him, no matter how indirect or subtle the opening.

According to a Karok myth, the sweathouse, its restriction to men, and the practice of gathering firewood for it were instituted in order that human beings might acquire and own dentalia.

The Yurok hold a strong conviction that dentalium money and the congress of the sexes stand in a relation of inherent antithesis. This is the reason given for the summer mating season: the shells would leave the house in which conjugal desires were satisfied, and it is too cold and rainy to sleep outdoors in winter. To preserve his money, in other words to prevent his becoming a spendthrift, a man bathes after contact with his wife, and is careful not to depart from the natural positions. Strangely enough, the Yurok have a saying that a man who can exercise his virility ten times in one night will become extraordinarily wealthy; but there are not wanting those who consider this ideal unattainable by modern human beings.

This is a case of typical blending of avarice and magic, as related by the Hupa. The grandchild of the rich man of Medilding had its mouth constantly open. A shaman finally saw and proclaimed the cause. An ancestor of the rich man had asked to kiss a dead friend or relative goodby. He descended into the grave and, bending over the corpse's face, used his lips to draw out from the nose the two dentalia that are inserted through the septum, concealing his booty in his mouth until the grave had been filled. According to report, the rich man admitted that an ancestor of his had actually risked this deed; and the shaman declared that it was the same dentalia that now kept the child's jaws apart.

A man who had borrowed a canoe and wished to buy it might report to the owner that he had broken it; but the possessor was likely to see through the ruse. This is a native instancing of the cupidity which seems to them natural and justifiable.

Gifts were sometimes made by the Yurok, but on a small scale; and while reciprocation of some sort was anticipated, it was generally smaller and could not be enforced. Presents were clearly a rich man's luxury. The host might say to a visitor whose friendship he considered worth strengthening: "You had better return by boat," thereby giving him a canoe. The guest in time would extend his invitation; and the visit would end with his presentation of a string or two of small money, or a quiver full of arrows. As the Yurok say, the first donor had to be satisfied with what he got, because he had given a gift.

MARRIAGE AND THE TOWN

The Yurok married where and whom they pleased, in the home village or outside, within their nation or abroad. The only bar was to kindred; but the kin of persons connected by marriage were not considered kin. The wife's daughter as well as her sister were regarded as suitable partners. The smaller villages were so often composed wholly of the branches of one family that they practiced exogamy of necessity. That such exogamy had not risen to native consciousness as something desirable in itself is shown by numerous endogamous marriages in the larger towns. This point deserves particular consideration because the organization of the Athabascans of the Oregon coast, which seems to have been identical with that of the Yurok, has been misportrayed, simple villages—as ungentile as our country towns—being represented as patrilinear clans, and the mere rule against the marriage of kindred construed as clan exogamy. The subjoined table illustrates the degree of endogamy at one of the larger Yurok towns, Weits-pus, and the following examples the distance to which its inhabitants were ready to go for wives when they pleased.

House 15 belonged to the daughter of the former owner. Her half-married husband is of a Karok father from Katimin and a Yurok woman of Ho'opeu. Kewik of Nohtsku'm half-married into Ertlerger, but quarreled with his wife's family, and, moving across the river with her, built himself house 3 in Weitspus, whose site his grandson still owned. The father of the owner of 9 had two wives: The first a Karok from Ashanamkarak, the second a Tolowa. An old man in 10 traded sisters with a Wahsekw man.

THE CRISES OF LIFE

Births occurred among the Yurok and their neighbors chiefly in spring. This was, of course, not because of any animal-like impulse to rut at a certain season, as has sometimes been imagined, but because of highly specialized ideas of property and magic. The Yurok had made the just psychological observation that men who think much of other matters, especially women, do not often become or remain wealthy. From this they inferred an inherent antipathy between money and things sexual. Since dentalia and valuables were kept in the house, a man never slept there with his wife, as already stated, for fear of becoming poor. The institution of the sweat-house rendered this easily possible. In summer, however, when the cold rains were over, the couple made their bed outdoors; with the result that it seems natural to the Yurok that children should be born in spring. A similar condition has been reported from the far-away Miwok region; but the responsible social circumstances, which were certainly different from those of the Yurok, are unknown.

As a girl's property value was greatly impaired if she bore a child before marriage, and she was subject to abuse from her family and disgrace before the community, abortion was frequently attempted. Hot stones were put on the abdomen, and the fœtus thrown into the river. There is little doubt that parents guarded their girls carefully, but the latter give the impression of having been more inclined to prudence than to virtue for its own sake. Probably habits differed largely according to the rank of the family. Poor girls had much less to lose by an indiscretion.

The prospective mother's wish was to bear a small child. Therefore she worked hard and ate sparingly. Difficulty in labor was thought to be caused by undue size of the child brought on by the mother's eating and sleeping too much.

In most of California women sit in childbirth. For the Hupa the same is reported, but the Yurok woman is said to have lain bracing her feet against an assistant. Her wrists were tied with pack straps to parts of the house frame. When the assistant commanded, she raised herself by these thongs. She must shut her mouth, else the child would not leave her body. Many formulas to assist childbirth were known. The most powerful of these, as their own content relates, were thought to become effective as soon as the reciter entered the house with her herb.

If the child during the first five or six days of its life were to take nourishment from its mother, the Yurok believe that its jaws would become affected and it would soon starve. During this period it is fed only a little water in which hazel or pine nuts have been rubbed, and which looks milky. For about the same number of days, or until the child's navel is healed, the father eats apart, touches no meat or fresh salmon, and drinks thin acorn soup instead of pure water. The mother is under the same restrictions for a longer period: fifty days, or sixty for a stillbirth. She spends this time in a separate hut.

The umbilical cord is severed with a piece of quartz clamped inside a split stick, and is carefully preserved in the house for about a year. When the child is about to be weaned the father takes the shred on a ridge, splits a living fir, inserts the little piece of preciousness, and binds the sapling together again. On his return the baby has its first meal other than milk.

If twins of opposite sexes were born, the Yurok smothered one of the pair, usually the girl. They had a dread of such births, which they explain on the ground that if the twins lived they might be incestuous. Boy twins were believed to quarrel all their lives, but were spared. Once triplets were born at Murekw. There was much excitement and much talk of killing them; but a Deerskin dance was made and warded off the sickness which the portent foreboded.

When a girl becomes mature she is called ukerhtsperek, and sits silent in her home for ten days with her back turned to the central fire pit. She moves as little as possible, and scratches her head only with a bone whittled and incised for the occasion. Once each day she goes to bring in firewood; on her way she looks neither to left nor right, and looks up at no one. The longer she fasts, the more food will she have in her life, it is believed. After four days she may eat, but only at a spot where the roar of the river confounds every other sound. Should she hear even a bird sing, she ceases at once. Each evening she bathes, once the first night, twice the second, and so increasingly until on the eighth she pours the water over herself eight times. The ninth night she bathes ten times; and on the tenth day, with declining day, once, squatting by the river, while the small children of the village, one after the other, wash her back. Her mother or another woman then places ten sticks on the sand and tells her she will bear so many sons, and places ten sticks in a row to represent her daughters. The girl's dress during the ten days is a skirt of shredded maple bark, such as shamans wear during their novitiate.

One in every several hundred Yurok men, on the average, preferred the life and dress of a woman, and was called wergern. This frame of mind, which appears to have a congenital or psychological basis well recognized by the psychiatrist, was not combated, but socially recognized by the Indians of California—in fact, probably by all the tribes of the continent north of Mexico. Only among the advanced peoples of that region did the law frown upon transvestites. The Yurok explanation of the phenomenon is that such males were impelled by the desire to become shamans. This is certainly not true, since men shamans were not unknown. It is a fact, however, that all the wergern seem to have been shamans and esteemed as such—a fact that illuminates the Yurok institution of shamanism. The wergern usually manifested the first symptoms of his proclivities by beginning to weave baskets. Soon he donned women's clothing and pounded acorns.

At death, the corpse is addressed: "Awok, tsutl [alas, goodby], look well and take with you the one who killed you with upunamitl" (a closure or pressing of internal organs produced magically). The body is then painted with soot, and the septum of the nose pierced for insertion of a dentalium shell. Elderberry sticks measure the length for the grave. This is lined with planks. Boards are removed from one side of the house and the body handed by two mourners inside to two outside. No living soul passes through the opening and the corpse does not leave by the door. The earth on which the person has lain in death is thrown away. At the grave the dead body is washed with water containing herbs or roots and then interred with its head downstream. No one in the town eats during the funeral, small children are taken aside, and all who have looked upon the dead bathe. Those of the mourners who have touched the corpse rub themselves with the grapevine with which the body has been lowered into the grave and hand it from one to the other, thereby passing on the contamination to the last one. This man for five days shuns all intercourse with human kind, does no work, sits in a corner of the house with his back turned, drinks no water, eats only thin acorn gruel, nightly makes a fire on the grave to keep his dead kinsman warm, and finally returns to communion with people by undergoing a washing purification of which the cardinal feature is a long formula.

Cemeteries adjoined towns; often lay in their very heart. Large settlements sometimes had two or three graveyards. Each family plot was small, so that in time numbers of bodies came to be buried in one grave. Old bones were always reinterred. At present each plot is neatly fenced with pickets and posts; but the Yurok say that even in the old days their graves were inclosed with boards. The clothing and some of the personal belongings of the dead were set or hung over the grave; but there was no extensive destruction of property, much less any subsequent offerings to fire, as among most California tribes. People dying away from home were, if possible, transported back for interment; or, a grave was purchased for them where they died.

The dead, called so'o or kesamui—the words are used alike for "ghost" and "skeleton"—were thought to go below. The entrance was pointed out at a small tree not far above the river just upstream from Sa'aitl, opposite Turip. The Coast Yurok knew a spot in their own territory, and the Karok made the path of the dead go up the ridge southeastward from the mouth of the Salmon. Underground, the dead Yurok came to a river, across which he was ferried by a Charon in a canoe. Occasionally the boat tipped over. Then the corpse revived on earth. Once the crossing had been accomplished, return was impossible. People killed with weapons went to a separate place in the willows; here they forever shouted and danced the war dance. Contentious and thievish men also remained apart: their place was inferior. A rich, peaceable man, on the other hand, who had constantly planned entertainment for dances, came to the sky. Long ago, a young man once followed his beloved, overtook her at the bank of the river, and in his anger broke the ferryman's boat, it is said. He brought back his bride, and for ten years while the canoe of the lower world was being repaired or rebuilt, no one died on earth.

If a person revived "after having died," a special dance, called wasurawits, was considered necessary to bring him back to human intelligence. This seems to have been a modified form of the brush dance, with similar step and positions, held indoors. Only a few feathers were used. All available dresses heavily fringed with haliotis were shaken to drown the voices of the ghosts which the patient had heard and which were rendering him insane. If he was violent, he was lifted on the drying frame within the house and held by two men; when his strength began to return, he was supported and made to dance to speed his recovery.

Should a person already buried make his way out of the grave, the Yurok believed him a monster, from whose insatiable desire for destruction they could only save themselves by killing him once more; but this was only to be accomplished by striking him with a bowstring!

NAMES

The Yurok avoid addressing each other by name, except sometimes in closest intimacy. It is the height of bad manners to call a person by name, and a Yurok who is so addressed by an American looks shocked. Of course, English names and nicknames do not count. It is not even proper to speak of an absent person by his name before his relatives. All sorts of circumlocution come into use, many of them known to all the Yurok: Ehkwiyer omewimar, "Ehkwiyer its old man"; Meta keryern, "the proud one of Meta"; Ra-hiwoi, "[he has his house] on the side of Ra [a streamlet in Murekw]"; and the like. An old man at Wahsekw was designated by the fact that his house faced upstream. Most of the following names of the women reputed about fifteen years ago the ablest shamans among the Yurok, are of this descriptive type.

At Wahsekw (farthest upstream of the towns mentioned): Petsi-metl (pets, "upstream").

At Sa'a: Sa'-wayo-metl.

At Murekw: Tsmeyowega and Mureku-tsewa.

At Sregon: Was-metl and Pekwisau.

At Wohtek: Kewei.

At Wohkero: Merit-mela (Merip, a town, presumably her birthplace).

At Sta'awin: Kosi-tsewa.

At Espau: Kairepu and O'men-mela (O'men, a town).

At Tsurau: Tsurau-tsewa.

Most of the true personal names of the Yurok are untranslatable in the present knowledge of the language, but may have meanings: Tsinso, Melotso, Ninowo, Penis, Woilo, Tskerker, O'pe'n, Wilets, Kwegetip ("yearling deer"), Petsuslo ("thrown upstream"). Nicknames like Segep ("coyote"), are of course transparent.

As in all California, an absolute taboo is laid on the names of the dead. The violation of this constitutes a mortal offense, voidable only by a considerable payment. We are wont to think of the hardship entailed by such a law on the unwitting and careless; but the Indian, reared since earliest recollection in the shadow of this regulation, makes no mistakes, and when he utters a dead man's name may justly be presumed to do so deliberately. De mortuis nil, the Yurok would paraphrase our saying, and live up to it with even greater emotional vehemence. A namesake drops his name at once. Even words that resemble a name are not used. When Tegis died, the common word tsis, "woodpecker scalps," was not uttered in the hearing of his relatives or by them. Other people, if no tell-tale ill-wishers were about, would be free from such scruple. Whatever may have been the original basis of the custom, it is clear that its force among the Yurok is now more social than religious. They no doubt hold that calling a ghost might bring it, but they hardly entertain such dread about the conversational mention of a dead person.

The name taboo has sometimes been invoked as a contributory explanation of the dialectic diversity of native California. It can not have had much influence. The custom prevails in the Great Basin, throughout whose broad extent no language is spoken but Shoshonean, and that in only three closely similar forms. Moreover, the Yurok, and with them apparently many other tribes of California, formally end the taboo at the end of a year, by bestowing the dead person's name on a younger relative or child of the same sex. A youth abandons his name to assume that of a dead brother, father's brother, or even mother's brother. This may happen to him several times; but after middle life he changes no more. Children remain unnamed until after they can walk; sometimes they are six or seven years old before a kinsman's name becomes vacant. Some sort of designation for them, of course, comes into use, but this appellation is "picked up" for them and not considered their name. The Yurok state that after a year the family that has lost a relative wishes his name to be out of taboo again.

WAR

No distinction of principle existed in the native mind between murder and war. It is rather clear that all so-called wars were only feuds that happened to involve large groups of kinsmen, several such groups, or unrelated fellow townsmen of the original participants. Whoever was not drawn into a war was as careful to remain neutral as in a private quarrel. When settlement came it was made on the sole basis known: all damage was compensated. Every man slain or hurt was paid for according to his value, all captive women and children restored, burned houses were paid for, seized property handed back. It seems that actual payments for the aggregate amounts due were made by each side instead of the lesser value being deducted from the greater and the net difference alone paid. This practice was perhaps necessitated by the fact that Yurok money with all its refinement of measurement was not really standardized in the same sense as our own, no two strings, generally speaking, being of exactly the same value. In any event the greater financial drain bore on the winner. There is no group of tribes in California better developed to enjoy tribute than the Yurok and their neighbors, and none to whom the idea was so utterly foreign. The *vae victis* of civilization might well have been replaced among the Yurok, in a monetary sense at least, by the dictum: "Woe to the victors."

When blood money was offered, the exact length of each string was shown by a rod of the precise dimension. This stick was kept by the payee, and subsequently measured against the row of dentalia. To the ends of the rod were lashed little tabs of buckskin, to make possible its being held between the fingers that clasped the string of shells. This device enabled the precise value of each string to be determined during the period when contact between the principals in conflict, or even handling of the property of one by the other, would have been precarious.

The Yurok took no scalps. They did not trouble to decapitate a fallen foe unless it was to make sure of his death. They held no scalp dance or formal victory celebration. They did have a war dance known as the wertlkerermer, the songs to which are of a lively if not stirring character. This was essentially a dance of settlement. The participants stood in a row, fully armed, with their faces painted black. A bowshot or less away their opponents performed. Before the actual dance took place, the money or property to be paid over by each side was "cooked." It was laid in baskets, held over the fire, blown upon, and sung over, while the party danced about. No doubt a formula was also recited over the money. The purpose of this practice was to insure that if the recipient of the pay continued to harbor thoughts of revenge against the payers, his wishes would recoil upon himself. After this came the war dance proper, performed by each side standing abreast, very much as in the great dances; and finally the payments by each side were actually handed over, provided the reconciliation had not broken up in a battle meanwhile. It seems that the same or a similar dance was also made as a preparation before war parties started out, but this is not certain.

The chief weapon was the bow. In close fighting, a short stone club, spatula shaped and blunt edged, was used for cracking heads. This was called okawaya. Spears were known, it appears, but very little employed. There were no shields, but two types of body armor. One was of thick elk hide, the other a strait jacket of rods wound together with string. Some men preferred not to be encumbered with so stiff a protection. Women are said sometimes to have rushed into a fight and seized men as if to allay the quarrel, but in reality to hold them for their brothers or husbands to smite.

The greatest war of which the Yurok know took place some years before the Americans came into the country, probably about 1830 or 1840. Some Weitspus men who had married Hupa wives were attacked while visiting there. The cause of the grievance has not been recorded. In the course of the resulting feud the Hupa attacked Weitspus. During the fight a woman was killed who was born of a Weitspus father and Rekwoi mother, and who was herself half-married, that is, living at her father's home. Her death angered her relatives at Rekwoi, it is said. At any rate they gathered their forces, to which were added a number of Tolowa. There were 84 altogether, including 6 women to cook for the party. This number shows conclusively that even this war was an affair of families or at most villages. If the Yurok as a whole had mustered against the Hupa they would have been able to assemble nearly ten times as strong. The party traveled toward Hupa by way of Redwood Creek or the hills above it. They journeyed three nights, resting during the day. Early in the morning they waited at Taki-mitlding. The first Hupa who emerged was killed. Then the fight was on. Many of the Hupa fell, the others fled, and the entire village was burned by the victors, who thereupon seized all the canoes and started homeward down the Trinity River. Two of the men had taken young women whom they intended to marry. But at Weitspus, where the party stopped, probably to eat after the morning's work and no doubt to recount its adventures, some people who pitied the girls enabled them to escape. These connivers may have been individuals with Hupa blood affiliations, perhaps even direct relatives of the two women.

About half a year later the Hupa retaliated. They were helped by their kinsmen up toward the south fork of the Trinity and by the Chilula. Nearly 100 of them are said to have gone. They descended by boat, traveling at night and drawing their canoes up into the brush during the day. Rekwoi was attacked and burned much as Takimitlding had been. Those who were not slain had difficulty living through the winter because their stores of food had been destroyed. The Hupa returned as they had come. This fact again indicates the private nature of the quarrel. Canoes must be laboriously poled and in some spots dragged upstream. Had the Yurok been possessed of any national sentiment in the matter, they could have easily mustered several hundred warriors to overwhelm the Hupa while these were occupied with their difficult navigation. As a matter of fact, the Yurok relate, the villages along the Klamath made no attempt to stop the war party. They concluded that scores being now substantially even, a settlement would soon follow. The Hupa indeed sent to ask for a settlement, and this took place, large amounts being paid on each side.

A feud of some note took place between Sregon and Ko'otep. When the leading man of Sregon lost his brother by sickness, he accused an inhabitant of Wohtek or Wohkero of having poisoned him. The suspect was soon killed from ambush. After this a Sregon man was attacked and killed at Ko'otep, which is only a short distance from Wohtek. This act involved the people of Ko'otep, which was at this time a large village. After a time, settlement was proposed, and the two parties met in an open place below Sregon to conclude the negotiations. Each side was ready to make the customary dance, when some one fired a shot. In the fight that resulted, a Meta ally of the Sregon people was killed. The headman of Sregon now went down river with his friends and lay in wait at an overhanging and bushy bank at Serper, where the current takes boats close in shore. When a canoe of his foes came up, he attacked it and killed four of the inmates. The feud went on for some time. Sregon, never a large village, fought, with only some aid from Meta, against Ko'otep, Wohtek, and Pekwan, but lost only 3 men to 10 of their opponents'. The headman at Sregon was sufficiently wealthy, when settlement came, to pay for all the satisfaction he had earned. He once said with reference to his experience in this and other feuds, that open battles often took place without anyone being killed. Somehow men are hard to hit, he philosophized: arrows have a way of flying past a human being when a hunter is sure to strike a deer at the same distance; as modern military handbooks also tell.

A small feud occurred between Meta and Pekwan. A number of families were camped along the river for fishing, when a man from Wohtek or Wohkero was killed by enemies from Meta. The grievance is not reported. Those who had slain him fled to Osegon, presumably because they had relatives there. The Wohkero kinsmen of the dead man followed them and a fight took place. An Osegon and a Meta man fell in this little battle. Subsequently another Meta man was killed. Afterwards settlement was made.

Many years ago, probably before the arrival of the Americans, Opyuweg, the largest village on Big Lagoon, became involved in a quarrel with the Wiyot, who attacked the town and killed a number of people. Opyuweg subsequently retaliated, but was unable to even the score, the Wiyot being too numerous. Consequently when settlement was made Opyuweg received a large balance. The village fought this feud alone.

Soon after 1860 the Chilula attacked Herwer on Stone Lagoon and killed 10 people. This was at the time the Chilula were in feud with the Americans and Herwer was very likely made to suffer for aid or information given the whites, or thought by the Chilula to have been given. The main grievance of the Chilula, as well as their danger, must have been from the Americans, but satisfaction was more easily taken against the Yurok.

Once there was sickness at Ko'otep. Three Orekw women married at Ko'otep were blamed. An attempt was made to kill them, but one of the Ko'otep men protected them against the others. This angered his fellow townsmen, who, with the aid of friends from Weitspus, succeeded in killing him when he was at Ayotl. One of his kinsmen, probably feeling himself impotent against the actual slayers, revenged himself by killing one of the three women from Orekw, whom he held responsible because it was on their account that his relative had become involved in the quarrel which resulted in his death. This act, of course, meant war between Orekw and Ko'otep. The two parties met several times to negotiate the difficulty before they succeeded. On each occasion some one became excited and fighting commenced over again. Several men were wounded in these skirmishes, but no one was killed. In the final settlement one of the two surviving Orekw women returned to her home, and the other was married by a housemate of the man who had lost his life through championing her cause.

Other wars were waged between Wetlkwau and Ho'opeu; between Rekwoi, aided by Oketo and Tsurau, against the Tolowa of Smith River; and by Weitspus, as an ally of the Karok of Orleans, against the Hupa and Chilula.

MODOC CHILDHOOD

by
Verne F. Ray

Parents expected an additional child every two to four years. Two years were considered the minimum time spacing between births. The infant mortality rate was relatively high; recorded data indicate that not more than two out of three survived the first few years. Consequently fraternities were not especially large; ten children were considered a very large family, perhaps the maximum. The mode was closer to five.

Children were never offered for adoption in order to reduce the size of a family. Adoption was limited to relatives and to cases where the child was an orphan or was neglected or deserted by a widower father. Adoption was not formal but the child was entitled to all the rights of a blood off-spring, including inheritance. Slave children were well treated but did not enjoy the status of the adopted child.

Deep parental affection for children was shown in many ways. When the first child was born it was not unusual for the parents to alternate in sitting up with the infant throughout the night. Being well aware of the high infant mortality they feared the child would become ill and not receive prompt enough attention. Even though the child slept well, the vigil might be kept for the first weeks at least. In winter one of the objects was to keep the fire burning so that there would be no danger of illness from exposure. The first and last children are said to have been the favorites of most parents. Fathers gave more objective evidences of love to children than did mothers; they had more time to do so. Frequently they fondled the youngsters, holding them, hugging them, and performing amusing antics. Mothers seldom or never did likewise. Fathers often cared for the children in the absence of the mothers, even though others were available for the task. A father might sit for hours at a time beside an ailing son or daughter.

The physical care of the older and apparently healthy child was often neglected, however. It was recognized that some of the skin diseases suf-fered by children were the result of allowing them to become too dirty.

Pp. 105–112 of *Primitive Pragmatists: The Modoc Indians of Northern California* (Seattle: University of Washington Press, 1963). By permission of the author and the University of Washington Press.

An ointment was applied to the skin, but little attention was given to correction of the cause. Children were never summoned for meals. This was not a mark of neglect but rather of recognition of the child's individuality and prerogatives. It was assumed that he would come at the proper hour if hungry. At any hour he was privileged to come to the house for any food available without preparation.

Older children were expected to supervise the activities of the younger ones. Even a child of cradle age was often tended or carried by a brother or sister only a few years older. The object was to free the mother for other efforts rather than to acquaint the child with adult responsibilities. Few formal tasks were assigned to the young child. Carrying wood and water was an incidental activity which a child was asked to do if older persons were otherwise occupied. Formal training in economic activities such as hunting and basket-making was not begun before adolescence. For example, it was rare for a young boy to accompany his father on a hunting expedition. Girls more often went with their mothers to seed-gathering or berry-picking grounds. They carried small baskets but these were principally for amusement since they seldom gathered many seeds or berries before they wandered away for play. They were not recalled to the task.

Children were permitted to watch adults at work as much as they cared to, and boys did, for example, learn to make respectable bows and arrows of small size; girls made passable baskets in miniature. When these were shown to parents praise was abundant and children were encouraged to persevere. The praise stemmed from true pride in the child's achievement; it was not a mechanism for stimulation. As phrased by one informant, "My parents were proud of me; and the prouder they were of me the more I wanted to work hard and the better I felt. So I was never lazy."

The small game killed by boys was never eaten by them, but only by adults. The first deer killed was left lying where it fell. Parents or other adults brought it to camp and it was dressed and eaten but the boy was given no share. Thereafter, however, he could eat flesh of game of any kind that he felled. There was no ritualization of this event.

Boys and girls were occasionally required to bathe in cold lakes or streams, even in winter, in order that they might become strong and brave. A child might be aroused in the middle of the night, without previous warning, and be taken or sent to a nearby body of water. Upon return home the child was permitted to warm himself by the fire. Emphasis upon this kind of training was very slight, a mere shadow of that found among tribes to the north.

The appearance of the first permanent tooth was used as a measure of age but no further significance was attributed to the phenomenon.

When a milk tooth became loose, it was pulled out with the fingers. At dusk the child threw the tooth away, toward the west, while facing the setting sun.

The activities and games of children are well portrayed in the reminiscent narratives of two informants, Peter Sconchin and Jennie Clinton. First, Sconchin reported as follows:

"When I was a child the first thing I did in the morning was to go out and play. I played around Tule Lake where the tules and grass grow thick on the north shore. Many of us boys played there together. We used to go out in the high tules, about seven of us. There three of us sat down and closed our eyes while the other three went off to hide. We covered our eyes with our hands but the seventh boy watched to see that no one stood up or opened his eyes. This boy didn't play. After a while we got up to look for the other boys. When we found them we went hiding and the others had to look for us.

"After we played this game for a while we went swimming in the lake. We had races to see who could swim farthest under water, or stay under longest. I played this game often when I was young.

"Every boy had bows and arrows that his father had made for him. The bows were made of young juniper. We used to go out in the tall grass of the lake and look for chub fish. When the chubs moved around the grass waved. Then we knew where to go; we pushed the grass aside and shot at the chubs with our arrows.

"I killed frogs, too, with small arrows that my father made for me. I also killed lots of watersnakes. I was afraid of them but I shot at them just the same.

"I used to go with the bigger boys to hunt chipmunks. I headed off the chipmunks while the bigger boys shot at them. At times I spent all day chasing chipmunks that ran from bush to bush.

"When wild rye was ripe the bigger boys would try to hit the stalks with their arrows. We used to see how many of them we could hit.

"After a while I played with rye-grass arrows. We used strips of bark as feathers. A big boy would sharpen the stalk to make a point. We played at dodging these rye-grass arrows. If you were hit by one it broke the skin. When you saw an arrow coming, you turned aside. If two or more arrows came you twisted around and jumped sideways.

"With several other boys I played a game of dodging a tule ball. We made up two sides. If I failed to dodge successfully I was out and a boy from the other side took my place. When I was hit it didn't hurt. But when I was hit behind the ear with it, it hurt.

"When we were about ten we got a long pole and tied a large ball to the end loosely, with tules. Then we gave a strong thrust to the pole, so that the ball left the pole. It was pretty hard to dodge that mud ball. Only a good quick boy could do that. About five or six boys played on each side, alternating as with the tule ball game.

"We also played at driving the other side away with long poles with mud balls on the ends. The poles were very flexible and had a good snap to them.

"We used to get a section of hard willow about a foot long, hollow on the inside. We made a ramrod of another stick. Then we split a stalk of tule, took out the pith, and twisted it tight and slender and about six inches long. We then stuffed it in the hollow willow pipe and gave a quick push with the ramrod. The twisted tule shot out like a bullet. We saw who could shoot farthest with it. We could only shoot eight or ten feet but it shot hard.

"Little boys used a similar hollow willow. They put juniper berries in them and blew on one end with their mouths. The berries went pretty far.

"We also played with a slingshot about three feet long. The pocket was about three inches wide and six inches long and made of buckskin. The strings were buckskin also. At the end of one of the strings was a small loop for the index finger. This side was never let go. A rock was put in the pocket and the other end drawn up and held in the same right hand. The sling was twirled a couple of times around the shoulder, and the rock let fly by letting go of the loose end. It would travel pretty far. We killed birds, squirrels, chipmunks, rabbits, and even ducks with this sling.

"In the springtime we ran races by hopping on one leg. We bet weasel hides on our races.

"Most of the time boys ran ordinary races every evening, and wrestled. I did this when I was old enough to wrestle. I wrestled until I was a man. I was a good wrestler.

"We used to play at dodging sling shots but when they hit they nearly broke your skull. They left bad bruises. We used to stand a long way off. When the boys shooting them came closer we would run off. They weren't easy to dodge.

"In winter I went hunting cottontails with my sling. But if I had a bow with me I would shoot them with that. If I only had a rock I would try to kill the rabbit with that. We saved the skins until we had enough to make a rabbitskin blanket.

"When I came back to lie down before going to sleep, I used to hear my father's mother tell stories of the mythological times.

"When we moved I had to walk. All young boys walked. While on the way I always wondered what sort of a place we would stop. I was always in a big hurry to get to our next place as quickly as possible. I couldn't wait."

Jennie Clinton reported the following: "We used to play a game in which we held hands and danced around a ring. We also played at trying to outdo one another in jumping while in a crouching position. And we would see who could jump farthest on one leg. That was certainly amusing; when a girl fell down we laughed and said that she did that because we were winning over her in the races.

"We climbed the mountains wherever we lived. It was difficult climbing. We had good times thus. We would say, 'Let's see who can go up first and get down first. The winner will be respected and will be a great person.' I used to fall down often when I tried to win. When I fell while going down the other shouted at me, 'Now that rolling down doesn't count!' I shouted back at them because I was angry.

"We used to try to make little baskets faster than each other. We would say, 'If someone is only half finished when the others are all finished we'll look down on that one as the poorest kind of person.' How tickled our parents were when they saw our little baskets!

"We never gambled when we were small. We had no bad habit of trying to win things from one another.

"Once we were sent to gather duck eggs, mudhen eggs, and any other eggs we could find in swampy places. We carried little burden baskets on our backs in which we put the eggs. The first girl to bring the egg back got a little wristlet of beads or a small necklace. People who had many beads used them to get the children to do these things."

In addition to the toys and games mentioned in the narratives, girls made dolls of tule and constructed houses of mud. Boys threw willow javelins at a sagebrush target. A moving target consisting of a disc of sagebrush about two inches in diameter was shot at with unfeathered arrows of rye grass, the point sharpened by burning. The disc was rolled along a smoothed section of ground. Balls of grass or tule were rolled along a similar playing area with the object of hitting a sagebrush target. Sides were chosen by the numerous children that played together at these games. A wooden ball was fashioned by further shaping a bolus cut from the trunk of a tree. This was used for tossing from one player to another. Boys and girls shared some games and were permitted to play together whenever they cared to do so, but most often they chose the company of their own sex.

The lack of pressure upon children to perform useful labor or to gain technical skills was mentioned above. However, from earliest infancy children were conscientiously trained in ethics, behavior, and tradition. Myths and anecdotes were told to them directly, or to the family group with the children as the significant auditors. Advice was frequently given respecting relations with other children and proper attitudes toward adults.

They were admonished not to fight with other children so that the parents might not have trouble. Respect and obedience to adults were strongly emphasized. Lying was not tolerated. Older children were forbidden to punish younger ones left in their care.

"A child that talked back to its elders," reported Jennie Clinton, "got a good whipping. Children were very obedient to all adults, whether they were relatives or strangers.

"If a boy were 'mean' his parents would try to whip it out of him. If he were caught lying they would give him double punishment. If a girl were mean she would be whipped in the same way. It's no wonder that children were good when they saw other children being lashed.

"Sometimes children were punished by being given very little to eat.

"At other times a child was put in a sweat house for punishment. The entrance was closed and the child couldn't get out. It certainly was hot when they did that to me! I had been disobedient and I thought I was going to die in that sweat house.

"Parents were insistent that they be obeyed. But children were not as bad as they are now.

"We were told, 'These mountains, these rivers hear what you say and if you are mean they will punish you.' As little children we used to hear the old people talk about what the earth did to them."

Young children were scolded or lightly punished — the pulling of an ear or switching on the legs — when they disobeyed, falsified, or caused damage in the home. But children above six or seven years of age were expected to know the rules of proper behavior. They were no longer punished for minor transgressions but were more severely handled for serious infractions. Severe fighting with other children was the most frequent action calling for punishment. Whipping with a heavy willow withe over the back and legs was the usual penalty. Either the mother or the father did the whipping, commonly the latter. Other relatives were not privileged to do so, although grandparents did not hesitate to give advice.

The more serious altercations between children and the consequences of such are discussed in the following remarks of Peter Sconchin. This informant's tendency to dramatize and exaggerate must be taken into account in judging his comments.

"Both boys and girls fought with the fists, but not like the whites. The fists, clenched, struck with a downward motion, rather than from the shoulder. They mostly pulled the hair and tried to throw the opponent down. They held the hair and kicked. They struck with rocks and sticks.

"Three girls, one larger than I, once whipped three of us boys. The big girl threw me down and hit me with a stick. We all ran away as soon as we could.

"Brothers fought with one another when small. Parents stopped such fights and talked at length to them, saying it was very bad to fight. If a boy was always fighting and couldn't be stopped his father told him to leave home and go to those with whom he could get along. The boy usually went to his father's brother's home or he could go to any relative's home that would have him.

"If a boy ran away they let him go. He had to find relatives, or even strangers, with whom to stay. Relatives asked the boy why he had run away. Then they decided whether to take him or not. They might send him away but they would never take him back. Where he stayed the boy had to help with the light work. After a while the father and mother might visit the boy, and if he talked convincingly they would take him back. He had to promise not to fight.

"In whipping a hard willow switch was used over the back and legs until the boy said, 'I will be a good boy.' While the boy was being whipped other boys came to jeer and make fun of him. After a boy was whipped he was very mad. He went out to hide where he couldn't be seen. There he cried and felt bad. Other boys were afraid to taunt him then because that might start a fight.

"Sometimes a big boy came while a small boy was being whipped and said 'Don't whip that boy any more; he'll be a good boy.' If the one being punished said that he would be a good boy and not do anything more bad, the parent might say, 'All right, I'll not whip you any more if you will keep your word.'

"Sometimes a boy didn't go out after being punished. His mother might give him something to eat and say, 'Now you be a good boy.' His father might sit beside him and say, 'Now don't do that any more.' He told him what he should do and what he should not do. The boy would say, 'All right, I'll do that.'

"If a boy was young he had to be cared for, and he had to be whipped until he said, 'I'll be a good boy.' If he wouldn't say it he was whipped until he did.

"Sometimes a boy killed his brother in a fight. My father said that his brother once killed a younger brother. Nothing was done to him. If a boy was considered good he wasn't whipped or sent away even if he killed a brother [since it must have been unintentional]. But if he should be whipped, either his father or mother did it. He was whipped until he was like dead on the floor.

"A boy's punishment was a family concern. Other people had nothing to do with it. Sometimes relatives or friends talked to the parents about a bad boy or talked to the boy to make him good."

MOHAVE WARFARE

by
Kenneth M. Stewart

The Mohave Indians of the Colorado River valley are by reputation a war-like tribe, although my informants insisted that the people as a whole were pacifically inclined. It was asserted that, while war was disliked by a majority of the Mohave, battle was the dominant concern of the kwanamis ("brave men"), who were responsible for the recurrent hostilities and over whom there was no effective control. Whether or not the mass of the population was averse to warfare, it is clear that the frequent warring expeditions were primarily the result of the existence among the Mohave of a distinct class of warriors with whom warfare was an obsession, who were set apart from other men by the nature of their dreams, and who were continually eager to join a war party to exercise the military powers conferred upon them by the spirits in those dreams. The Mohave were constant aggressors, and since they seldom plundered, economic motivation for war was inconsiderable. Prisoners were taken, but were a secondary objective in battle. Nor was territorial aggrandizement normally the reason for a military campaign, though it impelled the Mohave to drive the Halchidhoma out of what is now the Colorado River Indian Reservation.

The Mohave, in alliance with the Yuma, made a number of incursions into Maricopa territory, the Pima on occasion coming to the aid of the Maricopa. Similarly, the Yuma were at chronic enmity with the Cocopa, and they repeatedly called upon the Mohave to join them in expeditions against the latter tribe. The Halchidhoma are remembered as "Maricopa" who were driven out of the Parker region by the concerted efforts of Yuma and Mohave, but my informants knew nothing of hostilities with the Kohuana or Halyikwamai. There was no fighting with the Cahuilla or other southern California Shoshoneans, and the Kamia, Diegueño, Akwa'-

Southwestern Journal of Anthropology (1947), 3:257–278.

A charming and ethnographically authentic novel about the Mohave is Charles L. McNichols, *Crazy Weather* (Macmillan, 1944). Information of a more technical sort is given in L. Spier, *Cultural Relations of the Gila River and Lower Colorado Tribes,* Yale University Publications in Anthropology (1936), 3:1–22. See also A. L. Kroeber, "Earth Tongue, a Mohave," in Elsie Clews Parsons, ed., *American Indian Life* (1925), pp. 189–202; *idem,* "Preliminary Sketch of the Mohave Indians," *American Anthropologist,* n.s. (1902), 4:276–285. A real thriller is R. B. Stratton, *Captivity of the Oatman Girls* (New York, 1857).

ala, and Kiliwa were regarded as distant, rather unimportant tribes who were not enemies of the Mohave.

Relations with the Yuman tribes of Upland Arizona were on the whole friendly, with trade and some intermarriage. The Mohave never fought the Havasupai or Yavapai, and conflict with the Walapai was limited to a few minor encounters. The Shoshonean Chemehuevi were friends until after the establishment of Fort Mohave, when on several occasions they attacked the Mohave. The Paiute, likewise, were normally not enemies, but they joined the Chemehuevi in these forays, and there were isolated skirmishes between Mohave and Paiute in earlier times.

The following narrative of fighting with the Chemehuevi was told by Pete Lambert.

I heard of only two fights with the Chemehuevi. When the Whites were at Fort Mohave they gave the Mohave and Chemehuevi liquor. Before that time the Mohave and Chemehuevi were relations and friends. But then they started to kill one another in drunken fights. The Chemehuevi lost quite a few men that way, and they got sore at the Mohave. A bunch of Chemehuevi warriors came down early in the morning and killed several Mohave near Fort Mohave, and then the Chemehuevi ran to Sand Hill. The Mohave chased them and killed quite a few Chemehuevi at Sand Hill.

The other war with the Chemehuevi was also when the American troop was already here [1867]. The Mormons in Nevada wanted some Mohave women for wives, so they gave guns to about fifty Ute [?], Paiute, and Chemehuevi, and told them to go down and kidnap some Mohave girls for them. They came through up at Forty Nine Road, the old military road up above Ghost Mountain (Avikwame). They went through on the south side of the big wash by Hardyville. Then they came to a place called Moss Mine (Kawačuthomb). A lot of Mohave were gathered to fight over a piece of land at a place called Sand Hill (Anikočkwamb). So there were lots of Mohave there. They were camped and big dances were going on, singing nearly all night and day. At daylight the enemy attacked. Most of the Mohave were unarmed; so the Chemehuevi shot their guns and killed quite a few. They were old-time guns, and shot rocks, not lead. They never cleaned the barrels, and they shot so fast that the guns were not working so good. So they started to run. An unarmed Mohave kwanami ran after the Chemehuevi leader, and the Chemehuevi shot him through the shoulder, but he went right on. He grabbed the Chemehuevi by the hair and threw him down and broke his neck and killed him.

One man lost several relatives in the battle, and that made him reckless for revenge; so he chased after the retreating Chemehuevi all by himself. He caught up with them, and he killed five Chemehuevi by himself, and then the others killed him. When they killed him, they cut him into pieces, and set up poles and strung his flesh out.

While the fight was going on in the morning, the Mohave sent a messenger south to Topock for reinforcements. The kwanamis coming up from Topock did not go to the battlefield, but cut across the mesa to head off the Chemehuevi, and they got up to Hardyville about noon. Meanwhile the Chemehuevi kept on going, but they were exhausted from lack of food or sleep. Some of them fell down and died. The Mohave from Topock gave up the pursuit, or they could have caught and killed them all. The Chemehuevi crossed over to Nevada at a place called Avidunyor, a place where there are high cliffs with Indian designs on the rocks and a lot of bedrock mortars.

After that the soldiers gave the Mohave a gun apiece to protect themselves. They never fought the Chemehuevi again.

The wasauwič ("all the warriors") was an informal association of the kwanamis. Kwanamis, of whom there were forty or fifty in the tribe, were men who had received the proper dreams (sumač ahot) for power in war, and they constituted an amorphous warrior class. They were men of prestige, perhaps outranking even the tribal chief in this respect. The kwanamis were not the only men who went to war, since a war party of forty might include as few as six or seven kwanamis; but men who had unlucky dreams (sumač ačim) remained at home and served as guards during the absence of the warriors.

The dreams of a kwanami began at birth, or even while the unborn child was still in his mother's womb. In his dreams spirits appeared to him, conferring power, instructing him in proper modes of fighting, and teaching him how to avoid injury in combat. The kwanami dreamed of the hawk, a predatory bird whom he would later emulate in battle; and he dreamed of going through dust, which signified that he would come through war unscathed. He dreamed of fighting and killing such ferocious animals as mountain lions and bears. In his dreams he seized the animals by the legs and split them in two.

Kwanamis were unlike other Mohave. Their mode of living was Spartan: they were relatively insensible to cold and heat and were unconcerned about going four or five days without food. They ate little, taking only one meal a day, and they ate alone. They were uninterested in women and sex, few of them marrying until they had grown too old for combat. A kwanami did not farm, although he might hunt or fish, and he spent most of his time reclining in a secluded spot while meditating on the subject of warfare. The kwanamis are described as even tempered, little given to levity, and silent but not bashful. They "looked tough," but they were not necessarily large men, because "a small man might be a better fighter than a big man." The people believed that the eye of the kwanami was like the morning star, enabling him to discern the enemy in the distance. A kwanami was totally indifferent to death; his thinking was continually dominated by his supreme concern of battling the enemy.

In war the kwanamis competed among themselves to kill the first enemy.

Certain honors accrued to the man who was the first to kill, though I am not sure that the emoluments were of a tangible nature. Mrs. Lincoln stated that only kwanamis who had killed first were entitled to wear eagle feathers.

Two or three men in the tribe ranked as head kwanamis or war chiefs, for whom there was no name other than kwanami. Like other kwanamis, they theoretically attained their positions through proper dreaming. Each war party was conducted by a head kwanami, whose powers were minimal and not clearly formulated, although he was not responsible to the tribal chief. The head kwanami acted as a leader and officer on the war party, and when the party approached an enemy camp he stopped the warriors and gave them instructions relative to the attack. The tribal chief was not a kwanami and did not go to war.

Since boys learned what they needed to know in dreams, special training for war was regarded as superfluous. Boys between the ages of four and six were subjected to a series of tests or ordeals to determine whether or not they possessed sufficient fortitude to become kwanamis, which meant, in effect, to determine whether or not they were having the necessary dreams for power in war. A kwanami might push a boy into a bee's nest, or he might draw blood by sticking his fingernail into a boy's forehead. He might pinch the boy, or pull his ears, or lash him across the bare back with a switch. The boy who did not exhibit stoicism was not dreaming properly; but the boy who did not cry, but who fought back or merely stared unconcernedly at his tormenter, was the boy who would become a kwanami.

Boys who passed the ordeals became humar kwanamis ("half-grown warriors"). Between the ages of eight and ten they were taught to use bows and arrows, and they went hunting for practice in marksmanship. For conditioning they ran long distances, but they neither practiced dodging arrows, as did the Yuma boys, nor did they engage in sham battles.

The "brave boy" carried a warrior's bow rather than a hunting bow, and he seldom joined the other boys in archery games, since he thought only of going out to kill the enemy. If a brave boy entered an archery contest, he would put his war bow aside and tell the other boys not to touch it, and he would use a hunting bow. He would participate only for a short while, and other boys did not like to play with him, "he was too rough."

Four arrows were conferred upon the brave boy in his dreams, and these were named in sequence, enemy arrow, brave arrow, doctor arrow, and unbrave arrow. The boy preserved them carefully and shot them at the enemy in the above order on his first war party.

Occasionally a brave boy would go on a war party when he had reached the age of thirteen or fifteen. Such boys are said to have been cleverer in battle than older men. Once they had been to war, they became possessed with the desire to go out and fight again. Pete Lambert said that these boys were continually "keyed-up" like race horses; they slept little and were constantly straining to go out and kill. The majority of boys, however, did not go on a war party until they were nineteen or twenty, when they became known as mahai[y] kwanamis ("young warriors"). Fighting men were in their prime between the ages of twenty and thirty, and they continued to go to war until they were forty.

Members of a war party were naked save for breechclout and sandals. The long hair of the warriors was wrapped up and bound at the back of the head with rawhide. Just before the attack warriors applied war paint, delineating on their bodies red, black, and white designs identifying them as Mohave. The hair was painted red. Face paint was always black for war: usually the entire face was blackened, although sometimes a black stripe was painted across the eyes. Horses were not painted.

Eagle feathers were attached singly to the hair of men who had killed first in battle; the other warriors wore feather headdresses (hal[y]kwe). The headdress had a four-ply netting foundation made from black-eyed bean fibers, and a cord was tied under the chin to hold it in place. Wing and tail feathers of the hawk radiated from a central knot, projecting vertically and hanging down at the sides.

Each warrior carried a gourd canteen, five to eight inches in diameter, with a fiber stopper. The canteen was wrapped with ropes of willow fiber. There were horizontal ropes at the top, bottom, and in the middle, four vertical ropes, and a loop at the top by means of which the canteen was attached to the warrior's belt.

The principle weapons of the Mohave were long self bows (otisa) and mallet headed "potato-masher" clubs (halyawhai), the latter being the more lethal. The club, carved from a single piece of green mesquite or screw-bean wood, was used to advantage in hand-to-hand combat. Its overall length was approximately one foot, although a stronger warrior might carry a club of greater size. The handle measured seven or eight inches in length and two and a quarter inches in diameter, and the length of the cylindrical head averaged four or five inches, with a diameter of four inches across the top surface. A slight hollow was sometimes burned in the upper surface, leaving sharp edges which were made sharper still by carving. The top surface was painted red, and the remainder of the head and the handle were black. A wrist loop of buckskin or willow-bark fiber was passed through a hole three-eighths of an inch from the tip of the handle. Contrary to Yuma and Cocopa custom, the handle was not sharpened for stabbing.

The club was grasped near the cylinder rather than at the end of the handle, and it was usually smashed into the chin or face with an upward stroke. Occasionally the warrior struck downward at the enemy's temple. A warrior might seize an enemy by the hair and club him, then throwing the foe over his shoulder to men armed with heavy straight clubs (tokyeta), with which they cracked his skull.

Both hunting and war bows were plain self bows with a simple curve, and they were usually made of willow. Mesquite was sometimes used for war bows and was regarded as a superior material. The length of the bow varied with the height of the man who carried it, the ideal length being from the ground to the chin. Hunting bows were shorter than war bows, averaging from three and a half to four feet in length. The depth from string to belly averaged six inches, and the grip measured one inch by one and a half inches. Bowstrings were four-ply, and were made of horse or deer sinew. Fiber bowstrings were sometimes used on hunting bows, but never on war bows. The hunting bow was unpainted, while war bows were painted black on each end and red in the middle. The tips of the war bow were sometimes wrapped in sinew.

Each man made his own bow by the following process. A length of green willow, after drying in the sun, was split lengthwise and worked with stone knives. Willow bark which had been soaked in water was wrapped around half of the bow, and the wrapped end was thrust into a damp pile of earth on top of which a fire had been built. The bow was left in the hot earth for thirty minutes, after which the procedure was repeated with the other half of the bow. Next, the bow was bent back and forth over the knee to give even leverage and to ensure flexibility, and this resulted in a curving of the ends of the bow. Immediately after flexing, the bow was strung.

The Mohave occasionally reinforced their war bows by tying deer sinew on the back of the bow at the grip.

Bows were unstrung when not in use, since the Mohave had little fear of an enemy attack, and the bows could be strung in a matter of seconds. Warriors strung their bows only when nearing enemy country.

Warriors normally stood erect while shooting, holding the bow vertically. Hunters sometimes held the bow in a horizontal position. The bow was held in the left hand and grasped in the middle, although there were some lefthanded and ambidextrous archers. The Mohave knew the secondary arrow release, but the primary release was usually employed.

Arrows (ipa) were of arrowweed (*Pluchea*), although some use may also have been made of cane arrows: at least the latter were known for tribes to the south. Foreshafted arrows were denied, and Mohave arrows were invariably untipped. No arrow poison was used. The arrow was three-eighths of an inch in diameter and nearly three feet in length. The shaft was painted either red or black. War arrows were provided with three feathers; hunting arrows had four, and the arrows of children two feathers. The feathers of any kind of big bird, except the eagle or buzzard, were used, with those of the hawk and crane the most common. The feather was split in two with the teeth, the outer edges were trimmed, and the halves placed on the same arrow. No gum was used in fastening the feathers to the arrow; rather, sinew was wrapped around the top of the feather, brought down to the bottom, and tied. To identify the arrow as that of a Mohave, the shaft between the feathers was painted black on one side and red on the other.

Green arrowweeds destined for use as arrows were pulled up by the roots and placed in the sun to dry. The arrow was then heated, the bark was scraped off with a stone knife, and the end was whittled to a sharp point. The point was moistened and put in hot ashes for hardening.

No arrow straightener was used for arrowweed arrows, which were straightened only once. The arrow was heated over a fire to soften it, and it was straightened with the hands and teeth, the maker sighting along the shaft to determine degree of straightness. Cane arrows were sometimes straightened on a plain heated stone. War arrows were not decorated with pyrographic designs, although boys would peel the bark off of green arrowweeds, twine the bark around the arrow, and set it afire. The bark burned away, leaving a spiraling black design on the arrow.

The maximum flight of an arrow was two hundred yards, but no damage was inflicted at that distance. Arrow penetration varied from two to four inches, depending upon the distance from which the arrow was shot. The arrow was said to be painful if shot from about fifty yards, and at ten yards a direct hit on the heart could be fatal.

Warriors wore a deerhide bowguard on the wrist of the bow hand; sometimes the guard extended halfway up the arm. The hide was split on the ends and tied. Bark bowguards, braided and tied at each end, were worn by hunters and were discarded after they had been worn a few times.

Quivers (kupet) were usually of the whole skin of a fox, with the hair on the outside and the tail at the top. Coyote and wildcat skins were also used, and Mrs. Lincoln mentioned deerskin quivers. An arrowweed stick served as a reinforcing rod, with a sinew cord attached to each end of the stick so that the quiver could be slung over the back. The quiver was three feet long and three or four inches across, and it contained fifteen or twenty arrows. In battle, in order that arrows might be readily plucked out, the quiver was sometimes put under the arm and held in place with a willow bark cloth wrapped around the torso.

The tokyeta, a heavy straight club of mesquite wood, approximately two feet in length and two inches thick, was used for cracking skulls. Men with tokyetas followed the archers in battle formation, dispatching enemies who had been felled but not slain by warriors with halyawhai (the "potato-masher" club). Warriors wielded the tokyeta with one hand, beating the foe over the head until he died. The tokyeta was sometimes carried over the shoulder, suspended by a cord passing through a hole at the end of the club, and halyawhai-bearers might have as additional weapons tokyetas thrust through the belt.

Two or three warriors in a party of forty or fifty might carry spears (otat). These were five foot lengths of mesquite wood, sharpened at both ends, with a single feather attached to each end. They were ordinarily borne by horsemen.

Archers carried circular shields (sakol^y) of horsehide or deerskin, about two feet in circumference. These were used to protect the heart only. Two forms seem to have been in use: one with a rim of mesquite or screwbean wood over which a hide was stretched, the other rimless, with two hide disks sewn together around the peripheries with sinew. Two holes were punched in the middle of the shield, about four inches apart, with a sinew thong through which the hand was passed to hold the shield. The shield was not feathered, but was painted solidly in red or black. The Mohave did not paint the shield in four quarters as did the Maricopa and Cocopa.

Neither the sling nor the stone-headed club was used in battle. Occasionally a sharp bone or sharpened mesquite stick was used as a dagger, and stone knives (kemadj) were carried to battle but were seldom employed as weapons. The knife was a foot in length, unhafted, and sharpened on one edge only.

The Mohave lacked the curtain shield, and the strip of horsehide to protect the stomach was denied. Mrs. Lincoln said that warriors sometimes braided the vines of black-eyed beans and wrapped them around their stomachs for protection.

The feathered pike (okwil^y) was a three or four foot length of mesquite or willow wood, pointed at both ends, with chicken-hawk feathers tied onto the shaft in pairs. According to Lute Wilson, the usual number of feathers was forty. Usually an okwil^y was adorned with white feathers only, although occasionally one with black feathers was carried. The shaft of the okwil^y was painted either red or black.

The okwil^y functioned as a flag or standard, and no war party was without one. All informants insisted that there was ordinarily only one standard-bearer on a war party, although if several groups of warriors were attacking from different directions, each group would have an okwil^y. The okwil^y-bearer went into battle in front of the other warriors, going into the middle of the enemy and fighting with the pointed ends of the okwil^y. He carried no other weapons and no shield. He had nonflight obligations, and if he were killed the okwil^y was immediately picked up by another kwanami. There was a tendency, but not a rigid rule, for the same man to carry the okwil^y on each war party. The okwil^y might be borne by any kwanami, but the bearer was normally a man who had dreamed about feathers and carrying the okwil^y.

The huktharhueta, which has not been reported for other Yuman tribes, was infrequently substituted for the okwil^y, and it had an identical function. Both types of standard were not carried on the same war party. A huktharhueta in Pete Lambert's possession is a three foot shaft of screwbean wood, unpointed at the ends, with a single fox tail pendant from each end and one from the middle of the shaft.

There was a definite distinction between the small raiding party (hunyu), consisting of ten or twelve kwanamis, and the larger war party (kwanatme), which engaged in a pitched battle. Raiders went out whenever seized with the desire to fight. They departed secretly; there was no meeting or dance of incitement, nor were they obliged to ask the permission of the chief before leaving. They surprised outlying Maricopa camps, killed a few people, and ran away with corn, watermelons, and horses. The horses were killed on the way home; the meat was not eaten, but the hide was saved for sandals and bowstrings.

The war party, an undertaking of the tribe as a whole, had an average strength of forty or fifty men, although on rare occasions it comprised over a hundred warriors. A war party might go out once or twice a year, although usually the intervals between expeditions were longer.

War parties were invariably preceded by one or two scouts, who reconnoitered in the enemy country, locating trails, water holes, and hostile settlements. With his hair done up in a mud plaster as a disguise, a scout sometimes went among the Maricopa at night, even entering the houses and sitting among the enemy. The scout usually succeeded in slipping away before dawn undetected.

Several months often elapsed after the return of the scouts before a war party set out. A few days before the party was scheduled to leave the head kwanami would call a meeting, at which song cycles were sung, and at which warriors were given an opportunity to volunteer for the campaign. If the expedition was to be a joint undertaking with the Yuma, a messenger ran to a prearranged place near Parker, where he left for the Yuma messenger arrows on which were painted black and red signs designating the plate and date of attack. Sometimes a knotted string identical with one retained by the Mohave was substituted for the painted arrows, the messenger carrying it all the way to Yuma. The war parties of both Yuma and Mohave untied a knot each morning, and a simultaneous attack was thus ensured on the morning when the last knot was untied.

A dance of incitement was sometimes held before the departure of a war party. (The statements of my informants on the subject were vague and contradictory.) The dance lasted for one day and one night; the women dancing around scalps taken in previous battles; the men singing to the accompaniment of the gourd rattle. After the dance the warriors departed, leaving the women weeping.

There was no prohibition on sexual intercourse before a war party, nor were there food restrictions, although the warriors ate little. They carried with them a mere handful of ground parched wheat, which they consumed over a period of approximately two weeks.

The journey to the Maricopa country required six days. The party was guided by a scout who had previously made a reconnaissance of the territory to be traversed. The warriors at first traveled by day, walking along quietly in a group, talking little, but "feeling no sad feelings." A piece of willow or greasewood was chewed to keep the mouth from getting dry, and warriors could smoke if they wished. Nearing the country of the enemy, the warriors traveled by night and slept in concealment during the day. A sentry, posted about twenty yards from the sleeping warriors, investigated all noises, and he was said to be able to hear footsteps over a hundred yards away. It was an evil omen and a sign that the Mohave would lose the battle if an animal came into camp, but since kwanamis were indifferent to death the party did not turn back.

At home the people watched the sky at night for meteors; the direction in which a meteor fell foretold the winner of a battle. Those left behind were under no special restrictions, but it was deemed harmful to the warriors to think of them except on the day when it was known that they would have joined battle.

Some war parties included one or two women. Such women were from brave families; their fathers or brothers were kwanamis. They functioned chiefly as morale-builders, and they ordinarily did not enter the fray, although they were sometimes provided with tokyetas for self-defense. A number of women accompanied the warriors when the Mohave drove the Halchidhoma out of the Parker region, entering the fight and finishing off wounded enemies with their tokyetas.

On each war party there was at least one shaman. A doctor for arrow wounds (ipa sumadj) was always included in a party. There was sometimes a rattlesnake-bite doctor, and Lute Wilson mentioned a third specialist, a doctor for club wounds. En route the shaman made speeches to the warriors, relating his dreams, and admonishing them to conduct themselves with valor in battle. He attempted also to work magic against the enemy, trying to hypnotize them from a distance, so that they would go to sleep or fall unconscious. The rattlesnake doctor was able to locate drinking water.

The wounded were treated at the first night's encampment after the battle; the doctor singing and bathing the wounds. A rattlesnake shaman cured by singing and the laying on of hands, but neither he nor the wound doctor sucked or blew on the wound.

Informants without exception maintained that attacks were always by surprise; the enemy was never challenged or notified of an attack in advance. The Mohave crept up on an outlying enemy settlement under cover of darkness and fell upon the enemy at dawn, shrieking and whooping, with annihilation of the foe the aim. A man might escape and rouse other Maricopa settlements, in which case, if the Mohave advanced, they would find the foe drawn up in battle array, and a major engagement would commence.

Mohave warriors were divided in battle formation according to the weapons they bore. The bearer of the feathered pike went first, followed in that order by men with halyawhai, archers, and tokyeta-bearers. In some war parties from two to five horsemen, carrying bows and arrows or spears, rode on the flanks. A general mêlée ensued once the fray began, and the formation became confused. Warriors were not segregated according to their physical size, nor were there special names for the bearers of different weapons.

Warriors were sometimes separated into three or four groups, approximately equal in numerical strength, each group attacking from a different direction.

The head kwanami at times acted as a challenger before a pitched battle, hurling insults and imprecations at the enemy as he paraded up and down before the warriors. Single combat by champions was denied by all informants.

The duration of a battle was variable: it might last for an hour or two, for half a day, or rarely, an entire day. Lute Wilson said that occasionally the warriors would continue fighting without intermission for two days and nights, until one side was annihilated or until an agreement to suspend hostilities was reached. The Mohave head kwanami would talk to the enemy "face to face," saying, "Now we are returning. You don't have to be afraid of us tonight," and the enemy would reply, "You can go home, and you don't have to be afraid of us chasing you. We won't fight any more until the next time."

Pete Lambert estimated that in an average battle from five to seven Mohave were killed: fifteen dead was a great loss. Eight or ten Mohave might be wounded, some of them succumbing on the arduous return journey, but the majority recovered to fight again.

Time permitting, the dead were cremated on the field of battle, but frequently the bodies were left for the buzzards. A funeral was later held for the deceased; the houses and possessions of the dead warriors were burned and their horses slain.

Mohave warriors feared the magical potency of an enemy scalp; if a man should touch it he would go insane and "holler in the night." Consequently, scalping was performed only by a special scalper, the ahwe somadj ("dream[er] of foes"), who was a shaman rather than a warrior, and who, provided he underwent purification, was unharmed by contact with the scalp. The ahwe somadj, who dreamed his power to scalp, also doctored warriors who had fallen ill due to contact with the enemy.

The scalper went into battle with the warriors and watched for an enemy with "nice, long, heavy hair." There was no preference for the scalp of an enemy war leader. When the scalper spied an enemy with a desirable head of hair, he would knock him down, break his neck, and cut off the head with a stone knife. He ran off with the head to a near-by gulch, where he might hide and scalp undisturbed while the battle was still raging. The scalper made an incision at the outer edge of each eyebrow with a sharp stick of greasewood, and he cut back under the ears. He then made a cut down the face from the bridge of the nose, and ripped off the scalp, which included the ears. Only rarely did he go back into battle to obtain a second scalp. On the homeward journey the scalper would go off by himself at night and "tan" the scalp by rubbing in adobe.

The scalper fasted on the way home, and upon arrival he relinquished the trophy to its permanent keeper, the kohota (dance leader). Then, like the warriors, he purified himself by abstaining from meat and salt and bathing each morning for four days.

Not only enemy slayers but all members of a war party had to undergo purification, lest the maleficent influence of the enemy drive them insane. Those who had killed were not separated from the others on the return journey, but all the warriors slept little, drank little water, and fasted. When they reached home they immediately bathed in the river and the ablutions were repeated each morning for a period of either four or eight days. The four-day period was ordinarily observed, but it was considered more efficacious to undergo purification for eight days. During this time the warriors abstained from meat and salt, and they ate only a little cornmeal mush. Those undergoing lustration were not separated from their families, since relatives were likewise obliged to observe the food restrictions and to bathe each morning.

Now and then a warrior would be taken ill on the homeward journey as a result of the evil influence of the enemy, and he was doctored by the ahwe somadj. But he was regarded as potentially dangerous to his companions while in this condition, and if he were unable to walk the other warriors would not carry him.

After the battle a swift runner (konawowem) was sent ahead to bring tidings of casualties and to tell of the return of the warriors. The kohota then scheduled the scalp dance, fixing a date a day or two after the anticipated arrival of the fighting men. Word was sent to all the Mohave, for the scalp dance was a time of rejoicing and celebration, and since many marriages resulted from meetings of young people on such occasions, the ceremony was regarded as beneficial to the fertility of the tribe.

The kohota dressed and painted the scalp, and mounted it on a long cottonwood pole, which was planted in the ground for the dance. Four or five old scalps were brought out and prepared in like manner. For four days and nights men sang song cycles and women danced around the scalps. Although old women played a major role in the scalp dance, the aged were not the sole participants, since even little boys, painted like warriors and wearing feathers, were permitted to dance. The warriors did not take part in the festivities, but retired to their dwellings.

Women wore eagle feathers in their hair and were painted like kwanamis, with black paint on the face and red paint on the hair. While dancing around the scalp, they mimicked the actions of warriors, yelling and screaming, running and dodging with weapons, and shooting arrows at the scalps. They reviled the scalps; they talked "face to face" like rival challengers. They narrated their war exploits, telling how they had killed and scalped.

Prisoners were required to be present at the scalp dance, but were neither compelled nor permitted to dance. They were not tortured, though they might be insulted and might receive an occasional blow.

After the dance the scalps passed into the keeping of their permanent custodian, the kohota (also called kohot kusuman^y, or ahwe kusuman^y), who, like the scalper, was immune to the maleficent power of the scalp. The kohota had as many as fourteen or fifteen scalps sealed up with greasewood or arrowweed gum in a large gourd or olla which he kept in a corner of his dwelling.

The scalp dance was repeated at harvest time, the person with the largest crop announcing a dance and feast. The kohota prepared the scalps, washing and brushing them, dyeing the hair with boiled mesquite bark, and plastering it with mud, after which he painted the scalps and set them up on poles. The dance was the same as that following a battle, again lasting for four days and nights. After the dance the kohota and his family once more purified themselves by bathing and abstaining from salt for four days.

The Mohave took numerous captives (ahwethauk). These were young women and children, and rarely, adolescent boys; older people were never taken prisoner. Captives were seldom mistreated; and while boys were made slaves and forced to perform domestic tasks, the Mohave in time came to regard them as fellow tribesmen, and "thought more of them than their own sons." Upon reaching maturity the boys might marry Mohave girls, but a Mohave girl would never marry a youth who had grown up in an enemy tribe because "she was scared of him."

Prisoners were magically dangerous, and they underwent purification immediately upon arrival. A shaman washed them for four consecutive mornings with a mixture of soaproot and arrowweed, and during this period the captives, like returning warriors, were not permitted to eat meat and salt.

Since it was feared that such relations would cause insanity, women were not violated by their captors. Rather, they were given to old men as wives, partly as an insult to the enemy, and partly because it was felt that the old men had only a little longer to live and were indifferent to death. A child resulting from such a union was regarded as a half-breed.

Unlike the Yuma, Cocopa, and Maricopa, the Mohave did not sell prisoners to the Mexicans, and all informants denied that prisoners ever tried to escape, because "they were too well-treated."

Defensive warfare was little developed, since the Maricopa never came en masse to attack the Mohave, and only in later years were the Mohave raided by Chemehuevi. Sentries were rarely on guard in time of peace, but they were stationed out on the mesa while a war party was away.

To sum up, Mohave warfare was in the main the responsibility of the bellicose kwanamis, who derived their power in dreams. Warfare was an obsession with the kwanamis, and beginning in late adolescence they joined frequent warring expeditions in which the Mohave were allied with the Yuma against the Maricopa and Cocopa. Raiding parties of ten or twelve kwanamis went out at any time, but larger war parties were less frequent, and since they were tribal undertakings they involved somewhat more elaborate preparations. A war party sought to surprise enemy settlements, attacking in a battle formation in which warriors were segregated according to their weapons. The belief in the dangerous magical potency of the enemy, manifested by the presence in Mohave culture of the special scalper, the lustration of warriors, the purification of captives, and the special custodian of the scalp, was the dominant motif of all post-battle activities.

WAR STORIES FROM TWO ENEMY TRIBES

by
Walter Goldschmidt,
George Foster, and
Frank Essene

INTRODUCTION

The Yuki and the Nomlaki lived on opposite sides of the Coast Range in northern California. They were enemies. This is repeatedly indicated by off-hand statements of informants, but it gets its clearest expression in war stories from both sides, a collection of which is presented here. Linguistically the Nomlaki belong to the Penutian family, while the Yuki are the most numerous representatives of the Yukian stock. Both peoples subsisted on hunting, fishing, and gathering, and though there was a general similarity of culture, many specific differences existed. Some trade took place between the two tribes, but the Coast Range, rising to 7,500 feet, afforded a considerable barrier, so that contact was close only in summer when both peoples gathered food in the uplands.

The following accounts of Yuki-Nomlaki wars were obtained by the authors during the summers of 1935-1937. A comparison of their field notes indicated that joint treatment of the war stories might prove valuable. Three Yuki informants gave four stories, and four Nomlaki informants gave an additional five. The nine accounts which follow are presented approximately as recorded, in English; and in the conclusion the general points of comparison are discussed.

YUKI ACCOUNTS

1. A Yuki man and his woman became angry at their parents, so they left home and climbed up the mountains to the east, camping near the crest in Yuki territory [probably just below Black Butte]. Here they made a rough shelter in which to sleep. In the afternoon the woman looked up toward the summit and saw something move. She said to her husband, "Old man, let us go back; there are people above us." But the man said nothing; he was mad at everything and everybody, and didn't care even if he died. At

Journal of American Folk-Lore (1939), 52:141-154.

dusk they built a fire, ate, and went to bed. But the woman was restless. "Don't sleep. I feel uneasy," she said. But toward morning, both finally dozed off. Then something came into the shelter, stirred up the fire and sat down. The woman awakened and saw it, and awakened her man. He grabbed for his bow, but the stranger, who was an "Indian bear," jumped on him. This "Indian bear" was a Nomlaki doctor, covered by a thick bear hide which protected him from danger. He was naturally a very strong man. Both fought for a long time, and by and by the Yuki man became exhausted, and he turned to his woman who had been helping as best she could. "Go home. I'm done. Go home to your people." She was stubborn and wouldn't go home, but finally she slipped out of the shelter and hid herself to watch what was going on. Then the "bear" killed the Yuki and came out to look for the woman. He hunted everywhere, but she was hidden behind a tree and he couldn't find her. So he dragged the body of the Yuki man out of the shelter, and with his knife cut it all up. He took off the scalp and kept it, and spread the rest of the flesh, skin, and entrails over the ground and bushes. When this was all done, he went to the stream and took off his bear hide. Then he washed himself thoroughly, packed his hide on his back, and struck off over the mountain. Then it was that the woman knew it was an "Indian bear" and not a real grizzly bear. After this the woman went home to her people, and said, "My man was killed. A Nomlaki 'Indian bear' killed him, and hung him all over the ground and trees, and cut his guts out." So the warriors gathered, and she led them back to the spot, where they examined the remains which proved that the killer had been an "Indian bear." They gathered up the remains of the man and burned them, and took his ashes home for burial; after this they had a big "cry" [i.e., period of public mourning], for everyone felt very bad. Then after a few days they talked things over and sent word to the chief [war chief?]. He told them to get ready, to have plenty of arrows.

Then everyone started up the mountainside—everyone who could go, women and children too. They were afraid to stay at home for fear the Nomlaki would attack them while their men were away. At the top of the ridge at a place called č'ut [Government Flat] they stopped and sent word to the Nomlaki chief to come up there for a council. The Nomlaki chief asked what was wanted, and the messenger said that his chief wanted to talk about payments. So the Nomlaki chief came with all his warriors, and both sides drew up, with their chiefs in front.

Then the Yuki chief addressed the Nomlaki, and told them what had happened, and asked that they pay for the murder. The Nomlaki chief asked his people, "Did any of you do this?" One doctor answered, "Yes." But the Nomlaki refused to pay; three times they refused, so finally a Yuki warrior stabbed a Nomlaki, and the battle was on. It began in the evening, and lasted for most of the night. The Nomlaki chief and all of his people were killed, all except one young boy [Jim Halley] who escaped. Many women helped in the battle, too. Women who had lost their men were even more terrible as fighters than the men. Many Yuki were killed, but not so many as Nomlaki.

When the battle was ended, the Yuki gathered their dead and wounded, burying the former and carrying home on stretchers the latter. [Stretchers were made by lashing wild-grape vines between two poles.] They took the scalps and heads of the dead Nomlaki, and just let their bodies lie on the field. Scalping was done by cutting across the forehead and peeling to the rear. [Other accounts state that the cut was made on the neck, and the scalp peeled forward so as to include the entire face.] When they got home they had a big war dance, and danced with the scalps and heads on poles, carrying bows and spears and imitating shooting and stabbing the enemy. After this there was a big feast. The reservation was founded soon after this fight, so the Nomlaki, who were severely reduced in number, didn't have an opportunity to retaliate. But the two peoples have never gotten on very well in Round Valley, to which the Nomlaki were brought.

2. The Yuki used to trade with the Nomlaki. The Nomlaki brought in salt to trade for deerskins, beads, and pine nuts. Of course these trades led to arguments, fights, and eventually killings. Both men and women were involved. On one occasion a Yuki captain was nearly killed. This made the Yuki angry and they decided on a war with the Nomlaki.

The Mountain Yuki [Sukshaltatno'm] were the ones who had the trouble with the Nomlaki. The Mountain Yuki called together all the Yuki of Round Valley, Hull Valley, Eden Valley, and Dos Rios. The meeting was held in the fall of the year. They decided to make war on the Nomlaki and planned what they were going to do. Three men of the council were selected to go to Sacramento Valley and invite the Nomlaki to a big dance. There would also be grass games [the favorite gambling game of the California Indians] and everyone would have a big time. The celebration was to be held at Black Butte, the Yuki-Nomlaki boundary line.

People soon began to gather: the Nomlaki on the east side of the Butte, the Yuki on the west. It took two days and part of a night for all the people to get there. The last bunch of Yuki came after dark and circled around the Nomlaki. The Yuki encircled the Nomlaki with soldiers, five men deep. About midnight the Yuki attacked. The fight lasted that night, the next day, and another night. A little stream there became red with blood [a common simile to indicate the ferocity of the battle]. The Nomlaki would have run away if they could, but the Yuki had them surrounded and only a few got away. Only one Yuki was killed, but at least two thousand Nomlaki were killed or wounded!

After the battle was over the Yuki set a watch over the dead and wounded. When the Nomlaki tried to rescue one of their men, the Yuki would run them away. At last the Yuki got tired of watching and left the field. This was the last big war between the Yuki and Nomlaki. There were not enough Nomlaki left to carry on a war.

3. The Nomlaki came and camped at Rock Springs. Six Yuki men and one Wailaki went to visit them. The Nomlaki were not friendly, and talked among themselves in their own language. The Nomlaki headman got his spear and rushed at the Yuki. The Yuki man dodged away but one got cut in the back by the spearhead. The Yuki hurried home. They sent a woman out to tell all the people about the attack. The next day the woman came back with all the Yuki warriors and about ninety Wailaki. [The Wailaki are an Athabascan-speaking people who lived to the north of Yuki territory.] All got ready to fight the Nomlaki.

The Yuki and Wailaki started in double file up the mountain. They found all the Nomlaki in bed, asleep. The Yuki waited until the Nomlaki were up and ready to fight. The Yuki fought in pairs. [Two Yuki to one Nomlaki?] All the Nomlaki were killed except one little girl, who was seven or eight years of age. On the following night she sneaked through the brush and finally got home. The Yuki and Wailaki picked up everything that the Nomlaki had with them. Then they came back to Yuki country. They cooked up lots of food and gave a big dance. It lasted for two or three days. At the end of the dance, everyone went back to his own village.

4. A Yuki man and his wife lived at Devil's Jump-off. They lived all alone. One day they saw three men coming toward them. The woman knew they were enemies [i.e., Nomlaki]. She ran for help while her husband stayed to fight them. The Yuki man was a good fighter even though he had only one eye. He had a large basket shield to stop arrows with. The Nomlaki could not hit him. Soon he killed one Nomlaki, then two, and wounded the third. Just then an arrow struck him in his one good eye and killed him.

The woman had crossed the river and was calling for help. She brought three men back with her to help her husband. When they climbed back up the bluff they found him dead. Then they looked around and saw three Nomlaki. They chased the Nomlaki up the mountain. Near the top the Nomlaki hid in the thick brush. The Yuki could not find them.

The Yuki returned to where the man and wife had lived. The woman had gathered a big pile of brush. On top of the brush she had put all their baskets and everything they owned. The body of her husband was put on top of the pile and set on fire. The woman returned to her folks and lived with them after that.

NOMLAKI ACCOUNTS

5. In ancient times all Indian tribes had their own territory or hunting grounds. No other tribe was allowed on this land without special permission from the right officer. This is what happened on the Nomlaki hunting grounds many years ago. The Yuki at that time were a most warlike and vicious people. They often poached on Nomlaki territory and caused much disturbance and bloodshed. Often they would make raids on some of the Nomlaki camps, kill the men, and take away the young women. They robbed the camps of whatever seemed valuable to them. There were about four hundred of these bandits who ran in a gang all over the different Indian territories. The Yuki would take the scalps of the Nomlaki back to their own territory. There they would erect a pole about twenty feet high and put the scalps on the top. Then they would hold a wild war dance around the pole. While dancing around this pole, they would shoot at the scalps with bow and arrows. They had a great time over the victory. This went on for several years, and eventually the Nomlaki decided to try and put an end to it. So the captains of the foothills called a conference and talked the matter over very seriously. The officers agreed that they should stop these raids by the Yuki. On the following day they selected a large piece of ground and called every man from each village. Not a woman or child was allowed at this meeting. After the speeches at this big congregation, the men gladly organized into a small army.

The Nomlaki were not a warlike people, so in time of trouble they had to make preparations for war. They were obliged to get the men together, and the war chiefs lectured to them on warfare and made plans for the coming battle. The Yuki waged war all the time and had their trained men always on hand. The Yuki were the most warlike and vicious tribe of Indians in this part of the country. The Nomlaki, who were making preparations for war, lived in the foothills, while the Yuki lived over the mountains on the west side of the Coast Range.

The Yuki were not satisfied with their portion of ground on one side of the mountains. They wanted to rule both sides. The Nomlaki, who lived in the foothills, had some of their people by the Sacramento River. During this war preparation they had to go down to the river and call on these chiefs for men and help. In this district some of the white men who were married to Indian women learned all about what was going on. They spread the news to the white people who lived at Newville and the surrounding country. After the story was checked up, the white people hurriedly gathered all the rifles, shotguns, pistols, shot and powder they could find. They supplied the Nomlaki with this. This gave the Nomlaki a good chance of whipping the Yuki and breaking up this roving bandit gang. The whites did not have any too good a feeling about these Yuki anyhow. The river people understood very well how to use the white man's weapons, but the Nomlaki knew very little about guns, though they were very good shots with bows and arrows, and darts [spears?]. After everything was ready, the Nomlaki men, women, and children moved to the summit of the mountain where this combat was to take place. There were four hundred men on the Nomlaki side and the same number on the Yuki side. After the Nomlaki reached the summit and pitched camp, several smoke signs were given. This was a challenge for a fight. The fires were built along the side of the top of the mountain where the Yuki could get a good view of them. The fires were made of pine pitch with wet moss thrown on the top. This makes a thick, black smoke representing a dirty, black conflict.

The Yuki saw this, and they were ever ready, for they were bloodthirsty. They arrived the next morning. There was only one way to get to this place of battle. This was over the mountain on the old Indian trail. This trail led from the Yuki side over the mountain down a high ridge to the river on the Nomlaki side. There was another trail that led from the river on the Nomlaki side to the top of the mountain. This trail was used by the Nomlaki for gathering pine nuts. This was the trail that the Nomlaki army took. Some of the Nomlaki men hid themselves near the river and many hid themselves along the trail. Thus they could follow up the Yuki when they came.

The Yuki had to come over this mountain, down the ridge to the river, and up the other trail to where the foe was waiting. The Yuki came on, one by one, down the ridge to the river and up the trail on the opposite ridge. The hidden Nomlaki men watched them until the very last man passed by. The leading man of the Yuki, as he neared the top of the mountain, stopped and waited until his last man came up the trail.

They all assembled and were getting ready to make a charge and surround the Nomlaki camp. Then the Nomlaki opened fire on them. The Yuki heard the roar of guns and saw their men being mowed down. They became very frightened and fled down the trail into more gunshot. The Yuki were very afraid of the report of rifles. They thought that the United States army was after them. Nearly every Yuki was killed. Two young men were captured and taken to the Nomlaki camp, where they were fed and taken care of very well. These men were sent back to the remainder of the Yuki to tell the news so that they would come and take care of their dead and wounded.

Some time later, when the Nomlaki went to the top of the mountain to gather pine nuts, they saw where the Yuki had burned the dead, and also bows and arrows. This ended the Yuki bandits of four hundred strong. There was never any further trouble with the Yuki after this one battle with the Nomlaki.

6. One of the daughters of Dominic's grandfather went to gather seeds for the first time. The lookout was busy making rope, and the enemy [Yuki] came in and surrounded the gatherers, killing this old chief's daughter. The girl who took care of her ran back. She stripped off all her clothes and beads and got back. This group of gatherers wasn't large enough to attack the Yuki before they returned home. The Yuki were from Jump-off, and spies were sent after them. There was one Nomlaki who could talk Yuki and could come and go without being attacked, though he really belonged to our side. He was living with the Nomlaki at the time, and was sent to warn the girls who had been captured.

The chief asked the Stony Creek people, who were good warriors, to help him. In those times Indians would rather go to a war than to a dance, so they went. They never drank water or ate while going. The hunters would go ahead and get food together, and at camps the foretellers [diviners] would tell them what to do and what the outcome would be. This time the diviner told them to go on to the mountain and be ready early in the morning in order to rout the Yuki out at daybreak when their war dance would be over and everyone asleep. They had the scouts figure out the distance. They surrounded the village and gave a war whoop. The Yuki got excited and ran; they didn't put up a fight at all. Our people killed almost every Yuki.

Certain men had been detailed to go in for the Nomlaki girls, and these were brought back. They also brought back some Yuki boys, whom they raised to manhood and then sent home. Dominic's grandfather was a peacemaker, but he was mad and had this war. Only a few of our people were hurt, and none were killed.

7. The Nomlaki people used to go to Government Flat to gather sunflower seeds. The Yuki didn't know what salt was [i.e. didn't have any] and they traded seeds for salt and made friends with one another that way. A captain had gone with a son and a daughter to Government Flat where the Yuki sometimes went to hunt, and they were gone too long, so our

people suspected something. The Yuki had killed this group—scalped the boy and his parents and taken the girl into Round Valley. They cut up our people and made "jerky" of them. Our people learned of this and told the captain.

The next day our people started over the mountains. When they got to Government Flat they saw some Yuki carrying home deer, and some of the men wanted to kill them. But the captain, who wanted to find their home, wouldn't let them, and he had two men follow the Yuki hunters. They located the place at the fork of Williams Creek, I think, and returned to their captain.

They went back to the Yuki village in the evening, and saw the girl coming down to the creek to get water in a basket. One Nomlaki scout talked to her, and took her away. Toward morning our people surrounded the sweathouse where the Yuki were having a good time over the three scalps. They tried to get them out in the daylight, but the Yuki wouldn't come out. There was one old fellow in our tribe who talked Yuki, and he yelled to them that they should come out and face [the consequences of] what they had done. Our people killed every one of the Yuki—not a one got away. They took a lot of young girls with them, but no men.

There was a big tribe of Yuki in the country, and they gathered a party together and followed our people nearly to the valley. They were afraid, though, and went back. My grandfather was in charge of that war party. His white name was Thomson, and he was head man of the dolitewa group [lineage] from Newville. This was just before the white people came in.

8. The last fight with the Yuki happened after the whites had been in here three years. The Nomlaki were running away from the whites. They went to Howard Lake, over the summit, to catch salmon out of the Eel River and to gather nuts and seeds. That was over the border line. It was in the fall of the year that the Yuki from Round Valley found them there. They came into our camp in the morning and started killing our people. One woman ran up the summit and came down Log Spring Ridge; another came over Fork Ridge and crossed over by Bear Den Trail, and both ran to Lopom [a large village near the present Paskenta]. They both arrived there at about the same time—late in the afternoon. The people there had messengers whom they sent out. The next afternoon people came into Lopom from all over. They were going to the war. Their captains had sent them there. The captain from Lopom led them, and the people claim that the line was so long that its beginning was in the timber and the tail down in the valley. They ate lunch at Log Spring Ridge and went to Howard Lake, where they found the corpses of the people lying around. The Yuki had taken all the food that had been gathered up. The people sat and cried,

and were awfully mad. The captain said that the way was still long and that the Yuki were probably having a war dance; they should get there by early morning to fight. They went down the river to this side of Round Valley on the first ridge where they all sat down and watched the Yuki having a big war dance over the killing of the Nomlaki. The captain said that the boys could smoke, but that they would have to blow the smoke down squirrel holes to keep the Yuki watchmen from seeing it. Toward morning the Yuki quit dancing, and when they had gone to sleep the Nomlaki captain led his people down. One group was sent to the camp, another to get back the things that had been stolen. So they went down and set fire to the buildings and shot the Yuki with arrows, and speared them. They caught a bunch of young people and brought back eighteen girls and three boys after they were finished fighting late in the afternoon. All the rest were killed. They picked up all the food they could carry and brought it back along with the captives. They camped on Eel River one night and the next at Howard Lake, where they put their own dead in a gulch and threw earth over them. Then they came on home.

On Thomes' Creek they kept the girls a couple of years and made them work. They built a big sweathouse there. They set a war dance for the spring of the year, for they were going to kill those girls. The Nomlaki set a pole in the ground and attached crosspieces, like a ladder, so that they could make the girls climb up there. Then they dressed the girls in feathers, painted their lips and cheeks, and tied their hands in back of them. As they put each girl on the pole they tied her leg on each side of it and stood her up. They had gathered up a pile of small rocks and a lot of wood, and a big fire was built as soon as night fell. They started to yell and run around the girl they had up on the pole. They danced and made the other girls dance, too. They circled around her, stopping to give a whoop and to shoot arrows into her. They all took a shot at her, and she was quite a while dying. They didn't quit dancing until she died. Singers changed off and never stopped singing until she died. When she was dead they put another one up the same way. The girls that were to be killed were forced to dance, too. My grandfather had one of the boys who had learned to talk Nomlaki. He was a good boy, so my grandfather told him that he was to be killed in the same way. He sent the boy after water and told him to run away, and to stay in the canyons so they wouldn't find him. When the Nomlaki noticed that this boy was gone they told my grandfather, and made him go out to look for the boy with them. So he went out on a ridge and watched the trail on the summit by Log Springs, and when the boy came up the ride he told him to get down in the canyon. Then my grandfather returned and told the people he hadn't seen the boy, and they gave up the hunt.

After all had been killed they took the girls and the two boys and laid them down with the heads to the west and the feet to the east, on top of the ground. Then they took the white rocks and laid them on all around. That was the last fight they had with the Yuki. My grandmother was a young lady at the time. She danced in the war dance and showed me the place. The sweathouse and the rocks were still there.

9. They say that once they met twelve Yuki near Mountain House [Lopom]. The captain of the Yuki began to talk, when the Nomlaki found them. They couldn't understand one another except by gestures. The captain licked his hands and our people thought he meant he wanted salt. He showed his beads. One Yuki man kept looking at one of the Nomlaki. He had a spearing pole in his hand and he swung it around, saying, "leskoma," keeping his eye on this one man. Our people warned this Nomlaki fellow to be careful, but he didn't seem to pay any attention. All at once the Yuki thrust at this Nomlaki, who rolled over quickly so that the Yuki missed. Other Nomlaki shot the Yuki right in the rib. The captain paid no attention to this, as if nothing had happened. Our captain motioned to the Yuki to come to the village that night. The Yuki threw their man in the gulch and threw dirt on him and went down to camp. That night they went into the house and traded. They slept in there and were fed. The Yuki and the Nomlaki did big preaching [to give assurances of mutual good will] and then these men went home. They may really have wanted to trade, but they were found up in the hills.

CONCLUSION

The foregoing stories were related by informants as truthful accounts of historic happenings. Undoubtedly they did have their origins in actual conflicts, but beyond this assumption we must be very cautious in interpretation of the data.

The material can most easily be considered under three headings: (1) the folkloristic aspect, including the very marked "patterning" which occurs; (2) attitudes indicated; (3) ethnographic contents.

(1) Analysis shows that none of the stories can be accepted as accurate accounts of battles. Rather we find certain favored incidents appearing in varying but limited combinations. This combining leads to definite, stylized patterning, into which, presumably, any other war stories from these peoples should fit. Table 1 gives the principal traits in Yuki-Nomlaki war accounts, and their occurrence. A composite story would follow this approximate sequence: a small party is attacked (stories 1, 2, 3, 4, 6, 7, 8, 9) while

camping (stories 1, 3, 4), gathering (stories 6, 7), poaching (stories 5, 8), or trading (stories 2, 9). A woman or girl rushes back with the news (stories 1, 3, 4, 6, 8); a war party is formed (stories 1, 2, 3, 5, 6, 7, 8); a period of preparation follows (stories 1, 2, 5, 6, 8), culminating in a surprise attack (stories 2, 6, 7, 8), or a prearranged battle (stories 1, 5). All or nearly all of the enemy are killed (stories 1, 2, 3, 5, 6, 7, 8), while few or none of the narrator's party are slain (stories 2, 6). Scalps are taken (stories 1, 5, 7) and a victory dance follows (stories 1, 2, 7, 8). This is the last Yuki-Nomlaki fight (stories 1, 2, 5, 8).

It can be seen from the table that the patterns of the two tribes are quite similar, though there are several elements that are unique for one group

TABLE 1

DISTRIBUTION OF ELEMENTS IN YUKI-NOMLAKI WAR STORIES

	Yuki				Nomlaki				
	1	2	3	4	5	6	7	8	9
Cause of war an attack	x	x	x	x		x	x	x	x
Attacked party camping	x		x	x					
Attacked party gathering						x	x		
Attacked party poaching					x			x	
Attacked party trading		x							x
Woman or girl rushes back	x		x	x		x		x	
Period of war preparation	x	x			x	x		x	
War party formed	x	x	x		x	x	x	x	
Surprise attack on enemy		x				x	x	x	
Prearranged battle	x				x				
All-night fight	x	x							
Enemy cowards						x	x		
All or nearly all of enemy killed ..	x	x	x		x	x	x	x	
Few or none of own party killed ..		x				x			
Scalps taken	x				x		x		
Postwar victory dance	x		x				x	x	
Feast following dance	x		x						
Prisoners taken					x	x	x	x	
Last Yuki-Nomlaki fight	x	x			x			x	

only. Yuki stories alone record an attack upon camping persons, all-night fights, and a feast following the victory dance. Specific Nomlaki occurrences are attacks upon gathering parties, poaching upon the enemy's territory, enemy cowards, and prisoners taken.

Stories 4, 5, and 9 are most aberrant. Story 5 is weighted with invectives against the Yuki, and is also the least reliable. Stories 4 and 9 lack the decisive pitched battles of the other seven, and might more accurately be classified as "border incidents."

Thus we find that instead of historical verities we have mere folkloristic accounts, stylized and formalized, of what actually did occur. The reason for this transformation from true narration to idealized patterns is not difficult to find. All peoples love to relate stories of the bravery in war of their ancestors, and it is but natural that the glorifying elements come to take precedence over the less creditable ones. The farther removed the narrator is from first-hand acquaintance with the event, the fewer qualms he has in substituting fiction for fact. In the foregoing stories, war guilt is invariably attributed to the enemy, and justice and righteousness prevail in the form of victory. Size of war parties is fantastically increased, in one instance to 2,000 (two dozen would be a closer estimate), and frequently the enemy is destroyed. Further evidence of this tendency to boast is shown by a negative occurrence: no mention is made of the payment of compensation *by the victor* to the loser as a bribe against a counterattack, despite the fact that this practice is actually found among these tribes. Sagas of this nature, told to wide-eyed children and grandchildren, ending with "and there weren't enough of the enemy left," or the like, could scarcely be spoiled by adding, "and we paid them Indian gold and obsidian [highly valued objects] so they wouldn't attack us again."

The patterning becomes more evident when we compare it with that of our own stories of similar nature. In the stories recorded here, there is no mention of individual heroes of special abilities. Places are always carefully recorded, but the participants are, with rare exceptions, merely "the Yuki" and "the Nomlaki." There are no accounts of self-sacrifice, fighting against desperate odds, rescue by a relief force in the nick of time, and countless other elements which make up our own "historical" stories.

Another point raised by this analysis is the relative stability of various types of stories. It seems likely that narratives of this type, involving glorification of the tribe, would tend to be more quickly altered to conform to the socially idealized and accepted patterns than simple accounts of everyday life, such as a man's encounter with a ghost, a hunting trip, or the friendly meeting with members of another tribe for the purpose of trade. Further investigation along this line should prove interesting.

(2) These stories give us an interesting picture of certain attitudes held by the tribes toward each other. Such attitudes are indicated by the changes from truth to myth which have taken place; and they are emphasized by occasional derogatory phraseology, as, for instance, in story 5. A dominant theme in the Nomlaki accounts is that the Yuki were a "vicious and warlike tribe." All other sources (the related Huchnom to the south, the Kato to the west, and accounts of early settlers in the region) agree with this

statement. Stephen Powers bears eloquent testimony to this in his *Tribes of California:* "The inhabitants of this valley . . . were indisputably the worst tribe among the California Indians. . . . The unphilosophical and double-seeing Wintun at Red Bluff described the Yuki to me as terrific fellows, savage giants living in the Coast Range mountains, dwelling in caves and dens, horribly tattooed (which they are), and cannibals." The reference to the making of "jerky" in story 7 may be an implication of cannibalism. This attribute of the Yuki was believed by all their neighbors.

Another attitude, mentioned in the discussion of patterning above, is that of justice and righteousness on the part of the narrator's tribe and the unwarranted hostility of the enemy. Story 5 illustrates this most clearly, but the theme is apparent in nearly all.

(3) Though we cannot accept these stories as true history, there is no doubt that they do illustrate the general style of warfare and the underlying concepts. The prime cause of war—murder or assault—is not left in doubt. It appears, directly or implied, in all nine stories. A second cause of friction is based upon the concept of tribal property. Individual land ownership was of course unknown, but strict ideas with regard to the land of tribal and subtribal units were in force. Poaching as leading to war, is indicated in stories 5 and 8. The acceptance of wergild when feasible is illustrated in the first tale. This theme is widespread throughout California, and is merely the extension of the practice from interindividual to intertribal dealings. Prearranged battles are indicated in stories 1 and 5. There is likely an organic relationship between this practice and that of wergild. As in the first story, an unsuccessful palaver with armed warriors on each side might easily lead to fighting.

The taking of scalps (stories 1, 5, 7) was an important accessory to the victory dance (stories 1, 2, 7, 8) held at the conclusion of a successful campaign. The scalps were stretched on frames and erected on poles. In contrast to the popular conception of scalping, the taking of scalps by the Yuki and Nomlaki was not an end in itself. It served rather as a means by which the victors could give vent to their wrath, and at the same time shame the enemy. Being thus symbolic, only a few (even one) were sufficient, and thus not all fallen enemies were mutilated. When speaking off the record, both Yuki and Nomlaki informants admitted that sometimes one scalp was passed from village to village and dance to dance, until it was actually worn out. In the heat of the dance, grieving Yuki widows and orphans might seize the trophies and dance with them in their teeth. This practice observed by those who did not understand its significance, might well give rise to the charges of Yuki anthropophagy suggested in story 7, and by Powers.

Belief in the "Indian bear" (story 1) is common throughout much of

California. Here he is playing his culturally sanctioned role to perfection, that is, killing members of an enemy tribe. Other true elements that help complete the picture of warfare are the appropriation of the enemy's belongings (stories 3, 8), taking of captives (stories 5, 6, 7, 8), use of spies and scouts (stories 6, 7), prearranged battles (stories 1, 5), and surprise attacks (stories 2, 6, 7, 8). Curiously, these stories contain few references to actual fighting techniques, for example, how bows and arrows were carried, number of arrows, range of fire, formation of opposite sides. (Informants, however, are acquainted with these details.)

Summarizing briefly, we find that a comparative treatment of war stories of these two enemy tribes brings out the folkloristic nature of purported history, the stylized patterning to which the stories conform, the attitudes of the tribes toward each other, and makes it possible to identify correctly the ethnographical contents of "historical" tales.

ABORIGINAL CALIFORNIA AND GREAT BASIN CARTOGRAPHY

by
Robert F. Heizer

As seen on the map, the distribution of the Yuki seems irregular. This is not because their location ran counter to natural topography, but because it followed it. Their country lies wholly in the Coast Range mountains, which in this region are not, on the whole, very high, but are much broken. They contain some valleys, but the surface of the land in general is endlessly rugged. The Yuki habitat is, however, not defined, except incidentally, by limiting mountains and ranges, but is given in block by the drainage of such-and-such streams. The native did not think, like a modern civilized man, of his people owning an area circumscribed by a definite line, in which there might happen to be one or many watercourses. This would have been viewing the land through a map, whether drawn or mental, and such an attitude was foreign to his habit. What he did know was that the little town at which he was born and where he expected to die lay on a certain river or branch of a river; and that this stream, or a certain stretch of it, and all the creeks flowing into it, and all the land on or between these creeks, belonged to his people; whereas below, or above, or across certain hills, were other streams and tributaries, where other people lived, with whom he might be on visiting terms or intermarried, but who had proprietary rights of their own.

The passage quoted above is taken from A. L. Kroeber's *Handbook of the Indians of California*. The statement is important, for it established a generalization which has been applied in drawing up the detailed map of California tribes contained in Kroeber's book. Inspection of the large colored map in the *Handbook* will show how consistently stream drainages and watersheds served as tribal boundaries, and indeed, the same situation holds on the modern map of California county boundaries. The concept of drainage and watersheds as forming territorial boundaries of tribes has proved applicable beyond California, as, for example, in Kroeber's detailed map of American Indian tribes published in 1939 in *Cultural and Natural Areas of Native North America*.

As a student of California Indian culture, Kroeber's statement that, "viewing the land through a map, whether drawn or mental," was foreign to the California native may be, and probably is, true with reference to

Univ. of Calif. Arch. Survey Report, No. 41 (1958), pp. 1–9.

the Indian either visualizing or sketching a map of the territory occupied by his group. Dr. Kroeber, a person more intimately familiar with the California tribes, and an indefatigable researcher in ethnogeography, doubtless had good reason to state that such ideas were foreign to the native's habit, the implication being that, since there was no need or reason for such cartographic conceptions, they did not occur to the Indian. I can myself attest to the fact that even today non-map-oriented individuals are not rarities in California. Almost any archaeologist engaged in archaeological site reconnaissance has had the experience of hauling out a U.S.G.S. topographic quadrange, showing it to some provincial, and hearing him say, "I don't understand maps — never use 'em" or something of the sort. He is not familiar with maps, but he knows where he is, and he can direct you to a specific spot some miles away by citing natural features as guidemarks.

This brings me to the point of this article, *viz.*, that the California Indian may not have thought in terms of maps, but when he was asked for directions or requested to draw a map, he could often do so. There is abundant evidence of this fact in the historical documents which record the earliest meetings of Indians and Caucasians. It was the Indian who knew where he was, the Caucasian who was inquiring about what lay ahead. Answers to such inquiries were most often rendered in gestures and signs, but occasionally a native would draw a map on the earth.

The earliest instance seems to be that described by Fr. Juan Crespi on Sunday, August 6, 1769, when the Portola expedition was among the Fernandeño group of Gabrielino and the camp was visited by numbers of natives. Crespi says, "They had heard of the sailing of the packets to the coast and channel of Santa Barbara; they drew on the ground the shape of the channel with its islands, marking the route of the ships."

Frémont, while at Pyramid Lake, Nevada, on January 15, 1844, interrogated the local Northern Paiute people and reports, "We could obtain from them but little information respecting the country. They made on the ground a drawing of the [Truckee] river which they represented as issuing from another lake [Tahoe] in the mountains three or four days distant, in a direction a little west of south; beyond which, they drew a mountain [Sierra Nevadas]; and further still, two rivers [Sacramento and/or American or Feather or San Joaquin] on one of which [Sacramento?] they told us that people like ourselves travelled."

Frémont, on December 6, 1843, when somewhat south and east of Klamath Lake, Oregon, among the Klamath tribe says, "The stream we had struck [Pit River] issued from the mountain in an easterly direction, turning to the southward a short distance below; and, drawing a course upon the ground, they made us comprehend that it pursued its way for a long distance in that direction, uniting with many other streams, and gradually becoming a great river. Without the subsequent information, which confirmed the opinion, we became immediately satisfied that this water formed the principal stream of the Sacramento River."

In the journal of J. Goldsborough Bruff under the date of November 7, 1850, is the entry:

The older Hough related to me their first visit to Honey Lake, as they called it, from a sweet substance which they found exuding from the heads of wild oats in the basin. (I have named it L. Derby). An aged Indian visited their camp, and they made signs to him that they were in search of a deep-basined lake, where there was gold, and they showed him a small lump of the metal. The old savage, then took a pair of macheres (large flat leathers to throw over the saddle) and sprinkled sand over them, drew a model map of the country there, and beyond it, some distance. He heaped up sand, to form buttes, and ranges of mountains; and with a straw, drew streams, lakes and trails: then adjusted it to correspond with the cardinal points, and explained it. He pointed to the sun, and by signs made them understand, the number of day's travel from one point to another. On it he had traced (as I found on their explanation) Mary's Humboldt River, Carson River, Pyramid lake, and the emigrant routes — above and below. He moved his finger, explanatory of the revolutions of wagon wheels, and that white people travelled along, with guns, on the said routes. On his map, he had exhibited the lake they were then at, and another in a deep basin, with 3 buttes beside it, and said that gold was plentiful there; and also, that 10 months ago the whites had visited it, and fought with the Indians.

In 1849 A. J. McCall describes the making of a sand map by Northern Paiute at Lassen's Meadows: "While at the Meadows I met a friendly and intelligent Indian who made for me a map in the sand, a topographical map of the route over the [Sierra] Nevadas. The sand was piled up to indicate mountains and with his fingers he creased the heap to show the canyons and water courses. To indicate wood and timber he stuck in sprigs of sage, and spears of grass where grass was to be found, and made signs to inform us where the Indians were friendly or dangerous. It was really an ingenious affair and he was well acquainted with the country."

In 1853 Lt. A. W. Whipple encountered Chemehuevis near the Colorado River, and describes how one "drew a sketch of this country, giving the Pai-ute names of tribes, and the rivers where they dwell." In another section of the same report are reproduced three Indian maps, one a Tewa Pueblo map of the Rio Grande towns, another a Yuma map of the Colorado River with tribes located, and the third the Chemehuevi map of the Colorado showing tribal locations. It is presumably the Yuma map that is referred to by Kroeber (quoted above) as "the only native map ever published from California."

In Mallery's volume on North American Indian pictography occurs the following description of a sand map made by a Southern Paiute in Southern Nevada:

Dr. W. J. Hoffman states that when at Grapevine Springs, Nevada, in 1871, the Pai-Uta living at that locality informed the party of the exact location of Las Vegas, the objective point. The Indian sat upon the sand and with the palms of his hands formed an oblong ridge to represent Spring Mountains and southeast of this ridge, another gradual slope, terminating on the eastern side more abruptly; over the latter passed his fingers to represent the side valleys running eastward. He then took a stick and showed them the direction of the old Spanish trail running east and west over the lower portion of the last-named ridge. When this was completed the Indians looked at the members of the party, and with a mixture of English, Spanish and Pai-Uta, and gesture signs, told them that from where they were now they would have to go southward, east of Spring Mountain, to the camp of Pai-Uta Charlie, where they would have to sleep; then indicating a line southeastward to another spring (Stumps) to complete the second day; then he followed the line representing the Spanish trail to the east of the divide of the second ridge, above named, where he left it, and passing northward to the first valley, he thrust the short stick into the ground and said, "Las Vegas."

Stephen Powers records that, to illustrate a myth about how the Sierra Nevadas and Coast Ranges were formed, a Yokuts Indian "drew in the sand a long ellipse, representing quite accurately the shape of the two ranges." Whether this can be called a map as such is unclear, but the basic idea is present and for present purposes we shall consider this instance as evidence of the translation of topographic features into a plane map.

The instances cited above refer to the following tribes and dates: Fernandeño, 1769 (Crespi); Havasupai, 1775 (Escalante); Oregon Klamath, 1843 (Frémont); Pyramid Lake Paviotso, 1844 (Frémont); Honey Lake Paviotso, 1849, 1850 (Bruff, McCall); Chemehuevi and Yuma, 1853 (Mollhausen, Whipple); Southern Paiute, 1871 (Mallery); and Yokuts, 1877 (Powers). In these instances we may be reasonably or fully certain that the Indians' mapping technique was not acculturated, but was aboriginal. From more recent times there are at least two examples of Indian-made maps which might theoretically be ascribable to Caucasian influence, but even admitting the possibility, it seems unlikely. Kroeber reproduced a sketch map drawn between 1911 and 1916 by the famous Yahi, Ishi, and says this map "is of interest because it proves the California Indians to have been not totally devoid of faculty in this direction. They usually refuse pointblank to make even an attempt of this kind, alleging utter inability, and it is only in the extreme south of the State that some rudiments of a sense of tracing topography appear. The Mohave readily draw streams and mountains in the sand, and the only native map ever published from California is a sketch of this type. The Diegueño ground paintings also evince some elements of cartographic endeavor, although in ritualized form."

The second recent Indian map was drawn by an Owens Valley Paiute, and depicts the Big Pine creek drainage area. It was drawn some time between 1927 and 1931, is of modern date and hence may be suspect as representing a facility present among this group in pre-Caucasian times. The map was executed by a man then about 100 years old, which means that he was alive when the first whites were seen and was too old to have gone to school. I am inclined to think that these facts, together with the 1849 and 1850 sand maps of the same general Paiute group at Honey Lake, indicate the Owens Valley map as representing persistence of an old and original trait.

It will have occurred to the reader that there is a definite weighting of instances of sand-map making among groups who live in semiarid regions. Whether such maps were more used by the natives of the less well-watered portions of western North America, or whether, in the period of Caucasian discovery and exploration, it was in those less attractive regions that geographical advice was more deliberately sought and acquired from the natives, is something which I do not believe can be answered with the evidence at hand. Forest tribes, arctic coast dwellers, and plains peoples all make similar maps in the sand or draw them on bark or hide, so we can suppose no very absolute rule to obtain here as regards environmental determinism. If I were pressed to give my own opinion, I should say that the abundance of references attesting to sand maps among the Shoshonean peoples is probably a matter of historical and documentary chance, but I would not rule out the further possibility that the practice was emphasized by those thinly populated tribes who occupied the regions of deficient rainfall. At any rate, to such tribes these maps might often be of critical importance in the matter of arranging a rendezvous, or any number of other reasons which might theoretically apply.

This review of the cartographic ability of certain California and Great Basin Indians has served to illuminate, however imperfectly, one aspect of the natives' knowledge of the actual world. There is nothing remarkable in these little maps scratched in the sand, for primitive peoples all over the world can make such charts of areas known to them. In the extensive amount of intertribal trade and the involved network of trails of California Indians, such simple maps appear to have a rational functional context.

THE WORLD RENEWAL
CULT OF NORTHWEST
CALIFORNIA

by
A. L. Kroeber

We present herewith one of the closed systems of native American religion. It is a system comparable to the Kuksu cult of central California, the Chungichnish Datura religion of southern California, the Kachina cult of the Pueblos, the secret society of Hamatsa initiations and performances of Vancouver Island and northward. Every such system is pervaded by a definable pattern, which may appear endlessly varied in detail, but yet is felt, by both the participants in the cult and by outside observers, to constitute a single coherent scheme. Outside its frame, many elements of the system recur, both in other fields of the same cultures and beyond them in foreign cultures; but the pattern as such is no longer primarily operative. Internally, the various tribal or local expressions of the pattern are never identical, and may in fact vary quite considerably. It is the fact that in spite of such unlikenesses they are recognizable as being variants of one pattern, which constitutes them manifestations of a delimitable system.

How is such a system or its pattern recognized and "delimited"? By a synthetic perception, appraisal, or judgment, which is essentially intuitional —a subjective insight into qualities or qualitative relations; an apperception of forms having values, in short. This process does not exclude evidential validation, of course. And it must lead to rational results and be defensible by natural analysis and argument. But it seems that the evaluative act of pattern recognition and definition is not cardinally an act of reasoning so much as of organized apperception.

Basically, the ethnographer is responsible for his pattern recognitions, as a historian is for his. Now the historian takes into consideration the opinions of Pericles on the outbreak of the Peloponnesian War, or of Luther on the Reformation; though, if he restricted himself to reproducing their opinions, he would not be a historian but only a compiler. Just so, reflective and articulate native opinion is as much a part of the data which the ethnographer must use to develop his own formulation as are objectively observable acts of behavior and the paraphernalia of a system. Native opinion

Pp. 1–5 of A. L. Kroeber and E. W. Gifford, *World Renewal: A Cult System of Native Northwest California,* Univ. Calif. Publ. Anthro. Rec. (1949), 13:1–156.

may be volunteered or it may be stimulated by discussion or questioning; and sometimes it exists ready formulated in mythology. Such myth formulations are of course not analytical in the sense of modern science, and the world of scholarship does not take their statements as to origin as having any direct value. But their statements as to what does and does not belong together in the native culture, as to its organization or systematization, are certainly primary documents of the greatest significance, whether they be accepted outright or need revaluation.

Beyond what the native can formulate as to the pattern and purpose of his system of rituals lies a fringe of what the anthropologist can perceive or infer. This includes those aspects of the system which it has lately become fashionable to name "covert." Such are partial likenesses underlying surface unlikenesses within the system; inferences as to the historic development of the system and its external relations; and pertinent modes of behavior and motivations of which native participants remain unaware. Such "deeper" discoverable motivations do not seem to be many in this case: the Indians of northwest California are shrewd and suspicious psychologists of one another, on the *ad hoc* level. As to behavior, they put into the forefront of their attention the expected or "ideal" conduct; as well they ought to, in giving information: since without defined norm or standard, all deviations and penetrations beyond it are meaningless. Of discrepancies between ideal and practice they are potentially well aware, and sometimes, though not always, interested in them. Comparative analysis and historic inferences are not their business but the anthropologist's.

The name of the present system is coined, something like "Sun Dance"; just as Kuksu, Kachina, Hamatsa are actual native names for mere partial constituents, which ethnographers have extended to denote also the whole systems because the natives had no comprehensive designation for those. Around 1900–1905, some of the Karok, the nearer Yurok, and the few whites in the region called two or three of the Karok rites "New Years," in speaking English. The term "Pikiavish" was also beginning to be used, as an abbreviation of Isivsanen upikiavish, "world's restoration" or "repair" ("fixing"); and in the Karok region this word is now current, not only among white residents and Indians, but with tourists. The Yurok had no corresponding phrase, and spoke generally in terms of "dances" about their equivalent rites; the Hupa merely list the main parts of their corresponding unit complex, at any rate in English. The esoteric magic and avowed purpose of the focal ceremonies comprising the system include reëstablishment or firming of the earth, first-fruits observances, new fire, prevention of disease and calamity for another year or biennium. These several motivations, some of which are explicit or alluded to in each of the dozen local cults, appear to be conveniently suggested by our name "world renewal";

but, appropriate or otherwise, this is only a label which we have manufactured and applied.

Some of the features that recur through the dozen or so ceremonies of the system will now be reviewed—segregated for convenience into esoteric and exoteric traits.

The institutors are always believed to be individually nameless members of the prehuman spirit race, who departed or transformed themselves when human beings advanced to occupy the world. This is the race called ikhareya by the Karok, kihunnai by the Hupa, woge by the Yurok. The core of the esoteric rite is the recitation of a narrative or dialogue formula repeating the words of these spirits of the past, accompanied somewhat variably by acts of mimetic magic symbolic of their actions at that time. The formula is recited in segments at a series of specified spots in a fixed order, by a single priest or formulist, whose title sometimes varies, even within the same language, according to the particular rite which he conducts. He is purified by prolonged abstention from water, profane activities, sex contacts; by semifasting; and by sweating in the sweathouse. He blows tobacco crumbs to the spirits of old, or smokes tobacco, or burns angelica root as incense.

The acts performed by the formulist are the most variable parts of the ceremonies as these are made at different places. They include the partial rebuilding or repair of the timber structure sacred to the dance, as symbolic of restrengthening of the world; new fire kindling, with its smoke or flame tabooed to sight of the public; ceremonial taking or consuming of salmon or acorns in a first-fruit type of rite; long itineraries, or series of them, to spots at which sections of formulas or invocations are recited or firewood is cut or timbers are felled or fires built; watching or waking; directing the building of a weir; mock fishing with a pole and line for dentalium shells; and others more. These features of symbolic magic are not only numerous but quite diverse as between different ceremonies, though they are scrupulously prescribed and fixed for each. And they occur in the several ceremonies in varying frequency, emphasis, and combination.

The formulist in some rituals has with him a middle-aged male assistant; or one or two girls who may be married but have not yet had children; or a group of adults, men or women, young or old, whom the Yurok call tä:ʟ, who sing with him at night and in some cases accompany him on his itinerary.[1]

There is at least one structure sacred to each renewal rite or associated with it. This may be a dwelling actually inhabited at other times; or a sweathouse also used under less publicly sacred circumstances; or a special

---

[1] In this and other papers in the present volume the surd "l" is represented by a small capital ʟ.—Eds.

structure hybrid between house and sweathouse in its size and shape and used or entered only for the ceremony. If dancing takes place indoors, this occurs always only in one particular living house; and in that event a second specified living house serves to "tie up hair," that is, for the dancers to array themselves and practice. In one case, in Hupa, a lean-to fence of planks is erected to serve as a "house" for the ancient spirits. In one group of rites among the lower Yurok the symbolic magic of renewal is most fully expressed in the rebuilding of the sacred ritual structure. Even the weir building at Kepel may be allied in significance within this part of the pattern.

These ritual buildings represent the focus of an impulse toward localization which pervades the system and in fact the whole culture. Everything that is prescribed may and must be done only at a specified spot. This is true equally of indoor and outdoor, of esoteric and exoteric acts. Hence the formulists' itineraries to named places, the dancers' filing in to stand facing in one direction only under a particular tree or roof. Just as the inner, verbal part of each ceremony is attached to an ordained structure or group of structures in a settlement, and to a series of prayer and offering spots about or near the town, so the dance there is performed repetitively—and competitively as regards display—by several groups of dancers each representing a settlement or town close by—not more than a few miles away.

Strictly, perhaps, this providing of the equipment for a dance is the privilege of a family or house, or a related group of houses within a settlement, rather than of the undifferentiated town as a whole, since the town does not ordinarily function as a corporate unit. At any rate the privilege and responsibility of providing the equipment for a set of dancers is claimed as right by the descendants of certain houses. This device in one way concentrates recognized participation in the system, in another way spreads it. Of well over a hundred and perhaps nearly two hundred Karok, Yurok, and Hupa towns or settlements, only about a dozen held world-renewal rituals— only they might properly make them, in native belief. But these were on the whole the largest towns. Moreover, inclusion of the towns of next size, those which equipped contributory dances, would raise the number of participating settlements to around forty; and these forty would contain more or less half the total population of the three nationalities. Not all of the members of this total population were in publicly recognized personal relation to the ritual system; but they participated at least as minor kinsmen, affinals, neighbors, or friends of those having acknowledged functions.

The exoteric, public part of the world-renewal system consists of two dances, colloquially known in English as Jumping and Deerskin. The first alone was performed in six ceremonies; the second, in four; both together, in three. The two used different characteristic regalia—woodpecker-scalp headbands and dance baskets in the Jumping Dance; albino and other deerskins along with long flint and obsidian blades in the Deerskin. The prescribed steps were quite different, and the songs can always be told apart. However, there is a single word which denotes the performing of either dance in distinction from all other kinds or ways of dancing—a word, in short, meaning "world-renewal dance" or "major dance" only. The Jumping and Deerskin dances shared many of their accessory accoutrements; were both enacted by men standing abreast in one spot, and the whole rank invariably in a prescribed place; and were danced with a slow step to plaintive, wordless tunes sung only by the one to three dancers in the middle of the line. The regalia worn and carried in both were regarded as treasures and together with dentalium shells constituted the main wealth of the tribes, such as was also used in shamans' fees, bride prices, weregild, injury compensations, and inheritance of rank. The two dances gave the owners of the regalia their chief opportunity for public ostentation of treasures: they have accordingly been characterized as "wealth-displaying." By contrast, the dancers were little more than manikins exhibiting the treasures, and performed for the pleasure of participation—though the singers were chosen by informal public esteem for the quality of their voices or melodic inventiveness. Meanwhile, the hereditarily wealthy men of the town and of the customarily associated neighbor towns would be equipping and managing the several sets or parties of dancers. Their wealthy friends from a distance assisted them with voluntary—and reciprocated—contribution of dance-wear treasures. These coöperative arrangements were determined by personal and family connections; they were voluntary and might be abrogated; no one had any prescriptive right or duty to be responsible for a dance party at a distant ritual; but they often did participate as honored contributors visiting fifty miles and more away from home.

The two major dances always were repeated; usually for one or two or occasionally up to five days by the Karok, for ten to sixteen days among the Hupa and Yurok. Each song lasted perhaps three minutes, on the average. But each set or party ordinarily danced to three songs on each appearance; it might appear two or three times on one day; and there might be up to five parties participating. The number of separate dances—or songs —on one day might thus range from two or three to thirty or perhaps fifty. The considerable monotony of performance that might easily accumulate in a series of days was lessened by two factors. One of these was a slow but steady increase in the number of dancers, in the spiritedness of their performance, and in the gorgeousness of their apparel: everything worked toward a deferred climax of effect. The second device was the introduction of minor variations into the dance: such as changes of locale by means of progressive stations in a journey; or an approach made by dancing in boats; or a special figure or effect in a final dance.

Though the dances are rigorously bound by the sanctions of hallowed custom to particular manners, paraphernalia, and spots, there is almost nothing in these manners and features that is magically expressive, or symbolic, in the way that the esoteric parts of the rituals are symbolically magical. The dress and actions of the dancers, the wordless songs, are almost wholly "arbitrary," in the sense that they have no reference or ulterior meaning, either to the natives or ourselves. An occasional exception, such as the statement that the stamping of the dancers helps to firm and reëstablish the earth, seems secondary and is generic. All in all, the special characteristics of the dances have evidently been developed largely out of the technological, accumulative, and wealth-emphasizing tendencies of the culture, and have then become associated with its magico-symbolic system; the nexus or functional relation of the two remaining an extrinsic or accidental one; though apparently not less close and compelling on that account.

The differences between the thirteen rituals within the frame of the world-renewal system are evidently due to fortuitous or unexplained associations similar to this esoteric-exoteric association. Certain groupings of rituals within the system seem to be the result of local interinfluences and connections; though these have sometimes become interrupted.

Thus, as regards particularity, Hupa alone has a first-fruits feast for the acorn crop, a lean-to screen as "house" for its two separate Jumping dances, plus a Deerskin Dance—all associated with a sacred dwelling house in Takimiⅼding. There is also a first-salmon taking like those of WeⅬkwäu and Amaikiaram, but it is not associated with the same sacred house, and hence may be reckoned as outside the Takimiⅼding complex. All the Hupa features except the acorn feast have analogues elsewhere, but the combination of specificities is strictly local. The Takimiⅼding world renewal is rich in content, but its parts are very loosely aggregated and strung along over much of the year.

Kepel is featured by a "dam" or weir to take salmon—at the peak of the run, not at its beginning. This weir is the greatest mechanical undertaking of the tribes in question. Its building has afforded opportunities for many expressive acts of magic to be developed, and around these again there have grown up little playful dramatic enactments. Several items at Kepel seem Karok-derived. The Deerskin and concluding Jumping Dance follow on the dam construction, and appear to be but loosely connected with it, being actually held at other towns in the same reach of river.

Weitspus has dances that are very similar to those of Kepel, but it manifests a striking *minimum* of magical and esoteric ritual.

These three rites of the Hupa and upper Yurok geographically separate those made by the upstream Karok from another group made by the downriver and coastal Yurok and Wiyot. Of the four Karok ceremonies, three are definitely similar to one another; again, four lower Yurok ones form another uniform group; while one Karok and one Yurok enactment pair into a unit in being based on a first-salmon rite.

The three related Karok rituals are all called by the same name "irahiv," are interdetermined calendrically, and they most specifically emphasize new-year and world-renewal concepts. They include long and repeated itineraries by the formulist, target-shooting picnics by the uninitiated, a sacred new fire that may not be looked at, and a symbolic sand pile called yuhpīt. They are followed by a one- or two-day Deerskin Dance, but contain no trace of a Jumping Dance. Within this group, the Inā'm ritual, farthest upstream, is somewhat aberrant in having no sacred structure, and —with Katimīn—in permitting the War Dance and surrogate Deerskin dances; but these appear to be losses due to marginal situation within the system.

The four downriver and coast Yurok rituals have only Jumping dances, which are mostly made indoors and last for ten or more days. The world-reëstablishment aim is expressed most fully through the symbolism of the ritualized rebuilding of a sacred sweathouse, whose timbers, strangely enough, are several times treated as if they were a corpse. In this rebuilding the formulist is assisted by the group of men (and women) called tä:ʟ, who, moreover, sing with him through the night in a special hybrid structure called the tä:ʟ sweathouse. Indoor dances with headbands occur also among the coastal Tolowa and coastal Wiyot, though in associations which are not included by the Indians in the world-renewal system; and since indoor Jumping dances are not performed by the Yurok above Pekwon, it seems reasonable to construe the present group of world renewals as having grown out of a set of less specialized indoor dances and rites common to the coast region of northern California.

By contrast, the Deerskin Dance may have had a Karok origin; or, more likely, since the Karok use in it also wolf and otter skins, and keep the dancing relatively brief, they may have originated the first idea, which was then elaborated and standardized among the Hupa or upper Yurok.

A definite annual "first-fruits" rite for salmon was made in spring by the Yurok at Weʟkwäu at the mouth of the river and by the Karok at the fall at Amaikiaram. Both were esoteric performances by one formulist and his assistant. Among the Karok an outdoor Jumping Dance—the only Karok one—is associated with the Amaikiaram rite; although it follows it at several months' interval, and seems to have little of its own that is esoteric. The Yurok have both a myth and traditional "remembrance" of a Deerskin Dance that was associated with the first-salmon-rite house at Weʟkwäu. The tradition may have a basis of fact or of imagination; in any event the connection of salmon rite and dance was loose, as at Amaikiaram.

The Amaikiaram ritual, though possessing characteristic Karok features, such as taboo of the smoke of the new fire, is well set apart from the other Karok ceremonies; while its acceptance of the Jumping Dance and functioning of sweathouse singers corresponding to tä:ʟ suggest Yurok influencing. The Hupa have a definite first-salmon rite, also in spring, but it seems to lack intrinsic connection with the sacred house and associated renewal—dancing—first-fruits complex.

The one Wiyot new-year-type rite is so little known that it is included in our list only because the Yurok so reckon it. As the dance was held indoors with woodpecker-scalp bands, it may be assumed to have resembled the coast and lower river Yurok ceremonies.

The number of persons who were involved in the development and maintenance of this rich and varied ritual system was surprisingly small. There were about 2,500 Yurok; 2,000 Karok; 1,000 or 1,500 Hupa according to how far upstream one draws their boundary. Some 2,000 or 2,500 additional Wiyot, Tolowa, and Chilula may have participated as occasional dance spectators and contributors of regalia or treasures. This means that the total clientele of the system consisted of fewer than 10,000 individuals—probably around 6,000 to 8,000. These in turn would comprise 1,500 to 2,000 adult males; or an average of 120 to 150 men responsible for the maintenance of each rite. This number is small enough to give almost every man a sense of participation: occasionally in the esoteric ritual, either personally or vicariously through a kinsman; more often as at least a minor contributor of regalia or entertainer of visitors. On the other hand, when it is considered how particularized each rite is from the others in innumerable details, and often in fundamental features, one inevitably acquires a respect for the gradual inventiveness and innovating faculty of the little nationalities in question. It is evident from their own statements that they wanted their world small, compact, closed, stable, permanent, and fixed. They believed that these very renewal rites were specially efficacious in keeping it so. But their created product, as we encounter it, manifests abundant diversity—enough to show that the forces of change customary in culture were operative here too and much as usual.

YUROK GEOGRAPHICAL CONCEPTS

by
T. T. Waterman

The Yurok imagines himself to be living on a flat extent of landscape, which is roughly circular and surrounded by ocean. By going far enough up the river, it is believed that "you come to salt water again." In other words, the Klamath River is considered, in a sense, to bisect the world. This whole earth mass, with its forests and mountains, its rivers and sea cliffs, is regarded as slowly rising and falling, with a gigantic but imperceptible rhythm, on the heaving primeval flood. The vast size of the "earth" causes you not to notice this quiet heaving and settling. This earth, therefore, to their minds is not merely surrounded by the ocean but floats upon it. At about the central point of this "world" lies a place which the Yurok call *qe'nek*, on the southern bank of the Klamath, a few miles below the point where the Trinity comes in from the south. No Indian ever told me in plain words that this was the center of the world, but this seems to be the idea. Thus numerous mythical tales center here, and here the culture hero "grew" out of nothing, back in the myth days.

At this locality also the sky was made. A character called *we'sona-me' getoL*, "world-maker," fashioned the empyrean vault after the manner and pattern of a fishnet. Little else seems to be known of this deity. He plays no further part in myths. The story tells in detail how he took a rope and laid it down in an enormous circle, leaving one end loose at a certain place among the hills. Traveling off in a gigantic circuit and coming around from the south to the same spot again, he joined the two ends of the rope together. Then for days he journeyed back and forth over the hills, filling in and knotting the strands across each other. The song he sang to accompany his labors is still sung by people who work on fishnets or netted carrying bags. When the sky net was complete, the hero took hold of it in two places and "threw it up." As it sailed aloft it became solid, and now stretches over us as the great blue sky. Above this solid sky there is a sky country, *wo'noiyik*, about the topography of which the Yurok's ideas are almost as definite as are his ideas of southern Mendocino County, for

Pp. 189–198, 200, of T. T. Waterman, *Yurok Geography*. Univ. Calif. Publ. Amer. Arch. and Ethnol. (1920), 16:177–314.

instance. Downstream from *qe'nek*, at a place called *qe'nek-pul* ("qe'nek-down-stream"), is an invisible ladder leading up to the sky country. A great number of "myth people" who formerly congregated at *qe'nek* quite frequently went up this ladder to watch shinny games in the sky country. The ladder is still thought to be there. The sky vault is a very definite item in the Yurok's cosmic scheme.

In their theory this sky just described was constructed so as to come down into the ocean, all the way around. It lies far out, away from land. The powers who decide such matters arranged that it should not be in a state of rest, but should move up and down. It continually rises and plunges down again into the sea; hence the rollers which wash up on the world's shores. If you paddle far out where the sky comes down to the water, it is perfectly possible, by counting off the lifting and lowering, to slip through underneath. This is the way to get into the regions beyond the sky. The geese have a special exit of their own, a "sky-hole," a round opening where they enter and leave this world. They spend part of each season in outer space beyond the sky. When flock after flock of geese sail overhead toward the northwest they are headed for this opening. The structure, if I may so call it, consisting of the sky dome and the flat expanse of landscape and waters which it incloses, is known to the Yurok as *ki-we'-sona* (literally "that-which-exists"). I may repeat that the sky overhead is to the Indian as real and as concrete as is the earth he treads on. This sky, then, together with its flooring of landscape, constitutes "our world." I used to be puzzled at the Yurok confusing earth and sky, telling me, for example, that a certain gigantic redwood tree "held up the world." Their ideas are of course perfectly logical, for the sky is as much a part of the "world" in their sense as the ground is.

The Yurok believe that passing under the sky edge and voyaging still outward you come again to solid land. This is not our world, and mortals ordinarily do not go there; but it is good, solid land. What are breakers over here are just little ripples over there. Yonder lie several regions. To the north (in our sense) lies *pu'lekuk*, downstream at the north end of creation. A supernatural being called *qa-pu'loiyo* seems to be the presiding genius there. "In the beginning" there lived in his company a supernatural being called *pu'leku-kwe'rek*, "At-the-north-end-of-creation sharp-one." He came to "our" world and cleared it of all monsters and evil beings. "South" of *pu'lekuk* lies *tsi'k'tsik-ol*, "money lives," where the dentalium-shell, medium of exchange, has its mythical abode. Again, to the south there is a place called *kowe'tsik*, the mythical home of the salmon, where also all have a "house." About due west of the mouth of the Klamath lies *rkrgr'*, where lives the culture-hero *wo'xpa-ku-ma^w*, "across-the-ocean that widower." After a varied career here, he was taken *wo'xpa*, "across-the-sea," by a skate who tricked him through assuming the form of a woman. Every night "over there" in *rķrgr'* "they" have a deerskin dance. The frogs on summer evenings can be heard going down the Klamath in a canoe from far up-river, talking and laughing. The canoe is invisible, but you can hear it pass along with its cheerful crew. They go down the river and across the ocean and under the sky edge, to see the deerskin dance in *rķrgr'*; and they come home again early every morning.

Still to the south of *rķrgr'* there lies a broad sea, *ķiolaapopa'a*, which is half pitch (an Algonkian myth idea, by the way.) All of these solid lands just mentioned lie on the margin, the absolute rim of things. Beyond them the Yurok does not go even in imagination. In the opposite direction, he names a place *pe'tsķuķ*, "up-river-at," which is the upper "end" of the river but still in this world. He does not seem to concern himself much with the topography there.

Below our world is an underworld, *tso'r:eķ*, a sort of cellar, of unde-termined extent. This is the world of the dead, and is connected with "our" world. The dead are said to go to a lake. After going round and round and about they go down through this water into the underworld. Two widely separate points were mentioned to me as the very spot where the souls go down. I am uncertain whether the Yurok believes there are two such places or not. They are loath to discuss this subject.

The Yurok's conception of the world he lives in may be summed up in the accompanying diagram. This was not drawn by a native; I pieced it together myself from various allusions and references.

DIRECTION TERMS

The Yurok direction and position terms enter into the place names to some extent, and the ideas involved differ sufficiently from ours to warrant ex-plaining in some detail. The Yurok's conceptions of directions are quite different from our own. It is certain that they have no idea of our cardinal points north, east, south, and west. Instead, their world is bisected by the river; and the fundamental concepts are *pets*, "upriver," and *pul*, "down-river." The river is rather crooked, and hence *pets* may stand for almost anything in our terminology. The river enters the ocean after following a northwesterly course, and for this or for some other reason "down-stream" is applied to the direction north along the coast. Their "downriver" by an extension of the term, or of the idea, is equivalent to our "up the coast." *Puluķuķ*, "down-river-at," as the name of a mythical place, would be paraphrased in English "at the north of everything"; for there is nothing whatever beyond it.

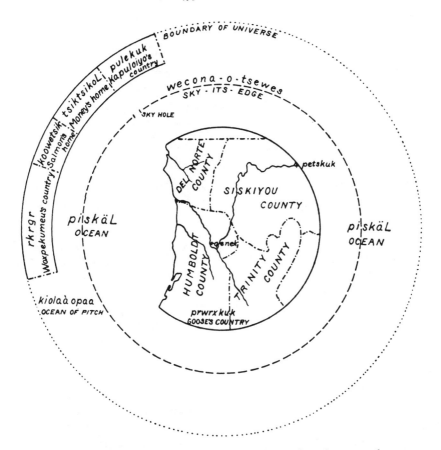

There exists in Yurok a term *hirq*, which is often, but not always, associated with the region north of the river. I have the feeling that it applies rather to the region than to the direction. It is sometimes translated by Indian informants (who speak very imperfect English) as "around in back," with a sweeping gesture northward. I may advance the opinion that in essence its implication is away from the river and a long way from it. A second word, *pr'kwr*, whose literal meaning seems to be "behind" or "in rear," is very frequently used with reference to the south. It is also used in defining positions within a village, or inside of a house, where the idea of direction in our sense is almost certainly not involved.

I can say definitely that in paddling down a twenty-mile stretch of river, as the current bears the canoe first in one direction, then in another, around promontories and down rapids, an Indian will almost box the compass in pointing *pul*, or *hirq*, for he has the course of the river channel as his fundamental idea, to which the others are relative.

The following list of direction terms and geographical expressions is not exhaustive, but it contains a number of elements very frequently used and may be of service from the comparative standpoint. (The Indian words have been deleted; only the English equivalents are given):

"This at" (here); at the edge of; at the end of; on the other side of; inside; in the water; above (overhead, up); near you; behind; further; away from the water (when on the ocean this term signifies ashore); at the head of (ahead); upriver; downriver; in the rear of (in back); from; on top of; downhill; oceanward; close; crosswise; in the ground; on the other side of the hill; facing backward; down below; yonder (not visible); across.

The following are some of the commonest geographical expressions (again the Indian words have been omitted and only the English equivalents given):

Salt water; where trails meet; acorn grounds; village; rapids; lake; lagoon; flat; where trail goes over; landing place; spring; high; a small creek; a cliff; creek; earthquake; echo; ocean; a knoll; a bar (submerged barrier in river); a promontory; upright; a cove; a slide; tributary; a low cliff; flat in front of a cliff ("bench"); a mountain; fork of a creek; limit of snaring rights (i.e. a boundary); ridge; mountain peak; a flat; entrance from ocean into lagoon.

PLACE NAMES

My impression is that local geography seems to mean rather more to the Yurok than is ordinarily the case with Indian tribes. The Yurok have a very large number of local names. The names listed herewith could readily be doubled if an investigator were to put in the necessary time and effort. In certain areas the separate place names crowd so thickly that it is difficult to find space for them on a map. In their nomenclature certain principles are very clearly visible, which it is interesting to point out, particularly with reference to those features in which the Yurok practice differs from our own.

The places having names exhibit in themselves a good deal of variety; for example, a place name in a given case may become attached to a flat of thirty acres, or to a village site, or to a boulder the size of a steamer trunk, or to a few elderberry bushes, or to a single tan-oak tree, while vast numbers of such places have no proper names at all. The spots which are "named" are to be found, in the great majority of cases, along the edge of the stream. In a sense, my maps showing place names are misleading, for I myself went along the river in a canoe, and naturally most readily secured the names of the places close at hand. I am, however, perfectly certain of the general fact. What place names are current in the hills away from the river show a marked disposition to group themselves along the important trails. Wherever possible I have indicated these trails on the maps, but I am unable to go into this matter systematically. The hills are not, however, so devoid of place names as they seem to be on glancing at the maps. I may remark also that many place names occurring in localities far removed from the river refer indirectly to some locality or landmark which is at the very edge of the stream. I believe that the map indicates fairly well the way in which the independent names crowd at the edge of the water. On the coast the same rule holds. A sea-stack the size of a piano will have a name, while a hill of two thousand feet elevation has none.

In our own practice stream names are considered fundamental. When a country is explored or newly charted the streams are named first. I should consider stream names the most important of all geographical names for use. The Yurok, speaking now in general terms, treat streams very differently. There is nothing which can be called a name for their main river, a fact which is not in itself surprising, for it is for them the "only" river. But, with a few exceptions, there are also no names for its tributaries. I do not mean that the Yurok never refer to the streams, but that the term applied to the stream is the name of some place on it or at its mouth. Such a stream as Blue Creek, for example, which in many regions would be looked upon as a moderately large river, is called *r'nr wroi'*, *r'nr* being the village site just west of its mouth. Tuley Creek is called *Oḵe'go wroi*, "Rapids" creek, the name referring to the great rapids in the main river, near where the creek enters. Examples of this trick of nomenclature could be supplied ad libitum.

Some exceptions to this general rule should be pointed out. There are a few cases in which the stream name is descriptive of the stream. The Trinity River is called *hu'pa-sr*, that is, "Hupa affluent." It flows for the last few miles of its course through the valley inhabited by this tribe of Indians. A stream known to the whites as Bluff Creek, in reference to numerous precipices on both the main stream and its tributaries, is called by the Indians *tsi'poi wroi'*, *tsi'poi* meaning "steep." A small stream on the coast runs for part of its course underground. I think a hillside slid over its channel, leaving the creek to find its way through the debris. It is called *lḵe'liḵ wroi'*, "earth" creek, or ground creek. Some stream names refer to mythical beliefs connected with the water itself. A brooklet above *o'segen* is called *sme'Rḵitur*, "toothless." There are supernatural influences assigned to it, and anyone who drinks the water loses his teeth. A small creek, one and a half miles below Blue Creek, mentioned above, flows in a gully which was made by the crawling of a gigantic horned serpent. The stream is called *ma' 'a-spu*, "never drink." Such names are obviously applied directly to the stream itself.

In some cases a stream name appears on the map, while the place name, from which it originated, does not. The reasons for this situation are various. The investigator inquires very carefully for all creek names, partly I suppose, because the creeks are not readily overlooked, most of them appearing on the commercial maps which are likely to be in his pocket. Place names which are applied to boulders, or small flats or clumps of buckeye trees, are, on the other hand, very easily missed. My maps, therefore, fail to illustrate with absolute fidelity what I nevertheless know to be a fact.

I remarked a moment ago that in exploring a country we name the streams first of all. We also apply names conscientiously to the elevations. A glance at the map of any state in the Union will show a great number of "named" mountains and hills. In this respect also the Yurok's interest is very different from our own. Broadly speaking, he does not name a whole mountain. A name may seem to the investigator to be applied to a mountain, but in most cases it will be found to designate some one particular spot on it. In explanation I may mention the case of two mountains. One of them, Rivet Mountain to the whites, lies near the upper end of the Yurok territory. It is a big cone-shaped elevation, lying in a great bend of the Klamath and culminating in a peak some 3500 feet in height. It is a conspicuous landmark for great distances and plays a picturesque role in myth. The name seems to be *ke'wet*. I have reason to believe, however, that this is really the name of one "myth" village, invisible to mortal eyes, which lies on a terrace on its upper slopes. Similarly, there is what are called by the white the Bald hills, a great grass-covered butte which I understood the Indians to refer to as *an'kau*. Closer inquiry seems to indicate that this term is the name of one particular spot on the mountain slope in front of a cliff where there is an echo. The Indian belief is that one goes there and "shouts" for supernatural help, and that the echo response tells whether or not the supernatural beings are favorable. I feel perfectly sure that the Yurok does not apply names to mountains or to regions on the scale that we do. He applied place names with meticulous care to a vast number of definite spots and objects, but the larger features of the relief and the drainage system go practically unnamed.

Certain descriptive elements occur very commonly in the place names mentioned by Indians. The commonest of these are *pul*, "downstream," *pets*, "upstream," already mentioned, *higwon*, "at a higher elevation" (above, in the sense of above on a hillside), and *hiqo*, "across from." Let us say that a boulder at the edge of the river has a name connected with some myth. Let us assume, which is often the case, that this rock is known by its own proper name to every Indian on the river. A place a short distance upstream, and another in a similar position downstream, a place across the river, and places on the hill slopes on both sides of the river—all are known variously as "upstream from" or "downstream from" or "opposite" or "above" this particular rock. In this way four or five additional place terms are often manufactured.

Geography and myth among the Yurok are closely associated. Mythical stories are frequently localized very definitely. The Yurok believe, like the Hupa, that in myth times the country was inhabited by "immortals" (*wo'ge* in Yurok, corresponding to the Hupa *kixunai*). These *wo'ge* are the actors in most of the mythical tales. When the Indians appeared they either turned into animals or left the country. Place names continually refer to these mythical predecessors of the Indians. Anything and everything that puzzles the Indian is ascribed to these *wo'ge*. Old village sites, where the Indian recognizes house pits or natural depressions resembling housepits but about which he has no information, are referred to as *wo'ge* towns. I found one addle-pated old informant to whom these *wo'ge* were so real that he sometimes bewildered me, making me think he was referring to real people. He would point out a "house pit," for example, and tell me about the structure (which way the door faced, how big it was, etc.), and would then remark, incidentally, that the people who lived in it were immortals. This localization of mythical stories is very marked in the tales of all the neighboring tribes also.

VILLAGE SHIFTS AND TRIBAL SPREADS IN CALIFORNIA PREHISTORY

by
Robert F. Heizer

Archaeologists are very conscious of the fact that the ethnographic record often lacks information on cultural details about recent peoples which is needed in order to interpret prehistoric materials. California ethnographers, for example, neglected to secure from informants, who had actually experienced the aboriginal life, information on how much of the various kinds of food were collected; and this deficiency of quantitative data (for which there is no solution since the old cultures are quite extinct) will forever plague all attempts to derive precise occupance duration or population numbers by the archaeological technique of refuse site constituent analysis.

The state of California was densely occupied by aboriginal peoples. Comprising about 1 percent of the land area of North America north of Mexico, California held about 250–300,000 persons. As may be expected in a region which was heavily occupied and used for a long time (at least eight or ten thousand years), there are large numbers of archaeological sites. My own guess as to the total number for California is 50,000 sites of all types, of which half this number are occupation sites. Living sites differ over the state in their size, location, and nature. Some are situated in very favorable positions and have been occupied for thousands of years by a succession of peoples; others are thin refuse deposits which show every indication of having been village sites which were lived on for a few score or hundreds of years and were then abandoned, never to be used again. One may ask what we know about why village sites were abandoned. The question is an important one since if we were able to answer it for archaeological sites it would help considerably in our efforts to interpret California's ancient history. While we have an abundance of ethnographic information on names and locations of village sites, we are rarely given data on numbers of inhabitants and even more seldom the cause of abandonment of dead villages.

T. T. Waterman, in referring to the Yurok of northwestern California, says:

Slightly revised version of article in *Southwest Museum Masterkey* (1962), 30:60–67.

Like most primitive people the Yurok change their places of abode very abruptly. No doubt the relative size and importance of towns has shifted from time to time. I think the Yurok may have been more prone to change their places of abode than the average tribe. In addition to all the usual causes of change of abode (disease, floods, attacks of enemies, bad dreams, and plain fidgetiness), the Yurok are extremely quarrelsome. Prominent among their traits is a certain sinful pride, a love of squabbling, and readiness to take offense. These result indirectly in the shifting of habitations. . . . If an individual commits a homicide . . . that individual is an uncomfortable person to have around. Unless his cause is so just, his character so upright, or his personality so winning that his townspeople are ready to join in his defense and make common cause with him, the village usually makes it so unpleasant for him that he leaves. While the quarrel is being patched up such a man is considered to be better living by himself in some lonely stretch of the [Klamath] river where his presence embarrasses nobody and compromises nobody. In most cases in which a man moves off in this way he begins sooner or later to "pay for" the man he has killed. The price for a homicide is pretty high, however, and a number of years are often occupied in making up the full sum, which is paid in installments. When he has completed his payments he often does not feel like moving back. If he makes his new home a permanent one, and raises a large family there, the addition of new houses gradually lends the place the character of a settlement. . . . Some very important towns are said to have started in this way, the town of Sregon, for example. . . . In cases of epidemics a whole village would readily be abandoned.

Waterman adds that "River towns are usually more than a hundred feet above the stream, which has in places an annual rise of more than seventy vertical feet. A tremendous flood in the winter of 1862 . . . somewhat changed the location of settlements; a good many towns were permanently moved to higher sites, and others where the houses were washed down the river were abandoned." The quotation from Waterman provides us, for one tribe and area, concrete causes for the abandonment or formation of new villages which we may list as: social fractionation, epidemics, and floods.

Fr. Palou tells of the attack in 1755 by Indians of a village near San Mateo on the inhabitants of a native village near the mission of San Francisco in which many of the latter were killed and wounded and the village burned. Being afraid to remain, the survivors built rush boats and crossed the bay where they established themselves in another settlement. The account does not state whether a new village was built or whether the San Francisco survivors were given refuge in an existing village of people with whom they had friendly relations.

A reported cause for failure to reoccupy a former village site (and therefore account for the absence of stratified deposits) is the religious one of dread of the ghosts or spirits of the former occupants.

Longinos, in 1792, speaks of Indians of northernmost Baja California moving out of a village because the fleas and other vermin were too annoying. Lewis and Clark mention the same cause for removal of villages on the Columbia River. M. Costanso and Fray Crespi on October 27, 1769, mention an abandoned village on the California coast whose empty dwellings were full of fleas, but they do not specifically state that these pests were the cause of the Indians leaving. S. Powers was told in the 1870s by the Sierra Nevada Maidu that on occasion villages had to be abandoned because they became so foul, and E. Voegelin was told by Tubatulabal informants that after ten years of use a winter house could no longer be lived in because it was so heavily infested with fleas.

Warfare among most California Indians was usually a reaction to trespass by people of neighboring villages collecting food and had, therefore, a fundamentally economic motive. Among the Yuman tribes of the Colorado River, however, a military spirit and activity was notably developed since war was organized on a tribal or national basis. Thus, in wars involving two tribal entities, the loser might be physically dispossessed of his territory. One such case is recorded, this being the Halchidhoma tribe which was forced to leave its home area along the middle section of the Colorado River's stretch which forms the California-Arizona border. The Mohave victors, having plenty of land, did not settle the vacated territory and this no-man's land was ultimately occupied by the Chemehuevi (Southern Paiute) who moved in from the desert to the west with the permission of the Mohave. Elsewhere in California we have records of villages abandoned because they were too vulnerable to attack by neighboring groups between whom there developed and prevailed unfriendly relations which on occasion manifested themselves in surprise attacks. The result of this is that tribal borders, while sharply delimited and usually acknowledged by both sides, were often unoccupied. A long stabilized border might be recognizable archaeologically from two lineal series of village sites situated with reference to some natural boundary feature showing evidence of continuous occupation over a considerable span of time. A border zone where the boundary had shifted through time might be recognized archaeologically by a series of village sites which show evidence of discontinuous habitation, presumably reflecting successive abandonments and reoccupations in response to temporary ascendancy or decline of tribal fortunes.

In further illustration we quote Kroeber on the Pomo Indians: "Often a settlement split: a petty quarrel, a shortening supply of some food in the vicinity, a death, or mere indifferent instability would lead to a living apart without any sense of a division having taken place. Thus, settlements of a few houses sprang up, decreased, or were totally abandoned and then, after the passage of a few years or a generation or two, when the memory of the omen or disaster or feud that had caused their desertion had weakened, might come to be reoccupied."

Kroeber records another Pomo instance of the abandonment of villages in the northern end of Ukiah valley. The area was held by the Northern Pomo among whom lived a famous shaman, Sikutsha, who was accused of having "poisoned" (by magical means) a man in one of the villages of a different tribelet to the south. The aggrieved tribelet attempted to take revenge by force, but the shaman escaped and went to live with friends in a distant village near Upper Lake. The people of Sikutsha's village had not been drawn into the quarrel, but they nevertheless felt uncomfortable; and not long after the attempt to seize Sikutsha they abandoned the settlement and moved north, finally establishing a new town in Scott Valley. This instance, so highly particular and revolving around a specific action concerning one individual, could obviously never be inferred from the archaeological record. But it is revealing of the tendency of California Indians to move their village location to a new site where they would feel more secure and less threatened.

In view of the undoubted fact of migrational movements and occupation of new territories by ethnic groups in pre-Caucasian times we should be able, in these instances where the causes, processes, and time of such spreads can be determined, to gain hints of how these might be traced from archaeological evidence. If archaeologists carried out field research specifically aimed at- detecting the archaeological evidences for known recent ethnic-linguistic expansions such as Western Mono (= Monache), Northern Paiute (= Paviotso), Yokuts, and Wintu, they might then be in a better position to try to identify older archaeological culture types with prehistoric tribal-linguistic entities. California offers any number of ideal situations for this kind of methodological examination of linguistic-material culture correlation. For example, let us take the Yuki-speaking tribes of west-central California. The Yuki group consists of four tribes, three of which (Yuki, Huchnom, and Coast Yuki) have a connected distribution with the fourth, Wappo, being geographically detached and lying about forty miles to the south. The Yuki and Huchnom exhibit an unusual and distinctive physical type which is easily recognizable both in the living and in skeletal vestiges. It is hard to escape the conclusion that anciently the distinctive Yuki physical type and equally distinctive Yuki language were correlated. By the opening of the period of Caucasian contact in the mid-nineteenth century, we have clear evidence that the language and physical type had become independent variables. Thus the Yuki-speaking Wappo are not of Yuki physical type but were of the Californian physical type, whereas the Athabascan-speaking Kato and Wailaki, who live immediately north of the Yuki-Huchnom group, are of the Yuki physical type. The Yuki physical type, first recognized and defined on the living, does occur in prehistoric sites in Round Valley, which is the center of Yuki territory, so that further excavation in this area should provide a known starting point for the tracing back in time of the variable histories of Yuki culture, language, and physical type. With this statement of a problem we have admittedly entered a new sphere, namely, culture contact on the prehistoric time level.

Translinguistic acculturation problems in California archaeology are easy to formulate because they are so abundant. Not the least interesting of these would be the unraveling of the history on the California scene of the northwestern California culture focus, where the linguistically separate Algonkian Yurok and Wiyot, Athabascan Hupa and Tolowa, and Hokan Karok all participated to a remarkably similar degree in a peculiarly distinctive local subpattern.

The ethnographic data on shifting of tribal territories of the Colorado River tribes has been reasonably well worked out and these movements might be traceable from archaeological investigation. Here again one might think that linguistic evidence of earlier periods of close contact between now-separated groups would be of very considerable importance in trying to trace the movements of groups.

These problems are very real ones, and some attention to them seems required of California archaeologists in the light of the growing body of findings by linguists interested in glottochronology. If separation dates for California languages are to become more than an hypothesis resulting from statistical manipulation of controlled linguistic comparisons, the archaeologists will have to devote themselves to excavation with an aim at discovering in their data something that is still generally considered unscientific speculation, namely, the ethnic identification of the authors. And ultimately it is only by such archaeological evidence that the lexicostatistic "dates" can be objectively verified or corrected. In this kind of archaeology the linguist's cooperation will be vital since the assessment of evidence must be considered always in the light of what the linguist considers as within the realm of probability.

PRINCIPAL LOCAL TYPES OF THE KUKSU CULT

by
A. L. Kroeber

The Kuksu system cults fall into two major types, a western and an eastern. To the former adhere the Pomo and Yukian groups, the Coast and Lake Miwok, and the Kato; to the latter, the Patwin, Salt Pomo, valley and presumably hill Maidu, valley Nisenan, and probably Plains Miwok. The line of division is marked by the main crest—not watershed—of the Coast Ranges. The two areas thus coincide exactly with portions of the Coast Range system and the Sacramento Valley.

The western form of Kuksu cult everywhere has two initiating societies. One of these nearly everywhere contains Kuksu and his companion shalnis, sometimes one or two other impersonations. The other society impersonates a class of spirits more or less identified with ghosts of the dead, but known by quite different names. The total number of impersonated spirits in the two societies thus is relatively small; and mostly ceremonies also are few. Initiations are generally stressed, including on the one hand "schools of instruction," and on the other "health-giving" rites for all small children. So far as there is differentiation between the Kuksu and the ghost society in exclusiveness or age of members, it is the Kuksu that takes in the fewer and older individuals, but may include women.

The cults of the eastern tribes vary from one to three in the number of their societies. The socially basic society is always the one that makes a great spectacular dance ceremony like the hesi, into which a varied array of spirits enter. Initiation into general membership of this society is largely by boys learning to dance; into directing membership, by private instruction for payment, usually within a hereditary line. Other societies are either merged into this hesi society, or exist alongside it as separate organizations of restricted, wholly adult membership, which in some tribes may include women. These additional societies impersonate either Kuksu or a ghost-like class of spirits, in other words equate with the two societies universal

Pp. 396–402, 408, 411, 417–420 of A. L. Kroeber, *The Patwin and Their Neighbors*, Univ. Calif. Publ. Am. Arch. and Ethn. (1932), 29:255–423.

The Kuksu cult is further discussed in three papers by E. M. Loeb in the same series: *Pomo Folkways* (1926), 19:149–405; *The Western Kuksu Cult* (1932), 33:1–137; *The Eastern Kuksu Cult* (1933), 33:139–232.

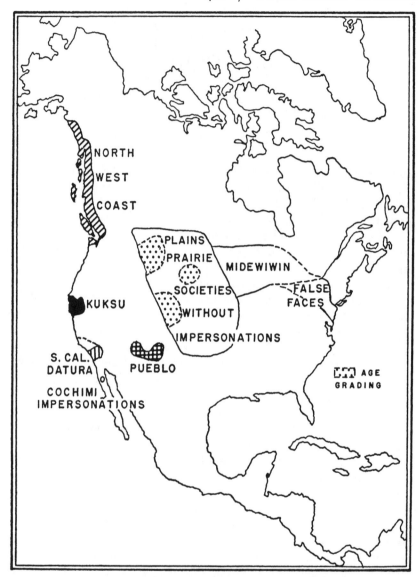

Map 15. Distribution of North American Cult Societies.

among the western tribes. The initiation into Kuksu and ghost among the eastern peoples is by a dangerous act, such as pretended wounding, sickening, or killing, often with the idea of temporary dementedness.

It is apparent that, in spite of numerous generic resemblances and specific identities, the eastern and western forms of the cults are fairly rigorously differentiated. To date no tribal cult is known which is so intermediate or transitional as to leave doubt as to which of the two forms it belongs to.

Within the eastern group, Loeb has suggested that a subdivision can be made between the Clear Lake and probably Russian River Pomo on the one hand, and the Coast Pomo, Yuki, Huchnom, and Coast Miwok on the other, the former having the more elaborate ceremonies and dances and somewhat more numerous kinds of spirit impersonations.

Among the peripheral eastern tribes, the Yuki and perhaps other northern groups can be set apart from the Coast Pomo, whom they resemble in general simplicity of system, by nonuse of the name Kuksu, identification of his substitute with the creator, emphasis on initiation, mythological instruction, and "school" features; and probably other traits.

Within the eastern or Sacramento Valley division of the system, there seem to be no outstanding areal segregations, except that the true valley people, Patwin, Maidu, and Nisenan, show definitely greater richness of system, in societies, ceremonies, spirits, dances, and costumes, than the northern hill Patwin and hill Maidu. At the same time, the valley peoples, while appearing to recognize one another's systems as equivalent, vary considerably in them, tribes with fewer societies sometimes possessing more ceremonies and impersonations and so on.

CAUSES OF LOCAL DIFFERENCES

A historical reconstruction of the course of development of the Kuksu system cults cannot as yet be carried very far on the basis of the data themselves. A general scheme of interpretation on a continental or world-wide basis might conceivably take one further. If for instance like Loeb one starts from the position that tribal initiations everywhere are due to a single, ancient diffusion with features like bull-roarer, mutilation, death and resurrection rites, spirit impersonations as original criteria, and that secret societies grew out of this substratum as secondary parallels, considerable headway can be made toward reconstructing the history of the California or any other system. Only, in that case, the evidence for the fundamental scheme is necessarily world-wide, and the local data become of interest chiefly for the degree of fit to and variation from the larger pattern of development, and the local or specific factors that have caused departures from it. The more modest problem whether an internal comparison of the Californian data by themselves throws any light on former events in the area, is likely to lead to more limited results.

As already said in connection with the description of the river Patwin cults, so basic a point as the sequence of development of the California societies is somewhat dubiously illuminated by the facts as to their number, nature, and relations. The one with simplest organization is the ghosts, but it is not known to be represented in the eastern part of the eastern division. The most widely distributed is the Kuksu. The most elaborate in number of officials, degrees, kinds of spirits, and introduced or associated dances is the hesi, which is limited to the eastern division. A natural hypothesis is that this elaborateness argues relative recency. Further, it would scarcely be expectable that, other things being reasonably equal, this elaboration took place among groups who were just beginning to organize rites into societies while neighboring groups had had societies longer. The inference then would be that the valley Patwin and Maidu and Nisenan had had ghost and Kuksu societies before they developed the hesi, and that after this commenced to luxuriate they began to suppress, or merge out of existence, one or both of these other organizations, though retaining certain features of their rituals, these now becoming attached to the hesi society. On this view the western or Pomo-Yuki division would be the one which on the whole preserved a more ancient phase of Kuksu development; among the easterners, the Patwin, the fullest development; the Maidu and Nisenan, the greatest degree of specialization, accompanied, however, by a smothering of the historic foundations of the whole growth.

All in all, a sequence of events like this seems not unlikely. It must, however, be held as a hypothesis only, and may therefore not be unduly strained by the piling on it of other hypotheses in order to attain more remote interpretations. Specific hypotheses may be regarded as normally being fractional certainties, and the interweaving of hypotheses a process of multiplying these fractions.

Further, there is the question of what may have caused the Pomo not to accept the new hesi-type developments while the Patwin did accept them, and the Maidu-Nisenan both accepted them and began to abandon their earlier ghost and perhaps Kuksu societies. I can think of only one local phenomenon that might explain this abandonment: the annual mourning memorial or "anniversary" cult. This, like the ghost society, has to do with the dead; and the distributions of the two, in the part of California in question, are mutually exclusive. Pomo, Yuki, Patwin have societies of ghost type but no communal anniversary ceremony for the actual dead. Maidu and Nisenan lack ghost societies but do commemorate the dead. It is conceivable that the two sets of cults were too alike in emotional import and too different in expressive approach, to be compatible. In favor of this view is the fact that the Kuksu society, which refers not to ghosts but to mythologic or ritual personages, is still present among the Nisenan and perhaps among the Maidu. Also, the mourning commemoration appears to be south Californian in origin, and reached its most northerly distribution, at any rate in normally full form, among the Maidu. Unless therefore it has undergone a shrinkage of territory, or held a stationary frontier for an unusually long time, of neither of which possibilities there is any specific indication, the mourning commemoration would presumably be a relatively recent practice among the Nisenan and Maidu; which would fit in with the hypothesis that the absence of the ghost society was due to a loss, in other words, a secondary phenomenon, among these peoples. Finally it might be mentioned that the strongest development of the mourning commemoration among the Nisenan and Maidu is among the hill divisions, while the society cults have their hold chiefly, and with the Nisenan wholly, in the valley. This fact bears only indirectly on the present hypothesis because it refers to societies in general instead of the ghost society. But it suggests a certain degree of incompatibility, historically accidental if not psychological, between societies and the commemoration; and even a partial tendency of this sort might have been sufficient to cause the obliteration of that one of the societies which was felt to conflict most with the commemoration.

It is for the reader to judge whether these considerations have been spun with undue fineness. I submit them as possible explanations.

As to the other problem raised by our first hypothesis, namely, why the hesi society does not occur among the Pomo or elsewhere in the western division, I have no specific explanation to suggest. The simplest answer would be that the hesi society originated late enough for it not to have spread to the Pomo. This is plausible enough; yet unless one were to assume the origin of the hesi to have been as recent as a century or two before 1850, there would certainly have been time for its diffusion to a prosperous neighboring people like the Clear Lake Pomo. Specific factors making for its nonacceptance by them would thus be called for by the situation; and such factors I cannot adduce. This fact I therefore leave unexplained, except so far as the general considerations to be taken up next may bear on it.

RELATIVE AGE OF THE SOCIETIES

The question may now be raised whether there is any internal indication as to the point and circumstances of origin and first steps of development of the Kuksu system as a whole. This problem involves: which society was the first; where and why, or how, it came into existence; and what caused it to differentiate into two or more. On these points the specific indications are particularly tenuous. We are dealing with things that may have happened a millennium or two ago. On the basis of the explanatory mechanism of productive focal centers and diffusions outward toward the margins of distribution, the river Patwin would be indicated as the most likely originators, because they alone possess the maximum number of three societies.

However, we are here concerned with a diffusion with a radius of only about seventy-five miles in a duration of perhaps ten or twenty times as many years. This unusual combination would obviously make a reconstructive search for the point of origin vain if not ludicrous if we were not dealing with populations of proved high sessility plus stability of adaptation to the soil. It is known from archaeology that the subsistence habits of the California Indians have remained materially unchanged for several thousand years. A given valley or stretch of river is therefore extremely likely to have had a larger and more concentrated population, with more leisure and greater incentive to order, wealth, and organized institutions, in 1 A. D. as well as 1770, and a hill population only twenty miles away to have remained equally backward for the same time. Of course, populations may have moved; but this would merely mean, so far as our problem is concerned, that the place of origin might theoretically be determinable even if the originating ethnic group were not. We might not be able to affirm that it was the Patwin rather than some antecedent people who were the originators of the cult, and yet be able to show that the point of origin was more likely to have been on the Sacramento River than elsewhere.

Now topographic considerations leave little doubt that it is the areas in which the historic Kuksu cult reached its greatest elaboration which would in the prehistoric period also have been most likely to hold a population living under conditions most favorable to the originating of a luxury development like this cult system. This means either the Sacramento Valley along its large streams, or the Clear Lake–Russian River area. As between these, a slight precedence must be accorded the Sacramento Valley, on account of its greater interconnected area. It must have held some fifty tribelets, against about ten on Clear Lake and perhaps twenty or twenty-five on the hill-broken stretch of Russian River.

A more or less simultaneous origin of distinct societies in these two centers, with subsequent exchange, seems logically improbable in so small an area. It might have happened if the system had had its origin and first differentiation outside, and had then been fragmentarily imported into the present Kuksu area, to undergo new growth there. But of this there is no evidence. Specific elements may well have filtered in in this way, but the specific fundamentals of the system, like the ghost concept or the Kuksu stabbing initiation, seem wholly restricted to the area.

As between these two societies, specific evidence for the priority of one over the other is very scant. The wider present distribution of Kuksu may be due to the already suggested crowding-out of the ghosts by the mourning commemoration in the east. Kuksu and his associates or substitutes are personages, the ghosts a class or race of spirits, in other words the more generalized concept of the two; especially in view of the universal Californian preoccupation with death. Nor does Kuksu enter importantly into mythology as such, except on the northwest margin, and there his name is replaced by that of the traveling creator. These indications seem to favor the priority of the ghost society; but the preferential probability is very slight. It would also remain to account for the replacement in the western Sacramento Valley of the ghosts-of-the-dead idea by that of a brood of insane running spirits. . . .

EXTERNAL RELATIONS OF THE KUKSU CULT

The external relations of the Kuksu cult are characterized by two facts. No other ritual or secret society cult existed within a long distance; but the neighboring non-Kuksu tribes shared many specific cult elements with the Kuksu tribes. Among such elements are the large earth-covered dance house; the half-log foot drum; the magpie-feather laya headdress and the feather capes on a net; the split-stick and cocoon rattles and bone whistle; and dances or dance personages like ghosts, condor, coyote, creeper, lole, hiwe, kilak. There can be no doubt that ritual material was both exported from and imported into the Kuksu area, respectively losing or acquiring its attachment to the society organization; and that this happened in ancient as well as recent times. Some of the elements may be older than the oldest society. Whether a given feature of wider distribution was evolved within or without the Kuksu area can by no means be judged offhand. In some cases a decision can no doubt ultimately be arrived at with reasonable probability, through intensive comparison. This task is outside the scope of the present study, though it will have to be performed before the history of Kuksu is unraveled as fully as it can be. Meanwhile it is essential to remember that adjacent Kuksu and non-Kuksu groups differ far less in the content of their ritual than in the formal organization of their religions.

The three areas nearest the Kuksu one in which ceremonial societies occur are the Northwest Coast, the Plains, and the Southwest. (See Map 15.) All three of these are separated by about 600 miles from the Kuksu cult, as against an area of this of not over 150 miles in any direction. The Northwest Coast societies die out about Puget Sound; those of the Plains lie east of the Rockies; the Southwestern ones end with the Hopi.

This situation would at once raise the presumption, even if no further data were available, that the Kuksu cult could have little specific content in common with these other society cults. Theoretically, not very much would normally have passed through the long intervening stretches without leaving some mark there. And such marks are not conspicuous among the intervening, societyless peoples. Nor are the specific features which the Kuksu cult shares with the Northwest, Southwest, or Eastern society cults either notable or numerous compared with those peculiar to each.

Is it then necessary to assume an independent local origin for the Kuksu cult? This can hardly be affirmed, at least not to the extent of denial of a considerable possibility of at least suggestions or stimuli having been introduced into California and resulting in the Kuksu development. Both the Northwestern and Southwestern society cults impersonate spirits and initiate; and one of these concepts or both, or one like them, might conceivably have been diffused and then have been developed into the formation of societies in north central California, whereas in the intervening stretches the practice died out again, perhaps just because it was not permanently reënforced by the crystallization of societies. This is about as far as it seems reasonable to go in delimiting the possibilities of historical connections as the cause of Kuksu origins. That societies once existed over the intermediate territory and then died out, is a logically permissible assumption, but somewhat gratuitous.

The safest approximation to a reconstruction of Kuksu origins then is the admission that certain specific ritual practices embodying concepts capable of serving as stimuli toward the formation of spirit-impersonating societies may have been transmitted to north central California from without, and that from these stimuli the cult then evolved locally through the utilization of ceremonial material already at hand among the organizing groups, plus other material subsequently taken over from their neighbors or invented by themselves. This view means in short that most of the specific course of Kuksu history was independent; its beginning, more likely induced from without.

As to which one of the three distant society cults furnished the first impulse, if any, toward Kuksu, the Plains system can be eliminated because it does not impersonate spirits. Also it is likely to be recent in the Plains, its roots lying to the south or east. As between the other two systems, the Southwest evidently merits preference. Not only are there the clues of the bull-roarer and the pole ceremony, but the Pueblo kachina are a race of spirits associated with and including the human dead, like the Kuksu cult ghosts. The shamanistic coloring of the Kuksu cult indeed has a parallel on the Northwest Coast, but also among the Pueblos, whose non-kachina societies are in part curative and seem historically to have replaced shamanism as a separate institution. There are also Pueblo parallels to the Californian practice of curing by a spirit impersonation people made sick by the

spirit. And above all, there exists at least a quasi-society territorially intermediate between Pueblos and Kuksu, in southern California; of which
more in a moment. . . .

SUMMARY OF INDICATED HISTORY OF KUKSU AND RELATED CULTS

The general outline of Kuksu developments then may be tentatively re-
constructed to have been this. At an early date, long before Pueblo cults
had taken their present specific form, certain ritual practices were diffused from an undetermined center which may have lain in Mexico, but
which, if in the United States, is most likely to have been situated among
the Pueblos. These rituals probably included initiations of boys (Loeb's
"tribal initiations"), or supernatural impersonations, or both; altars of
groundpainting type; fetish bundles; possibly the bull-roarer. The impersonations are likely to have been of two types: ghosts of the tribal dead or
a race of spirits more or less identified with them; and spirits of a superior
or special character, designable as deities and associated with the origin and
maintenance of the world. There may also have been the concept that the
impersonations, especially of the gods, served to cure illness. These practices
and ideas were diffused westward, and then south and north in the coast
region, as far as north central California, where they were checked by en-
countering a culture of fairly distinct origins and trends, that of the Northwest Coast. In each area reached, the transmissions became merged with
culture elements already established, and were still further modified by
the development of provincial traits consonant with the culture of the area.
Thus the cult houses, musical instruments, and performers' apparel largely
became specific, not generic or uniform, in the several regions where the
introductions flourished. These regions were those in which economic prosperity induced relatively concentrated living and inclinations toward organization. The organizing impulses resulted in the formation of societies,
perhaps at times *de novo*. These were essentially luxury growths. In other
regions subsistence was less favorable, or at least tended to more scattered
or seasonal residence, organization was blocked instead of encouraged,
societies did not form, and even the original impulse toward initiations or
impersonations, often died out again. New tendencies arose, or grew to
more strength than they had had before, in this area or that producing
greater local variety. Along the Colorado River, for instance, myth-dream
singing habits, with an essentially individualistic coloring, tended to
smother out not only concrete ritual, but any surviving impulses toward
initiation or impersonation. On the southern California coast, on the other

hand, the widespread trait of Datura intoxication, which quite probably had no original connection with the initiating and impersonating cults, was more and more emphasized, brought into connection with the local form of the cults, and modified these. The altar painting and fetish bundle were retained here along with initiation; impersonations faded away; a well organized society may never have been attained. In the environs of the Sacramento Valley, the altar and fetish were lost, new impersonations were created and became dominant, societies became strong, even one new one, at least, being formed; but impersonation of the dead languished and died away where it came in competition with the introduced mourning commemoration held for the specific and recent dead. Change, progressive and retrogressive, was still active at the time of Caucasian occupation. Even in the adverse environment of peninsular California some remnants of the original diffusion maintained themselves. Elements like the bull-roarer, a rattlesnake ceremony, eagle rearing, and the like, which variously occur and are absent both among initiating and noninitiating tribes, may be part of the original complex diffused, or may represent separate specific diffusions. Sporadically occurring traits like prayer feathers or feather sticks, meal offerings, or pole climbing may be due to the same causes or possibly to independent local invention. That this latter was at times an active process even among groups of simpler culture, is suggested by the composite pota ceremony of the hill Miwok. That invention was likely to be still more productive among groups with organization is shown by the valley Maidu, with their numerous ceremonies and spirit impersonations and the calendar sequence of these. To a less degree, the Nisenan and Patwin show specialization. Simplifying tendencies also operated: as evidently among the hill Patwin, and possibly among the coast Pomo and Yuki in relation to the Clear Lake Pomo. In the main, one line of growth seems to have been followed by the groups in the Sacramento Valley itself, another by those of the Coast Range region to the west. But almost every group had developed some positive peculiarities of its own. Many traits are common to several groups, and a great many extend beyond the limits of tribes with societies, so that long-continued reciprocal export and import of ritual material between Kuksu and non-Kuksu groups are indicated, and the detailed history of the system becomes exceedingly intricate.

In some such manner as here outlined, it seems to me, the Kuksu cult system must have grown up. The phenomena are highly complex, and demonstrable determinations will necessarily be fewer than probabilities in their historical reconstruction; and probabilities fewer than possibilities. But to deny that any historical significance can be extracted from the phenomena would be negativistic. There are enough specific and generic similarities between the Kuksu, southern California, and Pueblo cult systems to render pedantic an insistence on the wholly independent origin and parallel development of these. But there are a greater number of specific and even generic features which are dissimiar, and these, which constitute the bulk of the systems, cannot be brushed aside as secondary and negligible. They too constitute historic growths, to dismiss which as provincialisms in favor of those features which lend themselves to a simple unified scheme would be summary and contrary to the spirit of historic inquiry. Finally, there are the great territorial gaps between the cult system centers. These must have acted as filters and modifiers in transmission, and enforce extreme caution in reconstructive interpretation. Still, some conclusions more or less along the lines indicated, seem attainable and perhaps justified.

In closing this review I wish to reëmphasize the value of Loeb's contributions to the subject, precisely because my historical interpretations in part differ from his. He has sharply defined certain fundamental features of the cult, such as the ghost and the death-and-resurrection concepts, which had been inadequately recognized before. Also, he has envisaged the entire Kuksu complex in the light of more or less comparable phenomena elsewhere—perhaps mistakenly at some points but certainly with illumination at others. Whatever the foregoing pages may have contributed to the understanding of this interesting religious system, is very considerably due to the clarifying influence of his work and of my discussions with him.

THE 1870 GHOST DANCE

by
Cora Du Bois

A complicated series of interacting cults had developed as a consequence of the stimulus given by the 1870 Ghost Dance. The religious developments covered in this paper occurred during a period of sixty years beginning in 1871. It was a time of marked intra- and intertribal flux, during which Indian life underwent progressive disintegration. As a result, the early reactions which were resistive to white encroachments were gradually transformed into an acceptance of European habits and attitudes. These changes represent a closely integrated continuum in time and space. However, for descriptive purposes, it is convenient to set a series of categorical terms as points of reference on that continuum, if one bears in mind that the borders are blurred. In the title, Ghost Dance has been used as a general term to cover a series of generically related religious developments, but in the body of the paper the term will be applied only to the first phase of the whole growth. The early manifestations consisted largely of doctrinal stress on the return of the dead and the end of the world, which in some vague supernatural manner would entail the elimination of the white people. The adherents believed these changes were imminent. The Ghost Dance proper had two main strands of diffusion. The cult originated among the Paviotso of Walker Lake in Nevada and spread to the Washo, the Paviotso of Pyramid Lake, Klamath Reservation, and Surprise Valley, to the Modoc, Klamath, Shasta, and Karok tribes. It was transmitted by the Shasta to Siletz and Grand Ronde reservations in Oregon. From Siletz it was carried to the Tolowa and Yurok. The circle of this first strand of diffusion was completed in the vicinity of Orleans on the Klamath River when the Yurok movement going upstream met the Karok movement progressing downstream. A second but contemporaneous strand of the Ghost Dance proper spread from the Paviotso to the easternmost Achomawi, across Achomawi territory to the Northern Yana, the Wintun, and Hill Patwin.

Among the Wintun and Hill Patwin the second point of reference on

---

Pp. 1–3 of Cora Du Bois, *The 1870 Ghost Dance*, Univ. Calif. Publ. Anthro. Rec. (1939), 3:1–152.

The Ghost Dance religion as a whole is discussed by J. W. Mooney, *The Ghost Dance Religion*, Bureau of American Ethnology, *14th Annual Report 1892–1893*, Pt. 2 (1896).

the continuum was developed. It will be called the Earth Lodge cult, from its most characteristic feature. This cult was similar to the Ghost Dance proper in excitement over immediate supernatural phenomenon. But, whereas the Ghost Dance stressed the return of the dead, the Earth Lodge cult stressed the end of the world. The faithful were to be protected from the catastrophe by the subterranean houses which they built for that purpose. The Earth Lodge cult, like the Ghost Dance, had two main strands of diffusion. One spread to the north from the Wintun to the Wintu and then back over Achomawi territory and to the Klamath Reservation, while simultaneously the Wintu transmitted the Earth Lodge cult to the Shasta, from whom it was passed in turn to Siletz and Grand Ronde reservations. There it was known locally as the Warm House Dance. The Earth Lodge cult in its northern manifestations also had an abortive introduction to Oregon City by Klamath Indians. Some years later a Siletz Reservation Indian carried a form of Earth Lodge cult southward among the Oregon tribes as far as Coos Bay. This has been called Thompson's Warm House Dance after the principal proselytizer.

Meanwhile the second strand of Earth Lodge cult diffusion spread southwestward to the Pomo area, where seven earth lodges were built in which surrounding tribes and tribelets congregated.

Almost immediately after the Earth Lodge cult was introduced to the Wintun and Hill Patwin, there grew up an elaboration of it called the Bole-Maru. This is a compound term consisting respectively of the Patwin and Pomo words for the cult. The Bole-Maru abandoned gradually doctrines of imminent world catastrophe and stressed instead concepts of the afterlife and of the supreme being. Ceremonially its highest development occurred among the Patwin and Pomo. Each local dreamer had his own revelations and supernatural authority, which determined the particular form his cult activities should take. By and large, however, most dreamers used the following devices: (1) flagpole, from which a flag was flown in front of the dance house during the ceremony; (2) a secularized form of the old Patwin Hesi dance, which has been called Bole-Hesi; (3) cloth costumes, especially for women, which were often used in conjunction with a particular dance known as Bole or Maru depending upon the language area; and (4) a Ball dance.

The Bole-Maru probably originated with the Hill Patwin prophet, Lame Bill, who also supported the Earth Lodge cult. In less than a year the Bole-Maru overlaid the Earth Lodge cult in Pomo and adjacent territories. It also spread to the River Patwin and Chico Maidu, who had not been touched by previous movements. The Bole-Maru in a somewhat attenuated form also spread northward to the Wintun, Wintu, Shasta, and

Achomawi. The Wintun dreamers seem to have been particularly active in repeatedly sending out groups of dancers to northern neighbors.

From an early form of the Bole-Maru in Pomo territory still another cult detached itself, which has been called the Big Head cult. This traveled rapidly northward along the western slopes of the Coast Range to the Shasta, where its momentum was exhausted, but not before some knowledge of it had reached Siletz and Grand Ronde reservations.

At this point a preliminary idea of dating will clarify matters. The Ghost Dance probably originated among the Paviotso of Walker Lake in about 1869. Its diffusion, however, did not begin until 1871. Once under way, it spread with great rapidity. By the end of 1871, or early in 1872, the Earth Lodge cult was already in existence. In the spring of 1872 the Earth Lodge cult reached its climax among the Pomo. By the end of that same year it had diffused over most of northeastern California and the first forms of the Bole-Maru had already been created. The Bole-Maru, although constantly in flux, has persisted until the present, especially in the Patwin and Pomo areas.

Characteristic of all these movements was the appearance of local dreamers or prophets whenever an external impulse set a new religious form in motion. Each tribe had its own interpreters of the new cults, so that in the description of the religious developments of each tribe, a more or less complete list of local dreamers has been given in approximately chronological order. These local dreamers and interpreters represent a constant recrudescence of local authoritarianism, but always beneath this local authority can be discovered an external stimulus. It is as though taproots were constantly being sent down into the intense localism of the Californian tribelets. In most tribes, and for only the short period of the Ghost Dance and Earth Lodge cults, dreaming was epidemic. It soon subsided and concentrated in the hands of particular dreamers or "preachers."

The influence of these leaders was everywhere different and individualized, yet on the whole they seem to have been instrumental in reshaping shamanism, in furthering the development of the Bole-Maru, or breaking ground for further Christianization. Their influence has made possible the introduction and acceptance of the many marginal Christian sects which now flourish among the Indians of this region. The Indian Shaker church has recently made marked progress in northwest California. The Pentecostal church and Four Square Gospel have very real influence and are eliminating the last phases of the Bole-Maru among the Pomo. The Round Valley Reservation and Fall River (Achomawi) churches are being conducted by Indian ministers for Indian converts. Besides, everywhere in northern California are found flourishing churches whose members are both white and Indian. The revivalistic psychology of the Pentecostals, for instance, has made it peculiarly a well-fitted vehicle for the Christianization of those Indians who had had previous experience with the Ghost Dance and its proliferations. At the moment it represents one of the terminal points in a progressively Christianized ideology, for which the Ghost Dance and its subsequent cults were transitional factors.

Lastly, attention should be drawn to A. H. Gayton's treatment of the Ghost Dance in south-central California.[1] This publication is necessary to a complete picture of the 1870 Ghost Dance. . . . Although I speak of two main avenues of introduction for the Ghost Dance, the statement applies only to northern California. There was a third and completely independent one into the southern part of the state, which Gayton has described.

---

[1] *The Ghost Dance of 1870 in South-Central California,* Univ. Calif. Publ. Am. Arch. and Ethn., 27 (1930), 57–82.

DEATH AND BURIAL
AMONG THE
NORTHERN MAIDU

by
Roland B. Dixon

There is some difference in the customs relating to death and burial in different portions of the Maidu area. In the Sacramento Valley region the usual custom appears to have been burial, and not cremation. The body of the deceased was dressed in the best the family could afford, and decorated with strings of beads, and with feather ornaments of various sorts. It was placed on a bearskin, and, the knees being bent closely, so that the body was in a squatting position, it was then wrapped and roped up by some of the older men into a ball. Sometimes several skins were used, but, as a rule, one was all that could be afforded. The grave was dug generally close to the village, as, were it at a distance, enemies might dig up the body for the beads. The grave was usually from about a meter to a meter and a half in depth, and over it a mound of earth was heaped. Some food was placed in the grave with the body, as well as bow and arrows, pipe, and so on. The body being buried, all went back to the house and wailed for some time; and, although the wailing began at once after death, it was now continued with redoubled energy. In some cases a net was first put over the body before tying it up in the bear- or deerskins. Generally the objects put into the grave were broken. The body was placed in the grave in a sitting position, usually facing east. The persons who dug the grave, and roped up the body, are said not to have had to undergo any ceremonial purification. Bodies were burned only when the man died far from home. When cremated, the ashes were taken home and there buried. In mourning, the widow cut her hair short, and covered her head, face, neck, and breast with a mixture of pine pitch and charcoal obtained from charring the wild nutmeg or pepper nut. This pitch she was obliged to wear until it came off, generally many months. Often there was a longer period set, as a year or more, and it was then renewed. The widow must remain in the house continually during the daytime, and was allowed to come out only for a short time after dark. This she must continue until the time of the "burning." There are said to have been no food restrictions. A man in mourning

Pp. 241–259 of Roland B. Dixon, "The Northern Maidu," *Bulletin of the American Museum of Natural History* (1905), 17:119–346.

had to cut his hair short, and also wore the pitch. He must not gamble or dance till the "burning" was over. During the period while the widow remained in the house, she was constantly occupied in making baskets and other things which were to be burned for the deceased at the next "burning" that was held. Generally all relatives aided her in this.

In the foothill region the body was prepared in the same way; and although cremation was somewhat more in use, perhaps, than in the valley, yet burial appears to have been the prevailing method. The grave was dug with the aid of digging sticks, the earth being thrown out with the hands or with small baskets. As in this region there were regular burial grounds, usually near or the same as the "burning" ground, it was not uncommon for bones of previous burials to be found in the course of digging a grave. In case this occurred, the other bones were carefully laid aside, and when the grave was finished, they were thrown in first, and the body placed directly over them. The body was placed in a sitting position, and all the personal property of the person was buried with him. Occasionally, instead of burying all, some of it was burned. The body usually faced the west. Pieces of pine bark were often put over the body, so that the earth might not rest heavily on it. The house of the man was burned, and often the locality deserted for a while. In the case of a chief, the dance house was pulled down or burned, and a new one built. The same methods of mourning were in use here. The widow or widower wore a peculiar necklace of string and beads, on which the beads were arranged in different ways. This necklace was worn until the mourner stopped "burning" for the deceased, when the necklace was burned, as described hereafter, in discussing the ceremony of the "burning." Here, as elsewhere, the name of the dead must not be mentioned for at least a year after his death.

In the region occupied by the Northeastern Maidu, the bodies of the dead were decked with beads and feathers, and, if the family owned one, an otterskin was put about the body. It was then placed in a sitting or squatting position on a bearskin, other small things, personal property of the deceased, and gifts, added, and the whole roped and securely tied up in a ball. Sometimes the body was put first into a large basket, and the bearskin placed outside of this. The grave was dug as elsewhere, and the body placed in it lying on the back, with the head toward the east. Food and water were placed in the grave, which was then filled in. If the person were a chief or shaman, then wands (yo'koli), or sticks with pendant feathers, were set up over the grave. Generally the immediate relatives attended to the preparation of the body, and to getting the grave ready. Most of the man's property was buried with him here, as among the other members of the stock. The persons who attended to the preparation of the body and dug the grave had to undergo a ceremony of purification. The first time any one took part in these duties, he (or she) must fast, abstaining from meat and fish, for five days. During this time he had to use the scratching-stick, live quietly by himself, although not forced to leave his house, and, when the time was over, must bathe and swim. He must eat alone. The next time the period was only four days, the next three, and so on until it was reduced to one. After the death of a chief, the dance house was usually burned, and rebuilt at a short distance. The houses of other people were generally burned, but not always. For a child it would not be done. Persons were not carried out of the house to die. Most of a man's dogs were killed at his death. In mourning, widows cut their hair and wore pitch, as already described. Men rarely showed any outward signs of mourning unless in case of the death of their father, when the whole family, men and women, cut their hair and put on pitch. A man might do this in the case of the death of his mother, but it was not usual.

When a child of mature years died, if he had been a young man known for his ability, and was much beloved by his father, then the father would cut his hair and put on pitch; but for a young child, or an older one of less reputation, only the mother would do so. Occasionally a man would mourn thus for his wife, but not always. The hair cut off in mourning was, in any case, kept carefully for a time, and then secretly put away somewhere in the brush. It was never made into a belt and worn ceremonially, as was the case among the Achomawi and Shasta. Widows wore a necklace of beads of pitch on a buckskin thong. This was worn until the "burning."

When a mother died, leaving a very young child, the child, as a rule, was buried alive with the mother, lying on the mother's breast, as if nursing. If the child were old enough to wean, the grandmother or oldest sister took charge of it, and brought it up. If the body of the mother were burned, the infant was placed similarly on her breast, and burned with her. It is said that, throughout the region, persons who had been invalids for a long time were sometimes buried before death occurred, being roped up and prepared as described.

By far the most important of the ceremonials and customs in connection with death and burial among the Maidu, and one of the most important of all their ceremonials, was the annual so-called "burning," or ö'stu. The ceremony seems to have varied not a little in the different parts of the Maidu region, being developed to its fullest extent in the valley and foothill area, and being less elaborate, and more purely personal in its character, in the higher Sierra. The custom is still kept up to some extent in the mountains and foothills, and it is from the latter section that the best descriptions have been obtained.

In the foothill region every village, or small group of villages, has a burning ground. The selection of a site for this was largely determined by the topography of the region. As a rule, a position on some rising ground clear of brush was chosen, for a watch could then more easily be kept for an attack by some enemy. The time of the burning was formerly a favorite time for such attacks, as the excitement of the participants, and the great noise made, prevented the attacked from being aware of the approach of the enemy. The soil was also a matter to be considered, for, as in general the burning ground was also the burial place, soft earth was a necessity.

As a rule, a burning ground, once chosen, is used for many generations. Sometimes a burning ground is abandoned for lack of people, the village or villages to whom it belongs having largely died out. As a rule, however, the ground is kept up even when the number of survivors of a village is very small. A man always desired to be buried in the same place as his ancestors. Several villages generally have a burning ground in common. Should a man move away from home, he would, when he died, be buried in the burning ground of his native village. If any section should be practically depopulated, the ground would be abandoned; but if an old person should die who belonged there, he or she would be buried there, although no burning would be held for only two or three persons. There are no ceremonies when a new burning ground is chosen.

Every burning ground is ruled by one or more members (generally shamans) of the tribe or village in whose territory it is situated. In case of a death, the family may bury the deceased in the burning ground of their own village or village group, without asking permission of any one; or the body may be buried, if it is desired, in the ground of some other village; but, under any circumstances, the relatives may not take part in the burning until they have received a membership string or necklace for the ground in which the body was placed. After the body is buried, therefore, the mourners go to those who are in charge of the ground in question, and apply for such a string, so that they may take part in the next burning which is to be held. The owners or overseers of the burning ground then give the applicant a string, for which payment has to be made in beads, furs, food, or other things. The so-called "strings" are necklaces of beads and cord, the number of beads and their arrangement varying with every burning ground, so that from the string one can tell at once to what ground the person wearing it belongs. The arrangements of beads on the cord are varied thus:

0-0-00-0-0-00-0-0
00-0-00-0-00-0-00
000-0-000-0-000-0-000, etc.

Having received such a string, the recipient is entitled to burn (or "cry") for a period of five years. At the end of this time, if no other member of the family has died, the person may burn the string, or tell the one from whom it was received that he wishes it to be burned. When this occurs, he receives from the original giver the equivalent of the price paid for it. The strings are worn, while they are in the hands of the mourner, constantly as a necklace. Should other members of the family die before the five years are up, the string may be kept till five years from the date of the most recent death. It seems that strings are also given out under somewhat different conditions. From information obtained by Mr. S. A. Barrett, it appears that strings may be issued by the individual mourners, to any persons whom they wish to invite to come to the burning which they expect to hold for their dead. The recipient must give in return a few baskets or something of that sort, and is then entitled to attend all burnings by the issuer, until the latter redeems the string. This is done, as above described, by paying back to the person property equivalent in value to that which he originally gave for it. The string, thus redeemed, is then burned. The whole affair of redemption and burning of the string takes place at one of the regular burnings. In some cases, if the person issuing the strings is wealthy, he or she may give property to the recipient when issuing the string, in which case the recipient must pay this back, when the string is called for to be redeemed. The time of the burning is set by the votes of all who have strings for that particular ground. If a person has many relatives to burn for, the other members will not hasten the matter, but let the person have plenty of time to get things ready. The burning comes, however, as a rule, in the latter part of September, or early October, although it may be put off until somewhat later. Every family may hold one of these strings, but no more. They must be kept with great care, never given away or traded, and never sold.

The date being finally set by the members, as above stated, in consultation with the shaman, knotted strings are distributed to all who are to be present; and, in the usual manner, by untying or cutting off one knot every day, they all arrive together. The village in whose territory the affair is to occur has to supply the guests with food. Each member of the local group gives as much toward this general store as he can. All such food is then collected in baskets in a great pile. The whole number of guests having arrived, the shaman calls for the food to be brought, and then divides it among the people as he sees fit. Usually it is divided with regard to the size of the families, a family of six getting twice as much as one of three. In distributing the food, the chief or shaman calls the name of the oldest male member of that family, who then comes forward, and receives the share for the whole family, which he then divides among them. Any person who comes late, after the food has been distributed, must be looked out for by those who have already received food.

The whole party being assembled, the ceremony begins the evening before the actual burning. This preliminary ceremony is participated in only by the chief mourners. There is little regular order in the affair. About sunset they gather at the burning ground, and wail and mourn at the graves, crying thus for several hours. Often the graves are covered by the mourners with a thin layer of flour, and then of earth. Members begin and stop when they please, and drop away one by one, going back to the camp to sleep. The purpose of this preliminary cry is to give notice to the dead that the burning is to take place.

The following morning and early afternoon are spent in repairing the brush fences about the burning ground, and in gathering the poles to be used for the suspension of gifts. These brush fences or enclosures are usually from twenty to thirty meters in diameter, or less, and are made by piling up brush of any kind about a low, roughly circular earthen embankment about twenty centimeters high. The brush is leaned against poles running between crotched posts, and forms a fence from one to two meters in height. In this fence there are generally two openings left—one at the eastern and one at the western side, the latter generally the wider. Sometimes but one such opening is made, and then invariably on the western side. In the center a huge pile of wood is placed for the fire, which is lighted when the ceremony itself begins. The arrangement of the ground is shown in the accompanying figure.

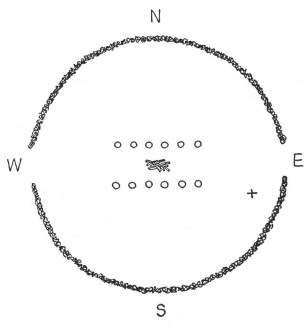

Plan of Burning-grounds.

The fences having been repaired, and plenty of wood gathered for the fire, all eat their dinner, the local residents partaking of their own supplies of food, the visitors depending on what had been given them, as already described. Each family eats by itself; and, although it may eat with others, it is not customary.

The meal over, the preparation of the poles is begun. Each mourner may have as many poles as he or she wishes and can fill; and each person will be given space according to the amount of property on the poles he has. Some have large quantities to burn, some but little, but the amount of goods does not increase the respect felt for the person. All the property to be burned by each mourner is brought to the burning ground the day before, but no display is made of it till the evening of the burning itself. If the night is bright, one is supposed to wait till dusk before beginning to prepare the poles and display the property. There is, however, complete individual freedom, and any person may begin to prepare his poles earlier if he desires. Each article which is to be burned in honor and for the use of the dead is, if possible, tied to a pole. Shirts have sticks placed in the arms to hold these out. The shirt is then hung to the pole by a string from the collar. The first shirt is tied at the top of the pole, and others successively below it till the pole is filled to within about one meter of the ground. In a similar manner other articles of clothing for men or women—skins, beads, necklaces, etc.—are tied to other poles. It is customary to have a separate pole for each sort of thing to be burned, all the shirts being on one pole or on several poles, all dresses on others, and so forth. People help each other in the preparation of their poles.

The poles are usually from five to eight meters long, and are either stripped of bark or not, as the person prefers. When these poles are all ready, each family carries its poles, with their loads of goods, to the center of the burning ground, and digs a hole about fifty centimeters deep for each group of from five to ten poles to stand in. The poles are then placed in the hole, and earth firmly stamped down about them. The groups of poles are arranged roughly in rows, on the north and south sides of the fire, as shown in the diagram. In 1904 one pole to which baskets were attached was not set in the ground, but thrust into the brush fence, so that the pole leaned inward at an angle of about 45°. The baskets on this pole were not used in the ceremony. The poles being thus set, the heavier articles, and such as could not well be attached to the poles, are piled on the ground at the foot. This would include such things as large baskets, flour, acorns, dried meat, fish, etc. . . . This all accomplished, each family gathers about its poles, and sits by them till all have finished. The large fire in the center has not yet been lighted, but many small fires are lighted outside the enclosure for cooking purposes and for light. There is usually one such fire for each family.

After some time, one of the members of the local tribe, holding a member's string for this burning ground, comes forward and lights the fire. The task is usually given to some old man. As soon as the fire is lighted, any member may, if he chooses, sell or exchange any articles he has brought for the burning; and there is often considerable bargaining among the people for a time. If no trading takes place, or, if trading occurs, when it is over, the chief or shaman makes the opening address. Of this the following, delivered in 1900, may serve as an example:

Don't fail to hear me! Don't fail to hear me! Light up the fire, it is not long till daylight. Our people are all ready. We have assembled here to mourn and cry again. We want no trouble. We are here to cry, and not for trouble. Do not drink whiskey. Hear me, all you boys! Do not drink any whiskey and get drunk. Come here, every one, and from every place, and help us cry! If you assist us, we, in our turn, will assist you. I, as your chief, will lead you in all things. Come, one and all! While we are here, if any one has a member string, and he has finished with it, I am ready to receive it. If no one has one to give up, we will begin.

As soon as this address has been made, the speaker begins crying, and this is the signal for the others to begin also. The chief or shaman, having begun the crying, throws on the fire a few pine nuts, acorns, pieces of dried meat or fish. In no case, however, is anything yet taken from any of the poles, or the piles at their bases. All present now join in the wailing. From time to time individuals throw bits of food and small offerings taken from the piles on the ground into the fire, and in this manner the night passes till nearly dawn. The mourners stand back to the fire; and after gently swinging the article to be burned to and fro before the body, it is then swung over the fire and dropped in, the right hand being at the same time thrown up above the head, or simply to the head. In wailing, some moan or wail in a low tone, others scream loudly, and all use different expressions and exclamations, which are addressed to the dead. Some of these are the following: "Pity my poor boy!" "Where are you, my darling girl?" "Why, oh why, did you die, my boy?" "Oh, my husband!" "Come back, my poor sister!" "Brother, brother, brother, no more!" "My child, my child!" "Father, father, father, pity me!" At early dawn the stripping of the poles begins. Any person may start when he wishes, without waiting for the others. The poles are lifted from the holes, and the articles removed, either by the person who is giving them or by any friend who is willing to assist. As the objects are removed, they are thrown into the fire, singly or in armfuls. This is done always by the person who is giving the things. At this stage in the ceremony generally, the member and invitation strings are redeemed. Baskets and other property for this purpose are brought and placed on poles, just as other property is. New strings are also given out at this time. As soon as any one thus starts to take down the poles, it serves as a signal for all to begin, and a general stripping of poles at once takes place. It is at this time that the ceremony reaches its climax of excitement and importance. The older men and women sway their bodies from side to side, and sing and wail, and there is intense excitement among all. The fire is often nearly smothered by the great amount of things thrown into it; and, under these circumstances, a halt must be called till the fire can burn up again. While the things from the poles are being put on the fire, and to a less extent during the earlier wailing, the mourners pat their heads rapidly with the hands, and blow forcibly every now and then, expelling the air from the lungs violently, as if to blow away unseen things. As the dawn approaches, and the last of the goods are being thrown into the fire, the wailing and moaning increase, if possible, in intensity, and the older women try to throw themselves into the fire, having to be restrained by the men. Old men are wiping away the tears that stream down their faces, and many are prostrated by the fatigue and excitement. As soon as all the poles are stripped, the remaining articles piled at the bases of the poles are thrown on; and this continues till all has been destroyed.

After a short interval, during which the assembly secures a little rest, the chief or shaman makes his closing address:

Don't fail to hear me! Our burning is ended. I command you all to go to the dance house. We are all tired. At the dance house we have food for all. There we will eat, for it is not well to go home hungry. You may gamble there. The fire is burning in the dance house, and the house awaits your coming. Gamble and make merry, but let us have no trouble or disturbance. Let us go! I will lead the way.

This speech over, the assembly adjourns to the dance house, and there, after a little food and sleep on the part of the men (the women being usually scattered about in the various other houses), there is for a day or more a constant succession of games, gambling, and feasts. Then one by one the visitors start for home, and the village returns to its former quiet life.

At the burning held at Mooretown in 1900 there were about a hundred and fifty poles filled with objects, so the amount of property sacrificed was not small. There were dresses, shirts, baskets, two poles of earrings, one of knitted caps, three bearhides, one coyote hide, one pole of raccoon skins, and one of chinchilla-cat skins, etc. There were about three hundred pounds of flour, birch-seed flour, pine nuts, dried eels, dried fish, etc. There were also a number of hats for boys, men and women. The approximate value of the goods burned was about two hundred dollars; the value in baskets destroyed was about equal; and in skins the money value was about thirty-five dollars. Thus nearly five hundred dollars' worth of property was burned at this single burning. In this same year there were burnings held at four or five other places in Maidu territory; and while the amount of property consumed was probably considerably smaller in all cases, yet the aggregate must have been over a thousand dollars.

The purpose of the whole ceremony is to supply the ghosts of the dead with clothing, property, and food in the other world. Each family gives to its dead what it can afford; and the whole ceremony is distinctly individual, in that there is no general offering for the dead as a body, but each family offers directly to its own relatives only. As already mentioned in speaking of the burial customs, there is considerable property placed with the body in the grave, and sometimes some is burned at the time of burial. The main reliance is, however, placed on the supplies offered at the annual burning. After sacrificing thus for three or four years, it seems to be felt that enough has been done; and, as a rule, the family does not continue to offer property for a relative at the burnings for more than four or five years. Occasionally, however, some will continue the offerings for a long period; and one case was noted of a woman who had burned for ten or twelve years for her husband, and she had declared that it was her intention to continue to "burn" every year until she should die.

In some cases the ceremony is considerably more elaborate. This is when use is made of an image representing the dead, for whom the offerings are made. The image is made only when the person offered to, if a man, was a member of the Secret Society, or, if a woman, if she were of wealth and importance. The figure was constructed, in the former case, of a lynx or wildcat skin stuffed with dry grass or leaves. If no wildcat or lynx skin could be had, the skin of a gray fox would be used, but never that of a red, black, or silver fox, all of which have white hairs on the tail. The nose of the skin is tucked down inside, a piece of otter or mink skin wound around to form the neck, and in place of the head is put a netted cap stuffed with grass. Around this, and over the place where the face would be, is placed one of the regular yellowhammer feather bands. Sometimes this is made, instead, from the feathers of the speckled woodpecker. The band is affixed only in the central portion, the ends being allowed to stand out from the head on either side. Bunches of hawk feathers are attached to the "head," also a vertical plume stick, and a horizontal one as well, these marking the individual's rank in the Secret Society. A bone whistle is hung about the neck. The claws are carefully removed from the fore-paws of the skin, and sticks put into the legs to make them stand out straight like arms. At the end of each arm is suspended a tiny basket containing acorn meal and birch-seed flour respectively; or a head plume is substituted for one of the baskets. The hind legs and tail of the skin are concealed from view. At the lower end of the skin a row of feathers is sometimes tucked in, which may be of any bird except the eagle or a bird with white feathers. These feathers form a sort of ruff or skirt. Images made for women differed considerably from that just described. . . . The differences are chiefly that the head is formed of stuffed buckskin in place of the netted cap; that the face is painted with stripes, representing the painting used by girls at their puberty dances; that the quail-plume ear ornaments are worn, as well as a pair of bone ones; that a woodpecker scalp headdress is used in place of a feather band; that a mass of shredded tule or maple bark is affixed to the back of the head, presumably to represent hair; that a much more elaborate necklace or necklaces are worn; that the feather belt is added; and that two sorts of yokoli are placed in the hands of the figure, which also carries a small burden basket on the back. There should be a feather rope running from one hand to the other to make the image complete. In the making of both sorts of images, considerable variety existed, wealthy families lavishing ornament where poor persons had to content themselves with but a few simple beads. The maker of an image must give a "soup" either when he begins work or after the image is finished.

The figure, when completed, is fastened to a stake, which is set up, facing the fire, inside the burning-ground enclosure. The figure is always placed either on the east or west side of the fire, near the opening in the fence (at the spot marked by a cross in the diagram, p. 505), and is generally put on the side nearest to the place where lived the person for whom it stands.

The greater part of the ceremony of the burning is the same, whether or not there is an image present. When the image is present, however, during the earlier part of the proceedings it is common for a member of the Secret Society to approach the figure, and act as if feeding it with acorn bread, saying, "Here is bread! eat it, old man." Then, breaking the bread in pieces, he holds it to the place where the mouth of the image should be. As a rule, there are several baskets of meal and food placed on the ground at the base of the pole which supports the figure. When the end of the burning comes near, the chief or shaman goes up to the image, followed by several members of the society. One of these takes the figure by the right arm, and another by the left; and thus they lead or carry the image to the fire, making it move as if walking. Should a bow be among the objects to be burned for the figure, one member walks in advance of the image, carrying the bow with arrow on the string, and jumping rapidly from side to side as he walks, aiming now here, now there, stopping frequently, stooping, crouching, hesitating, and trying for a better aim. All his motions are as if he were trying to shoot an unseen enemy. If a bearhide is to be burned, it is carried before the image by a member of the society, who holds it high above his head, and makes several circuits of the fire thus, crying loudly the while. Behind the image come other members of the society, carrying baskets of acorn flour, birch-seed flour, acorn bread, etc. As soon as the procession reaches the fire, the image is thrown on at once, and also the bow, bearskin, and food. This occurs always as the very final part of the ceremony, just as dawn is breaking, and is the signal for frantic bursts of wailing and crying.

The image is known as ku'kini bü'sdi ("spirit or ghost stays within"), and is regarded as having within it during the ceremony the spirit of the man for whom it was made. It may be made at any time previous to the evening of the burning, and by any member of the Secret Society. If the person who makes the image is not one of the local residents, he must be paid by the family of the person for whom he makes it. The image is regarded as very sacred, and any one offering an insult to it formerly paid the penalty with his life. On one occasion, still within the memory of middle-aged persons, over thirty Indians were killed as a result of some one having broken an image. At the burning held at Mooretown in 1900, a drunken half-breed boy fell against the figure, and he was obliged to give as penalty a big soup-dinner and feast to all present. At a burning where such an image is present, no gambling of any kind is allowed, and no one may clap the hands, under penalty of a heavy fine.

The ceremonial of the burning in the region of the Sacramento Valley was, so far as known, substantially the same as above described from the foothill area. The ceremony has at present, however, gone almost completely out of use. The member strings seem, perhaps, to have been somewhat differently arranged, the necklace being made by a brother of the deceased, and by him placed about the neck of the mourner, usually here a woman. She wears the necklace till the burning, or till a subsequent burning; and then the giver of the necklace cuts it off and burns it himself, paying to the woman beads, which she keeps for herself. A widow may not marry again till the first burning is over. She may do so, however, that very night.

The night after the burning a dance was held in the dancehouse. All persons took part in it: there was no special costume, and but one man sat at the drum to beat time. The dancers formed a ring about the fire, and danced four times around, in sinistral circuit. After this dance, the next day a feast and gambling party were held. If the deceased had been a chief, his successor was selected at this time.

In the higher Sierra, among the Northeastern Maidu, the burning is much simpler, and somewhat different. In both the Sacramento Valley and the foothills the ceremony is an annual one, and at it all who have lost relatives during the last few years take part together. It is otherwise among the Northeastern Maidu. Here the burning is a ceremony held for a single person alone, and occurs at an interval of a year or two after his death. It is held once, and then repeated the following year, when the matter is over, and no further offerings are made. Others than the immediate family of the deceased of course take part, but offerings are made, it appears, only to the single individual. A burning is not held, moreover, for a child or young person, and often not for an older person, the affair being rather restricted to those who have been notable, and, as the people say, "good Indians." A further point of difference is, that so far as ascertained, no image, or anything resembling it, is ever used. When held, the general ceremony is very similar to that described, the ground being prepared in the same way, the poles arranged, and the property thrown into the fire just before dawn. Similar addresses are also made by the shaman. Among this portion of the Maidu, thus, the burning shows quite a different type; and no ceremony may occur for several years, should there be a prolonged period during which no deaths occur. Among the rest of the stock in the north, however, it occurs regularly each year. It is to be regretted that more detailed information has not yet been secured in regard to the form of the ceremony in the Sacramento Valley region. Owing to the greater degree of civilization of the Indians in that region, however, and their consequent abandonment of the old custom earlier than in the mountains, together with the accompanying dislike to discuss the subject, it has not yet been possible to secure as much information as desired. When such material shall have been obtained, however, it is believed that it will show some points of difference from the form as described in the foothills—differences which, in the light of further study of the Wintun tribes, may lead to conclusions of some interest. The greater simplicity of the whole affair among the Northeastern Maidu connects this form of the ceremony with the ceremonials of the Southern Maidu. Here, again, unfortunately, the material is as yet rather fragmentary; but enough is known to show that there the burning becomes even more simple, keeping the while its character, more or less, of a purely individual offering, and along the southern limit of the stock fading by degrees into the type characteristic of the Moquelumnan peoples. To the north, among the Yana, Achomawi, and Shasta, the whole ceremony is unknown.

THE YOKUTS DANCE
FOR THE DEAD

by
Stephen Powers

While in Coarse Gold Gulch, it was my good fortune to witness the great dance for the dead (*ḳo-ti-wa-chil*), which was one of the most extraordinary human spectacles I ever beheld. It was not the regular annual dance, but a special one, held by request of Ko-lo-mus-nim, a subchief of the Chukchansi; but it was in all respects as strange, as awful, as imposing an exhibition of barbaric superstition and barbaric affection as is afforded by the formal anniversary. Not to my dying hour will the recollection of that frightful midnight pageant be effaced.

First, it will be well to explain that among the Yokuts the dance for the dead is protracted nearly a week. The first two or three nights, while they are waiting for the assembling of the tardy delegations, are occupied only in speech-making, story-telling, etc., until a late hour; but during the last three nights they dance throughout the night until morning, and on the third night, about daybreak, they burn the offerings consecrated to the dead. This happened to be the first of the last three nights, hence no burning occurred, but in every other respect it was complete, and all the exercises were conducted with more energy and with fuller choruses than they would have been after the Indians had become exhausted.

When Tueh, the Indian interpreter, and myself entered the camp it was already an hour after nightfall, but there were yet no indications of a beginning of the dark orgies that were to be enacted. We found about three hundred Indians assembled, in a place remote from any American habitations, and encamped in light, open booths of brushwood, running around three sides of a spacious quadrangle. This quadrangle had been swept and beaten smooth for a dancing floor, and near one of the inside corners there was a small, circular embankment, like a circus ring, with the sacred fire brightly burning in the center. Kolomusnim and his relatives, the chief mourners, occupied the corner booths near this ring; and near by was Sloknich, the head chief of the Chukchansi, by whose authority this assembly had been convened. Here and there a fire burned with a stag-

Pp. 384–391 of Stephen Powers, *Tribes of California*, Contributions to North American Ethnology, vol. 3 (1877).

gering, sleepy blaze just outside the quadrangle, faintly glimmering through the booths; at intervals an Indian moved stealthily across the half-illuminated space within; while every few minutes the atmosphere was rendered discordant and hideous, as indeed the whole night was, during the most solemn passages, by the yelping, snarling, and fighting of the hordes of dogs.

For fully half an hour we slowly sauntered and loitered about the quadrangle, conversing in undertones, but still nothing occurred to break the somber silence, save the ever-recurring scurries of yelps from the accursed dogs. Now and then an Indian slowly passed across and sat down on the circular embankment, while others in silence occasionally fed the sacred fire. But at last, from Kolomusnim's quarter, there came up a long, wild, haunting wail, in a woman's voice. After a few minutes it was repeated. Soon another joined in, then another, and another, slowly, very slowly, until the whole quarter was united in an eldritch, dirge-like, dismal chorus. After about half an hour it ceased, as slowly as it began; and again there was profound, death-like silence; and again it was broken by the ever-renewed janglings of the dogs.

Some time again elapsed before any further movement was made, and then Sloknich, a little, old man, but straight as an arrow, with a sharp face and keen, little, basilisk eyes, stepped forth into the quadrangle and began to walk slowly to and fro around its three sides, making the opening proclamation. He spoke in extremely short, jerky sentences, with much repetition, substantially as follows:

"Make ready for the mourning. Let all make ready. Everybody make ready. Prepare your offerings. Your offerings to the dead. Have them all ready. Show them to the mourners. Let them see your sympathy. The mourning comes on. It hastens. Everybody make ready."

He continued in this manner for about twenty minutes, then ceased and entered his booth; after which silence, funereal and profound, again brooded over the encampment. By this proclamation he had formally opened the proceedings, and he took no further part in them, except in a short speech of condolence. By this time the Indians had collected in considerable numbers on the embankment, and they kept slowly coming forward until the circle was nearly completed, and the fire was only visible shooting up above their heads. A low hum of conversation began to buzz around it, as of slowly awakening activity. The slow piston rod of aboriginal dignity was beginning to ply; the clatter and whizzing of the machinery were swelling gradually up. No women had yet come out, for they took no part in the earlier proceedings. It was now quite ten o'clock, and we were getting impatient.

Presently the herald, a short, stout Indian, with a most voluble tongue, came out into the quadrangle with a very long staff in his hand, and paced slowly up and down the lines of booths, proclaiming: "Prepare for the dance. Let all make ready. We are all friends. We are all one people. We were a great tribe once. We are little now. All our hearts are as one. We have one heart. Make ready your offerings. The women have the most money. The women have the most offerings. They give the most. Get ready the tobacco. Let us chew the tobacco."

This man spoke with an extraordinary amount of repetition. For instance, he would say: "The women—the women—the women—have the most— have the most—the most money— have the most money—the women—the women — have the most offerings — the most offerings — give the most — give the most — the women — the women — give the most."

He spoke fully as long as Sloknich had done, and while he was speaking they were preparing a decoction of Indian tobacco by the fire. When he ceased he took his place in the circle, and all of them now began to sip and taste the tobacco, which seemed to be intended as a kind of mortification of the flesh. Sitting along on the embankment, while the nauseous mess was passing around in a basket and others were tasting the boiled leaves, they sought to mitigate the bitter dose with jokes and laughter. One said, "Did you ever see the women gather tobacco for themselves?" This was intended as a jest, for no woman ever touches the weed, but nobody laughed at it. As the powerful emetic began to work out its inevitable effect, one Indian after another arose from the circle and passed slowly and silently out into the outer darkness, whence there presently came up to our ears certain doleful and portentous sounds, painfully familiar to people who have been at sea. After all the Indians in the circle, except a few tough stomachs, had issued forth into the darkness and returned to their places, about eleven o'clock, the herald went around as before, making a third proclamation: "Let all mourn and weep. O, weep for the dead. Think of the dead body lying in the grave. We shall all die soon. We were a great people once. We are weak and little now. Be sorrowful in your hearts. O, let sorrow melt your hearts. Let your tears flow fast. We are all one people. We are all friends. All our hearts are one heart."

For the last hour or so the mourners and their more intimate friends and sympathizers, mostly women, had been collecting in Kolomusnim's quarter, close behind the circle, and preparing their offerings. Occasionally a long, solitary wail came up, trembling on the cold night wind. At the close of the third proclamation they began a death dance, and the mourners crowded promiscuously in a great, open booth, and held aloft in their hands or on their heads, as they danced, the articles they intended to offer to the memory of the departed. It was a splendid exhibition of barbaric gewgaws. Glittering necklaces of Haliotis and other rare marine shells;

bits of American tapestry; baskets of the finest workmanship, on which they had toiled for months, perhaps for years, circled and furred with hundreds of little quail plumes, bespangled, scalloped, festooned, and embroidered with beadery until there was scarcely place for the handling; plumes; shawls; etc. Kolomusnim had a pretty plume of metallic-glistening ravens' feathers in his hand. But the most remarkable article was a great plume, nearly six feet long, shaped like a parasol slightly opened, mostly of ravens' feathers, but containing rare and brilliant plumage from many birds of the forest, topped with a smaller plume or kind of coronet, and lavishly bedecked through all its length with bulbs, shell-clusters, circlets of feathers, dangling festoons — a magnificent bauble, towering far above all, with its glittering spangles and nodding plume on plume contrasting so strangely with the tattered and howling savages over whom it gorgeously swayed and flaunted. Another woman had an image, rudely constructed of shawls and clothing, to represent the dead woman, sister to Kolomusnim.

The beholding of all these things, some of which had belonged to the departed, and the strong contagion of human sorrow, wrought the Indians into a frenzy. Wildly they leaped and wailed; some flung themselves upon the earth and beat their breasts. There were constant exhortations to grief. Sloknich, sitting on the ground, poured forth burning and piercing words: "We have all one heart. All our hearts bled with yours. Our eyes weep tears like a living spring. O, think of the poor, dead woman in the grave." Kolomusnim, a savage of a majestic presence, bating his garb, though a hesitating orator, was so broken with grief that his few sobbing words moved the listeners like a funeral knell. Beholding now and then a special friend in the circle, he would run and fall upon his knees before him, bow down his head to the earth, and give way to uncontrollable sorrow. Others of the mourners would do the same, presenting to the friend's gaze some object which had belonged to the lamented woman. The friend, if a man, would pour forth long condolences; if a woman, she would receive the mourner's head in her hands, tenderly stroke down her hair, and unite her tears and lamentations with hers. Many an eye, both of men and women, both of mourners and strangers, glistened in the flickering fire light with copious and genuine tears.

But amid all this heart-felt mourning there were occasional manifestations of purely mechanical grief that were amusing. The venerable Sloknich, though he was a gifted and thrilling orator, a savage Nestor, preserved a dry eye; but once in a while he would arise in his place and lift up his voice in mourning like a sandhill crane, then presently sit down and calmly light a cigarette. After smoking two or three, he would stand up and fire away again. Cigarettes were burning everywhere. An Indian would take one out of his mouth and give a prolonged and dolorous bellow, then take a few whiffs again.

Yet even these comical manifestations were so entirely in earnest that nobody thought of laughing at the time; and though one's sense of humor could not but make silent note of them the while, they were greatly overborne by the outpouring of genuine, unmistakable grief. So far even from smiling, one might, without being accused of sentimental weakness, have dropped a tear at the spectacle of these poor wretches, weeping not more perhaps for the loved and lost than over their own miserable and hapless destiny of extermination.

These demonstrations continued a long time, a very long time, and I began to be impatient again, believing that the principal occasion had passed. It appeared afterward that they are compelled by their creed and custom to prolong the proceedings until daylight; hence this extreme deliberation.

But now, at last, about one o'clock in the morning, upon some preconcerted signal, there was a sudden and tumultuous rushing from all quarters of the quadrangle, amid which the interpreter and myself were almost borne down. For the first time during the night the women appeared conspicuously on the scene, thronged into the sacred circle, and quickly formed a ring close around the fire — a single circle of maidens, facing inward. The whole multitude of the populous camp crowded about them in confusion, jostling and struggling. A choir of male singers took their position hard by and commenced the death song, though they were not audible except to the nearest listeners.

At the same instant the young women began their frightful dance, which consisted of two leaps on each foot alternately, causing the body to rock to and fro; and either hand was thrust out with the swaying, as if the offering it held were about to be consigned to the flames, while the breath was forced out with violence between the teeth, in regular cadence, with a harsh and grinding sound of "heh!" The blaze of the sacred fire flamed out between the bodies of the dancers, swaying in accord, while the disheveled locks of the leaping hags wildly snapping in the night wind, the blood-curdling rasp of their breath in concert, and the frightful ululations and writhings of the mourners, conspired to produce a terrible effect. At the sight of this weird, awful, and lurid spectacle, which was swung into motion so suddenly, I felt all the blood creep and tingle in my veins, and my eyes moisten with the tears of a nameless awe and terror. We were beholding now, at last, the great dance for the dead.

All the long remainder of that frenzied night, from one o'clock to two, to three, to four, to five, those women leaped in the maddening dance, through smoke, and choking dust, and darkness, and glaring light, and cold, and heat, amid the unceasing wail of the multitude, not knowing or heeding aught else on earth. Once in five or ten minutes, when the choir completed a chorus, there was a pause of a few seconds; but no one moved from her place for a moment. What wonder that only the strongest young maidens were chosen for the duty! What wonder that the men avoided this terrible ordeal!

About four o'clock, wearied, dinned, and benumbed with the cold of the mountains, I crept away to a friendly blanket and sought to sleep. But it was in vain, for still through the night air were borne up to my ears the far-off crooning, the ululations, and that slow-pulsing, horrid "heh!" of the leaping witches, with all the distant voices, each more distinct than when heard nearer, of the mourning camp. The morning star drew itself far up into the blue reaches of heaven, blinking in the cold, dry California air, and still all the mournful riot of that Walpurgis night went on.

Then slowly there was drawn over everything a soft curtain of oblivion; the distant voices blended into one undistinguishable murmur, then died away and were still; the mourning was ended; the dancers ceased because they were weary.

For half an hour, perhaps, I slept. Then awaking suddenly I stood up in my blankets and looked down upon the camp, now broadly flooded by the level sun. It was silent as the grave. Even the unresting dogs slept at last, and the Indian ponies ceased from browsing, and stood still between the manzanita bushes to let the first sunshine warm and mellow up their hides, on which the hair stood out straight. All that wonderful night seemed like the phantasmagoria of a fevered dream. But before the sun was three-quarters of an hour high that tireless herald was out again, and going the rounds with a loud voice, to waken the heavy sleepers. In a few minutes the whole camp was in motion; not one remained, though many an eyelid moved like lead. The choir of singers took their places promptly, squatting on the ground; and a great company of men and women, bearing their offerings aloft, as before, joined in the same dance as described, with the same hissing "heh!" only it was performed in a disorderly rush-round, raising a great cloud of dust. Every five minutes, upon the ceasing of the singers, all faced suddenly to the west, ran forward a few paces, with a great clamor of mourning, and those in the front prostrated themselves, and bowed down their faces to the earth, while others stretched out their arms to the west, and piteously wrung them, with imploring cries, as if beckoning the departed spirits to return, or waving them a last farewell. This is in accordance with their belief in a Happy Western Land. Soon, upon the singers resuming, they all rose and joined again in the tumultuous rush-round. This lasted about an hour; then all was ended for that day, and the weary mourners betook themselves to their booths and to sleep.

Perhaps the only feature that mars this wonderful exhibition, in a moral point of view, is the fact that any mourner, when about to consign a funeral plume or other ornament to the flames in honor of the dead, will accept money for it from a bystander (provided he is an Indian), if only enough is offered. But they have scruples against selling objects on these occasions to a white man.

THE MOURNING
CEREMONY OF THE
MIWOK, 1906

by

C. Hart Merriam

[*This is an account of a four-day ceremony of the Miwok taken from notes and an incomplete manuscript of Dr. C. Hart Merriam. The sequence of ceremonies described below is as follows: the nights of October 9 and 10, 1906, the* Yum-meh, *or* Nah-choo-wah (*mourning or "cry"*) *ceremony; the morning of October 11, the* Mo-lah-gum-sip (*washing*) *ceremony; the night of October 11, the* Kal-la-ah (*fandango or acorn dance*) *rite; the night of October 12, the* Wok-ke-la (*war dance*).]

During the nights of October 9 and 10, 1906, and the morning of the eleventh I had the good fortune to witness, in its entirety, the *Yum-meh*, the mourning ceremony of the Miwok. It was held at Ha-cha-nah (called by the whites Railroad Flat, after an abandoned mine), in the lower part of the yellow pine belt in Calaveras County, California.

I reached the place the night before the ceremony began — in time to witness the preparations and see the guests arrive.

The resident Indians and those from the neighboring rancheria at West Point were camped around the ceremonial house — or "roundhouse" — in temporary brush shelters of fresh green manzanita and oak boughs.

The ceremonial house, called *hang-e* by the Miwok, is a circular structure of variable size but usually about 40 feet in diameter. It consists of a single chamber formed by an enclosing wall of vertical boards or slabs 5 or 6 feet high, with a high conical roof supported from the inside by four tall posts, arranged in the form of a square, which serve to define an open central area, thus dividing the interior into an inner and an outer space. During the ceremonies and dances the performers occupy the smaller inner space, called *kal-loo-tah*, the spectators the larger outer space, called *et-chat*. The fireplace is in the center of the floor; and over it, in the peak of the conical roof, is a circular hole for the escape of the smoke. The door fronts the north or northeast.

Formerly the ceremonial house was partly underground and its roof was domed and covered with earth. In the Miwok territory this type is now

Pp. 49–61 of C. Hart Merriam, *Studies of California Indians* (Univ. of Calif. Press, 1955).

rare and is replaced by the conical structure here described. The modern form is easier to build and appears to be borrowed from the Ne-se-non tribe on the north.

Two of the resident women took forty dollars' worth of gold dust, obtained by washing the river gravels, to the nearest store and traded it for flour, sugar, tea, coffee, and crackers.

On the morning of the ninth a small group of women went to the *hung-oi-yah* — the place where the acorn flour is leached and the mush cooked — kindled a fire of manzanita wood, and covered it with stones to be heated. The acorn flour was put on the circular leaches, of which there were two, each about four feet in diameter, and warm water was poured on till the bitter was washed out. It was then cooked in large baskets by means of hot stones, in the usual way. Enough was made to fill four large and several small baskets. The large ones held from one to two bushels each, so the total quantity was considerable — and more was cooked each day for three days. Two kinds were made — the thin porridge called *oo-la,* and the thick mush called *nu-pah,* which jellies when cold.

The women who were not engaged in making the acorn mush were busy all day baking bread and preparing other food for the expected guests; and in the afternoon the men killed a beef and cut it up. Most of it was cut into strips.

For several hours the young men were occupied cutting and carrying into the ceremonial house armfuls of pine boughs, from which the old people inside tore off the tufts of long needles and scattered them over the earth floor until it was completely and thickly covered with the fresh green needles, filling the house with the welcome fragrance of the pines.

The guests began to arrive on the afternoon of the ninth. They came from the rancherias at or near Oleta, Mokelumne Hill, San Andreas, Sheep Ranch, Murphys, and one family from as far south as Bald Rock near Soulsbyville. As they arrived, they were housed in the ceremonial house, where most of them took places on the west side. Baskets of bread and acorn mush and vessels of tea and coffee were carried into the ceremonial house by the resident women and set before them. This was done not only when the guests arrived, but also three times a day during the four following days. All meals for the visitors were served inside the ceremonial house; but all food, except the meat, was cooked outside. The beef was distributed raw in strips, and the guests broiled theirs on the coals inside.

When eating the *oo-la,* the thin mush or porridge, three or four persons sat on the ground around each basket and ate it by dipping their fingers into it, the thumb folded back out of the way, the other fingers collectively making a sort of spatula which was turned in the porridge, rotated when lifted out, and thrust into the mouth.

FIRST NIGHT: THE YUM-MEH CEREMONY

The ceremony began before it was quite dark, about six o'clock, and lasted an hour and a half, when it was followed by sermons or harangues from the principal chiefs. The head chief of the tribe, a very old and rather feeble man known to the whites as "MacKenzie," officiated as master of ceremonies. He sat on the ground at the foot of the southwest post, which position he retained as his station throughout the ceremony. At the beginning the principal mourners, called *naw-chet-took* and *loo-wah-zuk*, were seated in a semicircle on the west side. When all was ready, the old chief spoke a few sentences that I did not understand, whereupon the mourners, without rising, immediately began to mourn and wail. In a few minutes the old chief arose, carrying a long staff in his right hand, entered the inner space, and began a slow march around the fire, taking very short trotting steps and uttering a prolonged sad cry in musical cadence, in which the others joined. The words most often repeated were, "Ha-ha-ha-yah, ha-ha-ha-yah," pronounced simultaneously and in perfect time by all. Some of the women mourners — the number varied from four to seven — now arose and followed the old chief in single file. They were soon joined by three mourning chiefs, and the procession continued to circle from left to right around the fire for an hour and a half with slight intervals, the old head chief always in the lead.

During the entire ceremony the Indians not engaged in the mourning chant occupied the outer space, sitting or reclining in little groups on the carpet of pine needles that covered the hard ground. Now and again a dusky figure arose and moved noiselessly from group to group or passed in or out of the gloom; at intervals sorrowing women burst forth in dismal cries, while solicitous mothers gave breast to eager children, and a hundred hungry dogs wandered back and forth to lie down sooner or later beside their silent masters.

Save the dull light from the fire, the smoke-blackened interior was absolutely dark, forming an appropriate background for the solemn rite. The smoke rose fitfully, at times diffusing itself through the room, at times ascending to the roof holes in a pulsating column, reddened intermittently by the glow of the coals. The flickering fire disclosed at intervals the forms of the people reclining in the outer circle and cast a dim and lurid light on the band of mourners as they continually circled round it. All was silence save the steady rhythmic chant of the marchers and an occasional muffled sob from the obscurity of the outer space.

At one time the march stopped and the mourners faced the west and cried; then they faced the north and cried, meanwhile wailing and swaying their bodies to and fro. At another time three women from the outer circle stepped forward and each took hold of one of the women marchers and led her to one of the four inner or central posts where they immediately sat down cross-legged in facing couples — one couple at the foot of each of three of the posts. They then grasped each other by the elbows or shoulders and swayed their bodies backward and forward, sometimes stopping to caress each other on the face and neck, but still sobbing and crying.

While this was going on the others continued the march. Sometimes the leader halted and seemed to utter commands, whereupon the marchers faced about, changed the words of the cry, and gesticulated in a different manner. At times the head chief looked down at the ground, with his arms and the palms of his hands extended toward a spot on the earth floor, around which he moved in a semicircle, addressing it as if speaking to a dead person or to a grave. Sometimes, all the women simultaneously extended their arms forward and slightly upward with open hands, as if in supplication, sobbing and wailing as they did so. One of the mourners, a woman with hair clipped short and face blackened in memory of the recent death of her husband, did not join the marchers but throughout the ceremony remained sitting on the west side of the outer circle with her face to the wall, uttering continually a peculiarly sad and at the same time plaintive musical lament, in slow rhythmical cadence. It was a beautiful strain, full of pathos and melody. She was very much in earnest and was so exhausted by the excitement and effort that, when the march was over, she fell on her side and remained motionless in that position for more than an hour.

When the march was over, the mourners retired to the outer circle, and So-pi-ye, the old blind chief from Murphys, delivered a solemn oration. His voice was remarkably loud, deep, and clear. Another chief, who sat on the ground at his side, joined in from time to time.

At daylight on the following morning, the head chief harangued the people again for a long time, speaking until he was completely exhausted. A kindly old woman brought him coffee and a small basket of food but it was a long time before she could persuade him to take anything.

SECOND NIGHT

On the second night, October 10, the proceedings began shortly after dark and lasted about two hours, when the old head chief fell from exhaustion and the affair came to an abrupt end.

The character of the performance differed materially from that of the first night. In the beginning, the head chief faced the south, standing with his staff in his right hand. He then turned and faced the north, speaking and exhorting. Then a woman on the east side of the outer circle began sobbing. Then two women on the south side stepped out and sat on the ground with their arms around one another, sobbing and crying. The head chief remained standing on the south side of the inner space, facing in; he then turned and faced out, continuing his exhortations. After this he moved to the east and kneeled by the side of So-pi-ye, the blind chief, who was sitting on the ground with his legs crossed. Immediately two other chiefs took places facing each other, squatting close together on the ground, and both couples moaned and cried. At the same time the women in the outer circle were wailing and sobbing. The chiefs who were squatting on the ground facing each other rested their hands on each other's arms and shoulders. The four chiefs then changed places and partners, everybody crying, after which three of the chiefs arose and began a slow dancing march back and forth from the west side of the inner space, singing, "Ha-ha-ha-ha, ha-ha-ha-ha." While this was going on the women mourners were squatting on the ground in facing couples, crying and sobbing as before.

The old head chief, leaning on his staff, next approached one of the couples to the south and seemed to address them personally, while another chief continued the dance alone, moving slowly around the fire. Then the wife of one of the chiefs went to So-pi-ye and sat down facing him; they placed their hands on each other's arms and shoulders. There were now three chiefs standing near the fire. Then another old woman danced once around the fire alone, slowly swaying her body and arms, and sat down facing one of the chiefs who was a mourner; so that there were two couples kneeling or squatting on the ground, each consisting of a chief and an old woman. At this time the old head chief was slowly moving around the fire with one of the subordinate chiefs. The march stopped and the head chief kneeled by an elderly woman mourner and placed his hands on her head and she hers on his shoulders, both kneeling and weeping. The local chief danced slowly around the fire alone, bending his body and pointing to the ground in various directions with his wand. He then squatted on the ground, and an old woman put one hand on his heart and reached over with the other and patted him on the back.

The three chiefs and three old women exchanged partners and continued to sway their bodies and mourn as before. Then the local chief arose and went to the fire, and three of the chiefs took places on the south side, facing outward. Another old man squatted by one of the old women as before, and the local chief danced slowly around the fire, facing first to the right, then to the left, motioning with his wand. He then sat cross-legged on the ground by the side of a visiting chief who was one of the mourners. This left the head chief the only man standing. He continued to face the south, speaking and gesticulating. Two women knelt by the visiting chief, who knelt down and placed a hand on the shoulder of each, and all three remained kneeling. The old head chief continued to exhort, still facing the south, but showed signs of great fatigue. Then the wife of a local chief approached the fire, stood close to it, and, swaying her body back and forth, pointed across it. Another woman began the slow dancing march around the fire alone. A young mother, not a mourner, went to a woman at the fire, led her away, and they sat down together, facing each other, sobbing and rubbing one another with their hands.

The local chief now faced the fire and exhorted. He was soon joined by two other chiefs and the three stood in a row, while one of the women continued the march alone, swaying her body and arms and sobbing. She was soon joined by another woman and the local chief took his place at the head; a third woman followed at the rear. The head chief beat time and moved slowly back and forth on the east side of the fire. He then, in spite of his obvious exhaustion, led the dancing march and was followed by two other chiefs, after which he again faced south and continued to exhort, while the local chief stooped low, with hands extended, facing alternately in different directions but continuing to move slowly around the fire. The old chief again led the march, then halted and called out; the others also halted and swayed their bodies and arms.

The old chief now moved alone to the north side of the inner space and exhorted, his voice becoming feebler and feebler. The others faced him, standing on the south side. A few minutes later seven persons were marching around the fire, when the head chief stopped them by putting his hands on the old women and men. Again he led off, and the marchers were joined by others, until there were in all eleven persons marching around the fire, the largest number at one time during the ceremony. The head chief then stopped and sang out, "Hi-ha-ho-ho," and everyone stood still. He then faced the west, and the women continued the march alone, soon joined however by two of the other chiefs, while the old head chief continued to exhort from the north side. The dancers fell away until only three were left. By this time the old head chief's strength was gone and he fell to the ground exhausted. He was carried to his place at the foot of the south-west post by a local chief and an old woman, and it was a long time before we were sure whether he would live or die. This put a stop to the proceedings.

At intervals throughout the ceremony of the second night, as on the first, the woman mourner with the cropped hair and blackened face, who sat on the east side of the outer circle with her back to the others, remained in her position and continued to wail, keeping up her peculiarly pathetic musical lament.

The Mo-lah-gum-sip

The ceremony of the second night, so abruptly ended, recommenced before daylight the following morning, when the final act, known as the *Mo-lah-gum-sip*, or "wash," was performed.

Since the old head chief was too ill to take part, his place was taken by a local chief, Pedro, who at half-past five addressed the mourners in the roundhouse. He finished sometime before daylight, after which there was an interval of silence. Shortly before sunrise, some of the women brought out a large basket, set it on the ground near a small fire about forty feet north of the entrance to the ceremonial house, filled it with water and heated the water in the usual way by means of hot stones which had previously been put into the fire. When the water was hot, the chief (*eph*) from the neighboring village at West Point and an old woman who had been designated for the place, each holding a cloth in the right hand, took positions facing one another, one on each side of the basket (called *choo-soo-ah*).

Then there was a stir inside the ceremonial house, and a local chief led out three of the women mourners and brought them to the basket. As each in turn leaned over it she was seized by one of the washers, who immediately proceeded to wash her face vigorously with the cloth, which was frequently dipped in the hot water. After the women's faces had been washed, their wrists and hands were treated in the same way, but were held outside so that the water would drip away from, not into, the basket. When these three had been washed, a chief and an old woman led out two old men chiefs, also mourners, and they were washed in the same way as the others. Then two more mourners, both old women, were led out and washed. After this one of the local chiefs went to a place in the chaparral, at some little distance, where a middle-aged couple were sleeping, grasped the woman by the hand, and led her all the way back to the *choo-soo-ah* or hot-water basket, where she was treated as the others had been.

This completed the ceremony of the *Mo-lah-gum-sip* or "wash," and was the last act of the *Yum-meh* or mourning ceremony. It also ended the period of mourning for those who had been washed, thus freeing them from the restrictions imposed upon them during its continuance.

It should be stated however that mourners who have lost a husband or wife a short time before the *Yum-meh* are not expected to accept liberty at that time but continue in mourning till the "cry" of the following year. A mourner who takes advantage of an opportunity to terminate the mourning period within two or three months after the death of husband or wife is not well thought of by the people.

In the ceremony under consideration, the woman mourner who took no part in the march but remained throughout facing the outer wall singing by herself in a remarkably sad and sweet voice was washed with the others at the *Mo-lah-gum-sip*, but declined her liberty and expects to give a *Yum-meh* at her own home next fall.

The ceremony being over, all returned to the ceremonial house, where they were harangued by So-pi-ye, the old blind chief from the settlement on the hill near Murphys.

The sun now rose above the mountains in the east, and the feeble old head chief got up slowly from his place at the foot of the southwest post and with his staff walked out to an open place on the west side of the ceremonial house, where he stood in silence for a long time, facing the sun.

After this, breakfast was served, consisting of coffee, acorn mush, and biscuit. I ate with the others. Each of the mourners who had been washed gave a silver fifty-cent piece to the local chief in charge of this part of the ceremony.

The chiefs, when speaking, shouted the first syllable of each sentence or clause, and sometimes of each word, thus: "TEN-ni-ah; NAT-too-na-tah, POO-soo-ne," and so on. This they did uniformly in all their addresses and sermons; So-pi-ye the blind chief did it with great vigor. At the close of each speech, and at some of the pauses, the audience sang out "Hoo-oo-oo."

So-pi-ye in his last address spoke of some of the old chiefs who had passed away — notably of Teniah of Yosemite Valley, whose youngest son was brutally murdered by the whites. He spoke also of various tribes from the village of Poosoone at the mouth of American River to the Natoonatah on lower Kings River.

At the end he said, "Me-chet me-chet-te, woo-te woo-te. Koo-nahs" — his voice falling with the last word. The words mean, "What shall we do, what shall we do? Let's go, let's go. That's all" or "I'm done."

The *Yum-meh* held at Ha-cha-nah October 9 to 11, 1906, consisted of three quite distinct parts: (1) the mourning march of the first night; (2) the mixed ceremony of the second night; and (3) the *Mo-lah-gum-sip*, or "wash," which took place at daybreak on the morning of the third day. The Indians say that the ceremony often occupies four nights instead of two.

In the ceremony I witnessed, the operations of the first night consisted mainly of a nearly continuous slow trotting march in single file around the fire, broken by two conspicuous acts — one in which the old head chief appeared to address the graves of the dead, the other in which the old women danced slowly around the inner space with their arms and hands held forward as in supplication. On the second night the marching was reduced to brief intervals and the principal part was made up of a number of separate acts, the most prominent of which were the frequent assembling of the chiefs and principal mourners in facing couples squatting, sitting, or kneeling on the ground; the dancing march of solitary individuals; the impressive act of the old woman who, bending forward, with outstretched arm and finger, pointed across the fire; the curious stooping dance of the old chief who, with body bent low and arms extended, faced out in different directions in turn while dancing slowly around the fire.

Throughout the period covered by the mourning ceremony and subsequent festivities the greatest respect and affection were shown the old head chief. His speeches and sermons and those by So-pi-ye, the blind chief from Murphys, are worthy of permanent record; but my knowledge of the language is so exceedingly meager that I was able to understand only disjointed fragments. It was evident however that the addresses were of two kinds — the one historical, dealing mainly with the distribution and relations of the tribes, the conditions under which they lived, and the succession and characteristics of the great chiefs; the other advisory, exhorting people to do right. The young men were admonished to let drink alone, to keep away from quarrelsome people, to be slow to anger; to avoid hasty replies, particularly when talking to white men who might say exasperating things; to be kind and good and follow the example of the old people.

The foregoing account is hardly more than an empty skeleton of the ceremony — a skeleton divested not only of the life, but also of the meaning of the several acts. It is submitted as a fragmentary contribution to the life history of a little known people.

THIRD NIGHT: THE KAL-LA-AH OR FANDANGO

The mourning ceremony of two nights' duration was immediately followed by the dancing ceremony, *Kal-la-ah*, also of two nights' duration. The first night of the dance, October 11 (the third night of the ceremony), the performers were as follows: one *too-mop-peh*, or drummer, who beat the large plank drum with his feet; one *mul-lip-peh*, or singer, who stood with his back to the dancers, facing the drummer and beating time with a pair of clappersticks of elderwood, about fifteen inches long; and eight *ƙol-lep-peh* or dancers, five of whom were men, three women.

The five men dancers wore *tum-mah-ƙe-lah* — broad red headbands made of the red shaft feathers from the tails of the red-shafted flicker (*Colaptes cafer*). These headbands are worn horizontally across the front part of the head and project on each side so far that, when the two flaps are brought forward, they meet on the middle of the forehead. Most of them were solid red, with a black border formed by the tips of the tail feathers. One was interrupted by black vertical bars, and all were black at the ends. Three of the dancers had, projecting horizontally from each side of the head, *chah-le-lah*, two large white feathers. The two remaining men dancers had other feathers standing up on the top or back of their heads, and one wore a white side feather also. The *so-pop-peh*, or head dancer, wore in addition a *sol-lah*, or large feather apron, which hung from his hips and reached nearly to the ground. It was made of feathers of hawks and turkeys, and had the tail of a red-tail hawk in the center. It was fastened on by a cord passing under the arms and around the back of the neck. To the sides of this cord were attached obliquely on each side several long, dark feathers, giving the appearance of ribs. Each dancer carried in his hand a sort of feather wand. (They complained that they should have had complete feather suits, but did not possess them.)

The three women dancers wore no feathers, but each had a handkerchief tied tightly around her head and each carried in her hand a long handkerchief or piece of cloth. The women stood in a line between two of the posts, at first between the two on the east side, later between the two on the west side. The men dancers occupied the space between the drum and the two rear or south posts, from which position they danced toward or around the fire and back, the inner circle being their dancing ground.

The first dance began at eight o'clock and lasted till ten-thirty. The three women dancers stood in a row between the two posts on the east side and did not move out of their places, their part consisting in swaying their bodies and heads and beating time with their feet, while, at the same time, they made curious movements with their hands. The handkerchief held in the hands was at first passed around behind the body, the ends held in the hands just over the hips. While the dance was going on, the hands were repeatedly pushed forward and downward, moving the handkerchief in a sawing motion across the back.

The women were not painted. The men dancers had their faces painted in horizontal black bands, but each dancer was decorated differently from the others. The leader had two broad black horizontal cheek bands, one passing backward in continuation of the moustache, the other about half an inch above it. Each band was about half an inch in width. Another dancer had a single black band passing entirely around the front of the head, just below the level of the eyes. The leader had two black rings painted around his ankles.

The singer stood with his back to the dancers, between them and the west end of the drum. He sang in a rather low voice and beat long clapper sticks, held in his right hand, against the palm of his left hand. The drummer beat time with his feet, keeping time with the singer. The men danced in perfect time and with remarkable vigor, stamping the ground hard with their bare feet; the pine needles that covered the ground had been swept away from the dancing circle immediately around the fire. During the first dance the men jumped with both feet together; during the others they usually danced two-step, stamping each foot twice, first one and then the other.

The leader was a ventriloquist, and from time to time uttered smothered sounds which led the audience to believe that a man was hidden in the hole under the drum. He and the others, when dancing, made a hissing, expiratory sound, said to be in imitation of the bone whistles they formerly used. All said repeatedly while dancing, "Hoo-hoo-hoo-e." Each dance was repeated four times, and at the end the dancers turned and faced the drum and danced for a short time longer, then stopped suddenly and all together; the time was perfect throughout. During the progress of the dance, which I shall not attempt to describe in detail, the leader often left the others and ran back and forth in a zigzag course about the fire, frequently crouching and leaping as if escaping from or pursuing an enemy. Once he danced for a few minutes by alternately squatting and leaping with great vigor, a very difficult procedure and one requiring great strength. At the close of each dance the audience, which occupied the outer circle where they sat cross-legged on the ground or reclined in various positions, uttered a low "Hoo-oo, hoo-oo-oo."

Before the dance the dancing circle was sprinkled with water, and one of the old women threw acorn meal into the fire and uttered four times a peculiar wailing cry, facing the drum as she did so.

The dance on the first night of the ceremony was borrowed from the north and is known collectively (for it consists of six or seven separate dances, each repeated four times) as the acorn dance. It is supposed to bring a good crop of acorns the following year. The original or aboriginal dances of the tribe were danced by couples, male and female, with a clown between each two couples. About one hundred people were present, in the outer circle.

FOURTH NIGHT: THE WOK-KE-LA OR WAR DANCE

The dancing space about the fire was carefully swept and sprinkled as before. Then a woman stepped forward and sprinkled acorn meal on the fire. After she had done this several times, an older woman, wife of the local chief, came forward and in like manner sprinkled acorn meal on the same meal. She then uttered a prolonged wail in a single key. This she repeated at intervals four times, sprinkling the dancers and casting meal into the fire. The dancers then crossed the ceremonial house and went outside for a few moments, each turning a complete circle just before he passed outside. Returning, each turned around again after entering the house before crossing to the place at the rear. This was done in order to propitiate the spirits and secure permission to open and use the feather dresses without danger of serious consequences. As one of the Indians told me, this war dance, called *Wok-ke-la*, is the most particular and dangerous of all the dances and has to be done just so or the dancers would be very sick.

Before the dance began (at 7:30) the door was tightly closed and a guard place beside it. Then the singer began to sing in a low voice and beat time with his clapper, holding the clapper in his right hand and striking the palm of the left hand. The drummer at once began to beat time on the plank drum with his feet in the usual manner, stamping hard and in perfect time, and the dancers followed singing "Hoo-e, hoo-e, hoo-e."

Five men and four women took part in the first dance. One woman stood alone between the posts on the east side, the other three in a row between the posts on the west side. The women held their hands in front, each holding her handkerchief between her hands. At first the leader of the men danced by the side of the solitary woman on the west side, the other four men dancing in two rows between the south posts, each man holding feathers in his hands and moving his hands tremulously (the feathers in the hand representing the bows and arrows formerly held during the dance). The leader carried a bunch of feathers, each of the others two white feathers in each hand. During the first dance the movements were made in a succession of jumps, both feet moving simultaneously, the heels striking the ground vigorously and keeping perfect time with the drum. The expiratory hiss in imitation of the bone whistle was prominent throughout this dance. During the second dance the lone woman on the east side did not take part; she reappeared in the third dance. Ventriloquial sounds were made by the leader at intervals.

Some of the dancing was done in a circle about the fire, but most of it back of the fire or between it and the drum. The women remained in their places throughout, swaying their bodies and moving their hands. Between the dances, the dancers sat in a semicircle between the drum and the rear posts, with their backs to the audience, and sang and beat with three or more sets of clappers. Originally this dance had to be continued for four nights.

YUROK SHAMANISM

by
Robert Spott and
A. L. Kroeber

The information contained in this group of stories necessitates some revision of the account of Yurok shamanism given in the *Handbook*. It also elucidates the set of customs.

First of all, it is clear that there is a guardian spirit in the customary American Indian sense, and that the spirit appears in a dream or during a trance: it is very difficult to distinguish the two states. This guardian spirit is the source of shamanistic power through his putting into the candidate one of the telogel or "pains" upon control of which the doctor's power rests. This spirit may be a dead person, presumably a woman who was herself a doctor in her day, or an animal like the chicken hawk [see p. 536] . . . or the whale.

However, after this first appearance the guardian spirit recedes into the background and the animate "pains" which the doctor has received into her body take its place. It is these pains that throw her into the trance state or unconsciousness and give her clairvoyant power; it is they that make her ill and have gradually to be mastered; and it is they that extract from a patient the disease-bringing pains in his body. It is to "cook" these pains, to accustom them to their new human abode, and to make them tractable, that the new doctor dances the remôhpo or "kick dance" for days before a fire in the sweathouse. When she can finally produce the pain and return it to her body at will, she has the necessary control and is ready to begin curing. . . .

What was also not clear before is that the pains always come in pairs, just as the pains which make a nondoctor ill are in pairs. A doctor's first pain may come to her unsought in a dream, but may also be acquired when she is dancing in solitude in order to obtain power. To get its mate she goes to one of the mountaintop half-enclosures of stone which the Yurok called tsektsel and which in English they often speak of as seats. There she dances again, still alone, but under guard and at night, until, the guardian spirit having put the second of the pair into her body, she goes out of her senses

Pp. 155–157 of Robert Spott and A. L. Kroeber, *Yurok Narratives*, Univ. Calif. Publ. Am. Arch. and Ethn. (1942), 35:143–256.

again and has once more to be taken down to the "cooking" remôhpo dance in the sweathouse. A strong doctor may ultimately acquire many pairs of pains; but the foundation of her ability and her strongest pains are the first two pairs.

The technique of curing has also become clearer. The larger telogeʟ pains rest in the doctor's body enveloped in a "blanket" (uka'a) of something like slime (slêyiʟ). When the doctor's power comes on her, one of her pains rises in her gorge, and its sleyiʟ helps her find the telogeʟ in the patient, as she moves her mouth over his body. She facilitates the egress of her pain by putting three or four fingers into her throat to retch it up. It then passes from her mouth, as she is "sucking" the patient, into the latter's body, and travels in this until it meets the pain which is causing the disease. The two slimy envelopes mingle and the doctor's pain returns to the doctor, drawing the other after it. Once the latter is safe in her body, she brings it up in the same manner as her own, and causes it to fly away to where it came from. The telogeʟ pains are little things, not bigger than a finger and often less, and are described as of various shapes and colors, although usually longitudinal.

There are other causes of illness besides pains. One is a soul loss, as we should call it, or taking away of the life—the "body," the Yurok put it. This is done by spirits and cannot be cured by doctors. It is treated by a special ritual. . . .

Another cause of sickness is sin. A person has secretly done something which is against custom law and is wrong. Years afterward he becomes ill; or perhaps it is his child or grandchild. Then confession is in order as the only way in which life can be saved. The doctor declares that there are no pains left in the sick person. He can become well only if he or a relative confesses having done something very wrong. Often the doctor half sees the sinful act and is able to suggest it sketchily. The patient or his suspected relative may call on his wife or a kinsman to confess; but the doctor has seen enough, while in her power, to know whether the confession is the pertinent one. If it is irrelevant to the cause of the illness, the patient will die. When the true and proper confession has been extorted, she accepts it, and blows the sickness away. It is a significant touch that the confession must be made in the hearing of others and thus become more or less common knowledge. The deed confessed to may be grave robbery, abortion, keeping a monster as a pet, attempting to poison or bewitch, approaching the supernatural while sexually unclean. Most often the act has to do with death, or intended death, or a dead body.

There are still other sicknesses which are not due to pains and therefore are not treated by shamanistic technique; rattlesnake bite, for instance. The Yurok know quite a list of troubles and ailments which fall into this category. They include insanity, sacroiliac slip, cuts, bruises, breaks, puerperal fever, or any illness within twenty days of parturition, and arrowhead or bullet wounds. The last two are treated by formula recitation with her medicine, plus sucking for the arrowhead by the formulist.

Doctoring was clearly a source of wealth—in successful cases, of great wealth. Young women wished to become doctors in order to be rich. Daughters who had already begun their career were held for a higher marriage price; or the father might insist on the husband's coming into the house as half-married so that the father himself instead of the husband—his house, at any rate—would receive the wealth that accrued. . . .

A DOCTOR ACQUIRES POWER [1]

This is how Fanny Flounder of Espeu became a doctor. She told me the story herself, at various times.

For several summers she danced at WogeL-otek, on a peak perhaps three miles from Espeu north of the creek. It looks out over the ocean. Then at last while she was sleeping here she dreamed she saw the sky rising and blood dripping off its edge. She heard the drops go "ts, ts" as they struck the ocean. She thought it must be Wes, ona olego', where the sky moves up and down, and the blood was hanging from it like icicles. Then she saw a woman standing in a doctor's maple-bark dress with her hair tied like a doctor. Fanny did not know her nor whether she was alive or dead, but thought she must be a doctor. The woman reached up as the edge of the sky went higher and picked off one of the icicles of blood, said "Here, take it," and put it into Fanny's mouth. It was icy cold.

Then Fanny knew nothing more. When she came to her senses she found she was in the wash of the breakers on the beach at Espeu with several men holding her. They took her back to the sweathouse to dance. But she could not: her feet turned under her as if there were no bones in them. Then the men took turns carrying her on their backs and dancing with her. Word was sent to her father and mother, who were spearing salmon on Prairie Creek. But her mother would not come: "She will not be a doctor," she said. Most of Fanny's sisters had become doctors before this. Her mother was a doctor, and her mother's mother also, but her mother had lost faith in her getting the power.

Now, after five days of dancing in the sweathouse, she was resting in the house. Then she felt a craving for crabmeat; so an old kinswoman, also a doctor, went along the beach until she found a washed-up claw (the Indians had no way of taking crabs in nets). She brought this back, roasted

---

[1] *Ibid.*, pp. 158–163.

it in the ashes, and offered it to Fanny. At the first morsel Fanny was nauseated. The old woman said, "Let it come out," and held a basket under her mouth. As soon as she saw the vomit, she cried, "Eya," because she saw the telogeʟ in it. Then everyone in Espeu heard the cry and came running and sang in the sweathouse, and Fanny danced there. She danced with strength as soon as the telogeʟ was out of her body. And her mother and father were notified and came as fast as they could. Then her mother said, "Stretch out your hands [as if to reach for the pain] and suck in your saliva like this: hlrr." Fanny did this and at last the pain flew into her again.

This pain was of blood. When she held it in her hands in the spittle in which it was enveloped you could see the blood dripping between her fingers. When I saw it in later years it was a black telogeʟ tipped red at the larger end. This, her first, is also her strongest pair of pains. About it other doctors might say "Skui k'etsêmin k'eʟ (Your pain is good)." They say that sort of thing to each other when one doctor has seen a pain in a patient but has been unable to remove it and the next doctor succeeds in sucking it out. The words of Fanny's song when she sucks out blood with her strongest power are: "Kitelk'el wes,ona-olego' kithônoksem" ("Where the sky moves up and down you are traveling in the air").

Now after a time an old kinsman at Espeu was sick in his knee. The other doctors there, who were also his kin, said, "Let the new doctor treat him." Her mother wanted her to undertake it but warned her not to try to sing in curing until she told her to. So she treated the old man without singing; and then she took on other light cases. Altogether she doctored seven times before she sang. Then her mother told her to try to sing, and the song came to her of itself.

Next summer she was at the same place on the hill, again dancing for more power. She was stretching out her hands in different directions when she saw a chicken hawk (tspegyī) soaring overhead. She became drowsy, lay down, and dreamed. She saw the chicken hawk alight and turn into a person about as tall as a ten-year-old boy, with a martenskin slung on his back. He said, "I saw you and came to help you. Take this." And he reached over his shoulder, took something out of his martenskin, and gave her something which she could not see; but she swallowed it. At once she became unconscious.

At Espeu they heard her coming downhill singing. As she ran past the sweathouse the people seized her and put her into it and she danced and came to her senses again. This telogeʟ took her less long to learn to control. It is her second strongest pain. After she had taken it out and reswallowed it she saw that it looked like a dentalium.

Now when she is called on to doctor, if she sees a chicken hawk overhead while she is on her way she knows she will be able to cure, even if she has not seen the patient. If she does not see a chicken hawk the case is serious and the patient may die.

The song she got from the chicken hawk is also about the ocean or something near it. When she is not in the trance state she can hardly remember the song, but when in a trance she sings it without knowing it.

When Fanny first told me about her power, she told me only about the chicken hawk. She was saving out how she got her first and strongest pain. That is the way doctors do: they do not give it all away. Nevertheless, other doctors soon find out that a doctor has additional pains, from what they see she can extract and they cannot.

All her other pains came to her later, and are smaller and weaker. She did not have to go to dance at WôgeL-otek for these; she dreamed and got them at home. That is the way it is with all doctors.

But after she had her first pain it was still necessary for her to "go inland" (heLkäu nusôton). This is like "passing an examination" or proving oneself. This she did only after she had had her first pain in and out several times and had it pretty well under control. She went up the peak on which WôgeL-otek is, but to another part of it on the south side called Tsektsêl otek. It is so called because there is a tsektsêL there—one of the seats or semicircular rock walls where the woge used to sit down and think. Besides doctors, men can go there to acquire luck. This tsektsêL is big enough to permit one to sit within it and stretch his legs in any direction. Its open side faces south.

Well, Fanny went up there with her mother, who was also a doctor. She wore her maple-bark dress. She stood aside until her mother had cleaned out the seat and built a fire in front of it. By it her mother laid down a new bark dress for her and a pipe in its case and a keyem basket. She told Fanny to put on the new dress and leave the old one. She built herself another little fire a short way off.

Then Fanny stepped into the tsektsêL and danced just as she had danced when first seeking power, stretching out her hands in all directions. All that night she did not stop dancing. Occasionally she shouted. When she danced more slowly she clapped her hands together. Her mother had told her, "When you shout you will hear all kinds of things from inland (heLkäu). But say, 'No, I did not come here for that.' Toward morning perhaps you will hear them singing the remôhpo from the mountains. Then say to them, 'That is what I am here for.'"

Then, as the night wore on, she danced harder and harder, and heard the sounds from inland more plainly and shouted, "I wish that when I doctor, any sick person will become well (wokteu niwa'a sôksipa). I am glad, you will give me the power."

Then at daylight she started straight for the sweathouse at Espeu. She knew nothing, but the woge led her there directly while she sang.

Her mother stayed behind, throwing the ashes from the fire aside, sweeping out the tsektsêL, and laying Fanny's old dress and basket in the first fork of the nearest tree, tying them against it with two or three strands of the dress so that they would stay there. It was the old basket into which she had spat out her first telogeL pain that her mother thus put away with her old dress. Fanny's old pipe she laid inside the tsektsêL at the back. Then she slapped her pipe sack five times, poured tobacco into her hand, rubbed it with her other, and blew it off inland toward the mountains. Then she slapped the sack five times more and poured tobacco on the ground before the bowl of Fanny's abandoned pipe. After they have led the novice to the sweathouse the woge take with them the life of the dress, the basket, and the pipe (wegwolotsik heLkäu wesôto). That is how doctors know that when they are dead they will go into the mountains, and each one while here has to make her path into the mountains. They go inland (heLkäu).

Then Fanny's mother went down to the sweathouse at Espeu.

When Fanny had arrived, they were already singing in the sweathouse. Others stood outside to keep away any menstruating women, because a woman who was an enemy and menstruating might deliberately come to stand near the sweathouse to spoil the new doctor's power. Also, these people outside may be needed to direct the doctor. Sometimes a novice runs straight to the sweathouse and dives in through the door headfirst. Others start to wander off and have to be led to the door. Now Fanny had jumped in and was dancing.

The second night, she felt as if she were dancing outdoors, not in the sweathouse. When people fell out from the singing to eat or rest, she also rested in the sweathouse. She felt weaker and weaker, but did not tell her mother. Then new people from the mouth of the river and up the river came in to sing, and they brought heavy songs (winôktsênoL). These are slow songs and not meant to be danced to, and her mother had told Fanny not to dance to them, but only to the proper remôhpo songs; but these heavy songs were good, and after them, when they went back to the remôhpo, she felt strong again and danced.

Now the rule is that each singer must sing four times before he passes the song on to the next one; and he goes on until the doctor begins to slow down her step and clap her hands; then he stops. On the third song of the first singer Fanny felt all her strength leaving her again. On the fourth song she did not get up until after he was going, and barely managed to stand up. Now most doctors close their eyes when they dance. But on the south corner of the sweathouse, where the sky had been showing between the planks, Fanny now saw that from time to time it looked as if it were covered. Then she clapped, the song stopped, she sat right down, and her mother came to her at once. She told her what she had seen. Then the mother told her husband to go outside and look around the south corner of the sweathouse. Tipsy looked and looked until he saw a piece of dry salmon stuck into the cracks between the planks. This was tspurawo ukä'm, menstruant woman's food. He did not touch it, but came back in and told his wife and she slipped out quietly and removed it while Tipsy told the singer.

Then Fanny danced again and her strength came back. On the third song of the new singer her pain came out and she handled it, both on the keyem basket and in her hand, and sucked it back in. Then she was in a trance again, but finished the song and clapped her hands. When they stopped, Fanny's mother whispered to her husband to put an end to the dancing for a while and find out who had secreted the impure salmon, so Tipsy said, "You visitors come to the house and eat." So they all filed out and ate. Meanwhile they summoned the menstruating women, but all made denial. Only one of them would not come, and she was a kinswoman, although a distant one. Then her husband sent a woman to tell her that he would beat her if she did not come. So she came and confessed she had put the impure salmon into the sweathouse in order to spoil Fanny's power, but she said she had done it to test how good a doctor she was. Then Fanny's mother told this woman's husband not to beat her, but they made her promise never to do anything like this again.

In the evening they sang for Fanny again in the sweathouse. Now everything went fine. She took her pain out four times during the night. In the morning she rested. This is done for ten nights; then the pains are settled and under control for good.

After this and after her experience with the chicken hawk Fanny had her roadway to heʟkäu established. From now on she could get her dreams and pains in her own house.

This account of how one of the most powerful of surviving doctors, a friend of both authors, acquired her powers, not only contains individual elements, but also illustrates the general method and attitudes. . . .

It is clear that shamanistic power is always wanted by the women who become doctors, and usually is overtly sought. Its possession definitely brings status and wealth. To successful doctors it brings great wealth. This is alluded to again and again, both in the biographies of persons and in legendary accounts. Also, the Yurok, unlike most California Indians, do not kill their doctors when they fail to cure, so that the advantages of the profession are not balanced by serious deterrents. The chief requisites seem to be possession of the necessary type of personality and willingness to undergo the somewhat arduous training of fasting, abstention from drinking, and dancing to the point of exhaustion. This training undoubtedly contributes to suggestibility as well as to direction of attention and concentration of will.

There appear to be four stages necessary to the acquiring and controlling of a pair of telogeʟ or pains. The first is the putting of a pain in the novice's body by the guardian spirit, be this an animal or a former doctor. Next is the taming of this pain—its "cooking," as the Yurok call it—by the remôhpo singing and dancing in a half-dismantled sweathouse in front of a concourse of people from whom only menstruant women and other impure persons are excluded. Then, the next summer, there follows the dancing in one of the stone half-enclosures on a mountaintop with an attendant or a guard near by. Here another pain is implanted. Unconsciousness follows and the doctor runs back to the river or ocean and again goes through the remôhpo dance as the last stage. The entire sequence may be repeated later.

It remains unexplained why the Yurok and a few of the neighboring tribes should have allotted doctoring power almost exclusively to women. In other regions women are usually not excluded, but the majority of doctors and the more powerful ones are men. Yurok men have several ways open to them to acquire power, but it is not the power to cure illness. The most usual method is to gather sweathouse wood ceremonially, that is, ascetically and with conscious direct willing. This brings luck, especially wealth, including sometimes wealth by gambling. Luck seekers and gamblers may also go to the stone enclosures on mountaintops, although this is less usual. Finally, a man who wishes to be brave and strong plunges into a lake or eddy, or under water in the hollow of a seastack, becomes unconscious, and is given the power he seeks by monsters or thunders. There is usually also the implication that a man acquires wealth power along with this fighting power; he would need it in settling for success in battle.

All these male procedures, however, differ from that for women in that no pain object is acquired, hence no power of curing illness, and that there is no remôhpo dance, nor any equivalent. When a man has secured his power he has it, and simply ends his practices.

The power to bewitch or "devil" is entirely distinct from the power of curing. It depends on an apparatus which can be transferred and usually is acquired by sale. Most often it is exercised by men. In fact, I do not know that women have ever practiced this power of "deviling." Such cases probably occur, but must be unusual.

Doctors are sometimes held responsible for deaths, but it is by sins of omission: they leave some of the pains (wo-telo) in and say nothing about them. This seems to be more often due to a desire for lucrative reemployment later on than to an attribution of malevolence. It is therefore logical that the Yurok do not kill doctors who lose cases, but content themselves with a refund of the payment if the patient dies within a year. The following is an account given by a [Yurok] shaman of repute of her acquisition of her powers.[2]

I began with a dream. At that time I was already married at Sregon. In the dream I was on Bald Hills. There I met a Chilula man who fed me deer meat which was black with blood. I did not know the man, but he was a short-nosed person. I had this dream in autumn, after we had gathered acorns.

In the morning I was ill. A doctor was called in to treat me and diagnosed my case. Then I went to the sweathouse to dance for ten nights. This whole time I did not eat. Once I danced until I became unconscious. They carried me into the living house. When I revived I climbed up the framework of poles for drying fish, escaped through the smoke hole, ran to another sweathouse, and began to dance there.

On the tenth day, while I was dancing, I obtained control of my first "pain." It came out of my mouth looking like a salmon liver, and as I held it in my hands blood dripped from it to the ground. This is what I had seen in my dream on Bald Hills. I then thought that it was merely venison. It was when I ate the venison that the pain entered my body.

On the eleventh day I began to eat again, but only a little.

All that winter I went daily high up on the ridge to gather sweathouse wood and each night I spent in the sweathouse. All this time I drank no water. Sometimes I walked along the river, put pebbles into my mouth and spat them out. Then I said to myself: "When I am a doctor I shall suck and the pains will come into my mouth as cool as these stones. I shall be paid for that." When day broke I would face the door of the sweat house and say: "A long dentalium is looking in at me." When I went up to gather wood, I kept saying: "The dentalium has gone before me; I see its tracks." When I had filled my basket with the wood, I said: "That large dentalium, the one I am carrying, is very heavy." When I swept the platform before the sweathouse clean with a branch, I said: "I see dentalia. I see dentalia. I am sweeping them to both sides of me." So whatever I did I spoke of money constantly.

My sleeping place in the sweathouse was atserger. This is the proper place for a doctor. I was not alone in the sweathouse. Men were present to watch, for fear I might lose my mind and do myself some harm.

Thus, once while the others slept, I dreamed I saw an uma'a coming. One of his legs was straight, the other bent at the knee, and he walked on this knee as if it were his foot, and had only one eye. Then I shouted, dashed out, and ran down along the river. My male relatives pursued me and brought me back unconscious. Then I danced for three nights

---

[2] Pp. 65–66 of A. L. Kroeber, *Handbook of the Indians of California*. Bureau of American Ethnology, Bulletin 78 (1925).

more. At this time I received my four largest pains. One of these is blue, one yellowish, another red, and the fourth white. Because I received these in dreaming about the uma'a they are the ones with which I cure sickness caused by an uma'a.

My smaller pains are whitish and less powerful. It is they that came to me in my first period of training. The pains come and go from my body. I do not always carry them in me. Today they are inside of me.

Again, not long after, I went to the creek which flows in above Nohtsku'm. I said to myself: "When people are sick, I shall cure them if they pay me enough." Then I heard singing in the gully. That same song I now sing in doctoring, but only if I am paid sufficiently. After this I danced again for ten days.

In my dancing I could see various pains flying above the heads of the people. Then I became beyond control trying to catch them. Some of the pains were very hard to drive away. They kept coming back, hovering over certain men. Such men were likely to be sick soon. Gradually I obtained more control of my pains, until finally I could take them out of myself, lay them in a basket, set this at the opposite end of the sweathouse, and then swallow them from where I stood. All this time I drank no water, gathered firewood for the sweathouse, slept in this, and constantly spoke to myself of dentalium money. Thus I did for nearly two years. Then I began to be ready to cure. I worked hard and long at my training because I wished to be the best doctor of all. During all this time, if I slept in the house at all, I put angelica root at the four corners of the fireplace and also threw it into the blaze. I would say: "This angelica comes from the middle of the sky. There the dentalia and woodpecker scalps eat its leaves. That is why it is so withered." Then I inhaled the smoke of the burning root. Thus the dentalia would come to the house in which I was. My sweating and refraining from water were not for the entire two years, but only for 10 days at a time again and again. At such periods I would also gash myself and rub in young fern fronds.

In the seventh moon, after nearly two years, I stopped my training. Then the ukwerhkwer teilogitl formula was made for me and we danced about the fire. This cooked me, cooked my pains in me, and after this I was done and did not train any more.

When I am summoned to a patient I smoke and say to myself: "I wish you to become well because I like what they are paying me." If the patient dies, I must return the payment. Then I begin to doctor. After I have danced a long time I can see all the pains in the sick person's body. Sometimes there are things like bulbs growing in a man, and they sprout and flower. These I can see but can not extract. Sometimes there are other pains which I can not remove. Then I refer the sick person to another doctor. But the other doctor may say: "Why does she not suck them out herself? Perhaps she wishes you to die." Sometimes a doctor really wishes to kill people. Then she blows her pains out through her pipe, sending them into the person that she hates.

A shaman is called kegeior; the pains, teinom or teilogitl; teilek or teile'm is "sick."

HUPA SORCERY

by
William J. Wallace
and Edith S. Taylor

The Hupa Indians of northwestern California entertain a strong belief that certain individuals possess supernatural or magical power which can be used to produce illness or death among fellow tribesmen. Bewitching is a practice open to anyone, male or female, who knows the correct procedure and is carried on by adults of all age groups. Men, however, seem to resort to it more often than women. A sorcerer usually directs his power against his own enemies, though he may occasionally, for a price, agree to attack another's foe. The power to bewitch is distinct from that of curing.

The motives for invoking black magic vary, though envy of possessions seems to be by far the most significant. Jealousy of success or possessions is strongly developed in Hupa culture, and an eminent or prosperous man is in constant danger of attack by an envious tribesman. A handsome well-liked child or the scion of an important family is also in continual peril, and such children are often victimized by the parents of a less well-endowed offspring.

The Hupa are a sensitive people, easily insulted, and retaliation for a personal slight often takes the form of a supernatural attack rather than overt aggression or a demand for financial compensation. A quarrel, a prolonged enmity, a personal grudge, or a thwarted design may also motivate a vindictive person to use sorcery against his rival.

Social recognition or power cannot be obtained through sorcery. Great secrecy surrounds the evil art, and a practitioner dare not boast of his deeds for fear of retaliation by the kinsmen of his victims.

The Hupa recognize several distinct types of witchery, ranging from the utterance of a simple curse or formula to the utilization of a diabolic device by which an invisible missile ("arrow") is shot into the victim's body. Common to all is the use of an incantation, the pronouncement of the name of the selected person, and the intrusion of a foreign object into his body. A practitioner of black magic need not encounter his victim face-to-face but can carry on his evil act from a distance.

Incantations. One of the most popular methods of sorcery is the recita-

Southwestern Journal of Anthropology (1950), 6:188–196. By permission of the authors.

tion or chanting of certain words which in themselves have power to harm. Sometimes the incantation takes the form of imitative magic, the mere saying the desired thing over and over again. More often, however, the words are in the form of a traditional formula, the knowledge of which has been obtained from a parent or other close relative. The burning of angelica root or the blowing of angelica root powder off the palm of the hand normally accompanies the recital.

Certain ritual actions may occur in association with the use of a verbal charm. For example, a formula may be spoken over a stick which is then placed on the trail where, if the victim steps over it, he soon succumbs. A dread form, occasionally invoked after a killing, involves the slashing open of the corpse of the slain man and the mixing of some of his blood with the footprints of the killer while an incantation is recited.

Evil spells must be narrated with fidelity and with a firm conviction in their power to produce the desired result. It is sometimes dangerous to employ them because they may react against the invoker, particularly if the intended victim possesses powerful countermagic.

Contagious magic (*choheksan*, "to put dirt in bad place"). A sorcerer can work evil by obtaining nail parings, hair, spittle, feces, or bits of clothing from the individual he wishes to harm. Such personal objects may be placed at a spot inhabited by a large number of rattlesnakes ("a rattlesnakes' den"), and the usual procedure of pronouncing the name of the person and uttering the correct formula followed. If a snake "eats" the offering, the victim immediately becomes ill and dies within the year. In a similar fashion the earth of a footprint may be taken to a rattlesnake, and the snake is told "what is wanted to happen."

An ill-wisher can also cause his personal enemy to be stricken by reciting a formula over his footprints and then burying close by a grave some of the earth from the impressions. Hair or clothing inhumed near a grave will achieve the same result. An article of clothing placed in a pool of water will cause the owner to waste away as the fabric rots.

The Hupa are careful to dispose of their personal leavings so that they will not fall into the hands of an evildoer. Children are instructed to dispose of all nail parings and hair-combings in the fire and to cover over spittle and feces. Adults carefully remove and put out of the way anything which might furnish a sorcerer with a starting point for his malpractices.

"Poisons" (*mil'kosa*, "put in mouth"). A number of "poisons" are administered by malevolent people, usually being placed in the selected victim's food or, in the case of a man, in his tobacco. One type is smeared upon an object which, when touched, causes injurious or deadly effects. Some of these are of plant origin, and a few may have actual lethal power, but most seem to depend upon the supernatural for their effectiveness.

A powder made from a portion of a human body, such as the finger bones, is used with fatal result, as are potions derived from snakes, lizards, frogs, and water dogs. All are prepared in much the same fashion as curative medicines.

The recipient of a dose of poison loses appetite and gradually wastes away. Death is inevitable unless a shaman can diagnose and remove the source of the trouble. Some poisons are said not to take effect until a year later. Children are frequently victimized. Poisons can be purchased for a high price though the trade in them is surrounded with great secrecy.

"Indian devil" (kitdongwe). The most dreaded practitioner of black magic is the "Indian devil," who strikes down his fellows with a supernatural instrument made from a sharpened human bone or with a miniature bow shaped from a fragment of human rib and strung with sinew procured from the wrist of a recently interred corpse. Under the cover of darkness and with his face painted black, he approaches a dwelling and, after reciting a formula and uttering the name of his enemy, shoots an invisible projectile which enters his prey's body. It is not necessary for a *kitdongwe* to see his victim although he may remove a board from the side of the house or look down the smoke hole in order to make sure that his quarry is inside. The sound of something moving about outside the dwelling, the excited barking of dogs, or other strange noises may indicate that an Indian devil is prowling around. Usually, however, he moves stealthily through the night, his presence revealed only by sparks flying up from his instrument of death which is carried under the arm.

An Indian devil can change himself at will into a wolf or bear, and often prowls about in one of these disguises. If some one sees a track "that looks like a bear or wolf track but isn't," it is assumed that a sorcerer has passed that way. If pursued, a *kitdongwe* presses his contrivance to his breast and travels at great speed ("he can jump 'way off, like flying"). An Indian devil can only operate at night ("he cannot devil in the daytime").

Death usually follows an attack by a *kitdongwe*, the afflicted person being seized with a severe headache and dying within a few minutes. Occasionally, however, the victim falls into a coma or becomes violently ill. A powerful shaman can cure the sufferer if called in time, but the mystic projectile must be removed rapidly if he is to recover.

After a killing, an Indian devil "has to get his power back from the dead man." He must visit the grave and carry away the clothing and implements placed thereon to regain his capacity for evil doing. The relatives of the deceased may, if they are courageous, lie in wait in the cemetery for his visit and slay him. It is generally believed that a sorcerer must strengthen his power from time to time by obtaining portions of fresh corpses. Any disturbance of a recent burial is attributed to the actions of a *kitdongwe*, and anyone observed near a fresh grave at night is suspected of being an Indian devil.

A chance nocturnal encounter with a *kitdongwe* usually results in bewitchment. Consequently most Hupa are reluctant to leave the house at night. A brave man, whose ceremonial strength protects him from black magic, may occasionally lie in wait and seize a sorcerer and demand a huge ransom for his release.

A *kitdongwe* attempts to keep his heinous profession a secret, even to members of his own family. His diabolic apparatus is carefully hidden when not in use. It may be concealed under a rock or in a hollow tree, or buried in the ground in a remote part of the forest. Even when completely covered, however, its presence is revealed at night by flashes of light. No attempt is made to steal it, because "it is dangerous to handle" and "no one dares to touch it." It seems doubtful that a *kitdongwe* succeeds in keeping his secret from his family, because his nocturnal absences and the various preparations necessary for bewitching would make any close relative suspicious. The evil pursuits of an Indian devil are a constant threat to the lives of his relatives — perhaps an even greater menace to them than to outsiders. His lethal instrument is always a potential danger and may cause sickness or death within his family, or the sorcerer may deliberately exercise its dreaded force against his own kind.

Occasionally, two or three *kitdongwe* may work together as "partners"; but there is no evidence that they ever all gather for a witches sabbath. Some villages are credited with harboring more Indian devils than others. Xonsadin, the northernmost Hupa village, has long had such a reputation. The Southfork Creek people, closely related to the Hupa in language and culture, are regarded as expert *kitdongwe*.

Sorcery is believed to be the cause of much, though not all nor even the majority of, disease and death. Natural causes for illness or demise are recognized, but if a sickness is long-continued or unusual in any way, the explanation is sought in the machinations of a malevolent human agent. Sudden seizures or deaths are interpreted in the same way. When several well-known men die in succession, suspicion is aroused that they are victims of black magic. A shaman called in to treat a patient will often ascribe the affliction to a supernatural object of "pain" sent by a sorcerer, and the diagnosis is readily accepted by the patient and his family.

A "pain" introduced by a vindictive person is more troublesome to remove than one caught accidentally from the air in the usual fashion, and a shaman has difficulty in extracting it. A shaman may fail to remove the disease-causing object if it has been in the sufferer's body too long or because he lacks the necessary power. If the "pain" is removed, the shaman carries it outside and places it on a block of wood, and covers it with a small basket. Most of the people of the village gather around, and the shaman calls out the name of a person suspected of causing the disease and lifts the basket. If the object is still there, that person is innocent, and it is again covered and another name is called. This continues until the disease-object disappears and the one whose name is last called is assumed to be the guilty party ("when the doctor hits the right one, the pain goes away"). The accused is given a chance to confess; his admission will hasten the sufferer's recovery. If he refuses to confess or protests innocence, he may be beaten or killed by relatives of the patient.

It is difficult to determine with any exactness the frequency of witchcraft among the Hupa, because it is never practiced openly and it is a subject which many people are unwilling to discuss. The Hupa are not obsessed with ideas of sorcery, though bewitching is feared and both men and women manifest anxiety concerning it. Though witchcraft is not a commonplace phenomenon, a fairly large number of incidents involving witchcraft in recent generations are recalled. Hupa mythology is not overburdened with tales or incidents of witchcraft.

It is equally hard to assess the efficacy of witchery in actually attaining its purpose. Direct poisoning may be effective when toxic plants are employed but other forms of sorcery, with the possible exception of the operations of the *kitdongwe*, are probably ineffectual, because, for the most part, the victim does not know or even suspect the sorcerer's intention. However, should a person fall ill and the affliction be diagnosed as the result of black magic, it may become effective psychologically. A patient who believes that he is under the spell of a sorcerer may wither away and die without any real or apparent physical reason.

There is no elaboration of techniques for countering the attacks of sorcerers, though many precautionary measures are taken. Children are cautioned against accepting food from others; personal offal is carefully disposed of; unnecessary trips into the night are avoided; a man is careful not to offend anyone unnecessarily lest animosities be stirred up which would lead to black magic being used against him; contacts with individuals suspected of controlling diabolic power are avoided where possible. In addition, leaves of the pepperwood tree or bits of angelica root are carried to ward off evil. A few people own protective songs or formulas. None of these is a sure defense, however.

A man who has obtained strong supernatural "power" through fasting, hardships, and religious contemplation is relatively immune from an attack. It is also believed that a person who has led an exemplary ("good") life and has participated in the great group ceremonials has a certain amount of security against the antagonistic actions of malevolent people.

A sorcerer is occasionally detected committing an evil act, but more often his identity is revealed by other means. The name-calling test carried on by a shaman results in detection, or a powerful shaman may perceive the evildoer in a revelation which occurs during the regular ritual of curing. The identity of a sorcerer may also be divulged to his victim. The sick man usually suspects one of his enemies and should this individual appear to him in a dream it is accepted as proof that he is the malefactor.

A person may inadvertently fall under suspicion of practicing witchcraft. A threat against an individual who subsequently falls ill, perhaps months or even years later, may be remembered and used as an indictment against him. Also anyone whose habits are unusual, or irregular ("who acts suspicious or not right") may acquire a reputation for witchery, particularly if seen wandering about at night or if observed doing strange things out in the forest. A close relative of a known sorcerer is always regarded with distrust because of the possibility that knowledge of the black art may have been passed on to him. Several individuals in each village are usually looked upon with suspicion and avoided when possible. Quite often these are ineffectual old people, poverty-stricken men or women who live alone and have few relatives.

An accused sorcerer is usually given an opportunity to confess his odious crime because, as already mentioned, an admission of guilt aids the recovery of the sufferer. The suspect often "confesses" perhaps because he fears violence if he refuses, or because the suggestion of the idea immediately produces a sense of reality, so that he is quite incapable of distinguishing what he has merely thought from what he has actually done. An individual may acknowledge the misdeed because he enjoys the attention or recognition. Torturing a suspect or submitting him to an ordeal is not known. If the afflicted recovers after an admission of sin, the sorcerer is usually not punished. However, if the suspect disavows guilt or if the patient dies following a confession, personal revenge is taken by the relatives of the victim. In cases of death from black magic, retribution is swift; and mere suspicion is usually enough to bring reprisal. The normal punishment is death, and is in no way mitigated when the accused happens to be a woman. The suspect is quickly executed by being shot from ambush with bow and arrow, or beaten to death with clubs and stones. Hanging is not practiced, and it seems doubtful that another sorcerer is ever hired to kill a suspect by witchcraft.

Relatives are not likely to stand solidly behind a kinsman accused of witchery. A family normally defends its members against outsiders, but in a case of witchcraft, the sorcerer's kin faces an aroused population, and they themselves consider sorcery as an abhorrent crime. Compensation, which is regularly demanded for a murdered kinsman, is usually not requested for an executed sorcery suspect because the burden of proof is placed upon the accused's relatives.

There is no special type of burial for a sorcerer and the soul of a deceased malefactor does not go to a different hereafter but to the underworld which is the final abode of the souls of ordinary men.

Witchcraft, although it is always looked upon as utterly bad and as an evil which cannot be sanctioned, nonetheless performs several distinct functions in Hupa culture. It is a factor which operates to influence and channel human conduct. A Hupa is careful not to offend anyone unnecessarily for fear that black magic may be used against him. He also seeks to avoid suspicion of being an evil practitioner by conforming to established norms of overt conduct instead of indulging in aberrant or idiosyncratic behavior.

Sorcery is also an outlet for an expression of hostility which cannot be exhibited directly. Insults, threats, or actual physical violence are avoided because they must all be compensated by money payments, and the average Hupa is extremely reluctant to squander any of his wealth in this manner. If a man cannot engage in overt aggression in face-to-face situations, he can, at least, injure his rival by sorcery. Thus he can give vent to his anger or jealousy with some feeling of satisfaction and without fear of financial loss or other retaliation.

The Hupa beliefs and usages connected with witchcraft are shared with minor variation by their close neighbors, the Yurok and Karok, and by the more distant Tolowa. Undoubtedly the practices of other tribes in this general area of northwestern California and southwestern Oregon are similar, but detailed data for them are lacking. Many of the traits seem to have a wide distribution in western North America, but more information on witchcraft is needed before any definitive statements on distributions and relationships can be made because facts on witchcraft in many tribes have not been collected as yet. There are some traits shared by the Hupa with their fellow Athabascan-speakers in the southwest, the Apache and Navaho, but these are probably general throughout the western part of the continent and do not represent a specific Athabascan heritage.

MIGRATION AND
URBANIZATION OF THE
INDIANS IN CALIFORNIA

by
S. F. Cook

I

The racial assimilation of the American Indian is a problem of interest not only to the demographer and geneticist but also to the student of human ecology. The profound disturbance in environmental conditions to which the primitive race was subjected has been manifested in several aspects. One of these is the territorial redistribution of the aboriginal groups as a whole and another the dispersion of individuals in conformity with pressures exerted by white society. The latter phenomenon, which may be termed "internal migration" is here considered.

II

Over most of the United States the survivors of the Indian population have been restricted to reservations or otherwise subjected to artificial constraint. Hence any natural tendency to move about has been sharply inhibited. The State of California has, however, constituted an exception and has provided an opportunity to observe what an Indian group would do if left largely to its own initiative. The causes of this anomalous situation are clear. The first lies in the fact that the majority of California Indians were never reservationized but were left to merge as best they might with the American civilization which surrounded them. The second factor lies in the peculiar manner in which the State was settled. From 1848 to 1860 the entire coastal region was suddenly overrun by whites who, to be sure, killed and starved large numbers of the natives but who left the survivors to persist in their ancestral habitat. The aborigines were thus submerged, rather than expelled or exterminated. The third factor was the very strong Spanish-Mexican tradition which persisted long after the American conquest. This tradition, strongly reinforced by the Catholic clergy, envisaged the Indian as an integral, even if subordinate, component of the social organism itself, rather than as an enemy to be segregated in isolation.

By virtue of another historical anomaly we come into possession of

Human Biology (February, 1943), 15:33–45.

population data pertaining to the Indians of California which do not exist for any other state.

According to a treaty made by Wozencraft in 1851 compensation was to be paid the California natives. Not until 1928 did Congress act to carry out its terms, at which late date it had become necessary to determine who the descendants were. Congress then authorized a census to be taken to list "all Indians who were residing in the State of California on July 1, 1852 and their descendants now living in said state."

This census was the most comprehensive and thorough that could be taken under the circumstances. For each individual it showed name, age, family relationship, degree of blood, tribal affiliation, residence and property owned. In all, 23,542 persons were recorded, and even if not absolutely complete, this record constituted the most thorough survey which could be secured.

With respect to coverage it is probable that practically all persons with an appreciable degree of Indian blood were counted. On the other hand it is likely that some individuals with very slight Indian blood who long since had come to regard themselves as wholly white were missed. With respect to correctness of statement there were undoubtedly errors introduced. Due to ignorance or design many persons were unable to state with utter fidelity degree of blood, age, and tribal affiliation. Considering the numbers involved, however, we may regard the general picture as correct in essence if not in minute detail. In certain instances particular items are left blank on the census sheets, due to admitted factual ignorance on the part of the persons involved. When compilations are made, therefore, these items cannot be included. As a result the totals for specific categories (such as age, degree of blood, residence, and so on) will always fall somewhat short of the general census total of 23,542. The sample, nevertheless, will usually be at least 90 per cent complete, thus rendering statistically insignificant the losses due to omissions.

The shift of individuals and hence groups may be determined by means of the present (1928) residence and the tribal descent. Since the tribal boundaries were originally very definite and since there has been no mass movement during the past century it is possible to specify, for any individual a *home territory,* within which he or his ancestors must have lived. Although certain inexactitudes are thereby introduced it is most feasible to delimit former tribal areas along modern county lines. Thus the Yurok once inhabited parts of both Humboldt and Del Norte counties. For present purposes, accordingly, it is necessary to consider the entire area of both these counties as home territory. Any shift of residence within such a restricted field could not be considered a significant change of habitat. A second group may then be recognized: those who are living outside the home counties, or *migrants*. The data do not permit a more refined classification since the domicile of migrants varies progressively from fairly close to quite distant. Moreover, no deduction is usually possible with respect to whether it was the living person or his forebears who actually moved outside the aboriginal tribal boundaries. A third group may also be distinguished, including parts of the previous two: those who are living in *cities* rather than in villages or remote rural sections. The line of demarcation is based upon the mailing address given under each name in the census which in numerous cases includes a street and number in some town or city. Now it may be assumed fairly that if a person has a street address in such a locality as Los Angeles, San Francisco, or even Stockton, Riverside, or Eureka, he is a city dweller. Naturally this fails to include itinerants and other casuals with no established residence who might frequent the towns. On the other hand it errs on the side of conservatism and restricts the city class to bona fide urbanites.

III

The aboriginal distribution of population followed very closely that of the food supply. Today the situation has completely altered. Diet as a determining factor has been replaced by others, among which is the density of the white population. By virtue of war, disease, and ineffectual economic competition the natives have tended to diminish most rapidly when and where the white men have been most numerous. This process reached its maximum intensity between 1848 and 1860 during which period the Indians of the mining regions were nearly obliterated. The long term influence of white settlement, moreover, can be detected in the census of 1928. By using counties as subdivisions the relation between the two races may be compared: the number of whites being taken directly from the United States Census of 1930 and that of the Indians being calculated from the 1928 census.

A direct test of association between absolute Indian and white population by counties yields a chi-square value of 2.19 which is below the limit of significance. If, however, we utilize the Indian home population (excluding migrants) the value is 5.86 which may be considered moderately although not strongly significant.

A better criterion of white influence than gross population per county is the density per county. The relation between this factor and the Indian population is expressed by a chi-square value of 11.79. Apparently, therefore, a tendency exists for the Indians to be most numerous in those regions where the whites are fewest.

As a final test we may employ the relative, rather than absolute Indian population, that is, the ratio of Indians to whites, since this term is an index to the reaction of the Indians to the white group over a long period of years and also tends to eliminate extraneous geographical factors. The association between this ratio and density of the whites is highly significant: chi-square equals 26.26. If the data are treated as a correlation the value of r is —.847, again definitely significant.

These results exemplify for California the generally recognized principle that an indigenous population thrives best over the period of transition in those regions where the density of the invading group, and hence the interracial conflict and competition, are at a minimum. The immediate response, therefore, to invasion by the foreign race, and one might say the fundamental inclination of the Indian population, was to remain as far out of contact with the whites as possible. Only thus could pure survival be achieved. However, with more settled conditions there has begun to appear the inevitable reaction and countertrend toward intermixture. One criterion of its extent is the number of Indians who have voluntarily forsaken the home territory and have gone to dwell in a purely white community. In 1928 the census shows that 13.2 per cent of the California Indians were in this category.

One would conclude at first sight that the total migration among the Indian group had been relatively small up to 1928. The closest comparison is with the native-born whites living in California at the same time. In 1930, 45.5 per cent of the latter had migrated from other states. If intercounty, rather than interstate movements could be checked we should probably find that well over half the white people in 1930 were living some distance from the county of birth or parental origin.

On the other hand California is notorious for the unsettled character of its population, and the enormous number of new immigrants. The Indian value of 13.2 per cent removals might be considered more fairly in relation to that of more stable white groups such as the native-born of Maine and South Carolina of which only 7.8 per cent were from outside the state. In brief, it is clear that the drift away from the ancestral habitat had definitely set in by 1928, and although it had not reached large dimensions, nevertheless was making headway against the basic inertia and conservatism of Indian tribal culture.

IV

We may now examine the conditions affecting migration, the direction of migration, and the character of the migrants. Certain factors may be distinguished which appear to have determined *the extent of migration*. These seem to have been chiefly historical, or long-term influences, rather than contemporary effects, and to have been concerned with the degree of inter-racial contact.

The intensity of former conflict is discernible in the reduction of numbers since the American occupation. The aboriginal populations by tribes have been carefully worked out by Kroeber. I have made a fairly accurate estimate of the values for the period 1845–1850. Finally, there are the modern data in the 1928 census. When the per cent of modern survivors by tribes (from 1848) is related to the per cent of migrants from those tribes, the chi-square value is 8.71, in the sense that the smaller the per cent of survivors the greater the proportion of these are migrants. Since the chi-square value is significant it is reasonable to conclude that serious depletion due to war and disease during the period of settlement operated to disintegrate tribal and geographic unity, thereby rendering the subsequent generation more prone to seek new habitats. The extremes of this process may be noted in a qualitative manner by considering the Yana and the Luiseño, both tribes which were exposed to strong white influence. In modern times the Yana have been reduced to about 1 per cent of their former number (a few mixed bloods), all of whom live well outside the original tribal territory. The Luiseño, on the other hand, who still retain 45 per cent of their aboriginal strength show only 3.3 per cent migrants.

In conjunction with the factors governing emigration from the ancestral habitat one indirect line of evidence is the age distribution of the home and migrant groups. These distributions may be expressed graphically but perhaps the most convenient index, for purposes of comparison, is the median age.

It is a principle of universal applicability that whenever a free emigration occurs from a stable population the younger element predominates. Moreover the internal age dispersion is less, owing to the reduced proportion of very old and very young persons. Following resettlement the migrant group tends to reacquire the features of the parent stock. In the present instance the home population of 19,076 persons had a median age of 21.93 years with a standard deviation from the median of ± 23.1 years. Since the equivalent values for 2,973 migrants were 19.97 and 19.2, the latter group as a whole appears to be relatively recent in origin.

The designated differences in median age and age dispersion are, however, not sufficiently great to suggest a uniform and homogeneous migratory impulse within recent years. It appeared desirable, therefore, to break down the entire population into a series of component groups. On a basis of past history and geographical location there seems to be a more or less natural subdivision as follows:

1. Tribes, untouched by Ibero-American culture, exposed since 1850 to strong Anglo-American influence, north and central cismontane Califor-

nia: Tolowa, Yurok, Wiyot, Hupa, Karok, Chimariko, Wylackie, Yuki, Athabascan remnants, Pomo, Shasta, Maidu, Yana, Miwok, Wintun, Yokuts, and Western Mono.

2. Tribes, untouched by Ibero-American culture, relatively isolated geographically from Anglo-American influence, tramontane and desert California: Achomawi, Paiute (including Eastern Mono and Tübatulabal) Washo, Shoshone (mainly Koso) and Yuma.

3. Tribes, ethnographically indistinct, which remain from the central coast missions as far south as Mission San Gabriel at Los Angeles, thoroughly impregnated with both Ibero- and Anglo-American cultures, since 1850 socially amalgamated with the surrounding white population.

4. Tribes, ethnographically distinct, which remain from the south coast missions (San Luis Rey, San Juan Capistrano, and San Diego plus the closely coterminous Cahuilla); differ from Group 3 in that they have been strongly under reservation influence and are socially somewhat isolated; considerably influenced by Ibero- and Anglo-American cultures but not so strongly as Group 4.

The pertinent data have been summarized in table 1. Certain features of this summary merit discussion. In the first place the median age of the geographically and politically isolated groups (2 and 4) is high, that of the intermediate group (1) is medium and that of the well assimilated group (3) is low. At the same time the per cent of each group which has migrated varies in the opposite direction.

The median age of the migrants is lowest for Group 2 and also differs by the greatest amount from that of the nonmigrants. Nearly the same situation exists for Group 4. According to the thesis mentioned above the inference may be advanced that the migration from these two groups is of relatively recent origin, an hypothesis supported by our general knowl-

TABLE 1

PER CENT MIGRANTS AND MEDIAN AGES IN FOUR INDIAN GROUPS

	Per cent migrants	Median age home group	Median age migrants	Median age city dwellers
Group 1	15.4	21.26	20.18	18.26
Group 2	6.3	23.13	19.58	17.83
Group 3	40.1	19.65	19.62	19.00
Group 4	6.5	23.64	20.50	20.32

edge of the peoples concerned. Group 1 again occupies an intermediate position implying that migration has been proceeding for a longer period. This is in conformity with the fact that during the latter half of the nineteenth century the northern and central tribes were subjected to severe dislocation by the invading miners and ranchers as well as by the armed forces. Group 3 shows no significant difference whatever in the median age of migrants and nonmigrants. This may be taken as reflecting the turmoil and disintegration of the postmission period, 1830–1850, and the disappearance of the mission Indians as a distinct social entity. The transition stage, however, has completely passed such that both components of the group have reached a new and probably stable equilibrium.

From the above findings we may conclude that whenever the native race, in California, has entered upon a period of intensified contact with the whites, there has been a response in the form of increased emigration, primarily on the part of the younger individuals. This response is by no means inconsistent with that previously discussed whereby the population subjected to intense conflict suffered more extensive loss in numbers than that which was permitted to remain in comparative isolation. Indeed, the two reactions are component parts of the same mass behavior pattern.

V

The *direction of migration* has been uniformly toward the centers of white population with the result that an Indian urban class has come into existence. To support this conclusion are various lines of evidence.

a) In any given county the relative number of Indian immigrants may be expressed as the ratio between immigrants and total Indians. This value may then be related to the density of white population. For the fifty-eight counties the association by chi-square is 8.48 and the correlation coefficient, r, is $+ 0.541$. There is a significant movement, therefore, toward regions of high population density.

b) The Indians as a whole tend to follow the degree of urbanization characteristic of the region. Thus there is a significant correlation ($r - 0.676$) between the ratio of Indians in cities to total Indians on the one hand, and the ratio of whites in cities to total whites on the other. That the phenomenon has reached considerable dimensions is attested by the fact that 11 per cent of the names recorded in the 1928 census had street addresses and were therefore definitely urbanized. Predominantly migrants have contributed to this group, for of the nonmigrants throughout the State 7.43 per cent were in cities, and of the migrants, 40.1 per cent. There can be no doubt, consequently, that urbanization is a process closely associated with migration.

c) The median ages of city dwellers (see table 1) throws further light on the situation. With Group 1 the median age of the urban component is definitely below that of the migrants. It is probable that this represents a secondary, more modern movement, for the earlier migrants were relatively primitive and preferred to remain in rural communities. With Group 2 the city dwellers appear to represent what might be called the progressive younger element, those migrants who went all the way to the larger centers of population, rather than remain in more remote districts. Group 4 shows an urban median age almost identical with that of the migrants, both being definitely below that of the nonmigrants. As contrasted with the mountain and desert tribes of Group 2, when the Indians of Group 4 left home, they had in effect no place to go save the Los Angeles metropolitan area, and as a result this region has absorbed most of them. With Group 3 the urban median age is a little, but not materially, below that of the migrants, due probably to a slight tendency in recent years for the younger people to gravitate to the nearby towns.

VI

Something concerning the *type of people* who make up the migrant and urban classes can be deduced from the census. It has already been pointed out that in the aggregate, with certain exceptions, they are more youthful than those who still remain in the old tribal habitat. An examination by sexes shows the male-female ratio to be highest for the home dweller (1.072), lower for migrants (0.890) and least for the urban class (0.798). For the total population the ratio is rather high: 1.045. A heavier migration by women, than by men, is thus indicated. From a breakdown of sex ratios by age (see table 2) it is apparent that among migrants and urbanites the great predominance of women is among those of early maturity and middle age. There are two factors which appear to be largely responsible for this phenomenon: (1) Many Indian women have married men of other races who have gone to the centers of agriculture and industry, whereas very few Indian men have married outside their own race; (2) numerous other Indian women and young girls have in the past gone to accept employment as domestic servants in white families. Such individuals have been likely to marry or otherwise permanently sever all ties with the ancestral home. The result has been a steady drain upon the females in the home localities. That this process is of no very recent origin is attested by the low sex ratio among the migrants over forty years of age.

If the sociogeographic groups discussed previously (see table 1) are examined the trend toward female predominance is found to be least in Group 3 (ratio for all ages of migrants is 1.092) and greatest in Group 2 (corresponding ratio is 0.717). This is in conformity with the fact that

TABLE 2

Sex Ratios by Age Group

Age in years	0–9	10–19	20–39	40–00	Total
Home	1.031	1.055	1.134	1.060	1.072
Migrants ...	1.114	0.915	0.726	0.827	0.890
Cities	1.117	1.036	0.586	0.582	0.798
Total	1.042	1.035	1.008	1.032	1.045

Group 3 has been in longest and closest contact with American civilization whereas Group 2 has been left in maximum isolation.

Another characteristic of migrants and urbanites is their consistently lower degree of Indian blood. The mean values for per cent Indian blood are, for the entire State: nonmigrants 68.3, migrants 40.7, city dwellers 36.9. This is true even in the highly assimilated Group 3 where the per cent of Indian blood among nonmigrants is 50.9 and among migrants is 29.7. Among the individual tribes it is possible to compare mean degree of Indian blood (per tribe) and per cent of migrants. We obtain a value of chi-square of 13.34 and for the correlation coefficient, r, of —.768, both indicating a very significant relationship. There is thus a consistent tendency for individuals and groups genetically farthest removed from the pure Indian strain to migrate to centers of white culture. The social and racial motivation of this trend is obvious and needs no comment.

In addition to age, sex, and degree of blood we can derive certain information from the 1928 census pertaining to the family relationship of migrants and urban population. The census undertakes to set forth the exact family status of each person—such as husband, wife, widow, son, daughter, father, mother, cousin, single, and so on. However, the relationships are social, rather than genetic. Thus there must invariably be a *head,* whether that individual is husband, widower, wife, widow, sister, brother, or unmarried mother. The remaining members of the social family unit are grouped around the head. As a result, mature men and women frequently are listed as sons or daughters, while children occasionally appear as single or even as head of the family. The term *single* is reserved strictly for persons who are living apart from any recognized social family, although it may be obvious from the names that they have numerous relatives in the vicinity. For present purposes it has seemed advisable to set up four main categories which are of clearer connotation than the minor subdivisions:

(1) *Head:* includes husband, wife, widower, widow, divorcée or illegitimate parent.

(2) *Child:* includes all progeny of a head who are actually living under the same roof as the latter.

(3) *Other relatives:* includes parents, aunts, uncles, nieces, grandchildren, etc., who are living with the designated head.

(4) *Single:* includes any individual living apart from a recognized family unit.

TABLE 3

A

FAMILY RELATIONSHIPS IN PER CENT OF TOTAL, INCLUDING BOTH SEXES

	Head	Child	Other relatives	Single
Home	40.9	48.1	2.9	8.0
Migrant	40.4	49.2	2.3	7.9
Urban	38.3	50.9	2.6	8.0

B

SEX RATIOS FOR THE CLASSIFICATION SHOWN ABOVE

	Head	Child	Other relatives	Single
Home	0.774	1.182	...	2.886
Migrant	0.475	1.187	...	1.950
Urban	0.402	1.190	...	1.164

For the State as a whole the distribution of these categories is shown in table 3A. It will be observed that the general constitution of the family, *irrespective of sex,* is nearly identical in the home, migrant, and urban groups. If, however, we segregate the categories according to sex certain deviations appear. In table 3B, it is shown that whereas the male-female ratio for children is almost identical for all three classes, the ratio for heads and single persons is markedly lower among the migrants and still lower among the urban class. In other words, wives predominate over husbands, and the relative number of single women becomes larger as the Indians move away from the primitive locality, or go to the cities. This result intensifies the previous impression derived from the age distribution of sex ratios that a greater number of females than males move into regions of high population density.

VII

The broad outline of migrational shift among the present Indian population in California now seems fairly clear. Beginning gradually to overcome a fundamental inertia developed during generations of strict localization these natives are showing a tendency to move out from their primitive habitats such that by 1928 some 13 per cent of their population were emigrants. This movement has been intensified whenever and wherever contact with the whites was brought to a high level of intensity. On the whole its direction has been toward rather than away from the regions of most dense American settlement. The active participants have been and still are predominantly persons in late youth or early middle age, with a considerable admixture of white blood. A large share of them have been females who have entered white society by the pathways of matrimony or economic employment. This process appears to have accelerated in recent years and probably will run to completion within a few generations.

CONFLICT BETWEEN THE CALIFORNIA INDIAN AND WHITE CIVILIZATION

by
S. F. Cook

THE AMERICAN INVASION, 1848–1870

When the California Indian was confronted with the problem of contact and competition with the white race, his success was much less marked with the Anglo-American than with the Ibero-American branch. To be sure, his success against the latter had been far from noteworthy; both in the missions and in the native habitat the aboriginal population had declined, and the Indian had been forced to give ground politically and racially before the advance of Spanish colonization.[1] However, the nonmission Indian had demonstrated a certain power of resilience and, in the realm of physical activity, had been able to evolve a new behavior pattern which, if he had been left alone, might have permitted him to cope on fairly even terms with the invading race. The valley and northern tribes were evincing a fair capacity for adaptation, in the strictly material sense, to the new environment imposed by the entrance of a new biological group. Furthermore, the native culture had by no means utterly collapsed. To a certain extent in the missions and predominantly in the aboriginal habitat the Indian had retained his primitive social and religious character and, indeed, had appropriated a few features of the white civilization, modifying them and incorporating them into his own system.

When the Indian was forced to withstand the shock and impact of the Anglo-Saxon invasion, his failure in all these respects was virtually complete. In the physical and demographic spheres his competitive inferiority was such as to come very close to bringing about his literal extermination. His social structure was not only utterly disorganized, but almost completely wiped out. Culturally, he has been forced to make a slow, painful adjustment, ending with the adoption of the alien system, and he has now lost all but fragments of the aboriginal pattern. The present study under-

Pp. 1–5 of S. F. Cook, *The Conflict between the California Indian and White Civilization: III. The American Invasion, 1848–1870*, Ibero-Americana, No. 23 (1943).

[1] See S. F. Cook, *The Conflict between the California Indian and White Civilization: I. The Indian versus the Spanish Mission, ibid.*, No. 21 (1943).

takes to describe some of the processes involved in this racial failure and some of the factors determining its extent.

Without embarking upon any attempt to analyze the differences between the Anglo-American and Ibero-American personality, social order, or culture, certain points of divergence between the two groups may be mentioned briefly in so far as they affected Indian relations in California. Perhaps these points may be allocated to two prime categories: differences in mode of colonization and differences in economic and social attitude toward the aborigine.

The divergent Indian reaction to Spanish clerical authority, as demonstrated by the mission neophytes, and to Spanish civil authority, as shown by the unconverted interior tribes, is clear evidence that the two modes of interracial contact were fundamentally different. The opinion may be advanced that the determining factor was aggregation versus dissemination. The fatal effects of the altruistic mission lay, first, in the removal of the native from his original habitat and, second, in his subjection to continuous close association with the foreign environment and race. The relative preservation of the gentile element was due to the failure of the Spanish actually to occupy the territory of the Indian. This same distinction in the type of interracial contact appears when the Spanish system as a whole is contrasted with the American.

The great interior of the State was penetrated many times by the Spaniards. Repeatedly they entered the lands of the Indians, but they did not settle and stay on these lands. Between the frequent but still temporary foreign incursions the natives were able to maintain their life and social order more or less unaltered. At least they were not called upon to make any continuous and permanent adjustment to a change in their own environment. When the Americans arrived, they took over the Indian habitat and made it their own. The aborigines were forced, therefore, to adapt themselves, on their own ground, to a new environment. The final effect was precisely the same as if they had been bodily removed and set down in a strange region. They were subjected not to invasion but to inundation.

Another factor of significance here is that of numbers. Other things being equal, the intensity of conflict and the weight thrown against the primitive group will roughly follow the numerical strength of the new or invading species. This general principle has been demonstrated repeatedly with the lower organisms in their parasite-host or predator-prey relationships, and it holds similarly for human beings. The Spanish type of colonization was such that the invading and ruling caste or race was always small in numbers. In California, for example, the whole coastal strip was taken and held by little more than one hundred persons. By 1845 the entire population of the *gente de razon* did not exceed 4,000. Against this may be set the native population of over 100,000. The Americans, on the other hand, entered the region in great numbers. Undoubtedly they would have continued to do so, for by 1848 they were already coming in by the hundreds. Owing to the fortuitous discovery of gold in that year, however, they poured in by thousands to flood the country. Furthermore, because of the nature of mining, they swarmed in hordes into those hill and mountain retreats which the Spaniards had never even penetrated. The Indians, therefore, were overwhelmed by tremendous numbers of aliens at all points and at much the same time. The conversion of their past primitive range and habitat into a group of civilized communities was thus accomplished in an incredibly short period.

Both branches of the white race arrived on the Pacific Coast with a heritage of long experience with the Indian; both had developed a well-formulated mental attitude and a definite policy with respect to the natives. But these attitudes and policies were conditioned by the widely differing pioneering and colonial experience of the two branches in the preceding centuries. Both Anglo-Saxons and Spanish had pursued an avowed course of exploitation of New World resources. The Spanish, however, had systematically availed themselves of human resources, whereas the English had tapped only material wealth. Whatever the causes of the divergence, by the nineteenth century the Ibero-Americans consistently followed the procedure of utilizing the natives and incorporating them in their social and economic structure, whereas the Anglo-Americans rigidly excluded them from their own social order. It followed, therefore, that in opening up California the Spanish system undertook as far as possible to employ the Indians, even by force, in useful pursuits. This in turn meant that the aboriginal race was an economic asset and as such was to be conserved. Destruction of individual life occurred only when and if the Indian actively resisted the process of amalgamation or definitely failed to conform to the conqueror's scheme of existence. Wholesale slaughter or annihilation was definitely undesirable.

The Anglo-American system, on the other hand, had no place for the Indian. If the latter could of his own initiative find subsistence within its framework, there was a priori nothing to prevent such adjustment. But if there was any conflict whatsoever with the system, the native was to be eliminated ruthlessly, either by outright extermination or the slower method of segregation in ghetto-like reservations. Accompanying this economic difference was another divergence of great social significance. The Spanish colonial system always envisaged the retention of the native as the basis of the population and simultaneously encouraged racial mixture. The result was naturally widespread hybridization, especially among the lower classes. Thorough and complete mestization, as in some parts of Spanish America, would have resulted in the disappearance of the California Indian as a pure line strain but would not have destroyed his race or eliminated it as a factor in the body politic. Nor would it necessarily have involved long and bloody physical conflict during the period of racial reorganization. The American civilization, on the contrary, viewed miscegenation with the greatest antipathy and relegated the mestizo, or half-breed, to the same status as his Indian parent. Consequently, no blood bond could ever become established which would mitigate the indifference and contempt with which the Indians were regarded.

These, and other differences, were reinforced by a powerful tradition relating to the Indian. Among the Ibero-Americans, the Indian was regarded, if not with definite attachment, at least with tolerance and sympathy, as perhaps not yet an equal but as a human being entitled to the rights and privileges of his class. His life was almost as sacred as that of a white man; his soul was entitled to salvation. He was permitted to testify in court. Theoretically, his property was inviolate. At best, he could participate in civic and political activity; at worst, he was deemed a child before the law. This fundamentally friendly attitude was seldom manifested by the Anglo-Americans. The latter, coming fresh from two centuries of bitter border warfare and intolerant aggression, brought with them an implacable hatred of the red race, which made no discrimination between tribes or individuals. All Indians were vermin, to be treated as such. It is therefore not surprising that physical violence was the rule rather than the exception. The native's life was worthless, for no American could even be brought to trial for killing an Indian. What little property the Indian possessed could be taken or destroyed at the slightest provocation. He had no civil or legal rights whatever. Finally, since the quickest and easiest way to get rid of his troublesome presence was to kill him off, this procedure was adopted as standard for some years. Thus was carried on the policy which had wiped out *en masse* tribe after tribe across the continent.

In comparing the objective effects wrought by the Ibero-American and Anglo-Saxon civilizations on the native population, it must not be supposed that the differences just mentioned were absolute, for human nature is much the same everywhere, despite policies and tradition. The Spanish at times certainly resorted to barbaric physical violence, and the Americans frequently treated their Indians with humanity and justice. Nevertheless, the broad tendencies were apparent and were reflected in the details of the two types of racial contact.

THE INDIAN RESPONSE [1]

We have dwelt at some length upon the shock to the native welfare which followed contact with Ibero-American civilization. . . . From this discussion one might gain the impression that the physical collapse of the interior tribes was complete, that the wild Indian was utterly unable to compete with the invading race and was doomed to early extinction. Such an impression would not be wholly justified.

In the first place, the actual numerical decline in population, although severe, was not as great as that suffered by the same or similar Indians either in the missions or under American domination. In a previous paper (*Population Trends,* 1940) I have shown that the total number of gentile baptisms in the missions was nearly 53,600. The neophytes living in the establishments at the close of the era were either these same gentiles or their descendants, and numbered, 14,900. The difference, 38,700, denotes, therefore, the decline suffered by this group or segment of California aborigines. Using relative values, we may calculate the decline, or ratio of reduction to original population, as 72 per cent. During the American period the decline was even greater. It may be calculated . . . that the estimated population of all California Indians north of the Tehachapi was 72,050 in 1848 and 12,500 in 1880. Hence the decline was about 82 per cent. For the six tribes affected by Spanish colonization from 1800 to 1848, the corresponding figures are 58,900 and 35,950, or a decline of only 31 per cent. Thus from the standpoint of population alone these tribes made a showing which, although in the absolute rather poor, was relatively better against the Spanish civil colonial system than against the mission system or the American settlement.

Not only in population changes do group reactions and group adaptation to new environmental factors become evident. Usually there may be observed physical activities carried on in unison by a sufficient number of individuals to warrant their being regarded as group responses. The direction of such an activity may be negative or positive, that is, tending to remove the affected group from the environment or, conversely, to remove certain components of the environment from the group. It has been pointed out with reference to the mission Indians that this type of response usually took the negative form. The Indians generally attempted to escape, thus generating the widespread phenomenon of fugitivism. Seldom was the activity positively directed, toward active physical resistance or insurrection.

---

[1] Pp. 30–37, *The Conflict between the California Indian and White Civilization: II. The Physical and Demographic Reaction of the Nonmission Indians in Colonial and Provincial California,* Ibero-Americana No. 22 (1943).

The wild Indians evinced a different type of behavior. With them the positive reaction predominated over the negative. With the exception of temporary flight to escape the ravages of an invading party, the interior natives held their ground and resisted the onslaught. Moreover, not only did they stand their ground over a large territory, but they actually, and with some success, took the offensive. Together with this active response they underwent considerable physical and military adaptation.

The evolution of the response of resistance or adaptation is quite clear cut. On their first appearances among new tribes and subtribes, the exploring expeditions found the natives peaceful and inclined to be friendly. The customary hospitality was shown, presents were exchanged, and the gospel was heard from the priests with sympathy. As party followed party, however, and the natives saw their people drawn off to the missions or heard more and more tales of mission life, their first favorable attitude changed to one of hostility and fear. At this stage, the explorers and convert hunters began to find the villages empty, or were greeted with showers of arrows as they approached. Retaliation and "chastisement" were then in order. Gentiles were carried off by force rather than persuasion, and atrocities began to occur. By the decade 1820–1830, the people of the interior valleys and hills had definitely embarked upon a policy of physical resistance, not through any political or cultural unification, but through a common response to a uniform style of treatment.

The general effect of these events was to bring about a shift in the entire social horizon of the natives, particularly that of the Yokuts, Miwok, and Wappo. The disruptive forces . . . had also the effect of generating an entirely new kind of civilization. To put it in essence: a peaceful, sedentary, highly localized group underwent conversion into a semiwarlike, seminomadic group. Obviously this process was by no means complete by 1848, nor did it affect all component parts of the native masses equally. But its beginnings had become very apparent.

We notice the inception of the change in a few rather sensational events, events which are indicative of the more fundamental, although much less obvious, changes going on underneath. In 1797 occurred the so-called "Raymundo affair." This individual, "Raymundo el Californio," took some forty neophytes on a fugitive hunt in Contra Costa County. They were set upon by gentiles and virtually destroyed, much to the horror and alarm of the local authorities. In 1807 over one hundred neophytes escaped from the missions to the rancherias of Carquinez Strait, where they were cut to pieces by gentiles, only thirty getting back to the mission. In 1813 Soto with twelve soldiers and one hundred auxiliaries was fought to a standstill in the marshes of the Delta by the consolidated rancherias of the region. At about this period, the Indians began to find leaders. Pomponio and Joscolo did excellently, and Estanislao, the Miwok, was a real genius. Expedition after expedition was broken up by this brave people, until Vallejo invaded their territory in 1829 with cavalry, artillery, and all the panoply of war. Even the final campaign, which took a heavy toll of life and did the Miwok great damage, utterly failed to subjugate them.

Meanwhile the Indians were learning new methods of defense. Their acquisition of firearms was slow. Indeed, it is doubtful whether they had secured any appreciable stock of firearms prior to 1848. Their failure in this respect is not to be ascribed to lack of knowledge or aggressiveness, but rather to the fact that there were no guns to be had. The Spanish themselves were very poorly outfitted. There were no large stocks which could be stolen, and powder was such a rarity that at one time the governor had to commandeer all private supplies in order to fit out an expedition. On the other hand, the natives very quickly learned the tactics of defense. Their original method was to stand up in masses and try to overwhelm the enemy with the fire power of swarms of arrows. But experience soon taught them that this weapon was relatively useless against Spanish leather armor, and the range was too short to enable them to hold up against gunfire. They then resorted to hit-and-run tactics—a heavy assault from ambush followed by a retreat into the impenetrable tule swamps or the chapparal, or else systematic sniping from cover. The Miwok under Estanislao developed a defense almost European in character. Against Sánchez and also Vallejo in 1829, Estanislao fortified a hill with brush breastworks and, if the word "fossas" can be so interpreted, an actual system of trenches. Against these defenses Sánchez failed completely, and Vallejo, even with a cannon, was not able to penetrate them until he resorted to a flank attack and covered his front by setting the chapparal on fire.

Considering that all available accounts of this early fighting come from Spanish-Mexican officialdom and from prejudiced survivors, it is clear that throughout the early decades of the nineteenth century the valley tribes put up a pretty good fight. Despite repeated small-scale incursions and full-dress campaigns by the military, in which they were often beaten, they held the Spanish settlement to the coast. This, after all, is the critical point, for the successful defense of an area demands that any permanent lodgement be prevented, rather than that every stabbing invasion be annihilated. Such relative success indicates that the Yokuts and Miwok were able, with sufficient rapidity, to make a drastic reorientation of their ideas of physical conflict.

But this reorientation did not stop with an improved defensive. By the time of secularization, the natives had begun to pass actually to the offensive. One reads in every general history of the times a great deal about the activity of the valley Indians, and to a lesser extent of those north of the Bay, in raiding and stealing domestic livestock, in particular cattle and horses. This phenomenon is one of great biological and cultural significance. It is mentioned here, however, only as it bears on offensive warfare.

Very early in mission history, outlying heathen began to slip in and run off stock. As the years went on, they learned two things, perhaps subconsciously. They learned that with the correct technique such raids were very easy to carry out, and that they were highly irritating to the white men. Furthermore, the acquisition of horses enabled the Indians to improve their methods by providing fast transportation. As the great herds of cattle and horses spread out from the coastal ranches, the opportunities increased, until by 1835 stock raiding was universal.

The acquisition of horses and the practice derived from years of experience wrought a further extension of their warfare, for it is but a short step from the quick dash to cut away stock to the serious armed cavalry assault on a fixed point, such as a ranch house or settlement. These developments follow rather naturally. The essential point in this discussion is that the valley people possessed sufficient mental agility and racial adaptive power to utilize their opportunity. Thus, from a race of slow, unwarlike, sedentary seed gatherers, these tribes were evolving rapidly into a group of fast, shifty, quite clever cavalrymen. This was a physical response, an adaptation to new conditions of the first order of magnitude.

As a result of this process, by 1845 the valley Indians had made inland expeditions and invasions very costly and dangerous, but, more important, they had also actually begun to drive in the Spanish frontier. The change of status becomes apparent from the official records after the Estanislao campaigns of 1829. During 1830 and 1831 there was a period of quiescence, but in 1833 complaints began to arise that the valley Indians were committing serious depredations. They seem in this to have been aided and perhaps organized by outside adventurers—American trappers and, particularly, New Mexicans who penetrated by way of the Colorado River. The following years saw an intensification of the same process. In 1834 M. G. Vallejo proposed an expedition to subjugate the Indians raiding San José and "lay a formal siege to the place where the natives are fortified." In 1836 conditions in San José had become so bad that the citizens had to petition the governor for help. In 1838 several rancheros were killed in raids in the Monterey district, and in 1839 the Indians attacked the grain storehouse at Santa Clara. In 1841, Mission San Juan was attacked, and hardly a ranch was spared from Santa Barbara to the Strait of Carquinez. The most spectacular raid occurred in 1840, when a band of heathen penetrated as far west as San Luis Obispo and ran off a thousand head of stock.

Meanwhile the government adhered to the old policy of counterattacking by expeditions. Dozens of these were sent out, but with very poor success. It is true that many Indians were killed and many villages destroyed, but the raiding continued. Finally a change of policy was contemplated, although not carried out. In 1840, the governor by decree established a force of twenty men to remain permanently on the border to act as military police and prevent the Indians from entering the passes of the coast range. Micheltorena, in 1843, proposed to build a stockade in Pacheco Pass, but the plan fell through. This shift in basic procedure from offensive to defensive is the best evidence we have that the Indian assault was really effective.

What would have happened if external conditions had not changed we can only conjecture. The Indian offensive reached its peak about 1845, or perhaps earlier, and then rapidly diminished. The reason for the diminution does not lie in any efforts put forth by the California government or its people (with the exception of the energetic action of Vallejo in the north). Indeed, the Spanish regime was showing no ability whatever to cope with the situation. Rather, the reason lies in the penetration of Americans and other foreigners into the valley itself on a basis of settlement, not mere expeditionary raiding. These men were able to attack the Indians from the rear, so to speak, and were present in numbers adequate to reduce the Indians' effectiveness. We see, therefore, that the adaptation of the natives to the Spanish type of colonization was not only sharp and clear in the qualitative sense, but was also of considerable magnitude. In fact, had the status of, say, 1840 remained unaltered, it is entirely possible that the response of the wild natives would have enabled them to establish a permanent physical equilibrium with Ibero-American civilization.

To sum up the foregoing discussion, it appears that the first effect of white impact on the native California Indian was to reduce his numbers through warfare, disease, and forced removal. The native racial response, however, was subsequently sufficiently powerful to minimize these influences and permit the evolution of a type of behavior calculated to insure his ultimate survival.

When we survey the racial conflict between the Ibero-American and the Indian, we cannot but be impressed by the far better showing made by the Indian in the wild than by the Indian in the mission. From the demographic standpoint there is no doubt that the Indian in his native environment withstood the shock of the new invasion better than he did when transported to the surroundings characteristic of mission life. He did so in spite of the fact that his numbers in the missions were not depleted by homicide and warfare, and that indeed he was protected quite effectively from physical competition. But perhaps this statement gives the wrong impression. Perhaps he survived better in the field because he was not protected, because he was forced to utilize his best adaptive power. Subjection to severe hardship and social disruption may well have been more potent agents in bringing out his full capacity than the easy existence and stable social order of the missions.

Other factors, however, may have been preponderant. It has been set forth at some length in a previous essay (*The Indian versus the Spanish Mission,* Ibero-Americana, No. 21 [1943]) how the racial fiber of the native decayed morally and culturally in the missions, how confinement, labor, punishment, inadequate diet, homesickness, sex anomalies, and other social or cultural forces, sapped his collective strength and his will to resistance and survival. Any detailed consideration of such matters cannot be undertaken here, but the suggestion may be advanced, at least tentatively, that the cultural aspects of mission existence largely account for the difference in behavior between the two similar groups of Indians. If this line of reasoning be granted, then the extremely important bearing of the cultural on the strictly biological becomes apparent. Indeed, one may go so far as to maintain that it is impossible to secure an adequate picture of the mechanism whereby primitive human races react physically and demographically without taking account of the social and psychological factors concerned. For analytical purposes, some distinction must be made; for synthetic purposes no separation is possible.

by
Robert F. Heizer and
M. A. Whipple

We have not been successful in finding in print a concise survey of present-day Indian numbers and distribution in California and their economic, educational, and health conditions. Rather than pass over the subject, we have extracted from a series of longer detailed published reports (cited in the reference bibliography under "The California Indian Today," p. 608) some information on the subject. The reader interested in more details can find these in the works referred to.

Who Is an Indian?

J. Forbes (1969) discusses this matter and says, "The only type of person in the United States who can be safely categorized as an 'American Indian' *under any and all circumstances* is an individual who is of unmixed or virtually unmixed United States native ancestry and who (1) resides in an Indian community, (2) is a member of a tribal organization, and (3) participates in the way of life of the group to which he belongs; or, (1) resides in an urban setting (usually temporarily), (2) maintains contacts with 'home,' and (3) participates in the activities of inter-tribal organizations or tribal clubs."

The U.S. census attempts to identify Indians as persons of native American origin who are "full blood," "half-blood," "quarter-blood," etc. Such definitions are as out of date as the practice of President Jefferson keeping black slaves on his Virginia plantation, but the federal government has thus far failed to utilize a *cultural* rather than racial identification. The government considers persons of "one-eighth blood" as non-Indian, and those of "one-quarter blood" or more as Indians.

The Sacramento Area Director of the Bureau of Indian Affairs, Leonard M. Hill, testified in a hearing in November, 1954, that "The government itself has . . . [been] trying to find some definition of an Indian. . . . You have to look at the purpose for which you're trying to define an Indian. . . . For some purposes, for giving health services, for instance, he must be a quarter blood and live on trust land. For educational purposes, to be eligible for educational loans, he must be a quarter blood or more . . . so that it is all a question of the purpose involved and what kind of subjects you are dealing with, as to whether an Indian is an Indian or whether he isn't. I just don't think that there is any definition that you can give to an Indian. . . . He is an Indian for some purpose and for other purposes he isn't an Indian, so there just isn't any clear definition."

Mr. Hill, when further pressed by a somewhat puzzled senator, A. W. Way, answered, "I am sorry, I cannot make a definition. I wish I knew one, too. It is a question which bothers a lot of people. We in the Indian Bureau are concerned with it also. We don't know how to define an Indian" (Senate Interim Committee, 1966, p. 408).

The 1960 U.S. Census observed the following definition: "American Indian. In addition to fullblooded American Indians, persons of mixed white and Indian blood are included in this category if they are enrolled on an Indian tribal or agency roll or if they are regarded as Indians in their community. A common requirement for such enrollment at present is that the proportion of Indian blood should be at least one-fourth."

We thus have the anomalous situation of the federal government, whose duty it is to assist Indians, confessing that its bureaus cannot agree on how to define an Indian.

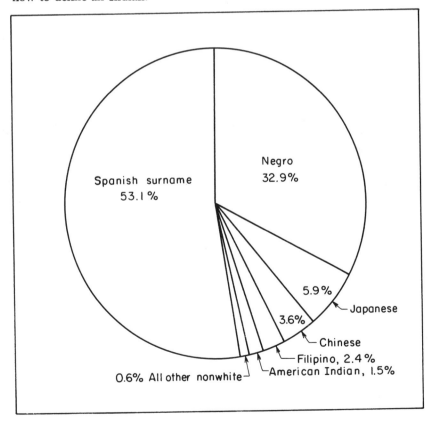

The California Indians as One of the Ethnic Minorities

In 1960 the non-Anglo population of California numbered 2,700,000 of the total population of 15,700,000. The pie diagram on p. 573 illustrates graphically the relative strength of the principal minorities.

Population Numbers and Distribution

The number of California Indians at the time of discovery by Europeans has been estimated by several people. S. Powers in 1877 calculated that the pre-Spanish population of California was about 750,000, a figure which has been considered too large by all later students of the subject. C. Hart Merriam in 1905 placed the number at about 250,000. A. L. Kroeber in 1925 thought the Merriam total to be excessive and proposed a figure of 125,000. S. F. Cook has on several occasions taken up this problem and in his latest publication (which is reprinted in the present volume) concludes that about 275,000 Indians lived in California at the time of discovery.

We provide here several population tables which are taken from the following sources (cited in full in the reference bibliography, p. 609 below): *Progress Report . . . by the State Advisory Commission on Indian Affairs*, 1966; *American Indians in California*, 1965; *Minority Groups in California*, 1966).

First is a table showing American Indian population by state according to the U.S. Bureau of the Census records for 1950 and 1960. Three states (Arizona, New Mexico, and Oklahoma) have more Indians than California.

TABLE 1

U.S. INDIAN POPULATION BY STATE, 1950 AND 1960

State	1950 Number	1950 Percent	1960 Number	1960 Percent
United States	357,499	100	551,669	100
Alabama	928	0.25	1,276	0.23
Alaska	*14,089	....	42,518	7.7
Arizona	65,761	18.4	83,387	15.1
Arkansas	533	0.14	580	0.10
California	19,947	5.6	39,014	7.1
Colorado	1,567	0.43	4,288	0.77
Connecticut	333	0.09	923	0.16
Delaware	....	....	597	0.10
District of Columbia	330	0.09	587	0.10
Florida	1,011	0.28	2,504	0.45
Georgia	333	0.09	749	0.13

TABLE 1 (continued)

State	1950		1960	
	Number	Percent	Number	Percent
Hawaii	....	... .	472	0.08
Idaho	3,800	1.1	5,231	0.94
Illinois	1,443	0.40	4,704	0.85
Indiana	438	0.12	948	0.17
Iowa	1,084	0.30	1,708	0.30
Kansas	2,381	0.66	5,069	0.91
Kentucky	234	0.06	391	0.07
Louisiana	409	0.11	3,587	0.65
Maine	1,522	0.42	1,879	0.34
Maryland	314	0.08	1,538	0.27
Massachusetts	1,201	0.33	2,118	0.38
Michigan	7,000	2.0	9,701	1.75
Minnesota	12,533	3.5	15,496	2.8
Mississippi	2,502	0.69	3,119	0.56
Missouri	547	0.15	1,723	0.31
Montana	16,606	4.6	21,181	3.8
Nebraska	3,954	1.1	5,545	1.0
Nevada	5,025	1.4	6,681	1.2
New Hampshire	74	0.02	135	0.02
New Jersey	621	0.17	1,699	0.3
New Mexico	41,901	11.7	56,255	10.2
New York	10,640	3.0	16,491	3.0
North Carolina	3,742	1.0	38,129	6.9
North Dakota	10,766	3.0	11,736	2.1
Ohio	1,146	0.32	1,910	0.34
Oklahoma	53,769	15.0	64,689	11.7
Oregon	5,820	1.6	8,026	1.5
Pennsylvania	1,141	0.31	2,122	0.38
Rhode Island	385	0.10	932	0.16
South Carolina	554	0.15	1,098	0.19
South Dakota	23,344	6.5	25,794	4.7
Tennessee	399	0.09	638	0.11
Texas	2,736	0.76	5,750	1.04
Utah	4,201	1.2	6,961	1.26
Vermont	30	0.008	57	0.01
Virginia	1,056	0.29	2,155	0.39
Washington	13,816	3.9	21,076	3.8
West Virginia	160	0.04	181	0.03
Wisconsin	12,196	3.4	14,297	2.6
Wyoming	3,237	0.90	4,020	0.7

*Includes only Athabascans.
SOURCE: U.S. Bureau of the Census, 1960, 1950.

American Indians in California numbered, by decade from 1890 to 1960 as follows:

TABLE 2

POPULATION OF AMERICAN INDIANS IN CALIFORNIA: 1890 TO 1960

Year	State Population	Indian		
		Population	Change over Previous Census (percent)	Percent of State Population
1960	15,717,204	39,014 (Urban 20,619) (Rural 18,395)	+95.6	.248
1950	10,586,223	19,947 (Urban 5,094) (Rural 14,853)	+6.8	.2
1940	6,907,387	18,675 (Urban 4,078) (Rural 14,597)	−2.8	.3
1930	5,677,251	19,212	+10.7	.3
1920.........................	3,426,861	17,360	+6.0	.5
1910.........................	2,377,549	16,371	+6.5	.7
1900	1,485,053	15,377	−7.5	1.0
1890	1,213,398	16,624	....	1.4
	State population increase 1960 = 48.5%			

SOURCE: U.S. Bureau of the Census, 1960, 1950.

As one of several minority ethnic groups, Indians in California rank sixth in number as shown by the following table. American Indians, have, however, shown the fastest rate of increase in the decade 1950–1960. This increase is in part due to growth of the resident California Indian stock, but probably in largest part to American Indians from other states who have emigrated to California.

TABLE 3

POPULATION OF CALIFORNIA BY ETHNIC GROUP, 1950 AND 1960

Ethnic Group	Population, California		Percent Change 1950–60
	1950	1960	
Total	10,586,223	15,717,204	+ 48.5
White, except Spanish surname	9,156,773	13,028,692	+ 42.3
Spanish surname	758,400	1,426,538	+ 88.1
Afro-American	462,172	883,861	+ 91.2
Japanese	84,956	157,317	+ 85.2
Chinese	58,324	95,600	+ 63.9
Filipino	40,424	65,459	+ 61.9
American Indian	19,947	39,014	+ 95.6
All other	5,227	20,723	+296.5

In late 1969, the estimated American Indian population of California is 100,000. The trend toward urban living of Indians has gone on at an ever accelerating pace. In 1950 26 percent of Indians in California lived in cities and towns; in 1960 this had doubled to 53 percent, and in 1969 the urban percentage is estimated at 65 percent. The following table shows urban-rural distribution of minorities as of 1960:

TABLE 4

PERCENT OF POPULATION RESIDING IN RURAL AND URBAN AREAS IN CALIFORNIA IN 1960

Ethnic Group	Rural Areas	Urban Areas
American Indian	47.1	52.9
Spanish surname	20.4	79.6
Japanese	13.5	86.5
Afro-American	5.6	94.4
Chinese	3.6	96.4

Education

In 1960 the educational attainment of California Indians was low. Forty-three percent of both Indian men and women had not gone beyond the eighth grade. About 5 percent of Indians in 1960 had had no schooling whatsoever.

TABLE 5

PERCENTAGE DISTRIBUTION OF SCHOOL LEVEL COMPLETED BY
CALIFORNIA INDIANS, 14 YEARS OLD OR MORE, 1960

School Level Completed		Male	Female
Elementary:	Grades 1-4	8.0	7.1
	Grades 5-6	8.1	7.9
	Grade 7	6.8	6.1
	Grade 8	16.0	17.4
High School:	Grades 9-11	30.0	29.0
	Grade 12	19.1	20.4
College:	1 to 3 years	5.8	5.3
	4 or more years	1.8	2.0
No schooling		4.4	4.8
		100.00	100.00

The California State Advisory Commission on Indian Affairs found in 1966 that while Indians are enrolled in elementary schools at the same ratio as non-Indians, the high-school dropout rate for Indians is 21 percent as against non-Indians whose dropout rate is 7 percent. Some schools reported the dropout rate for Indians as high as 75 percent.

Obstacles to achieving an adequate education include inadequate study facilities; an oppressive social environment due to crowded living conditions; inadequate family incomes leading to inability to secure proper clothing and allow participation in recreational or nonclassroom educational activities such as music programs, social events, sports and drama groups; lack of motivation and absence of encouragement to continue in school from parents; lack of preparation due to educational disabilities of parents and nonattendance in kindergarten; significantly lower quality of education provided for Indians because teachers are not encouraged to deal with the special problems of these socially and economically disadvantaged students.

Economic and Employment Conditions

California Indians in 1960 topped the list of ethnic minorities who were unemployed.

TABLE 6

UNEMPLOYMENT RATES OF ETHNIC MINORITIES IN CALIFORNIA, 1960

(*in percent*)

Ethnic Group	Unemployment Rates	
	Men	Women
American Indian	15.1	11.4
Afro-American	12.7	11.4
Filipino	12.7	11.4
Spanish surname*	7.8	13.6
Chinese	4.9	5.1
Japanese	2.6	3.1

*"Spanish surname" individuals are mostly Mexican Americans (sometimes called Chicanos) but this group includes a small number of persons of other national origin: Cuban, Puerto Rican, Central and South American, Spanish.

As regards income earned by Indians in California, we find them in 1959 to be the poorest of all ethnic minorities.

TABLE 7

MEDIAN ANNUAL INCOME IN 1959 OF PERSONS 14 YEARS OLD OR OVER, IN CALIFORNIA

Ethnic Group	Men	Women
White	$5,109	$1,812
Japanese	4,388	2,144
Spanish surname	3,849	1,534
Chinese	3,803	1,997
Afro-American	3,553	1,596
Filipino	2,925	1,591
American Indian	2,694	1,213

Table 8 indicates that Indians tend to have large families.

TABLE 8

POPULATION AND SIZE OF FAMILY BY ETHNIC GROUP IN CALIFORNIA, 1960

Characteristic	Spanish surname	Afro-American	Japanese	Chinese	Filipino	Amer. Indian
Population	1,426,538	883,861	157,317	95,600	65,459	39,014
Percent of total population	9.1	5.6	1.0	0.6	0.4	0.2
Size of family (percent)						
2 persons	21.1	32.1	20.5	19.1	21.2	17.5
3 "	18.6	21.0	20.5	20.1	17.2	16.2
4 "	20.0	16.2	23.1	22.1	17.5	15.4
5 "	16.2	11.6	17.6	17.8	14.6	14.0
6 "	10.6	7.8	10.3	11.4	12.0	11.5
7 "	13.5	11.3	8.0	9.5	17.5	25.4

Health Conditions

Federal health services for Indians in California was terminated in 1955. While the state of California agreed that local governmental agencies would be able most effectively to provide such health services, no state funds have been made available from 1955 to present to continue any of the terminated federal health services. The result has been an accelerated deterioration of the health conditions of Indians in California. In 1954–1955 the federal government spent $24,549,125 on Indian health programs; and of this $420,000 was allocated to California. For 1969–1970 the federal Indian health appropriation was $99,581,000. The California Indians' share would have been $1,693,000; but this amount was not allocated owing to federal withdrawal from all health, welfare, and educational benefits for California Indians. Some relief is finally promised as the result of passage of California Senate Bill 1397 which provides some funds for the State Department of Public Health to provide a minimum of the desperately needed health services for the Indians of California. Efforts are being made to encourage the federal government to reconsider its action of 1955 and reinstitute federal aid for Indian health programs.

Table 9 illustrates some aspects of Indian health conditions as reflected in known causes of death.

TABLE 9

CAUSES OF DEATH IN THE GENERAL CALIFORNIA POPULATION (I.E. WHITES),
AND INDIAN MEN AND INDIAN WOMEN, 1962

Cause of Death	California Non-Indians	Indian Men	Indian Women
Diseases of the heart	37.0	22.0	19.3
Accidents	5.9	25.6	13.3
All other causes	13.7	14.3	23.7
Malignant neoplasms (cancer)	16.3	4.8	11.1
Influenza, pneumonia	3.3	7.1	7.4
Cirrhosis of the liver	1.9	7.1	5.9
Vascular lesions affecting central nervous system	11.0	4.8	6.7
Diseases of early infancy	4.4	4.2	5.9
Tuberculosis	0.7	4.2	2.2
Congenital malformations	1.4	2.4	1.5
Arteriosclerosis	2.4	3.0	0.7
Suicide	1.9	0.6	2.2

The average age at death of American Indians in the United States is 42 years; that in the general (mainly white) population is 62 years. The Indian infant death rate is 41.8 per 1,000 live births which is 70 percent higher than in the general population. The Indian death rate from accidents, influenza, pneumonia, cirrhosis of the liver, tuberculosis, and congenital malformations is greater than in the general population.

Reservations

There exist 82 Indian reservations and "rancherias" (group homesites) in California. These are so widely scattered that trying to list them, their sizes, and their locations would run to too great length. The detailed information can be found in the U.S. Department of Interior, Bureau of Indian Affairs publications titled *U.S. Indian Population (1962) and Land (1963)*, issued in 1963.

Tribal and allotment lands in the reservations amount to 550,775 acres. In 1960 only 19 percent (7,400) of the California Indians lived on or adjacent to reservation lands. Only 18 of the 82 reservations were used as homesites of 100 or more Indians. The largest reservation, in terms of both population and acreage, is Hoopa Valley comprising 86,068 acres, where, 992 Indians lived in 1962.

REfERENCE BIBLIOGRAphy

LIST OF TOPICS

Abbreviations / 583
General Surveys of California Indian Culture / 584
Geographical Natural History and Historical Background / 586
The Indian in the Spanish and American Periods / 587
Tribal Locations and Boundaries; Native Languages / 589
Population Numbers; Ancient and Recent Physical Types / 589
Culture Areas: Northwestern California / 591
Culture Areas: Central California (Valley and Sierra Nevadas) / 592
Culture Areas: Southern California Coast and Desert / 593
Culture Areas: Colorado River / 595
Culture Areas: Northeastern California / 596
Archaeology: Statewide Surveys and Syntheses:
  General Studies, Dating of Cultures / 597
Archaeology: Northern and Central California / 598
Archaeology: Southern California / 600
Indian Arts: Basketry; Symbolism of Basket Designs / 602
Mythology and Folk Tales / 603
Psychoanalytic Interpretations of California Indian Culture / 604
Songs, Music, Prayers, Place Names of Indian Origin / 605
Rock Art: Petroglyphs and Pictographs / 607
Ishi, Last of the Mill Creek Yahi / 608
The California Indian Today and in the Recent Past / 608

ABBREVIATIONS

The following abbreviations have been used:

UCAS-R   University of California Archaeological Survey Reports (Berkeley)
UC-AR   University of California Anthropological Records
UC-PAAE   University of California Publications in American Archaeology and Ethnology

What follows is a selected list of references provided for persons interested in consulting original sources for details on California Indians and their culture. California-wide surveys of specific aspects of culture are listed in "General Surveys of California Indian Culture"; regional treatments of subjects and ethnographies of tribal groups are cited in the section divided geographically — i.e. northern, central, southern, Colorado River, and northeastern California. References to archaeological reports also follow a regional breakdown.

Information on nearly every tribe and further references can be found in A. L. Kroeber, *Handbook of the Indians of California*; S. Powers, *Tribes of California*; F. W. Hodge (ed.), *Handbook of American Indians*; and G. P. Murdock, *Ethnographic Bibliography of North America*, which are cited in full below under General Surveys.

GENERAL SURVEYS OF CALIFORNIA INDIAN CULTURE

Culley, J.
    1936. The California Indians: Their Medical Practices and Drugs. Journal of the American Pharmaceutical Association, 25:332–339.
Curtis, E. S.
    1907–1930. The North American Indian. Norwood, Mass. (Vol. 2, Mohave, Yuma; Vol. 13, Yurok, Hupa, Karok, Wiyot, Tolowa, Shasta, Achomawi, Klamath; Vol. 14, Kato, Wailaki, Yuki, Pomo, Wintun, Maidu, Miwok, Yokuts; Vol. 15, Washo, Diegueño).
Davis, J.
    1961. Trade Routes and Economic Exchange Among the Indians of California. UCAS-R, No. 54.
Driver, H. E.
    1941. Girl's Puberty Rites in Western North America. UC-AR, 6:21–90.
Durham, B.
    1960. Canoes and Kayaks of Western North America. Seattle.
Elsasser, A. B.
    1960. The History of Culture Classification in California. UCAS-R, No. 49, pp. 1–10.
Forbes, J. D.
    1969. Native Americans of California and Nevada. Naturegraph Publishers, Healdsburg, Calif.
Gayton, A. H.
    1930. The Ghost Dance of 1870. UC-PAAE, 28:57–82.
Gifford, E. W.
    1926. Miwok Lineages and the Political Unit in California. American Anthropologist, 28:389–401.
Goldschmidt, W. R.
    1948. Social Organization in Native California and the Origin of Clans. American Anthropologist, 50:444–456.
Gould, R. A.
    1963. Aboriginal California Burial and Cremation Practices. UCAS-R, No. 60, pp. 149–168.

Greengo, R. E.
1952. Shellfish Foods of the California Indians. Kroeber Anthropological Society, Paper No. 7, pp. 63–114. Berkeley.

Heizer, R. F.
1962. The California Indians: Archaeology, Varieties of Culture, Arts of Life. California Historical Society Quarterly, 41:1–28.

Heizer, R. F. and W. C. Massey
1953. Aboriginal Navigation off the Coasts of Upper and Baja California. Bureau of American Ethnology, Bulletin 151, pp. 285–311.

Heizer, R. F. and A. E. Treganza
1944. Mines and Quarries of the Indians of California. California Journal of Mines and Geology, 40:291–359.

Hodge, F. W. (ed.)
1907–1910. Handbook of American Indians. Bureau of American Ethnology, Bulletin 30 (Part I, A-M, 1907; Part II, N-Z, 1910).

Holmes, W. H.
1902. Anthropological Studies in California. Smithsonian Inst., United States National Museum Report for 1900, pp. 155–187.

Klimek, S.
1935. Culture Element Distributions: I, The Structure of California Indian Culture. UC-PAAE, Vol. 37, No. 1.

Kroeber, A. L.
1904. Types of Indian Culture in California. UC-PAAE, Vol. 21, No. 3.
1907. The Religion of the Indians of California. UC-PAAE, Vol. 4, No. 6.
1920. California Culture Provinces. UC-PAAE, Vol. 17, No. 2.
1920. Games of the Indians of California. American Anthropologist, 22: 272–277.
1925. Handbook of the Indians of California. Bureau of American Ethnology, Bulletin 78.
1936. Area and Climax. UC-PAAE, Vol. 37, No. 3.
1955. Nature of the Land-Holding Group [in Aboriginal California]. Ethnohistory, 2:303–314.
1962. The Anthropology of California. UCAS-R, No. 56, pp. 1–18 (reprinted, with annotations from original article of 1908).
1962. The Nature of Land-Holding Groups in Aboriginal California. UCAS-R, No. 56, pp. 19–58.

Merriam, C. H.
1955. Studies of California Indians. Berkeley and Los Angeles: University of California Press (reprinted without change, 1962).
1966. Ethnographic Notes on California Indian Tribes. Compiled and edited by R. F. Heizer. UCAS-R, No. 68, Parts I–III. (Part I, pp. 1–166; Part II, pp. 167–256, Ethnological Notes on Northern and Southern California Indian Tribes; Part III, pp. 257–448, Ethnological Notes on Central California Indian Tribes.)

Murdock, G. P.
1960. Ethnographic Bibliography of North America. Behavior Science Bibliographies, Human Relations Area Files, New Haven, Conn. 3rd

edition. (For California tribes see pp. 77, 79, 80–106, 109–111, 387–388.)

Powers, S.

1877. Tribes of California. Contributions to North American Ethnology, Vol. 3. U.S. Dept. of Interior, Washington, D.C.

Romero, J. B.

1954. The Botanical Lore of the California Indians. New York.

Sherwin, J.

1963. Face and Body Painting Practices Among California Indians. UCAS-R, No. 60, pp. 81–148.

Squier, R.

1953. The Manufacture of Flint Implements by the Indians of Northern and Central California. UCAS-R, No. 19, pp. 15–32.

Willoughby, N. C.

1963. Division of Labor Among the Indians of California. UCAS-R, No. 60, pp. 1–80.

Yates, L. G.

1896. Aboriginal Weapons of California. Overland Monthly, Ser. 2, 27: 337–342.

GEOGRAPHICAL NATURAL HISTORY AND HISTORICAL BACKGROUND

Bolton, H. E.

1926. Historical Memoirs of New California by Fr. Francisco Palou. Berkeley: University of California Press.

1927. Fray Juan Crespi, Missionary Explorer on the Pacific Coast. Berkeley: University of California Press.

1930. Anza's California Expeditions. Vols. I–IV. Berkeley: University of California Press.

1931. Font's Complete Diary. Berkeley: University of California Press.

Coues, E.

1900. On the Trail of a Spanish Pioneer; the Diary and Itinerary of Francisco Garces, 1775–1776. Vols. I–II. New York. (More recent edition translated and edited by John Galvin, A Record of Travels in Arizona and California. San Francisco: John Howell, 1965.)

Cutter, D. C.

1969. The California Coast: Documents from the Sutro Collection. Norman, Oklahoma: University of Oklahoma Press.

Drake, N. F.

1897. The Topography of California. Journal of Geology, 5:563–578.

Durrenburger, R. W.

1959. The Geography of California in Essays and Readings. Brewster Publications, Los Angeles.

Grinnell, J.

1935. A Revised Life Zone Map of California. University of California Publications in Zoology, Vol. 40, No. 7.

Hall, H. M. and J. Grinnell
  1919. Life-Zone Indicators in California. Proceedings of the California Academy of Sciences, 4th ser., Vol. 9, No. 2.
Heizer, R. F.
  1947. Francis Drake and the California Indians, 1579. Berkeley and Los Angeles: University of California Press.
Hinds, N. E. A.
  1952. Evolution of the California Landscape. Calif. Division of Mines, Bulletin 158, San Francisco.
Ingles, L. G.
  1954. Mammals of California and its Coastal Waters. Stanford: Stanford University Press.
Jenkins, O. P.
  1938. Geologic Map of California. California State Division of Mines.
Munz, P. A.
  1959. A California Flora. Berkeley and Los Angeles: University of California Press.
Priestley, H. I.
  1937. A Historical, Political and Natural Description of California, by Pedro Fages. Berkeley: University of California Press.
Russell, R. J.
  1926. Climates of California. University of California Publications in Geography, Vol. 2, No. 4 (with map).
Smith, J. P.
  1916. The Geologic Formations of California with Reconnaissance Geological Map. California State Mining Bureau, Bulletin 72.
Sprague, M.
  1941. Climate of California. In Climate and Man (pp. 783–792). U.S. Dept. of Agriculture, Washington, D.C.
Wagner, H. R.
  1929. Spanish Voyages to the Northwest Coast of America in the Sixteenth Century. California Historical Society, Special Publication No. 4 (Journals of Cabrillo, Cermeno, and Vizcaino in 1542, 1595, and 1602.)
Wieslander, A. E. and H. A. Jensen
  1946. Timber Areas, Timber Volumes, and Vegetation Types in California. California Forest and Range Experiment Station, Forest Release No. 4. Berkeley.
Zierer, C. M.
  1956. California and the Southwest. New York: John Wiley.

THE INDIAN IN THE SPANISH AND AMERICAN PERIODS

[No single book covers this large subject. H. H. Bancroft's *History of California, 1542–1890* (7 vols., San Francisco, 1884–1890) remains a basic source of information, though it is not organized for convenient reference.]

Bleeker, S.
  1956. The Mission Indians of California. New York.
Caughey, J. W.
  1952. The Indians of California in 1852. San Marino (report of B. D. Wilson on Indians of Southern California, 1852).
Cook, S. F.
  1941. The Mechanism and Extent of Dietary Adaptation Among Certain Groups of California and Nevada Indians. Ibero-Americana, No. 18.
  1943. The Conflict Between the California Indian and White Civilization: I, The Indian versus the Spanish Misson. Ibero-Americana, No. 21.
  1943. The Conflict Between the California Indian and White Civilization: II, The Physical and Demographic Reaction of the Nonmission Indians in Colonial and Provincial California. Ibero-Americana No. 22.
  1943. The Conflict Between the California Indian and White Civilization: III, The American Invasions, 1848–1870. Ibero-Americana No. 23.
  1943. The Conflict Between the California Indian and White Civilization: IV, Trends in Marriage and Divorce Since 1850. Ibero-Americana No. 24.
  1955. The Epidemic of 1830–1833 in California and Oregon. UC-PAAE, Vol. 43, No. 3.
Cutter, D. C.
  1960. The California Franciscans as Anthropologists. Southwest Museum Masterkey, 34:88–94.
Dale, E. E.
  1949. The Indians of the Southwest. Norman, Oklahoma: University of Oklahoma Press. (Contains excellent summary of early reservations in California.)
Ellison, W. H.
  1922. The Federal Indian Policy in California, 1846–1860. Mississippi Valley Historical Review, Vol. 9.
Forbes, J. D.
  1969. Native Americans of California and Nevada. Naturegraph Publishers, Healdsburg, California.
Geary, G. J.
  1934. The Secularization of the California Indian Missions. Catholic University of America, Studies in American Church History, Vol. 17.
Goodrich, C. S.
  1926. The Legal Status of the California Indian. California Law Review, 14: 83–100, 157–187.
Hoopes, A. W.
  1932. Indian Affairs and Their Administration, with Special Reference to the Far West, 1849–1860. Philadelphia.
Webb, E. B.
  1952. Indian Life at the Old Missions. Los Angeles.

TRIBAL LOCATIONS AND BOUNDARIES; NATIVE LANGUAGES

Bright, W.
  1964. Studies in California Linguistics. University of California Publications in Linguistics, Vol. 34.
Dixon, R. B. and A. L. Kroeber
  1903. The Native Languages of California. American Anthropologist, 5: 1–26.
  1919. Linguistic Families of California. UC-PAAE, Vol. 16, No. 3.
Forbes, J. D.
  1969. Native Americans of California and Nevada. Naturegraph Publishers, Healdsburg, California (listing of native languages, tribal groups, and map, pp. 181–191).
Heizer, R. F.
  1941. Alexander S. Taylor's Map of California Indian Tribes, 1864. California Historical Society Quarterly, 20:171–180 (with reproduction of Taylor's map).
  1966. Languages, Territories and Names of California Indian Tribes. Berkeley and Los Angeles: University of California Press. (Survey of the history of study and classification of California Indian languages; linguistic classification of A. L. Kroeber with a detailed map of tribal territories; linguistic classification of C. Hart Merriam with a detailed map of tribal territories; list of published maps showing areas occupied by individual tribes, pp. 31–34.)
Kroeber, A. L.
  1904. The Languages of the Coast of California South of San Francisco Bay. UC-PAAE, Vol. 2, No. 2.
  1911. The Languages of the Coast of California North of San Francisco Bay. UC-PAAE, Vol. 9, No. 3.
  1911. Phonetic Constituents of the Native Languages of California. UC-PAAE, Vol. 2, No. 2.
  1925. Handbook of the Indians of California. Bureau of American Ethnology, Bulletin 78.
Lee, D. D.
  1938. Conceptual Implications of an Indian Language [Wintu]. Philosophy of Science, 5:89–102.

POPULATION NUMBERS; ANCIENT AND RECENT PHYSICAL TYPES

Baumhoff, M. A.
  1963. Ecological Determinants of Aboriginal California Populations. UC-PAAE, Vol. 49, No. 2.

Boas, F.
  1905. Anthropometry of Central California. American Museum of Natural History, Bulletin, 27:347–380. (Contains some excellent photographs of Indians.)
Brown, A.
  1967. The Aboriginal Population of the Santa Barbara Channel. UCAS-R, No. 69.
Cook, S. F.
  1940. Population Trends Among the California Mission Indians. Ibero-Americana, No. 17.
  1943. The Conflict Between the California Indian and White Civilization: I. Ibero-Americana, No. 21. (The whole work treats the population question in California. The appendix is a careful inquiry into the aboriginal population figure.)
  1943. The Conflict Between the California Indian and White Civilization: II. Ibero-Americana, No. 22. (Table 1, Indian population from the end of Mission times to the modern period.)
  1955. The Aboriginal Population of the San Joaquin Valley, California. UC-AR, Vol. 16, No. 2.
  1956. The Aboriginal Population of the North Coast of California. UC-AR, Vol. 16, No. 3.
  1957. The Aboriginal Population of Alameda and Contra Costa Counties, California. UC-AR, Vol. 16, No. 4.
Cook, S. F. and R. F. Heizer
  1965. The Quantitative Approach to the Relation Between Population and Settlement Size. UCAS-R, No. 64. (An attempt to determine prehistoric population numbers in California using archaeological data.)
  1968. Relationships Among Houses, Settlement Areas, and Population in Aboriginal California. In K. C. Chang (ed.), Settlement Archaeology (National Press, Palo Alto), pp. 79–116. (An essay in determining prehistoric numbers using ethnographic information and archaeological site data.)
Gifford, E. W.
  1926. California Anthropometry. UC-PAAE, Vol. 22, No. 2. (The largest and most comprehensive work of the kind on this subject. Contains excellent pictures of both living and skeletal types.)
Hrdlicka, A.
  1906. Contribution to the Physical Anthropology of California. UC-PAAE, Vol. 4, No. 2.
Klimek, S.
  1935. The Structure of California Indian Culture. Culture Element Distributions: I. UC-PAAE, Vol. 37, No. 1. (On pp. 31–33 are data on physical types.)
Kroeber, A. L.
  1921. The Aboriginal Population of California. Science, 54:162–163.

1925. Handbook of the Indians of California. Bureau of American Ethnology, Bulletin 78. (Pp. 880–891, aboriginal population.)

1957. California Indian Population About 1910. UC-PAAE, Vol. 47, No. 2, pp. 218–225.

Kroeber, T. and R. F. Heizer

1968. Almost Ancestors: the First Californians. Sierra Club, San Francisco. (Text and numerous photographs of Indians.)

Leigh, R. W.

1928. Dental Pathology of Aboriginal California. UC-PAAE, Vol. 23, No. 10. (A study of prehistoric Indian teeth.)

Merriam, C. H.

1905. The Indian Population of California. American Anthropologist, 7: 594–606.

Newman, R.

1957. A Comparative Analysis of Prehistoric Skeletal Remains from the Lower Sacramento Valley. UCAS-R, No. 39, pp. 1–66.

CULTURE AREAS: NORTHWESTERN CALIFORNIA

Baumhoff, M. A.

1958. California Athabascan Groups. UC-AR, Vol. 16, No. 5.

Dixon, R. B.

1907. The Shasta. American Museum of Natural History Bulletin, 17:381–498.

Driver, H. E.

1939. Culture Element Distributions: X, Northwest California. UC-AR, Vol. 1, No. 6.

Drucker, P.

1937. The Tolowa and their Southwest Oregon Kin. UC-PAAE, Vol. 36, No. 7.

Elmendorf, W. W. and A. L. Kroeber

1960. The Structure of Twana Culture with Comparative Notes on the Structure of Yurok Culture. Research Studies, Monographic Supplement No. 2, Washington State University, Pullman, Wash.

Erikson, E. H.

1943. Observations on the Yurok: Childhood and World Image. UC-PAAE, Vol. 35, No. 10.

Goldschmidt, W.

1951. Ethics and the Structure of Society: an Ethnological Contribution to the Sociology of Knowledge. American Anthropologist, 53:506–524.

Goldschmidt, W. and H. Driver

1940. The Hupa White Deerskin Dance. UC-PAAE, Vol. 35, No. 8.

Goddard, P. E.

1903. Life and Culture of the Hupa. UC-PAAE, Vol. 1, No. 1.

Harrington, J. P.
    1932. Tobacco Among the Karuk Indians of California. Bureau of American Ethnology, Bulletin 94.
Heizer, R. F. and J. Mills
    1952. The Four Ages of Tsurai. Berkeley and Los Angeles: University of California Press.
Holt, C.
    1946. Shasta Ethnography. UC-AR, Vol. 3, No. 4.
Kelly, I. T.
    1930. The Carver's Art of the Indians of Northwestern California. UC-PAAE, Vol. 24, No. 7.
Kroeber, A. L. and S. A. Barrett
    1960. Fishing Among the Indians of Northwestern California. UC-AR, Vol. 21, No. 1.
Kroeber, A. L. and E. W. Gifford
    1949. World Renewal: A Cult System of Native Northwest California. UC-AR, Vol. 13, No. 1.
Nomland, G. A.
    1938. Bear River Ethnography. UC-AR, Vol. 2, No. 2.
Schenck, S. M. and E. W. Gifford
    1952. Karok Ethnobotany. UC-AR, Vol. 13, No. 6.
Spott, R. and A. L. Kroeber
    1942. Yurok Narratives. UC-PAAE, Vol. 35, No. 9.
Thompson, L.
    1916. To the American Indian. Eureka, California. (An account of Yurok culture written by a Yurok woman.)
Waterman, T. T.
    1920. Yurok Geography. UC-PAAE, Vol. 16, No. 5.

CULTURE AREAS: CENTRAL CALIFORNIA (VALLEY AND SIERRA NEVADAS)

Barrett, S. A.
    1908. The Ethno-Geography of the Pomo and Neighboring Indians. UC-PAAE, Vol. 16, No. 1.
    1917. The Washo Indians. Bulletin of the Public Museum, City of Milwaukee, 2:1–52.
    1917. Ceremonies of the Pomo Indians. UC-PAAE, Vol. 12, No. 10.
    1919. The Wintun Hesi Ceremony. UC-PAAE, Vol. 14, No. 4.
    1952. Material Aspects of Pomo Culture. Bulletin of the Public Museum, City of Milwaukee, Vol. 20, parts I, II.
Beals, R. L.
    1933. Ethnology of the Nisenan. UC-PAAE, Vol. 31, No. 6.
Dixon, R. B.
    1905. The Northern Maidu. American Museum of Natural History, Bulletin, 17:119–346.

Downs, J. F.
  1966. The Two Worlds of the Washo. New York: Holt, Rinehart and Winston.
DuBois, C.
  1935. Wintu Ethnography. UC-PAAE, Vol. 36, No. 1.
Gayton, A. H.
  1930. Yokuts-Mono Chiefs and Shamans. UC-PAAE, 24:361–420.
  1945. Yokuts and Western Mono Social Organization. American Anthropologist, 47:409–426.
  1948. Northern Foothill Yokuts and Western Mono. UC-AR, Vol. 10, Nos. 1, 2. (Part I, Tulare Lake, Southern San Joaquin Valley, Central Foothill Yokuts; Part II, Northern Foothill Yokuts and Western Mono.)
Gifford, E. W.
  1916. Miwok Moieties. UC-PAAE, Vol. 12, No. 4.
  1926. Clear Lake Pomo Society. UC-PAAE, Vol. 18, No. 2.
  1926. Miwok Cults. UC-PAAE, Vol. 18, No. 3.
  1932. The Northfork Mono. UC-PAAE, Vol. 31, No. 2.
Goldschmidt, W.
  1951. Nomlaki Ethnography. UC-PAAE, Vol. 42, No. 4.
Kroeber, A. L.
  1932. The Patwin and Their Neighbors. UC-PAAE, Vol. 29, No. 4.
Latta, F. F.
  1949. Handbook of Yokuts Indians. Kern County Museum, Bakersfield.
Loeb, E. M.
  1926. Pomo Folkways. UC-PAAE, Vol. 19, No. 2.
  1932. The Western Kuksu Cult. UC-PAAE, Vol. 33, No. 1.
Lowie, R. H.
  1939. Ethnographic Notes on the Washo. UC-PAAE, Vol. 36, No. 5.
Noble, W. B.
  1904. A Day with the Mono Indians. Out West, 20:413–421.
Price, J. A.
  1962. Washo Economy. Nevada State Museum, Anthropological Papers No. 6. Carson City, Nevada.
Stewart, O. C.
  1944. Washo-Northern Paiute Peyotism. UC-PAAE, Vol. 40, No. 3.
Voegelin, E. W.
  1938. Tubatulabal Ethnography. UC-AR, Vol. 2, No. 1.

CULTURE AREAS: SOUTHERN CALIFORNIA COAST AND DESERT

Anderson, E.
  1964. A Bibliography of the Chumash and Their Predecessors. UCAS-R, No. 61, pp. 24–74.
Caughey, J.
  1952. Indians of Southern California in 1852. Huntington Library, San Marino. (Report on Indians of Southern California by B. D. Wilson.)

Coville, F. V.
  1892. The Panamint Indians of California. American Anthropologist, 5: 351–361.
Drucker, P.
  1937. Culture Element Distributions: V, Southern California. UC-AR, Vol. 1, No. 1.
DuBois, C. G.
  1905. Religious Ceremonies and Myths of the Mission Indians. American Anthropologist, 7:620–629.
  1908. The Religion of the Luiseño Indians of Southern California. UC-PAAE, Vol. 8, No. 3.
Gifford, E. W.
  1931. The Kamia of Imperial Valley. Bureau of American Ethnology, Bulletin 97.
Heizer, R. F. (ed.)
  1938. The Plank Canoe of the Santa Barbara Region. Ethnological Studies, 7:193–229. Gothenburg, Sweden.
  1952. California Indian Linguistic Records; the Mission Indian Vocabularies of Alphonse Pinart. UC-AR, Vol. 15, No. 1. (Deals mainly with the Chumash; with annotations.)
  1955. California Indian Linguistic Records: the Mission Indian Vocabularies of H. W. Henshaw. UC-AR, Vol. 15, No. 2. (Mainly concerns Chumash; abundantly annotated by notes from Henshaw and the editor.)
  1968. The Indians of Los Angeles County: Hugo Reid's Letters of 1852. Southwest Museum, Los Angeles. (These 22 letters have been printed several times. One version, although not complete and not annotated is *in* S. B. Dakin, A Scotch Paisano. Berkeley: University of California Press, 1939.)
Hooper, L.
  1920. The Cahuilla Indians. UC-PAAE, Vol. 16, No. 6.
James, H. C.
  1960. The Cahuilla Indians. Westernlore Press, Los Angeles.
Johnson, B. E.
  1962. California's Gabrielino Indians. Southwest Museum, Los Angeles.
Kroeber, A. L.
  1908. The Ethnography of the Cahuilla Indians. UC-PAAE, Vol. 8, No. 2.
Landberg, L.
  1965. The Chumash Indians of Southern California. Southwest Museum, Los Angeles.
Lee, M. H.
  1937. Indians of the Oaks. San Diego.
Robinson, E.
  1942–43. Plank Canoes of the Chumash. Southwest Museum Masterkey, 16: 202–209; 17:13–19.

Robinson, W. W.
   1952. The Indians of Los Angeles: Story of the Liquidation of a People. Los Angeles.
Sparkman, P. S.
   1908. The Culture of the Luiseño Indians. UC-PAAE, Vol. 8, No. 1.
Spier, L.
   1923. Southern Diegueño Customs. UC-PAAE, Vol. 20, pp. 297–358.
Strong, W. D.
   1929. Aboriginal Society in Southern California. UC-PAAE, Vol. 26, No. 1.
Walker, E. F.
   1937–43. Indians of Southern California. Southwest Museum Masterkey, 11:184–194; 12:24–29; 17:201–216.
Waterman, T. T.
   1910. The Religious Practices of the Diegueño Indians. UC-PAAE, Vol. 8, No. 6.
White, R. C.
   1957. The Luiseño Theory of "Knowledge." American Anthropologist, 59: 1–19.
   1963. Luiseño Social Organization. UC-PAAE, Vol. 48, No. 2.

CULTURE AREAS: COLORADO RIVER

Bourke, J. G.
   1889. Notes on the Cosmogony and Theogony of the Mohave Indians of the Rio Colorado, Arizona. Journal of American Folk-Lore, 2:169–189.
Castetter, E. W. and W. H. Bell
   1951. Yuman Indian Agriculture. Albuquerque: University of New Mexico Press.
Densmore, F.
   1932. Yuman and Yaqui Music. Smithsonian Institution, Bureau of American Ethnology, Bulletin 110. (Mainly about music, but contains a large amount of ethnographic detail.)
Devereux, G.
   1950. Amusements and Sports of Mohave Children. Southwest Museum Masterkey, 24:143–152.
Fathauer, G. H.
   1954. The Structure and Causation of Mohave Warfare. Southwestern Journal of Anthropology, 10:97–118.
Forbes, J.
   1965. Warriors of the Colorado. Norman, Oklahoma: University of Oklahoma Press.
Forde, C. D.
   1931. Ethnography of the Yuma Indians. UC-PAAE, Vol. 28, No. 4.

Kroeber, A. L.

    1902. A Preliminary Sketch of the Mohave Indians. American Anthropologist, 4:276–285.

    1920. Yuman Tribes of the Lower Colorado. UC-PAAE, Vol. 16, No. 8.

Kroeber, A. L. and M. J. Harner

    1955. Mohave Pottery. UC-AR, Vol. 16, No. 1.

Putnam, G. R.

    1895. A Yuma Cremation. American Anthropologist, O.S., 8:264–267.

Smith, G. A.

    1966. The Mohaves. San Bernardino County Museum Association Quarterly, Vol. 14, No. 1.

Stewart, K. M.

    1947. Mohave Warfare. Southwestern Journal of Anthropology, 3:257–278.

Taylor, E. S. and W. J. Wallace

    1947. Mohave Tattooing and Face-Painting. Southwest Museum Leaflet, No. 20.

Trippel, E. J.

    1889. The Yuma Indians. Overland Monthly, 2nd series, 14:1–11.

Wallace, W. J.

    1953. Tobacco and Its Use Among the Mohave Indians. Southwest Museum Masterkey, 27:193–202.

CULTURE AREAS: NORTHEASTERN CALIFORNIA

Barrett, S. A.

    1910. The Material Culture of the Klamath Lake and Modoc Indians. UC-PAAE, Vol. 5, No. 4.

Curtin, J.

    1909. Achomawi Myths. Journal of American Folk-Lore, 22:283–287.

Dixon, R. B.

    1905. The Mythology of the Shasta-Achomawi. American Anthropologist, 7:607–612.

    1908. Achomawi and Atsugewi Tales. Journal of American Folk-Lore, 21:159–177.

    1908. Notes on the Achomawi and Atsugewi of Northern California. American Anthropologist, 10:208–220.

Garth, T.

    1953. Atsugewi Ethnography. UC-AR, Vol. 14, No. 2.

Gatschet, A. S.

    1890. The Klamath Indians of Southwestern Oregon. Contribs. to North American Ethnology, Vol. 2, parts 1, 2. Washington. (This work includes information on the Modoc.)

Kelly, I.

    1932. Ethnography of the Surprise Valley Paiute. UC-PAAE, Vol. 31, No. 3.

Kniffen, F.
　1928. Achomawi Geography. UC-PAAE, Vol. 23, No. 5.
Kroeber, A. L.
　1925. Handbook of the Indians of California. Bureau of American Ethnology, Bulletin 78, chapters 21, 22. (Achomawi, Atsugewi, Modoc.)
Merriam, C. H.
　1926. The Classification and Distribution of the Pit River Indian Tribes of California. Smithsonian Miscellaneous Collections, Vol. 78, No. 3.
Miller, J.
　1873. Life Amongst the Modocs. London.
Murray, K. A.
　1965. The Modocs and Their Wars. Norman, Oklahoma.
Ray, V. F.
　1963. Primitive Pragmatists: The Modoc Indians of Northern California. Seattle: University of Washington Press.

ARCHAEOLOGY: STATEWIDE SURVEYS AND SYNTHESES: GENERAL STUDIES, DATING OF CULTURES

Antevs, E.
　1952. Climatic History and the Antiquity of Man in California. UCAS-R, No. 16, pp. 23–31.
Baumhoff, M. A. and A. B. Elsasser
　1956. Summary of Archaeological Survey and Excavation in California. UCAS-R, No. 33, pp. 1–27. (A bibliographic guide to excavations and surveys in each county; map showing areas surveyed and sites excavated.)
Bennyhoff, J. A.
　1950. California Fish Spears and Harpoons. UC-AR, Vol. 9, No. 4.
Bright, M.
　1965. California Radiocarbon Dates. Annual Report of the Archaeological Survey, Dept. of Anthropology, Univ. of Calif., Los Angeles, pp. 367–374.
Gifford, E. W.
　1940. California Bone Artifacts. UC-AR, Vol. 3, No. 2.
　1947. California Shell Artifacts. UC-AR, Vol. 9, No. 1.
Greengo, R. W.
　1951. Molluscan Species in California Shell Middens. UCAS-R, No. 13.
Heizer, R. F.
　1948. A Bibliography of Ancient Man in California. UCAS-R, No. 2.
　1949. A Bibliography of the Archaeology of California. UCAS-R, No. 4.
　1949. Curved Single-Piece Fishhooks of Shell and Bone in California. American Antiquity, 15:89–97.
　1952. A Survey of Cave Archaeology in California. UCAS-R, No. 15, pp. 1–12.

1952. A Review of Problems in the Antiquity of Man in California. UCAS-R, No. 16, pp. 3–17.

1958. Radiocarbon Dates from California of Archaeological Interest. UCAS-R, No. 44, pp. 1–16.

1964. The Western Coast of North America. *In* J. Jennings and E. Norbeck (eds.), Prehistoric Man in the New World, Chicago, pp. 117–118.

Kroeber, A. L.

1909. The Archaeology of California. Putnam Anniversary Volume, New York, pp. 1–42.

1936. Prospects in California Prehistory. American Antiquity, 2:108–116.

Lowie, R. H.

1923. The Cultural Connection of Californian and Plateau Shoshonean Tribes. UC-PAAE, 20:145–156.

Meighan, C.

1959. Californian Cultures and the Concept of an Archaic Stage. American Antiquity, 24:289–305.

1965. Pacific Coast Archaeology. *In* H. E. Wright and D. G. Frey (eds.), The Quaternary of the United States. Princeton: Princeton University Press, pp. 709–719.

Owen, R. C.

1964. Early Milling Stone Horizon (Oak Grove), Santa Barbara County, California: Radiocarbon Dates. American Antiquity, 30:210–213.

Willey, G. R.

1966. An Introduction to American Archaeology. Vol. I, North and Middle America. New York: Prentice-Hall. (Chapter 6, pp. 361–379, deals with California archaeology.)

ARCHAEOLOGY: NORTHERN AND CENTRAL CALIFORNIA

Baumhoff, M. A.

1957. An Introduction to Yana Archaeology. UCAS-R, No. 40.

Beardsley, R. K.

1954. Temporal and Areal Relationships in Central California Archaeology. UCAS-R, No. 24 (Part I); UCAS-R, No. 25 (Part II).

Bennyhoff, J. A.

1956. An Appraisal of the Archaeological Resources of Yosemite National Park. UCAS-R, No. 34.

1958. The Desert West: A Trial Correlation of Culture and Chronology. UCAS-R, No. 42, pp. 98–112 (with chronological chart).

Cook, S. F. and R. F. Heizer

1951. The Physical Analysis of Nine Indian Mounds of the Lower Sacramento Valley. UC-PAAE, Vol. 40, No. 7.

Davis, J. T.

1960. The Archaeology of the Fernandez Site, a San Francisco Bay Region Shellmound. UCAS-R, No. 49, pp. 1–52.

Davis, J. T. and A. E. Treganza
1959. The Patterson Mound: A Comparative Analysis of the Archaeology of Site Ala-328. UCAS-R, No. 47.

Elsasser, A. B.
1960. The Archaeology of the Sierra Nevada in California and Nevada. UCAS-R, No. 51.

Elsasser, A. B. and R. F. Heizer
1966. Excavation of Two Northwestern California Coastal Sites. UCAS-R, No. 67, pp. 1–149.

Gifford, E. W. and W. E. Schenck
1926. Archaeology of the Southern San Joaquin Valley. UC-PAAE, Vol. 23, No. 1.

Gould, R. A.
1966. Archaeology of the Point St. George Site, and Tolowa Prehistory. University of California Publications in Anthropology (formerly UC-PAAE), Vol. 4.

Heizer, R. F.
1941. The Direct Historical Approach in Central California Archaeology. American Antiquity, 7:98–122.

1949. The Archaeology of Central California: I, The Early Horizon. UC-AR, Vol. 12, No. 1.

Heizer, R. F. (ed.)
1953. The Archaeology of the Napa Region. UC-AR, Vol. 12, No. 6.

Heizer, R. F. and A. B. Elsasser
1953. Some Archaeological Sites and Cultures of the Central Sierra Nevada. UCAS-R, No. 21.

1964. Archaeology of Hum-67, the Gunther Island Site in Humboldt Bay, California. UCAS-R, No. 62, pp. 1–122.

Heizer, R. F. and J. E. Mills
1952. The Four Ages of Isurai: A Documentary History of the Indian Village on Trinidad Bay. Berkeley and Los Angeles: University of California Press.

Hewes, G. W.
1941. Archaeological Reconnaissance of the Central San Joaquin Valley. American Antiquity, 7:123–133.

Hindes, M. G.
1962. The Archaeology of the Huntington Lake Region in the Southern Sierra Nevada, California. UCAS-R, No. 58.

Holmes, W. H.
1901. Review of the Evidence Relating to Auriferous Gravel Man in California. Smithsonian Institution, Annual Report for 1899, pp. 419–472.

Lanning, E. P.
1963. Archaeology of the Rose Spring Site, Iny-372. UC-PAAE, Vol. 49, No. 3.

Loud, L. L.
   1918. Ethnography and Archaeology of the Wiyot Territory. UC-PAAE, Vol. 14, No. 3.
Meighan, C. W.
   1955. Archaeology of the North Coast Ranges, California. UCAS-R, No. 30, pp. 1–39.
Nelson, N. C.
   1909. Shellmounds of the San Francisco Bay Region. UC-PAAE, Vol. 7, No. 4.
Riddell, F.
   1960. The Archaeology of the Karlo Site (Las-7), California. UCAS-R, No. 53.
Schenck, W. E.
   1926. The Emeryville Shellmound; Final Report. UC-PAAE, Vol. 23, No. 3.
Schenck, W. E. and E. J. Dawson
   1929. Archaeology of the Northern San Joaquin Valley. UC-PAAE, Vol. 25, No. 4.
Treganza, A. D.; C. E. Smith; and W. D. Weymouth
   1950. An Archaeological Survey of the Yuki Area. UC-AR, Vol. 12, No. 3.
Walker, E. F.
   1947. Excavation of a Yokuts Indian Cemetery. Kern County Historical Society, Bakersfield.
Wedel, W. R.
   1941. Archaeological Investigations at Buena Vista Lake, Kern County, California. Bureau of American Ethnology, Bulletin No. 130.

ARCHAEOLOGY: SOUTHERN CALIFORNIA

Brainerd, G. W.
   1952. On The Study of Early Man in Southern California. UCAS-R, No. 16, pp. 18–22.
Campbell, E. W. C.
   1931. An Archaeological Survey of the Twenty-Nine Palms Region. Southwest Museum Papers, No. 7.
Campbell, E. W. C. and W. H. Campbell
   1935. The Pinto Basin Site. Southwest Museum Papers, No. 9.
Campbell, E. W. C. et al.
   1937. The Archaeology of Pleistocene Lake Mohave. Southwest Museum Papers, No. 11.
Curtis, F.
   1963. Arroyo Sequit. State of California, Resources Agency, Department of Parks and Recreation, Archaeological Report, No. 9, Sacramento.
Harrington, J. P.
   1928. Exploration of the Burton Mound at Santa Barbara, California. Bureau of American Ethnology, Annual Report, No. 44, pp. 23–168.

Heizer, R. F.
   1965. Problems in Dating Lake Mohave Artifacts. Southwest Museum Masterkey, 39:125–134.
Jones, P. M.
   1956. Archaeological Investigations on Santa Rosa Island in 1901. UC-AR, Vol. 17, No. 2.
Orr, P. C.
   1943. Archaeology of Mescalitan Island and Customs of the Canaliño. Santa Barbara Museum of Natural History, Occasional Papers, No. 5.
Owen, R. C.
   1967. Assertions, Assumptions, and Early Horizon (Oak Grove) Settlement Patterns in Southern California: A Rejoinder. American Antiquity 32:236–241.
Rogers, D. B.
   1929. Prehistoric Man of the Santa Barbara Coast. Santa Barbara Museum of Natural History.
Rogers, M. J.
   1929. Stone Art of the San Dieguito Plateau. American Anthropologist, 31:454–467.
   1939. Early Lithic Industries of the Lower Basin of the Colorado River and Adjacent Desert Areas. San Diego Museum Papers, No. 3.
   1945. An Outline of Yuman Prehistory. Southwestern Journal of Anthropology, 1:167–198.
   1966. Ancient Hunters of the Far West. San Diego.
Shumway, G., C. L. Hubbs, and J. R. Moriarty
   1961. Scripps Estate Site, San Diego, California: A La Jolla Site Dated 5460 to 7370 Years Before the Present. Annals of the New York Academy of Sciences, 93:37–132.
Treganza, A. E.
   1942. An Archaeological Reconnaissance of Northeastern Baja California and Southeastern California. American Antiquity, 8:152–163.
Treganza, A. E. and A. Bierman
   1958. The Topanga Culture: Final Report on Excavations, 1948. UC-AR, Vol. 20, No. 2.
Tuthill, C. and A. A. Allanson
   1954. Ocean Bottom Artifacts. Southwest Museum Masterkey, 28:222–232.
Walker, E. F.
   1951. Five Prehistoric Archaeological Sites in Los Angeles County, California. Southwest Museum, Los Angeles.
Wallace, W. J.
   1962. Prehistoric Cultural Development in the Southern California Deserts. American Antiquity, 28:172–180.
Warren, C. B.
   1967. The Southern California Milling Stone Horizon: Some Comments. American Antiquity, 32:233–236.

Warren, C. N. and D. L. True
  1961. The San Dieguito Complex and Its Place in California Prehistory. University of California Archaeological Survey, Los Angeles, Annual Report for 1960–61, pp. 246–338.

INDIAN ARTS: BASKETRY; SYMBOLISM OF
BASKET DESIGNS

Barrett, S. A.
  1908. Pomo Indian Basketry. UC-PAAE, Vol. 7, No. 3.
Cody, B. P.
  1940. California Indian Baby Cradles. Southwest Museum Masterkey, 14:129–148.
Dawson, L. and J. Deetz
  1965. A Corpus of Chumash Basketry. Archaeological Survey, Annual Report for 1965, Department of Anthropology, UCLA, pp. 193–276.
Dixon, R. B.
  1902. Basketry Designs of the Maidu Indians of Northern California. American Museum of Natural History Bulletin, Vol. 17, Part 1.
  1904. Basketry Designs of the Maidu Indians of California. American Anthropologist, 2:266–276.
Heizer, R. F.
  1968. One of the Oldest Known California Indian Baskets. Southwest Museum Masterkey, 42:70–74.
Hudson, J. W.
  1893. Pomo Basket Makers. Overland Monthly, 21:561–578.
James, G. W.
  1909. Indian Basketry, and How to Make Indian and Other Baskets. 4th ed. New York. (Contains abundant references to California baskets and their makers.)
Kroeber, A. L.
  1905. Basket Designs of the Indians of Northwestern California. UC-PAAE, Vol. 2, No. 4.
  1909. California Basketry and the Pomo. American Anthropologist, 11:233–249.
  1922. Basket Designs of the Mission Indians of California. American Museum of Natural History Anthropological Papers, 20:149–183.
Mason, O. T.
  1904. Aboriginal American Basketry. Annual Report of the United States National Museum for 1902, pp. 171–548. (The basic work on the subject; California is amply treated.)
Merrill, R. E.
  1923. Plants Used in Basketry by the California Indians. UC-PAAE, 20:215–242.

O'Neale, L. M.
    1932. Yurok-Karok Basket Weavers. UC-PAAE, Vol. 32, No. 1.
Purdy, C.
    1902. Pomo Indian Baskets and Their Makers. Out West Company Press,
        Los Angeles. (Also appeared in Out West, 1901–1902, 15:438–449;
        16:9–19, 151–158, 262–273.)
Roseberry, V. M.
    1915. Illustrated History of Indian Baskets and Plates Made by California
        Indians. (No publisher listed. This is a souvenir catalogue of the
        Lassen County exhibit at the 1915 Panama-Pacific International Ex-
        position.)
Swartz, B. K.
    1958. A Study of Material Aspects of Northeastern Maidu Basketry. Kroe-
        ber Anthropological Society Papers, No. 19, pp. 67–84.

MYTHOLOGY AND FOLK TALES

d'Angulo, J.
    1953. Indian Tales. Hill and Wang, New York.
Barrett, S. A.
    1919. Myths of the Southern Sierra Miwok. UC-PAAE, Vol. 16, No. 1.
    1933. Pomo Myths. Bulletin of the Public Museum, City of Milwaukee,
        Vol. 15.
Clark, C. and T. B. Williams
    1954. Pomo Indian Myths. New York.
Curtin, J.
    1898. Creation Myths of Primitive America. Boston.
Dixon, R. B.
    1902. Maidu Myths. American Museum of Natural History, Bulletin, Vol.
        17, Part 2.
Dubois, C. and D. Demetracopoulou
    1931. Wintu Myths. UC-PAAE, Vol. 28, No. 5.
Du Bois, C. G.
    1901. Mythology of the Diegueño. Journal of American Folk-Lore, 14:181–
        185.
    1906. Mythology of the Mission Indians. Journal of American Folk-Lore,
        19:52–60, 145–164.
Fisher, A.
    1957. Stories California Indians Told. Berkeley.
Gayton, A. H.
    1935. Area Affiliations of California Folktales. American Anthropologist,
        37:582–599.
Gayton, A. H. and S. S. Newman
    1940. Yokuts and Western Mono Myths. UC-AR, Vol. 5, No. 1.

Gifford, E. W.
  1917. Miwok Myths. UC-PAAE, Vol. 12, No. 8.
Gifford, E. W. and G. H. Block
  1930. Californian Indian Nights Entertainment. Glendale.
Harrington, J. P.
  1908. Yuma Account of Origins. Journal of American Folk-Lore, 21:324–348.
Heizer, R. F.
  1955. Two Chumash Legends. Journal of American Folk-Lore, 68:34, 56.
James, G. F.
  1903. The Legend of Tahquitch and Algoot. Journal of American Folk-Lore, 16:153–159.
Kroeber, A. L.
  1906. Wishosk (Wiyot) Myths. Journal of American Folk-Lore, 19:85–107.
  1906. Two Myths of the Mission Indians of California. Journal of American Folk-Lore, 19:309–321.
  1907. Indian Myths of South Central California. UC-PAAE, Vol. 4, No. 4.
  1932. Yuki Myths. Anthropos, 27:905–940.
  1948. Seven Mohave Myths. UC-AR, Vol. 11, No. 1.
  1951. A Mohave Historical Epic. UC-AR, Vol. 11, No. 2.
Kroeber, T.
  1963. The Inland Whale: Nine Stories from California Indian Legends. University of California Press.
Merriam, C. H.
  1910. The Dawn of the World: Myths and Weird Tales Told by the Mewan Indians of California. Cleveland: Arthur H. Clark.
  1928. An-nik-a-del: The History of the Universe as Told by the Mod-des-se Indians of California. Boston.
Rush, E. M.
  1930. Legends of the Paiutes of the Owens River Valley. El Palacio, 28:72–87.
Spott, R. and A. L. Kroeber
  1942. Yurok Narratives. UC-PAAE, Vol. 35, No. 9.
Steward, J. H.
  1936. Myths of the Owens Valley Paiute, UC-PAAE, Vol. 34, No. 5.
Waterman, T. T.
  1909. Analysis of the Mission Indian Creation Story. American Anthropologist, 11:41–55.

PSYCHOANALYTIC INTERPRETATIONS OF CALIFORNIA INDIAN CULTURE

Aginsky, B. W.
  1939. Psychopathic Trends in Culture. Character and Personality, 7:331–343.

1940. The Socio-Psychological Significance of Death Among the Pomo Indians. American Imago, Vol. 1, No. 3, pp. 1–18.

Devereux, G.
1939. Mohave Culture and Personality. Character and Personality, 8:91–109.
1947. Mohave Orality: An Analysis of Nursing and Weaning Customs. Psychoanalytic Quarterly, 16:519–546.
1951. Cultural and Characterological Traits of the Mohave Related to the Anal State of Psychosexual Development. Psychoanalytic Quarterly, 20:398–422.
1961. Mohave Ethnopsychiatry and Suicide: The Psychiatric Knowledge and the Psychic Disturbances of an Indian Tribe. Bureau of American Ethnology, Bulletin No. 175.

Erickson, E. H.
1943. Observations on the Yurok: Childhood and World Image. UC-PAAE, Vol. 35, No. 1. (Concludes that the Yurok exhibit the "oral character" as described by Freud and Abraham.)
1945. Childhood and Tradition in Two American Indian Tribes. Psychoanalytic Study of the Child, 1:319–350.

Goldschmidt, W. R.
1951. Ethics and the Structure of Society: An Ethnological Contribution to the Sociology of Knowledge. American Anthropologist, 53:506–524.

Kroeber, A. L.
1959. Yurok National Character. UC-PAAE, Vol. 47, No. 3, pp. 236–240.

Lee, D. D.
1951. Notes on the Concept of Self Among the Wintu Indians. Journal of Abnormal and Social Psychology, 45:538–543.

Posinsky, S. H.
1956. Yurok Shell Money and "Pains": a Freudian Interpretation. Psychiatric Quarterly, 30:598–632.
1957. The Problem of Yurok Anality. American Imago, 14:3–31.

Toffelmeier, G. and K. Luomela
1936. Dreams and Dream Interpretation of the Diegueño Indians. Psychoanalytic Quarterly, 5:195–225.

Wallace, W. W.
1947. The Dream in Mohave Life. Journal of American Folk-Lore, 60:252–258.

SONGS, MUSIC, PRAYERS, PLACE NAMES
OF INDIAN ORIGIN

d'Angulo, J. and R. d'Harcourt
1931. La musique chez les Indiens de la Californie du Nord. Journal de la Société des Americanistes de Paris, 23:189–228.

Cason, G. R.
n.d. An Introduction to the Study of California Indian Music. Unpublished M.A. thesis, University of California, Berkeley.

Demetracopoulou, D.

    1935. Wintu Songs. Anthropos, 30:483–494.

Densmore, F.

    1932. Yuman and Yaqui Music. Bureau of American Ethnology, Bulletin 110.

    1939. Musical Instruments of the Maidu Indians. American Anthropologist, 41:113–118.

    1958. Music of the Maidu Indians of California. Southwest Museum, Los Angeles.

Du Bois, C. G.

    1906. Two Types or Styles of Diegueño Religious Dancing. Proceedings of the 15th International Congress of Americanists, 2:135–138.

Gatschet, A. S.

    1894. Songs of the Modoc Indians. American Anthropologist, O.S., 7:26–31.

Gudde, E.

    1969. California Place Names. 3rd ed. Berkeley and Los Angeles: University of California Press.

Hall, J. C. and B. Nettl

    1955. Musical Style of the Modoc. Southwestern Journal of Anthropology, 11:58–66.

Hanna, P. T.

    1946. The Dictionary of California Land Names. Los Angeles.

Hatch, J.

    1958. Tachi Yokuts Music. Kroeber Anthropological Society, Paper No. 19, pp. 47–66.

Herzog, G.

    1928. The Yuman Musical Style. Journal of American Folk-Lore, 41:183–231.

Kroeber, A. L.

    1916. California Place Names of Indian Origin. UC-PAAE, Vol. 12, No. 2.

Kroeber, A. L. and E. W. Gifford

    1949. World Renewal: A Cult System of Native Northwest California. UC-AR, Vol. 13, No. 1 (Appendix VI contains a number of transcriptions of World Renewal Cult songs.)

Merriam, A. P. and W. d'Azevedo

    1957. Washo Peyote Songs. American Anthropologist, 59:615–641.

Nomland, G.

    1931. A Bear River Shaman's Curative Dance. American Anthropologist, 33:38–41.

Pietroforte, A.

    1965. Songs of the Yokuts and Paiutes. Naturegraph Publishers, Healdsburg, Calif.

Roberts, H.

    1933. Form in Primitive Music. New York. (Deals with Luiseño and Gabrieliño songs.)

1936. Musical Areas in North America. Yale University Publications in Anthropology No. 12. (Includes California.)

Sanchez, N. V.

1922. Spanish and Indian Place Names of California. San Francisco.

Steward, J. H.

1933. Ethnography of the Owens Valley Paiute. UC-PAAE, Vol. 33, No. 3. (Pp. 278–285, transcriptions of Paiute songs.)

Waterman, T. T.

1908. Native Musical Instruments of California. Out West, 28:276–286.

ROCK ART: PETROGLYPHS AND PICTOGRAPHS

Fenenga, F.

1949. Methods of Recording and Present Status of Knowledge Concerning Petroglyphs in California. UCAS-R, No. 3.

Grant, C.

1961. Ancient Art in the Wilderness. Pacific Discovery, 14:12–19.

1964. California Cave Paintings. Desert Magazine, Vol. 27, No. 5, pp. 16–20.

1964. California's Legacy of Indian Rock Art. Natural History, Vol. 73, No. 6, pp. 32–41.

1965. The Rock Paintings of the Chumash. Berkeley and Los Angeles: University of California Press.

1967. Rock Art of the American Indian. Thomas Y. Crowell, New York.

Grant, C., J. W. Baird, and J. K. Pringle

1968. Rock Drawings of the Coso Range. Maturango Museum, Publication 4, China Lake.

Heizer, R. F. and M. A. Baumhoff

1962. Prehistoric Rock Art of Nevada and Eastern California. Berkeley and Los Angeles: University of California Press.

Momyer, G.

1937. Indian Picture Writing in Southern California. San Bernardino.

Payen, L. A.

1959. Petroglyphs of Sacramento and Adjoining Counties, California. UCAS-R, No. 48, pp. 66–83.

Smith, V.

1944. Sheep Hunting Artists of Black Canyon Walls. Desert Magazine (March), 8:5–7.

Steward, J. H.

1929. Petroglyphs of California and Adjoining States. UC-PAAE, Vol. 24, No. 2.

Swift, R. H.

1931. Prehistoric Paintings at Santa Barbara. Bulletin of the Southern California Academy of Sciences, No. 30, pp. 35–38.

True, D.
  1954. Pictographs of the San Luis Rey Basin, California. American Antiquity, 20:68–72.
Van Blom, J. L.
  1929. Rock Writings of the Owens Valley. Touring Topics, Vol. 21, No. 5, pp. 14–17, 51.
Von Werlhof, J. C.
  1965. Rock Art of Owens Valley, California. UCAS-R, No. 65.
Yates, L. G.
  1896. Indian Petroglyphs in California. Overland Monthly, 2nd ser., 28:657–661.

ISHI, LAST OF THE MILL CREEK YAHI

Anderson, R. A.
  1909. Fighting the Mill Creeks. Chico Record Press, Chico.
Carson, A. T.
  1915. Captured by the Mill Creek Indians. Chico (?).
Kroeber, T.
  1961. Ishi in Two Worlds. University of California Press.
  1962. The Hunter, Ishi. The American Scholar, 31:408–418.
  1964. Ishi, Last of His Tribe. Parnassus Press, Berkeley.
Moak, S.
  1923. The Last of the Mill Creeks. Chico.
Nelson, N. C.
  1916. Flint Working by Ishi. Holmes Anniversary Volume, Washington, D.C., pp. 397–402.
Pope, S. T.
  1913. Making Indian Arrow Heads. Forest and Stream, Dec. 20, pp. 796–797.
  1918. Yahi Archery. UC-PAAE, Vol. 13, No. 3.
  1920. The Medical History of Ishi. UC-PAAE, Vol. 13, No. 5.
Waterman, T. T.
  1915. The Last Wild Tribe of California. Popular Science Monthly (March), pp. 233–244.
  1917. Ishi, the Last Yahi. Southern Workman (Hampton Normal and Agricultural Institute), 46:528–537.
  1918. The Yana Indians. UC-PAAE, Vol. 13, No. 2.
Weston, E. B.
  1913. Ishi the Archer. Forest and Stream, Nov. 22, 1913.

THE CALIFORNIA INDIAN TODAY AND IN THE RECENT PAST

Ablon, J.
  1963. Relocated American Indians in the San Francisco Bay Area: Con-

cepts of Acculturation, Success, and Identity in the City. Unpub. Ph.D. Dissertation, University of Chicago.

Ad Hoc Committee on California Indian Education
1967. California Indian Education: Report of the First All-Indian Statewide Conference on California Indian Education. Modesto.

Anonymous
1966. Minority Groups in California. Monthly Labor Review, Vol. 89, No. 9, pp. 978–983. U.S. Dept. of Labor, Bureau of Statistics.

Armsby, E. R. and J. G. Rockwell
1948. New Directions Among Northern California Indians. The American Indians, Vol. 4, No. 3, pp. 12–23.

Bee, R. L.
1963. Changes in Yuma Social Organization. Ethnology, 2:207–227.

Cook, S. F.
1941. The Mechanism and Extent of Dietary Adaptation Among Certain Groups of California and Nevada Indians. Ibero-Americana, No. 18. University of California Press.
1943. The Conflict Between the California Indian and White Civilization: IV, Trends in Marriage and Divorce Since 1850. Ibero-Americana No. 24. University of California Press.
1943. Migration and Urbanization of the Indians of California. Human Biology, 15:33–45.
1943. Racial Fusion Among the California and Nevada Indians. Human Biology, 15:153–165.

Forbes, J. D.
1969. Native Americans of California and Nevada. Naturegraph Publishers, Healdsburg.

MacGregor, G.
1940. The Social and Economic Adjustment of the Indians of the Sacramento Jurisdiction in California. Proceedings of the Sixth Pacific Science Congress, 4:53–58.

State of California
1955. Progress Report to the Legislature by the Senate Interim Committee on California Indian Affairs (Senate Resolution No. 115). Sacramento.
1965. American Indians in California. State of California Department of Industrial Relations, Division of Fair Employment Practices. San Francisco.
1966. Progress Report to the Governor and Legislature by the State Advisory Commission on Indian Affairs (Senate Bill No. 1007) on Indians in Rural and Reservation Areas. Sacramento.
1969. California Indian Health Status. California State Department of Public Health, Bureau of Maternal and Child Health. 9 pp., mimeographed. Berkeley, September, 1969.

index

Achomawi: material culture, 7, 9, 12, 24; basketry, 15, 320, 321, 324; social culture, 26, 33, 34, 35, 39, 52; religion, 41, 53, 56, 58, 496, 498; knowledge, 61, 63; population estimates, 69; physical type, 100

Acorns: storage, 24, 339–340; as food, 74, 76, 77, 80, 117, 305n, 521; importance, 87, 89, 91; preparation and use, 265–266, 298, 301–304, 521

Adolescence rites, 19; girls', 44, 49–52, 118, 416–417; boys', 52

Adoption, 424

Agriculture, 87, 88, 89, 122

Algonkians, 62, 111n, 117, 119, 227, 229

Ancestral home, 375, 376, 377

Anglo-American invasion, 562–565

Animals, domesticated, 87

Anza expedition of 1776, 70

Archaeological sites: lake basins, 133–134; radiocarbon dated, 133–142 passim; northwestern California, 142–143, 225, 226; central California, map, 160; southern California, 189–190, 196–197, 198 (Malaga Cove), 189–191 (San Dieguito), 194 (coast); Santa Barbara area, 206–209, 212–215, 213 (table), 215–218 passim; number of, 480

Archaeology: nature of evidence, 126–128; problems of dating, 133, 135–136, 181; central California area, 158–184; techniques of analysis, 159, 175. See also Archaeological sites; Archaeology, Santa Barbara area excavations; Cultural development; Cultural traits; Cultures

Archaeology, Santa Barbara area excavations: frequency of objects, 209–216 (tables, 210, 214, 216); materials (tables), 210, 213; age of sites, 212–215 (table, 213), 215–218 passim; in cemeteries, 215–218 (tables, 216, 217)

Armor, 39, 421

Arrows, 14–15, 180, 263, 436–437; straightening of, 15, 347, 362–363, 437; children's, 426, 427, 434

Assembly or dance house, 58, 491; Miwok, 334–337, 338–339, 520–521; burning of, 502

Astronomical knowledge, 62–63

Athabascans: social culture, 50, 58, 369; knowledge, 62; population estimates, 68–69; language, 108, 111n; origins, 119, 227, 228, 229; basketry, 320, 322

Atsugewi, 12, 33; basketry, 15, 320, 321; population estimates, 69

Baked clay objects, 174–175

Balsa raft, 9–12 passim, 118

Barnett, H. G., 228

Barrett, S. A., 332–340

Barrows, David Prescott, 306–314

Basketry and baskets: techniques, 5, 6, 15–18 passim, 320–325; forms, 15, 16 17, 24; materials, 15, 16, 17, 316, 319–320, 322–323; of northernmost tribes, 15–16; of central California, 16–18; of southern California, 16; decoration and design, 16, 319, 322–323, 325–330; used for storage, 24; economic and artistic value of, 89–90, 93; in four culture periods, 117–118, 119, 120, 121, 124; Santa Barbara area, 221; Yurok, 264; made by men, 327

Basketry hat, 5–6, 16, 18, 121

Basketry complex, 15, 16, 18

Basketry mortar hopper, 16, 17, 18

Beals, R. L., 73–83

Bear doctor, 42–43

Beardsley, R. K., 158–185

Black magic. See Sorcery and sorcerers

Blankets, 4, 18

Blood money, 399–400, 403, 420

Boats, 9–12, 123. See also Canoes

Bole-Maru cult, 497–498

Bows, 14–15, 114, 117, 180; Yurok, 263; children's, 426, 427; Mohave, 435, 436

British Columbia, influence of, 7

Brown, Charlie (Carl Detman), and San Nicolas Island woman, 278–281

Bruff, J. Goldsborough, on map making, 461

Buckeye (Aesculus californica), uses, 146

Burial, 35–36; position, 167, 179; customs, 170, 500–502; ceremony, 260; before death, 502. See also Disposal of the dead

Burial sites: analysis of, 159, 175; importance of data, 162; central California, 164; Early Horizon, 167

Burning: of property for the dead, 49; of dance house, 502

Burning ceremony (Maidu mourning anni-

versary), 502–512; time of, 504, 511, 512; preliminaries, 504–507; addresses, 507, 508; the crying and the burning, 507–508; purpose of, 509; images used in, 509–511
Burning ground (Maidu): site, 502–503; use of, 503; membership string, 503–504, 511; plan of, 505

Cahuilla (Coahuilla), 5, 18, 351, 359; social culture, 30, 32, 377, 382; religion, 40, 44; population estimates, 71–72; food preparation, 303, 306, 307, 308, 310; food resources, 306–314; basketry, 320, 324, 326
Calendar, 59–61, 121
Canoes, 9–12, 119, 120, 220; sea-going plank, 10, 11, 76, 132
Captives, 431, 443–444, 451, 453
Carrying: net, 32, 121; frame, 24
Cartography. See Map making
Census 1928: coverage, 552; summaries of data, 552–560 passim
Central California: natural setting described, 165–166; archaeology, 166–182
Ceremonial objects, 180. See also Charmstones; Images; Musical instruments
Ceremonial traits, 174
Charmstones, 167, 174, 180
Chemehuevi: material culture, 5, 6, 8, 18; basketry, 16, 322, 324; social culture, 35, 58, 423–433
Chief, 26, 27–28, 118; as war leader, 28, 248–249, 258–259, 434; Yuma, 248–249; Chumash, 258–259; Yurok, 266
Chieftainship, hereditary aspects, 27, 375, 377, 380, 381, 382
Childbirth, 33–34, 256, 415–416
Children: care of, 424–426; activities, games, toys, 425–428; training, 425, 428; punishment, 429–430; mourning for, 502
Chimariko: language, 105–111 passim; food preparation, 303, 304
Chronology: of four culture periods, 113–128 passim; and archaeology, 125–128
Chukchansi: food, 300
Chumash: houses, 6, 7, 255; material culture, 10, 12, 13, 14, 21, 22; basketry, 16, 322, 324; tools and implements, 23, 257; food resources, 24, 256–257, 260; social organization, 26, 27, 380; social culture, 35, 255, 256, 259, 260, 261; religion, 53, 255, 259; knowledge, 63, 64; population estimates, 70–71; language, 105, 107, 108, 111; rock art, 239–241; clothing and ornament, 255–256, 259, 261; history, 255–

261; occupations, 257, 260, 355; marriage, 259
Chumash territory: natural setting described, 208–209, 257, 261
Chungichnish cult, 62, 124, 464
Clans, 29, 30, 31, 32, 377, 380
Climate, 84–94 passim
Clothing, 3–6; Yumas, 247, 250; Chumash, 255–256, 259; Yurok, 263, 264; of feathers, 280, 284
Clubs, 38, 263, 435–436, 437–438
Coiffure. See Hair, treatment of
Colorado River tribes: material culture, 5, 7, 8, 12, 13, 16, 18, 19, 24, 25; attitude toward property, 29; clans, 29, 30, 32; religion, 39, 40, 42, 44, 47, 122, 493; social culture, 50, 61, 122; knowledge, 61; agriculture and food, 122, 306–307. See also names of tribes: Mohave; Yuma
Communication and transportation, 95
Cook, S. F., 66–72, 176, 202–205, 551–571
Costanoans: material culture and economy, 12, 17, 22, 23, 303; social culture, 26, 53, 54, 58; knowledge, 62, 63; population estimates, 69–70; language, 105–111 passim
Costume: standardized, 121; dancers', 529
Counting methods, 61–64
Couvade, 33
Cremation, 35–36, 179, 500, 501, 502
Crespi, Father: 71
Cults, 43–48; distribution (map), 45; development, 124; patterns and purposes, 464–465; distribution of societies, North America (map), 486. See also names of cults: Bole-Maru; Earth Lodge; Ghost Dance; Jimsonweed; Kuksu
Cultural climax, 92–96, 181, 183
Cultural development, 117–125, 131, 132
Cultural development, central California, 137–142, 158–185; Early Horizon, 166–169; Middle Horizon, 169–177; Late Horizon, 177–182
Cultural development, Santa Barbara area, 191, 193, 212–224
Cultural development, southern California coast, 186–201; natural setting, 186–187; early period, 188–191; milling-stone assemblage phase, 191–193 (table, 192); intermediate period, 193–195; late prehistoric period, 195–199
Cultural traits, 136–137, 163–164, 171–177, 178–182, 192, 195, 196–197 (table), 199; geographical and temporal relationships diagrammed, 114–117
Culture(s): dating of, 126, 177; external in-

fluences, 131–132; Lake Mohave-Playa, 133–134, 134n; Death Valley, 134; California Desert, 134, 137; Pinto Basin, 134; San Dieguito, 134; La Jolla, 135, 136, 194; Santa Barbara area, 136, 198; San Francisco Bay region, 139, 156–157; disappearance of Indian, 178, 182; Oak Grove, 191; northwestern coast, 227

Cupeño, 18, 62; social organization, 30, 32, 378–380; lineages (table), 379

Curing. See "Pains" and shamanism; Rattlesnake doctor; Shamanism; Shamans and doctors

Dance(s), 48, 49, 50, 53, 118, 123, 261, 343–344; scalp or victory, 37–38, 123, 443, 447, 449, 453, 457; war, 37–38, 44, 123, 439–440, 531–532; shaman's or "doctor's," 40–41, 44, 533–542 passim; Deerskin, 53, 64, 403, 467–470 passim; Kuksu cult, 93, 491; Jumping, 467–471 passim; Yokuts, for the dead, 513–519; Miwok acorn, 528–530. See also Ghost Dance

Dance house. See Assembly and dance houses

Death, causes of (1962), 581 (table)

Deerskins as wealth items, 397–398

Dentalia, 20, 21, 123; sizes and names of shells, 394 (table), 395; source, 394; valuation, 394, 395, 396; as ornaments, 395

Descent: matrilineal, 29, 31; patrilineal, 29, 118, 120

Detman, Carl. See Brown, Charlie

Dialects, 369, 370, 373

Diegueño: material culture, 6, 12, 18, 20, 24; social organization, 30, 377–378, 380; social culture, 34, 38, 49; religion, 42, 44, 48; knowledge, 60, 61, 63; paintings, 242; food preparation, 303, 304, 305; basketry, 320, 323, 324; earthquake myth, 352

Disposal of the dead, 35–36, 118, 120, 199, 351, 441; Yurok, 417–418; Maidu area, 500–502. See also Burial; Cremation

Divorce, Yurok, 401–402

Dixon, R. B., 105–111, 500–512

Dreams and dreaming: in religion, 40, 47, 122, 125, 497, 498; and Mohave warrior class, 431, 433, 434

Dress. See Clothing; Ornaments

Drucker, P., 228

Drum(s). See Musical instruments

Du Bois, Cora, 496–499

Early man, evidences of, 132–133, 188–191

Earth Lodge cult, 497, 498

Earthquakes, explanation of, 352

Ecological types, 73–83; difficulties in formulating, 73–74; range and nature of environment, 74–82 passim; subsistence staples, summary, 74; variations within subtypes, 74; tidelands gatherers, 74–75; sea hunters and fishers, 74, 75–76; riverine, 74, 76–78; lake, 74, 78; valley, 74, 78–79; foothill, 74, 80–81; desert hunters and gatherers, 74, 81–82; desert farmers, 74, 82; variance from characteristic pattern, 83

Economic conditions: median annual income (1959), table, 579; unemployment rates (1960), 579 (table)

Economy, basic collecting and hunting, 87–92 passim

Education: school levels completed (1960), 578 (table)

Ellis Landing shellmound, age of, 202–205

Elsasser, A. B., 225–230

Emeryville site, 176

Essig, E. O., 315–318

Esselen: population estimates, 69–70; language, 105, 108, 111

Essene, Frank, 445–458

Exogamy and totemism, 29–32, 121, 375

Explorers' accounts, 123

Fages, Pedro, 255–261

Fages expedition, 70, 79

Family: size, 424; constitution, 559–560

Famine, 298

Fernandeño: knowledge, 62; map making, 460

Ferrying, 12, 406–407

Fetish, 41; bundles, 221, 493, 494

Fire, use and significance, 152, 250, 265

Fire making, 257–258, 281, 344–345

First-fruits rites. See World-renewal rites

Fishing implements and methods, 13–14, 89–90, 167, 172, 180, 257, 299; fishhooks, 13, 132, 210, 212, 213–217 passim; harpoon, 13, 118; nets, 13–14, 118; poison, 14

Fishing privileges, 405–406

Font, Pedro, 247–254

Food resources, 87, 117, 248, 256–257, 260, 281, 342–343; of ecologic types, 73–82 passim; methods of obtaining, 89–91, 298–299; of central California, 90, 94–95; preparation, 117, 306–311 passim; buckeye, 146; diversity of, 297; of the desert, 306–314; mesquite (algaroba), 306–307, 313; agave, 307–308, 314; yucca, 308–309, 313, 314; wild plum, 309, 314; cactus, 311–313; chia, 311, 314; insects, 316–318. See also Acorns; Pine nut; Salmon

Food storage, 24, 314, 339–340

Food taboos, 268, 300

Foster, George, 445–458
Frémont, John, on Indian map-making, 460–461

Gabrielino, 19, 37, 50; religion, 44, 48; knowledge, 61, 62, 63; food, 303, 304; artisan class, 355, 357
Geography: regional, 84–96; Yurok concepts of, 472–479; direction and position terms (Yurok), list, 474–476; expressions, list of, 476; Yurok place names, 476–478
Geomorphology, 85
Ghost Dance, 6, 54–59, 114, 496–499
Gifford, E. W., 29, 91, 97–104, 127, 176, 202–205, 301–305, 332–340, 375–384
Goldschmidt, W. R., 226, 445–458
Grant, Campbell, 231–243
Grave goods: occurrence, 170–171; Late Horizon, 179–180
Great Basin: influence of cultures, 6, 23, 81, 121, 131
Grinding implements, 119, 171, 194–195, 196, 210–219 passim; prehistoric, illustrated, 354
Ground painting, 47, 52, 121, 122, 124, 493, 494
Guardian spirit, 39–40, 533, 540

Hair, treatment of, 251–252, 255, 259, 262
Haliotis, 22
Hammerstones, 171
Hardacre, Emma, 272–284
Headdress: caps and hats, 5–6, 16, 18, 121; net, 6; feather, 491
Health conditions, 580–581
Heizer, R. F., 95, 131–143, 177, 225–230, 346–359, 459–463, 480–484, 572–581
Hesi cult society, 124, 485, 488, 489
Hester, Jr., J. A., 73–83
Hokans, 64, 111 and n, 117, 119, 227
Houses, 6–8, 118, 120, 222, 255; forms of, 6–7, 196; separate, for women, 7–8; Yuma, 249–250; Yurok, 265, 387–388; Miwok, kinds of, 332–340; Miwok terms applied to, 332–339 passim; semisubterranean, 333–337 passim. See also Assembly or dance house
Huchnom, 64, 367, 368, 487
Hunting: culture traits, 193–194; magic, 237, 238; methods, 277–278, 299
Hupa, 25, 34, 38, 226; material culture, 4, 6, 7, 9, 19, 22, 394; religion, 41, 43, 44, 49, 53, 56, 58, 465–471 passim; knowledge, 62, 63; population estimates, 68–69; food, 301, 303, 304; basketry, 320, 324,

326, 328, 330; character, 544, 550; sorcery, 544–550

Images, ceremonial, 509–511, 516
Impersonations, supernatural, 485, 487, 492, 493, 494
Indian, American: definition of, 572–573
Influences, external. See British Columbia; Great Basin; North Pacific coast tribes; Oceania; Plains tribes; Pueblo; Southwest; Zuni
Inheritance, 28, 30, 410–411
Initiation: into cult societies, 44–46, 52, 485, 486, 493; tribal, 487
Insects: in legend, 315–316; as food, 316–318; uses, 316
Irrigation, 87, 88
Ishi, the last Yahi, 285, 288–293
Iskoman language family, 111

Jacobs, M., 227–228, 229
Jeffries, Thomas, and San Nicolas Island, 276–277
Jimsonweed cult (toloache), 43, 44, 45, 48, 52, 62; development, 121, 124; and rock art, 242
Jones, S. J., 84–96
Juaneño, 27, 28, 34; knowledge, 60, 61, 62; paintings, 242

Kamia, 303, 304, 359
Karok, 7, 9, 19, 25, 100; religion, 53, 55, 58, 465–471 passim, 496; population estimates, 68–69; language, 107, 108, 111; basketry, 320, 324, 328, 330; laws and customs, 395–413 passim
Kato: material culture, 6, 15; social culture, 33, 34, 227, 485
Kawaiisu, 16, 31, 52, 241
Kinship: taboos, 34–35, 121; Yurok claims of, 392–393
Kitanemuk, 14, 22
Klamath River tribes: material culture, 4, 12, 15; religion, 58, 496, 497; famine among, 298
Klimek, S., 92–93
Kroeber, A. L., 3–65, 73, 89–90, 105–119, 132, 229, 297–300, 319–331, 367–374, 385–423, 464–471, 485–495, 533–543; estimates of aboriginal population, 66–72 passim; quoted, 459, 482–483
Kuksu cults, 6, 7, 8, 19, 28, 43–46, 48, 52, 53, 56, 58; in central California culture, 93, 95; origins and development, 121, 124, 487–492, 493–495; local types, 485–495; ghost, 485, 488, 489, 491; hesi, 485, 488,

489; Kuksu, 485, 488; cause of local differences, 487–498; relative age of, 489–491; external relations, 491–493; ritual material, 491

Land ownership, 406
Language(s), 103, 132, 370; of ecologic types, 75–82; separation of, 227, 229, 483–484; housing terms, Miwok, 332–340 passim
Language families, 97, 105–111; shared stems (table), 108; paired by resemblances (table), 109; basis of new names, 110–111; recognized at present, 111n
Lassik, 4, 49
Laws, Yurok, 391–393
Leaching process, 302–303. See also Acorns
Levirate, 33, 118, 402
Lineage(s), 375–384 passim; as autonomous political unit, 375–378; as part of body politic, 378–384; amalgamation of, 376, 378, 379, 380; Cupeño, 379 (table)
Loeb, E. M., 495
Luiseño: material culture, 8, 12, 14, 15, 18, 19, 20, 23, 52; society, 30, 32, 34, 50, 52; religion, 44, 46, 47, 48, 58, 59; knowledge, 60–64 passim; paintings, 242; food, 303, 304; basketry, 320, 324; lineages, 380; migration, 555
Lutuamians, 108, 111n. See also Modoc

McCall, A. J., 461
Maidu: material culture, 8, 12, 15, 18, 20–25 passim; basketry, 15, 16, 17, 124, 320–323 passim, 325, 326, 328; social organization, 25, 368–369; social culture, 33, 34, 37, 39, 49, 53; disposal of the dead, 35, 500–502; religion, 39–48 passim, 53, 54, 56, 58; knowledge, 59, 61, 62, 63; population estimates, 69; cultural climax, 92, 93; language, 105, 107–111 passim; food, 303, 304; and Kuksu cult, 485, 487, 488, 494, 497; mourning ceremonies ("burning"), 500–512
Maize, cultivation of, 87, 88
Map making: aboriginal, California and Great Basin, 459–463; recent, 462, 463; sand maps, 462, 463
Marriage, 32–33, 118, 250, 259, 266, 392–393, 400–403; by purchase, 32, 119, 123, 266, 399, 400–403 passim; levirate, 33, 118; sororate, 33, 118
Merriam, C. Hart, 520–532
Meyer, Carl, 262–271
Migration, fish-trap theory of, 132
Migration, internal, 551–561; conditions affecting, 554–557; age distribution and ra-

tios, 555–557 (table, 556); direction of, 557–558; type of people, 558–560
Milling Stone Horizon, 135, 191–193
Mineral springs, use of, 350–351
Minerals, chemical processes used with, 348–349
Mines and quarries, 346–359; ownership of, 124, 352, 355–356; principal function, 353; laws, 356; location, 357–359; techniques and tools, 357–359
Mission Indians, 56, 566–571 passim
Missions, effect of, 76, 95
Miwok: material culture, 4, 12, 20, 21, 24; houses, 7, 332–340; basketry, 17, 322, 324, 325, 326; social organization and culture, 26–34 passim, 375–382 passim; religion, 41, 58, 485, 487, 494; mourning ceremonies, 48, 336, 338, 339, 520–528; knowledge, 62, 63, 64; population estimates, 68–69; language, 105–111 passim; food taboos, 300; food preparation, 303, 304, 521; myths, 352; land ownership, 376; washing ceremony, 526; acorn dance, 528–530; war dance, 531–532; and white man, 567, 568
Modoc: material culture, 4, 6, 7, 9, 12, 13, 22, 23; basketry, 15, 18, 320, 324; society, 26, 35, 39; religion and knowledge, 56, 58, 60, 496; population estimates, 69; childhood, 424–430
Modoc War, 56
Mohave: material culture, 8, 12, 18, 20; society, 25, 26, 27, 28, 37, 49, 50, 371; warfare, 36–37, 431–444; weapons, 38, 435–438, 441; religion, 46, 48, 49, 58, 59; knowledge, 63, 64; physical type, 100; famine among, 298; and insects, 315, 316; basketry, 322, 323. See also Colorado River tribes
Moieties, 28–32 passim, 121; and lineage, 375–383 passim
Money, 20–22, 123, 181, 394–397. See also Blood money; Dentalia; Valuations
Mono, 8, 18, 24; society, 31, 34, 35, 36, 38, 58, 378; population estimates, 69; food preparation, 303, 304; basketry, 322, 324
Mortuary complex (Late Horizon), 197
Mortuary data (central California), table, 162
Mourning customs and ceremonies, 32, 33, 48–49, 120, 121, 125, 488, 489, 491, 494; Miwok, 336, 338, 339, 520–528; Yurok, 408–410; Maidu, 500–512; Yokuts, dance for the dead, 513–519
Murder for revenge, 123
Musical instruments, 19–20; drums, 19, 20,

334–335, 337, 491; rattles, 19, 20, 50, 52, 261, 316, 491; bull-roarer, 20, 487, 493, 494; flute, 20, 261; whistles, 20, 491
Myths and legends, 47, 121, 132, 348, 351–352, 400; astronomical, 60–61; about insects, 315–316; and Yurok wealth, 396–397; and geography, 472–473, 479

Names: Yurok, 270, 388, 418–410, 476–478; of tribes, 370; of dead, taboo on use of, 410, 419–420, 501
Navahos, 7, 47
Nelson, N. C., 126, 127, 144–157, 176, 202–205
New year rites, 47, 53, 64, 123. See also World-renewal rites
Nidiver, George, and San Nicolas Island woman, 275–284 passim
Nisenan: cultural climax, 92, 94; food, 303; religion, 485, 487, 489, 494
Nomlaki, war stories of, 445–457
Nongatl, 43
North Pacific coast tribes, influence of, 6, 29, 39, 46, 47, 60, 118–120, 122, 131, 227; on cults, 491, 494, 493
Numeration, 61–65

Obsidian, 174, 347, 348; as wealth, 21, 123, 397–398
Oceania, influence of, 131–132, 224
Ocher, red, occurrence of, 168, 170, 174
Offerings, memorial, 515–516
Olson, 206–224
Ornament(s), 22, 33, 123, 173, 174, 256, 261, 262, 264, 389; beads, 120, 167, 173, 174, 179, 181, 197, 251, 395, 396; Early Horizon, 167–168; Middle Horizon, 173–174; pendants, 197, 251; face and body paint, 251, 256, 263, 316, 350, 435, 443, 529–530
Orr, P. C., 132

"Pains" and shamanism, 536–542 passim, 547–548
Paintings. See Rock art
Paiute (Northern), 12, 56, 58
Panamints, 8, 14, 58, 310, 312
Patwin, 9, 303, 304; cultural climax, 92–95 passim; religion, 485, 487, 488, 494, 496, 497
Paviosto, 496, 497
Penutians, 62, 111 and n, 117, 119, 373
Peor es Nada (schooner), 274, 275, 276
Petroglyphs. See Rock art
Physical characteristics: face form, 97, 99, 101; head form, 97, 98, 100; nose form,

97, 100; stature, 97, 100; compared with other races, 100, 101; color of skin, eyes, hair, 101; face and head, 101–102; compared with other North American Indians, 104
Physical types, 97, 167, 170, 178, 249, 483; Western Mono, 98, 102, 103, 104; Yuki, 100–104 passim; Californian, 102, 103, 104; probable distribution, 102–103; and language, 103
Pine nut (piñon), 310–311, 314
Pipes, 22, 343, 347, 348
Pitch, use of, 35
Plains tribes: comparison with, 4, 29, 38, 46, 47, 52; influence of, 9
Political organization, 25–27, 375–384 passim
Pomo: material culture, 5, 7, 8, 9, 12, 14, 20–24 passim; basketry, 17, 124, 319–331; social organization, 25, 355, 357, 368–374 passim, 381, 482–483; social culture, 31–37 passim; religion, 41, 42, 43, 49, 54, 56, 58; knowledge, 61, 62, 63, 64; population estimates, 68–69; agricultural practices, 87; cultural climax, 93, 94, 96; language, 107–111 passim; food, 301, 303, 304; control of mines and quarries, 356; and Kuksu cult, 485, 487, 488, 494, 497, 498
Population: density, 80, 81, 89; stability, 97; census (1928), 552; sex ratios of (tables), 558, 559, 560
Population, aboriginal: methods of computation of, 66–68; estimates of, by area, 66–72; sources of information, 66–71 passim; southern coast ranges area, 71–72, 480
Population, California: nature of, 554; Spanish, 564; non-Anglo (1960), 574; by ethnic groups, 1950, 1960 (table), 577; minorities in rural and urban areas, 1960 (table), 577; family size by ethnic groups, 1960 (table), 580
Population, Indian, 140, 357, 564, 566; influence of whites on, 553; pre-Spanish, 574; U.S., by state, in 1950, 1960 (table), 574–575; in California, 1890–1960 (table), 576. See also Census 1928; Migration, internal; Urbanization
Portola expedition, 71
Pottery, 18–19, 121–122, 221
Power, supernatural, 544, 546, 548. See also Shamanism; Shamans and doctors
Powers, Stephen, 112, 513–519
Priests, 28, 466
Prisoners. See Captives

Projectile points, 167, 171–172, 196
Property, 29, 119, 120, 406; burning of, as mourning rite, 49, 506–509
Pueblos: comparison with, 8, 16, 40, 47; influence of, 38, 60, 119, 131; kachina cult, 492
Purification rites and requirements, 442–444, 500, 501–502
Putnam, F. W., 132

Quartz crystal, 348

Raft, tule balsa, 9–12, 118
Rain doctor, 42
Rattles. See Musical instruments
Rattlesnake doctor, 42
Ray, Verne F., 424–430
Redding, George H. H., 341–345
Religion, 32, 39–59, 120, 121, 124, 249, 255; dreaming as an element in, 40, 47, 497, 498; Yurok, 268–269, 271; Christianization, 498–499; world-renewal cult, 464–471. See also Cults; Ghost Dance; Shamanism; Shamans and doctors; and names of individual tribes and cults
Reservations (1960s), 581
Ritual numbers, 61, 63
Ritwan language family, 111
Rock art, 137, 231–243; motivation, 137, 232, 237, 239, 242; designs and subject matter, 231, 237, 238, 239, 241; age of, 232, 238, 239, 242; rock types, 232, 237–242 passim; colors, 239
Rock art methods: pecked, 232–239; incised, 238–239; painted, 239–243
Rock art styles: major concentrations, 232; Great Basin, 232–237 (abstract), 237–238 (representational); pit-and-groove, 238–239; abstract, 238–239 (curvilinear), 239–241 (polychrome), 241–243 (rectilinear)
Rocks in shellmounds, 152

Salinan: material culture, 17, 19, 21, 300, 303, 304; social culture, 26, 31, 35, 43, 63, 64; population estimates, 69–70; language, 105, 107, 108, 111
Salmon, importance of as food resource, 76–77, 79, 94
San Nicolas Island, 277; natives of, 273–274, 275
San Nicolas Island, lone woman of, 275–284; discovery and rescue, 279–280; culture, 280–283; life and death on mainland, 282–284
Santa Barbara area: natural setting, 208–209; cultural changes and developments, 218–

220, 222–224; islands and islanders, 272, 273
Santa Barbara area, archaeology of, 206–224. See also Archaeological sites; Archaeology, Santa Barbara area
Scalp dance. See Dances
Scalp taking, 37–38, 442, 443, 447, 457
Schenck, W. Egbert, 91, 176
Schumacher, Paul, 360–363
Seashells. See Money; Ornaments; Trade
Serrano, 18, 30, 32, 44, 54, 377
Shamanism, 39–43, 46–47, 119, 120, 533–543
Shamans and doctors: acquisition of power, 28, 39–40, 118, 119, 533, 535–543; functions of, 39, 42, 118, 119, 120; techniques of curing, 39, 43, 534–535, 542–543; dances, 40–41, 533–542 passim; killing of, 41; women, 123, 535, 539, 540; and rock art, 232, 237; legal status among Yurok, 407–408; in warfare, 440–441, 446; and "pains," 536–542 passim; singing of, 532–542 passim; and sorcery, 547–548
Shasta: material culture, 6, 7, 9, 12, 23, 24; social culture, 33, 38, 39, 52, 53; religion, 41, 42, 56, 58, 496, 497; food preparation, 301, 302, 303, 304; basketry, 320
Shastan tribes: population estimate, 69; language, 105–111 passim
Shellmounds, San Francisco Bay region: age of, 126–127, 139, 176–177, 202–205; limitations of evidence therein, 126–127; distribution, 144–152; disappearance of, 145, 147–148; size and form, 146–147; collections containing artifacts from, 148; relation to shore line and sea level, 149–150; composition and internal structure, 152–156; molluscan remains in, 153–155; vertebrate fauna remains in, 155–156; Emeryville site, 176
Shields, 38–39, 438
Shoshoneans, 10, 26, 27, 62, 117; basketry, 16, 322; language, 108, 109, 110, 111n, 119; origin and movement, 119, 120, 238; rock art, 237, 241–
Singing, in shamanism, 536–542 passim
Sinkyone, 8, 15, 19, 38, 49, 61, 63
Slavery, 28, 123, 404–405; valuation of slaves, 395–396, 399
Slings, 38
Social classes, 28–29, 411–412
Social organization, 25–32, 66–67, 83, 93, 121, 123, 375–384 passim. See also Lineages; Moieties; Villages
Society, native: general survey of, 25–39
Sodomy, 250, 259

Song-myth cycles or series, 44, 45, 47
Sorcery and sorcerers, Hupa, 544–550; motives, 544; types of, 544–547; as cause of death and diseases, 546; detection and reprisal, 548–549; efficacy of, 548; precautions against, 548; cultural functions, 550
Sororate, 33, 118
Southwest: comparison with, 24, 38, 40, 61; influence of, 29, 30, 46, 47, 54, 60, 118–120, 121, 122; influence on cults, 491, 492, 493. *See also* Pueblos
Spanish colonization: effects of, 562–565 *passim*; Indian responses to, 566–570
Spears, 38, 172
Steatite, 347, 358, 362
Steward, Julian, 73, 133, 231, 242
Stewart, Kenneth M., 431–444
Stones: as weapons, 38; perforated, 220–221; knowledge of, 346–351. *See also* Minerals; Mines and Quarries; Obsidian; Ornaments; Projectile points; Tools and implements; Valuables; Weapons
String materials, 23
Sweathouse, 8–9, 118, 337–338, 343

Taboos, 32, 50; kinship, 34–35, 121; birth and death, 118, 120; food, 268, 300; on use of name of dead, 410, 419–420, 501
Tannic acid, removal of, 301–305, 350
Tatooing, 263
Taylor, Edith S., 544–550
Textiles, 15–18, 320. *See also* Basketry and baskets
Time, concept of, 59
Tobacco, 22–23, 54, 87, 342, 515
Toloache cult. *See* Jimsonweed cult
Tolowa, 19, 23; religion, 53, 55, 58, 496; knowledge, 61, 62, 63; population estimates, 68–69; basketry, 320, 324
Tools and implements, 23, 118, 167, 257; domestic, 24–25, 179–180; bone and antler, 172–173, 257; chipped stone, 197. *See also* Fishing implements and methods; Grinding implements; Weapons
Torture, 37
Toys and games, 38, 426–428
Trade, 75, 181, 204, 353–355, 447, 451
Transvestites as shamans, 417
Treganza, A. E., 346–359
"Tribe" as a term, 25, 368
Tribes, 25–26, 87, 88; nature and organization, 367–374; name endings, 370; nature of boundaries, 459, 482; spread of, 482–484
Tübatulabal: material culture, 12, 16, 18, 22; social culture, 31, 35, 110, 241, 300; population estimates, 69

Twins, 34, 416

Uhle, Max, 176
Umbilical cord, 34
Urbanization, 553, 556, 557–561 *passim*
Uto-Aztekan language family, 110, 111n

Vallejo, M. G., 568, 569, 570
Valuables, 21, 397–398, 467, 468
Valuations, list of Yurok, 398–399
Villages, 25–26, 368–374, 376–380 *passim*, 480–483

Wailaki, 6, 39, 58; basketry, 15, 321, 324
Wallace, W. J., 186–201, 544–550
Wappo, 24, 31, 63, 64, 110, 567; population estimates, 68–69; basketry, 324, 326
War stories: Yuki accounts, 445–449; Nomlaki accounts, 449–455; analysis of, 454–458; patterning of, 455–456; distribution of elements in (table), 455; attitudes of tribes shown in, 456–457
Warfare, 36–39, 122; causes, 41, 356, 457, 482; Mohave, 371, 431–444; Yurok, 420–423; post-battle activities, 422–444; Indian and white, 567–570
Warrior class, Mohave, 431, 433–434
Washing ceremony, Miwok, 526
Washo, 9, 24; basketry, 17, 124, 322; social culture, 49, 58, 108, 496
Waterman, T. T., 229, 285–293, 472–479, 481
Wealth, 27, 28–29. *See also* Money; Valuables; Yurok attitude toward wealth
Weapons, 38–39, 249, 255, 263–264, 435, 436, 450; in rock art, 238; manufacture, of stone, 360–363. *See also* Arrows; Bows; Clubs; Spears
Wells, deep water, 359
Weregild. *See* Blood money
Whilkut, 58
Whipple, A. W., 461, 572–581
White man: attitudes and policies toward Indians, 563–565; Indian responses to invasion by, 566–571
Widows and widowers, mourning of, 33, 500, 501, 502, 511, 523, 525, 526–527
Windmiller site, 166–168
Wintun: material culture, 12, 21, 22, 24; basketry, 15, 320–326 *passim*; social culture, 33, 35, 38, 352; religion, 41, 42, 49, 56, 58, 496, 497; knowledge, 62, 63, 64; population estimates, 69; language, 105–111 *passim*; food, 304, 342–343; natural setting, 341–343; fire making, 344–345
Witchcraft. *See* Sorcery and sorcerers

Wiyot, 43, 62, 63, 226, 228; population estimates, 68–69; language, 107, 108, 111; basketry, 320, 322, 324

Women: separate huts for, 7–8; as shamans and doctors, 41, 123, 390, 535, 539, 540; in cults, 485; in dance for the dead, 517–518; migration of, 558, 560

Woodpecker scalps, value of, 397

Woodworking, 118, 119

World-renewal rites, 53, 123, 387, 464–471; purpose, 465; formulist in, 466; sacred structures of, 466–467, 469, 470; first-fruit rites, 469, 470, 471

Yahi, 15, 22, 35, 286–287, 288; population estimates, 69; history of, 285–288

Yana, 9, 34, 69, 555; basketry, 15, 321, 322, 324; religion, 58, 496; language, 107, 108, 109, 111

Yokuts: material culture, 6, 7, 8, 12, 14, 15, 18, 20–24 passim, 303; basketry, 16, 17, 124, 322, 324, 326; social organization, 26, 27–28, 369–370, 381; social culture, 31–37 passim, 49; taboos, 34, 300; religion, 39, 41, 42, 43, 48, 54, 56, 58, 59; knowledge, 61, 62, 63; population estimates, 69; territory, 89, 90, 91, 370; food resources, 90, 91, 303; language, 105–111 passim, 370; paintings, 231, 239, 241; myths, 316, 351; mourning (dance for the dead), 513–519; and white man, 567, 568

Yuki, 35, 49; material culture, 7, 8, 12, 21, 23; basketry, 15, 16, 17, 321–326; social organization, 25, 368–369; religion, 41, 42, 43, 46, 47, 49, 487, 488, 494; knowledge, 63, 64; population estimates, 68–69; physical characteristics, 100, 101; food preparation, 301, 303, 304; distribution of, 367–368, 459; war stories, 445–457

Yukian language family, 108, 109, 110, 111n, 483–484, 485

Yumans, 52; language, 105, 108, 111; social organization, 26–27, 30, 369, 382–383.

See also Colorado River tribes; Diegueño; Mohave; Yumas

Yumas, 247–254; material culture and economy, 8, 18, 249–250, 252; warfare and weapons, 15, 36–37, 38, 249; social culture and organization, 25, 50, 250, 251, 252; chieftainship, 28, 248–249; religion, 48, 249; knowledge, 61, 63; clothing and ornament, 247, 250, 251–252; natural setting, 247–248; physical type, 249

Yurok, 9, 20, 22; clothing and ornament, 4, 262, 263, 264, 389; houses, 6, 7, 265, 387–388; social organization, 25, 266–267, 369, 374, 381–382; attitude toward wealth, 28, 381–382, 386, 387, 412–414, 535; rites and ceremonies, 38, 49, 53, 267–268, 387, 416–417, 421; religion, 40, 41, 46, 49, 56, 58, 268, 465–471 passim, 496; knowledge, 59, 60, 62, 63; population estimates, 68–69, 385; language, 107, 108, 111, 269–270; culture of Coast, 226, 228; physical type, 262; basketry, 264, 320, 322, 324, 326, 327, 328, 330, 380; character and temperament, 264, 385–390; food, 265–266 (resources), 301, 303, 304 (preparation); marriage, 266, 392–393, 400–403, 414–415; warfare, 267, 420–423; names, 270, 388, 418–420, 476–478 (local place); taboos, 300, 419–420; weapons, 360–363, 421; disposal of the dead, 389, 417–418; women, 389–390, 393; custom and law, 391–423; standards of conduct, 391–393; claims of kinship, 392–393; money, 394–397; treasure besides money, 397–398; valuations, list of, 398–399; adultery and seduction, compensation for, 399, 403; divorce, 401–402; land ownership, 406; social classes, 411–412; magic, 413, 415; concepts of geography, 472–479; concepts of the world, 472–475 (diagram, 475); shamanism, 533–543; acquisition of power (men), 540

Zuni, influence of, 60